صحيح البخاري

The Translation of the Meanings of

Sahih Al-Bukhari

Arabic-English

Vol. VI

By

Dr. Muhammad Muhsin Khan

Islamic University, Medina Al-Munawwara

CM01116870

TAB BHAVAN

ew Delhi-110002

DEDICATED TO
THE CAUSE OF ALLAH

Reprinted 1987
Revised Edition

ISBN 81-7151-013-2 (SET)
ISBN 81-7151-019-1 (Vol. VI)

Printed in India at :
Lahoti Fine Art Press, Suiwalan, Delhi - 2 [India]

Published by :
Nusrat Ali Nasri for Kitab Bhavan
1784, Kalan Mahal, Darya Ganj, New Delhi - 2 [India]

In the Name of Allāh, the Most Beneficent, the Most Merciful

Praise be to Allāh, the Lord of the Worlds, and Peace be upon the Master of the Apostles, his Family and Companions.

We, the undersigned, have read this translation of the Meanings of "Ṣaḥīḥ al-Bukhāri" achieved by Dr. Muḥammed Muḥsin Khan and have done our best to revise and correct it from its beginning to its end so that, with the ability and efforts available, it has come near to correctness as much as possible.

We thank Allāh, the Elevated, for the success of this beneficial project and ask Him to bountifully reward all those who have undertaken it or participated in it — Allāh's Pleasure being our aim, and it is He who guides us on the right path.

Shākir Naṣīf Al-Ubaydī:
M.A. English, Vanderbilt Univ., U.S.A.;
Teacher of English:
Baghdad Univ., & College of Education, Mecca.

Dr. Maḥmūd Hamad Naṣr:
Graduate of Khartum Univ.
Physician, King Hospital, Medina.

Dr. Muḥammad Taqiy-ad-Dīn Al-Hilālī:
Ph.D. Berlin Univ., Germany; Professor;
Muḥammad V Univ., Morocco; Islamic Univ., Medina.

I have persued a little portion of this translation and found that the translator has succeeded in rendering the meanings of "Al-Jami'As-Ṣaḥīḥ" (Ṣaḥīḥ al-Bukhāri) into English in a simple comprehensible style free from complications. I have also noticed that he has chosen successfully the best and most authentic interpretation of some Ḥadīths that are interpreted differently by different scholars.

Dr. Maḥmūd Ḥamad As-Sūdani did his best to check the whole translation. The second revision was done by Mr. Shākir Naṣīf Al-Ubaydī. Finally, Dr. Muḥammad Taqiy-ad-Dīn Al-Hilālī checked the translation with the translator Dr. M.M. Khan thoroughly and minutely, doing his utmost to correct the minor mistakes he detected, till the translation acquired a high degree of precision.

May Allāh bountifully reward whoever has participated in this benevolent work; and may He make people benefit by it.

I am perfectly sure that the translation, with Allāh's help and after all the great efforts exerted in its production, has neared perfection.

In Allāh's Hands are all means of success. And Praise be to Allāh, the Lord of the Worlds.

MUḤAMMAD AMĪN AL-MISRĪ
Ph.D. Cambridge Univ.,
Advisor & Head of Shari'a Department
College of Shari'a and Islāmic Studies,
Mecca Al-Mukarrama.

بسم الله الرحمن الرحيم

الحمد لله رب العالمين والصلاة والسلام على سيد المرسلين و على آله و أصحابه الغر الميامين و بعد : فاننا نحن الموقعين ادناه قد عملنا على قراءة هذه الترجمة التى قام بها الدكتور محمد محسن خان لمعانى كتاب صحيح البخارى ولقد بذلنا الوسع فى مراجعتها و تصحيحها بدقة تامة من البداية الى النهاية حتى اصبحت الترجمة اقرب ما يمكن الى الصواب فى حدود طاقتنا و جهدنا -

و اننا نحمد الله على ما وفق من انجاز هذا المشروع الطيب و نسأله ان يجزل المثوبة للذين قاموا به و اسهموا فيه جميعا والله من وراء القصد و هوالهادى الى سواء السبيل -

الاستاذ شاكر نصيف العبيدى
ماجستير فى اللغة الانكليزية من جامعة فاند زيلت الامريكية واستاذ اللغة الانكليزية فى جامعة بغداد ثم استاذ اللغة الانكليزية فى كلية التربية بمكة المكرمة

الدكتور محمود حمد نصر
خريج جامعة الخرطوم و طبيب مستشفى الملك بالمدينة المنورة

الدكتور محمد تقى الدين الهلالى
دكتوراه من جامعة برلين المانيا استاذ فى جامعة بغداد سابقا و حاليا استاذ فى جامعة محمد الخامس بالمغرب و استاذ منتدب فى الجامعة الاسلامية بالمدينة المنورة

لقد اطلعت على جزء يسير من هذه الترجمة و قد وجدت القائم على الترجمة قد وفق الى نقل معانى الجامع الصحيح الى اللغةالانكليزية با سلوب سهل ميسر قريب خال من التعقيد كما انى وجدته قد وفق الى احسن الاقوال و ارجحها فى تفسير معانى بعض الاحاديث المختلف فيها و قد تسلم العمل بتمامه الدكتور محمود حمد نصر السودانى فبذل فيه غاية وسعه و راجعه مراجعة اولى من اوله الى آخره ثم قام بمراجعته مراجعة ثانية الاستاذ شاكر نصيف العبيدى . ثم راجعه الدكتور محمد تقى الدين الهلالى مع مؤلفه الدكتور محمد محسن خان مراجعة فحص و تدقيق و بذل جهده فى اصلاح ما ظهر له من خطأ قليل حتى ظهرت الترجمة فى غاية التحقيق -

و نسأل الله ان يجزل ثواب كل من شارك فى هذا العمل المبرور و ان ينفع به . و انى واثق تمام الثقة ان الترجمة بعون الله بعد كل ما بذل لها من جهد اصبحت اقرب الى الصواب -

والله ولى التوفيق والحمد لله رب العالمين -

محمد امين المصرى

دكتوراه من جامعة كمبرج . المستشار و رئيس قسم الشريعة فى كلية الشريعة والدراسات الاسلامية فى مكة المكرمة

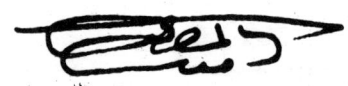

بسم الله الرحمن الرحيم

المملكة العربية السعودية
الجامعة الإسلامية
بالمدينة المنورة

الرقم
التاريخ ١٠/٤/١٣٩٨
التوابع

لمن يهمه الأمر

الدكتور محمد تقي الدين الهلالي :

الدكتور محمد محسن خان :

تقرر الامانة العامة للجامعة الاسلامية بالمدينة المنورة ان المذكورين بعاليه كانا من ضمن العاملين بالجامعة . وانهما قد قاما أثناء ذلك بترجمة معاني القرآن الكريم باللغة الانجليزية وترجمة صحيح البخاري بها أيضا .

ولقد سدت بحمد الله فراغا كبيرا يحتاج العالم الاسلامي لمثله . كما أن المذكورين يمتازان بحسن العقيدة السليمة من الشوائب . وبالصفات الحميدة .

وبناء على الرغبة اعطيها هذه الشهادة ، والله ولي التوفيق .

وصلى الله وسلم وبارك على نبينا محمد وعلى آله وصحبه .

الامين العام للجامعة

عمر محمد فلاته

GLOSSARY

'Ammā Ba'du : An expression used for separating an introductory from the main topics in a speech; the introductory being usually concerned with Allāh's praises and glorification. Literally it means "Whatever comes after".

An-Najwa : The private talk between Allāh and each of His slaves on the Day of Resurrection.

Fadak : A town near Medīna.

Ghīra : This word covers a wide meaning; jealousy as regards women, and also, it is a feeling of great anger and fury when one's honour and prestige is injured or challenged.

Ghazwa : (plural: Ghazawāt); A holy battle in the cause of Allāh, consisting of a large army unit with the Prophet ﷺ himself leading the army.

Iqāmat-aṣ-Ṣalāt : (i.e., the offering of prayers perfectly). This is not understood by many Muslims. It means that:— (A) All the members of a family or a group etc., of a town or a village etc., must offer the prayers; all males in the mosque for the five congregational prayers, and all the females in their houses, both young and old from seven years of age upwards (and no member of the family is to be excused) at the five fixed stated hours for the five compulsory prayers. If any member intentionally did not offer the prayer, then even if the others prayed, they did not establish the prayers. Each chief (of the family or a town or a village etc.) is responsible for it before Allāh.

: (B) To offer the prayers in a way just as the Prophet ﷺ offered it with all its rules and regulations (Please see Ḥadīth No. 785, 786, 788 of the First volume in order to know the Prophet's way of Praying.)

Khalīl : The one whose love is mixed with one's soul, and it is superior than a friend or a beloved. The Prophet ﷺ had only one Khalīl, i.e., Allāh but he had many friends.

Li'ān : An oath which is taken by both wife and husband when the latter accuses his wife of illegal sexual intercourse. (See Qur'ān, Sūrat-an-Nūr 24: 6–9).

Maqām-al-Maḥmūd : The most highest place in Paradise which will be granted to the Prophet Muḥammad ﷺ and none else.
(See 6th Vol., Ḥadīth 242.)

Moḥkam : Qur'ānic Verses which are not abrogated.

Mulā'ana : The act of performing Li'ān.

Mutashābihāt : Qur'ānic Verses which are difficult to understand.

Mu'wwidhāt : i.e., the Sūrat-al-Falaq (113) and Sūrat-an-Nās (114).

Qasāma : The oath taken by some people (50 men) of a tribe of a person who is being accused of killing somebody.

Qiṣāṣ : The law of equality in punishment.

Ribā' : Usury which is of two major kinds; (A) Ribā' Nasī'a, i.e., interest on lent money;
(B) Ribā' Faḍl, i.e., taking a superior thing of the same kind of goods and giving more of the same kind of goods of inferior quality, e.g., dates of superior quality for dates of inferior quality of greater amount.

Rouḥ-ul-Lāh : According to the early religious scholars from among the companions of the Prophet ﷺ and their students and the Mujtahadīn, there is a rule to distinguish between the two nouns composed as genitives:— (A) One of that is Allāh, and the other is a person or a thing, e.g., (i) Allāh's House (Bait-ul-Lāh بيت الله) (ii) Allāh's Messenger (Rasūl-lullāh رسول الله); (iii) Allāh's slave ('Abdullāh عبد الله); (iv) Allāh's Soul (Rouḥ-ul-Lāh روح الله); etc. The rule for the above words is that the second noun, e.g., house, apostle, slave, soul, etc., is created by Allāh and is honourable in His Sight, and similarly Allāh's Soul or Spirit may be understood as the Spirit or Soul of Allāh, i.e., Jesus. And it was His Word: Be! And it "was" (i.e. Jesus was created like Adam.) (B) But when one of the two is Allāh and the second is neither a person nor a thing, then it is not a created thing but is a quality of Allāh, e.g., (i) Allāh's Knowledge ('Ilmullāh علم الله); (ii) Allāh's Life (Ḥayātullāh حيات الله); (iii) Allāh's Statement (Kalāmullāh كلام الله); (iv) Allāh's Self (Dhātullāh ذات الله) etc.

Sab'a-Al-Mat͟hānī : The seven repeatedly recited Verses, i.e., Sūrat-al-Fātiḥa.

Sakīna : Tranquillity, calmness, etc.

Sariya : An army which is not led by a commander-in-chief. The army which was sent by the Prophet ﷺ without his participating in it, was called Sariya.

Sawik : A meal made of powdered roasted wheat or barley (also with sugar and dates).

Tas͟hahud : "I testify that none has the right to be worshipped but Allāh, and that Muḥammad ﷺ is His Messenger."

Tauḥīd : is of four aspects (a) Unity of Lordship, "Tauḥīd-al-Rabūbiya; to believe that there is only one Lord for the whole universe and whatever is in it, its Creator, its Maintainer and that is Allāh.

(b) Unity of Worship; "Tauḥīd-al-ulūhiya", to believe that none has the right to be worshipped but Allāh, e.g., praying, fasting, slaughtering and giving Zakāt (i.e. all kinds of worship).

(c) Unity of Names and the Qualities of Allāh "Tauḥīd-al-Asmā-Waṣ-ṣifāt." To believe that:

(i) none can be named or qualify Allāh except with what He and His Messenger ﷺ have named or qualified Him .

(ii) none can be named or qualified with the names and qualifications of Allāh, e.g., Al-Karīm,

(iii) we must confirm all Allāh's qualifications which Allāh has stated in His Book (Qur'ān) or mentioned through his Messenger ﷺ without twisting the meaning and giving resemblance to any of the created thing.

(a) (b) (c): These three aspects of Tauḥīd are included in the meaning, "None has the right to be worshipped but Allāh."

(d) Unity of following Allāh's Messenger (Muḥammad ﷺ) "Tauḥīd-al-Itibā", and this is included in the meaning of, I testify that (Muḥammad ﷺ) is Allāh's Messenger and that means: None has the right to be followed after Allāh's Book (Qur'ān), but Allāh's Messenger (Muḥammad ﷺ).

GENERAL CONTENTS

VOLUME I

1. How the Divine Inspiration started
2. The book of Belief (Faith)
3. The book of Knowledge
4. The book of Wuḍū (Ablution)
5. The book of Ghusl (Bathing)
6. The book of Menses (Menstrual Periods)
7. The book of Tayammum (Rubbing hands and face with earth)
8. The book of the Ṣalāt (Prayers)
9. The book of Sutra of Muṣallā
10. The book of the Times of the Prayers
11. The book of the Ādhān (The Call to Prayer)
12. The book of the Characteristics of Prayer

VOLUME II

13. The book of the Jumu'a (Friday) Prayer
14. The book of the Fear Prayer
15. The book of the two 'Īd Festivals
16. The book of the Witr Prayer
17. The book of Al-Istisqā' Prayer
18. The book of the Eclipse Prayer
19. Prostrations during Recitation of the Qur'ān
20. The book of At-Taqṣīr (Shortened) Prayers
21. The book of Tahajjud (Night) Prayer
22. Actions while praying
23. The book of Al-Janā'iz (Funerals)
24. The book of Zakāt, (i.e. obligatory charity)
25. Zakāt-al-Fiṭr
26. The book of Ḥajj (Pilgrimage)

VOLUME III

27. The book of 'Umra ....
28. The Muḥṣar (One, prevented from Ḥajj or 'Umra) ....
29. The Penalty for Hunting by a Muḥrim ....
30. The Virtues of Medīna ....
31. The book of Fasting ....
32. The book of Tarāwīḥ Prayers ....
33. The book of I'tikāf ....
34. The book of Sales (Bargains) ....
35. The book of As-Salām (Paid goods to be delivered later) ....
36. The book of Renting ....
37. The book of Al-Ḥawāla (Transference of debt) ....
38. The book of Representation (Authorization) ....
39. The book of Agriculture ....
40. Distribution of Water ....
41. Loans, Payment of Loans, Freezing of Property, Bankruptcy ....
42. The book of Luqaṭa (Lost things picked up) ....
43. The book of Oppression ....
44. Partnership ....
45. Mortgaging ....
46. Manumission of Slaves ....
47. The book of Gifts ....
48. The book of Witnesses ....
49. Peacemaking (Reconciliation) ....
50. The book of Conditions ....

VOLUME IV

51. The book of Wills and Testaments (Waṣāya) ....
52. The book of Jihād (Fighting for Allāh's Cause) ....
53. The Obligation of Khumus ....
54. The book of the Beginning of Creation ....
55. The book of the Prophets ....
56. The Virtues and Merits of the Prophet and his companions ....

VOLUME V

57. The Virtues and Merits of the companions of the Prophet ....
58. The Merits of the Anṣār ....
59. The book of Al-Maghāzī (The Military Expeditions) ....

VOLUME VI

60. The book of Commentary (Interpretation of the Qur'ān) ....
61. The book of the Virtues of the Qur'ān ....

VOLUME VII

62. The book of Nikāḥ (Wedlock) ....
63. The book of Divorce ....
64. The book of Provision (Outlay) ....
65. The book of food (Meals) ....
66. The book of 'Aqīqa ....
67. The book of Slaughtering and Hunting ....
68. The book of Aḍaḥī (Sacrifice slaughtered on 'Īd-al-Aḍḥā) ....
69. The book of Drinks ....
70. The book of Patients ....
71. The book of Medicine ....
72. The book of Dress ....

VOLUME VIII

73. The book of Al-Āḍāb (Good Manners) ....
74. The book of Asking Permission ....
75. The book of Invocations ....
76. The book of Ar-Riqāq (i.e., the Ḥadīth that makes the heart tender by affecting the emotions and feelings of the one who hears it) ....
77. The book of Al-Qadar (Divine Fore-ordainment) ....
78. The book of Oaths and Vows ....
79. The book of Expiation for Unfulfilled Oaths ....
80. The book of Al-Farā'iḍ (The Laws of Inheritance) ....

81. The book of Ḥudūd (Allāh's set limits and punishment for those who violate them) ....
82. The book of (the punishment of) those who wage war (against Allāh and His Apostle) from the unbelievers and of those who have reverted from Islām....

VOLUME IX

83. The book of Ad-Diyāt (Blood Money)..
84. The book of Obliging the Reverters from Islām (Apostates) to repent, and those who refuse the truth obstinately (though they know that it is the truth) and to fight against them ....
85. The book of Ikrāh (Coertion) i.e., saying something under compulsion......
86. The book of Tricks ....
87. The book of the Interpretation of Dreams ....
88. The book of Afflictions ....
89. The book of Aḥkām (Judgements) ....
90. The book of Wishes ....
91. Regarding the acceptance of the information given by one truthful person concerning the Ādhān, the prayer, the fasting and all other obligations and laws prescribed by Allāh ....
92. The book of Holding fast to the Qur'ān and the Tradition (of the Prophet ﷺ). ....
93. The book of Tauḥīd (i.e. monotheism, the belief in the Oneness of Allāh)....

END OF ṢAḤĪḤ-AL-BUKHĀRĪ

Volume VI

CONTENTS

Pages

Glossary . . . . vii - ix
General Contents. . . . . x - xiii
Contents . . . . xiv - xxiii

LX. THE BOOK OF COMMENTARY (Interpretation of the Holy Qur'ān): CHAPTERS:–

1. 'Fātiḥatul-Kitāb (The Opening Chapter of the Book) 1
2. 'Not (the path) of those who earn Your anger ...' (1:7). 2
3. 'And He (Allāh) taught Adam all the names.' (2:31) 3
4. 'With their devils,' (2:14) 5
5. 'Then set not up rivals unto Allāh...' (2:22) 6
6. 'And We caused the clouds to overshadow you.' (2:57) 7
7. 'We said: "Enter this town and eat..." ' (2:58). 7
8. 'Whoever is an enemy to Gabriel...' (2:97) 8
9. 'Whatever Verse (revelation) do We abrogate...' (2:106) 10
10. 'They say: "Allāh has begotten offspring..." ' (2:116) 10
11. 'Take you (people) the station of Abraham...' (2:125). 11
12. 'Remember when Abraham and Ishmael were raising...' (2:127). 12
13. 'Say (O Muslims): "We believe in Allāh...' (2:136) 13
14. 'The fools among the people will say:...' (2:142) 14
15. 'Thus We have made you a just nation...' (2:143) 15
16. 'We made the Qibla (Prayer Direction)...' (2:143). 15
17. 'We see the turning of your faces...' (2:144) 16
18. 'Even if you were to bring to the people...' (2:145) 16
19. 'Those to whom We gave the Scripture...' (2:146). 17
20. 'For every nation, there is a direction...' (2:148). 18
21. 'Verily! (the mountains) Ṣafā and Marwa...' (2:158). 19
22. 'Yet of mankind are some who take others...' (2:165) 21
23. '....the law of Al-Qiṣāṣ (equality in punishment) is made compulsory' (2:178) 22
24. '....Fasting is made compulsory for you...' (2:183) 24
25. '(Fasting) for a fixed number of days...' (2:184). 25
26. 'So whoever of you is present (at his home)...' (2:185). 27
27. 'To have sexual relation with your wives is permitted...' (2:187) 27
28. 'And eat and drink until the white thread...' (2:187) 28
29. 'And it is not righteousness that you enter...' (2:189). 30

Pages

30. 'And fight them until there is no affliction...' (2:193) 30
31. 'And spend in the Cause of Allāh...' (2:195) 32
32. 'And whoever of you is ill...' (2:196) 33
33. 'And whoever preformed the 'Umra...' (2:196) 34
34. 'There is no harm for you if you seek of the bounty...' (2:198) 34
35. 'Then depart from the place...' (2:199) 35
36. '.....those who say: "O Lord! Give us good...' (2:201) 36
37. 'Yet he is the most quarrelsome...' (2:204) 37
38. 'Your wives are as a tilth unto you...' (2:223) 38
39. 'And when you have divorced women...' (2:232) 39
40. 'Those of you who die and leave wives...' (2:234) 40
41. 'Guard strictly your (five obligatory) prayers...' (2:238) 43
42. 'Stand before Allāh in obedience...' (2:238) 44
43. 'If you fear (an enemy), pray on foot...' (2:239) 44
44. 'Those of you who die and leave wives behind.' (2:240) 46
45. 'When Abraham said: "My Lord show...' (2:260) 47
46. 'Do any of you wish to have...' (2:266) 47
47. 'They do not beg of people at all...' (2:273) 48
48. 'But Allāh has permitted bargaining and has forbidden Ribā.' (2:275) 49
49. 'Allāh will destroy Ribā.' (2:276) 49
50. 'Take notice of war from Allāh...' (2:279) 50
51. 'And be afraid of a day when you shall be brought back' (2:281) 51
52. 'Whether you show what is in your minds...' (2:284) 51
53. 'The Messenger ﷺ believes in what has been revealed.' (2:285) 51
54. 'And I seek refuge with You (Allāh) for her...' (3:35) 54
55. **'Verily! Those who Purchase a small gain...' (3:77)** 54
56. 'Say: "O the people of the Scripture ...' (3:64) 56
57. 'By no means shall you attain righteousness...' (3:92) 62
58. 'Say: "Bring here the Torah and recite it.." ' (3:93) 63
59. 'You are the best of peoples...' (3:110) 64
60. 'When two parties from among you ...' **(3:122)** 65
61. 'Not for you is the decision.' (3:128) 65
62. 'And the Apostle in your rear was calling...' (3:153) 67
63. ' He sent down security...' (3:154) 67
64. 'Those who answered (the call of) Allāh...' (3:174) 68
65. '...the people have gathered against you...' (3:173) 68
66. 'Let not those who covetously withhold...' (3:180) 69
67. 'And you shall certainly hear much...' (3:186) 70
68. 'Think not that those who rejoice...' (3:188) 72
69. 'In the creation of the Heavens and the Earth...' (3:90) 74
70. 'Those who remember Allāh...' (3:191) 75
71. 'Our Lord! Verily whom You admit...' (3:192) 76

Pages
72. 'Our Lord! Verily We have heard the call...' (3:193) .... .77
73. 'If you fear that you shall not be able...' (4:3) .... .79
74. '(If the guardian is) poor...' (4:6) .... .81
75. '...at the time of division...' (4:8) .... .81
76. 'Allāh commands you...' (4:11).. .82
77. 'In what your wives leave, your share is half.' (4:12)................. .82
78. '...you are forbidden to inherit women...' (4:19)....................... .83
79. '...We have appointed heirs...' (4:33)..................................... .84
80. 'Allāh wrongs not...' (4:40)... .85
81. 'How, then when We bring from each nation a witness...' (4:41) ...... .87
82. 'And if you are ill or on a journey...' (4:43) .... .88
83. 'Obey Allāh and obey the Apostle...' (4:59) .... .89
84. '...they have no faith until...' (4:65) .... .89
85. '...are in the company of those on whom...' (4:69) .... .90
86. 'And why should you not fight...' (4:75) .... .91
87. 'Why should you be divided into two parties...' (4:88) .... .92
88. 'When there comes to them some matter...' (4:83) .... .92
89. 'And whoever kills a believer intentionally...' (4:93)................. .93
90. 'And say not to anyone who offers you peace...' (4:94) .... .93
91. 'Not equal are those believers who sit (at home)...' (4:95) .... .94
92. 'Whom the angels take (in death)...' (4:97) .... .96
93. 'For those there is hope...' (4:99) .... .97
94. 'But there is no blame on you...' (4:102) .... .98
95. 'They ask your instructions concerning women...' (4:127) .... .98
96. 'The hypocrites will be in the lowest depths...' (4:145)............. .100
97. 'We have sent you inspiration...' (4:163)................................. .100
98. 'They ask you for a legal decision...' (4:176)............................ .101
99. 'You have nothing.' (5:68) .... .102
100. 'This day I have perfected your religion...' (5:3) .... .102
101. 'And (if) you find no water...' (5:6) .... .103
102. 'Go you and your Lord and fight...' (5:24) .... .105
103. 'The only reward of those who wage war...' (5:33) .... .106
104. 'And wounds...' (5:45) .... .108
105. '...preach that which has been sent down.' (5:67) .... .109
106. 'Allāh will not punish you...' (5:89) .... .109
107. '...do not make unlawful the good things...' (5:87) .... .110
108. 'Alcoholic drinks and gambling and Anṣāb...' (5:90)................. .111
109. (A) '...there is no blame for what they ate...' (5:93) .... .113
109. (B) '...ask not questions about things (5:101) .... .113
110. 'Allāh has not instituted Baḥīra or Sā'iba...' (5:103) .... .115
111. 'And I was a witness over them while...' (5:117)...................... .116
112. 'If You do punish them... (5:118) .... .117

Pages

196. 'The angels say We descend not...' (19:64) 227
197. 'Have you then seen him... (19:77) 228
198. 'Has he known the Unseen...' (19:78) 228
199. 'Nay! We shall record what he says..' (19:79) 229
200. **'And we shall inherit from him all that he talks of...' (19:80)** 230
201. 'And I have chosen you for Myself...' (20:41) 232
202. 'We inspired Moses...' (30:77-79) 233
203. 'So let him not get you both...' (20:117) 233
204. 'As We began the first creation...' (21:104) 235
205. 'And you shall see mankind...' (22:2) 237
206. 'And among men is he who worships...' (22:11) 238
207. **'These two opponents ...'** (22:19) 239
208. 'As for those who accuse their wives...' (24:6) 242
209. 'And the fifth testimony...' (24:7) 244
210. 'But it would avert the punishment...' (24:8) 245
211. 'And the fifth (testimony) should be...' (24:9) 247
212. 'They who spread the slander...'(24:11) 247
213. 'Why did not the believers...' (24:12-13) 248
214. 'Had it not for the Grace and Mercy of Allāh...' (24:14) 257
215. 'When you welcomed it...' (24:15) 258
216. 'And why did you not, when you heard it...' (24:16) 258
217. 'Allāh admonished you...' (24:17) 259
218. 'And Allāh makes the signs plain to you...' (24:18) 260
219. 'Those who like that slander...' (24:19-20) 261
220. 'They should cover their bosoms...' (24:31) 267
221. 'Those who will be gathered to Hell...' (25:34) 268
222. 'Those who invoke not with Allāh...' (25:68) 269
223. **'The torment will be doubled to him on the day of Resurrection...' (25:69)** 271
224. 'Except those who repent, believe and ...' (25:70) 272
225. 'So the torment will be ...' (25:77) 273
226. 'And disgrace me not...' (26:87) 275
227. 'And warn your tribe of near kinsmen...' (26:214-215) 275
228. 'You will not be able to guide those...' (28:56) 278
229. 'Verily, He, Who has given you the Qur'ān...' (28:85) 280
230. 'There be no change in the religion of Allāh.' (30:30) 283
231. (O my son) join not in worship others with Allāh..' (31:13) 284
232. 'Verily, the knowledge of the Hour...' (31:34) 285
233. 'No soul knows what is kept hidden...' (32:17) 288
234. 'The Prophet is closer to the believers...' (33:6) 289
235. 'Call them (by the names of) their father ...' (33:5) 290
236. '...Who have been true to their covenant...' (33:23) 290
237. 'O Prophet! Say to your wives...' (33:28) 292

Pages
238. 'But if you seek Allāh...' (33:29) 292
239. 'But you did hide in your mind...' (33:37) 294
240. 'You can postpone...' (33:51) 294
241. 'Enter not the Prophet's houses...' (33:53-54) 296
242. 'Whether you reveal anything...' (33:54-55) 301
243. 'Allāh sends Blessings...' (33:56) 302
244. 'Be you not like those who annoyed...' (33:69) 304
245. 'Yet when fear is banished...' (34:23) 306
246. 'He is only a warner...' (33:46) 307
247. 'And the sun runs its course...' (36:38) 308
248. 'Verily! Jonah was one of the Apostles...' (37:139) 311
249. 'Grant me a kingdom...' (38:35) 313
250. 'Nor am I a person who pretends things which do not exist...' (38:86) 314
251. 'O My slaves who have trangressed...' (39:53) 316
252. 'They have made of Allāh...' (39:67) 317
253. 'On the Day of Resurrection the whole of the earth...' (39:67) 318
254. 'And the trumpet will be blown...' (39:68) 318
255. 'There will be no kinship...' (23:101) 321
256. 'You did not seek to hide...' (41:22) 324
257. 'And that thought of yours...' (41:23) 325
258. 'Then if they have patience...' (41:24) 326
259. 'Except to be kind to me...' (42:23) 327
260. 'They will call: "O Malik!...' (43:77) 329
261. 'Then watch for the Day...' (44:10) 331
262. 'Covering the people: This... **(44:11)** 331
263. 'Our Lord! Remove the punishment...' (44:12) 333
264. 'How can there be ...' **(44:13)** 334
265. 'Then they had turned away from him... '**(44:14)** 335
266. 'On the Day when we shall seize you... '**(44:16)** 336
267. 'And nothing destroys us but Time'. (45:24) 337
268. 'But he who says to his parents...' (46:17) 338
269. 'Then when they saw a cloud...' (46:24) 339
270. 'And sever your ties of kith and kin., '(47:22) 340
271. 'Verily, We have granted you a manifest victory.' (48:1) 342
272. 'That Allāh may forgive your faults...' (48:2) 344
273. 'Truly We have sent you as a witness...' (48:8) 345
274. 'It is He Who sent down tranquillity...' (48:4) 346
275. 'When they swore allegiance to you... '(48:18) 346
276. 'Raise not your voices above the voice...' (49:2) 349
277. 'Those who shout out to you...' (49:4) 351
278. 'If only they had patience until...' (49:5) 352

Pages

279. 'It will say: "Are there anymore...' (50:30) .353
280. 'And celebrate the praises...' (50:39) .354
281. 'And that was at a distance...' (53:9) .360
282. 'So did Allāh convey the inspiration...' (53:10) .360
283. 'For truly did he see the signs...' (53:18) .361
284. 'Have you seen the Lāt and the 'Uzza?' (53:19) .361
285. 'And Manāt the third.' (53:20) .362
286. 'So fall you down in prostration to Allāh and worship Him.' (53:62) .363
287. 'And the moon is cleft assunder...' (54:1-2) .365
288 'Floating under Our Eyes... '(54:14-15) .366
289. 'And We have indeed made the Qur'ān...' (54:17) .367
290. 'And they became like the dry stubble...: (54:31-32) .368
291. 'Their multitude will be put to flight...' (54:45) .369
292. 'Nay, but the Hour (of Judgement) is their...' (54:46) .369
293. 'And beside these two...' (55:62) .373
294. 'Beautiful females restrained in the pavilions.' (55:72) .374
295. 'The shade long extended.' (56:30) .376
296. 'Whether you cut down...' (59:5) .378
297. 'What Allāh has given as booty...' (59:7) .379
298. 'And what the Messenger gives you.' (59:7) .379
299. 'But those who, before them, had homes...' (59:9) .381
300. 'But they prefer (the emigrants)...' (59:9) .382
301. 'Take not my enemies and your enemies as friends.' (60:1) .383
302. 'When there come to you believeing women...' (60:12) .385
303. 'O Prophet! When believeing women...' (60:12) .386
304. 'And He has sent him (Muḥammad ﷺ)...' (62:3) .390
305. 'But when they see some bargain...' (62:11) .391
306. 'When the hypocrites come to you...' (63:1) .391
307. 'They have made their oaths...' (63:1-2) .393
308. 'This is because they believed...' (63:3) .394
309. 'When you look at them...' (63:4) .395
310. 'And when it is said to them...' (63:5) .396
311. 'It is equal to them whether you ask... (63:6) .397
312. 'These are the ones who say...' (67:3) .398
313. 'They say: "If we return to Medīna...' (63:8) .399
314. 'For those who are pregnant...' (64:5) .402
315. 'O Prophet! Why do you ban that which...' (66:1) .403
316. 'You seek to please your wives...' (66:2) .405
317. 'When the Prophet disclosed a matter...' (66:3) .408
318. 'If you two turn in repentance...' (66:4) .409
319. 'It may be, if he divorced you all...' (66:5) .410

Pages

320. 'Cruel after all that...' (68:13) 411
321. The day that when the severest Hour will be fall...'(68:42) 412
322. 'Forsake not Wadd nor Suwa...' (71:23) 414
323. 'And magnify your Lord...' (74:3) 418
324. 'And keep your garments pure.' (74:4) 420
325. 'And desert the idols.' (74:5) 420
326. 'Move not your tongue...' (75:16) 421
327. 'It is for Us to collect (it in your mind)...' (75:17) 422
328. 'When We have revealed it to you...' (75:18) 423
329. 'Indeed, it throws about sparks...' (77:32) 427
330. 'As if they were yellow camels...'(77:33) 427
331. 'That will be a Day when...' (77:35) 428
332. 'The Day that the trumpet will be blown...' (78:18) 429
333. 'A Day when all mankind will stand before...' (83:6) 433
334. 'His account will be taken...' (84:8) 434
335. 'You shall surely travel...' (84:19) 435
336. 'By the day as it.' (92:2) 440
337. 'By Him Who created male and female.' (92:3) 441
338. 'As for He Who gives...' (92:5) 442
339. '....and believes in the best.' (92:6) 443
340. 'We will indeed make smooth for him...' (92:7) 443
341. 'But he who is a greedy miser...' (92:8) 444
342. 'And disbelieves the Best...' (92:9) 445
343. 'We will make smooth for him...' (92:10) 446
344. 'Your Lord has not forsaken you...' (93:3) 447
345. 'Your Lord has not forsaken you...' (93:3) 450
346. '(He) created man out of a clot...' (96:2) 453
347. 'Read! And your Lord is Most Generous.' (96:3) 454
348. 'Who teaches (his slaves) by the pen.' (96:4) 454
349. 'Let him beware if he does not cease...' (96:15-16) 455
350. 'So whoever does good...' (99:7) 457
351. 'And Whoever does evil...' (99:8) 459
352. 'And (when) you see the people...' (110:2) 464
353. 'Celebrate the praises of your Lord...' (110:3) 465
354. 'Perish he! No profit to him...' (111:1-2) 468
355. 'He (Abū Lahb) will be burnt...' (111:3) 468
356. 'His wife too, who carries the wood...' (111:4) 469
357. 'Allāh, the Self-Sufficient Master Whom all creatures need...' (112:3) 470
358. 'He does not beget...' (112:3-4) 470

LXI. THE BOOK OF THE VIRTUE OF THE QUR'ĀN:

Pages

1. How the Divine Inspiration used to be revealed 473
2. The Qur'ān was revealed in the language of Quraish 475
3. The collection of the Qur'ān 476
4. The scribe of the Prophet 480
5. Recitation in seven different ways 481
6. The compilation of the Qur'ān 483
7. Gabriel recited the Qur'ān 485
8. The Qurrā' among the Companions 486
9. The superiority of Fātiḥa-al-Kitāb 489
10. The superiority of Sūrat-al-Baqara 491
11. The superiority of Sūrat-al-Kahf 492
12. The superiority of Sūrat-al-Fatḥ 492
13. The superiority of Sūrat-al-Ikhlāṣ 493
14. The superiority of Sūrat-al-Falaq & Sūrat-an-Nās 495
15. The descent of tranquillity and Angels on recitation 496
16. The Prophet ﷺ did not leave anything after his death except the Qur'an 497
17. The superiority of the Qur'ān 497
18. To recommend the Book of Allāh 499
19. Recitation in a pleasant tone 499
20. Wish to be the like of the reciter 500
21. Learn the Qur'ān and teach it 501
22. Reciting the Qur'ān by heart 503
23. Reciting Qur'ān repeatedly 504
24. Reciting Qur'ān on an animal 506
25. Teaching the Qur'ān to children 506
26. Forgetting the Qur'ān 507
27. Saying "Sūrat-al-Baqara" etc. 508
28. Recitation in a slow, clear, rhythmic tone 510
29. Prolonging certain sounds 512
30. Recitation in an attractive vibrating tone 513
31. Recitation in a charming voice 514
32. Listening to the recitationof the Qur'ān 514
33. Saying of recitation: "Enough!" 515
34. The proper period for reciting the whole Qur'ān 515
35. Weeping while reciting the Qur'ān 518
36. Reciting the Qur'ān to show off 519
37. Recite and study the Qur'ān together 521

In the name of Allāh,
the Most Beneficent, the Most Merciful.

بِسْمِ اللهِ الرَّحْمٰنِ الرَّحِيمِ

LX. BOOK OF COMMENTARY:
(Interpretation of the Holy Qur'ān:—

كتاب التفسير

The words 'Ar-Raḥmān', 'Ar-Raḥīm' (i.e. The Most Beneficent, the Most Merciful) are two words derived from 'Ar Raḥma' (i.e. Mercy). and the words 'Ar-Raḥīm' and 'Ar-Rāḥim' have one meaning as the words 'Al-Ālim' and 'Al-Ālim' have one and the same meaning (i.e. the Cognizant One).

الرَّحْمَنُ الرَّحِيمُ : اسْمَانِ مِنَ الرَّحْمَةِ . الرَّحِيمُ وَالرَّاحِمُ بِمَعْنًى وَاحِدٍ ، كَالعَلِيمِ وَالعَالِمِ .

In the Name of Allāh,
The Most Beneficent, the Most Merciful

بِسْمِ اللهِ الرَّحْمٰنِ الرَّحِيمِ

SŪRAT-AL-FĀTIḤA (1)

سورة الفاتحه

(1) CHAPTER. What has been said about Fātiḥa-tul-Kitāb (1) (i.e. The Opening of the Book). It is also called Um-ul-Kitāb (i.e. The Mother of the Book), i.e. because it is the first Sūra that has been written in the copies of the Qur'ān, and it is also the first Sūra to be recited in prayer.

بابُ ما جاءَ في فاتحةِ الكتابِ . وسُمِّيَتْ أُمَّ الكتابِ أنَّهُ يُبْدَأُ بكتابتِها في المَصاحِفِ . ويُبْدَأُ بقراءتِها في الصَّلاةِ . الدِّينُ : الجزاءُ في الخيرِ والشَّرِّ ، كما تَدِينُ تُدانُ . وقالَ مُجاهِدٌ : بالدِّينِ : بالحِسابِ . مَدِينِينَ : مُحاسَبِينَ .

1. Narrated Abū Sa'īd bin Al-Mu'allā: While I was praying in the Mosque, Allāh's Messenger ﷺ called me but I did not respond to him. Later I said, "O Allāh's Messenger! I was praying." He said, "Didn't Allāh say'—

١ - حدَّثنا مُسَدَّدٌ : حدَّثنا يَحيى ، عن شُعبةَ ، قالَ : حدَّثني خُبَيبُ بنُ عبدِ الرَّحمنِ ، عن حفصِ ابنِ عاصمٍ ، عن أبي سعيدِ بنِ المُعَلَّى

(1) First Sūra in the Holy Qur'ān.

'I am not fit for this undertaking.' He will remember his appeal to his Lord to do something of which he had no knowledge, then he will feel ashamed thereof and will say, 'Go to the Khalīl-Ar-Raḥmān (1) (i.e. Abraham).' They will go to him and he will say, 'I am not fit for this undertaking. Go to Moses, the slave to whom Allāh spoke (directly) and gave him the Torah.' So they will go to him and he will say, 'I am not fit for this undertaking.' and he will mention (his) killing a person who was not a killer, and so he will feel ashamed thereof before his Lord, and he will say, 'Go to Jesus, Allāh's Slave, His Messenger and Allāh's Word and a Spirit coming from Him. (2) Jesus will say, 'I am not fit for this undertaking, go to Muḥammad ﷺ the Slave of Allāh whose past and future sins were forgiven by Allāh.' So they will come to me and I will proceed till I will ask my Lord's Permission and I will be given permission. When I see my Lord, I will fall down in Prostration and He will let me remain in that state as long as He wishes and then I will be addressed.' (Muḥammad!) Raise your head. Ask, and your request will be granted; say, and your saying will be listened to; intercede, and your intercession will be accepted.' I will raise my head and praise Allāh with a saying (i.e. invocation) He will teach me, and then I will intercede. He will fix a limit

مِنْ مَكَانِنَا هَذَا، فَيَقُولُ: لَسْتُ هُنَاكُمْ وَيَذْكُرُ ذَنْبَهُ فَيَسْتَحِي، ائْتُوا نُوحًا فَإِنَّهُ أَوَّلُ رَسُولٍ بَعَثَهُ اللهُ إِلَى أَهْلِ الأَرْضِ فَيَأْتُونَهُ فَيَقُولُ: لَسْتُ هُنَاكُمْ وَيَذْكُرُ سُؤَالَهُ رَبَّهُ مَا لَيْسَ لَهُ بِهِ عِلْمٌ فَيَسْتَحِي، فَيَقُولُ: ائْتُوا خَلِيلَ الرَّحْمَنِ. فَيَأْتُونَهُ فَيَقُولُ لَسْتُ: هُنَاكُمْ، ائْتُوا مُوسَى عَبْدًا كَلَّمَهُ اللهُ وَأَعْطَاهُ التَّوْرَاةَ. فَيَأْتُونَهُ فَيَقُولُ: لَسْتُ هُنَاكُمْ وَيَذْكُرُ قَتْلَ النَّفْسِ بِغَيْرِ نَفْسٍ فَيَسْتَحِي مِنْ رَبِّهِ فَيَقُولُ: ائْتُوا عِيسَى عَبْدَ اللهِ وَرَسُولَهُ وَكَلِمَةَ اللهِ وَرُوحَهُ، فَيَقُولُ لَسْتُ: هُنَاكُمْ، ائْتُوا مُحَمَّدًا صلى الله عليه وسلم عَبْدًا غَفَرَ اللهُ لَهُ مَا تَقَدَّمَ مِنْ ذَنْبِهِ وَمَا تَأَخَّرَ. فَيَأْتُونِي فَأَنْطَلِقُ حَتَّى أَسْتَأْذِنَ عَلَى رَبِّي فَيُؤْذَنُ، فَإِذَا رَأَيْتُ رَبِّي وَقَعْتُ سَاجِدًا فَيَدَعُنِي مَا شَاءَ اللهُ ثُمَّ يُقَالُ: ارْفَعْ رَأْسَكَ وَسَلْ تُعْطَهُ، وَقُلْ يُسْمَعْ، وَاشْفَعْ تُشَفَّعْ. فَأَرْفَعُ رَأْسِي فَأَحْمَدُهُ بِتَحْمِيدٍ يُعَلِّمُنِيهِ. ثُمَّ أَشْفَعُ فَيَحُدُّ لِي حَدًّا فَأُدْخِلُهُمُ الجَنَّةَ. ثُمَّ أَعُودُ إِلَيْهِ فَإِذَا

(1) The intimate friend of the Beneficent (Allāh).

(2) This may be understood as the Spirit or Soul of Allāh, in fact, it is a soul created by Allāh, i.e. Jesus. It was His Word: 'Be,' and it was created like the creation of Adam. Please see the word 'Rouḥ-ullāh' in the glossary for further details.

for me (to intercede for) whom I will admit into Paradise. Then I will come back again to Allāh, and when I see my Lord, the same thing will happen to me. And then I will intercede and Allāh will fix a limit for me to intercede whom I will admit into Paradise, then I will come back for the third time; and then I will come back for the fourth time, and will say, 'None remains in Hell but those whom the Qur'ān has imprisoned (in Hell) and who have been destined to an eternal stay in Hell.' " (The compiler) Abū 'Abdullāh said: 'But those whom the Qur'ān has imprisoned in Hell,' refers to the Statement of Allāh تعالى :-

'To dwell therein forever.' (16:29)

رَأَيْتُ رَبِّي مِثْلَهُ ثُمَّ أَشْفَعُ فَيَحُدُّ لِي
حَدًّا فَأُدْخِلُهُمُ الْجَنَّةَ. ثُمَّ أَعُودُ
الثَّالِثَةَ، ثُمَّ أَعُودُ الرَّابِعَةَ فَأَقُولُ مَا
بَقِيَ فِي النَّارِ إِلَّا مَنْ حَبَسَهُ الْقُرْآنُ
وَوَجَبَ عَلَيْهِ الْخُلُودُ. قَالَ أَبُو عَبْدِ اللهِ :
إِلَّا مَنْ حَبَسَهُ الْقُرْآنُ : يَعْنِي قَوْلَ اللهِ
تَعَالَى - خَالِدِينَ فِيهَا -

(4) CHAPTER. Mujāhid said.

" 'With their devils.' (2:14)

means their companions from the hypocrites and the pagans." (Qur'ānic vocabulary not translated.)

بَابٌ - قَالَ مُجَاهِدٌ - إِلَى شَيَاطِينِهِمْ -
أَصْحَابِهِمْ مِنَ الْمُنَافِقِينَ وَالْمُشْرِكِينَ -
مُحِيطٌ بِالْكَافِرِينَ - اللهُ جَامِعُهُمْ - صِبْغَةَ -
دِينٌ - عَلَى الْخَاشِعِينَ - عَلَى الْمُؤْمِنِينَ
حَقًّا، قَالَ مُجَاهِدٌ : بِقُوَّةٍ يَعْمَلُ بِمَا

فيه . وقال أبو العالية - مرض - شك
وما خلفها عبرة لمن بقي - لاشية -
لا بياض وقال غيره - يسومونكم -
يولونكم . الولاية : مفتوحة مصدر
الولاء وهي الربوبية ، وإذا كسرت
الواو فهي الإمارة . وقال بعضهم :
الحبوب التي تؤكل كلها فوم ، وقال
قتادة - فباءوا - فانقلبوا . وقال غيره -
يستفتحون - يستنصرون - شروا -
باعوا - راعنا - من الرعونة إذا أرادوا
أن يحمقوا إنسانا قالوا راعنا - لا تجزي -
لا تغني - خطوات - من الخطو والمعنى
آثاره . - ابتلى - اختبر .

(5) CHAPTER. The Statement of Allāh تعالى :-

'Then do not set up rivals unto Allāh (in worship) while you know (that He Alone has the right to be worshipped).' (2:22)

باب قوله تعالى - فلا تجعلوا لله أندادا وأنتم تعلمون - .

4. Narrated 'Abdullāh رضي الله عنه : I asked the Prophet ﷺ, "What is the greatest sin in the Sight of Allāh?" He said, "That you set up a rival unto Allāh though He Alone created you." I said, "That is indeed a great sin." Then I asked, "What is next?" He said, "To kill your son lest he should share your food with you." I asked, "What is next?" He said, "To commit illegal sexual intercourse with the wife of your neighbour."

٤ - حدثنا عثمان بن أبي شيبة :
حدثنا جرير ، عن منصور ، عن أبي
وائل ، عن عمرو بن شرحبيل ،
عن عبد الله قال : سألت النبي صلى
الله عليه وسلم : أي الذنب أعظم عند
الله ؟ قال : أن تجعل لله ندا وهو
خلقك ، قلت : إن ذلك لعظيم ، قلت :

ثُمَّ أيٌّ ؟ قالَ : وأنْ تقتُلَ ولَدَكَ تخافُ أنْ يطْعَمَ معَكَ ، قُلْتُ : ثُمَّ أيٌّ ؟ قالَ : أنْ تُزانِيَ حَلِيلَةَ جارِكَ .

(6) CHAPTER. 'And We caused the clouds to overshadow you and sent down on you Manna and Salwā (i.e. Quails)..............but they harmed their own souls.'

(2:57)

Mujāhid said,"Manna is a kind of sweet gum, and "Salwa", a kind of bird (i.e. Quail).

باب - وظَلَّلْنا علَيْكُمُ الغَمامَ وأنزَلْنا علَيْكُمُ المَنَّ والسَّلْوَى - إلى - يَظْلِمونَ - . وقالَ مُجاهِدٌ : المَنُّ : صَمْغَةٌ . والسَّلْوَى : الطَّيْرُ .

5. Narrated Sa'īd bin Zaid : Allāh's Messenger said, "The Kam'a (i.e. a kind of edible fungus) is like the Manna (in that it is obtained without effort) and its water is a (medicine) cure for eye trouble."

٥ - حدَّثَنا أبو نُعَيْمٍ : حدَّثَنا سُفْيانُ : عَنْ عَبْدِ المَلِكِ ، عَنْ عَمْرِو ابنِ حُرَيْثٍ ، عَنْ سَعِيدِ بنِ زَيْدٍ رَضِيَ اللهُ عَنْهُ قالَ : قالَ رَسُولُ اللهِ صلى اللهُ عليهِ وسلَّم : الكَمْأةُ مِنَ المَنِّ وماؤُها شِفاءٌ للعَيْنِ .

(7) CHAPTER. 'And (remember) when We said: Enter this town(Jerusalem) and eat bountifully therein wherever you wish.' (2:58)

بابٌ - وإذْ قُلْنا ادْخُلوا هذِهِ القَرْيَةَ فَكُلُوا مِنْها حَيْثُ شِئْتُمْ - الآيَةَ - رَغَدًا - واسِعًا كَثِيرًا .

6. Narrated Abū Huraira : The Prophet said, "It was said to the children of Israel, 'Enter the gate (of the town), prostrate (in humility) and say: Ḥiṭṭatun (i.e. repentance) i.e. O Allāh!

٦ - حدَّثَنا مُحَمَّدٌ : حدَّثَني عَبْدُ الرَّحْمَنِ بنُ مَهْدِيٍّ ، عَنْ ابنِ المُبارَكِ ، عَنْ مَعْمَرٍ ، عَنْ هَمَّامِ بنِ

Forgive our sins.' But they entered by dragging themselves on their buttocks, so they did something different (from what they had been ordered to do) and said, 'Ḥiṭṭatun,' but added, "A grain in a hair.' " (1)

مُنَبِّهٍ ، عَنْ أَبِي هُرَيْرَةَ رَضِيَ اللهُ عَنْهُ ، عَنِ النَّبِيِّ صلى الله عليه وسلّم قالَ : قِيلَ لِبَنِي إِسْرَائِيلَ ادْخُلُوا البَابَ سُجَّدًا وَقُولُوا حِطَّةٌ فَدَخَلُوا يَزْحَفُونَ عَلَى أَسْتَاهِهِمْ فَبَدَّلُوا وَقَالَ حِطَّةٌ : حَبَّةٌ فِي شَعْرَةٍ .

(8) CHAPTER. 'Whoever is an enemy to Gabriel...' (2:97)

بابٌ - مَنْ كانَ عَدُوًّا لِجِبْرِيلَ -

'Ikrima said, "Each of the words: Jabrā and Mīka and Sarāf means 'slave', and (the word) 'īl means Allāh." (2)

وقالَ عِكْرِمَةُ : جَبْرَ ، ومِيكَ ، وسَرَافِ : عَبْدٌ ، إِيلْ : اللهُ .

7. Narrated Anas ﷺ : 'Abdullāh bin Salām heard the news of the arrival of Allāh's Messenger ﷺ (at Medīna) while he was on a farm collecting its fruits. So he came to the Prophet ﷺ and said, "I will ask you about three things which nobody knows unless he be a prophet. Firstly, what is the first portent of the Hour? What is the first meal of the people of Paradise? And what makes a baby look like its father or mother?'. The Prophet ﷺ said, "Just now Gabriel has informed me about that." 'Abdullāh said, "Gabriel?" The Prophet ﷺ said, "Yes." 'Abdullāh said, "He, among the angels is

٧ - حَدَّثَنَا عَبْدُ اللهِ بنُ مُنِيرٍ : سَمِعَ عَبْدَ اللهِ بنَ بَكْرٍ ، حَدَّثَنَا حُمَيْدٌ ، عَنْ أَنَسٍ قالَ : سَمِعَ عَبْدُ اللهِ بنُ سَلَامٍ بِقُدُومِ رَسُولِ اللهِ صلى الله عليه وسلّم وَهُوَ فِي أَرْضٍ يَخْتَرِفُ ، فَأَتَى النَّبِيَّ صلى الله عليه وسلّم فَقَالَ : إِنِّي سَائِلُكَ عَنْ ثَلَاثٍ لا يَعْلَمُهُنَّ إِلَّا نَبِيٌّ ، فَمَا أَوَّلُ أَشْرَاطِ السَّاعَةِ ؟ وَمَا أَوَّلُ طَعَامِ أَهْلِ الجَنَّةِ ؟ وَمَا يَنْزِعُ الوَلَدُ

(1) They said so just to redicule Allāh's Order as they were disobedient to Him.

(2) Thus Jibrāīl (i.e. Gabriel), Mīkā'īl (i.e. Michael) and 'Esrāfīl (i.e. Sarafil) each means Allāh's Slave.

the enemy of the Jews." On that the Prophet ﷺ recited this Holy Verse:—

> 'Whoever is an enemy to Gabriel (let him die in his fury!) for he has brought it (i.e. Qur'ān) down to your heart by Allāh's permission. (2:97)

Then he added, "As for the first portent of the Hour, it will be a fire that will collect the people from the East to West. And as for the first meal of the people of Paradise, it will be the caudite (i.e. extra) lobe of the fish liver. And if a man's discharge preceeded that of the woman, then the child resembles the father, and if the woman's discharge preceeded that of the man, then the child resembles the mother." On hearing that, 'Abdullāh said, "I testify that None has the right to be worshipped but Allāh, and that you are the Apostle of Allāh, O, Allāh's Messenger; the Jews are liars, and if they should come to know that I have embraced Islām, they would accuse me of being a liar." In the meantime some Jews came (to the Prophet ﷺ) and he asked them, "What is 'Abdullāh's status amongst you?" They replied, "He is the best amongst us, and he is our chief and the son of our chief." The Prophet ﷺ said, "What would you think if 'Abdullāh bin Salām embraced Islām?" They replied, "May Allāh protect him from this!" Then 'Abdullāh came out and said, "I testify that None has the right to be worshipped but Allāh and that Muḥammad ﷺ is the Messenger of Allāh." The Jews then said, "Abdullāh is the worst of us and the son of the worst of us," and disparaged him. On that 'Abdullāh said, "O Allāh's Messenger! This is what I was afraid of!"

إلى أبيه أو إلى أمه؟ قال: أخبرني بهن جبريل آنفا، قال: جبريل؟ قال: نعم، قال: ذاك عدو اليهود من الملائكة. فقرأ هذه الآية - من كان عدوا لجبريل فإنه نزله على قلبك - أما أول أشراط الساعة فنار تحشر الناس من المشرق إلى المغرب، وأما أول طعام أهل الجنة فزيادة كبد الحوت، وإذا سبق ماء الرجل ماء المرأة نزع الولد، وإذا سبق ماء المرأة نزعت. قال: أشهد أن لا إله إلا الله، وأشهد أنك رسول الله. يا رسول الله، إن اليهود قوم بهت، وإنهم إن يعلموا بإسلامي قبل أن تسألهم يبهتوني. فجاءت اليهود، فقال النبي صلى الله عليه وسلم: أي رجل عبد الله فيكم؟ قالوا: خيرنا وابن خيرنا، وسيدنا، وابن سيدنا. قال: أرأيتم إن أسلم عبد الله بن سلام؟ فقالوا: أعاذه الله من ذلك. فخرج عبد الله فقال: أشهد أن لا إله إلا الله، وأن محمدا رسول الله. فقالوا: شرنا وابن شرنا، وانتقصوه. قال: فهذا الذي كنت أخاف يا رسول الله.

(9) CHAPTER. "Whatever verse (Revelations) do We abrogate or cause to be forgotten but We bring a better one or similar to it. . . . . . (2:106)

بابُ قَوْلِهِ - ما نَنْسَخْ مِنْ آيَةٍ
أوْ نُنْسِهَا نَأْتِ بِخَيْرٍ مِنْهَا أوْ مِثْلِهَا - .

8. Narrated Ibn 'Abbās: 'Umar said, "Our best Qur'ān reciter is Ubai and our best judge is 'Alī; and in spite of this, we leave some of the statements of Ubai because Ubai says, 'I do not leave anything that I have heard from Allāh's Messenger while Allāh said:—

'Whatever verse (Revelations) do We abrogate or cause to be forgotten but We bring a better one or similar, to it. (2:106)

٨ - حدَّثَنَا عَمْرُو بنُ عليّ: حدَّثَنا
يَحْيَى: حدَّثَنا سُفْيانُ، عَنْ حَبِيبٍ،
عَنْ سَعِيدِ بنِ جُبَيْرٍ، عَنِ ابنِ عَبَّاسٍ
قالَ: قالَ عُمَرُ رَضِيَ اللهُ عَنْهُ:
أقْرَؤُنا أُبَيٌّ، وأقْضَانا عَلِيٌّ. وإنَّا لَنَدَعُ
مِنْ قَوْلِ أُبَيٍّ وَذَاكَ أنَّ أُبَيًّا يَقُولُ:
لا أدَعُ شَيْئًا سَمِعْتُهُ مِنْ رَسُولِ اللهِ
صلى اللهُ عليهِ وسلَّم وَقَدْ قالَ اللهُ تَعالى - ما
نَنْسَخْ مِنْ آيَةٍ أوْ نُنْسِهَا -

(10) CHAPTER. 'They say: Allāh has begotten offspring.
Glory be to Him . . . Nay,' (2:116)

بابٌ - وَقَالُوا اتَّخَذَ اللهُ وَلَدًا
سُبْحانَهُ - .

9. Narrated Ibn 'Abbās (رضي الله عنهما): The Prophet (ﷺ) said, "Allāh said, 'The son of Adam tells a lie against me though he has no right to do so, and he abuses Me though he has no right to do so. As for his telling a lie against Me, it is that he claims that I cannot recreate him as I created him before; and as for his abusing Me, it is his statement that I have offspring. No! Glorified be Me! I am far from taking a wife or offspring.' "

٩ ـ حدَّثَنا أبو اليَمانِ : أخبَرَنا شُعَيبٌ ، عَنْ عبدِ اللهِ بنِ أبي حُسَينٍ : حدَّثنا نافِعُ بنُ جُبَيرٍ ، عَنِ ابنِ عبّاسٍ رَضِيَ اللهُ عَنهُما ، عَنِ النَّبيِّ صلى الله عليه وسلَّم قالَ : قالَ اللهُ : كَذَّبَني ابنُ آدَمَ ولَمْ يَكُنْ لَهُ ذَلِكَ ، وشَتَمَني ولَمْ يَكُنْ لَهُ ذَلِكَ . فأمّا تَكذِيبُهُ إيّايَ فزَعَمَ أنّي لا أقدِرُ أنْ أُعيدَهُ كما كانَ . وأمّا شَتمُهُ إيّايَ فقَولُهُ لي وَلَدٌ فسُبحاني أنْ أتَّخِذَ صاحِبَةً أو وَلَدًا .

(11) CHAPTER. 'Take you (people) the station of Abraham as a place of prayer (for some of your prayers, e.g. 2 Rak'āts after the Ṭawāf of Ka'ba).(2:125)

باب ـ واتَّخِذُوا مِنْ مَقامِ إبراهيمَ مُصَلّى ـ مَثابَةً : يَثُوبُونَ . يَرجِعُونَ .

10. Narrated Anas: 'Umar (رضي الله عنه) said, "I agreed with Allāh in three things," or said, "My Lord agreed with me in three things. I said, 'O Allāh's Messenger! Would that you took the station of Abraham as a place of prayer.' I also said, 'O Allāh's Messenger! Good and bad persons visit you! Would that you ordered the Mothers of the believers to cover themselves with veils.' So the Divine Verses of Al-Ḥijāb (i.e. veiling of the women) were revealed. I came to know that the Prophet (ﷺ) had blamed some of his wives so I entered upon them and said, 'You should either stop (troubling the Prophet (ﷺ)) or else Allāh will give His Messenger (ﷺ) better wives than you.' When I came to one of his wives, she said to me,

١٠ ـ حدَّثَنا مُسَدَّدٌ : عَنْ يَحيى ابنِ سَعيدٍ ، عَنْ حُمَيدٍ ، عَنْ أنَسٍ قالَ : قالَ عُمَرُ رَضِيَ اللهُ عَنهُ : وافَقتُ اللهَ في ثَلاثٍ ، أوْ وافَقَني رَبّي في ثَلاثٍ . قُلتُ : يا رَسولَ اللهِ لَوِ اتَّخَذْتَ مِنْ مَقامِ إبراهيمَ مُصَلّى ، وقُلتُ : يا رَسولَ اللهِ يَدخُلُ عَلَيكَ البَرُّ والفاجِرُ فلَوْ أمَرتَ أُمَّهاتِ المُؤمِنينَ بالحِجابِ ، فأنزَلَ اللهُ آيةَ الحِجابِ . قالَ : وبَلَغَني مُعاتَبَةُ النَّبيِّ صلى الله عليه وسلَّم بَعضَ نِسائهِ فدَخَلتُ عَلَيهِنَّ قُلتُ إنِ انتَهَيتُنَّ أوْ لَيُبَدِّلَنَّ

١٢

'O 'Umar! Does Allāh's Messenger ﷺ haven't what he could advise his wives with, that you try to advise them?' " Thereupon Allāh revealed:—

> 'It may be, if he divorced you (all) his Lord will give him instead of you, wives better than you muslims (who submit to Allāh)..........' (66:5)

اللهُ رَسُولَهُ صلى الله عليه وسلَّم خَيْراً مِنْكُنَّ حتَّى أتَيْتُ إحْدَى نِسائِهِ قالَتْ : يا عُمَرُ ، أما فى رَسُولِ اللهِ صلى اللهُ عليه وسلَّم ما يَعِظُ نِساءَهُ حتَّى تَعِظَهُنَّ أنْتَ ؟ فأنْزَلَ اللهُ - عَسَى رَبُّهُ إنْ طَلَّقَكُنَّ أنْ يُبْدِلَهُ أزْواجا خَيْراً مِنْكُنَّ مُسْلِماتٍ - الآيَةَ . وقالَ ابنُ أبي مَرْيَمَ : أخْبَرَنا يَحْيَى بنُ أيُّوبَ : حدَّثَنِي حُمَيْدٌ : سَمِعْتُ أنَسا ، عَنْ عُمَرَ .

(12) CHAPTER. And (remember) when Ābraham and Ishmael were raising the foundations of the House (saying):— Our Lord! Accept (this service) from us, verily!
You are the All-Hearer, the All-Knower.' (2:127)

باب - وَإذْ يَرْفَعُ إبْراهِيمُ القَواعِدَ مِنَ البَيْتِ وَإسْماعِيلُ رَبَّنا تَقَبَّلْ مِنّا إنَّكَ أنْتَ السَّمِيعُ العَلِيمُ - القَواعِدُ : أساسُهُ وَاحِدَتُها قاعِدَةٌ . والقَواعِدُ مِنَ النِّساءِ : وَاحِدُها قاعِدٌ .

11. Narrated 'Āisha (رضي الله عنها), the wife of the Prophet ﷺ : Allāh's Messenger ﷺ said, "Don't you see that when your people built the Ka'ba, they did not build it on all Abraham's foundations?" I said, "O Allāh's Messenger! Why don't you rebuild it on Abraham's foundations?" He said, "Were your people not so close to (the period of Heathenism, i.e. the period between their being Muslims and being infidels), I would do so." The sub-narrator, 'Abdullāh bin 'Umar said,

١١ - حدَّثَنا إسْماعِيلُ قالَ : حدَّثَنِي مالِكٌ ، عَنِ ابنِ شِهابٍ ، عَنْ سالِمِ بنِ عَبْدِ اللهِ : أنَّ عَبْدَ اللهِ بنَ مُحَمَّدِ بنِ أبي بَكْرٍ أخْبَرَ عَبْدَ اللهِ بنَ عُمَرَ ، عَنْ عائِشَةَ رَضِيَ اللهُ تعالى عَنْها زَوْجِ النَّبِيِّ صلى اللهُ عليه وسلَّم أنَّ رَسُولَ اللهِ صلى اللهُ عليه وسلَّم قالَ : ألَمْ تَرَيْ أنَّ قَوْمَكِ بَنَوُا الكَعْبَةَ

"'Āisha had surely heard Allāh's Messenger ﷺ saying that, for I do not think that Allāh's Messenger ﷺ left touching the two corners of the Ka'ba facing Al-Ḥijr except because the Ka'ba was not built on all Abraham's foundations."

وَاقْتَصَرُوا عَنْ قَوَاعِدِ إِبْرَاهِيمَ ؟ فَقُلْتُ : يَا رَسُولَ اللهِ ، أَلَا تَرُدُّهَا عَلَى قَوَاعِدِ إِبْرَاهِيمَ ؟ قَالَ : لَوْلَا حِدْثَانُ قَوْمِكِ بِالْكُفْرِ . فَقَالَ عَبْدُ اللهِ بْنُ عُمَرَ : لَئِنْ كَانَتْ عَائِشَةُ سَمِعَتْ هَذَا مِنْ رَسُولِ اللهِ صلى اللهُ عليهِ وسلَّم مَا أُرَى رَسُولَ اللهِ صلى اللهُ عليه وسلَّم تَرَكَ اسْتِلَامَ الرُّكْنَيْنِ اللَّذَيْنِ يَلِيَانِ الْحِجْرَ إِلَّا أَنَّ الْبَيْتَ لَمْ يُتَمَّمْ عَلَى قَوَاعِدِ إِبْرَاهِيمَ .

(13) CHAPTER. 'Say (O Muslims): We believe in Allāh and what is revealed to us......' (2:136)

بَابٌ - قُولُوا آمَنَّا بِاللهِ وَمَا أُنْزِلَ إِلَيْنَا -

12. Narrated Abū Huraira (رضي الله عنه): The people of the Scripture (Jews) used to recite the Torah in Hebrew and they used to explain it in Arabic to the Muslims. On that Allāh's Messenger ﷺ said, "Do not believe the people of the Scripture or disbelieve them, but say:—

> 'We believe in Allāh and what is revealed to us.' " (2:136)

١٢ - حَدَّثَنَا مُحَمَّدُ بْنُ بَشَّارٍ : حَدَّثَنَا عُثْمَانُ بْنُ عُمَرَ : أَخْبَرَنَا عَلِيُّ ابْنُ الْمُبَارَكِ ، عَنْ يَحْيَى بْنِ أَبِي كَثِيرٍ ، عَنْ أَبِي سَلَمَةَ ، عَنْ أَبِي هُرَيْرَةَ رَضِيَ اللهُ عَنْهُ قَالَ : كَانَ أَهْلُ الْكِتَابِ يَقْرَءُونَ التَّوْرَاةَ بِالْعِبْرَانِيَّةِ وَيُفَسِّرُونَهَا بِالْعَرَبِيَّةِ لِأَهْلِ الْإِسْلَامِ . فَقَالَ رَسُولُ اللهِ صلى اللهُ عليه وسلَّم : لَا تُصَدِّقُوا أَهْلَ الْكِتَابِ وَلَا تُكَذِّبُوهُمْ - وَقُولُوا آمَنَّا بِاللهِ وَمَا أُنْزِلَ إِلَيْنَا - الْآيَةَ .

(14) CHAPTER. The Statement of

بَابٌ قوله تعالى - سَيَقُولُ السُّفَهَاءُ

Allah ﷻ :–

'The fools among the people will say:
What has turned them (Muslims) from the Prayer direction towards Jerusalem to which they were used to face in prayer. (2:142)

مِنَ النَّاسِ مَا وَلَّاهُمْ عَنْ قِبْلَتِهِمْ - الآيَةَ .

13. Narrated Al-Bara' ﷺ : The Prophet ﷺ prayed facing Bait-ul-Maqdis (i.e. Jerusalem) for sixteen or seventeen months but he wished that his Qibla would be the Ka'ba (at Mecca). (So Allah Revealed (2:144) and he offered 'Asr prayers (in his Mosque facing Ka'ba at Mecca) and some people prayed with him. A man from among those who had prayed with him, went out and passed by some people offering prayer in another mosque, and they were in the state of bowing. He said, "I, (swearing by Allah,) testify that I have prayed with the Prophet ﷺ facing Mecca." Hearing that, they turned their faces to the Ka'ba while they were still bowing. Some men had died before the Qibla was changed towards the Ka'ba. They had been killed and we did not know what to say about them (i.e. whether their prayers towards Jerusalem were accepted or not). So Allah revealed:–

'And Allah would never make your faith (i.e. prayer) to be lost (i.e. your prayers offered (towards Jerusalem). Truly Allah is Full of Pity, Most Merciful towards mankind.' (2:143)

١٣ - حدَّثنا أبو نُعَيْم : سَمِعَ زُهَيْرًا ، عَنْ أبي إسحاقَ ، عَنِ البَرَاءِ رَضِيَ اللهُ عَنْهُ أنَّ النَّبِيَّ صلى اللهُ عليه وسلَّم صَلَّى إلى بَيْتِ المَقْدِسِ سِتَّةَ عَشَرَ شَهْرًا أوْ سَبْعَةَ عَشَرَ شَهْرًا . وكانَ يُعْجِبُهُ أنْ تَكُونَ قِبْلَتُهُ قِبَلَ البَيْتِ ، وَإنَّهُ صَلَّى أوْ صَلاَّهَا صَلاةَ العَصْرِ وَصَلَّى مَعَهُ قَوْمٌ فَخَرَجَ رَجُلٌ مِمَّنْ كانَ صَلَّى مَعَهُ فَمَرَّ عَلَى أهْلِ المَسْجِدِ وهُمْ رَاكِعُونَ ، قالَ : أشْهَدُ بِاللهِ لَقَدْ صَلَّيْتُ مَعَ النَّبِيِّ صلى اللهُ عليه وسلَّم قِبَلَ مَكَّةَ فَدَارُوا كَمَا هُمْ قِبَلَ البَيْتِ وكانَ الَّذِي ماتَ عَلَى القِبْلَةِ قَبْلَ أنْ تُحَوَّلَ قِبَلَ البَيْتِ رِجالٌ قُتِلُوا لَمْ نَدْرِ ما نَقُولُ فِيهِمْ . فأنْزَلَ اللهُ - وَمَا كانَ اللهُ لِيُضِيعَ إيمانَكُمْ إنَّ اللهَ بِالنَّاسِ لَرَءُوفٌ رَحِيمٌ - .

(15) CHAPTER. The Statement of Allāh تعالى :–

'Thus We have made of you a just and the best nation
that you may be witnesses over mankind,
and the Messenger (Muhammad ﷺ)
will be a witness over yourselves.. (2:143)

باب قوله تعالى - وكذلك جعلناكم أمة وسطا لتكونوا شهداء على الناس ويكون الرسول عليكم شهيدا -.

14. Narrated Abū Sa'īd Al-Khudrī رضي الله عنه : Allāh's Messenger ﷺ said, "Noah will be called on the Day of Resurrection and he will say, 'Labbaik and Sa'daik, O my Lord!' Allāh will say, 'Did you convey the Message?' Noah will say, 'Yes.' His nation will then be asked, 'Did he convey the Message to you?' They will say, 'No Warner came to us.' Then Allāh will say (to Noah), 'Who will bear witness in your favour?' He will say, 'Muhammad and his followers. So they (i.e. Muslims) will testify that he conveyed the Message. And the Messenger (Muhammad ﷺ) will be a witness over yourselves, and that is what is meant by the Statement of Allāh عز وجل :–

'Thus We have made of you a
just and the best nation that you may be witnesses over mankind and the Messenger (Muhammad ﷺ) will be a witness over yourselves.' .. ...
(2:143)

'Wasaṭ 'means just'.

١٤ - حدثنا يوسف بن راشد : حدثنا جرير وأبو أسامة واللفظ لجرير، عن الأعمش، عن أبي صالح. وقال أبو أسامة : حدثنا أبو صالح، عن أبي سعيد الخدري قال : قال رسول الله صلى الله عليه وسلم : يدعى نوح يوم القيامة فيقول : لبيك وسعديك يا رب. فيقول : هل بلغت؟ فيقول : نعم، فيقال لأمته : هل بلغكم؟ فيقولون : ما أتانا من نذير، فيقول : من يشهد لك؟ فيقول : محمد وأمته، فيشهدون أنه قد بلغ - ويكون الرسول عليكم شهيدا - فذلك قوله عز وجل - وكذلك جعلناكم أمة وسطا لتكونوا شهداء على الناس ويكون الرسول عليكم شهيدا - والوسط : العدل.

(16) CHAPTER. The Statement of

باب قول الله تعالى - وما جعلنا

Allāh تعالى 'And We made the Prayer Directions towards Jerusalem which you used to face, only to test, those who followed the Messenger (Muḥammad ﷺ) from those who would turn on their heels.....' (2:143)

القِبْلَةَ الَّتي كُنْتَ عَلَيْها إلاَّ لِنَعْلَمَ مَنْ يَتَّبِعُ الرَّسُولَ ـ الآيَةَ .

15. Narrated Ibn 'Umar رضي الله عنهما: While some people were offering Fajr prayer in the Qubā' mosque, some-one came and said, "Allāh has revealed to the Prophet ﷺ Qur'ānic instructions that you should face the Ka'ba (while praying) so you too, should face it." Those people then turned towards the Ka'ba.

١٥ ـ حدَّثنا مُسَدَّدٌ : حدَّثنا يَحْيى ، عَنْ سُفْيانَ ، عَنْ عَبْدِ اللهِ بنِ دينارٍ ، عَنِ ابنِ عُمَرَ رَضِيَ اللهُ تعالى عَنْهُما : بَيْنا النَّاسُ يُصَلُّونَ الصُّبْحَ في مَسْجِدِ قُباءٍ إذْ جاءَ جاءٍ فَقالَ : أنْزَلَ اللهُ عَلَى النَّبِيِّ صلى اللهُ عليهِ وسلَّم قُرآنا أنْ يَسْتَقْبِلَ الكَعْبَةَ فاستَقْبِلُوها ، فتَوَجَّهوا إلى الكَعْبَةِ .

(17). CHAPTER. The Statement of Allāh تعالى :–

بابٌ ـ قَوْلُهُ تعالى ـ قَدْ نَرَى تَقَلُّبَ وَجْهِكَ في السَّماءِ ـ الآيَةَ .

Verily! We see the turning of your (Muḥammad's ﷺ) face towards the Heaven.' (2:144)

16; Narrated Anas رضي الله عنه: None remains of those who prayed facing both Qiblas (that is, Jerusalem and Mecca) except myself.

١٦ ـ حدَّثنا عَلِيُّ بنُ عَبْدِ اللهِ : حدَّثنا مُعْتَمِرٌ ، عَنْ أبيهِ ، عَنْ أنَسٍ رَضِيَ اللهُ تَعالى عَنْهُ قالَ : لَمْ يَبْقَ مِمَّنْ صَلَّى القِبْلَتَيْنِ غَيْري .

(18) CHAPTER. 'And even if you

بابٌ ـ وَلَئِنْ أتَيْتَ الَّذينَ أُوتُوا

were to bring to the people of the Scripture (Jews and Christians), all the signs (together) they would not follow your Qibla (i.e. Prayer-Direction).' (2:145)

الكتاب بكل آية ما تبعوا قبلتك - الآية .

17. Narrated Ibn 'Umar : While some people were offering morning prayer at Qubā', a man came to them and said, "A Qur'ānic Order has been revealed to Allāh's Messenger ﷺ tonight that he should face the Ka'ba at Mecca (in prayer), so you too should turn your faces towards it." At that moment their faces were towards Shā'm (i.e. Jerusalem) (and on hearing that) they turned towards the Ka'ba (at Mecca).

١٧ - حدثنا خالد بن مخلد : حدثنا سفيان قال : حدثني عبد الله ابن دينار ، عن ابن عمر رضي الله عنهما : بينما الناس في الصبح بقباء جاءهم رجل فقال : إن رسول الله صلى الله عليه وسلم قد أنزل عليه الليلة قرآن وقد أمر أن يستقبل الكعبة ، ألا فاستقبلوها وكان وجه الناس إلى الشام فاستداروا بوجوههم إلى الكعبة .

(19) CHAPTER. 'Those to whom We gave the Scripture (i.e. Jews and Christians) recognise him (i.e. Muḥammad ﷺ) as they recognise their own sons.' (2: 146)

باب - الذين آتيناهم الكتاب يعرفونه كما يعرفون أبناءهم - .

18. Narrated Ibn 'Umar : While some people were offering Fajr prayer at Qubā' (mosque), some-one came to them and said, "Tonight some Qur'ānic Verses have been revealed to the Prophet ﷺ and he has been ordered to face the Ka'ba (at Mecca) (during prayers), so you too should turn your faces towards it." At that time their faces were

١٨ - حدثنا يحيى بن قزعة : حدثنا مالك ، عن عبد الله بن دينار ، عن ابن عمر قال : بينا الناس بقباء في صلاة الصبح إذ جاءهم آت فقال : إن النبي صلى الله عليه وسلم قد أنزل عليه الليلة قرآن ، وقد أمر أن

towards Shā'm (Jerusalem) so they turned towards the Ka'ba (at Mecca).

يستقبل الكعبة فاستقبلوها، وكانت وجوههم إلى الشام فاستداروا إلى الكعبة.

(20) CHAPTER. 'For every nation there is a direction to which they face (in their prayers)..........' (2:148)

باب - ولكل وجهة هو موليها - الآية.

19. Narrated Al-Barā' : We prayed along with the Prophet facing Jerusalem for sixteen or seventeen months. Then Allāh ordered him to turn his face towards the Qibla (in Mecca):–

> 'And from whence-so-ever you start forth (for prayers) turn your face in the direction of (the Sacred Mosque of Mecca) Al-Masjid-ul-Ḥarām......' (2:149)

١٩ - حدثنا محمد بن المثنى قال: حدثنا يحيى، عن سفيان: حدثني أبو إسحاق قال: سمعت البراء رضي الله تعالى عنه قال: صلينا مع النبي صلى الله عليه وسلم نحو بيت المقدس ستة عشر أو سبعة عشر شهرا، ثم صرفه نحو القبلة - ومن حيث خرجت فول وجهك شطر المسجد الحرام - الآية. شطره: تلقاؤه.

20. Narrated Ibn 'Umar : While some people were at Qubā' (offering) morning prayer, a man came to them and said, "Last night Qur'ānic Verses have been revealed whereby the Prophet has been ordered to face the Ka'ba (at Mecca), so you too should face it." So they, keeping their postures, turned towards the Ka'ba. Formerly the people were facing Shā'm (Jerusalem) (Allāh said):–

٢٠ - حدثنا موسى بن إسماعيل: حدثنا عبد العزيز بن مسلم: حدثنا عبد الله بن دينار قال: سمعت ابن عمر رضي الله تعالى عنهما يقول: بينما الناس فى الصبح بقباء إذ جاءهم رجل فقال: أنزل الليلة قرآن فأمر أن يستقبل الكعبة فاستقبلوها

'And from whence-so-ever you start forth (for prayers), turn your face in the direction of the Sacred Mosque of Mecca (Al-Masjid-ul-Ḥarām), and whence-so-ever you are, turn your face towards it (when you pray). (2:150)

فاستداروا كهيئتهم فتوجهوا إلى الكعبة وكان وجه الناس إلى الشام - ومن حيث خرجت فول وجهك شطر المسجد الحرام وحيثما كنتم فولوا وجوهكم شطره ..

21. Narrated Ibn 'Umar :
While some people were offering Fajr prayer at Qubā' mosque, someone came to them and said, "Qur'ānic literature" has been revealed to Allāh's Messenger - tonight, and he has been ordered to face the Ka'ba (at Mecca) so you too, should turn your faces towards it. Their faces were then towards Shā'm (Jerusalem), so they turned towards the Qibla (i.e. Ka'ba at Mecca)."

٢١ - حدثنا قتيبة بن سعيد : عن مالك عن عبد الله بن دينار ، عن ابن عمر قال : بينما الناس في صلاة الصبح بقباء إذ جاءهم آت فقال : إن رسول الله صلى الله عليه وسلم قد أنزل عليه الليلة وقد أمر أن يستقبل الكعبة فاستقبلوها وكانت وجوههم إلى الشام ، فاستداروا إلى القبلة .

(21) CHAPTER. The Statement of Allāh :–

'Verily, Safā and Marwa (i.e. two mountains at Mecca) are among the Symbols of Allāh.' (2:158)

باب قوله تعالى - إن الصفا والمروة من شعائر الله - شعائر : علامات ، واحدتها شعيرة . وقال ابن عباس : الصفوان : الحجر ، ويقال الحجارة الملس التي لا تنبت شيئا والواحدة صفوانة بمعنى الصفا . والصفا للجميع .

22. Narrated 'Urwa: I said to

٢٢ - حدثنا عبد الله بن يوسف :

أخبرنا مالك، عن هشام بن عروة، عن أبيه أنه قال: قلت لعائشة زوج النبي صلى الله عليه وسلم وأنا يومئذ حديث السن: أرأيت قول الله تبارك وتعالى - إن الصفا والمروة من شعائر الله فمن حج البيت أو اعتمر فلا جناح عليه أن يطوف بهما - فما أرى على أحد شيئا أن لا يطوف بهما، فقالت عائشة: كلا لو كانت كما تقول كانت فلا جناح عليه أن لا يطوف بهما، إنما أنزلت هذه الآية في الأنصار كانوا يهلون لمناة وكانت مناة حذو قديد، وكانوا يتحرجون أن يطوفوا بين الصفا والمروة. فلما جاء الإسلام سألوا رسول الله صلى الله عليه وسلم عن ذلك فأنزل الله - إن الصفا والمروة من شعائر الله فمن حج البيت أو اعتمر فلا جناح عليه أن يطوف بهما -.

'Āisha, the wife of the Prophet ﷺ, and I was at that time, a young boy, "How do you interpret the Statement of Allāh تبارك وتعالى :—

> 'Verily, Ṣafā and Marwa (i.e. two mountains at Mecca) are among the Symbols of Allāh.'

So it is not harmful of those who perform the Ḥajj to the House of Allāh) or perform the 'Umra, to ambulate (Ṭawāf) between them. In my opinion it is not sinful for one not to ambulate (Ṭawāf) between them." 'Āisha said, "Your interpretation is wrong for as you say, the Verse should have been: "So it is not harmful of those who perform the Ḥajj or 'Umra to the House, not to ambulate (Ṭawāf) between them.' This Verse was revealed in connection with the Anṣār who (during the Pre-Islāmic Period) used to visit Manāt (i.e. an idol) after assuming their Iḥrām, and it was situated near Qudaid (i.e. a place at Mecca), and they used to regard it sinful to ambulate between Ṣafā and Marwa (1) after embracing Islām. When Islām came, they asked Allāh's Messenger ﷺ about it, whereupon Allāh revealed:—

> 'Verily, Ṣafā and Marwa (i.e. two mountains at Mecca) are among the Symbols of Allāh. So it is not harmful of those who perform the Ḥajj of the House (of Allāh) or perform the 'Umra, to ambulate (Ṭawāf) between them.' "
> (2:158)

(1) Because at Safā and Marwa there were placed two idols belonging to other nations.

23. Narrated 'Āsim bin Sulaimān: I asked Anas bin Mālik about Ṣafā and Marwa. Anas replied, "We used to consider (i.e. going around) them a custom of the Pre-Islāmic period of Ignorance, so when Islām came, we gave up going around them. Then Allāh revealed:

> 'Verily, Ṣafā and Marwa (i.e. two mountains at Mecca) are among the Symbols of Allāh. So it is not harmful of those who perform the Ḥajj of the House (of Allāh) or perform the 'Umra to ambulate (Ṭawāf) between them.' "
>
> (2:158)

٢٣ - حدثنا محمد بن يوسف: حدثنا سفيان، عن عاصم بن سليمان قال: سألت أنس بن مالك رضي الله عنه عن الصفا والمروة، فقال: كنا نرى أنهما من أمر الجاهلية فلما كان الإسلام أمسكنا عنهما فأنزل الله تعالى - إن الصفا والمروة من شعائر الله فمن حج البيت أو اعتمر فلا جناح عليه -.

(22) CHAPTER. The Statement of Allāh تعالى :–

> 'And of mankind are some who take (for worship), others besides Allāh as rivals (to Allāh); They love them as they love Allāh.'
>
> (2:165)

"Andād" is a plural of "Nidd" and it means opponent, or rival, etc.

باب قوله تعالى - ومن الناس من يتخذ من دون الله أندادا يحبونهم كحب الله - يعني أضدادا، واحدها ند.

24. Narrated 'Abdullāh رضي الله عنه : The Prophet ﷺ said one statement and I said another. The Prophet ﷺ said-

٢٤ - حدثنا عبدان: عن أبي حمزة، عن الأعمش، عن شقيق،

"Whoever dies while still invoking anything other than Allāh as a rival to Allāh, will enter Hell (Fire)." And I said, "Whoever dies without invoking anything as a rival to Allāh, will enter Paradise."

عَنْ عَبْدِ اللهِ قالَ : قالَ النَّبِيُّ صلى اللهُ عليه وسلَّمَ كَلِمَةً وَقُلْتُ أُخْرَى ، قالَ النَّبِيُّ صلى اللهُ عليه وسلَّم : مَنْ ماتَ وَهُوَ يَدْعُو مِنْ دُونِ اللهِ نِدًّا دَخَلَ النَّارَ ، وَقُلْتُ أنا : مَنْ ماتَ وَهُوَ لا يَدْعُو لله نِدًّا دَخَلَ الجَنَّةَ .

(23) CHAPTER 'O you who believe! The law of Al-Qiṣāṣ (i.e. equality in punishment) is prescribed to you.' (2:178)

بابٌ - يا أَيُّها الَّذِينَ آمَنُوا كُتِبَ عَلَيْكُمُ القِصَاصُ - الآيَة . عُفِيَ : تُرِكَ .

25. Narrated Ibn 'Abbās :
The law of Qiṣāṣ (i.e. equality in punishment) was prescribed for the children of Israel, but the Diya [i.e. blood money (was not ordained for them). So Allāh said to this Nation (i.e. Muslims):—

> 'O you who believe! The law of Al-Qiṣāṣ (i.e. equality in punishment) is prescribed for you in cases of murder: The free for the free, the slave for the slave, and the female for the female. But if the relatives (or one of them) of the killed (person) forgive their brother (i.e. the killer) something of Qiṣāṣ (i.e. not to kill the killer by accepting bloodmoney in the case of intentional murder)——then the relatives (of the killed person) should demand blood-money in a reasonable manner and the killer must pay with handsome gratitude. This is an alleviation and a Mercy from your Lord, (in comparison to what

٢٥ - حدَّثنا الحُمَيْدِيُّ : حدَّثنا سُفْيانُ : حدَّثنا عَمْرٌو قالَ : سَمِعْتُ مُجاهِدًا قالَ : سَمِعْتُ ابنَ عَبَّاسٍ رَضِيَ اللهُ عَنهما يَقُولُ : كانَ فى بَنِي إِسْرائيلَ القِصَاصُ وَلَمْ تَكُنْ فِيهِمُ الدِّيَةُ فَقالَ اللهُ تَعالى لِهَذِهِ الأُمَّةِ - كُتِبَ عَلَيْكُمُ القِصَاصُ فى القَتْلَى الحُرُّ بالحُرِّ والعَبْدُ بالعَبْدِ والأُنْثَى بالأُنْثَى فَمَنْ عُفِيَ لَهُ مِنْ أَخِيهِ شَيْءٌ - فالعَفْوُ أَنْ يَقْبَلَ الدِّيَةَ فى العَمْدِ - فاتِّباعٌ بالمَعْرُوفِ وأَداءٌ إِلَيْهِ بإِحْسانٍ - يَتَّبِعُ بالمَعْرُوفِ وَيُؤَدِّي بإِحْسانٍ - ذَلِكَ تَخْفِيفٌ مِنْ رَبِّكُمْ وَرَحْمَةٌ - مِمَّا كُتِبَ عَلَى مَنْ كانَ قَبْلَكُمْ - فَمَنِ اعْتَدَى بَعْدَ ذَلِكَ فَلَهُ عَذابٌ أَلِيمٌ - قَتَلَ بَعْدَ قَبُولِ الدِّيَةِ .

was prescribed for the nations before you).

"So after this, whoever trangresses the limits (i.e. to kill the killer after taking the blood-money) shall have a painful torment.'

(2:178)

26. Narrated Anas : The Prophet said, "The prescribed Law of Allāh is the equality in punishment (i.e. Al-Qiṣāṣ)." (In cases of murders, etc.)

٢٦ - حدثنا محمد بن عبد الله الأنصاري: حدثنا حميد أن أنسا حدثهم عن النبي صلى الله عليه وسلم قال: كتاب الله: القصاص.

27. Narrated Anas that his aunt, Ar-Rubai' broke an incisor tooth of a girl. My aunt's family requested the girl's relatives for forgiveness but they refused; then they proposed a compensation, but they refused. Then they went to Allāh's Messenger and refused everything except Al-Qiṣāṣ (i.e. equality in punishment). So Allāh's Messenger passed the judgement of Al-Qiṣāṣ (i.e. equality of punishment). Anas bin Al-Nadr said, "O Allāh's Messenger! Will the incisor tooth of Ar-Rubai be broken? No, by Him Who sent you with the Truth, her incisor tooth will not be broken." Allāh's Messenger said, "O Anas! The prescribed law of Allāh is equality in punishment (i.e. Al-Qiṣāṣ.)" Thereupon those people became satisfied and forgave her. Then Allāh's Messenger said, "Among Allāh's Worshippers there

٢٧ - حدثني عبد الله بن منير: سمع عبد الله بن بكر السهمي: حدثنا حميد، عن أنس: أن الربيع عمته كسرت ثنية جارية، فطلبوا إليها العفو فأبوا، فعرضوا الأرش فأبوا، فأتوا رسول الله صلى الله عليه وسلم وأبوا إلا القصاص، فأمر رسول الله صلى الله عليه وسلم بالقصاص، فقال أنس بن النضر: يا رسول الله، أتكسر ثنية الربيع؟ لا والذي بعثك بالحق لا تكسر ثنيتها، فقال رسول الله صلى الله عليه وسلم: يا أنس، كتاب الله القصاص، فرضي القوم فعفوا،

are some who, if they took Allāh's Oath (for something), Allāh fulfils their oaths."

فَقَالَ رَسُولُ اللهِ صلى اللهُ عليه وسلَّمَ ، إنَّ مِنْ عِبادِ اللهِ مَنْ لَوْ أقْسَمَ عَلَى اللهِ لأَبَرَّهُ .

(24) CHAPTER. 'O you who believe! Fasting is prescribed for you as it was prescribed for those before you that you may be righteous.' (2: 183)

بابٌ - يا أيُّها الَّذِينَ آمَنُوا كُتِبَ عَلَيْكُمُ الصِّيامُ كَمَا كُتِبَ عَلَى الَّذِينَ مِنْ قَبْلِكُمْ لَعَلَّكُمْ تَتَّقُونَ - .

28. Narrated Ibn 'Umar : Fasting was observed on the day of 'Āshūrā' (i.e. 10th of Muḥarram) by the people of the Pre-Islāmic Period. But when (the order of compulsory fasting in) the month of Ramaḍān was revealed, the Prophet said, "It is up to one to fast on it (i.e. day of 'Āshūrā') or not."

٢٨ - حَدَّثَنَا مُسَدَّدٌ : حَدَّثَنَا يَحْيى ، عَنْ عُبَيْدِ اللهِ قَالَ : أخْبَرَنِي نافِعٌ ، عَنِ ابنِ عُمَرَ رَضِيَ اللهُ عَنْهُما قَالَ : كانَ عاشُوراءُ يَصُومُهُ أهْلُ الجاهِلِيَّةِ ، فَلَمَّا نَزَلَ رَمَضانُ قالَ : مَنْ شاءَ صامَهُ وَمَنْ لَمْ يَشَأْ لَمْ يَصُمْهُ .

29. Narrated 'Āisha : The people used to fast on the day of 'Āshūrā' before fasting in Ramaḍān was prescribed, but when (the order of compulsory fasting in) Ramaḍān was revealed, it was up to one to fast on it (i.e. 'Āshūrā') or not.

٢٩ - حَدَّثَنِي عَبْدُ اللهِ بنُ مُحَمَّدٍ : حَدَّثَنا ابنُ عُيَيْنَةَ ، عَنِ الزُّهْرِيِّ ، عَنْ عُرْوَةَ ، عَنْ عائِشَةَ رَضِيَ اللهُ تَعالى عَنْها قالَتْ : كانَ عاشُوراءُ يُصامُ قَبْلَ رَمَضانَ فَلَمَّا نَزَلَ رَمَضانُ مَنْ شاءَ صامَ وَمَنْ شاءَ أفْطَرَ .

30. Narrated 'Abdullāh that

٣٠ - حَدَّثَنِي مَحْمُودٌ : أخْبَرَنا

Al-Ash'ath entered upon him while he was eating. Al-Ash'ath said, "Today is 'Āshūrā.' " I said (to him), "Fasting had been observed (on such a day) before (the order of compulsory fasting in) Ramaḍān was revealed. But when (the order of fasting in) Ramaḍān was revealed, fasting (on 'Āshūrā') was given up, so come and eat."

عُبَيْدُ اللهِ ، عَنْ إِسْرائِيلَ ، عَنْ مَنْصُورٍ ، عَنْ إِبْرَاهِيمَ ، عَنْ عَلْقَمَةَ عَنْ عَبْدِ اللهِ قَالَ : دَخَلَ عَلَيْهِ الأَشْعَثُ وَهُوَ يَطْعَمُ فَقَالَ : الْيَوْمُ عَاشُورَاءُ ، فَقَالَ : كَانَ يُصَامُ قَبْلَ أَنْ يَنْزِلَ رَمَضَانُ فَلَمَّا نَزَلَ رَمَضَانُ تُرِكَ فَادْنُ فَكُلْ .

31. Narrated 'Āisha (رضي الله عنها): During the Pre-Islāmic Period of ignorance the Quraish used to observe fasting on the day of 'Āshūrā', and the Prophet (ﷺ) himself used to observe fasting on it too. But when he came to Medīna, he fasted on that day and ordered the Muslims to fast on it. When (the order of compulsory fasting in) Ramaḍān was revealed, fasting in Ramaḍān became an obligation, and fasting on 'Āshūrā' was given up, and who ever wished to fast (on it) did so, and whoever did not wish to fast on it, did not fast.

٣١ - حَدَّثَنَا مُحَمَّدُ بْنُ الْمُثَنَّى : حَدَّثَنَا يَحْيَى : حَدَّثَنَا هِشَامٌ قَالَ : أَخْبَرَنِي أَبِي عَنْ عَائِشَةَ رَضِيَ اللهُ تَعَالَى عَنْهَا قَالَتْ : كَانَ يَوْمُ عَاشُورَاءَ تَصُومُهُ قُرَيْشٌ فِي الْجَاهِلِيَّةِ وَ كَانَ النَّبِيُّ صلى الله عليه وسلم يَصُومُهُ فَلَمَّا قَدِمَ الْمَدِينَةَ صَامَهُ وَ أَمَرَ بِصِيَامِهِ ، فَلَمَّا نَزَلَ رَمَضَانُ كَانَ رَمَضَانُ الْفَرِيضَةَ وَتُرِكَ عَاشُورَاءُ فَكَانَ مَنْ شَاءَ صَامَهُ وَمَنْ شَاءَ لَمْ يَصُمْهُ .

(25) CHAPTER. The Statement of Allāh (تعالى) :–

> '(Fasting) for a fixed number of days; but
> if any of you is ill, or on a journey,
> the same number (should be made up)
> from other days. And as for those who can fast they had a choice, either fast or feed a poor for

بَابُ قَوْلِهِ تَعَالَى - أَيَّامًا مَعْدُودَاتٍ فَمَنْ كَانَ مِنْكُمْ مَرِيضًا أَوْ عَلَى سَفَرٍ فَعِدَّةٌ مِنْ أَيَّامٍ أُخَرَ ، وَعَلَى الَّذِينَ يُطِيقُونَهُ فِدْيَةٌ طَعَامُ مِسْكِينٍ فَمَنْ تَطَوَّعَ خَيْرًا فَهُوَ خَيْرٌ لَهُ وَ أَنْ تَصُومُوا خَيْرٌ لَكُمْ إِنْ كُنْتُمْ تَعْلَمُونَ - وَقَالَ عَطَاءٌ : يُفْطِرُ مِنَ الْمَرَضِ كُلِّهِ

every day. But whoever does good of his own accord, it is better for him. And that your fast is better for you, if you only knew.' (2:184)

(Note: The order of this Verse has been abrogated by the next Verse (i.e. 2:185 with few exceptions i.e. very old person, pregnancy etc). 'Aṭā' said, "One may stop fasting if one is suffering from any kind of disease, as Allāh says."

Concerning nursing or pregnant women, Al-Ḥasan and Ibrāhīm said, "If they are afraid of harming themselves or their babies, they can give up fasting for the time being and make up for the missed fasts later on. If an old man has no strength to fast (he can feed a poor person daily). When Anas bin Mālik became old, he used to provide a poor person with bread and meat everyday while he gave up fasting during the last one or two years of his life."

كَمَا قَالَ اللهُ تَعَالَى . وَقَالَ الحَسَنُ وَإِبْرَاهِيمُ فِى المُرْضِعِ والحَامِلِ : إِذَا خَافَتَا عَلَى أَنْفُسِهِمَا أَوْ وَلَدِهِمَا تُفْطِرَانِ ثُمَّ تَقْضِيَانِ . وَأَمَّا الشَّيْخُ الكَبِيرُ إِذَا لَمْ يُطِقِ الصِّيَامَ فَقَدْ أَطْعَمَ أَنَسُ بْنُ مَالِكٍ بَعْدَ مَا كَبِرَ عَامًا أَوْ عَامَيْنِ ، كُلَّ يَوْمٍ مِسْكِينًا خُبْزًا وَلَحْمًا وَأَفْطَرَ ، قِرَاءَةُ العَامَّةِ : يُطِيقُونَهُ وَهُوَ أَكْثَرُ .

32. Narrated 'Aṭā' that he heard Ibn 'Abbās reciting the Divine Verse: —

'And for those who can fast they had a choice either fast, or feed a poor for every day (2:184) Ibn 'Abbās said, "This Verse is not abrogated, but it is meant for old men and old women who have no strength to fast, so they should

٣٢ - حَدَّثَنِى إِسْحَاقُ : أَخْبَرَنَا رَوْحٌ : حَدَّثَنَا زَكَرِيَّاءُ بْنُ إِسْحَاقَ : حَدَّثَنَا عَمْرُو بْنُ دِينَارٍ ، عَنْ عَطَاءٍ : سَمِعَ ابْنَ عَبَّاسٍ يَقُولُ - وَعَلَى الَّذِينَ يُطَوَّقُونَهُ فِدْيَةٌ طَعَامُ مِسْكِينٍ - قَالَ ابْنُ عَبَّاسٍ : لَيْسَتْ بِمَنْسُوخَةٍ ، هُوَ

feed one poor person for each day of fasting (instead of fasting)."

الشَّيْخُ الكَبِيرُ والمَرْأَةُ الكَبِيرَةُ لا يَسْتَطِيعانِ أنْ يَصُوما فَلْيُطْعِمانِ مَكانَ كُلِّ يَوْمٍ مِسْكِينا .

(26) CHAPTER. 'So whoever of you is present (at his home), then he should fast the month. (2:185)

بابٌ - فَمَنْ شَهِدَ مِنْكُمُ الشَّهْرَ فَلْيَصُمْهُ -

33. Narrated Nāfi': Ibn 'Umar recited:—

They had a choice, either fast or feed a poor for every day... ....

and added, "This Verse is abrogated."

٣٣ - حدَّثَنا عَيَّاشُ بنُ الوَلِيدِ : حدَّثَنا عَبْدُ الأعْلَى : حدَّثَنا عُبَيْدُ اللهِ ، عَنْ نافِعٍ ، عَنِ ابنِ عُمَرَ رَضِيَ اللهُ عَنْهُما : أنَّهُ قَرَأَ - فِدْيَةٌ طَعامُ مَساكِينَ - قالَ : هِيَ مَنْسُوخَةٌ .

34. Narrated Salama: When the Divine Revelation:—

'For those who can fast, they had a choice either fast, or feed a poor for every day,' (2:184)

was revealed, it was permissible for one to give a ransom and give up fasting, till the Verse succeeding it was revealed and abrogated it.

٣٤ - حدَّثَنا قُتَيْبَةُ : حدَّثَنا بَكْرُ ابنُ مُضَرَ ، عَنْ عَمْرِو بنِ الحارِثِ ، عَنْ بُكَيْرِ بنِ عَبْدِ اللهِ ، عَنْ يَزِيدَ مَوْلَى سَلَمَةَ بنِ الأكْوَعِ ، عَنْ سَلَمَةَ قالَ : لَمَّا نَزَلَتْ - وَعَلَى الَّذِينَ يُطِيقُونَهُ فِدْيَةٌ طَعامُ مِسْكِينٍ - كانَ مَنْ أرادَ أنْ يُفْطِرَ وَيَفْتَدِي حَتَّى نَزَلَتِ الآيَةُ الَّتِي بَعْدَها فَنَسَخَتْها . قالَ أبُو عَبْدِ اللهِ : ماتَ بُكَيْرٌ قَبْلَ يَزِيدَ .

(27) CHAPTER. It is made lawful for you to have sexual relation with your wives on the night of the fasts ....and seek that which Allāh has ordained for you (i.e. offspring.).' (2: 187)

بابٌ - أُحِلَّ لَكُمْ لَيْلَةَ الصِّيامِ الرَّفَثُ إلى نِسائِكُمْ - إلى قَوْلِهِ - وَابْتَغُوا ما كَتَبَ اللهُ لَكُمْ - .

مِنَ الفَجْرِ - فَعَلِمُوا أنَّما يَعْنِى اللَّيْلَ
مِنَ النَّهارِ .

(29) CHAPTER. 'And it is not righteousness that you enter the houses from the back, but the righteous man is he who fears Allāh, obeys His Orders and keeps away from what He has forbidden. So enter houses through their doors.' (2:189)

باب - ولَيْسَ البِرُّ بأنْ تَأتُوا
البُيُوتَ مِنْ ظُهُورِها ولَكِنَّ البِرَّ مَنِ
اتَّقَى - الآيَة .

39. Narrated Al-Barā' رضي الله عنه :In the Pre-Islāmic Period when the people assumed Iḥrām, they would enter their houses from the back. So Allāh revealed:—

'And it is not righteousness that you enter houses from the back, but the righteous man is he who fears Allāh , obeys His Orders and keeps away from what He has forbidden. So enter houses through their doors.' (2:189)

٣٩ - حدَّثَنا عُبَيْدُ اللهِ بنُ مُوسَى :
عَنْ إسْرَائيلَ ، عَنْ أبي إسحاقَ ، عَنِ
البَرَاءِ قالَ : كانُوا إذَا أحْرَمُوا فى
الجاهِلِيَّةِ أتَوُا البَيْتَ مِنْ ظَهْرِهِ ،
فأنزَلَ اللهُ - ولَيْسَ البِرُّ بأنْ تأتُوا
البُيُوتَ مِنْ ظُهُورِها ولَكِنَّ البِرَّ مَنِ
اتَّقَى وأتُوا البُيُوتَ مِنْ أبْوَابِها -

(30) CHAPTER. Allāh's Statement:—
'And fight them until there is no more affliction (i.e. no more worshipping of others along with Allāh) and (all and every kind of) worship is for Allāh (Alone).
But if they cease, then let there be no transgression except against wrong-doers.' (2:193)

باب قَوْلِهِ - وقاتِلُوهُمْ حتَّى لا
تَكُونَ فِتْنَةٌ ويَكُونَ الدِّينُ لِلهِ فإنِ
انْتَهَوْا فَلا عُدْوَانَ إلاَّ عَلَى الظَّالِمِينَ - .

40. Narrated Nāfi': During the affliction of Ibn Az-Zubair, two men came to Ibn 'Umar and said, "The people are lost, and you are the son of

٤٠ - حدَّثَنا مُحَمَّدُ بنُ بَشَّارٍ :
حدَّثَنا عَبْدُ الوَهَّابِ : حدَّثَنا عُبَيْدُ اللهِ ،

'Umar, and the companion of the Prophet ﷺ, so what forbids you from coming out?" He said, "What forbids me is that Allāh has prohibited the shedding of my brother's blood." They both said, "Didn't Allāh say, 'And fight them until there is no more affliction?'" He said, "We fought until there was no more affliction and the worship became for Allāh (Alone) while you want to fight until there is affliction and until the worship becomes for other than Allāh."

Narrated Nāfi' (through another group of sub-narrators): A man came to Ibn 'Umar and said, "O Abū Abdur-Raḥmān! What made you perform Ḥajj in one year and 'Umra in another year and leave the Jihād for Allāh's Cause though you know how much Allāh recommends it?" Ibn 'Umar replied, "O son of my brother! Islām is founded on five principles, i.e. belief in Allāh and His Messenger ﷺ, the five compulsory prayers, the fasting of the month of Ramaḍān, the payment of Zakāt, and the Ḥajj to the House (of Allāh)." The man said, "O Abū Abdur-Raḥmān! Won't you listen to what Allāh has mentioned in His Book:—

> 'If two groups of believers fight each other, then make peace between them, but if one of them transgresses beyond bounds against the other, then you all fight against the one that transgresses.' (49:9)

and:—

'And fight them till there is no more affliction (i.e. no more worshipp-

عن نافع، عن ابن عمر رضي الله
عنهما: أتاه رجلان في فتنة ابن الزبير
فقالا: إن الناس قد ضيعوا وأنت ابن
عمر وصاحب النبي صلى الله عليه وسلم
فما يمنعك أن تخرج؟ فقال:
يمنعني أن الله حرم دم أخي، قالا:
ألم يقل الله - وقاتلوهم حتى لا تكون
فتنة - فقال: قاتلنا حتى لم تكن
فتنة وكان الدين لله، وأنتم تريدون
أن تقاتلوا حتى تكون فتنة ويكون
الدين لغير الله. وزاد عثمان بن
صالح، عن ابن وهب قال: أخبرني
فلان وحيوة بن شريح، عن بكر
ابن عمرو المعافري: أن بكير بن
عبد الله حدثه عن نافع: أن رجلا
أتى ابن عمر فقال: يا أبا عبد الرحمن،
ما حملك على أن تحج عاما وتعتمر
عاما وتترك الجهاد في سبيل الله عز وجل
وقد علمت ما رغب الله فيه؟ قال:
يا ابن أخي، بني الإسلام على خمس:
إيمان بالله ورسوله، والصلاة الخمس،
وصيام رمضان، وأداء الزكاة، وحج
البيت. قال: يا أبا عبد الرحمن، ألا
تسمع ما ذكر الله في كتابه - وإن
طائفتان من المؤمنين اقتتلوا فأصلحوا
بينهما فإن بغت إحداهما على
الأخرى فقاتلوا التي تبغي حتى تفيء

(33) CHAPTER. And whosoever performed the 'Umra in the months of Ḥajj before (performing) the Ḥajj he must slaughter. . . . . (2:196)

باب ـ فمن تمتع بالعمرة إلى الحج ـ.

43. Narrated 'Imrān bin Ḥuṣain : The Verse of Ḥajj-at-Tamatu' was revealed in Allāh's Book, so we performed it with Allāh's Messenger and nothing was revealed in Qur'ān to make it illegal, nor did the Prophet prohibit it till he died. But the man (who regarded it illegal) just expressed what his own mind suggested.

٤٣ ـ حدثنا مسدد: حدثنا يحيى، عن عمران بن أبى بكر: حدثنا أبو رجاء، عن عمران بن حصين رضى الله تعالى عنه قال: نزلت آية المتعة فى كتاب الله ففعلناها مع رسول الله صلى الله عليه وسلم ولم ينزل قرآن يحرمه ولم ينه عنها حتى مات، قال رجل برأيه ما شاء.

(34) CHAPTER. 'There is no harm for you if you seek of the Bounty of your Lord (during Ḥajj).' (2:198)

باب ـ ليس عليكم جناح أن تبتغوا فضلا من ربكم ـ.

44. Narrated Ibn 'Abbās : 'Ukāz, Mijanna and Dhul-Majāz were markets during the Pre-Islāmic Period. They (i.e. Muslims) considered it a sin to trade there during the Ḥajj time (i.e. season), so this Verse was revealed:—

> 'There is no harm for you if you seek of the Bounty of your Lord during the Ḥajj season.' (2:198)

٤٤ ـ حدثنى محمد قال: أخبرنا ابن عيينة، عن عمرو، عن ابن عباس رضى الله تعالى عنهما قال: كانت عكاظ ومجنة وذو المجاز أسواقا فى الجاهلية فتأثموا أن يتجروا فى المواسم فنزلت ـ ليس عليكم جناح أن تبتغوا فضلا من ربكم فى مواسم الحج ـ.

(35) CHAPTER. 'Then depart from the place whence all the people depart and ask for Allah's Forgiveness.'... (2:199)

بابٌ - ثُمَّ أفيضُوا مِنْ حَيْثُ أفاضَ النَّاسُ -

(45) Narrated 'Aisha : The Quraish people and those who embraced their religion, used to stay at Muzdalifa and used to call themselves Al-Hums, while the rest of the Arabs used to stay at 'Arafat. When Islam came, Allah ordered His Prophet to go to 'Arafat and stay at it, and then pass on from there, and that is what is meant by the Statement of Allah :–

> 'Then depart from the place whence all the people depart ......' (2:199)

٤٥ - حدَّثنا عليُّ بنُ عبدِ اللهِ : حدَّثنا مُحمَّدُ بنُ حازمٍ : حدَّثنا هِشامٌ ، عَنْ أبيهِ ، عَنْ عائشةَ رَضِيَ اللهُ تعالى عَنْها قالَتْ : كانَتْ قُرَيْشٌ وَمَنْ دانَ دينَها يَقِفونَ بالمُزْدَلِفَةِ وكانُوا يُسَمَّوْنَ الحُمْسَ ، وكانَ سائرُ العَرَبِ يَقِفونَ بعَرَفاتٍ ، فَلَمَّا جاءَ الإسْلامُ أمَرَ اللهُ نَبيَّهُ صلى اللهُ عليهِ وسلَّمَ أنْ يأتيَ عَرَفاتٍ ثُمَّ يَقِفَ بِها ثُمَّ يُفيضَ مِنْها ، كَذلِكَ قَوْلُهُ تعالى - ثُمَّ أفيضُوا مِنْ حَيْثُ أفاضَ النَّاسُ -.

46. Narrated Ibn 'Abbas : A man who wants to perform the Hajj (from Mecca) can perform the Tawaf around the Ka'ba as long as he is not in the state of Ihram till he assumes the Ihram for Hajj. Then, if he rides and proceeds to 'Arafat, he should take a Hadi (i.e. animal for sacrifice), either a camel or a cow or a sheep, whatever he can afford; but if he cannot afford it, he should fast for three days during the Hajj before the day of 'Arafat, but if the third day of his fasting happens to be the day of 'Arafat (i.e. 9th of Dhul-Hijja) then it is no sin for him (to fast on it). Then he should proceed

٤٦ - حدَّثني مُحمَّدُ بنُ أبي بَكْرٍ : حدَّثنا فُضَيْلُ بنُ سُلَيْمانَ : حدَّثنا مُوسى بنُ عُقْبَةَ : أخبرَني كُرَيْبٌ ، عَنِ ابنِ عبَّاسٍ قالَ : يَطوفُ الرَّجُلُ بالبَيْتِ ما كانَ حَلالاً حتَّى يُهِلَّ بالحَجِّ ، فإذا رَكِبَ إلى عَرَفَةَ فَمَنْ تَيَسَّرَ لَهُ هَدِيَّةٌ مِنَ الإبِلِ أوِ البَقَرِ أوِ الغَنَمِ ما تَيَسَّرَ لَهُ مِنْ ذَلِكَ أيَّ ذَلِكَ شاءَ غيرَ إنْ لَمْ يَتَيَسَّرْ لَهُ فعلَيْهِ ثَلاثَةُ أيَّامٍ في الحَجِّ وَذَلِكَ قَبْلَ يَوْمِ عَرَفَةَ ،

to 'Arafāt and stay there from the time of the 'Aṣr prayer till darkness falls. Then the pilgrims should proceed from 'Arafāt, and when they have departed from it, they reach Jam' (i.e. Al-Muzdalifa) where they ask Allāh to help them to be righteous and dutiful to Him, and there they remember Allāh greatly or say Takbīr (i.e. Allāh is Greater) and Tahlīl (i.e. None has the right to be worshipped but Allāh) repeatedly before dawn breaks. Then, after offering the morning (Fajr) prayer you should pass on (to Minā) for the people used to do so and Allāh said:–

> 'Then depart from the place whence all the people depart. And ask for Allāh's Forgiveness. Truly! Allāh is Oft-Forgiving, Most Merciful.' (2:199)

Then you should go on doing so till you throw pebbles over the Jamra.

فإنْ كانَ آخرُ يومٍ منَ الأيامِ الثلاثةِ يومَ عرفةَ فلا جناحَ عليهِ، ثمَّ لينطلقْ حتى يقفَ بعرفاتٍ منْ صلاةِ العصرِ إلى أنْ يكونَ الظلامُ ثمَّ ليدفعوا منْ عرفاتٍ فإذا أفاضوا منها حتى يبلغوا جمعًا الذى يتبررُ فيهِ، ثمَّ ليذكروا اللهَ كثيرًا أو أكثروا التكبيرَ والتهليلَ قبلَ أنْ تصبحوا ثمَّ أفيضوا فإنَّ الناسَ كانوا يفيضونَ. وقالَ اللهُ تعالى - ثمَّ أفيضوا منْ حيثُ أفاضَ الناسُ، واستغفروا اللهَ إنَّ اللهَ غفورٌ رحيمٌ - حتى ترموا الجمرةَ.

(36) CHAPTER. 'And of them is he who says Our Lord! Give us in this world that, which is good and in the Hereafter that, which is good...' (2:201)

باب - ومنهمْ منْ يقولُ ربَّنا آتنا فى الدنيا حسنةً وفى الآخرةِ حسنةً - الآيةَ.

47. Narrated Anas: The Prophet used to say, "O Allāh! Our Lord! Give us in this world that, which is good and in the Hereafter that,

٤٧ - حدثنا أبو معمرٍ: حدثنا عبدُ الوارثِ، عنْ عبدِ العزيزِ، عنْ أنسٍ قالَ: كانَ النبىُّ صلى اللهُ عليهِ وسلمَ

which is good and save us from the torment of the Fire." (2:201)

يقول: اللهم ربنا آتنا في الدنيا حسنة وفي الآخرة حسنة وقنا عذاب النار.

(37) CHAPTER. 'Yet he is the most quarrelsome.' (2:204)

باب - وهو ألد الخصام - وقال عطاء: النسل: الحيوان.

48. Narrated 'Āisha: The Prophet ﷺ said, "The most hated man in the Sight of Allāh is the one who is the most quarrelsome."

Narrated 'Āisha: The Prophet ﷺ said, "Or do you think that you shall enter Paradise without such (trials) as came to those who passed away before you?" (2:214)

٤٨ - حدثنا قبيصة: حدثنا سفيان، عن ابن جريج، عن ابن أبي مليكة، عن عائشة ترفعه: أبغض الرجال إلى الله الألد الخصم. وقال عبد الله: حدثنا سفيان: حدثني ابن جريج، عن ابن أبي مليكة، عن عائشة رضي الله تعالى عنها، عن النبي صلى الله عليه وسلم - أم حسبتم أن تدخلوا الجنة ولما يأتكم مثل الذين خلوا من قبلكم - الآية.

49. Narrated Ibn Abū Mulaika: Ibn 'Abbās recited: '(Respite will be granted) until when the Messengers gave up hope (of their people) and thought that they were denied (by their people). There came to them Our Help ......,' (12:110) reading 'Kudhibu' without doubling the sound 'dh', and that was what he understood of the Verse. Then he went on reciting.

"...even the Messenger and those who believed along with him said: When

٤٩ - حدثني إبراهيم بن موسى: أخبرنا هشام، عن ابن جريج قال: سمعت ابن أبي مليكة يقول: قال ابن عباس رضي الله عنهما - حتى إذا استيأس الرسل وظنوا أنهم قد كذبوا - خفيفة، ذهب بها هناك. وتلا - حتى يقول الرسول والذين آمنوا معه

(will come) Allāh's Help? Yes, verily, Allāh's Help is near.' (2: 214)

مَتَى نَصْرُ اللهِ أَلا إِنَّ نَصْرَ اللهِ قَرِيبٌ. فَلَقِيتُ عُرْوَةَ بنَ الزُّبَيرِ فَذَكَرْتُ لَهُ ذَلِكَ فَقَالَ: قَالَتْ عَائِشَةُ: مَعَاذَ اللهِ، وَاللهِ مَا وَعَدَ اللهُ رَسُولَهُ مِنْ شَيءٍ قَطُّ إِلاَّ عَلِمَ أَنَّهُ كَائِنٌ قَبْلَ أَنْ يَمُوتَ، وَلَكِنْ لَمْ يَزَلِ البَلاءُ بِالرُّسُلِ حَتَّى خَافُوا أَنْ يَكُونَ مَنْ مَعَهُمْ يُكَذِّبُونَهُمْ فَكَانَتْ تَقْرَؤُهَا: وَظَنُّوا أَنَّهُمْ قَدْ كُذِّبُوا مُثَقَّلَةً.

Then I met 'Urwa bin Az-Zubair and I mentioned that to him. He said, "Āisha said, 'Allāh forbid! By Allāh, Allāh never promised His Messenger ﷺ anything but he knew that it would certainly happen before he died. But trials were continuously presented before the Apostles till they were afraid that their followers would accuse them of telling lies. So I used to recite:—

'Till they (come to) think that they were treated as liars.'

reading 'Kudh-dhibū' with double 'dh.'

(38) CHAPTER. 'Your wives are a tilth unto you; so go to your tilth when or how you will.' (2:223)

بَابُ نِسَاؤُكُمْ حَرْثٌ لَكُمْ فَأْتُوا حَرْثَكُمْ أَنَّى شِئْتُمْ.

50. Narrated Nāfi': Whenever Ibn 'Umar recited the Qur'ān, he would not speak to anyone till he had finished his recitation. Once I held the Qur'ān and he recited Sūrat-al-Baqara from his memory and then stopped at a certain Verse and said, "Do you know in what connection this Verse was revealed?" I replied, "No." He said, "It was revealed in such-and-such connection." Ibn 'Umar then resumed his recitation.

Nāfi' added regarding the Verse:—

٥٠ - حَدَّثَنِي إِسْحَاقُ: أَخْبَرَنَا النَّضْرُ بنُ شُمَيلٍ: أَخْبَرَنَا ابنُ عَوْنٍ، عَنْ نَافِعٍ قَالَ: كَانَ ابنُ عُمَرَ رَضِيَ اللهُ عَنْهُمَا إِذَا قَرَأَ القُرآنَ لَمْ يَتَكَلَّمْ حَتَّى يَفْرُغَ مِنْهُ. فَأَخَذْتُ عَلَيْهِ يَوْماً فَقَرَأَ سُورَةَ البَقَرَةِ حَتَّى انْتَهَى إِلى مَكَانٍ قَالَ: تَدْرِي فِيمَ أُنْزِلَتْ؟ قُلْتُ: لا، قَالَ: أُنْزِلَتْ فِي كَذَا وَكَذَا

ثُمَّ مَضَى. وَعَنْ عَبْدِ الصَّمَدِ: حَدَّثَنِي أَبِي: حَدَّثَنِي أَيُّوبُ، عَنْ نَافِعٍ، عَنِ ابْنِ عُمَرَ - فَأْتُوا حَرْثَكُمْ أَنَّى شِئْتُمْ - قَالَ: يَأْتِيهَا فِي، رَوَاهُ مُحَمَّدُ بْنُ يَحْيَى ابْنِ سَعِيدٍ عَنْ أَبِيهِ، عَنْ عُبَيْدِ اللهِ، عَنْ نَافِعٍ، عَنِ ابْنِ عُمَرَ.

'So go to your tilth when or how you will,'

Ibn 'Umar said, "It means one should approach his wife in......"(1)

٥١ - حَدَّثَنَا أَبُو نُعَيْمٍ: حَدَّثَنَا سُفْيَانُ، عَنِ ابْنِ الْمُنْكَدِرِ: سَمِعْتُ جَابِرًا رَضِيَ اللهُ عَنْهُ قَالَ: كَانَتِ الْيَهُودُ تَقُولُ: إِذَا جَامَعَهَا مِنْ وَرَائِهَا جَاءَ الْوَلَدُ أَحْوَلَ، فَنَزَلَتْ - نِسَاؤُكُمْ حَرْثٌ لَكُمْ فَأْتُوا حَرْثَكُمْ أَنَّى شِئْتُمْ -.

51. Narrated Jābir (رضي الله عنه) : Jews used to say: "If one has sexual intercourse with his wife from the back, then she will deliver a squint-eyed child." So this Verse was revealed:—

'Your wives are a tilth unto you; so go to your tilth when or how you will.' (2:223)

باب - وَإِذَا طَلَّقْتُمُ النِّسَاءَ فَبَلَغْنَ أَجَلَهُنَّ فَلَا تَعْضُلُوهُنَّ أَنْ يَنْكِحْنَ أَزْوَاجَهُنَّ -

(39) CHAPTER. 'And when you have divorced women and they have fulfilled the term of their prescribed period ('Iddat, i.e. three months), do not prevent them from marrying their (former) husbands.' (2:232)

٥٢ - حَدَّثَنَا عُبَيْدُ اللهِ بْنُ سَعِيدٍ: حَدَّثَنَا أَبُو عَامِرٍ الْعَقَدِيُّ: حَدَّثَنَا عَبَّادُ ابْنُ رَاشِدٍ: حَدَّثَنَا الْحَسَنُ قَالَ:

52. Narrated Al-Ḥasan: The sister of Ma'qal bin Yasār was divorced by her husband who left her till she had fulfilled her term of 'Iddat (i.e. the period which should elapse before she can re-

(1) Al-Bukhārī left a blank space here because he was not sure of what Ibn 'Umar had said.

marry) and then he wanted to remarry her but Ma'qal refused, so this Verse was revealed:—

'Do not prevent them from marrying their (former) husbands.'

(2:232).

حدَّثني معقلُ بنُ يسارٍ قالَ: كانتْ لي أُختٌ تُخطَبُ إليَّ. وقالَ إبراهيمُ، عنْ يونسَ، عنِ الحسنِ: حدَّثني معقلُ بنُ يسارٍ: حدَّثنا أبو معمرٍ: حدَّثنا عبدُ الوارثِ: حدَّثنا يونسُ، عنِ الحسنِ: أنَّ أُختَ معقلِ بنِ يسارٍ طلَّقها زوجُها فتركَها حتَّى انقضتْ عدَّتُها فخطبَها فأبى معقلٌ فنزلتْ ـ فلا تعضُلوهُنَّ أنْ ينكِحنَ أزواجَهنَّ ـ.

(40) CHAPTER. 'Those of you who die and leave wives behind, they (the wives) shall wait (as regards their marriage) for four months and ten days. When they have fulfilled their term, there is no blame on you if they (the wives) dispose of themselves (i.e. to be married) in a just and honourable manner (i.e. they can marry) And Allāh is Well-acquainted with what you do.'

(2:234)

باب ـ والذينَ يُتوفَّونَ منكُمْ ويذَرونَ أزواجًا يتربَّصنَ بأنفسِهنَّ أربعةَ أشهرٍ وعشرًا ـ فإذا بلغنَ أجلَهنَّ فلا جُناحَ عليكُمْ فيما فعلنَ في أنفسِهنَّ بالمعروفِ واللهُ بما تعملونَ خبيرٌ ـ يعفُونَ: يهَبنَ.

53. Narrated Ibn Az-Zubair: I said to 'Uthman bin 'Affān (while he was collecting the Qur'ān) regarding the Verse:—

'Those of you who die and leave wives ...... (2:240)

"This Verse was abrogated by an other Verse. So why should you write it? (Or leave it in the Qur'ān) ?" 'Uthmān said. "O son of my brother! I will not shift anything of it from its place."

٥٣ ـ حدَّثني أُميَّةُ بنُ بسطامٍ: حدَّثنا يزيدُ بنُ زُرَيعٍ، عنْ حبيبٍ، عنِ ابنِ أبي مُليكةَ: قالَ ابنُ الزُّبيرِ: قُلتُ لعثمانَ بنِ عفَّانَ ـ والذينَ يُتوفَّونَ منكُمْ ويذَرونَ أزواجًا ـ قالَ: قدْ نسختْها الآيةُ الأُخرى فلِمَ تكتُبُها أوْ تدَعُها؟ قالَ: يا ابنَ أخي،

لا أغير شيئا منه من مكانه.

54. Narrated Mujāhid (regarding the Verse):—

> Those of you who die and leave wives behind. They - (their wives) — shall wait (as regards their marriage) for four months and ten days).' (2:234)

The widow, according to this Verse, was to spend this period of waiting with her husband's family, so Allāh revealed

> 'Those of you who die and leave wives (i.e. widows) should bequeath for their wives, a year's maintenance and residences without turning them out, but if they leave (their residence), there is no blame on you for what they do with themselves provided it is honourable.' (i.e. lawful marriage) (2:240).

So Allāh entitled the widow to be bequeathed extra maintenance for seven months and twenty nights, and that is the completion of one year. If she wished she could stay (in her husband's home) according to the will, and she could leave it if she wished, as Allāh says:—

> '...without turning them out, but if they leave (the residence), there is no blame on you.'

So the 'Idda (i.e. four months and ten days as it) is obligatory for her.

'Aṭā said: Ibn 'Abbās said, "This Verse, i.e. the Statement of Allāh ﷻ :—

> . ...without turning them out......'

cancelled the obligation of staying for the waiting period in her dead husband's house, and she can complete this period

٥٤ - حدثني إسحاق: حدثنا روح: حدثنا شبل، عن ابن أبي نجيح، عن مجاهد - والذين يتوفون منكم ويذرون أزواجا - قال: كانت هذه العدة تعتد عند زوجها واجب، فأنزل الله - والذين يتوفون منكم ويذرون أزواجا وصية لأزواجهم متاعا إلى الحول غير إخراج فإن خرجن فلا جناح عليكم فيما فعلن في أنفسهن من معروف - قال: جعل الله لها تمام السنة بسبعة أشهر وعشرين ليلة وصية، إن شاءت سكنت في وصيتها، وإن شاءت خرجت، وهو قول الله تعالى - غير إخراج فإن خرجن فلا جناح عليكم. فالعدة كما هي واجب عليها، زعم ذلك عن مجاهد. وقال عطاء، قال ابن عباس: نسخت هذه الآية عدتها عند أهلها فتعتد حيث شاءت وهو قول الله تعالى: - غير إخراج - قال عطاء: إن شاءت اعتدت عند أهله وسكنت في وصيتها، وإن شاءت خرجت لقول الله تعالى - فلا جناح عليكم فيما فعلن - قال عطاء: ثم

wherever she likes." 'Aṭā'said: If she wished, she could complete her 'Idda by staying in her dead husband's residence according to the will or leave it according to Allāh's Statement:–

'There is no blame on you for what they do with themselves.'

'Aṭā' added: Later the regulations of inheritance came and abrogated the order of the dwelling of the widow (in her dead husband's house), so she could complete the 'Idda wherever she likes. And it was no longer necessary to provide her with a residence. Ibn 'Abbās said, "This Verse abrogated her (i.e. widow's) dwelling in her dead husband's house and she could complete the 'Idda (i.e. four months and ten days) wherever she liked, as Allāh's Statement says:–

'......without turning them out...'

جاءَ الميراثُ فنسخَ السُّكنى فتعتدُّ حيثُ شاءَتْ ولا سُكنى لها. وعَنْ مُحمّدِ بنِ يوسفَ: حدَّثنا ورْقاءُ، عَنِ ابنِ أبي نجيحٍ، عَنْ مُجاهدٍ بهذا. وعَنِ ابنِ أبي نجيحٍ، عَنْ عطاءٍ، عَنِ ابنِ عبّاسٍ قالَ: نسخَتْ هذهِ الآيةُ عِدَّتَها في أهلِها فتعتدُّ حيثُ شاءَتْ لقولِ اللهِ تعالى - غيرَ إخراجٍ - نحوَهُ.

55. Narrated Muḥammad bin Sīrīn: I sat in a gathering in which the chiefs of the Anṣār were present, and Abdur-Raḥmān bin Abū Lailā was amongst them. I mentioned the narration of 'Abdullāh bin 'Utba regarding the question of Subai'a bint Al-Ḥāriṯh. Abdur-Raḥmān said, "But 'Abdullāh's uncle used not to say so." I said, "I am too brave if I tell a lie concerning a person who is now in Al-Kūfa," and I raised my voice. Then

٥٥ - حدَّثني حبّانُ: أخبرَنا عبدُ اللهِ: أخبرَنا عبدُ اللهِ بنُ عونٍ، عَنْ مُحمّدِ بنِ سيرينَ قالَ: جلستُ إلى مجلسٍ فيهِ عُظْمٌ منَ الأنصارِ وفيهِم عبدُ الرّحمنِ بنُ أبي ليلى. فذكرْتُ حديثَ عبدِ اللهِ بنِ عُتبةَ في شأنِ سُبَيْعةَ بنتِ الحارثِ فقالَ

I went out and met Mālik bin 'Āmir or Mālik bin 'Auf, and said, "What was the verdict of Ibn Mas'ūd about the pregnant widow whose husband had died?" He replied, "Ibn Mas'ūd said, 'Why do you impose on her the hard order and don't let her make use of the leave? The shorter Sūra of women (i.e. Sūrat-aṭ-Ṭalāq) was revealed after the longer Sūra (i.e. Sūrat-al-Baqara). ' " (i.e. Her 'Idda is uptill she delivers.)

عبدُ الرحمنِ : ولكنْ عمهُ كانَ لا يقولُ ذلكَ . فقلتُ : إنى لجرىءٌ إنْ كذبتُ على رجلٍ فى جانبِ الكوفةِ ، ورفعَ صوتهُ قالَ : ثمَّ خرجتُ فلقيتُ مالكَ بنَ عامرٍ ، أوْ مالكَ بنَ عوفٍ ، قلتُ : كيفَ كانَ قولُ ابنِ مسعودٍ فى المتوفَّى عنها زوجُها وهى حاملٌ ؟ فقالَ : قالَ ابنُ مسعودٍ : أتجعلونَ عليها التغليظَ ولا تجعلونَ لها الرخصةَ ؟ أُنزلتْ سورةُ النساءِ القُصرى بعدَ الطولى . وقالَ أيوبُ ، عنْ محمدٍ : لقيتُ أبا عطيةَ مالكَ بنَ عامرٍ .

(41) CHAPTER. 'Guard strictly the (five obligatory) prayers (their offering at their stated times), especially the middle (the Best) Prayer (i.e. 'Aṣr).' (2:238)

باب - حافظوا على الصلواتِ والصلاةِ الوسطى -

56. Narrated 'Alī : The Prophet said (as below).

٥٦ - حدثنى عبدُ اللهِ بنُ محمدٍ : حدثنا يزيدُ : أخبرنا هشامٌ ، عنْ محمدٍ ، عنْ عبيدةَ ، عنْ علىٍّ رضىَ اللهُ تعالى عنهُ : قالَ النبىُّ صلى اللهُ عليهِ وسلَّمَ .

57. Narrated 'Alī : on the day

٥٧ - حدثنى عبدُ الرحمنِ : حدثنا

of Al-Khandaq (the battle of the Trench). the Prophet ﷺ said, "They (i.e. pagans prevented us from offering the middle (the Best) Prayer till the sun had set. May Allāh fill their graves, their houses (or their bodies) with fire...... ......

يحيى بن سعيد قال هشام : حدثنا محمد عن عبيدة عن على رضى الله تعالى عنه أن النبى صلى الله عليه وسلم قال يوم الخندق : حبسونا عن صلاة الوسطى حتى غابت الشمس ، ملأ الله قبورهم وبيوتهم أو أجوافهم نارا ، شك يحيى

(42) CHAPTER. 'And stand before Allāh with obedience (and not to speak to others during the prayers),'(1) (2:238)

باب - وقوموا لله قانتين - أى مطيعين .

58. Narrated Zaid bin Arqam: We used to speak while in prayer. One of us used to speak to his brother (while in prayer) about his need, till the Verse was revealed:—

> 'Guard strictly the (five obligatory) prayers, especially the middle (the Best) ('A ṣr) Prayer and stand before Allāh with obedience (and not to speak to others during the prayers).' Then we were ordered not to speak in the prayers. (2 : 238)

٥٨ - حدثنا مسدد : حدثنا يحيى ، عن إسماعيل بن أبى خالد ، عن الحارث بن شبيل ، عن أبى عمرو الشيبانى ، عن زيد بن أرقم قال : كنا نتكلم فى الصلاة ، يكلم أحدنا أخاه فى حاجته حتى نزلت هذه الآية - حافظوا على الصلوات والصلاة الوسطى وقوموا لله قانتين - فأمرنا بالسكوت .

(43) CHAPTER. Allāh's Statement:— 'If you fear (an enemy), pray on foot, or riding (as may be most convenient), but when you are in safety......' (2:239)

باب - قوله - فإن خفتم فرجالا أو ركبانا فإذا أمنتم - الآية . وقال ابن جبير : كرسيه : علمه ، يقال

(1) See "Iqāmat-aṣ-Ṣalāt" in glossary.

بَسْطَةً : زِيَادَةً وَفَضْلاً. أَفْرِغْ : أَنْزِلْ. وَلا يَؤُودُهُ : لا يُثْقِلُهُ ، آدَنِي أَثْقَلَنِي : والآدُ والأَيْدُ : القُوَّةُ . السِّنَةُ : النُّعاسُ ، لَمْ يَتَسَنَّهْ : لَمْ يَتَغَيَّرْ . فَبُهِتَ : ذَهَبَتْ حُجَّتُهُ . خاوِيَةٌ : لا أَنِيسَ فِيها . عُرُوشُها : أَبْنِيَتُها . نُنْشِرُها : نُخْرِجُها . إِعْصارٌ : رِيحٌ عاصِفٌ تَهُبُّ مِنَ الأَرْضِ إِلى السَّماءِ كَعَمُودٍ فِيهِ نارٌ . وَقالَ ابْنُ عَبّاسٍ : صَلْداً : لَيْسَ عَلَيْهِ شَيْءٌ . وَقالَ عِكْرِمَةُ : وابِلٌ : مَطَرٌ شَدِيدٌ . الطَّلُّ : النَّدَى . وَهَذا مَثَلُ عَمَلِ المُؤْمِنِ . يَتَسَنَّهْ : يَتَغَيَّرْ .

59. Narrated Nāfi': Whenever 'Abdullāh bin 'Umar was asked about Ṣalāt-al-Khauf (i.e. prayer of fear) he said, "The Imām comes forward with a group of people and leads them in a one-Rak'a prayer while another group from them who has not prayed yet, stay between the praying group and the enemy. When those who are with the Imām have finished their one-Rak'a, they retreat and take the positions of those who have not prayed but they will not finish their prayers with Taslīm. Those who have not prayed, come forward to offer a Rak'a with the Imām (while the first group covers them from the enemy). Then the Imām, having offered two Rak'āt, finishes his prayer. Then each member of the two groups offer the second Rak'a alone after the Imām has

٥٩ - حَدَّثَنا عَبْدُ اللهِ بنُ يُوسُفَ : أَخْبَرَنا مالِكٌ ، عَنْ نافِعٍ : أَنَّ عَبْدَ اللهِ ابنَ عُمَرَ رَضِيَ اللهُ تَعالَى عَنْهُما كانَ إِذا سُئِلَ عَنْ صَلاةِ الخَوْفِ قالَ : يَتَقَدَّمُ الإِمامُ وَطائِفَةٌ مِنَ النّاسِ فَيُصَلِّي بِهِمُ الإِمامُ رَكْعَةً وَتَكُونُ طائِفَةٌ مِنْهُمْ بَيْنَهُمْ وَبَيْنَ العَدُوِّ لَمْ يُصَلُّوا ، فَإِذا صَلَّوْا الَّذِينَ مَعَهُ رَكْعَةً اسْتَأْخَرُوا مَكانَ الَّذِينَ لَمْ يُصَلُّوا وَلا يُسَلِّمُونَ . وَيَتَقَدَّمُ الَّذِينَ لَمْ يُصَلُّوا فَيُصَلُّونَ مَعَهُ رَكْعَةً ثُمَّ يَنْصَرِفُ الإِمامُ وَقَدْ صَلَّى رَكْعَتَيْنِ ، فَيَقُومُ كُلُّ واحِدٍ مِنَ الطّائِفَتَيْنِ فَيُصَلُّونَ

finished his prayer. Thus each one of the two groups will have offered two Rak'āt. But if the fear is too great, they can pray standing on their feet or riding on their mounts, facing the Qibla or not."

Nāfi' added: I do not think that 'Abdullāh bin 'Umar narrated this except from Allāh's Messenger ﷺ (See Hadīth No. 451, Vol 5 to know exactly "The Fear Prayer.")

لأنفسهم ركعة بعد أن ينصرف الإمام، فيكون كل واحد من الطائفتين قد صلى ركعتين. فإن كان خوف هو أشد من ذلك صلوا رجالاً قياماً على أقدامهم أو ركباناً مستقبلي القبلة أو غير مستقبليها.
قال مالك: قال نافع: لا أرى عبد الله ابن عمر ذكر ذلك إلا عن رسول الله صلى الله عليه وسلم.

(44) CHAPTER. 'Those of you who die and leave wives behind.' (2: 240)

باب - والذين يتوفون منكم ويذرون أزواجا -

60. Narrated Ibn Az-Zubair: I said to 'Uthmān, "This Verse which is in Sūrat-al-Baqara:

'Those of you who die and leave widows behind......
without turning them out.'

has been abrogated by an other Verse. Why then do you write it (in the Qur'ān)?" 'Uthmān said. "Leave it (where it is), O the son of my brother, for I will not shift anything of it (i.e. the Qur'ān) from its original position."

٦٠ - حدثني عبد الله بن أبي الأسود: حدثنا حميد بن الأسود ويزيد بن زريع قالا: حدثنا حبيب ابن الشهيد، عن ابن أبي مليكة قال: قال ابن الزبير: قلت لعثمان: هذه الآية التي هي في البقرة - والذين يتوفون منكم ويذرون أزواجا - إلى قوله - غير إخراج - قد نسختها الآية الأخرى فلم تكتبها؟ قال: تدعها يا ابن أخي، لا أغير شيئا منه من مكانه. قال حميد: أو نحو هذا.

(45) CHAPTER. 'And (remember) when Abraham said: My Lord! Show me how You give life to the dead.'
(2:260)

باب ـ وإذ قال إبراهيم رب أرني كيف تحيي الموتى ـ فصرهن: قطعهن.

61. Narrated Abū Huraira : Allāh's Messenger said, "We have more right to be in doubt than Abraham when he said, 'My Lord! Show me how You give life to the dead.' He said, 'Do you not believe?' He said, 'Yes (I believe) but to be stronger in Faith.' "
(2:260)

٦١ ـ حدثنا أحمد بن أبي صالح: حدثنا ابن وهب: أخبرني يونس، عن ابن شهاب، عن أبي سلمة وسعيد، عن أبي هريرة رضي الله تعالى عنه قال: قال رسول الله صلى الله عليه وسلم: نحن أحق بالشك من إبراهيم ـ إذ قال رب أرني كيف تحيي الموتى، قال أو لم تؤمن قال بلى ولكن ليطمئن قلبي ـ.

(46) CHAPTER. 'Do any of you wish that he should have a garden with date-palms and vines...... that you may give thought." (2:266)

باب قوله ـ أيود أحدكم أن تكون له جنة من نخيل وأعناب ـ إلى قوله ـ لعلكم تتفكرون ـ.

62. Narrated 'Ubaid bin 'Umair: Once 'Umar (bin Al-Khaṭṭāb) said to the companions of the Prophet "What do you think about this Verse:—

'Does any of you wish that he should have a garden?' "

They replied, "Allāh knows best." 'Umar became angry and said, "Either say that you know or say that you do not know!" On that Ibn 'Abbās said,

٦٢ ـ حدثنا إبراهيم: أخبرنا هشام، عن ابن جريج: سمعت عبد الله بن أبي مليكة يحدث عن ابن عباس قال: وسمعت أخاه أبا بكر بن أبي مليكة يحدث عن عبيد بن عمير قال عمر رضي الله تعالى عنه يوما لأصحاب النبي صلى الله

"O chief of the believers! I have something in my mind to say about it." 'Umar said, "O son of my brother! Say, and do not under-estimate yourself." Ibn 'Abbās said, 'In this Verse there has been put forward an example for deeds." 'Umar said, "What kind of deeds?" Ibn 'Abbās said, "For deeds." 'Umar said, "This is an example for a rich man who does good deeds out of obedience to Allāh and then Allāh sends him Satan whereupon he commits sins till all his good deeds are lost."

عليه وسلم : فيم ترون هذه الآية نزلت ؟ - أيود أحدكم أن تكون له جنة - قالوا : الله أعلم ؛ فغضب عمر ، فقال : قولوا نعلم أو لا نعلم . فقال ابن عباس : في نفسي منها شيء يا أمير المؤمنين ، قال عمر : يا ابن أخي ، قل ولا تحقر نفسك . قال ابن عباس : ضربت مثلا لعمل . قال عمر : أي عمل ؟ قال ابن عباس : لعمل . قال عمر : لرجل غني يعمل بطاعة الله عز وجل ثم بعث الله له الشيطان فعمل بالمعاصي حتى أغرق أعماله . فصرهن : قطعهن .

(47) CHAPTER. 'They do not beg of people at all.' (2:273)

باب - لا يسألون الناس إلحافا - يقال : ألحف علي وألح وأحفاني بالمسألة .

63. Narrated Abū Huraira : The Prophet ﷺ said, "The poor person is not the one for whom a date or two or a morsel or two (of food) is sufficient but the poor person is he who does not (beg or) ask the people (for something) or show his poverty at all. Recite if you wish, (Allāh's Statement):–

'They do not beg of people at all.' (2:273)

٦٣ - حدثنا ابن أبي مريم : حدثنا محمد بن جعفر قال : حدثني شريك بن أبي نمر : أن عطاء بن يسار وعبد الرحمن بن أبي عمرة الأنصاري قالا : سمعنا أبا هريرة رضي الله عنه يقول : قال النبي صلى الله عليه وسلم : ليس المسكين الذي ترده التمرة والتمرتان ولا

اللُّقْمَةُ وَلا اللُّقْمَتَانِ . إِنَّمَا المِسْكِينُ الَّذِى يَتَعَفَّفُ ، اقْرَءُوا إِنْ شِئْتُمْ ، يَعْنِى قَوْلَهُ تَعَالَى - لا يَسْأَلُونَ النَّاسَ إِلْحَافًا -.

(48) CHAPTER. 'But Allāh has permitted trade and forbidden usury (1) (2:275)

بَاب - وَأَحَلَّ اللهُ البَيْعَ وَحَرَّمَ الرِّبَا - المَسُّ : الجُنُونُ .

64. Narrated 'Āisha: When the Verses of Sūrat-al-Baqara regarding usury (i.e. Ribā) were revealed, Allāh's Messenger ﷺ recited them before the people and then he prohibited the trade of alcoholic liquors.

٦٤ - حَدَّثَنَا عُمَرُ بْنُ حَفْصِ بْنِ غِيَاثٍ : حَدَّثَنَا أَبِى : حَدَّثَنَا الأَعْمَشُ : حَدَّثَنَا مُسْلِمٌ ، عَنْ مَسْرُوقٍ ، عَنْ عَائِشَةَ رَضِىَ اللهُ عَنْهَا قَالَتْ : لَمَّا نَزَلَتِ الآيَاتُ مِنْ آخِرِ سُورَةِ البَقَرَةِ فِى الرِّبَا فَقَرَأَهَا رَسُولُ اللهِ صلى اللهُ عليه وسلَّمَ عَلَى النَّاسِ . ثُمَّ حَرَّمَ التِّجَارَةَ فِى الخَمْرِ .

(49) CHAPTER. 'Allāh will destroy usury (i.e. Ribā) (2:276) (i.e. will make it lost).

بَاب - يَمْحَقُ اللهُ الرِّبَا - يُذْهِبُهُ .

65. Narrated 'Āisha: When the last Verses of Sūrat-al-Baqara were revealed. Allāh's Messenger ﷺ went out and recited them in the Mosque and

٦٥ - حَدَّثَنَا بِشْرُ بْنُ خَالِدٍ : أَخْبَرَنَا مُحَمَّدُ بْنُ جَعْفَرٍ ، عَنْ شُعْبَةَ ، عَنْ سُلَيْمَانَ : سَمِعْتُ أَبَا الضُّحَى

(1) See Glossary of Vol 1 for "Ribā".

prohibited the trade of alcoholic liquors.

يُحَدِّثُ عَنْ مَسْرُوقٍ ، عَنْ عَائِشَةَ ، أَنَّهَا قَالَتْ : لَمَّا أُنْزِلَتِ الآيَاتُ الأَوَاخِرُ مِنْ سُورَةِ البَقَرَةِ ، خَرَجَ رَسُولُ اللهِ صلى اللهُ عليه وسلَّمَ فَتَلاهُنَّ فى المَسْجِدِ ، فَحَرَّمَ التِّجَارَةَ فى الخَمْرِ .

(50) CHAPTER. 'Then be aware of taking a notice of war from Allāh and His Messenger'.' (2:279)

بَاب ـ فَأْذَنُوا بِحَرْبٍ مِنَ اللهِ وَرَسُولِهِ ـ فَاعْلَمُوا .

66. Narrated 'Āisha : When the last Verses of Sūrat-al-Baqara were revealed, the Prophet read them in the Mosque and prohibited the trade of alcoholic liquors. If the debtor is in difficulty, grant him time till it is easy for him to repay......' (2 : 280)

Narrated 'Āisha : When the last Verses of Sūrat-al-Baqara were revealed, Allāh's Messenger stood up and recited them before us and then prohibited the trade of alcoholic liquors.

٦٦ ـ حدَّثنى مُحَمَّدُ بنُ بَشَّارٍ : حدَّثنا غُنْدَرٌ : حدَّثنا شُعْبَةُ ، عَنْ مَنْصُورٍ ، عَنْ أَبى الضُّحَى ، عَنْ مَسْرُوقٍ ، عَنْ عائشَةَ ، قَالَتْ : لَمَّا أُنْزِلَتِ الآيَاتُ مِنْ آخِرِ سُورَةِ البَقَرَةِ قَرَأَهُنَّ النَّبِىُّ صلى اللهُ عليه وسلَّمَ فى المَسْجِدِ وَحَرَّمَ التِّجَارَةَ فى الخَمْرِ ـ وَإِنْ كَانَ ذُو عُسْرَةٍ فَنَظِرَةٌ إلى مَيْسَرَةٍ ـ الآيَةَ . وَقَالَ مُحَمَّدُ بنُ يُوسُفَ ، عَنْ سُفْيَانَ ، عَنْ مَنْصُورٍ وَالأَعْمَشِ عَنْ أَبى الضُّحَى ، عَنْ مَسْرُوقٍ ، عَنْ عائشَةَ قَالَتْ : لَمَّا أُنْزِلَتِ الآيَاتُ مِنْ آخِرِ سُورَةِ البَقَرَةِ قَامَ رَسُولُ اللهِ صلى اللهُ عليه وسلَّمَ فَقَرَأَهُنَّ عَلَيْنَا ثُمَّ حَرَّمَ التِّجَارَةَ فى الخَمْرِ .

(51) CHAPTER. 'And fear a day when you shall be brought back to Allāh.'

(2 : 281)

باب - واتقوا يوما ترجعون فيه إلى الله -

67, Narrated Ibn 'Abbās ؓ: The last Verse (in the Qur'ān) revealed to the Prophet ﷺ was the Verse dealing with usury (i.e. Ribā').

٦٧ - حدثنا قبيصة بن عقبة: حدثنا سفيان، عن عاصم، عن الشعبي، عن ابن عباس رضي الله عنهما قال: آخر آية نزلت على النبي صلى الله عليه وسلم آية الربا.

(52) CHAPTER. 'Whether you show what is in your minds or conceal it......'

(2: 284)

باب - وإن تبدوا ما فى أنفسكم أو تخفوه - الآية.

68. Narrated Ibn 'Umar ؓ: This Verse: –

'Whether you show what is in your minds or conceal it......' (2:284) was abrogated.

٦٨ - حدثنا محمد: حدثنا النفيلي: حدثنا مسكين: حدثنا شعبة، عن خالد الحذاء، عن مروان الأصفر، عن رجل من أصحاب النبي صلى الله عليه وسلم وهو ابن عمر أنها قد نسخت - وإن تبدوا ما فى أنفسكم أو تخفوه - الآية.

(53) CHAPTER. 'The Messenger (ﷺ) believes in what has been revealed to him from his Lord. (2:285)

باب - آمن الرسول بما أنزل إليه من ربه - وقال ابن عباس: إصرا: عهدا. ويقال: غفرانك: مغفرتك، فاغفر لنا.

69. Narrated Marwān Al-Asghar: A man from the companions of Allāh's Messenger ﷺ who I think, was Ibn 'Umar said, "The Verse:–

'Whether you show what is in your minds or conceal it. . . . . .'

was abrogated by the Verse following it."

٦٩ - حدَّثَني إسحاقُ بنُ مَنْصُور: أخبرَنا رَوْحٌ: أخبرَنا شُعْبَةُ، عَنْ خالد الحذَّاءِ، عَنْ مَرْوانَ الأصْغَرِ، عَنْ رَجُلٍ منْ أصحابِ رَسُولِ اللهِ صلى اللهُ عليهِ وسلَّم، قالَ: أحْسبهُ ابنَ عُمَرَ - إنْ تُبْدُوا ما فى أنفُسِكمْ أوْ تُخفُوهُ - قالَ: نَسَختْها الآيةُ التى بَعْدَها.

In the Name of Allāh,
the Most Beneficent, the Most Merciful

بِسْمِ اللهِ الرَّحْمَنِ الرَّحيمِ

SŪRAT-ĀL – 'IMRĀN (3)

سورة آل عمران

تَقاةٌ وتَقيةٌ واحدةٌ، صِرٌّ: بَرْدٌ. شَفا حُفْرَةٍ: مِثْلُ شَفا الرَّكيَّةِ وَهُوَ حَرْفُها. تُبَوِّئُ: تَتَّخِذُ مُعَسْكَرًا. رِبِّيُّونَ: الجُمُوعُ، واحدُها رِبِّيٌّ. تَحُسُّونَهمْ: تَسْتأصِلونَهمْ قَتْلاً. غُزًّا: واحدُها غازٍ. سَنَكْتُبُ ما قالُوا: سَنَحْفَظُ. نُزُلاً: ثَوابًا. ويَجُوزُ مُنْزَلٌ مِنْ عِنْدِ اللهِ كقَوْلكَ أنْزَلْتُهُ. والخَيْلِ المُسَوَّمَةِ: المُسَوَّمُ الَّذى لَهُ سِيماءُ بعَلامَةٍ أوْ بِصُوفَةٍ أوْ بِمَا كانَ. وَقالَ مُجاهِدٌ - والخَيْلِ المُسَوَّمَةِ - المُطَهَّمَةُ الحِسانُ. وَقالَ سَعيدُ بنُ جُبَيْرٍ وَعَبْدُ اللهِ ابنُ عَبْدِ الرَّحْمَنِ بنِ أبْزَى: الرَّاعِيَةُ: المُسَوَّمَةُ. وَقالَ ابنُ جُبَيْرٍ - وَحَصُورًا - لا يأتى النِّساءَ. وَقالَ عِكْرِمَةُ مِنْ فَوْرِهِمْ: غَضَبِهِمْ يَوْمَ بَدْرٍ. وَقالَ

مُجاهِدٌ: يُخْرِجُ الحَيَّ مِنَ المَيِّتِ: النُّطْفَةَ تَخْرُجُ مَيْتَةً، وَيُخْرِجُ مِنْها الحَيَّ. الإِبْكارُ: أَوَّلُ الفَجْرِ. والعَشِيُّ: مَيْلُ الشَّمْسِ إلى أنْ تَغْرُبَ - مِنْهُ آياتٌ مُحْكَماتٌ - قالَ مُجاهِدٌ: الحَلالُ والحَرامُ - وأُخَرُ مُتَشابِهاتٌ - يُصَدِّقُ بَعْضُها بَعْضًا كَقَوْلِهِ تَعالى - وَما يُضِلُّ بِهِ إلاَّ الفاسِقِينَ - وكَقَوْلِهِ جَلَّ ذِكْرُهُ - ويَجْعَلُ الرِّجْسَ عَلى الَّذينَ لا يَعْقِلُونَ - وكقوله تَعالى - وَالَّذينَ اهْتَدَوْا زادَهُمْ هُدًى وآتاهُمْ تَقْواهُمْ - زَيْغٌ: شَكٌّ - فَيَتَّبِعُونَ ما تَشابَهَ مِنْهُ ابْتِغاءَ الفِتْنَةِ المُشْتَبِهاتِ - والرّاسِخُونَ فى العِلْمِ - يَعْلَمُونَ تأويلَهُ - وَيَقُولُونَ آمَنّا بِهِ -.

٧٠ - حدَّثَنا عَبْدُ اللهِ بنُ مَسْلَمَةَ: حدَّثَنا يَزِيدُ بنُ إبْراهِيمَ التُّسْتَرِيُّ، عَنِ ابنِ أبي مُلَيْكَةَ، عَنِ القاسِمِ بنِ مُحَمَّدٍ، عَنْ عائِشَةَ رَضِيَ اللهُ عَنْها قالَتْ: تَلا رَسُولُ اللهِ صلى اللهُ عليه وسلَّم هَذِهِ الآيَةَ - هُوَ الَّذى أنزَلَ عَلَيْكَ الكِتابَ مِنْهُ آياتٌ مُحْكَماتٌ هُنَّ أُمُّ الكِتابِ وأُخَرُ مُتَشابِهاتٌ فَأَمّا الَّذينَ فى قُلُوبِهِمْ زَيْغٌ فَيَتَّبِعُونَ ما تَشابَهَ مِنْهُ ابْتِغاءَ الفِتْنَةِ وَابْتِغاءَ تأويلِهِ وَما يَعْلَمُ تأويلَهُ إلاَّ اللهُ والرّاسِخُونَ فى العِلْمِ يَقُولُونَ آمَنّا بِهِ كُلٌّ مِنْ عِنْدِ

70. Narrated 'Āisha' ; Allāh's Messenger recited the Verse:—

'It is He who has sent down to you the Book. In it are Verses that are entirely clear, they are the foundation of the Book, others not entirely clear. So as for those in whose hearts there is a deviation (from the Truth). follow thereof that is not entirely clear seeking affliction and searching for its hidden meanings; but no one knows its hidden meanings but Allāh. And those who are firmly grounded in knowledge say: "We believe in it (i.e. in the Qur'ān) the whole of it (i.e. its clear and unclear Verses) are from our Lord."

And none receive admonition except men of understanding.'

(3:7)

Then Allāh's Messenger ﷺ said, "If you see those who follow thereof that is not entirely clear, then they are those whom Allāh has named [as having deviation (from the Truth)] 'So beware of them'."

رَبِّنَا وَمَا يَذَّكَّرُ إِلاَّ أُولُو الأَلْبَابِ ـ
قَالَتْ: قَالَ رَسُولُ اللهِ صلى اللهُ عليه وسلَّم:
فَإِذَا رَأَيْتَ الَّذِينَ يَتَّبِعُونَ مَا تَشَابَهَ
مِنْهُ فَأُولَئِكَ الَّذِينَ سَمَّى اللهُ
فَاحْذَرُوهُمْ.

(54) CHAPTER. 'And I seek Refuge with You (Allāh) for her and her offspring from Satan, the outcast (3:36)

باب ـ وإنِّي أُعِيذُهَا بِكَ وَذُرِّيَّتَهَا
مِنَ الشَّيْطَانِ الرَّجِيمِ ـ

71. Narrated Sa'id bin Al-Musaiyab: Abū Huraira رضي الله عنه said, "The Prophet ﷺ said, 'No child is born but that, Satan touches it when it is born where upon it starts crying loudly because of being touched by Satan, except Mary and her Son.' " Abū Huraira then said, "Recite, it you wish:—

'And I seek Refuge with You (Allāh) for her and her offspring from Satan, the outcast.' " (3 :36)

٧١ ـ حدَّثَنِي عَبْدُ اللهِ بنُ مُحَمَّدٍ:
حدَّثَنَا عَبْدُ الرَّزَّاقِ: أَخْبَرَنَا مَعْمَرٌ، عَنِ
الزُّهْرِيِّ، عَنْ سَعِيدِ بنِ المُسَيَّبِ،
عَنْ أَبِي هُرَيْرَةَ رَضِيَ اللهُ تَعَالَى عَنْهُ:
أَنَّ النَّبِيَّ صلى اللهُ عليه وسلَّم قالَ: مَا مِنْ
مَوْلُودٍ يُولَدُ إِلاَّ وَالشَّيْطَانُ يَمَسُّهُ
حِينَ يُولَدُ فَيَسْتَهِلُّ صَارِخاً مِنْ مَسِّ
الشَّيْطَانِ إِيَّاهُ إِلاَّ مَرْيَمَ وَابْنَهَا، ثُمَّ
يَقُولُ أَبُو هُرَيْرَةَ: وَاقْرَؤُوا إِنْ شِئْتُمْ ـ
وَإِنِّي أُعِيذُهَا بِكَ وَذُرِّيَّتَهَا مِنَ
الشَّيْطَانِ الرَّجِيمِ ـ.

(55) CHAPTER. 'Verily' those who purchase a small gain at the cost of Allāh's Covenant and their oaths, they shall have no portion (i.e. no good) in the Hereafter..........and they shall have a painful torment.' (3:77)

باب ـ إِنَّ الَّذِينَ يَشْتَرُونَ بِعَهْدِ
اللهِ وَأَيْمَانِهِمْ ثَمَناً قَلِيلاً أُولَئِكَ لا
خَلاقَ لَهُمْ: لاخَيْرَ لَهُمْ ـ فِي الآخِرَةِ
وَلَهُمْ عَذَابٌ أَلِيمٌ ـ مُؤْلِمٌ مُوجِعٌ مِنَ
الأَلَمِ وَهُوَ فِي مَوْضِعِ مُفْعِلٍ.

72. Narrated Abū Wā'il: 'Abdullāh bin Mas'ūd said, "'Allāh's Messenger said, 'Whoever takes an oath when asked to do so, in which he may deprive a Muslim of his property unlawfully, will meet Allāh Who will be angry with him.' So Allāh revealed in confirmation of this statement:—

> 'Verily! Those who Purchase a small gain at the cost of Allāh's Covenant and oaths, they shall have no portion in the Hereafter...' "
> (3: 77)

Then entered Al-Ash'ath bin Qais and said, "What is Abū 'Abdur-Rahmān narrating to you?" We replied, "So-and-so." Al-Ash'ath said, "This Verse was revealed in my connection. I had a well in the land of my cousin (and he denied my possessing it). On that the Prophet said to me, 'Either you bring forward a proof or he (i.e. your cousin) takes an oath (to confirm his claim).' I said, 'I am sure he would take a (false) oath, O Allāh's Messenger.' He said, 'If somebody takes an oath when asked to do so through which he may deprive a Muslim of his property (unlawfully) and he is a liar in his oath, he will meet Allāh Who will be angry with him.' "

٧٢ - حدثنا حجاج بن منهال: حدثنا أبو عوانة، عن الأعمش، عن أبي وائل، عن عبد الله بن مسعود رضي الله تعالى عنه قال: قال رسول الله صلى الله عليه وسلم: من حلف يمين صبر ليقتطع بها مال امرئ مسلم لقي الله وهو عليه غضبان. فأنزل الله تصديق ذلك - إن الذين يشترون بعهد الله وأيمانهم ثمنا قليلا أولئك لا خلاق لهم فى الآخرة - إلى آخر الآية، قال: فدخل الأشعث بن قيس وقال: ما يحدثكم أبو عبد الرحمن؟ قلنا: كذا وكذا، قال: فيّ أنزلت، كانت لى بئر فى أرض ابن عم لى، قال النبي صلى الله عليه وسلم: بينتك أو يمينه، فقلت: إذا يحلف يا رسول الله. فقال النبي صلى الله عليه وسلم: من حلف على يمين صبر يقتطع بها مال امرئ مسلم وهو فيها فاجر لقي الله وهو عليه غضبان.

73. Narrated 'Abdullāh bin Abū Aufā: A man displayed some merchandise in the market and took an oath that he had been offered a certain price for it while in fact he had not, in order to cheat a man from the Muslims.

٧٣ - حدثنا علي هو ابن أبي هاشم: سمع هشيما: أخبرنا العوام بن حوشب، عن إبراهيم بن عبد الرحمن، عن عبد الله بن أبي أوفى رضي الله

So then was revealed:—

> 'Verily! Those who purchase a small gain at the cost of Allāh's Covenant and their oaths .....'
> (3: 77)

تعالى عنهما: أن رجلا أقام سلعة فى السوق فحلف فيها لقد أعطى بها ما لم يعطه ليوقع فيها رجلا من المسلمين، فنزلت: إن الذين يشترون بعهد الله وأيمانهم ثمنا قليلا- إلى آخر الآية.

74. Narrated Ibn Abū Mulaika: Two women were stitching shoes in a house or a room. Then one of them came out with an awl driven into her hand, and she sued the other for it. The case was brought before Ibn 'Abbās, Ibn 'Abbās said, "Allāh's Messenger ﷺ said, 'If people were to be given what they claim (without proving their claim) the life and property of the nation would be lost.' Will you remind her (i.e. the defendant), of Allāh and recite before her:—

> Verily! Those who purchase a small gain at the cost of Allāh's Covenant and their oaths......' "
> (3:77)

So they reminded her and she confessed. Ibn 'Abbās then said, "The Prophet ﷺ said, 'The oath is to be taken by the defendant (in the absence of any proof against him).' "

٧٤ - حدثنا نصر بن على بن نصر: حدثنا عبد الله بن داود، عن ابن جريج، عن ابن أبى مليكة: أن امرأتين كانتا تخرزان فى بيت وفى الحجرة فخرجت إحداهما وقد أنفذ باشفى فى كفها فادعت على أخرى فرفع إلى ابن عباس فقال ابن عباس: قال رسول الله صلى الله عليه وسلم: لو يعطى الناس بدعواهم لذهب دماء قوم وأموالهم، ذكروها بالله واقرءوا عليها - إن الذين يشترون بعهد الله - فذكروها فاعترفت. فقال ابن عباس: قال النبى صلى الله عليه وسلم: اليمين على المدعى عليه.

(56) CHAPTER. 'Say: O people of the Scripture (Jews & Christians)! Come to a

باب - قل يا أهل الكتاب تعالوا إلى كلمة سواء بيننا وبينكم أن لا

word common to you and us that we worship None but Allāh.' (3: 64)

75. Narrated Ibn 'Abbās : Abū Sufyān narrated to me personally, saying, "I set out during the Truce that had been concluded between me and Allāh's Messenger . While I was in Shā'm, a letter sent by the Prophet was brought to Heraclius. Diḥya Al-Kalbī had brought and given it to the governor of Buṣra, and the latter forwarded it to Heraclius. Heraclius said, 'Is there anyone from the people of this man who claims to be a prophet?' The people replied, 'Yes,' So I along with some of Quraishī men were called and we entered upon Heraclius, and we were seated in front of him. Then he said, 'Who amongst you is the nearest relative to the man who claims to be a prophet?' So they made me sit in front of him and made my companions sit behind me. Then he called upon his translator and said (to him). 'Tell them (i.e. Abū Sufyān's companions) that I am going to ask him (i.e. Abū Sufyān) regarding that man who claims to be a prophet. So, if he tell me a lie, they should contradict him (instantly).' By Allāh, had I not been afraid that my companions would consider me a liar, I would have told lies. Heraclius then said to his translator, 'Ask him: What is his (i.e. the Prophet's) family status amongst you? I said, 'He belongs to a noble family amongst us." Heraclius said, 'Was any of his ancestors a king?' I said, 'No.' He said, 'Did you ever accuse him of telling lies before his saying what he has said?' I said, 'No.' He said, 'Do the nobles follow him or the poor people?' I said,

نَعْبُدَ إِلاَّ اللهَ - سَوَاءٍ: قَصْدًا .

٧٥ - حَدَّثَنِي إِبْرَاهِيمُ بْنُ مُوسَى: عَنْ هِشَامٍ، عَنْ مَعْمَرٍ. وَحَدَّثَنِي عَبْدُ اللهِ بْنُ مُحَمَّدٍ: حَدَّثَنَا عَبْدُ الرَّزَّاقِ: أَخْبَرَنَا مَعْمَرٌ، عَنِ الزُّهْرِيِّ: أَخْبَرَنِي عُبَيْدُ اللهِ بْنُ عَبْدِ اللهِ بْنِ عُتْبَةَ: حَدَّثَنِي ابْنُ عَبَّاسٍ: حَدَّثَنِي أَبُو سُفْيَانَ مِنْ فِيهِ إِلَى فِيَّ قَالَ: انْطَلَقْتُ فِي الْمُدَّةِ الَّتِي كَانَتْ بَيْنِي وَبَيْنَ رَسُولِ اللهِ صلى اللهُ عليهِ وسلَّم قَالَ: فَبَيْنَا أَنَا بِالشَّامِ إِذْ جِيءَ بِكِتَابٍ مِنَ النَّبِيِّ صلى اللهُ عليهِ وسلَّم إِلَى هِرَقْلَ، قَالَ: وَكَانَ دِحْيَةُ الْكَلْبِيُّ جَاءَ بِهِ فَدَفَعَهُ إِلَى عَظِيمِ بُصْرَى، فَدَفَعَهُ عَظِيمُ بُصْرَى إِلَى هِرَقْلَ. قَالَ: فَقَالَ هِرَقْلُ: هَلْ هُنَا أَحَدٌ مِنْ قَوْمِ هَذَا الرَّجُلِ الَّذِي يَزْعُمُ أَنَّهُ نَبِيٌّ؟ فَقَالُوا: نَعَمْ، قَالَ: فَدُعِيتُ فِي نَفَرٍ مِنْ قُرَيْشٍ فَدَخَلْنَا عَلَى هِرَقْلَ فَأُجْلِسْنَا بَيْنَ يَدَيْهِ فَقَالَ: أَيُّكُمْ أَقْرَبُ نَسَبًا مِنْ هَذَا الرَّجُلِ الَّذِي يَزْعُمُ أَنَّهُ نَبِيٌّ؟ فَقَالَ أَبُو سُفْيَانَ: فَقُلْتُ: أَنَا، فَأَجْلَسُونِي بَيْنَ يَدَيْهِ وَأَجْلَسُوا أَصْحَابِي خَلْفِي. ثُمَّ دَعَا

'It is the poor who followed him.' He said, 'Is the number of his followers increasing or decreasing?' I said, 'They are increasing.' He said, 'Does anyone renounce his religion (i.e. Islām) after embracing it, being displeased with it?' I said, 'No.' He said, 'Did you fight with him?' I replied, 'Yes.' He said, 'How was your fighting with him?' I said, 'The fighting between us was undecided and victory was shared by him and us by turns. He inflicts casualties upon us and we inflict casualties upon him.' He said, 'Did he ever betray?' I said, 'No, but now we are away from him in this truce and we do not know what he will do in it.' " Abū Sufyān added, "By Allāh, I was not able to insert in my speech a word (against him) except that. Heraclius said, 'Did anybody else (amongst you) ever claimed the same (i.e. Islām) before him? I said, 'No.' Then Heraclius told his translator to tell me (i.e. Abū Sufyān), 'I asked you about his family status amongst you, and you told me that he comes from a noble family amongst you. Verily, all Apostles come from the noblest family among their people. Then I asked you whether any of his ancestors was a king, and you denied that. Thereupon I thought that had one of his fore-fathers been a king, I would have said that he (i.e. Muhammad ﷺ) was seeking to rule the kingdom of his fore-fathers. Then I asked you regarding his followers, whether they were the noble or the poor among the people, and you said that they were only the poor (who follow him). In fact, such are the followers of the Apostles. Then I asked you whether you have ever accused him of telling lies before he said what he said, and your reply was in the negative. There-

بترجمانه فقال: قل لهم: إني سائل عن هذا الرجل الذي يزعم أنه نبي، فإن كذبني فكذبوه. قال أبو سفيان: وايم الله لولا أن يؤثروا علي الكذب لكذبت. ثم قال لترجمانه: سله كيف حسبه فيكم؟ قال: قلت: هو فينا ذو حسب. قال: فهل كان من آبائه ملك؟ قال: قلت: لا، قال: فهل كنتم تتهمونه بالكذب قبل أن يقول ما قال؟ قلت: لا، قال: أيتبعه أشراف الناس أم ضعفاؤهم؟ قال: قلت: بل ضعفاؤهم. قال: يزيدون أو ينقصون؟ قال: قلت: لا بل يزيدون، قال: هل يرتد أحد منهم عن دينه بعد أن يدخل فيه سخطة له؟ قال: قلت: لا، قال: فهل قاتلتموه؟ قال: قلت: نعم. قال: فكيف كان قتالكم إياه؟ قال: قلت: تكون الحرب بيننا وبينه سجالاً يصيب منا ونصيب منه، قال: فهل يغدر، قال: قلت: لا، نحن منه في هذه المدة لا ندري ما هو صانع فيها. قال: والله ما أمكنني من كلمة أدخل فيها شيئا غير هذه، قال.

fore, I took for granted that a man who did not tell a lie about others, could ever tell a lie about Allāh. Then I asked you whether anyone of his followers had renounced his religion (i.e. Islām) after embracing it, being displeased with it, and you denied that. And such is Faith when it mixes with the cheerfulness of the hearts. Then I asked you whether his followers were increasing or decreasing. You claimed that they were increasing. That is the way of true faith till it is complete. Then I asked you whether you had ever fought with him, and you claimed that you had fought with him and the battle between you and him was undecided and the victory was shared by you and him in turns; he inflicted casualties upon you and you inflicted casualties upon them. Such is the case with the Messengers; they are out to test and the final victory is for them. Then I asked you whether he had ever betrayed; you claimed that he had never betrayed. Indeed, Apostles never betray. Then I asked you whether anyone had said this statement before him; and you denied that. Thereupon I thought if somebody had said that statement before him, then I would have said that he was but a man copying some sayings said before him.' " Abū Safyān said, "Heraclius then asked me, 'What does he order you to do?' I said, 'He orders us (to offer) prayers and (to pay) Zakāt and to keep good relationship with the kith and kin and to be chaste.' Then Heraclius said, 'If whatever you have said, is true, he is really a prophet, and I knew that he (i.e. the Prophet ﷺ) was going to appear, but I never thought that he would be from amongst you. If I were certain that I can reach him, I would like to meet him

فَهَلْ قَالَ هَذَا القَوْلَ أَحَدٌ قَبْلَهُ ؟ قُلْتُ : لا ، ثُمَّ قَالَ لِتَرْجُمانِهِ : قُلْ لَهُ إنِّى سَأَلْتُكَ عَنْ حَسَبِهِ فِيكُمْ فَزَعَمْتَ أَنَّهُ فِيكُمْ ذُو حَسَبٍ ، وكَذَلِكَ الرُّسُلُ تُبْعَثُ فى أَحْسَابِ قَوْمِها . وَسَأَلْتُكَ هَلْ كَانَ فى آبائِهِ مَلِكٌ فَزَعَمْتَ أَنْ لا . فَقُلْتُ لَوْ كَانَ مِنْ آبائِهِ مَلِكٌ ، قُلْتُ رَجُلٌ يَطْلُبُ مُلْكَ آبائِهِ . وَسَأَلْتُكَ عَنْ أَتْباعِهِ أَضُعَفاؤُهُمْ أَمْ أَشْرافُهُمْ . فَقُلْتَ بَلْ ضُعَفاؤُهُمْ ، وَهُمْ أَتْباعُ الرُّسُلِ . وَسَأَلْتُكَ : هَلْ تَتَّهِمُونَهُ بالكَذِبِ قَبْلَ أَنْ يَقُولَ ما قالَ ، فَزَعَمْتَ أَنْ لا ، فَعَرَفْتُ أَنَّهُ لَمْ يَكُنْ لِيَدَعَ الكَذِبَ عَلَى النَّاسِ ثُمَّ يَذْهَبَ فَيَكْذِبَ عَلَى اللهِ . وَسَأَلْتُكَ هَلْ يَرْتَدُّ أَحَدٌ مِنْهُمْ عَنْ دِينِهِ بَعْدَ أَنْ يَدْخُلَ فِيهِ سَخْطَةً لَهُ ، فَزَعَمْتَ أَنْ لا ، وكَذَلِكَ الإِيمانُ إذا خالَطَ بَشاشَةَ القُلوبِ . وَسَأَلْتُكَ : هَلْ يَزِيدونَ أَمْ يَنْقُصُونَ ؟ فَزَعَمْتَ أَنَّهُمْ يَزِيدُونَ وكَذَلِكَ الإِيمانُ حَتَّى يَتِمَّ . وَسَأَلْتُكَ هَلْ قاتَلْتُمُوهُ ، فَزَعَمْتَ أَنَّكُمْ قاتَلْتُمُوهُ فَتَكُونُ الحَرْبُ بَيْنَكُمْ وَبَيْنَهُ سِجالاً ، يَنالُ مِنْكُمْ وَتَنالُونَ

and if I were with him, I would wash his feet; and his kingdom will expand (surely) to what is under my feet.' Then Heraclius asked for the letter of Allāh's Messenger ﷺ and read it wherein was written:

In the Name of Allāh,
the Most Beneficent, the Most Merciful.

(This letter is) from Muḥammad, Apostle of Allāh, to Heraclius... the sovereign of Byzantine...... Peace be upon him who follows the Right Path. Now then, I call you to embrace Islām. Embrace Islām and you will be saved (from Allāh's Punishment); embrace Islām, and Allāh will give you a double reward, but if you reject this, you will be responsible for the sins of all the people of your kingdom (Allāh's Statement):–

'O the people of the Scripture (Jews and Christians) ! Come to a word common to you and us that we worship None but Allāh......bear witness that we are Muslims.' (3:64)

When he finished reading the letter, voices grew louder near him and there was a great hue and cry, and we were ordered to go out." Abū Sufyān added, "While coming out, I said to my companions, 'The situation of Ibn Abū Kabsha (1) (i.e. Muḥammad ﷺ) has become strong; even the king of Banu Al-Aṣfar is afraid of him.' So I continued to believe that Allāh's Messenger ﷺ would be victorious, till Allāh made me embrace Islām." Az-Zuhri said, "Heraclius then invited all the chiefs of the Byzantines and had them assembled in his house and said, 'O group of Byzantines! Do you wish to have a permanent suc-

٦٠

مِنْهُ ، وكَذَلكَ الرُّسُلُ تُبْتَلى ثُمَّ تَكونُ لَهُمُ العاقِبَةُ . وَسألْتُكَ : هَلْ يَغْدِرُ فزَعَمْتَ أنهُ لايَغْدِرُ ، وكَذَلكَ الرُّسُلُ لا تَغْدِرُ . وَسألْتُكَ : هَلْ قالَ أحَدٌ هَذَا القَوْلَ قَبْلَهُ فزَعَمْتَ أنْ لا . فَقُلْتُ : لَوْ كانَ قالَ هَذَا القَوْلَ أحَدٌ قَبْلَهُ ، قُلْتُ رَجُلٌ ائتَمَّ بقَوْلٍ قِيلَ قَبْلَهُ . قالَ : ثُمَّ قالَ : بِمَ يأمُرُكمْ ؟ قالَ : قُلْتُ : يأمُرُنا بالصَّلاةِ والزَّكاةِ والصِّلَةِ والعَفافِ ، قالَ : إنْ يَكُ ما تَقُولُ فِيهِ حَقًّا فإنهُ نَبيٌّ وَقَدْ كُنْتُ أعْلَمُ أنهُ خارِجٌ ولمْ أكُ أظُنُّهُ مِنْكمْ ، وَلَوْ أنِّي أعْلَمُ أنِّي أخْلُصُ إلَيْهِ لأحْبَبْتُ لِقاءَهُ . وَلَوْ كُنْتُ عِنْدَهُ لَغَسَلْتُ عَنْ قَدَمَيْهِ . وَلَيَبْلُغَنَّ مُلْكُهُ ما تَحْتَ قَدَمَيَّ . قالَ : ثُمَّ دَعا بِكِتابِ رَسُولِ اللهِ صلى اللهُ عليهِ وسلَّم فَقَرَأهُ فإذَا فِيهِ :

بِسْمِ اللهِ الرَّحْمَنِ الرَّحِيمِ ، مِنْ مُحَمَّدٍ رَسُولِ اللهِ إلى هِرَقْلَ عَظِيمِ الرُّومِ : سَلامٌ عَلى مَنِ اتَّبَعَ الهُدَى . أمَّا بَعْدُ : فإنِّي أدْعُوكَ بدِعايَةِ الإسْلامِ ، أسْلِمْ تَسْلَمْ ، وأسْلِمْ يُؤْتِكَ اللهُ أجْرَكَ مَرَّتَيْنِ . فإنْ تَوَلَّيْتَ فإنَّ عَلَيْكَ إثْمَ

(1) Abū Kabsha was not the father of the Prophet ﷺ but it was a mockery done by Abū Sufyān out of hostility against the Prophet ﷺ

cess and guidance and that your kingdom should remain with you?' (Immediately after hearing that), they rushed towards the gate like onagers, but they found them closed. Heraclius then said, 'Bring them back to me.' So he called them and said, 'I just wanted to test the strength of your adherence to your religion. Now I have observed of you that which I like.' Then the people fell in prostration before him and became pleased with him.''

(See Hadīth No. 6,Vol I)

الأَرِيسِيِّينَ . ـ يا أَهْلَ الكِتابِ تَعالَوْا إلى كَلِمَةٍ سَواءٍ بَيْنَنا وَبَيْنَكُمْ أَنْ لا نَعْبُدَ إلاَّ اللهَ ـ إلى قولِهِ ـ اشْهَدُوا بأنّا مُسْلِمونَ ـ فَلَمّا فَرَغَ مِنْ قِراءَةِ الكِتابِ ارْتَفَعَتِ الأَصْواتُ عِنْدَهُ وكَثُرَ اللَّغَطُ ، و أُمِرَ بِنا فأُخْرِجْنا ، قالَ : فَقُلْتُ لأَصحابِي حِينَ خَرَجْنا : لَقَدْ أَمِرَ أَمْرُ ابنِ أبي كَبْشَةَ ، إنَّهُ لَيَخافُهُ مَلِكُ بَنِي الأَصْفَرِ . فَما زِلْتُ مُوقِنًا بأَمْرِ رَسُولِ اللهِ صلى اللهُ عليهِ وسلمَ أَنَّهُ سَيَظْهَرُ حتى أَدْخَلَ اللهُ عَلَيَّ الإسلامَ ، قالَ الزُّهْرِيُّ : فَدَعا هِرَقْلُ عُظَماءَ الرُّومِ فَجَمَعَهُمْ في دارٍ لَهُ فَقالَ : يا مَعْشَرَ الرُّومِ ، هَلْ لَكُمْ في الفَلاحِ و الرَّشَدِ آخِرَ الأَبَدِ وأَنْ يَثْبُتَ لَكُمْ مُلْكُكُمْ ؟ قالَ : فَحاصُوا حَيْصَةَ حُمُرِ الوَحْشِ إلى الأَبْوابِ فَوَجَدُوها قَدْ غُلِّقَتْ ، فَقالَ : عَلَيَّ بِهِمْ ، فَدَعا بِهِمْ فَقالَ : إنِّي إنَّما اخْتَبَرْتُ شِدَّتَكُمْ عَلى دِينِكُمْ فَقَدْ رَأَيْتُ مِنْكُمُ الَّذِي أَحْبَبْتُ فَسَجَدُوا لَهُ وَرَضُوا عَنْهُ .

(57) CHAPTER. 'By no means shall you attain righteousness unless you spend (in charity) of that which you love. (3:92)

76. Narrated Anas bin Mālik ﷺ: Out of all the Anṣār, living in Medina, Abū Ṭalḥa had the largest number of (datepalm trees) gardens, and the most beloved of his property to him was Bairuḥa garden which was standing opposite the Mosque (of the Prophet ﷺ). Allāh's Messenger ﷺ used to enter it and drink of its good water. When the Verse:—

'By no means shall you attain righteousness unless you spend (in charity) of that which you love.' (3:92)

Abū Ṭalḥa got up and said, "O Allāh's Messenger, Allāh says:—

'By no means shall you attain righteousness unless you spend (in charity) of that which you love.' (3:92)

and the most beloved of my property to me is the Bairuḥa garden, so I give it (as a charitable gift) in Allāh's Cause

باب ـ لَنْ تَنَالُوا البِرَّ حَتَّى تُنْفِقُوا مِمَّا تُحِبُّونَ ـ الآيَةَ.

٧٦ ـ حَدَّثَنَا إِسْمَاعِيلُ قَالَ: حَدَّثَنِي مَالِكٌ، عَنْ إِسْحَاقَ بْنِ عَبْدِ اللهِ ابنِ أَبِي طَلْحَةَ: أَنَّهُ سَمِعَ أَنَسَ بْنَ مَالِكٍ رَضِيَ اللهُ عَنْهُ يَقُولُ: كَانَ أَبُو طَلْحَةَ أَكْثَرَ أَنْصَارِي بِالمَدِينَةِ نَخْلاً، وَكَانَ أَحَبَّ أَمْوَالِهِ إِلَيْهِ بَيْرُحَاءَ وَكَانَتْ مُسْتَقْبِلَةَ المَسْجِدِ، وَكَانَ رَسُولُ اللهِ صَلَّى اللهُ عَلَيْهِ وَسَلَّمَ يَدْخُلُهَا وَيَشْرَبُ مِنْ مَاءٍ فِيهَا طَيِّبٍ، فَلَمَّا أُنْزِلَتْ ـ لَنْ تَنَالُوا البِرَّ حَتَّى تُنْفِقُوا مِمَّا تُحِبُّونَ ـ. قَامَ أَبُو طَلْحَةَ، فَقَالَ: يَا رَسُولَ اللهِ إِنَّ اللهَ يَقُولُ ـ لَنْ تَنَالُوا البِرَّ حَتَّى تُنْفِقُوا مِمَّا تُحِبُّونَ ـ. وَإِنَّ أَحَبَّ أَمْوَالِي إِلَيَّ بَيْرُحَاءَ وَإِنَّهَا صَدَقَةٌ لِلهِ أَرْجُو بِرَّهَا وَذُخْرَهَا عِنْدَ اللهِ، فَضَعْهَا

and hope to receive good out of it, and to have it stored for me with Allāh. So, O Allāh's Messenger! Dispose it of (i.e. utilize it) in the way Allāh orders you (to dispose it of)." Allāh's Messenger ﷺ said, "Bravo! That is a fruitful property! That is a fruitful property! I have heard what you have said and I think that you should distribute that (garden) amongst your relatives." The Abū Ṭalḥa distributed that garden amongst his relatives and his cousins.

يا رسول الله حيث أراك الله . قال رسول الله صلى الله عليه وسلم : بخ ذلك مال رابح . ذلك مال رابح . وقد سمعت ما قلت ، وإني أرى أن تجعلها في الأقربين . قال أبو طلحة : أفعل يا رسول الله ، فقسمها أبو طلحة في أقاربه وبني عمه . قال عبد الله بن يوسف وروح بن عبادة : ذلك مال رابح .

77. Narrated Yaḥyā bin Yaḥyā: I learnt from Mālik, "......a fruitful property."

٧٧ ـ حدثنا يحيى بن يحيى قال : قرأت على مالك : مال رابح .

78. Narrated Anas (رضي الله عنه): Abū Ṭalḥa distributed the garden between Ḥassan and Ubai, but he did not give me anything thereof although I was a nearer relative to him.

٧٨ ـ حدثنا محمد بن عبد الله الأنصاري : حدثنا أبي ، عن ثمامة ، عن أنس رضي الله عنه قال : فجعلها لحسان وأبي وأنا أقرب إليه ولم يجعل لي منها شيئا .

(58) CHAPTER. 'Say: (O Muḥammad!) Bring here the Torah and recite it if you are truthful.' (3:93)

باب ـ قل فأتوا بالتوراة فاتلوها إن كنتم صادقين ـ .

79. Narrated 'Abdullāh bin 'Umar (رضي الله عنهما): The Jews brought to the Prophet ﷺ a man and a woman from among them who had committed illegal sexual

٧٩ ـ حدثني إبراهيم بن المنذر : حدثنا أبو ضمرة : حدثنا موسى بن عقبة ، عن نافع ، عن عبد الله

intercourse. The Prophet ﷺ said to them, "How do you usually punish the one amongst you who has committed illegal sexual intercourse?" They replied, "We blacken their faces with coal and beat them," He said, "Don't you find the order of Ar-Rajm (i.e. stoning to death) in the Torah?" They replied, "We do not find anything in it." 'Abdullāh bin Salām (after hearing this conversation) said to them. "You have told a lie! Bring here the Torah and recite it if you are truthful." (So the Jews brought the Torah). And the religious teacher who was teaching it to them, put his hand over the Verse of Ar-Rajm and started reading what was written above and below the place hidden with his hand, but he did not read the Verse of Ar-Rajm. 'Abdullāh bin Salām removed his (i.e. the teacher's) hand from the Verse of Ar-Rajm and said, "What is this?" So when the Jews saw that Verse, they said, "This is the Verse of Ar-Rajm." So the Prophet ﷺ ordered the two adulterers to be stoned to death, and they were stoned to death near the place where biers used to be placed near the Mosque. I saw her companion (i.e. the adulterer) bowing over her so as to protect her from the stones.

ابنِ عُمَرَ رَضِيَ اللهُ عَنْهُمَا : أنَّ اليَهُودَ جاءُوا إلى النَّبِيِّ صلى اللهُ عليه وسلَّم برَجُلٍ مِنْهُمْ وَامْرأةٍ قَدْ زَنَيا فقالَ لَهُمْ : كَيْفَ تَفْعَلُونَ بِمَنْ زَنَى مِنْكُمْ ؟ قالُوا : نُحَمِّمُهُما وَنَضْرِبُهُما ، فقالَ : لا تَجِدُونَ فِي التَّوْرَاةِ الرَّجْمَ ؟ فقالُوا : لا نَجِدُ فيها شَيْئًا ، فقالَ لَهُمْ عَبْدُ اللهِ بنُ سَلامٍ : كَذَبْتُمْ فأْتُوا بالتَّوْرَاةِ فاتْلُوها إنْ كُنْتُمْ صادِقِينَ . فوَضَعَ مِدْرَاسُها الذي يُدَرِّسُها مِنْهُمْ كَفَّهُ عَلَى آيَةِ الرَّجْمِ فَطَفِقَ يَقْرَأُ مادُونَ يَدِهِ وَما وَرَاءَها وَلا يَقْرَأُ آيَةَ الرَّجْمِ ، فنَزَعَ يَدَهُ عَنْ آيَةِ الرَّجْمِ فقالَ : ما هَذِهِ ؟ فَلَمَّا رأوْا ذَلِكَ قالُوا : هِيَ آيَةُ الرَّجْمِ فأمَرَ بِهما فَرُجِما قَرِيبًا مِنْ حَيْثُ مَوْضِعُ الجَنائِزِ عِنْدَ المَسْجِدِ . فَرَأيْتُ صاحِبَها يَجْنَأُ عَلَيْها يَقِيها الحِجارَةَ .

(59) CHAPTER. 'You (i.e. true Muslims) are the best of peoples ever raised up for mankind.' (3:110)

باب ـ كُنْتُمْ خَيْرَ أُمَّةٍ أُخْرِجَتْ لِلنَّاسِ ـ .

80. Narrated Abū Huraira ﷺ:
The Verse:—
'You (true Muslims) are the best of peoples ever raised up for mankind.' means, the best of peoples for the people, as you bring them with chains on their necks till they embrace Islām.

٨٠ - حدّثنا محمّد بن يوسف : عن سفيان، عن ميسرة، عن أبي حازم، عن أبي هريرة رضي الله عنه - كنتم خير أمة أخرجت للناس - قال : خير الناس للناس، تأتون بهم فى السلاسل فى أعناقهم حتّى يدخلوا فى الاسلام .

(60) CHAPTER. 'When two parties from among you were about to lose heart . . . (3:122)

باب - إذ همّت طائفتان منكم أن تفشلا -

81. Narrated Jābir bin 'Abdullāh ﷺ: The Verse:—
'When two parties from among you were about to lose heart, but Allāh was their Protector,' (3:122)
was revealed concerning us, and we were the two parties, i.e. Banū Ḥāritha and Banū Salama, and we do not wish (that it had not been revealed) or I would not have been pleased (if it had not been revealed), for Allāh says:—
'......Allāh was their Protector.'

٨١ - حدّثنا علي بن عبد الله : حدّثنا سفيان قال : قال عمرو : سمعت جابر بن عبد الله رضي الله عنهما يقول : فينا نزلت - إذ همّت طائفتان منكم أن تفشلا والله وليهما - قال : نحن الطائفتان، بنو حارثة وبنو سلمة، وما نحب . وقال سفيان مرة : وما يسرني أنها لم تنزل لقول الله - والله وليهما - .

(61) CHAPTER. 'Not for you (O Muḥammad) (but for Allāh) is the decision........' (3:128)

باب - ليس لك من الأمر شيء -

82. Narrated Sālim's father that he heard Allāh's Messenger on raising his head from the bowing in the last Rak'a in the Fajr prayer, saying, "O Allāh, curse such-and-such person and such-and-such person, and such-and-such person," after saying, "Allāh hears him who sends his praises to Him, O our Lord, all praise is for you." So Allāh revealed:—

'Not for you (O Muḥammad) (but for Allāh) is the decision ..Verily they are indeed wrongdoers.' (3:128)

٨٢ - حدَّثنا حِبَّانُ بنُ مُوسَى : أخبرَنا عَبْدُ اللهِ : أخبرَنا مَعْمَرٌ ، عَنِ الزُّهْرِيِّ قالَ : حدَّثني سالمٌ عَنْ أبيهِ أنَّهُ سَمِعَ رَسُولَ اللهِ صلى اللهُ عليهِ وسلَّمَ إذَا رَفَعَ رأسَهُ في الرُّكُوعِ في الرَّكْعَةِ الآخِرَةِ مِنَ الفَجْرِ يقُولُ : اللَّهُمَّ الْعَنْ فُلاناً وفُلاناً وفُلاناً بَعْدَ مايَقُولُ : سَمِعَ اللهُ لِمَنْ حَمِدَهُ ، رَبَّنا ولَكَ الحَمْدُ . فأنزَلَ اللهُ - لَيْسَ لكَ مِنَ الأمْرِ شَيْءٌ - إلى قولِهِ - فإنَّهُمْ ظالِمُونَ - رَوَاهُ إسحَاقُ بنُ رَاشِدٍ ، عَنِ الزُّهْرِيِّ .

83. Narrated Abū Huraira: Whenever Allāh's Messenger intended to invoke evil upon somebody or invoke good upon somebody, he used to invoke (Allāh) after bowing (in the prayer). Sometimes after saying, "Allāh hears him who sends his praises to Him, all praise is for You, O our Lord," he would say, "O Allāh. Save Al-Wālid bin Al-Walīd and Salama bin Hishām, and 'Aiyāsh bin Abū Rabī'a. O Allāh! Inflict Your Severe Torture on Muḍar (tribe) and strike them with (famine) years like the years of Joseph." The Prophet used to say in a loud voice, and he also used to say in some of his Fajr prayers, "O Allāh! Curse so-and-so and so-and-so." naming some of the Arab tribes till Allāh revealed:—

'Not for you (O Muḥammad) (but

٨٣ - حدَّثنا مُوسَى بنُ إسْماعِيلَ : حدَّثنا إبرَاهِيمُ بنُ سَعْدٍ : حدَّثنا ابنُ شِهابٍ ، عَنْ سَعِيدِ بنِ المُسَيَّبِ وأبي سَلَمَةَ بنِ عَبْدِ الرَّحْمَنِ ، عَنْ أبي هُرَيْرَةَ رَضِيَ اللهُ عَنْهُ : أنَّ رَسُولَ اللهِ صلى اللهُ عليهِ وسلَّمَ كانَ إذَا أرَادَ أنْ يَدْعُوَ عَلَى أحَدٍ أوْ يَدْعُوَ لأحَدٍ قَنَتَ بَعْدَ الرُّكُوعِ فَرُبَّما قالَ إذَا قالَ سَمِعَ اللهُ لِمَنْ حَمِدَهُ : اللَّهُمَّ رَبَّنا لَكَ الحَمْدُ . اللَّهُمَّ أنْجِ الوَلِيدَ ابنَ الوَلِيدِ ، وسَلَمَةَ بنَ هِشامٍ ، وعَيَّاشَ بنَ أبي رَبِيعَةَ . اللَّهُمَّ اشْدُدْ وَطْأتَكَ عَلَى مُضَرَ واجْعَلْها

for Allāh) is the decision.' (3:128)

سنين كسني يوسف، يجهر بذلك، وكان يقول في بعض صلاته في صلاة الفجر: اللهم العن فلانا وفلانا لأحياء من العرب حتى أنزل الله - ليس لك من الأمر شيء -

(62) CHAPTER. The Statement of Allāh ﷻ :–

'And the Messenger in your rear was calling you back.' (3:153)

Ibn 'Abbās said, " 'One of the two best things,' (9:52) means either victory or martyrdom."

باب قوله تعالى - والرسول يدعوكم في أخراكم - وهو تأنيث آخركم. وقال ابن عباس: إحدى الحسنيين فتحا أو شهادة.

84. Narrated Al-Barā' bin 'Āzib (رضي الله عنه): The Prophet ﷺ appointed 'Abdullāh bin Jubair as the commander of the infantry during the battle of Uhud. They returned defeated, and that is what is meant by:–

'And the Messenger was calling them back in the rear.'

None remained with the Prophet ﷺ then, but twelve men.

٨٤ - حدثنا عمرو بن خالد: حدثنا زهير: حدثنا أبو إسحاق قال: سمعت البراء بن عازب رضي الله عنهما قال: جعل النبي صلى الله عليه وسلم على الرجالة يوم أحد عبد الله ابن جبير وأقبلوا منهزمين فذاك - إذ يدعوهم الرسول في أخراهم - ولم يبق مع النبي صلى الله عليه وسلم غير اثني عشر رجلا.

(63) CHAPTER. Allāh's Statement:–

'He sent down security for you. Slumber overtook a party of you, ...' (3:154)

باب قوله - أمنة نعاسا.

85. Narrated Abū Ṭalḥa: Slumber overtook us during the battle of Uḥud while we were in the front files. My sword would fall from my hand and I would pick it up, and again it would fall down and I would pick it up again.

٨٥ - حدثني إسحاق بن إبراهيم ابن عبد الرحمن أبو يعقوب: حدثنا حسين بن محمد: حدثنا شيبان، عن قتادة: حدثنا أنس: أن أبا طلحة قال: غشينا النعاس ونحن في مصافنا يوم أحد، قال: فجعل سيفي يسقط من يدي وآخذه، ويسقط وآخذه.

(64) CHAPTER. The Statement of Allāh ﷻ :–

'Those who answered (the Call of) Allāh and the Messenger (Muḥammad ﷺ) after being wounded, for those of them who did good deeds and refrain from wrong, there is a great reward.' (3:172)

باب قوله تعالى - الذين استجابوا لله والرسول من بعد ما أصابهم القرح للذين أحسنوا منهم واتقوا أجر عظيم - القرح: الجراح. استجابوا: أجابوا، يستجيب: يجيب.

(65) CHAPTER. His Statement:–

'Those unto whom people said, "Verily; the people have gathered against you (a great army), therefore, fear them.'" (3: 173)

باب قوله - الذين قال لهم الناس إن الناس قد جمعوا لكم فاخشوهم -

86. Narrated Ibn 'Abbās رضي الله عنهما : 'Allāh is Sufficient for us and He is the Best Disposer of affairs," was said by Abrahām when he was thrown into the fire; and it was said by Muḥammad ﷺ when they (i.e. hypocrites) said, "A great army is gathering against you, therefore, fear them," but it only increased their faith and they said:

٨٦ - حدثنا أحمد بن يونس أراه قال حدثنا: أبو بكر، عن أبي حصين، عن أبي الضحى، عن ابن عباس: حسبنا الله ونعم الوكيل - قالها إبراهيم عليه السلام حين ألقي في النار، وقالها محمد صلى الله عليه وسلم

'Allāh is Sufficient for us, and He is the Best Disposer (of affairs, for us). (3:173)

حِينَ قَالُوا - إِنَّ النَّاسَ قَدْ جَمَعُوا لَكُمْ فَاخْشَوْهُمْ فَزَادَهُمْ إِيمَانًا وَقَالُوا حَسْبُنَا اللهُ وَنِعْمَ الْوَكِيلُ -.

87. Narrated Ibn 'Abbās : The last statement of Abraham when he was thrown into the fire was:—

'Allāh is Sufficient for me and He is the Best Disposer (of my affairs)'.

٨٧ - حدَّثنا مالكُ بنُ إسماعيلَ : حدَّثنا إسرائيلُ ، عَنْ أبي حَصِينٍ ، عَنْ أبي الضُّحَى ، عَنِ ابنِ عَبَّاسٍ قالَ : كانَ آخِرَ قَوْلِ إبراهيمَ حِينَ أُلْقِيَ في النَّارِ حَسْبِيَ اللهُ وَنِعْمَ الوَكِيلُ .

(66) CHAPTER. 'Let not those who covetously withhold of that which Allāh has bestowed upon them of His Bounty ....shall be tied to their necks like a collar.' (3:180)

بابٌ - وَلا يَحْسَبَنَّ الَّذِينَ يَبْخَلُونَ بِمَا آتاهُمُ اللهُ مِنْ فَضْلِهِ - الآيَةَ - سَيُطَوَّقُونَ - كَقَوْلِكَ طَوَّقْتُهُ بِطَوْقٍ .

88. Narrated Abū Huraira : Allāh's Messenger said, "Anyone whom Allāh has given wealth but he does not pay its Zakāt, then, on the Day of Resurrection, his wealth will be presented to him in the shape of a bald-headed poisonous male snake with two poisonous glands(1) in its mouth and it will encircle itself round his neck and bite him over his cheeks and say, "I am your wealth; I am your treasure.' " Then the Prophet recited this Divine Verse:—

'And let not those who covetously withhold of that which Allāh has

٨٨ - حدَّثني عَبْدُ اللهِ بنُ مُنِيرٍ : سَمِعَ أبا النَّضْرِ : حدَّثنا عَبْدُ الرَّحْمَنِ هُوَ ابنُ عَبْدِ اللهِ بنِ دينارٍ ، عَنْ أبيهِ ، عَنْ أبي صالحٍ ، عَنْ أبي هُرَيْرَةَ قالَ : قالَ رَسُولُ اللهِ صلى اللهُ عليهِ وسلَّمَ : مَنْ آتاهُ اللهُ مالاً فَلَمْ يُؤَدِّ زَكاتَهُ مُثِّلَ لَهُ مالُهُ شُجاعاً أقْرَعَ لَهُ زَبِيبَتانِ يُطَوَّقُهُ يَوْمَ القِيامَةِ يأخُذُ بِلِهْزِمَتَيْهِ ، يَعْني بِشِدْقَيْهِ يَقُولُ : أنا مالُكَ - أنا كَنْزُكَ ، ثُمَّ تَلا هذِهِ الآيَةَ - وَلا يَحْسَبَنَّ

(1) Feteh-Al-Bārī.

bestowed upon them of His Bounty. (3:180)

الَّذِينَ يَبْخَلُونَ بِمَا آتَاهُمُ اللهُ مِنْ فَضْلِهِ - إلى آخرِ الآيَةِ .

(67) CHAPTER. 'And you shall certainly hear much that will grieve you from those who received the Scripture before you and from the pagans.' (3:186)

باب - وَلَتَسْمَعُنَّ مِنَ الَّذِينَ أُوتُوا الكِتَابَ مِنْ قَبْلِكُمْ وَمِنَ الَّذِينَ أَشْرَكُوا أَذًى كَثِيرًا - .

89. Narrated Usāma bin Zaid : Allāh's Messenger ﷺ rode a donkey, equipped with a thick cloth-covering made in Fadak and I was riding behind him. He was going to pay visit to Sa'd bin 'Ubāda in Banū Al-Ḥārith bin Al-Khazraj; and this incident happened before the battle of Badr. The Prophet ﷺ passed by a gathering in which 'Abdullāh bin Ubai bin Salūl was present, and that was before 'Abdullāh bin Ubai embraced Islām. Behold in that gathering there were people of different religions: there were Muslims, pagans, idol-worshippers and Jews, and in that gathering 'Abdullāh bin Rawāḥa was also present. When a cloud of dust raised by the donkey reached that gathering, 'Abdullāh bin Ubai covered his nose with his garment and then said, "Do not cover us with dust." Then Allāh's Messenger ﷺ greeted them and stopped and dismounted and invited them to Allāh (i.e. to embrace Islām) and recited to them the Holy Qur'ān. On that, 'Abdullāh

٨٩ - حدَّثنا أبو اليَمانِ : أخبرَنا شُعَيْبٌ ، عَنِ الزُّهْرِيِّ : أخبرَني عُرْوَةُ ابنُ الزُّبَيرِ أنَّ أُسامَةَ بنَ زَيْدٍ رَضِيَ اللهُ عَنْهُما أخبرَهُ أنَّ رَسُولَ اللهِ صلى الله عليهِ وسلَّمَ رَكِبَ عَلَى حِمارٍ عَلَى قَطِيفَةٍ فَدَكِيَّةٍ وأرْدَفَ أُسامَةَ بنَ زَيْدٍ وَرَاءَهُ يَعُودُ سَعْدَ بنَ عُبادَةَ فِي بَنِي الحارِثِ بنِ الخَزْرَجِ قَبلَ وَقْعَةِ بَدْرٍ ، قالَ : حتَّى مَرَّ بِمَجْلِسٍ فيهِ عَبْدُ اللهِ ابنُ أُبيٍّ ابنُ سَلولَ وَذَلكَ قَبْلَ أنْ يُسْلِمَ عَبْدُ اللهِ بنُ أُبيٍّ ، فإذَا فِي المَجْلِسِ أخلاطٌ مِنَ المُسْلِمِينَ والمُشْرِكِينَ وَعَبَدَةِ الأوْثانِ وَاليَهُودِ والمُسْلِمِينَ ، وفي المَجْلِسِ عَبْدُ اللهِ ابنُ رَوَاحَةَ . فَلَمَّا غَشِيَتِ المَجْلِسَ عَجاجَةُ الدَّابَّةِ خَمَّرَ عَبْدُ اللهِ بنُ أُبيٍّ أنْفَهُ بِرِدائِهِ ثُمَّ قالَ : لا تُغَبِّرُوا عَلَيْنا ، فَسَلَّمَ رَسُولُ اللهِ صلى اللهُ عليهِ وسلَّمَ

bin Ubai bin Salūl said, "O man! There is nothing better than that what you say. If it is the truth, then do not trouble us with it in our gatherings. Return to your mount (or residence) and if somebody comes to you, relate (your tales) to him." On that 'Abdullāh bin Rawāḥa said, "Yes, O Allāh's Messenger! Bring it (i.e. what you want to say) to us in our gathering, for we love that." So the Muslims, the pagans and the Jews started abusing one another till they were on the point of fighting with one another. The Prophet ﷺ kept on quietening them till they became quiet, whereupon the Prophet ﷺ rode his animal (mount) and proceeded till he entered upon Sa'd bin 'Ubāda. The Prophet ﷺ said to Sa'd, "Did you not hear what 'Abū Ḥubāb said?" He meant 'Abdullāh bin Ubai. "He said so-and-so." On that Sa'd bin 'Ubāda said, "O Allāh's Messenger! Excuse and forgive him, for by Him Who revealed the Book to you, Allāh brought the Truth which was sent to you at the time when the people of this town (i.e. Medīna) had decided unanimously to crown him and tie a turban on his head (electing him as chief). But when Allāh opposed that (decision) through the Truth which Allāh gave to you, he (i.e. 'Abdullāh bin Ubai) was grieved with jealously, and that caused him to do what you have seen." So Allāh's Messenger ﷺ excused him, for the Prophet ﷺ and his companions used to forgive the pagans and the people of Scripture as Allāh had ordered them, and they used to put up with their mischief with patience. Allāh تعالى said:—

'And you shall certainly hear much that will grieve you from those who

عليهم ثم وقف فنزل فدعاهم إلى الله، وقرأ عليهم القرآن. فقال عبد الله ابن أبي ابن سلول: أيها المرء إنه لا أحسن مما تقول. إن كان حقا فلا تؤذنا به في مجالسنا. ارجع إلى رحلك، فمن جاءك فاقصص عليه. فقال عبد الله بن رواحة: بلى يا رسول الله فاغشنا به في مجالسنا فإنا نحب ذلك. فاستب المسلمون والمشركون واليهود حتى كادوا يتثاورون فلم يزل النبي صلى الله عليه وسلم يخفضهم حتى سكنوا ثم ركب النبي صلى الله عليه وسلم دابته فسار حتى دخل على سعد بن عبادة، فقال له النبي صلى الله عليه وسلم: يا سعد ألم تسمع ما قال أبو حباب؟ يريد عبد الله بن أبي. قال كذا وكذا، قال سعد بن عبادة: يا رسول الله اعف عنه واصفح عنه، فوالذي أنزل عليك الكتاب لقد جاء الله بالحق الذي أنزل عليك، ولقد اصطلح أهل هذه البحرة على أن يتوجوه فيعصبوه بالعصابة فلما أبى الله ذلك بالحق الذي أعطاك الله شرق بذلك، فذلك فعل به ما رأيت، فعفا عنه رسول الله صلى الله عليه وسلم وكان النبي صلى الله عليه وسلم وأصحابه

received the Scripture before you and from the pagans........'

(3:186)

And Allāh also said:--

Many of the people of the Scripture wish if they could turn you away as disbelievers after you have believed, from selfish envy........'

(2:109)

So the Prophet ﷺ used to stick to the principle of forgiveness for them as long as Allāh ordered him to do so till Allāh permitted fighting them. So when Allāh's Messenger ﷺ fought the battle of Badr and Allāh killed the nobles of Quraish infidels through him, Ibn Ubai bin Salūl and the pagans and idolaters who were with him, said, "This matter (i.e. Islām) has appeared (i.e. became victorious)." So they gave the pledge of allegiance (for embracing Islām) to Allāh's Messenger ﷺ and became Muslims.

يَعْفُونَ عَنِ المُشْرِكِينَ وأَهْلِ الكِتَابِ
كَمَا أَمَرَهُمُ اللهُ وَيَصْبِرُونَ عَلَى الأَذَى،
قَالَ اللهُ تعالى - وَلَتَسْمَعُنَّ مِنَ الَّذِينَ
أُوتُوا الكِتَابَ مِنْ قَبْلِكُمْ وَمِنَ
الَّذِينَ أَشْرَكُوا أَذًى كَثِيرًا - الآيَة.
وَقَالَ اللهُ - وَدَّ كَثِيرٌ مِنْ أَهْلِ الكِتَابِ
لَوْ يَرُدُّونَكُمْ مِنْ بَعْدِ إِيمَانِكُمْ كُفَّارًا
حَسَدًا مِنْ عِنْدِ أَنْفُسِهِمْ - إلى آخِرِ
الآيَةِ. وكانَ النَّبِيُّ صلى اللهُ عليهِ وسلَّم
يَتَأَوَّلُ العَفْوَ ما أَمَرَهُ اللهُ بِهِ حَتَّى أَذِنَ
اللهُ فِيهِمْ، فَلَمَّا غَزَا رَسُولُ اللهِ صلى اللهُ
عليهِ وسلَّم بَدْرًا فَقَتَلَ اللهُ بِهِ صَنَادِيدَ
كُفَّارِ قُرَيْشٍ قَالَ ابنُ أُبَيٍّ ابنُ سَلُولَ
وَمَنْ مَعَهُ مِنَ المُشْرِكِينَ وَعَبَدَةِ
الأَوْثَانِ: هَذَا أَمْرٌ قَدْ تَوَجَّهَ، فَبَايِعُوا
الرَّسُولَ صلى اللهُ عليهِ وسلَّم عَلَى الإِسْلَامِ
فَأَسْلَمُوا.

(68) CHAPTER.. "Think not that

بابُ لاتَحْسَبَنَّ الَّذِينَ يَفْرَحُونَ.

those who rejoice in what they have done.

(3:188)

90: Narrated Abū Sa'īd Al-Khudrī رضي الله عنه : During the lifetime of Allāh's Messenger ﷺ , some men among the hypocrites used to remain behind him (i.e. did not accompany him) when he went out for a Ghazwa and they would be pleased to stay at home behind Allāh's Messenger ﷺ , When Allāh's Messenger ﷺ returned (from the battle) they would put forward (false) excuses and take oaths, wishing to be praised for what they had not done. So there was revealed:—

'Think not that those who rejoice in what they have done, and love to be praised for what they have not done......' (3:188)

٩٠ - حدثنا سعيد بن أبي مريم: حدثنا محمد بن جعفر قال: حدثني زيد بن أسلم، عن عطاء بن يسار، عن أبي سعيد الخدري رضي الله عنه: أن رجالا من المنافقين على عهد رسول الله صلى الله عليه وسلم كان إذا خرج رسول الله صلى الله عليه وسلم إلى الغزو تخلفوا عنه وفرحوا بمقعدهم خلاف رسول الله صلى الله عليه وسلم، فإذا قدم رسول الله صلى الله عليه وسلم اعتذروا إليه وحلفوا وأحبوا أن يحمدوا بما لم يفعلوا، فنزلت: - لا تحسبن الذين يفرحون بما أتوا ويحبون أن يحمدوا بما لم يفعلوا -.

91. Narrated 'Alqama bin Waqqāṣ: Marwān said to his gatekeeper, "Go to Ibn 'Abbās, O Rafi, and say, 'If everybody who rejoices in what he has done, and likes to be praised for what he has not done, will be punished, then all of us will be punished.' " Ibn 'Abbās said, "What connection have you with this

٩١ - حدثني إبراهيم بن موسى: أخبرنا هشام: أن ابن جريج أخبرهم. عن ابن أبي مليكة أن علقمة بن وقاص أخبره: أن مروان قال لبوابه: اذهب يا رافع إلى ابن عباس فقل: لئن كان كل امرىء فرح بما أوتي وأحب أن يحمد بما لم يفعل معذبا

case? (1) It was only that the Prophet ﷺ called the Jews and asked them about something, and they hid the truth and told him something else, and showed him that they deserved praise for the favour of telling him the answer to his question, and they became happy with what they had concealed.

Then Ibn 'Abbās recited:—

'(And remember) when Allāh took a Covenant from those who were given the Scripture...and those who rejoice in what they have done and love to be praised for what they have not done.' (3:187-188)

لَتُعَذَّبُنَّ أَجْمَعُونَ. فَقَالَ ابْنُ عَبَّاسٍ: مَا لَكُمْ وَلِهَذِهِ؟ إِنَّمَا دَعَا النَّبِيُّ صلى الله عليه وسلم يَهُودًا فَسَأَلَهُمْ عَنْ شَيْءٍ فَكَتَمُوهُ إِيَّاهُ وَأَخْبَرُوهُ بِغَيْرِهِ، فَأَرَوْهُ أَنْ قَدِ اسْتَحْمَدُوا إِلَيْهِ بِمَا أَخْبَرُوهُ عَنْهُ فِيمَا سَأَلَهُمْ، وَفَرِحُوا بِمَا أَتَوْا مِنْ كِتْمَانِهِمْ. ثُمَّ قَرَأَ ابْنُ عَبَّاسٍ - وَإِذْ أَخَذَ اللهُ مِيثَاقَ الَّذِينَ أُوتُوا الْكِتَابَ - كَذَلِكَ حَتَّى قَوْلِهِ - يَفْرَحُونَ بِمَا أَتَوْا وَيُحِبُّونَ أَنْ يُحْمَدُوا بِمَا لَمْ يَفْعَلُوا - تَابَعَهُ عَبْدُ الرَّزَّاقِ عَنِ ابْنِ جُرَيْجٍ.

92. Narrated Humaid bin 'Abdur-Rahman bin 'Auf that Marwan had told him (the above narration No. 91).

٩٢ - حَدَّثَنَا ابْنُ مُقَاتِلٍ: أَخْبَرَنَا الْحَجَّاجُ، عَنِ ابْنِ جُرَيْجٍ، أَخْبَرَنِي ابْنُ أَبِي مُلَيْكَةَ، عَنْ حُمَيْدِ بْنِ عَبْدِ الرَّحْمَنِ بْنِ عَوْفٍ: أَنَّهُ أَخْبَرَهُ أَنَّ مَرْوَانَ بِهَذَا.

(69) CHAPTER. Allāh's Statement:—

'Verily! In the creation of the Heavens and the Earth, and in the alteration of night and day, there are indeed signs for men of understanding.' (3:190)

بَابُ قَوْلِهِ - إِنَّ فِي خَلْقِ السَّمَوَاتِ وَالأَرْضِ وَاخْتِلَافِ اللَّيْلِ وَالنَّهَارِ لَآيَاتٍ لِأُولِي الأَلْبَابِ -.

(1) According to the knowledge of understanding the meaning of the Qur'ān and Hadīth, we must consider the general meaning of the verse and not only the cause for which the verse was revealed.

93. Narrated Ibn 'Abbās: I stayed overnight in the house of my aunt Maimūna. Allāh's Messenger talked with his wife for a while and then went to bed. When it was the last third of the night, he got up and looked towards the sky and said:

> 'Verily! In the creation of the Heavens and the Earth and in the alteration of night and day, there are indeed signs for men of understanding.' (3:190)

Then he stood up, performed ablution, brushed his teeth with a Siwāk, and then prayed eleven Rak'āt. Then Bilāl pronounced the Adhān (i.e. call for the Fajr prayer). The Prophet then offered two Rak'āt (Sunna) prayer and went out (to the Mosque) and offered the (compulsory congregational) Fajr prayer.

٩٣ - حَدَّثَنَا سَعِيدُ بنُ أبي مَرْيَمَ: أخبَرَنا مُحَمَّدُ بنُ جَعْفَرٍ قالَ: أخبَرَنِي شَرِيكُ بنُ عَبْدِ اللهِ بنِ أبي نَمِرٍ، عَنْ كُرَيْبٍ، عَنِ ابنِ عَبَّاسٍ رَضِيَ اللهُ عَنْهُما قالَ: بِتُّ عِنْدَ خالَتي مَيْمُونَةَ فَتَحَدَّثَ رَسُولُ اللهِ صلى اللهُ عليه وسلَّم مَعَ أهْلِهِ ساعَةً ثُمَّ رَقَدَ. فَلَمَّا كانَ ثُلُثُ اللَّيْلِ الآخِرِ قَعَدَ فَنَظَرَ إلى السَّماءِ فَقالَ - إنَّ في خَلْقِ السَّمَوَاتِ والأرْضِ وَاخْتِلافِ اللَّيْلِ والنَّهارِ لآياتٍ لأُولي الألْبابِ - ثُمَّ قامَ فَتَوَضَّأَ وَاسْتَنَّ: فَصَلَّى إحْدَى عَشْرَةَ رَكْعَةً، ثُمَّ أذَّنَ بِلالٌ فَصَلَّى رَكْعَتَيْنِ ثُمَّ خَرَجَ فَصَلَّى الصُّبْحَ

(70) CHAPTER. 'Those who remember Allāh (by praying), standing, sitting, and lying down on their sides and think deeply in the creation of the Heavens and the Earth......' (3:191)

بابُ - الَّذِينَ يَذْكُرُونَ اللهَ قِياما وَقُعُوداً وَعَلَى جُنُوبِهِمْ وَيَتَفَكَّرُونَ في خَلْقِ السَّمَوَاتِ والأرْضِ - الآيَةَ.

94. Narrated Ibn 'Abbās: (One night) I stayed overnight in the house of my aunt Maimūna, and said to myself, "I will watch the prayer of Allāh's Messenger." My aunt placed a cushion for Allāh's Messenger and he slept on it in its length-wise direction and

٩٤ - حَدَّثَنا عَلِيُّ بنُ عَبْدِ اللهِ: حَدَّثَنا عَبْدُ الرَّحْمَنِ بنُ مَهْدِيٍّ، عَنْ مالِكِ بنِ أنَسٍ، عَنْ مَخْرَمَةَ بنِ سُلَيْمانَ، عَنْ كُرَيْبٍ عَنِ ابنِ عَبَّاسٍ رَضِيَ اللهُ تَعالى عَنْهُما قالَ: بِتُّ عِنْدَ

(woke-up) rubbing the traces of sleep off his face and then he recited the last ten Verses of Sūrat-āl-'Imran till he finished it. Then he went to a hanging waterskin and took it, performed the ablution and then stood up to offer the prayer. I got up and did the same as he had done, and stood beside him (by his left side). He put his hand on my head and held me by the ear and twisted it (pulled me, and made me stand by his right side). He offered two Rak'āt, then two Rak'āt, then two Rak'āt, then two Rak'āt, then two Rak'āt, then two Rak'āt and finally the Witr (i.e. one Rak'a) prayer.

خالتي ميمونة فقلت لأنظرن إلى صلاة رسول الله صلى الله عليه وسلم فطرحت لرسول الله صلى الله عليه وسلم وسادة ، فنام رسول الله صلى الله عليه وسلم في طولها فجعل يمسح النوم عن وجهه . فقرأ الآيات العشر الأواخر من آل عمران حتى ختم . ثم أتى سقاء معلقا . فأخذه فتوضأ ثم قام يصلي . فقمت فصنعت مثل ما صنع ، ثم جئت فقمت إلى جنبه . فوضع يده على رأسي ثم أخذ بأذني فجعل يفتلها . ثم صلى ركعتين ، ثم صلى ركعتين ، ثم صلى ركعتين ، ثم صلى ركعتين ، ثم صلى ركعتين ، ثم صلى ركعتين ، ثم أوتر .

(71) CHAPTER. Our Lord! (Verily) whom You admit to the Fire, truly, You have disgraced him and never will wrong-doers find any helpers.

(3:192)

باب ـ ربنا إنك من تدخل النار فقد أخزيته ، وما للظالمين من أنصار ـ.

95. Narrated 'Abdullāh bin 'Abbās that once he stayed overnight (in the house) of his aunt Maimūna. the wife of the Prophet ﷺ. He added: I lay on the cushion transversally in its breadthwise direction and Allāh's Messenger ﷺ lay along with his wife in its lengthwise direction. Allāh's Messenger ﷺ slept till the

٩٥ ـ حدثنا علي بن عبد الله : حدثنا معن بن عيسى ، عن مالك ، عن مخرمة بن سليمان ، عن كريب مولى عبد الله بن عباس : أن عبد الله ابن عباس أخبره أنه بات عند ميمونة

middle of the night, either a bit before or a bit after it, and then woke up rubbing the traces of sleep off his face with his hands and then he recited the last ten Verses of Sūrat-al-'Imrān, got up and went to a hanging waterskin. He then performed the ablution from it, and it was perfect ablution, and then stood up to offer the prayer. I too did the same as he had done, and then went to stand beside him (on his left side). Allāh's Messenger ﷺ put his right hand on my head and held and twisted my right ear (pulled me, and made me to stand by his right side). He then offered two Rak'āt, then two Rak'āt, then two Rak'āt, then two Rak'āt, then two Rak'āt, then two Rak'āt, and finally one Rak'a, the witr. Then he lay down again till the Mu'adhdhin (i.e. the call-maker) came to him, whereupon he got up and offered a light two-Rak'āt prayer, and went out (to the Mosque) and offered the (compulsory congregational) Fajr prayer.

(72) CHAPTER. 'Our Lord! We have heard the call of one (i.e. Muḥammad ﷺ) calling (us) to Faith...' (3:193)

زَوْجِ النَّبِيِّ صلى الله عليه وسلم وَهِيَ خَالَتُهُ. قَالَ: فَاضْطَجَعْتُ فِي عَرْضِ الْوِسَادَةِ، وَاضْطَجَعَ رَسُولُ اللهِ صلى الله عليه وسلم وَأَهْلُهُ فِي طُولِهَا. فَنَامَ رَسُولُ اللهِ صلى الله عليه وسلم حَتَّى انْتَصَفَ اللَّيْلُ أَوْ قَبْلَهُ بِقَلِيلٍ أَوْ بَعْدَهُ بِقَلِيلٍ ثُمَّ اسْتَيْقَظَ رَسُولُ اللهِ صلى الله عليه وسلم فَجَعَلَ يَمْسَحُ النَّوْمَ عَنْ وَجْهِهِ بِيَدَيْهِ، ثُمَّ قَرَأَ الْعَشْرَ الْآيَاتِ الْخَوَاتِمَ مِنْ سُورَةِ آلِ عِمْرَانَ. ثُمَّ قَامَ إِلَى شَنٍّ مُعَلَّقَةٍ فَتَوَضَّأَ مِنْهَا فَأَحْسَنَ وُضُوءَهُ، ثُمَّ قَامَ يُصَلِّي فَصَنَعْتُ مِثْلَ مَا صَنَعَ. ثُمَّ ذَهَبْتُ فَقُمْتُ إِلَى جَنْبِهِ فَوَضَعَ رَسُولُ اللهِ صلى الله عليه وسلم يَدَهُ الْيُمْنَى عَلَى رَأْسِي وَأَخَذَ بِأُذُنِي الْيُمْنَى يَفْتِلُهَا. فَصَلَّى رَكْعَتَيْنِ، ثُمَّ رَكْعَتَيْنِ، ثُمَّ رَكْعَتَيْنِ، ثُمَّ رَكْعَتَيْنِ، ثُمَّ رَكْعَتَيْنِ، ثُمَّ رَكْعَتَيْنِ، ثُمَّ أَوْتَرَ، ثُمَّ اضْطَجَعَ حَتَّى جَاءَهُ الْمُؤَذِّنُ. فَقَامَ فَصَلَّى رَكْعَتَيْنِ خَفِيفَتَيْنِ ثُمَّ خَرَجَ فَصَلَّى الصُّبْحَ.

بابٌ - رَبَّنَا إِنَّنَا سَمِعْنَا مُنَادِيًا يُنَادِي لِلْإِيمَانِ ـ الْآيَةَ.

96. Narrated Ibn 'Abbās that once he stayed overnight in the house of his aunt, the wife of the Prophet ﷺ - He added: I lay on the cushion transversally in its breadthwise direction while Allāh's Messenger ﷺ lay along with his wife in its lengthwise direction. Allāh's Messenger ﷺ slept till the middle of the night, either a bit before or a bit after it, and then woke up rubbing the traces of sleep off his face with his hands, and then recited the last ten Verses of Sūrat-āl-I-'Imrān. Then he got up and went to a hanging waterskin, performed ablution from it- -and performed it perfectly. Then he stood up to perform the prayer. I also did the same as he had done and then went to stand beside him (on his left side). Allāh's Messenger ﷺ put his right hand on my head and held and twisted my right ear (pulled me and made me to stand by his right side). He then offered two Rak'āt, then two Rak'āt, then two Rak'āt, then two Rak'āt, then two Rak'āt, then two Rak'āt, and finally, one Rak'a the witr. Then he lay down again till the Mu'adhdhin (i.e. the call-maker) came to him, whereupon he got up and offered a light two-Rak'āt prayer, and went out (to the Mosque) and offered the (compulsory congregational) Fajr prayer.

٩٦ - حدَّثنا قُتَيْبَةُ بنُ سَعِيدٍ: عَنْ مالكٍ: عَنْ مَخْرَمَةَ بنِ سُلَيْمانَ، عَنْ كُرَيْبٍ مَوْلَى ابنِ عَبَّاسٍ: أنَّ ابنَ عَبَّاسٍ رَضِيَ اللهُ عَنْهُما أخْبَرَهُ أنَّه باتَ عِنْدَ مَيْمُونَةَ زَوْجِ النَّبِيِّ صلى الله عليه وسلَّم وَهِيَ خالَتُهُ قالَ: فاضْطَجَعْتُ فى عَرْضِ الوِسادَةِ وَاضْطَجَعَ رَسُولُ اللهِ صلى اللهُ عليه وسلَّم وَأهْلُهُ فى طُولِها. فنامَ رَسُولُ اللهِ صلى اللهُ عليه وسلَّم حتَّى إذا انْتَصَفَ اللَّيْلُ أوْ قَبْلَهُ بِقَليلٍ أوْ بَعْدَهُ بِقَليلٍ، ثُمَّ اسْتَيْقَظَ رَسُولُ اللهِ صلى اللهُ عليه وسلَّم فَجَعَلَ يَمْسَحُ النَّوْمَ عَنْ وَجْهِهِ بِيَدِهِ، ثُمَّ قَرأ العَشْرَ الآياتِ الخَواتِيمَ مِنْ سُورَةِ آلِ عِمْرانَ. ثُمَّ قامَ إلى شَنٍّ مُعَلَّقَةٍ فَتَوَضَّأ مِنْها فأحْسَنَ وُضُوءَهُ، ثُمَّ قامَ يُصَلِّى. قالَ ابنُ عَبَّاسٍ: فَقُمْتُ فَصَنَعْتُ مِثْلَ ما صَنَعَ، ثُمَّ ذَهَبْتُ فَقُمْتُ إلى جَنْبِهِ فَوَضَعَ رَسُولُ اللهِ صلى اللهُ عليه وسلَّم يَدَهُ اليُمْنَى عَلَى رأسِي وأخَذَ بأُذُنِي اليُمْنَى يَفْتِلُها. فَصَلَّى رَكْعَتَيْنِ، ثُمَّ رَكْعَتَيْنِ، ثُمَّ رَكْعَتَيْنِ، ثُمَّ رَكْعَتَيْنِ، ثُمَّ رَكْعَتَيْنِ، ثُمَّ رَكْعَتَيْنِ، ثُمَّ أوْتَرَ، ثُمَّ اضْطَجَعَ حتَّى جاءَهُ المُؤَذِّنُ فقامَ فَصَلَّى رَكْعَتَيْنِ خَفِيفَتَيْنِ، ثُمَّ خَرَجَ فَصَلَّى الصُّبْحَ.

SŪRAT-AN-NISĀ' IV

**In the Name of Allāh,
the Most Beneficent, the Most Merciful**

سورة النساء

بِسْمِ اللهِ الرَّحْمٰنِ الرَّحِيمِ

قَالَ ابْنُ عَبَّاسٍ: يَسْتَنْكِفْ: يَسْتَكْبِرُ، قَوَّامًا: قِوَامُكُمْ، مِنْ مَعَايِشِكُمْ. لَهُنَّ سَبِيلًا: يَعْنِى الرَّجْمَ لِلثَّيِّبِ وَالجَلْدَ لِلبِكْرِ. وَقَالَ غَيْرُهُ - مَثْنَى وَثُلَاثَ وَرُبَاعَ - يَعْنِى اثْنَتَيْنِ وَثَلَاثًا وَأَرْبَعًا. وَلَا تُجَاوِزُ العَرَبُ رُبَاعَ.

(73) CHAPTER. 'If you fear that you shall not be able to deal justly with the orphan girls . . . (4:3)

بَابٌ - وَإِنْ خِفْتُمْ أَنْ لَا تُقْسِطُوا فِى اليَتَامَى -.

97. Narrated 'Āisha : There was an orphan (girl) under the care of a man. He married her and she owned a datepalm (garden). He married her just because of that and not because he loved her. So the Divine Verse came regarding his case:—

'If you fear that you shall not be able to deal justly with the orphan girls......' (4:3)

[The sub-narrator added: I think he (i.e. another sub-narrator) said, "That orphan girl was his partner in that datepalm (garden) and in his property."]

٩٧ - حَدَّثَنِى إِبْرَاهِيمُ بْنُ مُوسَى: أَخْبَرَنَا هِشَامٌ، عَنِ ابْنِ جُرَيْجٍ قَالَ: أَخْبَرَنِى هِشَامُ بْنُ عُرْوَةَ، عَنْ أَبِيهِ، عَنْ عَائِشَةَ رَضِىَ اللهُ عَنْهُمَا: أَنَّ رَجُلًا كَانَتْ لَهُ يَتِيمَةٌ فَنَكَحَهَا وَكَانَ لَهَا عِذْقٌ وَكَانَ يُمْسِكُهَا عَلَيْهِ وَلَمْ يَكُنْ لَهَا مِنْ نَفْسِهِ شَىْءٌ، فَنَزَلَتْ فِيهِ - وَإِنْ خِفْتُمْ أَنْ لَا تُقْسِطُوا فِى اليَتَامَى - أَحْسِبُهُ قَالَ: كَانَتْ شَرِيكَتَهُ فِى ذَلِكَ العِذْقِ وَفِى مَالِهِ.

98. Narrated 'Urwa bin Az-Zubair

٩٨ - حَدَّثَنَا عَبْدُ العَزِيزِ بْنُ

that he asked 'Āisha regarding the Statement of Allāh تعالى :–

> 'If you fear that you shall not be able to deal justly with the orphan girls . . . . (4:3)

She said, "O son of my sister! An Orphan girl used to be under the care of a guardian with whom she shared property. Her guardian, being attracted by her wealth and beauty, would intend to marry her without giving her a just Mahr, i.e. the same Mahr as any other person might give her (in case he married her). So such guardians were forbidden to do that unless they did justice to their female wards and gave them the highest Mahr their peers might get. They were ordered (by Allāh) to marry women of their choice other than those orphan girls." 'Āisha added," The people asked Allāh's Messenger his instructions after the revelation of this Divine Verse whereupon Allāh revealed:-

> They ask your instruction regarding women.' (4:127)

'Āisha further said, "And the Statement of Allāh تعالى :–

> 'And yet whom you desire to marry.' (4:127)

as anyone of you refrains from marrying an orphan girl (under his guardianship) when she is lacking in property and beauty." 'Āisha added, "So they were forbidden to marry those orphan girls for whose wealth and beauty they had a desire unless with justice, and that was because they would refrain from marrying them if they were lacking in property and beauty."

عَبْدِ اللهِ : حدَّثنا إبْرَاهيمُ بنُ سَعْدٍ ، عَنْ صَالِحِ بنِ كَيْسَانَ . عَنِ ابنِ شِهابٍ قالَ : أخبرَني عُرْوَةُ بنُ الزُّبَيْرِ : أنَّهُ سألَ عائشةَ عَنْ قَوْلِ اللهِ تعالى - وَإنْ خِفْتُمْ أنْ لا تُقْسِطُوا في اليَتامَى - فَقالَتْ : يا ابنَ أُخْتي ، هَذهِ اليَتيمَةُ تَكونُ في حَجْرِ وَلِيِّها تُشْرِكُهُ في مالِهِ ويُعْجِبُهُ مالُها وَجمالُها فيُريدُ وَليُّها أنْ يتزوَّجَها بغيرِ أنْ يُقْسِطَ في صَداقِها ، فيُعْطيَها مِثْلَ ما يُعْطيها غيرُهُ : فنُهُوا عَنْ ذَلكَ إلا أنْ يُقْسِطوا لهُنَّ ويَبْلُغوا لهُنَّ أعلى سُنَّتِهِنَّ ، فأُمِروا أنْ يَنْكِحوا ماطابَ لهُمْ مِنَ النِّساءِ سِواهُنَّ . قالَ عُرْوَةُ : قالَتْ عائشةُ : وَإنَّ النَّاسَ اسْتَفْتَوا رَسولَ اللهِ صلى اللهُ عليهِ وسلَّم بَعْدَ هَذهِ الآيَةِ فأنْزَلَ اللهُ وَيَسْتَفْتُونَكَ في النِّساءِ قالَتْ عائشةُ : وَقَوْلُ اللهِ تَعالى في آيَةٍ أُخْرَى :- وَتَرْغَبُونَ أنْ تَنْكِحوهُنَّ - رَغْبَةُ أحَدِكُمْ عَنْ يَتيمَتِهِ حينَ تَكونُ قَليلَةَ المالِ عَمَّنْ رَغِبوا في مالِهِ وَجمالِهِ في يَتامَى النِّساءِ إلاَّ بالقِسْطِ مِنْ أجْلِ رَغْبَتِهِمْ عَنْهُنَّ إذا كُنَّ قَليلاتِ المالِ والجَمالِ .

(74) CHAPTER. "But if he (the guardian) is poor, let him have for himself what is just and reasonable (according to his work). And when you release their property to them, take witnesses in their presence; and Allāh is All-Sufficient in taking account.' (4:6)

بابٌ - وَمَنْ كانَ فَقِيرًا فَلْيَأْكُلْ بِالمَعْرُوفِ فَإِذَا دَفَعْتُمْ إِلَيْهِمْ أَمْوالَهُمْ فَأَشْهِدُوا عَلَيْهِمْ وَكَفَى بِاللهِ حَسِيبًا - وَبِدَارًا: مُبادَرَةً. أَعْتَدْنا: أَعْدَدْنا، أَفْعَلْنا مِنَ العَتادِ.

99. Narrated 'Āisha regarding the Statement of Allāh :–

'And whoever amongst the guardian is rich, he should take no wages, but if he is poor, let him have for himself what is just and reasonable (according to his work).

This Verse was revealed regarding the orphan's property. If the guardian is poor, he can take from the property of the orphan, what is just and reasonable according to his work and the time he spends on managing it.

٩٩ - حَدَّثَنِي إِسْحاقُ: أَخْبَرَنا عَبْدُ اللهِ بنُ نُمَيْرٍ: حَدَّثَنا هِشامٌ، عَنْ أَبِيهِ، عَنْ عائِشَةَ رَضِيَ اللهُ عَنْها في قَوْلِهِ تَعالى. وَمَنْ كانَ غَنِيًّا فَلْيَسْتَعْفِفْ وَمَنْ كانَ فَقِيرًا فَلْيَأْكُلْ بِالمَعْرُوفِ - أَنَّها نَزَلَتْ في مالِ اليَتِيمِ إِذا كانَ فَقِيرًا أَنَّهُ يَأْكُلُ مِنْهُ مَكانَ قِيامِهِ عَلَيْهِ بِمَعْرُوفٍ.

(75) CHAPTER. 'And when the relatives, or orphans, or poor people are present at the time of division......' (4:8)

بابٌ - وَإِذا حَضَرَ القِسْمَةَ أُولُو القُرْبَى وَاليَتامَى وَالمَساكِينُ - الآيَةَ.

100. Narrated 'Ikrama: Ibn 'Abbās said (regarding the verse), "And when the relatives and the orphans and the poor

١٠٠ - حَدَّثَنا أَحْمَدُ بنُ حُمَيْدٍ: أَخْبَرَنا عُبَيْدُ اللهِ الأَشْجَعِيُّ، عَنْ

are present at the time of division,"..This verse and its order is valid and not abrogated."

سفيان ، عن الشيباني ، عن عكرمة ، عن ابن عباس رضي الله تعالى عنهما - وإذا حضر القسمة أولو القربى واليتامى والمساكين - قال : هي محكمة وليست بمنسوخة . تابعه سعيد بن جبير ، عن ابن عباس .

(76) CHAPTER. 'Allāh commands you as regards your children's (inheritance).' (4:11)

باب - يوصيكم الله في أولادكم - .

101. Narrated Jābir (رضي الله عنه): The Prophet ﷺ and Abū Bakr came on foot to pay me a visit (during my illness) at Banū Salama's (dwellings). The Prophet ﷺ found me unconscious, so he asked for water and performed the ablution from it and sprinkled some water over me. I came to my senses and said,"O Allāh's Messenger! What do you order me to do as regards my wealth?" So there was revealed:–

'Allāh commands you as regards your children's (inheritance):– (4:11)

١٠١ - حدثني إبراهيم بن موسى : أخبرنا هشام : أن ابن جريج أخبرهم قال : أخبرني ابن المنكدر عن جابر رضي الله تعالى عنه قال : عادني النبي صلى الله عليه وسلم و أبو بكر في بني سلمة ماشيين فوجدني النبي صلى الله عليه وسلم لا أعقل فدعا بماء فتوضأ منه ثم رش علي فأفقت فقلت ما تأمرني أن أصنع في مالي يا رسول الله ؟ فنزلت - يوصيكم الله في أولادكم - .

(77) CHAPTER. 'In what your wives leave, your share is a half.' (4:12)

باب قوله - ولكم نصف ما ترك أزواجكم - .

102. Narrated Ibn 'Abbās (رضي الله عنهما):

١٠٢ - حدثنا محمد بن يوسف :

(In the Pre-Islāmic Period) the children used to inherit all the property but the parents used to inherit only through a will. So Allāh cancelled that which He liked to cancel and decreed that the share of a son was to be twice the share of a daughter, and for the parents one-sixth for each one of them. (1) or one third (2), and for the wife one-eighth (1) or one-fourth (2), and for the husband one-half (2), or one-fourth (1).

عن ورقاء، عن ابن أبي نجيح، عن عطاء، عن ابن عباس رضي الله عنهما قال: كان المال للولد وكانت الوصية للوالدين، فنسخ الله من ذلك ما أحب فجعل للأبوين لكل واحد منهما السدس والثلث، وجعل للمرأة الثمن والربع، وللزوج الشطر والربع.

(78) CHAPTER. 'O you who believe! You are forbidden to inherit women against their will. And you should not treat them with harshness that you may take back part of the dower (i.e. Mahr) you have given them . .' (4:19)

باب - لا يحل لكم أن ترثوا النساء كرها ولا تعضلوهن لتذهبوا ببعض ما آتيتموهن - الآية. ويذكر عن ابن عباس: لا تعضلوهن: لا تقهروهن. حوبا: إثما. تعولوا: تميلوا. نحلة: فالنحلة المهر.

103. Narrated Ibn 'Abbās regarding the Divine Verse:–

> 'O you who believe! You are forbidden to inherit women against their will, and you should not treat them with harshness that you may take back part of the (Mahr) dower you have given them.' (4:19)

(Before this revelation) if a man died, his relatives used to have the right to inherit his wife, and one of them could

١٠٣ - حدثنا محمد بن مقاتل: أخبرنا أسباط بن محمد: حدثنا الشيباني، عن عكرمة، عن ابن عباس، قال الشيباني: وذكره أبو الحسن السوائي، ولا أظنه ذكره إلا عن ابن عباس - يا أيها الذين آمنوا لا يحل لكم أن ترثوا النساء كرها ولا تعضلوهن

(1) If the deceased had a child.
(2) If the deceased had no child.

marry her if he would, or they would give her in marriage if they wished, or, if they wished, they would not give her in marriage at all, and they would be more entitled to dispose her, than her own relatives. So the above Verse was revealed in this connection.

لِتَذْهَبُوا بِبَعْضِ ما آتَيْتُمُوهُنَّ - قالَ: كانُوا إذا ماتَ الرَّجُلُ كانَ أوْلِياؤُهُ أحَقَّ بِامْرَأتِهِ. إنْ شاءَ بَعْضُهُمْ تَزَوَّجَها وَإنْ شاءُوا زَوَّجُوها، وَإنْ شاءُوا لَمْ يُزَوِّجُوها وَهُمْ أحَقُّ بِها مِنْ أهْلِها، فَنَزَلَتْ هٰذِهِ الآيَةُ في ذٰلِكَ.

(79) CHAPTER. 'To everyone, We have appointed heirs of that (property) left by parents and relatives. To those, also, to whom your right hands have pledged, give them their due portion. Truly, Allāh is ever Witness over all things.' (4:33)

Ma'mar said, "Mawālī means the heirs. That whom your right hands have pledged is the ally. A parternal uncle's son is called Mawlā, so also a manumitter of a slave, a freed slave, a king, or a religious master."

باب - وَلِكُلٍّ جَعَلْنا مَوالِيَ مِمّا تَرَكَ الوالِدانِ وَالأقْرَبُونَ وَالَّذِينَ عاقَدَتْ أيْمانُكُمْ فَآتُوهُمْ نَصِيبَهُمْ إنَّ اللهَ كانَ عَلى كُلِّ شَيْءٍ شَهِيدًا - وَقالَ مَعْمَرٌ: مَوالِيَ: أوْلِياءَ وَرَثَةً. عاقَدَتْ أيْمانُكُمْ: هُوَ مَوْلَى اليَمِينِ: وَهُوَ الحَلِيفُ. وَالمَوْلَى أيْضًا ابْنُ العَمِّ، وَالمَوْلَى المُنْعِمُ المُعْتِقُ وَالمَوْلَى: المُعْتَقُ، وَالمَوْلَى: المَلِيكُ، وَالمَوْلَى مَوْلًى في الدِّينِ.

104. Narrated Ibn 'Abbās رضي الله عنهما:

Regarding the Verse:–

'To everyone, We have appointed heirs.' (4:33)

'Mawālī' means heirs. And regarding:–

'And those to whom your right hands have pledged.'

When the Emigrants came to Medīna, an Emigrant used to be the heir of an Anṣārī with the exclusion of the latter's relatives, and that was because of the bond of brotherhood which the Prophet ﷺ had

١٠٤ - حَدَّثَنا الصَّلْتُ بْنُ مُحَمَّدٍ: حَدَّثَنا أبُو أُسامَةَ، عَنْ إدْرِيسَ، عَنْ طَلْحَةَ بْنِ مُصَرِّفٍ، عَنْ سَعِيدِ بْنِ جُبَيْرٍ، عَنِ ابْنِ عَبّاسٍ رَضِيَ اللهُ عَنْهُما - وَلِكُلٍّ جَعَلْنا مَوالِيَ - قالَ: وَرَثَةً - وَالَّذِينَ عاقَدَتْ أيْمانُكُمْ - كانَ المُهاجِرُونَ لَمّا قَدِمُوا المَدِينَةَ يَرِثُ المُهاجِرِيُّ الأنْصارِيَّ دُونَ

established between them (i.e. the Emigrants and the Ansār). So when the Verses:—

> 'To everyone We have appointed heirs.'

was revealed, (the inheritance through bond of brotherhood) was cancelled. Ibn 'Abbās then said:—

> 'And those to whom your right hands have pledged.'

is concerned with the covenant of helping and advising each other. So allies are no longer to be the heir of each other, but they can bequeath each other some of their property by means of a will.

ذَوِي رَحِمِهِ لِلأُخُوَّةِ الَّتِي آخَى النَّبِيُّ صلى الله عليه وسلم بَيْنَهُمْ. فَلَمَّا نَزَلَتْ - وَلِكُلٍّ جَعَلْنَا مَوَالِيَ - نُسِخَتْ، ثُمَّ قَالَ - وَالَّذِينَ عَاقَدَتْ أَيْمَانُكُمْ - مِنَ النَّصْرِ وَالرِّفَادَةِ وَالنَّصِيحَةِ. وَقَدْ ذَهَبَ الْمِيرَاثُ وَيُوصِي لَهُ. سَمِعَ أَبُو أُسَامَةَ إِدْرِيسَ، وَسَمِعَ إِدْرِيسُ طَلْحَةَ.

(80) CHAPTER. 'Surely! Allāh wrongs not even of the weight of an atom (or a smallest ant.') . . . .(4:40)

بَابُ قَوْلِهِ - إِنَّ اللَّهَ لَا يَظْلِمُ مِثْقَالَ ذَرَّةٍ - يَعْنِي زِنَةَ ذَرَّةٍ.

105. Narrated Abū Sa'īd Al-Khudrī (رضي الله عنه): During the lifetime of the Prophet ﷺ some people said, "O Allāh's Messenger! Shall we see our Lord on the Day of Resurrection?" The Prophet ﷺ said, "Yes; do you have any difficulty in seeing the sun at midday when it is bright and there is no cloud in the sky?" They replied, "No." He said, "Do you have any difficulty in seeing the moon on a fullmoon night when it is bright and there is no cloud in the sky?" They replied, "No." The Prophet ﷺ said, "(Similarly) you will have no difficulty in seeing Allāh عَزَّوَجَلَّ on the Day of Resurrection as you have no difficulty in seeing either of them. On the Day of Resurrection, a call-maker will announce,

١٠٥ - حَدَّثَنَا مُحَمَّدُ بْنُ عَبْدِ الْعَزِيزِ: أَخْبَرَنَا أَبُو عُمَرَ حَفْصُ بْنُ مَيْسَرَةَ، عَنْ زَيْدِ بْنِ أَسْلَمَ، عَنْ عَطَاءِ بْنِ يَسَارٍ، عَنْ أَبِي سَعِيدٍ الْخُدْرِيِّ رَضِيَ اللَّهُ عَنْهُ: أَنَّ أُنَاسًا فِي زَمَنِ النَّبِيِّ صلى الله عليه وسلم قَالُوا: يَا رَسُولَ اللَّهِ، هَلْ نَرَى رَبَّنَا يَوْمَ الْقِيَامَةِ؟ قَالَ النَّبِيُّ صلى الله عليه وسلم: نَعَمْ. هَلْ تُضَارُّونَ فِي رُؤْيَةِ الشَّمْسِ بِالظَّهِيرَةِ ضَوْءٌ لَيْسَ فِيهَا سَحَابٌ؟ قَالُوا: لَا، قَالَ: وَهَلْ تُضَارُّونَ فِي رُؤْيَةِ الْقَمَرِ لَيْلَةَ الْبَدْرِ.

'Let every nation follow that which they used to worship.' Then none of those who used to worship anything other than Allāh like idols and other deities but will fall in Hell (Fire), till there will remain none but those who used to worship Allāh, both those who were obedient (i.e. good) and those who were disobedient (i.e. bad) and the remaining party of the people of the Scripture. Then the Jews will be called upon and it will be said to them, 'Who do you use to worship?' They will say, 'We used to worship 'Ezra, the son of Allāh.' It will be said to them, 'You are liars, for Allāh has never taken anyone as a wife or a son. What do you want now?' They will say, 'O our Lord! We are thirsty, so give us something to drink.' They will be directed and addressed thus, 'Will you drink,' whereupon they will be gathered unto Hell (Fire) which will look like a mirage whose different sides will be destroying each other. Then they will fall into the Fire. Afterwards the Christians will be called upon and it will be said to them, 'Who do you use to worship?' They will say, 'We used to worship Jesus, the son of Allāh.' It will be said to them, 'You are liars, for Allāh has never taken anyone as a wife or a son,' Then it will be said to them, 'What do you want?' They will say what the former people have said. Then, when there remain (in the gathering) none but those who used to worship Allāh (Alone, the real Lord of the Worlds), whether they were obedient or disobedient. Then (Allāh) the Lord of the worlds will come to them in a shape nearest to the picture they had in their minds about Him. It will be said, 'What are you waiting for?' Every nation have followed what they

ضوء ليس فيها سحاب؟ قالوا: لا، قال النبى صلى الله عليه وسلم: ما تضارون فى رؤية الله عز وجل يوم القيامة إلا كما تضارون فى رؤية أحدهما. إذا كان يوم القيامة أذن مؤذن: تتبع كل أمة ما كانت تعبد. فلا يبقى من كان يعبد غير الله من الأصنام والأنصاب إلا يتساقطون فى النار حتى إذا لم يبق إلا من كان يعبد الله بر أو فاجر وغبرات أهل الكتاب. فيدعى اليهود، فيقال لهم: ما كنتم تعبدون؟ قالوا: كنا نعبد عزير ابن الله، فيقال لهم: كذبتم ـ ما اتخذ الله من صاحبة ولا ولد ـ فماذا تبغون؟ فقالوا: عطشنا ربنا فاسقنا. فيشار ألا تردون، فيحشرون إلى النار كأنها سراب يحطم بعضها بعضا فيتساقطون فى النار. ثم يدعى النصارى فيقال لهم: ما كنتم تعبدون؟ قالوا: كنا نعبد المسيح ابن الله، فيقال لهم كذبتم ـ ما اتخذ الله من صاحبة ولا ولد ـ فيقال لهم: ماذا تبغون؟ فكذلك مثل الأول. حتى إذا لم يبق إلا من كان يعبد الله من بر أو فاجر، أتاهم رب العالمين فى أدنى صورة من التى رأوه فيها، فيقال: ماذا تنتظرون؟ تتبع كل أمة ما

used to worship.' They will reply, 'We left the people in the world when we were in great need of them and we did not take them as friends. Now we are waiting for our Lord Whom we used to worship.' Allāh will say, 'I am your Lord.' They will say twice or thrice, 'We do not worship any besides Allāh.' " (See Ḥadīth No. 532(B), Vol 9.)

كانت تعبد، قالوا: فارقنا الناس فى الدنيا على أفقر ما كنا إليهم ولم نصاحبهم ونحن ننتظر ربنا الذى كنا نعبد، فيقول: أنا ربكم، فيقولون: لا نشرك بالله شيئا، مرتين أو ثلاثا.

(81) CHAPTER. How (will it be) then when We bring from each nation a witness and We bring you (O, Muḥammad) as a witness against these people? (4:41)

باب - فكيف إذا جئنا من كل أمة بشهيد وجئنا بك على هؤلاء شهيدا. المختال والختال واحد. نطمس وجوها: نسويها حتى تعود كأقفائهم. طمس الكتاب: محاه. بجهنم سعيرا: وقودا.

106. Narrated 'Abdullāh (bin Mas'ūd): Allāh's Messenger said to me, "Recite (of the Qur'ān) for me," I said, "Shall I recite it to you although it had been revealed to you?" He said, "I like to hear (the Qur'ān) from others." So I recited Sūrat-an-Nisā' till I reached:—

١٠٦ - حدثنا صدقة: أخبرنى يحيى، عن سفيان، عن سليمان، عن إبراهيم، عن عبيدة، عن عبد الله: قال يحيى بعض الحديث عن عمرو بن مرة قال: قال لى رسول الله صلى الله عليه وسلم: اقرأ على،

'How (will it be) then when We bring from each nation a witness, and We bring you (O Muḥammad) as a witness against these people?
(4:41)

Then he said, "Stop!" And behold, his eyes were overflowing with tears."

قُلْتُ آقْرَأُ عَلَيْكَ وَعَلَيْكَ أُنْزِلَ ؟ قالَ: فإنى أُحِبُّ أنْ أسْمَعَهُ مِنْ غَيْرِى. فَقَرَأْتُ عليهِ سُورَةَ النِّساءِ حتّى بَلَغْتُ - فَكَيْفَ إذَا جِئْنا مِنْ كُلِّ أُمَّةٍ بِشَهِيدٍ وَجِئْنا بِكَ عَلَى هَؤُلاءِ شَهِيدًا - قالَ: أمْسِكْ فإذا عَيْناهُ تَذْرِفانِ.

(82) CHAPTER. 'And if you are ill or on a journey or one of you comes after answering the call of nature.....'
(4:43)

The word 'Sa'īdan' means the surface of the earth. And Jābir said, "The Tawāghīt (i.e. false deities) whom the people used to go for judgment in their disputes (were numerous): One in Juhaina, one in Aslam, and one in every (other) tribe. Those were soothsayers whom Satan used to inspire."

'Umar said, " 'Al-Jibt' means magic, and 'Ṭāghūt' means Satan."

'Ikrima said, " ' Al-Jibt' in the Ethiopian language means Satan, and 'Ṭāghūt' means a fore-teller."

باب قَوْلِهِ - وإنْ كُنْتُمْ مَرْضَى أوْ عَلَى سَفَرٍ أوْ جاءَ أحَدٌ مِنْكُمْ مِنَ الغائِطِ - صَعِيدًا . وَجْهَ الأرْضِ . وقالَ جابِرٌ: كانَتِ الطَّواغِيتُ التى يَتَحاكَمُونَ إلَيْها فى جُهَيْنَةَ واحِدٌ، وفى أسْلَمَ واحِدٌ، وفى كلِّ حَىٍّ واحِدٌ. كُهّانٌ يَنْزِلُ عَلَيْهِمُ الشَّيْطانُ . وقالَ عُمَرُ: الجِبْتُ: السِّحْرُ، والطّاغُوتُ: الشَّيْطانُ . وقالَ عِكْرِمَةُ: الجِبْتُ بِلِسانِ الحَبَشَةِ شَيْطانٌ . والطّاغُوتُ: الكاهِنُ .

107. Narrated 'Āisha : The necklace of Asmā' was lost, so the Prophet sent some men to look for it. The time for the prayer became due and they had not performed ablution and could not find water, so they offered the prayer without ablution. Then Allāh revealed (the Verse of Tayammum)

١٠٧ - حَدَّثَنِى مُحَمَّدٌ: أخْبَرَنا عَبْدَةُ، عَنْ هِشامٍ، عَنْ أبِيهِ، عَنْ عائشةَ رَضِىَ اللهُ عَنْها قالَتْ: هَلَكَتْ قِلادَةٌ لأسْماءَ فَبَعَثَ النَّبِىُّ صلى اللهُ عليه وسلّم فى طَلَبِها رِجالاً فَحَضَرَتِ

الصَّلاةُ وَلَبِسُوا عَلَى وُضُوءٍ وَلَمْ يَجِدُوا مَاءً فَصَلَّوْا وَهُمْ عَلَى غَيْرِ وُضُوءٍ ؛ فَأَنْزَلَ اللهُ تَعَالَى ، يَعْنِي آيَةَ التَّيَمُّمِ .

(83) CHAPTER. 'Obey Allāh and obey the Messenger (Muhammad ﷺ) and those of you (Muslims) who are in authority. (4:59)

بابٌ - أَطِيعُوا اللهَ وَأَطِيعُوا الرَّسُولَ وَأُولِي الأَمْرِ مِنْكُمْ - ذَوِي الأَمْرِ .

108. Narrated Ibn 'Abbās رضي الله عنهما : The Verse:—

'Obey Allāh and Obey the Messenger (ﷺ) and those of you (Muslims) who are in authority. (4:59)

was revealed in connection with 'Abdullāh bin Ḥudhāfa bin Qais bin 'Adī' when the Prophet ﷺ appointed him as the commander of a Sariyya (army detachment). (1)

١٠٨ - حَدَّثَنَا صَدَقَةُ بْنُ الفَضْلِ : أَخْبَرَنَا حَجَّاجُ بْنُ مُحَمَّدٍ ، عَنِ ابْنِ جُرَيْجٍ ، عَنْ يَعْلَى بْنِ مُسْلِمٍ ، عَنْ سَعِيدِ بْنِ جُبَيْرٍ ، عَنِ ابْنِ عَبَّاسٍ رَضِيَ اللهُ تَعَالَى عَنْهُمَا . أَطِيعُوا اللهَ وَأَطِيعُوا الرَّسُولَ وَأُولِي الأَمْرِ مِنْكُمْ - قَالَ : نَزَلَتْ فِي عَبْدِ اللهِ بْنِ حُذَافَةَ بْنِ قَيْسِ بْنِ عَدِيٍّ إِذْ بَعَثَهُ النَّبِيُّ صَلَّى اللهُ عَلَيْهِ وَسَلَّمَ فِي سَرِيَّةٍ .

(84) CHAPTER. But no, by your Lord, they can have no faith until they make you judge in all disputes between them.' (4:65)

بابٌ - فَلا وَرَبِّكَ لا يُؤْمِنُونَ حَتَّى يُحَكِّمُوكَ فِيمَا شَجَرَ بَيْنَهُمْ - .

109. Narrated 'Urwa: Az-Zubair

١٠٩ - حَدَّثَنَا عَلِيُّ بْنُ عَبْدِ اللهِ :

(1) See footnote of Ḥadīth No. 91.

quarrelled with a man from the Anṣār because of a natural mountainous stream at Al-Ḥarra. The Prophet ﷺ said, "O Zubair! Irrigate (your land) and then let the water flow to your neighbour." The Anṣār said, "O Allāh's Messenger! (This is because) he (Zubair) is your cousin?" At that, the Prophet's face became red (with anger) and he said, "O Zubair! Irrigate (your land) and then withhold the water till it fills the land up to the walls and then let it flow to your neighbour." So the Prophet ﷺ enabled Az-Zubair to take his full right after the Anṣārī provoked his anger. The Prophet ﷺ had previously given an order that was in favour of both of them. Az-Zubair said, "I don't think but this Verse was revealed in this connection:–

> 'But no, by your Lord, they can have no faith, until they make you judge in all disputes between them.' " (4:65)

حَدَّثَنَا مُحَمَّدُ بْنُ جَعْفَرٍ: أَخْبَرَنَا مَعْمَرٌ، عَنِ الزُّهْرِيِّ، عَنْ عُرْوَةَ قَالَ: خَاصَمَ الزُّبَيْرُ رَجُلاً مِنَ الأَنْصَارِ فِي شَرِيجٍ مِنَ الْحَرَّةِ، فَقَالَ النَّبِيُّ صلى الله عليه وسلم: اسْقِ يَا زُبَيْرُ ثُمَّ أَرْسِلِ الْمَاءَ إِلَى جَارِكَ. فَقَالَ الأَنْصَارِيُّ: يَا رَسُولَ اللهِ أَنْ كَانَ ابْنَ عَمَّتِكَ؟ فَتَلَوَّنَ وَجْهُهُ ثُمَّ قَالَ: اسْقِ يَا زُبَيْرُ ثُمَّ احْبِسِ الْمَاءَ حَتَّى يَرْجِعَ إِلَى الْجَدْرِ، ثُمَّ أَرْسِلِ الْمَاءَ إِلَى جَارِكَ. وَاسْتَوْعَى النَّبِيُّ صلى الله عليه وسلم لِلزُّبَيْرِ حَقَّهُ فِي صَرِيحِ الْحُكْمِ حِينَ أَحْفَظَهُ الأَنْصَارِيُّ وَكَانَ أَشَارَ عَلَيْهِمَا بِأَمْرٍ لَهُمَا فِيهِ سَعَةٌ. قَالَ الزُّبَيْرُ: فَمَا أَحْسِبُ هَذِهِ الآيَاتِ إِلاَّ نَزَلَتْ فِي ذَلِكَ - فَلاَ وَرَبِّكَ لاَ يُؤْمِنُونَ حَتَّى يُحَكِّمُوكَ فِيمَا شَجَرَ بَيْنَهُمْ -.

(85) CHAPTER. "Then they will be in the company of those on whom is the Grace of Allāh — — — of the prophets.' (4:69)

بَابٌ - فَأُولَئِكَ مَعَ الَّذِينَ أَنْعَمَ اللهُ عَلَيْهِمْ مِنَ النَّبِيِّينَ -.

110. Narrated 'Āisha رضي الله عنها : I heard Allāh's Messenger ﷺ saying, "No prophet gets sick but he is given the choice to select either this world or the Hereafter." 'Āisha added: During his fatal illness, his voice became very

١١٠ - حَدَّثَنَا مُحَمَّدُ بْنُ عَبْدِ اللهِ بْنِ حَوْشَبٍ: حَدَّثَنَا إِبْرَاهِيمُ بْنُ سَعْدٍ، عَنْ أَبِيهِ، عَنْ عُرْوَةَ، عَنْ عَائِشَةَ رَضِيَ اللهُ تَعَالَى عَنْهَا قَالَتْ: سَمِعْتُ

husky and I heard him saying: "In the company of those whom is the Grace of Allāh, of the prophets, the Ṣiddīqīn (those followers of the prophets who were first and foremost to believe in them), the martyrs and the pious.' (4:69)
And from this I came to know that he has been given the option.

رَسُولَ اللهِ صلى الله عليه وسلّم يَقُولُ :
ما مِنْ نَبِيٍّ يَمْرَضُ إلاَّ خُيِّرَ بَيْنَ
الدُّنْيا والآخِرَةِ ، وكانَ في شَكْواهُ الَّذي
قُبِضَ فِيهِ أخَذَتْهُ بُحَّةٌ شَدِيدَةٌ
فَسَمِعْتُهُ يَقُولُ : مَعَ الَّذِينَ أنْعَمَ اللهُ
عَلَيْهِمْ مِنَ النَّبِيِّينَ والصِّدِّيقِينَ والشُّهَداءِ
والصّالِحِينَ ، فعَلِمْتُ أنَّهُ خُيِّرَ .

(86) CHAPTER. And what is wrong with you that you fight not in the Cause of Allāh....whose people are oppressors.' (4:75)

باب - وَما لَكُمْ لا تُقاتِلُونَ في
سَبِيلِ اللهِ - إلى - الظّالِمِ أهْلُها -

111. Narrated Ibn 'Abbās :
My mother and I were among the weak and oppressed (Muslims at Mecca).

١١١ - حدَّثنا عَبْدُ اللهِ بنُ مُحَمَّدٍ :
حدَّثنا سُفْيانُ ، عَنْ عُبَيْدِ اللهِ قالَ :
سَمِعْتُ ابنَ عَبّاسٍ قالَ : كُنْتُ أنا
وأُمِّي مِنَ المُسْتَضْعَفِينَ .

112. Narrated Ibn Abi Mulaika:
Ibn 'Abbās recited:–

'Except the weak ones among men women and children,' (4:98)

and said, "My mother and I were among those whom Allāh had excused."

١١٢ - حدَّثنا سُلَيْمانُ بنُ حَرْبٍ :
حدَّثنا حَمّادُ بنُ زَيْدٍ : عَنْ أيُّوبَ ،
عَنِ ابنِ أبي مُلَيْكَةَ : أنَّ ابنَ عَبّاسٍ
تَلا - إلاَّ المُسْتَضْعَفِينَ مِنَ الرِّجالِ
والنِّساءِ والوِلْدانِ - قالَ : كُنْتُ أنا
وأُمِّي مِمَّنْ عَذَرَ اللهُ . ويُذْكَرُ عَنِ
ابنِ عَبّاسٍ : حَصِرَتْ : ضاقَتْ ، تَلْوُوا
ألْسِنَتَكُمْ : بالشَّهادَةِ . وقالَ غَيْرُهُ :
المُراغَمُ : المُهاجَرُ ، راغَمْتُ : هاجَرْتُ
قَوْمِي . مَوْقُوتاً : مُوَقَّتاً وَقْتَهُ عَلَيْهِمْ .

(87) CHAPTER. Then what is the matter with you that you are divided into two parties about the hypocrites? Allāh has cast them back (to disbelief) because of what they have earned.' (4:88)

بابٌ - فَمَا لَكُمْ فِى المُنَافِقِينَ فِئَتَيْنِ وَاللهُ أَرْكَسَهُمْ بِمَا كَسَبُوا - قالَ ابنُ عبَّاسٍ : بَدَّدَهُمْ . فِئَةٌ : جماعةٌ .

113. Narrated Zaid bin Thābit : Regarding the Verse:-- Then what is the matter with you that you are divided into two parties about the hypocrites?' (4:88)
Some of the companions of the Prophet returned from the battle of Uhud (i.e. refused to fight) whereupon the Muslims got divided into two parties; one of them was in favour of their execution and the other was not in favour of it. So there was revealed:—'Then what is the matter with you that you are divided into two parties about the hypocrites?' (4:88)

Then the Prophet said, "It (i.e. Medīna) "Ṭayyabah is (good) it expels impurities as the fire expels the impurities of silver."

١١٣ - حدَّثنى مُحمَّدُ بنُ بَشَّارٍ : حدَّثَنا غُنْدَرٌ وعَبْدُ الرَّحمنِ قالا : حدَّثنا شُعْبَةُ ، عَنْ عدىٍّ ، عَنْ عبدِ اللهِ ابنِ يزيدَ ، عَنْ زيدِ بنِ ثابتٍ رضىَ اللهُ تعالى عَنْهُ - فَمَا لَكُمْ فِى المُنَافِقِينَ فِئَتَيْنِ - رَجَعَ ناسٌ مِنْ أصحابِ النبىِّ صلى اللهُ عليهِ وسلَّمَ مِنْ أُحُدٍ وكانَ النَّاسُ فيهِمْ فِرْقَتَيْنِ : فريقٌ يقولُ اقتُلْهُمْ ، وفريقٌ يقولُ لا ، فنزلَتْ - فَمَا لَكُمْ فِى المُنَافِقِينَ فِئَتَيْنِ - وقالَ : إنَّها طَيْبَةُ تَنْفِى الخَبَثَ كما تَنْفِى النَّارُ خَبَثَ الفِضَّةِ .

(88) CHAPTER. 'When there comes to them some matter touching (public) safety or fear, they make it known.' (4:83)

بابٌ - وَإِذَا جَاءَهُمْ أَمْرٌ مِنَ الأَمْنِ أَوِ الخَوْفِ أَذَاعُوا بِهِ - أى أفشَوْهُ . يَسْتَنْبِطُونَهُ : يستخرجونَهُ . حَسِيبًا : كافيًا . إِلاَّ إِنَاثًا : يعنى المَوَاتَ حَجَرًا أو مَدَرًا وما أشبهَهُ . مَرِيدًا : مُتَمَرِّدًا .

فَلْيُبَتِّكُنَّ: بَتَّكَهُ: قَطَعَهُ. قِيلاً وَقَوْلاً وَاحِدٌ. طَبَعَ خَتَمَ.

(89) CHAPTER. 'And whoever kills a believer intentionally, his recompense is Hell." (4:93)

بابٌ ـ وَمَنْ يَقْتُلْ مُؤْمِنًا مُتَعَمِّدًا فَجَزَاؤُهُ جَهَنَّمُ ـ.

114. Narrated Sa'īd bin Jubair: The people of Kūfa disagreed (disputed) about the above Verse. So I went to Ibn 'Abbās and asked him about it. He said, "This Verse:—

> 'And who-so-ever kills a believer intentionally, his recompense is Hell.' (4:93)

was revealed last of all (concerning premeditated murder) and nothing abrogated it."

١١٤ ـ حدَّثنا آدمُ بنُ أبي إياسٍ: حدَّثنا شُعْبةُ: حدَّثنا مُغيرةُ بنُ النُّعمانِ قالَ: سَمِعتُ سَعيدَ ابنَ جُبَيرٍ قالَ: آيةٌ اختَلَفَ فيها أهلُ الكوفةِ فرَحَلتُ فيها إلى ابنِ عبَّاسٍ فسأَلتُهُ عنها فقالَ: نزَلَتْ هذهِ الآيةُ ـ وَمَنْ يَقْتُلْ مُؤْمِنًا مُتَعَمِّدًا فَجَزَاؤُهُ جَهَنَّمُ ـ هيَ آخِرُ ما نزَلَ وَما نسَخَها شيءٌ.

(90) CHAPTER. 'And say not to anyone who greets you (by embracing Islām): You are not a believer.' (4: 94)

بابٌ ـ وَلا تَقُولُوا لِمَنْ أَلْقَى إِلَيْكُمُ السَّلامَ لَسْتَ مُؤْمِنًا ـ السَّلَمُ والسَّلامُ والسِّلْمُ وَاحِدٌ.

115. Narrated Ibn 'Abbās regarding the Verse:—

> 'And say not to anyone who greets you (by embracing Islam), You are not a believer.'

There was a man amidst his sheep. The Muslims pursued him, and he greets them by saying : As-Salamu-Alaikum (peace be upon you)." But they killed him and took over his sheep. Thereupon Allah revealed in that concern, the

١١٥ ـ حدَّثني عليُّ بنُ عبدِ اللهِ: حدَّثنا سُفيانُ، عن عَمرٍو، عن عطاءٍ، عن ابنِ عبَّاسٍ رضيَ اللهُ عنهما ـ وَلا تَقُولُوا لِمَنْ أَلْقَى إِلَيْكُمُ السَّلامَ لَسْتَ مُؤْمِنًا ـ قالَ: قالَ ابنُ عبَّاسٍ: كانَ رجُلٌ في غُنَيمةٍ لهُ فلَحِقَهُ المُسلِمونَ فقالَ: السَّلامُ عليكُم،

above Verse up to:—

'......seeking the perishable good of this life.' (4:94)

i.e. those sheep.

فقتلوه وأخذوا غنيمته. فأنزل الله فى ذلك إلى قوله - عرض الحياة الدنيا - تلك الغنيمة. قال: قرأ ابن عباس السلام.

(91) CHAPTER. 'Not equal are those of the believers who sit (at home). (4:95)

باب - لا يستوى القاعدون من المؤمنين - الآية.

116. Narrated Zaid bin Thābit that the Prophet ﷺ dictated to him:—

'Not equal are those of the believers who sit (at home) and those who strive and fight in the Cause of Allāh.'

Zaid added: Ibn Um Maktūm came while the Prophet ﷺ was dictating to me and said, "O Allāh's Messenger! By Allāh, if I had the power to fight (in Allāh's Cause), I would," and he was a blind man. So Allāh revealed to his Messenger ﷺ while his thigh was on my thigh, and his thigh became so heavy that I was afraid it might fracture my thigh. Then that state of the Prophet ﷺ passed and Allāh revealed:—

'Except those who are disabled (by injury or are blind or lame etc).' (4:95)

١١٦ - حدثنا إسماعيل بن عبد الله قال: حدثنى إبراهيم بن سعد عن صالح، عن ابن شهاب قال: حدثنى سهل بن سعد الساعدى أنه رأى مروان بن الحكم فى المسجد فأقبلت حتى جلست إلى جنبه فأخبرنا أن زيد بن ثابت أخبره أن النبى صلى الله عليه وسلم أملى عليه - لا يستوى القاعدون من المؤمنين والمجاهدون فى سبيل الله - فجاءه ابن أم مكتوم وهو يملها علىّ. قال: يا رسول الله، والله لو أستطيع الجهاد لجاهدت وكان أعمى. فأنزل الله على رسوله صلى الله عليه وسلم وفخذه على فخذى فثقلت علىّ حتى خفت أن ترض فخذى ثم سرى عنه فأنزل الله - غير أولى الضرر -.

117. Narrated Al-Barā' رضي الله عنه :When

١١٧ - حدثنا حفص بن عمر:

the Verse:—

'Not equal are those of the believers who sit (at home)' (4:95)

was revealed, Allāh Messenger called for Zaid who wrote it. In the meantime Ibn Um Maktūm came and complained of his blindness, so Allāh revealed:—

'Except those who are disabled (by injury or are blind or lame etc.) (4:95)

حدثنا شعبة، عن أبي إسحاق، عن البراء رضي الله عنه قال: لما نزلت ـ لا يستوي القاعدون من المؤمنين ـ دعا رسول الله صلى الله عليه وسلم زيدا فكتبها فجاء ابن أم مكتوم فشكا ضرارته، فأنزل الله غير أولي الضرر ـ.

118. Narrated Al-Barā' :When the Verse:—

'Not equal are those of the believers who sit (at home),' (4:95)

was revealed, the Prophet said, "Call so-and-so." That person came to him with an inkpot and a wooden board or a shoulder scapula bone. The Prophet said (to him), "Write: 'Not equal are those believers who sit (at home) and those who strive and fight in the Cause of Allāh.'" Ibn Um Maktūm who was sitting behind the Prophet then said, "O Allāh's Messenger! I am a blind man." So there was revealed in the place of that Verse, the Verse:—

"Not equal are those of the believers who sit (at home) except those who are disabled (by injury, or are blind or lame etc.) and those who strive and fight in the Cause of Allāh.' (4:95)

١١٨ ـ حدثنا محمد بن يوسف، عن إسرائيل، عن أبي إسحاق، عن البراء قال: لما نزلت ـ لا يستوي القاعدون من المؤمنين ـ قال النبي صلى الله عليه وسلم: ادعوا فلانا، فجاءه ومعه الدواة واللوح أو الكتف فقال: اكتب ـ لا يستوي القاعدون من المؤمنين والمجاهدون في سبيل الله ـ وخلف النبي صلى الله عليه وسلم ابن أم مكتوم فقال: يا رسول الله أنا ضرير، فنزلت مكانها ـ لا يستوي القاعدون من المؤمنين غير أولي الضرر والمجاهدون في سبيل الله ـ.

119. Narrated Ibn 'Abbās :
Not equal are those believers who sat (at home) and did not join the Badr battle and those who joined the Badr battle.

١١٩ - حدثنا إبراهيم بن موسى: أخبرنا هشام: أن ابن جريج أخبرهم ح. وحدثني إسحاق: أخبرنا عبد الرزاق: أخبرنا ابن جريج: أخبرني عبد الكريم: أن مقسما مولى عبد الله بن الحارث أخبره أن ابن عباس رضي الله عنهما أخبره - لا يستوى القاعدون من المؤمنين عن بدر والخارجون إلى بدر -

(92) CHAPTER. 'Verily! As for those whom the angels take (in death) while they are wronging themselves (by staying among the disbelievers). They (Angels) say: 'In what (plight) were you?.....'
(4:97)

إن الذين توفاهم الملائكة ظالمي أنفسهم قالوا فيم كنتم: الآية.

120. Narrated Muhammad bin 'Abdur-Rahmān Abū Al-Aswad: The people of Medīna were forced to prepare an army (to fight against the people of Shā'm during the caliphate of 'Abdullāh bin Az-Zubair at Mecca), and I was enlisted in it; Then I met 'Ikrima, the freed slave of Ibn 'Abbās, and informed him (about it), and he forbade me strongly to do so (i.e. to enlist in that army), and then said, "Ibn 'Abbās informed me that some Muslim people were with the pagans, increasing the number of the pagans against Allāh's Messenger ﷺ. An arrow used to be shot which would hit one of them (the Muslims in the company of the pagans)

١٢٠ - حدثنا عبد الله بن يزيد المقرئ. حدثنا حيوة وغيره قالا: حدثنا محمد بن عبد الرحمن أبو الأسود قال: قطع على أهل المدينة بعث فاكتتبت فيه فلقيت عكرمة مولى ابن عباس أخبرته فنهاني عن ذلك أشد النهي ثم قال: أخبرني ابن عباس أن ناسا من المسلمين كانوا مع المشركين يكثرون سواد المشركين على رسول الله صلى الله عليه وسلم يأتي السهم يرمى به فيصيب

and kill him, or he would be struck and killed (with a sword)." Then Allāh revealed:—

> 'Verily! as for those whom the angels take (in death) while they are wronging themselves (by staying among the disbelievers) (4:97)

Abū Aswad added,

> 'Except the weak ones among men, women,........'
>
> (4:98)

أحَدَهُمْ فَيَقْتُلُهُ أوْ يُضْرَبُ فَيُقْتَلُ . فأنزَلَ اللهُ - إنَّ الذينَ تَوَفَّاهُمُ المَلائكَةُ ظالِمي أنفُسِهِمْ - الآيَة . رَوَاهُ اللَّيْثُ عَنْ أبي الأسْوَدِ - إلاَّ المُسْتَضْعَفِينَ مِنَ الرِّجالِ والنِّساءِ - الآيَة .

121. Narrated Ibn 'Abbās :-

> 'Except the weak ones (4:98)

and added: My mother was one of those whom Allāh excused.

١٢١ - حدَّثَنا أبو النُّعْمان : حدَّثَنا حَمَّادٌ ، عَنْ أيُّوبَ ، عَنْ ابنِ أبي مُلَيْكَةَ ، عَنِ ابنِ عَبَّاسٍ رَضِيَ اللهُ عَنْهُما - إلاَّ المُسْتَضْعَفِينَ - قالَ : كانَتْ أُمِّي مِمَّنْ عَذَرَ اللهُ .

(93) CHAPTER. 'For these there is hope that Allāh will forgive them........'

(4:99)

بابُ قَوْلِهِ - فأُولَئِكَ عَسَى اللهُ أنْ يَعْفُوَ عَنْهُمْ - الآيَة .

122. Narrated Abū Huraira : While the Prophet ﷺ was offering the 'Ishā' prayer, he said, "Allāh hears him who sends his praises to Him," and then said before falling in prostration, "O Allāh, save 'Aiyāsh bin Rabī'a. O Allāh, save Salama bin Hishām. O Allāh, save Al-Walīd bin Al-Walīd. O Allāh, save the weak ones among the believers. O Allāh, let Your punishment be severe on the tribe of Muḍar. O

١٢٢ - حدَّثَنا أبو نُعَيْمٍ : حدَّثَنا شَيْبانُ ، عَنْ يَحْيَى ، عَنْ أبي سَلَمَةَ ، عَنْ أبي هُرَيْرَةَ رَضِيَ اللهُ عَنْهُ قالَ : بَيْنا النَّبِيُّ صلى اللهُ عليهِ وسلَّم يُصَلِّي العِشاءَ إذْ قالَ : سَمِعَ اللهُ لِمَنْ حَمِدَهُ ، ثُمَّ قالَ قَبْلَ أنْ يَسْجُدَ : اللَّهُمَّ نَجِّ عَيَّاشَ بنَ رَبِيعَةَ اللَّهُمَّ نَجِّ

Allāh, inflict upon them years (of famine) like the years of Joseph."

سلمة بن هشام، اللهم نج الوليد بن الوليد، اللهم نج المستضعفين من المؤمنين. اللهم اشدد وطأتك على مضر، اللهم اجعلها سنين كسني يوسف.

(94) CHAPTER. 'But there is no blame on you (if you put away your arms) because of the inconvenience of rain...........: (4:102)

باب - ولا جناح عليكم إن كان بكم أذى من مطر - الآية.

123\. Narrated Ibn 'Abbās regarding the Verse:—

'Because of the inconvenience of rain or because you are ill.'(4:102)

(It was revealed in connection with) 'Abdur-Raḥmān bin 'Auf who was wounded.

١٢٣ - حدثنا محمد بن مقاتل أبو الحسن: أخبرنا حجاج، عن ابن جريج قال: أخبرني يعلى، عن سعيد ابن جبير، عن ابن عباس رضي الله عنهما - إن كان بكم أذى من مطر أو كنتم مرضى - قال عبد الرحمن ابن عوف وكان جريحا.

(95) CHAPTER. Allāh's Statement:— 'They ask your instruction concerning women. Say: Allāh instructs you about them, and about what is recited unto you in the Book concerning orphan girls.' (4:127)

باب قوله - ويستفتونك في النساء قل الله يفتيكم فيهن وما يتلى عليكم في الكتاب في يتامى النساء -.

124\. Narrated 'Āisha regarding

١٢٤ - حدثنا عبيد بن إسماعيل:

the Verse:—

> 'They ask your instruction concerning the women. Say: Allāh instructs you about them..........and yet whom you desire to marry.'
> (4:127)

(has been revealed regarding the case of) a man who has an orphan girl, and he is her guardian and her heir. The girl shares with him all his property, even a date-palm (garden), but he dislikes to marry her and dislikes to give her in marriage to somebody else who would share with him the property she is sharing with him, and for this reason that guardian prevents that orphan girl from marrying. So, this Verse was revealed: (And Allāh's statement:—)

> "If a woman fears cruelty or desertion on her husband's part.'
> (4:128)

حدَّثَنا أبو أُسامَةَ قالَ: حدَّثَنا هِشامُ بنُ عُرْوَةَ، عَنْ أبيهِ، عَنْ عائِشَةَ رَضِيَ اللهُ عَنْها - وَيَسْتَفْتُونَكَ في النِّساءِ قُلِ اللهُ يُفْتيكُمْ فيهِنَّ - إلى قَوْلِه - وَتَرْغَبونَ أنْ تَنْكِحوهُنَّ - قالَتْ عائِشَةُ: هُوَ الرَّجُلُ تَكونُ عِنْدَهُ اليَتيمَةُ هُوَ وَلِيُّها وَوارِثُها فأشْرَكَتْهُ في مالِهِ حتَّى في العَذْقِ فيَرْغَبُ أنْ يَنْكِحَها وَيَكْرَهُ أنْ يُزَوِّجَها رَجُلاً فيَشْرَكُهُ في مالِهِ بِما شَرِكَتْهُ فيَعْضُلُها فنَزَلَتْ هَذِهِ الآيَةُ - وَإنِ امْرَأةٌ خافَتْ مِنْ بَعْلِها نُشُوزًا أوْ إعْراضًا - قالَ ابنُ عَبَّاسٍ: شِقاقٌ: تَفاسُدٌ - وَأُحْضِرَتِ الأنْفُسُ الشُّحَّ - قالَ هَواهُ في الشَّيْءِ يَحْرِصُ عَلَيْهِ كالمُعَلَّقَةِ لا هِيَ أيِّمٌ وَلا ذاتُ زَوْجٍ. نُشُوزًا: بُغْضًا.

125. Narrated 'Āisha (may Allah be pleased with her) regarding the Verse:—

> 'If a woman fears cruelty or desertion on her husband's part.'
> (4:128)

It is about a man who has a woman (wife) and he does not like her and wants to divorce her but she says to him, "I make you free as regards myself."
So this Verse was revealed in this connection.

١٢٥ - حدَّثَنا مُحَمَّدُ بنُ مُقاتِلٍ: أخْبَرَنا عَبْدُ اللهِ: أخْبَرَنا هِشامُ بنُ عُرْوَةَ، عَنْ أبيهِ، عَنْ عائِشَةَ رَضِيَ اللهُ عَنْها - وَإنِ امْرَأةٌ خافَتْ مِنْ بَعْلِها نُشُوزًا أوْ إعْراضًا - قالَتِ: الرَّجُلُ تَكونُ عِنْدَهُ المَرْأةُ لَيْسَ بِمُسْتَكْثِرٍ مِنْها يُريدُ أنْ يُفارِقَها، فتَقولُ أجْعَلُكَ مِنْ شأني في حِلٍّ. فنَزَلَتْ هَذِهِ الآيَةُ في ذَلِكَ.

(96) CHAPTER. Verily, the hypocrites will be in the lowest depths of the Fire.' (4:145)

بابٌ - إنَّ المُنافِقِينَ فى الدَّرْكِ الأَسْفَلِ مِنَ النَّارِ - وقالَ ابنُ عبَّاسٍ : أسفَلَ النَّارِ . نفَقًا : سرَبًا .

126. Narrated Al-Aswad: While we were sitting in a circle in 'Abdullāh's gathering, Ḥudhaifa came and stopped before us, and greeted us and then said, "People better than you became hypocrites." Al-Aswad said: I testify the uniqueness of Allāh! Allāh says:— Verily! The hypocrites will be in the lowest depths of the Fire.' (4:145)

On that 'Abdullāh smiled and Ḥudhaifa sat somewhere in the Mosque. 'Abdullāh then got up and his companions (sitting around him) dispersed. Ḥudhaifa then threw a pebble at me (to attract my attention). I went to him and he said, "I was surprised at 'Abdullāh's smile though he understood what I said. Verily, people better than you became hypocrite and then repented and Allāh forgave them."

١٢٦ - حدَّثنا عُمَرُ بنُ حفْصٍ : حدَّثنا أبى : حدَّثنا الأعمَشُ قالَ : حدَّثنى إبْرَاهِيمُ ، عَنِ الأسْوَدِ قالَ : كُنَّا فى حَلَقَةِ عَبْدِ اللهِ فَجاءَ حُذَيفَةُ حتَّى قامَ علَيْنا فَسلَّمَ ثُمَّ قالَ : لَقَدْ أُنْزِلَ النفاقُ علَى قَوْمٍ خَيرٍ مِنكُم ، قالَ الأسْوَدُ : سُبْحانَ اللهِ ، إنَّ اللهَ يَقُولُ - إنَّ المُنافِقِينَ فى الدَّرْكِ الأَسْفَلِ مِنَ النَّارِ - فَتَبَسَّمَ عَبْدُ اللهِ وَجلَسَ حُذَيفَةُ فى ناحِيَةِ المَسْجِدِ . فقامَ عَبْدُ اللهِ فَتَفَرَّقَ أصحابُهُ فَرَمانى بالحَصا ، فأتَيْتُهُ فَقالَ حُذَيفَةُ : عَجِبْتُ مِنْ ضَحِكِهِ وَقدْ عرَفَ ما قُلْتُ ، لَقَدْ أُنْزِلَ النِّفاقُ علَى قَوْمٍ كانُوا خَيرًا مِنكُمْ ثُمَّ تابُوا فَتابَ اللهُ علَيْهِمْ .

(97) CHAPTER' Allāh's Statement:— Verily We have inspired you, (O Muḥammad) as We inspired Noah .... and Jonah, Aaron and Solomon.' (4:163)

بابُ قَوْلِهِ - إنَّا أوْحَيْنا إلَيْكَ كمَا أوْحَيْنا إلى نُوحٍ - إلى قَوْلِهِ - ويُونُسَ وَهارُونَ وَسُلَيْمانَ

127; Narrated 'Abdullāh: The

١٢٧ - حدَّثنا مُسَدَّدٌ : حدَّثنا

Prophet ﷺ said, "None has the right to say that I am better than Jonah bin Matta."

يَحْيَى ، عَنْ سُفْيَانَ قَالَ : حَدَّثَنِي الأَعْمَشُ ، عَنْ أَبِي وَائِلٍ ، عَنْ عَبْدِ اللهِ عَنِ النَّبِيِّ صلى اللهُ عليه وسلَّم قالَ : ما يَنْبَغِي لأَحَدٍ أَنْ يَقُولَ أَنا خَيْرٌ مِنْ يُونُسَ ابنِ مَتَّى .

128. Narrated Abū Huraira ؓ : The Prophet ﷺ said, "Whoever says that I am better than Jonah bin Matta, is a liar."

١٢٨ ـ حَدَّثَنا مُحَمَّدُ بنُ سِنانٍ : حَدَّثَنا فُلَيْحٌ : حَدَّثَنا هِلالٌ ، عَنْ عَطاءِ ابنِ يَسارٍ ، عَنْ أَبي هُرَيْرَةَ رَضِيَ اللهُ عَنْهُ ، عَنِ النَّبِيِّ صلى اللهُ عليه وسلَّم قالَ : مَنْ قالَ أَنا خَيْرٌ مِنْ يُونُسَ ابنِ مَتَّى فَقَدْ كَذَبَ .

(98) CHAPTER. 'They ask you for a legal verdict Say:—

> Allāh directs (thus) about, those who leave no descendants or ascendants as heirs. If it is a man that dies, leaving a sister but no child. she shall have half the inheritance. If (such a deceased was) a woman who left no child, her brother takes her inheritance.
>
> (4:176)

Al-Kalāla is the one who has no father or any son to be his heir.

باب ـ يَسْتَفْتُونَكَ قُلِ اللهُ يُفْتِيكُمْ فِي الكَلالَةِ إِنْ امْرُؤٌ هَلَكَ لَيْسَ لَهُ وَلَدٌ وَلَهُ أُخْتٌ فَلَهَا نِصْفُ ما تَرَكَ وَهُوَ يَرِثُها إِنْ لَمْ يَكُنْ لَها وَلَدٌ ـ والكَلالَةُ مَنْ لَمْ يَرِثْهُ أَبٌ أَوِ ابنٌ ، وَهُوَ مَصْدَرٌ مِنْ تَكَلَّلَهُ النَّسَبُ .

129; Narrated Al-Barā ؓ : The last Sūra that was revealed was Barā'a, and the last Verse that was revealed was:

١٢٩ ـ حَدَّثَنا سُلَيْمانُ بنُ حَرْبٍ : حَدَّثَنا شُعْبَةُ ، عَنْ أَبِي إِسْحاقَ : سَمِعْتُ البَرَاءَ رَضِيَ اللهُ تَعالى عَنْهُ قالَ : آخِرُ

سُورَةٍ نَزَلَتْ بَرَاءَةٌ، آخِرُ آيَةٍ نَزَلَتْ - يَسْتَفْتُونَكَ قُلِ اللهُ يُفْتِيكُمْ فِي الكَلالَةِ -.

'They ask you for a legal verdict, Say: Allāh's directs (thus) about those who leave no descendants or ascendants as heirs.'
(4:176)

بِسْمِ اللهِ الرَّحْمَنِ الرَّحِيمِ

In the Name of Allāh,
the Most Beneficent, the Most Merciful

تفسير سورة المائدة

The explanation of SŪRAT-AL-MĀ'IDA. V

بابُ - وأَنْتُمْ حُرُمٌ - وَاحِدُهَا حَرَامٌ - فَبِمَا نَقْضِهِمْ مِيثَاقَهُمْ - بِنَقْضِهِمِ التى كَتَبَ اللهُ. تَبُوءُ: تَحْمِلُ. دَائِرَةٌ: دَوْلَةٌ. وَقَالَ غَيْرُهُ: الإِغْرَاءُ: التَّسْلِيطُ، أُجُورَهُنَّ: مُهُورَهُنَّ. المُهَيْمِنُ: الأَمِينُ. القُرآنُ أَمِينٌ عَلَى كُلِّ كِتَابٍ قَبْلَهُ. وَقَالَ سُفْيَانُ: مَا فِى القُرآنِ آيَةٌ أَشَدُّ عَلَىَّ مِنْ - لَسْتُمْ عَلَى شَيْءٍ حَتَّى تُقِيمُوا التَّوْرَاةَ والإِنجِيلَ وَمَا أُنزِلَ إِلَيْكُمْ مِنْ رَبِّكُمْ - مَخْمَصَةٌ: مَجاعَةٌ. مَنْ أَحْيَاهَا: يَعْنِى مَنْ حَرَّمَ قَتْلَهَا إِلاَّ بِحَقٍّ. حَيِىَ النَّاسُ مِنْهُ جَمِيعًا. شِرْعَةً وَمِنْهَاجًا: سَبِيلاً وَسُنَّةً. فَإِنْ عُثِرَ: ظَهَرَ. الأَوْلَيَانِ: وَاحِدُهُمَا أَوْلَى.

(99) CHAPTER. Sufyān said: There is no Verse harder on me in the entire Qur'ān than this Verse: (' Say:" O people of the Scripture)!

'You have nothing (as regards guidance) till you act according to the Torah, the Gospel and all that which has been sent down to you (Muḥammad) from your Lord (including this Qur'ān)'. (5:68)

باب قَوْلِهِ - اليَوْمَ أَكْمَلْتُ لَكُمْ

(100) CHAPTER. Allāh's Statement:—

'This day I have perfected your religion for you.' (5:3)

دينكم - وقال ابن عباس: مخمصة: مجاعة.

130. Narrated Tāriq bin Shihāb: The Jews said to 'Umar, "You (i.e. Mulsims) recite a Verse, and had it been revealed to us, we would have taken the day of its revelation as a day of celebration." 'Umar said, "I know very well when and where it was revealed, and where Allāh's Messenger ﷺ was when it was revealeu. (It was revealed on) the day of 'Arafāt (Hajj Day), and by Allāh, I was at 'Arafāt." Sufyān, a subnarrator said: I am in doubt whether the Verse:—

'This day I have perfected your religion for you.'

was revealed on a Friday or not.

١٣٠ - حدثني محمد بن بشار: حدثنا عبد الرحمن: حدثنا سفيان، عن قيس، عن طارق بن شهاب: قالت اليهود لعمر: إنكم تقرءون آية لو نزلت فينا لاتخذناها عيدا، فقال عمر: إني لأعلم حيث أنزلت، وأين أنزلت؟ وأين رسول الله صلى الله عليه وسلم حيث أنزلت يوم عرفة وإنا والله بعرفة. قال سفيان: وأشك كان يوم الجمعة أم لا؟ - اليوم أكملت لكم دينكم -.

(101 CHAPTER, Allāh's Statement:—

'and you find no water, then go to clean earth..............(perform Tayammum)........' (5:6)

باب قوله - فلم تجدوا ماء فتيمموا صعيدا طيبا - تيمموا: تعمدوا، آمين: عامدين. أممت وتيممت واحد. وقال ابن عباس: لمستم، وتمسوهن، واللاتي دخلتم بهن. والإفضاء: النكاح.

131. Narrated 'Āisha رضي الله عنها the wife of the Prophet ﷺ : We set out with Allāh's Messenger ﷺ on one of his journeys, and when we were at Baidā' or at Dhāt-al-Jaish, a necklace of mine

١٣١ - حدثنا إسماعيل قال: حدثني مالك، عن عبد الرحمن بن القاسم، عن أبيه، عن عائشة رضي

was broken (and lost). Allāh's Messenger ﷺ stayed there to look for it, and so did the people along with him. Neither were they at a place of water, nor did they have any water with them. So the people went to Abū Bakr Aṣ-Ṣiddīq and said, "Don't you see what 'Āisha has done? She has made Allāh's Messenger ﷺ and the people, stay where there is no water and they have no water with them." Abū Bakr came while Allāh's Messenger ﷺ was sleeping with his head on my thigh. He said (to me), "You have detained Allāh's Messenger ﷺ and the people where there is no water, and they have no water with them." So he admonished me and said what Allāh wished him to say, and he hit me on my flanks with his hand. Nothing prevented me from moving (because of pain) but the position of Allāh's Messenger ﷺ on my thigh. So Allāh's Messenger ﷺ got up when dawn broke and there was no water, so Allāh revealed the Verse of Tayammum. Usaid bin Ḥuḍair said, "It is not the first blessing of yours, O the family of Abū Bakr." Then we made the camel on which I was riding, got up, and found the necklace under it.

اللهُ عنها زوجِ النبيِّ صلى اللهُ عليه وسلم قالت: خرجنا مع رسولِ الله صلى الله عليه وسلم في بعضِ أسفارِه حتى إذا كنا بالبيداءِ أو بذاتِ الجيشِ انقطع عقدٌ لي. فأقام رسولُ الله صلى الله عليه وسلم على التماسِه وأقام الناسُ معه وليسوا على ماءٍ وليس معهم ماءٌ، فأتى الناسُ إلى أبي بكرٍ الصديقِ فقالوا: ألا ترى ما صنعت عائشةُ؟ أقامت برسولِ الله صلى الله عليه وسلم وبالناسِ وليسوا على ماءٍ وليس معهم ماءٌ. فجاء أبو بكرٍ ورسولُ الله صلى الله عليه وسلم واضعٌ رأسَه على فخذي قد نام، فقال: حبستِ رسولَ الله صلى الله عليه وسلم والناسَ وليسوا على ماءٍ وليس معهم ماءٌ. قالت عائشةُ: فعاتبني أبو بكرٍ وقال ما شاء اللهُ أن يقولَ وجعل يطعنني بيدِه في خاصرتي، ولا يمنعني من التحركِ إلا مكانُ رسولِ الله صلى الله عليه وسلم على فخذي. فقام رسولُ الله صلى الله عليه وسلم حين أصبح على غيرِ ماءٍ فأنزل اللهُ آيةَ التيممِ فقال أسيدُ بنُ حضيرٍ: ما هي بأولِ بركتكم يا آلَ أبي بكرٍ. قالت: البعيرَ الذي كنتُ عليه فإذا العقدُ تحتَه.

132. Narrated 'Āisha . A necklace of mine was lost at Al-Baidā' and we were on our way to Medīna. The Prophet made his camel kneel down and dismounted and laid his head on my lap and slept. Abū Bakr came to me and hit me violently on the chest and said, "You have detained the people because of a necklace." I kept as motionless as a dead person because of the position of Allāh's Messenger , (on my lap) although Abū Bakr had hurt me (with the slap). Then the Prophet woke up and it was the time for the morning (prayer). Water was sought, but in vain; so the following Verse was revealed:–

'O you who believe! When you intend to offer prayer........' (5:6)

Usaid bin Ḥudair said, "Allāh has blessed the people for your sake, O the family of Abū Bakr. You are but a blessing for them."

١٣٢ ـ حدثنا يحيى بن سليمان قال: حدثني ابن وهب قال: أخبرني عمرو أن عبد الرحمن ابن القاسم حدثه عن أبيه عن عائشة رضي الله عنها: سقطت قلادة لي بالبيداء ونحن داخلون المدينة، فأناخ النبي صلى الله عليه وسلم ونزل فثنى رأسه في حجري راقدا، أقبل أبو بكر فلكزني لكزة شديدة وقال: حبست الناس في قلادة فبي الموت لمكان رسول الله صلى الله عليه وسلم وقد أوجعني، ثم إن النبي صلى الله عليه وسلم استيقظ وحضرت الصبح، فالتمس الماء فلم يوجد، فنزلت ـ يا أيها الذين آمنوا إذا قمتم إلى الصلاة ـ الآية، فقال أسيد بن حضير، لقد بارك الله للناس فيكم يا آل أبي بكر، ما أنتم إلا بركة لهم.

(102) CHAPTER. The Statement of Allāh :–

'So go you and your Lord and fight you two, we are sitting here.' (5:24)

باب قوله ـ فاذهب أنت وربك فقاتلا إنا هاهنا قاعدون ـ.

133. Narrated 'Abdullāh (bin Mas'ūd): On the day of Badr, Al-Miqdād said, "O Allāh's Messenger! We do not say to you as the children of

١٣٣ ـ حدثنا أبو نعيم: حدثنا إسرائيل، عن مخارق، عن طارق بن

Israēl said to Moses, 'Go you and your Lord and fight you two; we are sitting here, (5:24) but (we say). 'Proceed, and we are with you.' " That seemed to delight Allāh's Messenger ﷺ greatly.

شهاب : سمعت ابن مسعود رضي الله عنه قال : شهدت من المقداد ح. وحدثني حمدان بن عمر : حدثنا أبو النضر : حدثنا الأشجعي ، عن سفيان ، عن مخارق ، عن طارق ، عن عبد الله قال : قال المقداد يوم بدر : يا رسول الله إنا لا نقول لك كما قالت بنو إسرائيل لموسى - فاذهب أنت وربك فقاتلا إنا هاهنا قاعدون - ولكن امض ونحن معك ، فكأنه سرى عن رسول الله صلى الله عليه وسلم. ورواه وكيع عن سفيان عن مخارق عن طارق أن المقداد قال ذلك للنبي صلى الله عليه وسلم.

(103) CHAPTER. 'The only reward of those who wage war against Allāh and His Messenger, and do mischief through the land is execution or crucifixion. . . .(5:33) To wage war against Allāh means to reject faith in Him.

باب إنما جزاء الذين يحاربون الله ورسوله ويسعون في الأرض فسادا - الآية .. المحاربة لله : الكفر به .

134. Narrated Abū Qilāba that he was sitting behind 'Umar bin 'Abdul 'Azīz and the people mentioned and mentioned (about Al-Qasāma) and they said (various things), and said that the Caliphs had permitted it. 'Umar bin 'Abdul 'Azīz turned towards Abū Qilāba who was behind him and said. "What do you say, O 'Abdullāh bin Zaid?" or said, "What do you say, O

١٣٤ - حدثنا علي بن عبد الله : حدثنا محمد بن عبد الله الأنصاري : حدثنا ابن عون قال : حدثني سلمان أبو رجاء مولى أبي قلابة عن أبي قلابة أنه : كان جالسا خلف عمر بن عبد العزيز فذكروا وذكروا ، فقالوا

Abū Qilāba?" Abū Qilāba said, "I do not know that killing a person is lawful in Islām except in three cases: a married person committing illegal sexual intercourse, one who has murdered somebody unlawfully, or one who wages war against Allāh and His Messenger." 'Anbasa said, "Anas narrated to us such-and-such." Abū Qilāba said, "Anas narrated to me in this concern, saying, some people came to the Prophet ﷺ and they spoke to him saying, 'The climate of this land does not suit us.' The Prophet ﷺ said, 'These are camels belonging to us, and they are to be taken out to the pasture. So take them out and drink of their milk and urine.' (1) So they took them and set out and drank of their urine and milk, (1) and having recovered, they attacked the shepherd, killed him and drove away the camels.' Why should there be any delay in punishing them as they murdered (a person) and waged war against Allāh and His Messenger and frightened Allāh's Messenger ﷺ ?' " 'Anbasa said, "I testify the uniqueness of Allāh!" Abū Qilāba said, "Do you suspect me?" 'Anbasa said, "No, Anas narrated that (Ḥadīth) to us." Then 'Anbasa added, "O the people of such-and-such (country), you will remain in good state as long as Allāh keeps this (man) and the like of this (man) amongst you."

وَقالوا قَدْ أفادَتْ بِها الخُلَفاءُ . فالتَفَتَ إلى أبي قِلابَةَ وَهُوَ خَلْفَ ظَهْرِهِ فَقالَ : ما تَقولُ يا عَبْدَ اللهِ بنَ زَيْدٍ ؟ أوْ قالَ ما تَقولُ يا أبا قِلابَةَ ؟ قُلْتُ ما عَلِمْتُ نَفْسًا حَلَّ قَتْلُها في الإسْلامِ إلاَّ رَجُلٌ زَنى بَعْدَ إحْصانٍ ، أوْ قَتَلَ نَفْسًا بِغَيْرِ نَفْسٍ ، أوْ حارَبَ اللهَ وَرَسولَهُ صلى اللهُ عليهِ وسلَّم . فَقالَ عَنْبَسَةُ : حدَّثنا أنَسٌ بِكَذا وكَذا ، قُلْتُ : إيّايَ حَدَّثَ أنَسٌ ، قالَ : قَدِمَ قَوْمٌ عَلى النَّبِيِّ صلى اللهُ عليهِ وسلَّم فَكَلَّموهُ فَقالوا : قَدِ اسْتَوْخَمْنا هَذِهِ الأرْضَ فَقالَ : هَذِهِ نَعَمٌ لَنا تَخْرُجُ فاخْرُجوا فيها فاشْرَبوا مِنْ ألْبانِها وأبْوالِها ، فَخَرَجوا فيها فَشَرِبوا مِنْ أبْوالِها وألْبانِها واسْتَصَحّوا وَمالوا عَلى الرّاعي فَقَتَلوهُ وَاطَّرَدوا النَّعَمَ فَما يُسْتَبْطَأُ مِنْ هَؤُلاءِ ، قَتَلوا النَّفْسَ وَحارَبوا اللهَ وَرَسولَهُ وَخَوَّفوا رَسولَ اللهِ صلى اللهُ عليهِ وسلَّم . فَقالَ سُبْحانَ اللهِ فَقُلْتُ : تَتَّهِمُني ؟ قالَ : حدَّثنا بِهَذا أنَسٌ قالَ : وَقالَ يا أهْلَ كَذا إنَّكُمْ لَنْ تَزالوا بِخَيْرٍ ما أبْقى اللهُ هَذا فيكُمْ ، وَمِثْلُ هَذا .

(1) As a medicine for their disease.

(104) CHAPTER. Allāh's Statement:— 'And (punishment for) wounds, equal for equal (Qiṣāṣ i.e. equality in punishment).' (5:45)

بابُ قوْلِهِ ـ والجُرُوحُ قِصَاصٌ ـ .

135. Narrated Anas (bin Mālik): Ar-Rubai' (the paternal aunt of Anas bin Mālik) broke the incisor tooth of young Anṣārī girl. Her family demanded the Qiṣāṣ (1) and they came to the Prophet who passed the judgement of Qiṣāṣ. Anas bin An-Naḍr (the paternal uncle of Anas bin Mālik) said, "O Allāh's Messenger! By Allāh, her tooth will not be broken." The Prophet said, "O Anas! (The law prescribed in) Allāh's Book is Qiṣāṣ." But the people (i.e. the relatives of the girl) gave up their claim and accepted a compensation. On that Allāh's Messenger said, "Some of Allāh's worshippers are such that if they take an oath, Allāh will fulfill it for them."

١٣٥ ـ حدَّثَنِي مُحَمَّدُ بنُ سَلامٍ : أخبرَنا الفَزَارِيُّ ، عَنْ حُمَيْدٍ : عَنْ أنَسٍ رَضِيَ اللهُ تعالى عَنْهُ قالَ : كَسَرَتِ الرُّبَيِّعُ وَهِيَ عَمَّةُ أنَسِ بنِ مالكٍ ثَنِيَّةَ جارِيَةٍ مِنَ الأنْصَارِ فَطَلَبَ القَوْمُ القِصَاصَ فأتَوُا النَّبِيَّ صلى اللهُ عليهِ وسلَّم فأمَرَ النَّبِيُّ صلى اللهُ عليهِ وسلَّم بالقِصَاصِ ، فقَالَ أنَسُ بنُ النَّضْرِ عَمُّ أنَسِ بنِ مالكٍ : لا واللهِ لا تُكْسَرُ سِنُّها يا رَسُولَ اللهِ ، فقالَ رَسُولُ اللهِ صلى اللهُ عليهِ وسلَّم : يا أنَسُ ، كِتابُ اللهِ القِصَاصُ ، فرَضِيَ القَوْمُ وَقَبِلُوا الأرْشَ فقَالَ رَسُولُ اللهِ صلى اللهُ عليهِ وسلَّم : إنَّ مِنْ عِبادِ اللهِ مَنْ لَوْ أقْسَمَ عَلى اللهِ لأبَرَّهُ .

(1) Qiṣāṣ: The Law of equality in punishment.

(105) CHAPTER. 'O Messenger (Muḥammad)! Proclaim (the Message) which has been sent down to you from your Lord.' (5:67)

بابٌ ـ يا أيُّها الرَّسُولُ بَلِّغْ ما أُنزِلَ إلَيْكَ مِنْ رَبِّكَ ـ .

136. Narrated 'Āisha : Whoever tells that Muḥammad concealed part of what was revealed to him, is a liar, for Allāh says:—

'O Messenger (Muḥammad)! Proclaim (the Message) which has been sent down to you from your Lord.' (5:67)

١٣٦ ـ حدَّثنا مُحمَّدُ بنُ يُوسُفَ : حدَّثَنا سُفْيانُ ، عَنْ إسْماعِيلَ ، عَنِ الشَّعْبِيِّ ، عَنْ مَسْرُوقٍ عَنْ عائشَةَ رَضِيَ اللهُ عَنْها قالَتْ : مَنْ حدَّثَكَ أنَّ مُحَمَّدًا صلى اللهُ عليهِ وسلَّم كَتَمَ شَيْئًا مِمَّا أُنزِلَ عَلَيْهِ فَقَدْ كَذَبَ ، واللهُ يَقُولُ ـ يا أيُّها الرَّسُولُ بَلِّغْ ما أُنزِلَ إلَيْكَ مِنْ رَبِّكَ ـ الآيَةَ .

(106) CHAPTER. Allāh's Statement:—

'Allāh will not punish you for what is unintentional in your oaths.' (5:89)

بابُ قولِهِ ـ لا يُؤاخِذُكُمُ اللهُ باللَّغْوِ في أيمانِكُمْ ـ .

137. Narrated 'Āisha : This Verse:—

'Allāh will not punish you for what is unintentional in your oaths.' (5:89)

was revealed about a man's statement (during his talk), "No, by Allāh," and "Yes, by Allāh."

١٣٧ ـ حدَّثنا عَلِيُّ بنُ عَبْدِ اللهِ : حدَّثَنا مالِكُ بنُ سُعَيْرٍ : حدَّثنا هِشامٌ ، عَنْ أبيهِ ، عَنْ عائشَةَ رَضِيَ اللهُ عَنْها : أُنزِلَتْ هٰذِهِ الآيَةُ ـ لا يُؤاخِذُكُمُ اللهُ باللَّغْوِ في أيمانِكُمْ ـ في قَوْلِ الرَّجُلِ لا واللهِ ، وبَلَى واللهِ .

138. Narrated 'Āisha that her

١٣٨ ـ حدَّثنا أحْمَدُ بنُ أبي رَجاءٍ :

father (Abū Bakr) never broke his oath till Allāh revealed the order of the legal expiation for oath. Abū Bakr said, "If I ever take an oath (to do something) and later find that to do something else is better, then I accept Allāh's permission and do that which is better, (and do the legal expiation for my oath)".

حدَّثنا النَّضرُ، عن هشامٍ قالَ: أخبرني أبي، عن عائشةَ رضيَ اللهُ عنها: أنَّ أباها كانَ لا يحنثُ في يمينٍ حتَّى أنزلَ اللهُ كفارةَ اليمينِ. قالَ أبو بكرٍ: لا أرى يمينا أرى غيرَها خيرًا منها إلاَّ قبلتُ رخصةَ اللهِ وفعلتُ الذي هوَ خيرٌ.

(107) CHAPTER. The Statement of Allāh (تعالى) :–

'O you who believe! Do not make unlawful the good things which Allāh has made lawful for you.'
(5:87)

باب قولِهِ تعالى - يا أيُّها الذينَ آمنُوا لا تحرِّموا طيِّباتِ ما أحلَّ اللهُ لكُم -.

139. Narrated 'Abdullāh (رضي الله عنه) : We used to participate in the holy wars carried on by the Prophet (ﷺ) and we had no women (wives) with us. So we said (to the Prophet (ﷺ)). "Shall we castrate ourselves?" But the Prophet (ﷺ) forbade us to do that and thenceforth he allowed us to marry a woman (temporarily) by giving her even a garment, and then he recited:

'O you who believe! Do not make unlawful the good things which Allāh has made lawful for you.' (1)

١٣٩ - حدَّثنا عمرُو بنُ عونٍ: حدَّثنا خالدٌ، عن إسماعيلَ، عن قيسٍ، عن عبدِ اللهِ رضيَ اللهُ تعالى عنهُ قالَ: كُنَّا نغزُو معَ النَّبيِّ صلى اللهُ عليهِ وسلَّم وليسَ معَنا نساءٌ فقُلنا: ألا نختصي؟ فنهانا عن ذلكَ فرخَّصَ لنا بعدَ ذلكَ أن نتزوَّجَ المرأةَ بالثوبِ ثمَّ قرأَ - يا أيُّها الذينَ آمنُوا لا تحرِّموا طيِّباتِ ما أحلَّ اللهُ لكُم -.

(1) Temporary marriage (Mut'a) was allowed in the early days of Islām, but later, at the time of the Khaibar Battle, it was prohibited. (Allāh knows it better.)

(108) CHAPTER. Allāh's Statement:– 'Alcoholic drinks and gambling and Anṣāb (1) (i.e. erected posts for worship) and (seeking good luck by) arrows are an abomination of Satan's handiwork.' (5:90)

باب قوله - إنما الخمر والميسر والأنصاب والأزلام رجس من عمل الشيطان - وقال ابن عباس: الأزلام: القداح يقتسمون بها فى الأمور. والنصب: أنصاب يذبحون عليها. وقال غيره: الزلم القدح لاريش له وهو واحد الأزلام. والاستقسام: أن يجيل القداح، فإن نهته انتهى، وإن أمرته فعل ما تأمره به. يجيل: يدير. وقد أعلموا القداح أعلاما بضروب يستقسمون بها، وفعلت منه قسمت. والقسوم المصدر.

140. Narrated Ibn 'Umar : (The Verse of) prohibiting alcoholic drinks was revealed when there were in Medīna five kinds of (alcoholic) drinks, none of which was produced from grapes. (2)

١٤٠ - حدثنا إسحاق بن إبراهيم: أخبرنا محمد بن بشر: حدثنا عبد العزيز ابن عمر بن عبد العزيز قال: حدثنى نافع، عن ابن عمر رضى الله تعالى عنهما قال: نزل تحريم الخمر وإن فى المدينة يومئذ لخمسة أشربة ما فيها شراب العنب.

141. Narrated Anas bin Mālik : We had no alcoholic drinks except that which was produced from

١٤١ - حدثنا يعقوب بن إبراهيم: حدثنا ابن علية: حدثنا عبد العزيز

(1) Anṣāb is the plural of 'Naṣb' which means a stone at which sacrifices used to be slaughtered for an idol.

(2) Those drinks were produced from honey, dates, wheat, barley and corn.

dates and which you call Fadīkh. While I was standing offering drinks to Abū Ṭalḥa and so-and-so and so-and-so, a man came and said, "Has the news reached you?" They said, "What is that?" He said. "Alcoholic drinks have been prohibited." They said, "Spill (the contents of) these pots, O Anas! "Then they neither asked about it (alcoholic drinks) nor returned it after the news from that man.

ابنُ صُهَيْبٍ قالَ: قالَ أنسُ بنُ مالكٍ رَضِيَ اللهُ عنهُ: ما كانَ لنا خَمْرٌ غَيْرَ فَضِيخِكُمْ هذا الذي تُسَمُّونَهُ الفَضِيخَ، فإنِّي لقائمٌ أسقِي أبا طَلْحَةَ وفُلاناً وفُلاناً إذْ جاءَ رَجُلٌ فقالَ: وهَلْ بَلَغَكُمُ الخَبَرُ؟ فقالُوا: وما ذاكَ؟ قالَ حُرِّمَتِ الخَمْرُ، قالُوا: أهْرِقْ هذهِ القِلالَ يا أنسُ. قالَ فما سألُوا عنها ولا راجَعُوها بعدَ خَبَرِ الرَّجُلِ.

142. Narrated Jābir : Some people drank alcoholic beverages in the morning (of the day) of the Uḥud battle and on the same day they were killed as martyrs, and that was before wine was prohibited.

١٤٢ - حدَّثنا صَدَقَةُ بنُ الفَضْلِ: أخبرَنا ابنُ عُيَيْنَةَ، عنْ عَمْرٍو، عنْ جابرٍ قالَ: صَبَّحَ أُناسٌ غَدَاةَ أُحُدٍ الخَمْرَ فقُتِلُوا مِنْ يَوْمِهِمْ جميعاً شُهَدَاءَ وذلكَ قبلَ تَحْرِيمِها.

143. Narrated Ibn 'Umar : I heard 'Umar while he was on the pulpit of the Prophet , saying, "Now then O people! The revelation about the prohibition of alcoholic drinks has revealed; and alcoholic drinks are extracted from five things: Grapes, dates, honey, wheat and barley. And the alcoholic drink is that which confuses and stupifies the mind."

١٤٣ - حدَّثنا إسحاقُ بنُ إبراهيمَ: أخبرَنا عيسى وابنُ إدريسَ، عنْ أبي حَيَّانَ، عنِ الشَّعْبِيِّ، عنِ ابنِ عُمَرَ قالَ: سَمِعْتُ عُمَرَ رَضِيَ اللهُ عنهُ على مِنْبَرِ النَّبِيِّ صلى اللهُ عليهِ وسلَّمَ يقولُ: أمَّا بعدُ أيُّها النَّاسُ، إنَّهُ نَزَلَ تَحْرِيمُ الخَمْرِ وهيَ مِنْ خَمْسَةٍ: مِنَ العِنَبِ، والتَّمْرِ، والعَسَلِ والحِنْطَةِ، والشَّعِيرِ. والخَمْرُ: ما خامَرَ العَقْلَ.

(109) CHAPTER. (A) 'On those who believe and do good deeds there is no blame for what they ate (in the past). ...... (5:93)

باب - ليس على الذين آمنوا وعملوا الصالحات جناح فيما طعموا - الآية.

144. Narrated Anas : The alcoholic drink which was spilled was Al-Fadikh. I used to offer alcoholic drinks to the people at the residence of Abū Talḥa. Then the order of prohibiting Alcoholic drinks was revealed, and the Prophet ordered somebody to announce that: [Abū Ṭalḥa said to me, "Go out and see what this voice (this announcement) is." I went out and (on coming back) said, "This is somebody announcing that]"alcoholic beverages have been prohibited." Abū Ṭalḥa said to me, "Go and spill it (i.e. the wine)," Then it (alcoholic drinks) was seen flowing through the streets of Medina. At that time the wine was Al-Fadikh. The people said, "Some people (Muslims) were killed (during the battle of Uhud) while wine was in their stomachs." So Allāh revealed:—

> 'On those who believe and do good deeds there is no blame for what they ate (in the past)." (5:93)

١٤٤ - حدثنا أبو النعمان: حدثنا حماد بن زيد: حدثنا ثابت، عن أنس رضي الله عنه: أن الخمر التي هريقت الفضيخ. وزادني محمد البيكندي، عن أبي النعمان قال: كنت ساقي القوم في منزل أبي طلحة فنزل تحريم الخمر فأمر مناديا فنادى، فقال أبو طلحة: اخرج فانظر ما هذا الصوت. قال: فخرجت فقلت هذا مناد ينادي: ألا إن الخمر قد حرمت، فقال لي: اذهب فأهرقها، قال: فجرت في سكك المدينة. قال: وكانت خمرهم يومئذ الفضيخ، فقال بعض القوم: قتل قوم وهي في بطونهم، قال: فأنزل الله - ليس على الذين آمنوا وعملوا الصالحات جناح فيما طعموا -.

(109) CHAPTER. (B) Allāh's Statement:—

> 'Ask not about things which if made plain to you, may cause you trouble.' (5:101)

باب قوله - لا تسألوا عن أشياء إن تبد لكم تسؤكم -.

145. Narrated Anas ﷺ: The Prophet ﷺ delivered a sermon the like of which I had never heard before. He said, "If you but knew what I know then you would have laughed little and wept much." On hearing that, the companions of the Prophet ﷺ covered their faces and the sound of their weeping was heard. A man said, "Who is my father?" The Prophet ﷺ said, "So-and-so." So this Verse was revealed:—
'Ask not about things which, if made plain to you, may cause you trouble.'
(5:101)

146. Narrated Ibn 'Abbās ﷺ: Some people were asking Allāh's Messenger ﷺ questions mockingly. A man would say, "Who is my father?" Another man whose she-camel had gone astray would say, "Where is my she-camel?" So Allāh revealed this Verse in this connection:—
'O you who believe! Ask not about things which, if made plain to you, may cause you trouble.'
(5:101)

١٤٥ - حدَّثنا مُنذرُ بنُ الوَليدِ ابنِ عبدِالرَّحمنِ الجارُودِي: حدَّثنا أبي: حدَّثنا شعبةُ، عن موسى بنِ أنسٍ، رَضِيَ اللهُ تعالى عنهُ قالَ: خَطبَ النبيُّ صلى الله عليه وسلَّم خُطبةً ما سمِعتُ مِثلها قَطُّ، قال: لَوْ تَعلمونَ ما أعلمُ لَضَحِكتُم قَليلا ولَبَكيتُم كَثيرا، قالَ: فَغطَّى أصحابُ رسولِ الله صلى الله عليه وسلم وجوهَهُم لَهُم حَنينٌ، فقالَ رَجلٌ: مَنْ أبي؟ قال فُلانٌ، فَنَزَلَتْ هَذِهِ الآيةُ ـ لاتَسألُوا عَنْ أشياءَ إنْ تُبدَ لكُم تَسُؤْكُم ـ رَواهُ النَّضرُ ورَوْحُ بنُ عُبادَةَ عَنْ شُعْبَةَ.

١٤٦ - حدَّثني الفَضلُ بنُ سَهلٍ قالَ: حدَّثنا أبو النَّضرِ: حدَّثنا أبو خَيْثَمَةَ: حدَّثنا أبو الجُوَيْرِيَةِ عنِ ابنِ عبَّاسٍ رَضِيَ اللهُ عَنهُما قالَ: كانَ قَومٌ يَسألُونَ رسولَ اللهِ صلى اللهُ عليه وسلَّم استِهزاءً فَيقولُ الرَّجلُ: مَنْ أبي؟ ويَقولُ الرَّجلُ تَضِلُّ ناقتُهُ: أينَ ناقتي؟ فأنزَلَ اللهُ فيهِم هذهِ الآيةَ ـ يا أيُّها الذينَ آمنُوا لاتَسألُوا عَنْ أشياءَ إنْ تُبدَ لكم تَسُؤْكُم ـ حتى فَرغَ مِنَ الآيةِ كُلِّها.

(110) CHAPTER. 'Allāh has not instituted things (like those of) Baḥīra or Sā'iba, or Waṣīla or Ḥām.' (1) (5:103)

بابٌ - ما جَعَلَ اللهُ مِنْ بَحِيرَةٍ وَلا سائِبَةٍ وَلا وَصِيلَةٍ وَلا حامٍ - وَإذْ قالَ اللهُ - يَقُولُ قالَ اللهُ، وَإذْ هاهُنا صِلَةٌ. المائِدَةُ أصلُها مَفعولَةٌ، كَعِيشَةٍ راضِيَةٍ، وَتَطْلِيقَةٍ بائِنَةٍ. والمَعْنَى مِيدَ بِها صاحِبُها مِنْ خَيرٍ، يُقالُ مادَنِي يَمِيدُنِي. وَقالَ ابنُ عَبّاسٍ: مُتَوَفِّيكَ: مُمِيتُكَ.

147. Narrated Sa'īd bin Al-Musaiyab : 'Baḥīra' was a she-camel whose milk used to be spared for the idols and nobody was allowed to milk it : 'Sā'iba' was a she-camel which they (i.e. infidels) used to set free for their gods and nothing was allowed to be carried on it. Abū Huraira said : Allāh's Messenger ﷺ said, "I saw 'Amr bin 'Āmir Al-Khuza'i (in a dream) dragging his intestines in the Fire, and he was the first person to establish the tradition of setting free the animals (for the sake of their false deities)", 'Waṣīla' was a she-camel which gave birth to a she-camel as its first delivery, and then gave birth to an other she-camel as its second delivery. People (in the pre-islāmic periods of ignorance) used to let that she-camel loose for their idols if it gave birth to two she-camels successively without giving birth to a male camel in between. 'Ḥām' was a stallion camel which was used for copulation. When it had finished the number of copulations assigned for it,

١٤٧ - حدَّثنا موسَى بنُ إسْماعِيلَ: حدَّثنا إبْراهِيمُ بنُ سَعْدٍ، عَنْ صالِحِ ابنِ كَيْسانَ، عَنِ ابنِ شِهابٍ، عَنِ ابنِ المُسَيَّبِ قالَ: البَحِيرَةُ التي يُمْنَعُ دَرُّها للطَّواغِيتِ فَلا يَحْلُبُها أحَدٌ مِنَ النّاسِ. والسّائِبَةُ كانُوا يُسَيِّبُونَها لآلِهَتِهِمْ فَلا يُحْمَلُ عَلَيْها شَيْءٌ. قالَ: وَقالَ أبو هُرَيْرَةَ: قالَ رَسُولُ اللهِ صلى اللهُ عليهِ وسلَّم: رَأيْتُ عَمْرَو بنَ عامِرٍ الخُزاعِيَّ يَجُرُّ قُصْبَهُ في النّارِ، كانَ أوَّلَ مَنْ سَيَّبَ السَّوائِبَ. والوَصِيلَةُ: النّاقَةُ البِكْرُ تُبَكِّرُ في أوَّلِ نِتاجِ الإبِلِ بِأُنْثَى ثُمَّ تُثَنِّي بَعْدُ بِأُنْثَى، وكانُوا يُسَيِّبُونَهُمْ لِطَواغِيتِهِمْ إنْ وَصَلَتْ إحْداهُما بالأُخْرَى لَيْسَ

(1) See the meanings of these terms in the following Ḥadīth (No. 147)

they would let it loose for their idols and excuse it from burdens so that nothing would be carried on it, and they called it the 'Ḥāmi.' Abū Huraira said, "I heard the Prophet ﷺ saying so."

بَيْنَهُما ذَكَرٌ . والحامِ : فَحْلُ الإِبِلِ يَضْرِبُ الضِّرَابَ المَعْدُودَ فإذا قَضَى ضِرَابَهُ وَدَعُوهُ للطَّواغيتِ وأَعْفَوْهُ مِنَ الحَمْلِ فَلَمْ يُحْمَلْ عَلَيْهِ شَيْءٌ ، وسَمَّوْهُ الحَامِي . وقالَ لي أبُو اليَمَانِ : أخبرَنا شُعَيْبٌ ، عنِ الزُّهْرِيِّ : سَمِعْتُ سَعيدًا يُخْبِرُهُ بِهَذَا . قالَ : وَقالَ أبو هُرَيْرَةَ : سَمِعْتُ النَّبيَّ صلى اللهُ عليهِ وسلَّم نَحْوَهُ ؛ وَرَوَاهُ ابنُ الهَادِ ، عَنِ ابنِ شِهابٍ ، عَنْ سَعيدٍ ، عَنْ أبي هُرَيْرَةَ رَضِيَ اللهُ عَنْهُ : سَمِعْتُ النَّبيَّ صلى اللهُ عليهِ وسلَّم .

148. Narrated 'Āisha رضي الله عنها : Allāh's Messenger ﷺ said, "I saw Hell and its different portions were consuming each other and saw 'Amr dragging his intestines (in it), and he was the first person to establish the tradition of letting animals loose (for the idols)."

١٤٨ - حدَّثَني مُحَمَّدُ بنُ أبي يَعْقُوبَ أبو عَبْدِ اللهِ الكِرْمانيُّ : حدَّثنا حَسَّانُ ابنُ إبْراهيمَ : حدَّثنا يُونُسُ ، عَنِ الزُّهْرِيِّ ، عَنْ عُرْوَةَ : أنَّ عائشةَ رَضِيَ اللهُ عَنْها قالَتْ : قالَ رَسُولُ اللهِ صلى اللهُ عليهِ وسلَّم : رَأَيْتُ جَهَنَّمَ يَحْطِمُ بَعْضُها بَعْضًا ، وَرَأَيْتُ عَمْرًا يَجُرُّ قُصْبَهُ ، وَهُوَ أوَّلُ مَنْ سَيَّبَ السَّوائبَ .

(111) CHAPTER. 'And I was a witness over them while I dwelt amongst them; when You took me up, You were the Watcher over them, and You are a Witness to all things. (5:117)

بابٌ - وكُنْتُ عَلَيْهِمْ شَهيدًا ما دُمْتُ فيهِمْ فَلَمَّا تَوَفَّيْتَني كُنْتَ أنتَ الرَّقيبَ عَلَيْهِمْ وأنتَ على كُلِّ شَيْءٍ شَهيدٌ .

149. Narrated Ibn 'Abbās ﷺ: Allāh's Messenger ﷺ delivered a sermon and said, "O people! You will be gathered before Allāh bare-footed, naked and not circumcised." Then (quoting Qur'ān) he said:—

> 'As We began the first creation, We shall repeat it. A promise We have undertaken: Truly we shall do it........' (21:104)

The Prophet ﷺ then said, "The first of the human beings to be dressed on the Day of Resurrection, will be Abraham. Lo! Some men from my followers will be brought and then (the angels) will drive them to the left side (Hell-Fire). I will say. 'O my Lord! (They are) my companions!' Then a reply will come (from Almighty), 'You do not know what they did after you.' I will say as the pious slave (the Prophet Jesus) said:

> And I was a witness over them while I dwelt amongst them. When You took me up. You were the Watcher over them and You are a Witness to all things.' (5:117)

Then it will be said, 'These people have continued to be apostates since you left them.' "

١٤٩ - حدَّثنا أبو الوَليدِ : حدَّثنا شُعْبَةُ : أخبرَنا المُغيرَةُ بنُ النُّعمانِ قالَ : سَمِعْتُ سَعيدَ بنَ جُبَيرٍ ، عَنِ ابنِ عبَّاسٍ رَضِيَ اللهُ تَعالى عَنْهُما قالَ : خَطَبَ رَسُولُ اللهِ صلى اللهُ عليهِ وسلَّم فقالَ : يا أيُّها النّاسُ إنَّكمْ مَحْشُورُونَ إلى اللهِ حُفاةً عُراةً غُرْلاً ، ثُمَّ قالَ - كمَا بَدَأنا أوَّلَ خَلْقٍ نَعيدُهُ وَعْداً عَلَيْنا إنّا كُنّا فاعِلينَ - إلى آخرِ الآيَةِ . ثُمَّ قالَ : ألا وَإنَّ أوَّلَ الخَلائقِ يُكْسَى يَوْمَ القيامَةِ إبْراهيمُ ، ألا وإنَّهُ يُجاءُ برِجالٍ مِنْ أُمَّتي فيُؤْخَذُ بِهِمْ ذاتَ الشِّمالِ فأقولُ : يا رَبِّ أُصَيْحابي ، فيُقالُ : إنَّكَ لا تَدْري ما أحْدَثُوا بَعْدَكَ ، فأقُولُ كمَا قالَ العَبْدُ الصّالحُ - وكُنْتُ عَلَيْهِمْ شَهيداً مادُمْتُ فيهِمْ فلَمّا تَوَفَّيْتَني كُنْتَ أنتَ الرَّقيبَ عَلَيْهِمْ - فيُقالُ إنَّ هؤُلاءِ لَمْ يَزالُوا مُرْتَدِّينَ عَلى أعْقابِهِمْ مُنْذُ فارَقْتَهُمْ .

(112) CHAPTER. Allāh's Statement:—

بابُ قَولِهِ - إنْ تُعَذِّبْهُمْ فإنَّهُمْ

'If You punish them, they are Your slaves.' (5:118)

عِبادُكَ ـ الآيَةَ .

150. Narrated Ibn 'Abbās ﷺ : The Prophet ﷺ said, "You will be gathered (on the Day of Resurrection) and some people will be driven (by the angels) to the left side (and taken to Hell) whereupon I will say as the pious slave (Jesus) said:—

'And I was a witness over them while I dwelt amongst them.. ... the All-Mighty, the All-Wise. (5:117-118)

١٥٠ ـ حدَّثَنا مُحَمَّدُ بنُ كَثِيرٍ : حدَّثَنا سُفْيانُ : حدَّثَنا المُغِيرَةُ بنُ النُّعْمانِ قالَ: حدَّثَني سَعيدُ ابنُ جُبَيرٍ ، عَنِ ابنِ عَبّاسٍ ، عَنِ النَّبِيِّ صلى اللهُ عليهِ وسلَّم قالَ : إنكُمْ مَحْشُورُونَ وإنَّ ناسًا يُؤْخَذُ بِهِمْ ذاتَ الشِّمالِ فأقُولُ كما قالَ العَبْدُ الصّالحُ ـ وكُنْتُ عَلَيْهِمْ شَهِيدًا ما دُمْتُ فيهِمْ ـ إلى قَوْلِهِ ـ العَزِيزُ الحَكِيمُ ـ.

In the Name of Allāh, the Most Beneficent, the Most Merciful

بِسْمِ اللهِ الرَّحْمَنِ الرَّحِيمِ

SŪRAT-AL-AN'ĀM. VI

سورة الأنعام

قالَ ابنُ عَبّاسٍ : ثُمَّ لمْ تَكُنْ فِتْنَتُهُمْ : مَعْذِرَتُهُمْ . مَعْرُوشاتٍ : ما يُعْرَشُ مِنَ الكَرْمِ وغَيرِ ذَلكَ . حَمُولَةً : ما يُحْمَلُ عَلَيْها . ولَلَبَسْنا : لَشَبَّهْنا. لأُنْذِرَكُمْ بهِ : أهْلُ مَكَّةَ . ويَنْأَوْنَ : يَتَباعَدونَ . تُبْسَلُ : تُفْضَحُ . أُبْسِلُوا : أُفْضِحوا. باسِطوا أيْدِيهِمْ : البَسْطُ : الضَّرْبُ . اسْتَكْثَرْتُمْ : أضْلَلْتُمْ كَثِيرًا. مِمّا ذَرَأَ مِنَ الحَرْثِ : جَعَلُوا للهِ مِنْ ثَمَراتِهِمْ ومالِهِمْ نَصِيبًا وللشَّيْطانِ والأوْثانِ نَصِيبًا . أكِنَّةً : واحِدُها كِنانٌ .

١١٩

أمَّا اشتَمَلَتْ : يَعْنِي هَلْ تَشْتَمِلُ إلاَّ عَلَى ذَكَرٍ أوْ أُنْثَى ؟ فَلِمَ تُحَرِّمُونَ بَعْضًا وتُحِلُّونَ بَعْضًا ؟ مَسْفُوحًا : مُهْرَاقًا. صَدَفَ : أعْرَضَ. أُبْلِسُوا : أُويِسُوا. أُبْسِلُوا : أسْلِمُوا. سَرْمَدًا : دائمًا. اسْتَهْوَتْهُ : أضَلَّتْهُ. تَمْتَرُونَ : تَشُكُّونَ. وَقْرًا : صَمَمٌ، وأمَّا الوِقْرُ فإنَّهُ الحِمْلُ. أساطِيرُ : وَاحِدُها أُسْطُورَةٌ وإسْطَارَةٌ وَهِيَ التُّرَّهَاتُ. البَأْسَاءُ : مِنَ البَأْسِ، وَيَكُونُ مِنَ البُؤْسِ. جَهْرَةً : مُعَايَنَةً. الصُّوَرُ : جَماعَةُ صُورَةٍ. كقَوْلِهِ سُورَةٌ وسُوَرٌ، مَلَكُوتٌ ومُلْكٌ. رَهَبُوتٌ : رَحَمُوتٌ، وَتَقُولُ تُرْهَبُ خَيْرٌ مِنْ أنْ تُرْحَمَ. جَنَّ : أظْلَمَ. تَعالى : عَلا. وإنْ تَعْدِلْ : تُقْسِطْ، لا يُقْبَلُ مِنْها فِي ذَلِكَ اليَوْمِ. يُقَالُ عَلَى اللهِ حُسْبانُهُ. أي حِسابُهُ. وَيُقَالُ حُسْبانًا مَرَامِيَ وَرُجُومًا للشَّياطِينِ. مُسْتَقِرٌّ فِي الصُّلْبِ وَمُسْتَوْدَعٌ فِي الرَّحِمِ. القِنْوُ : العِذْقُ، وَالاثْنانِ قِنْوانِ، وَالجَماعَةُ أيضًا قِنْوانٌ، مِثْلُ صِنْوانٍ وصِنْوانٌ.

(113) CHAPTER. 'With Him are the Keys of the Unseen, none knows them but He.' (6:59)

بابٌ ـ وَعِنْدَهُ مَفَاتِيحُ الغَيْبِ لا يَعْلَمُها إلاَّ هُوَ ـ.

151. Narrated 'Abdullāh ﷺ :

١٥١ ـ حدَّثَنا عَبْدُ العَزِيزِ بنُ

Allāh's Messenger ﷺ said, "The keys of the Unseen are five: Verily with Allāh (Alone) is the knowledge of the Hour, He sends down the rain and knows what is in the wombs. No soul knows what it will earn tomorrow, and no soul knows in what land it will die. Verily, Allāh is All-Knower, All-Aware."

(31: 34)

عَبْدِ اللهِ : حدَّثَنا إبْرَاهِيمُ بنُ سَعْدٍ ، عَنِ ابنِ شِهابٍ ، عَنْ سالِمِ ابنِ عَبْدِ اللهِ ، عَنْ أبيهِ : أنَّ رَسُولَ اللهِ صلى اللهُ عليه وسلَّم قالَ : مَفاتِيحُ الغَيْبِ خَمْسٌ : إنَّ اللهَ عِنْدَهُ عِلْمُ السَّاعَةِ ، وَيُنَزِّلُ الغَيْثَ . وَيَعْلَمُ ما في الأرْحامِ . وَما تَدْرِي نَفْسٌ ماذَا تَكْسِبُ غَداً ، وَما تَدْرِي نَفْسٌ بِأيِّ أرْضٍ تَمُوتُ إنَّ اللهَ عَلِيمٌ خَبِيرٌ - .

(114) CHAPTER Say: He has power to send torment on you from above......' (6:65)

بابٌ قُلْ هُوَ القادِرُ عَلى أنْ يَبْعَثَ عَلَيْكُمْ عَذَابا مِنْ فَوْقِكُمْ - الآيَة . يَلْبِسَكُمْ : يَخْلِطَكُمْ مِنَ الالْتِباسِ . يَلْبِسُوا : يخْلِطُوا . شِيَعاً : فِرَقاً .

152. Narrated Jābir ﷺ : When this Verse was revealed:

'Say: He has power to send torment on you from above.'

(6:65)

Allāh's Messenger ﷺ said, "O Allāh! I seek refuge with Your Face (from this punishment)." And when the verse: "or send torment from below your feet," (was revealed),

Allāh's Messenger ﷺ said, "(O Allāh!) I seek refuge with Your Face (from this punishment))." (But when there

١٥٢ - حدَّثَنا أبو النُّعْمانِ : حدَّثَنا حَمَّادُ بنُ زَيْدٍ ، عَنْ عَمْرِو بنِ دِينارٍ ، عَنْ جابِرٍ رَضِيَ اللهُ عَنْهُ قالَ : لمَّا نَزَلَتْ هذِهِ الآيَةُ - قُلْ هُوَ القادِرُ عَلى أنْ يَبْعَثَ عَلَيْكُمْ عَذَابا مِنْ فَوْقِكُمْ - قالَ رَسُولُ اللهِ صلى اللهُ عليه وسلَّم : أعُوذُ بِوَجْهِكَ : - أوْ مِنْ تَحْتِ أرْجُلِكُمْ - قالَ : أعُوذُ بِوَجْهِكَ - أوْ يَلْبِسَكُمْ شِيَعاً وَيُذِيقَ بَعْضَكُمْ بَأسَ بَعْضٍ - قالَ رَسُولُ اللهِ صلى اللهُ عليه

was revealed):

> 'Or confuse you in party strife and make you to taste the violence of one another.' (6:65)

Allāh's Messenger ﷺ said, "This is lighter (or, this is easier)."

وسلم : هذا أهون، أو هذا أيسر.

(115) CHAPTER. '(It is those who believe) and confuse not their belief with wrong (worshipping others besides Allāh)........ (6:82)

باب - ولم يلبسوا إيمانهم بظلم -.

153. Narrated 'Abdullāh رضي الله عنه: When:–

> ....and confuse not their belief with wrong.' (6:82)

was revealed, the Prophet's companions said, "Which of us has not done wrong?" Then there was revealed:–

> 'Verily joining others in worship with Allāh is a tremendous wrong indeed. (31:13)

١٥٣ - حدثني محمد بن بشار : حدثنا ابن أبي عدي، عن شعبة، عن سليمان، عن إبراهيم، عن علقمة، عن عبد الله رضي الله عنه قال : لما نزلت - ولم يلبسوا إيمانهم بظلم - قال أصحابه : وأينا لم يظلم؟ فنزلت - إن الشرك لظلم عظيم -.

(116) CHAPTER. The Statement of Allāh: 'And Jonah and Lot, and each one of them We preferred above the peoples (of their times) .... (6:86)

باب قوله - ويونس ولوطا وكلا فضلنا على العالمين -.

154. Narrated Ibn 'Abbās رضي الله عنهما: The Prophet ﷺ said, "Nobody has

١٥٤ - حدثنا محمد بن بشار : حدثنا ابن مهدي : حدثنا شعبة، عن

the rights to say that I am better than Jonah bin Matta."

قتادة، عن أبي العالية قال: حدثني ابن عم نبيكم، يعني ابن عباس رضي الله عنهما، عن النبي صلى الله عليه وسلم قال: ما ينبغي لعبد أن يقول أنا خير من يونس بن متى.

155. Narrated Abū Huraira : The Prophet said, "Nobody has the right to say that I am better than Jonah bin Matta."

١٥٥ - حدثنا آدم بن أبي إياس: حدثنا شعبة: أخبرنا سعد بن إبراهيم قال: سمعت حميد ابن عبد الرحمن ابن عوف، عن أبي هريرة رضي الله عنه، عن النبي صلى الله عليه وسلم قال: ما ينبغي لعبد أن يقول أنا خير من يونس ابن متى.

(117) CHAPTER. The Statement of Allāh:–

> 'Those are they whom Allāh had guided. So follow their guidance.'
> (6:90)

باب قوله - أولئك الذين هدى الله فبهداهم اقتده -.

156. Narrated Mujāhid that he asked Ibn 'Abbās, "Is there a prostration in Sūrat-al-Ṣād?"(38:24) (1) Ibn 'Abbās said, "Yes," and then recited:

> 'We gave.......So follow their guidance.' (6:85,90)

Then he said, "He (David) is one of

١٥٦ - حدثني إبراهيم بن موسى: أخبرنا هشام: أن ابن جريج أخبرهم قال: أخبرني سليمان الأحول: أن مجاهدا أخبره: أنه سأل ابن عباس

(1) 'And David guessed that We had tried him; he sought forgiveness of his Lord, and he fell down, prostrate, and turned (to Allāh in repentance).' (38:24)

them (i.e. those prophets)." Mujāhid narrated: I asked Ibn 'Abbās (regarding the above Verse). He said, "Your Prophet (Muḥammad ﷺ) was one of those who were ordered to follow them."

أفي ص سجدة؟ فقال: نعم، ثم تلا - ووهبنا - إلى قوله - فبهداهم اقتده. ثم قال: هو منهم. زاد يزيد بن هارون، ومحمد ابن عبيد، وسهل بن يوسف، عن العوام، عن مجاهد: قلت لابن عباس، فقال: نبيكم صلى الله عليه وسلم ممن أمر أن يقتدي بهم.

(118) CHAPTER. Allāh's Statement:— And unto those who are Jews We forbade every (animal) with undivided hoof." (6:146)

Ibn 'Abbās said: Every (animal) with undivided hoof' means the camel and the ostrich.

باب قوله - وعلى الذين هادوا حرمنا كل ذي ظفر الاية - وقال ابن عباس: كل ذي ظفر: البعير والنعامة. الحوايا: المبعر، وقال غيره: هادوا: صاروا يهودا، وأما قوله هدنا: تبنا، هائد: تائب.

157. Narrated Jābir bin 'Abdullāh (رضي الله عنه); The Prophet ﷺ said, "May Allāh curse the Jews! When Allāh forbade them to eat the fat of animals, they melted it and sold it, and utilized its price!"

١٥٧ - حدثنا عمرو بن خالد: حدثنا الليث، عن يزيد بن أبي حبيب: قال عطاء: سمعت جابر بن عبد الله رضي الله عنهما: سمعت النبي صلى الله عليه وسلم قال: قاتل الله اليهود لما حرم الله عليهم شحومها جملوها ثم باعوها فأكلوها. وقال أبو عاصم: حدثنا عبد الحميد حدثنا يزيد: كتب إلي عطاء: سمعت جابرا، عن النبي صلى الله عليه وسلم.

(119) CHAPTER The Statement of Allāh ﷻ :–

'Do not come near to shameful sins (Illegal sexual intercourse etc.), whether committed openly or secretly, -------- (6:151)

بابٌ قولِهِ تعالى - وَلا تَقرَبُوا الفَوَاحِشَ ما ظَهَرَ مِنها وَما بَطَنَ - .

158 Narrated Abū Wā'il: 'Abdullāh (bin Mas'ūd) said, "None has more sense of ghaira (1) than Allāh therefore, **He has prohibited** shameful sins (illegal sexual intercourse, etc.) whether committed openly or secretly. And none loves to be praised more than Allāh does, and for this reason He praises Himself." I asked Abū Wā'il, "Did you hear it from 'Abdullāh?" He said, "Yes," I said, "Did 'Abdullāh ascribe it to Allāh's Messenger ﷺ ?" He said, "Yes."

١٥٨ - حدَّثنا حَفْصُ بنُ عُمَرَ : قال حدَّثنا شُعْبَةُ ، عَنْ عَمْرٍو ، عَنْ أبي وَائِلٍ ، عَنْ عَبْدِ اللهِ رَضِيَ اللهُ تَعالى عَنْهُ قالَ : لا أحَدَ أغْيَرُ مِنَ اللهِ ، وَلِذَلِكَ حَرَّمَ الفَوَاحِشَ ما ظَهَرَ مِنها وَما بَطَنَ . وَلا شَيْءَ أحَبُّ إلَيْهِ المَدْحُ مِنَ اللهِ ، وَلِذَلِكَ مَدَحَ نَفْسَهُ . قُلْتُ : سَمِعْتَهُ مِنْ عَبْدِ اللهِ ؟ قالَ : نَعَمْ ، قُلْتُ : وَرَفَعَهُ ؟ قالَ : نَعَمْ . وكِيلٌ . حَفِيظٌ ومُحِيطٌ بِهِ . قُبُلاً جَمْعُ قَبِيلٍ . والمَعْنى أنَّهُ ضُرُوبٌ لِلْعَذابِ كُلُّ ضَرْبٍ مِنها قَبِيلٌ . زُخْرُفَ القَوْلِ : كُلُّ شَيْءٍ حَسَّنْتَهُ وَزَيَّنْتَهُ وَهُوَ باطِلٌ فَهُوَ زُخْرُفٌ . وَحَرْثٌ حِجْرٌ : حَرَامٌ ، وكُلُّ مَمْنُوعٍ فَهُوَ حِجْرٌ . مَحْجُورٌ . والحِجْرُ : كُلُّ بِناءٍ بَنَيْتَهُ وَيُقالُ للأُنْثى مِنَ الخَيْلِ حِجْرٌ . وَيُقالُ للعَقْلِ حِجْرٌ وَحِجى . وأمَّا الحِجْرُ فَمَوْضِعُ ثَمُودَ ، وَما حَجَّرْتَ عَلَيْهِ

(1) Ghaira: See the glossary of Vol. 4.

مِنَ الأرْضِ فَهُوَ حِجْرٌ. وَمِنْهُ سُمِّيَ حَطِيمُ البَيْتِ حِجْرًا كأنَّهُ مُشْتَقٌّ مِنْ مَحْطُومٍ، مِثْلَ قَتِيلٍ مِنْ مَقْتُولٍ. وأمَّا حَجَرُ اليَمَامَةِ فَهُوَ مَنْزِلٌ.

(120) CHAPTER. The Statement of Allāh:—

Say: Bring forward your witnesses, (6:150)

باب قوله - قُلْ هَلُمَّ شُهَدَاءَكُمْ. لُغَةُ أهْلِ الحِجَازِ هَلُمَّ لِلْوَاحِدِ وَالاثْنَيْنِ والجَمْعِ.

(121) CHAPTER. 'No good will it do to a soul to believe." (6:158)

باب - لا يَنْفَعُ نَفْسًا إيمَانُهَا.

159. Narrated Abū Huraira: Allāh's Messenger said, "The Hour will not be established until the sun rises from the West: and when the people see it, then whoever will be living on the surface of the earth will have faith, and that is (the time) when no good will it do to a soul to believe then, if it believed not before." (6:158)

١٥٩ - حدَّثَنا مُوسَى بنُ إسْمَاعِيلَ: حدَّثَنا عَبْدُ الوَاحِدِ: حدَّثَنا عُمارَةُ: حدَّثَنا أبو زُرْعَةَ: حدَّثَنا أبو هُرَيْرَةَ رَضِيَ اللهُ عَنْهُ قالَ: قالَ رَسُولُ اللهِ صلى اللهُ عليه وسلَّم: لا تَقُومُ السَّاعَةُ حَتَّى تَطْلُعَ الشَّمْسُ مِنْ مَغْرِبِها فإذَا رَآها النَّاسُ آمَنَ مَنْ عَلَيْهَا فَذَاكَ - حِينَ لا يَنْفَعُ نَفْسًا إيمانُها لَمْ تَكُنْ آمَنَتْ مِنْ قَبْلُ -

160. Narrated Abū Huraira: Allāh's Messenger said, "The hour will not be established till the sun rises from the West; and when it rises (from the West) and the people see it, they all will believe. And that is (the time) when

١٦٠ - حدَّثَنِي إسْحاقُ: أخْبَرَنا عَبْدُ الرَّزَّاقِ: أخْبَرَنا مَعْمَرٌ، عَنْ هَمَّامٍ، عَنْ أبي هُرَيْرَةَ رَضِيَ اللهُ عَنْهُ قالَ: قالَ رَسُولُ اللهِ صلى اللهُ عليه وسلَّم:

no good will it do to a soul to believe then." Then he recited the whole Verse. (6:158) (1)

لاتَقومُ السّاعةُ حتّى تطلُعَ الشمسُ منْ مَغرِبها ، فإذا طلَعتْ ورآها النّاسُ آمَنُوا أجمَعُونَ ، وَذَلكَ - حِينَ لايَنفَعُ نَفسا إيمانُها - ثُمَّ قرأ الآيَة .

SŪRAT AL-A'RĀF. VII

سورة الأعراف

In the Name of Allāh, the Most Beneficent, the Most Merciful

بِسْمِ اللهِ الرَّحْمَنِ الرحيم

(1) (6:158) Are they waiting for anything other than that the angels should come to them or that your Lord (Allāh) should come or that some of the signs of your Lord should come (i.e. Protents of the Hour e.g. arising of the sun from the west etc)! The Day that some of the signs of your Lord do come, no good will it do to a soul to believe then , if it believed not before nor earned good (by deeds of righetousness) by its Faith, say "Wait you: we (too) are waiting."

قالَ ابنُ عبّاسٍ : وَرِياشا : المَالُ . إنّهُ لايُحبُّ المُعتَدينَ فى الدُّعاءِ وفى غيرِهِ . عَفَوْا : كَثُرُوا . الفَتّاحُ : القاضِي ، افتَحْ بَيْنَنا : اقْضِ بيْنَنا . نَتَقْنا الجبَلَ : رَفَعْنا . انبَجَسَتْ : انفَجرَتْ . مُتَبَّرٌ : خُسْرانٌ . آسَى : أحزَنُ . تأْسَ : تَحزَنْ . ما مَنَعَكَ أنْ لاتَسْجُدَ - يقولُ : ما مَنَعَكَ أنْ تَسْجُدَ . يخْصِفانِ : أخَذا الخِصافَ منْ وَرَقِ الجنّةِ ، يُؤَلِّفانِ الوَرَقَ : يَخْصِفانِ الوَرَقَ بعْضَهُ إلى بعْضٍ . سَوْآتِهِما : كِنايَةٌ عَنْ فَرْجَيْهِما . وَمَتاعٌ إلى حِينٍ : هُوَ هاهُنا إلى يَوْمِ القيامَةِ ، والحِينُ عِنْدَ العرَبِ مِنْ ساعَةٍ إلى ما لايُحْصَى عَدَدُها . الرِّياشُ والرِّيشُ وَاحِدٌ وَهُوَ ما ظَهَرَ مِنَ اللِّباسِ . قَبِيلُهُ جِيلُهُ الّذى هُوَ مِنهُمْ . ادّارَكُوا : اجتَمَعُوا . وَمَشاقُّ الإنسانِ والدّابّةِ كُلُّها يُسَمّى سُمُوما

وَاحِدُها سَمٌّ، وَهِيَ عَيْناهُ وَمَنْخِرَاهُ وفَمُهُ وأُذُناهُ وَدُبُرُهُ وإحْلِيلُهُ. غَوَاشٍ: ما غُشُّوا بِهِ. نُشُرًا: مُتَفَرِّقَةً. نَكِدًا: قَلِيلا. يَغْنَوْا: يَعِيشُوا. حَقِيقٌ: حَقٌّ. اسْتَرْهَبُوهُمْ، مِنَ الرَّهْبَةِ. تَلْقَفُ: تَلْقَمُ. طائِرُهُمْ: حَظُّهُمْ. طُوفانٌ: مِنَ السَّيْلِ، وَيُقالُ لِلمَوْتِ الكَثِيرِ الطُّوفانُ. القُمَّلُ: الحُمْنانُ شِبهُ صِغارِ الحَلَمِ. عُرُوشٌ وعَرِيشٌ: بِناءٌ. سُقِطَ: كلُّ مَنْ نَدِمَ فَقَدْ سُقِطَ فى يَدِهِ. الأَسْباطُ: قَبائِلُ بَنى إسْرائِيلَ. يَعْدُونَ فى السَّبْتِ: يَتَعَدَّوْنَ لَهُ، يجاوِزُونَ. تَعْدُ: تُجاوِزْ. شُرَّعًا: شَوَارِعَ. بَئِيسٍ: شَدِيدٍ. أَخْلَدَ إلى الأرْضِ: قَعَدَ وتَقاعَسَ. سَنَسْتَدْرِجُهُمْ: نَأْتِيهِمْ مِنْ مَأْمَنِهِمْ كَقَوْلِهِ تَعالى - فَأَتاهُمُ اللهُ مِنْ حَيْثُ لَمْ يَحْتَسِبُوا - مِنْ جِنَّةٍ: مِنْ جُنُونٍ. أَيَّانَ مُرْساها: مَتى خُرُوجُها. فَمَرَّتْ بِهِ: اسْتَمَرَّ بِها الحَمْلُ فَأَتَمَّتْهُ. يَنْزَغَنَّكَ: يَسْتَخِفَّنَّكَ. طَيْفٌ مُلِمٌّ: بِهِ لَمَمٌ، وَيُقالُ طائِفٌ وَهُوَ وَاحِدٌ. يَمُدُّونَهُمْ: يُزَيِّنُونَ: وَخِيفَةً: خَوْفًا. وَخِيفَةً مِنَ الإخْفاءِ. والآصالِ: وَاحِدُها أَصِيلٌ، وَهُوَ ما بَيْنَ العَصْرِ إلى المَغْرِبِ كَقَوْلِهِ: بُكْرَةً وأَصِيلا.

(122) CHAPTER. The Statement of Allāh :–

'Say (O Muhammad): But the things that my Lord has indeed forbidden are great sins (e.g. unlawful sexual intercourse etc.) whether committed openly or secretly, sins (of all kinds), unrighteous oppression, to join partners (in worship) with Allāh for which He has given no authority, and saying things about Allāh of which you have no knowledge.' (7:33)

بابُ قَوْلِ اللهِ عَزَّ وَجَلَّ - قُلْ إِنَّما حَرَّمَ رَبِّيَ الفَوَاحِشَ ما ظَهَرَ مِنْها وَما بَطَنَ -.

161. Narrated 'Abdullāh (bin Mas'ūd) : Allāh's Messenger said, "None has more sense of ghaira (1) than Allāh, and for this He has forbidden shameful sins whether committed openly or secretly, and none loves to be praised more than Allāh does, and this is why He Praises Himself."

١٦١ - حدَّثَنا سُلَيْمانُ بنُ حَرْبٍ: حدَّثَنا شُعْبَةُ، عَنْ عَمْرِو بنِ مُرَّةَ، عَنْ أبي وَائِلٍ، عَنْ عَبْدِ اللهِ رَضِيَ اللهُ عَنْهُ قالَ: قُلْتُ: أَنْتَ سَمِعْتَ هذَا مِنْ عَبْدِ اللهِ؟ قالَ: نَعَمْ، وَرَفَعَهُ قالَ: لا أَحَدَ أَغْيَرُ مِنَ اللهِ فَلِذَلِكَ حَرَّمَ الفَوَاحِشَ ما ظَهَرَ مِنْها وَما بَطَنَ، وَلا أَحَدَ أَحَبُّ إِلَيْهِ المِدْحَةُ مِنَ اللهِ فَلِذَلِكَ مَدَحَ نَفْسَهُ.

(123) CHAPTER. 'When Moses came at the time and place appointed by Us, and his Lord spoke to him, he said, "O my Lord! Show me (Yourself) that I may look upon You.'" (7:143)

بابٌ - وَلَمَّا جاءَ مُوسَى لِمِيقاتِنا وَكَلَّمَهُ رَبُّهُ قالَ رَبِّ أَرِنِي أَنْظُرْ إِلَيْكَ - الآيَةَ. قالَ ابنُ عَبَّاسٍ: أَرِنِي أَعْطِنِي.

162. Narrated Abū Sa'īd Al-Khudrī : A man from the Jews, having

١٦٢ - حدَّثَنا مُحَمَّدُ بنُ يُوسُفَ: حدَّثَنا سُفْيانُ، عَنْ عَمْرِو بنِ يَحْيَى

(1) Ghaira: See the glossary.

been slapped on his face, came to the Prophet ﷺ and said, "O Muḥammad! A man from your companions from the Anṣār has slapped me on my face!" The Prophet ﷺ said, "Call him." When they called him, the Prophet ﷺ said, "Why did you slap him?" He said, "O Allāh's Messenger! While I was passing by the Jews, I heard him saying, 'By Him Who selected Moses above the human beings,' I said, 'Even above Muḥammad?' I became furious and slapped him on the face." The Prophet ﷺ said, "Do not give me superiority over the other prophets, for on the Day of Resurrection the people will become unconscious and I will be the first to regain consciousness. Then I will see Moses holding one of the pillars of the throne. I will not know whether he has come to his senses before me or that the shock he had received at the Mountain, (during his worldly life) was sufficient for him.

المازني، عن أبيه، عن أبي سعيد الخدري رضي الله عنه قال: جاء رجل من اليهود إلى النبي صلى الله عليه وسلم قد لطم وجهه وقال: يا محمد إن رجلا من أصحابك من الأنصار لطم في وجهي، قال: ادعوه فدعوه قال: لم لطمت وجهه؟ قال: يا رسول الله، إني مررت باليهود فسمعته يقول: والذي اصطفى موسى على البشر، فقلت: وعلى محمد؟ وأخذتني غضبة فلطمته، قال: لا تخيروني من بين الأنبياء فإن الناس يصعقون يوم القيامة فأكون أول من يفيق فإذا أنا بموسى آخذ بقائمة من قوائم العرش، فلا أدري أفاق قبلي أم جزي بصعقة الطور؟

المن والسلوى.

163. Narrated Sa'īd Ibn Zaid: The Prophet ﷺ said, "Al-Kam'ā is like the Mann (sweet resin or gum) (in that it grows naturally without human care) and its water is a cure for the eye diseases."

١٦٣ - حدثنا مسلم: حدثنا شعبة، عن عبد الملك، عن عمرو ابن حريث، عن سعيد ابن زيد، عن النبي صلى الله عليه وسلم قال: الكمأة من المن وماؤها شفاء العين.

(124) CHAPTER. 'Say (O Muḥammad): O Mankind: Verily I am sent to you all as the Messenger of Allāh, to Whom belongs the dominion of the Heavens and the Earth. None has the right to be worshipped but Him. It is He Who gives life and causes death; so believe in Allāh and His Messenger, the Prophet who can neither read nor write (Muḥammad ﷺ) who believes in Allāh and His Words (this Qur'an); follow him so that you may be guided.' (7:158)

بابُ - قُلْ يا أيُّها النّاسُ إنى رَسُولُ اللهِ إلَيْكُمْ جميعا الّذى لَهُ مُلْكُ السَّمَوَاتِ والأرْضِ لا إلَهَ إلاَّ هُوَ يُحْيِى ويُمِيتُ فآمِنُوا باللهِ وَرَسُولِه النَّبِىِّ الأُمِّىِّ الّذى يُؤْمِنُ باللهِ وكَلِماتِه وَاتَّبِعوهُ لَعَلَّكُمْ تَهْتَدُونَ.

164. Narrated Abū Ad-Dardā': There was a dispute between Abū Bakr and 'Umar, and Abū Bakr made Umar angry. So 'Umar left angrily. Abū Bakr followed him, requesting him to ask for giveness (of Allāh) for him, but 'Umar refused to do so and closed his door in Abū Bakr's face. So Abū Bakr went to Allāh's Messenger ﷺ while we were with him. Allāh's Messenger ﷺ said, "This friend of yours must have quarrelled (with somebody)." In the meantime 'Umar repented and felt sorry for what he had done, so he came, greeted (those who were present) and sat with the Prophet ﷺ and related the story to him. Allāh's Messenger ﷺ became angry and Abū Bakr started saying, "O Allāh's Messenger! By Allāh, I was more at fault (than Umar)." Allāh's Messenger ﷺ said, "Are you (people) leaving for me my companion? (Abū Bakr), Are you (people) leaving for me my companion? When I said, 'O people I am sent to you all as the Messenger of Allāh,' you said, 'You tell a lie.' while

١٦٤ - حدَّثنى عَبْدُ اللهِ: حدَّثَنا سُلَيْمانُ بنُ عَبْدِ الرَّحْمَنِ وَمُوسَى بنُ هارُونَ قالا: حدَّثَنا الوَليدُ ابنُ مُسْلِمٍ: حدَّثَنا عَبْدُ اللهِ بنُ العلاءِ بنِ زَبْرٍ قالَ: حدَّثَنِى بُسْرُ بنُ عُبَيْدِ اللهِ قالَ: حدَّثَنِى أبو إدْرِيسَ الخَوْلانِىُّ قالَ: سَمِعْتُ أبا الدَّرْداءِ يَقولُ: كانَتْ بَيْنَ أبى بَكْرٍ وعُمَرَ مُحاوَرَةٌ فأغْضَبَ أبو بَكْرٍ عُمَرَ، فانْصَرَفَ عَنْهُ عُمَرُ مُغْضَبًا فاتَّبَعَهُ أبو بَكْرٍ يَسْألُهُ أنْ يَسْتَغْفِرَ لَهُ فَلَمْ يَفْعَلْ حَتَّى أغْلَقَ بابَهُ فى وَجْهِهِ. فأقْبَلَ أبو بَكْرٍ إلى رَسُولِ اللهِ صلى اللهُ عليهِ وسلَّم فَقالَ أبو الدَّرْداءِ ونَحْنُ عِنْدَهُ: فَقالَ رَسُولُ اللهِ صلى اللهُ عليهِ وسلَّم: أمَّا صاحِبُكُمْ هَذا فَقَدْ غامَرَ، قالَ: وَنَدِمَ عُمَرُ

عَلى ما كانَ مِنهُ فأقبَلَ حتَّى سَلَّمَ وَجَلَسَ إلى النَّبِيِّ صلى اللهُ عليهِ وسلَّمَ وقَصَّ عَلى رَسُولِ اللهِ صلى اللهُ عليهِ وسلَّمَ الخَبَرَ، قالَ أبو الدَّرْداءِ: وَغَضِبَ رَسُولُ اللهِ صلى اللهُ عليهِ وسلَّمَ وَجَعَلَ أبو بَكْرٍ يَقُولُ: وَاللهِ يا رَسُولَ اللهِ لأنا كُنْتُ أظْلَمَ: فَقالَ رَسُولُ اللهِ صلى اللهُ عليهِ وسلَّمَ: هَلْ أنتُمْ تارِكُولي صاحِبي؟ هَلْ أنتُمْ تارِكُولي صاحِبي؟ إني قُلْتُ - يا أيُّها النَّاسُ إني رَسُولُ اللهِ إلَيْكُمْ جميعاً - فَقُلْتُمْ كَذَبْتَ وقالَ أبو بَكْرٍ صَدَقْتَ. قالَ أبو عَبْدِ اللهِ: غامَرَ: سَبَقَ بالخَيْرِ.

Abū Bakr said, 'You have spoken the truth.' "

بابُ قَوْلِهِ حِطَّةٌ.

(125) CHAPTER. Allāh's Saying:— 'Ḥiṭatun.' (7:161) (i.e. (O Allāh) forgive our sins)

١٦٥ - حدَّثَني إسحاقُ: أخبَرَنا عَبْدُ الرَّزَّاقِ: أخبَرَنا مَعْمَرٌ، عَنْ هَمَّامِ ابنِ مُنَبِّهٍ: أنَّهُ سَمِعَ أبا هُرَيْرَةَ رَضِيَ اللهُ عَنْهُ يَقُولُ: قالَ رَسُولُ اللهِ صلى اللهُ عليهِ وسلَّمَ: قِيلَ لِبَني إسْرائيلَ - ادْخُلُوا البابَ سُجَّداً وَقُولُوا حِطَّةٌ نَغْفِرْ لَكُمْ خَطاياكُمْ فَبَدَّلُوا - فَدَخَلُوا يَزْحَفُونَ عَلى أسْتاهِهِمْ وَقالُوا: حَبَّةٌ في شَعَرَةٍ.

165. Narrated Abū Huraira ﷺ: Allāh's Messenger ﷺ said, "It was said to the children of Israel, 'Enter the gate in prostration and say Ḥiṭatun. (7:161) We shall forgive you, your faults.' But they changed (Allāh's Order) and entered, dragging themselves on their buttocks and said, 'Ḥabatun (a grain) in a Sha'ratin (hair).' "

(126) CHAPTER. 'Hold to forgiveness; command what is right: and leave (don't punish) the foolish.' (7:199)

166. Narrated Ibn 'Abbās :
'Uyaina bin Ḥiṣn bin Ḥudhaifa came and stayed with his nephew Al-Ḥurr bin Qais who was one of those whom 'Umar used to keep near him, as the Qurrā' (learned men knowing Qur'ān by heart) were the people of 'Umar's meetings and his advisors whether they were old or young. 'Uyaina said to his nephew, "O son of my brother! You have an approach to this chief, so get for me the permission to see him." Al-Ḥurr said, "I will get the permission for you to see him." So Al-Ḥurr asked the permission for 'Uyaina and 'Umar admitted him. When 'Uyaina entered upon him, he said, "Beware! O the son of Al-Khaṭṭāb! By Allāh, you neither give us sufficient provision nor judge among us with justice." Thereupon 'Umar became so furious that he intended to harm him, but Al-Ḥurr said, "O chief of the Believers! Allāh said to His Prophet :—

'Hold to forgiveness; command what is right; and leave (don't punish) the foolish, (7:199) and this (i.e. 'Uyaina) is one of the foolish." By Allāh, 'Umar did not overlook that Verse when Al-Ḥurr recited it before him; he observed (the orders of) Allāh's Book strictly.

بابٌ ـ خُذِ العَفْوَ وَأْمُرْ بِالعُرْفِ وَأَعْرِضْ عَنِ الجَاهِلِينَ ـ العُرْفُ: المَعْرُوفُ

١٦٦ ـ حَدَّثَنَا أَبُو اليَمَانِ: حَدَّثَنَا شُعَيْبٌ، عَنِ الزُّهْرِيِّ: أَخْبَرَنِي عُبَيْدُ اللهِ بْنُ عَبْدِ اللهِ بْنِ عُتْبَةَ: أَنَّ ابْنَ عَبَّاسٍ رَضِيَ اللهُ عَنْهُمَا قَالَ: قَدِمَ عُيَيْنَةُ بْنُ حِصْنِ بْنِ حُذَيْفَةَ فَنَزَلَ عَلَى ابْنِ أَخِيهِ الحُرِّ بْنِ قَيْسٍ، وَكَانَ مِنَ النَّفَرِ الَّذِينَ يُدْنِيهِمْ عُمَرُ، وَكَانَ القُرَّاءُ أَصْحَابَ مَجَالِسِ عُمَرَ وَمُشَاوَرَتِهِ كُهُولًا كَانُوا أَوْ شُبَّانًا، فَقَالَ عُيَيْنَةُ لِابْنِ أَخِيهِ: يَا ابْنَ أَخِي، لَكَ وَجْهٌ عِنْدَ هَذَا الأَمِيرِ فَاسْتَأْذِنْ لِي عَلَيْهِ، قَالَ: سَأَسْتَأْذِنُ لَكَ عَلَيْهِ، قَالَ ابْنُ عَبَّاسٍ: فَاسْتَأْذَنَ الحُرُّ لِعُيَيْنَةَ فَأَذِنَ لَهُ عُمَرُ، فَلَمَّا دَخَلَ عَلَيْهِ قَالَ: هِيْ يَا ابْنَ الخَطَّابِ، فَوَاللهِ مَا تُعْطِينَا الجَزْلَ وَلَا تَحْكُمُ بَيْنَنَا بِالعَدْلِ. فَغَضِبَ عُمَرُ حَتَّى هَمَّ بِهِ، فَقَالَ لَهُ الحُرُّ: يَا أَمِيرَ المُؤْمِنِينَ، إِنَّ اللهَ تَعَالَى قَالَ لِنَبِيِّهِ صَلَّى اللهُ عَلَيْهِ وَسَلَّمَ: خُذِ العَفْوَ وَأْمُرْ بِالعُرْفِ وَأَعْرِضْ عَنِ الجَاهِلِينَ ـ وَإِنَّ هَذَا مِنَ الجَاهِلِينَ، وَاللهِ مَا جَاوَزَهَا

عُمَرَ حِينَ تَلاهَا عَلَيْهِ وَكَانَ وَقَّافًا عِنْدَ كِتَابِ اللَّهِ .

167. Narrated 'Abdullāh bin Az-Zubair: (The Verse):—

> 'Hold to forgiveness; command what is right...'

was revealed by Allāh except in connection with the character of the people. 'Abdullāh bin Az-Zubair said: Allāh ordered His Prophet ﷺ to forgive the people their misbehaviour (towards him).

١٦٧ ـ حَدَّثَنِي يَحْيَى : حَدَّثَنَا وَكِيعٌ ، عَنْ هِشَامٍ ، عَنْ أَبِيهِ ، عَنْ عَبْدِ اللَّهِ بْنِ الزُّبَيْرِ ـ خُذِ الْعَفْوَ وَأْمُرْ بِالْعُرْفِ ـ قَالَ : مَا أَنْزَلَ اللَّهُ إِلاَّ فِي أَخْلاقِ النَّاسِ . وَقَالَ عَبْدُ اللَّهِ بْنُ بَرَّادٍ : حَدَّثَنَا أَبُو أُسَامَةَ : قَالَ هِشَامٌ ، عَنْ أَبِيهِ ، عَنْ عَبْدِ اللَّهِ بْنِ الزُّبَيْرِ قَالَ : أَمَرَ اللَّهُ نَبِيَّهُ صلى اللهُ عليهِ وسَلَّم أَنْ يَأْخُذَ الْعَفْوَ مِنْ أَخْلاقِ النَّاسِ أَوْ كَمَا قَالَ .

In the Name of Allāh.
the Most Beneficent, the Most Merciful

بِسْمِ اللَّهِ الرَّحْمَنِ الرَّحِيمِ

SŪRAT-AL-AN-FĀL
(Spoils of war); No. VIII

سُورَةُ الأَنْفَالِ

(127) CHAPTER. The Statement of Allāh ﷻ :—

> 'They ask you (O Muḥammad) concerning Al-Anfāl (things taken as) spoils of war. Say: (Such) spoils are at the disposal of Allāh

قَوْلُهُ ـ يَسْأَلُونَكَ عَنِ الأَنْفَالِ قُلِ الأَنْفَالُ لِلَّهِ وَالرَّسُولِ فَاتَّقُوا اللَّهَ وَأَصْلِحُوا ذَاتَ بَيْنِكُمْ ـ قَالَ ابْنُ عَبَّاسٍ : الأَنْفَالُ : الْمَغَانِمُ . قَالَ قَتَادَةُ : رِيحُكُمْ : الْحَرْبُ ، يُقَالُ نَافِلَةٌ : عَطِيَّةٌ .

and the Messenger . So fear Allāh and adjust the matters of your differences and obey Allāh and His Messenger, if you are believers.---------
(8:1)

Ibn 'Abbās said: 'Al-Anfāl' means war booty.

168. Narrated Sa'īd bin Jubair: I asked Ibn 'Abbās regarding Sūrat-al-Anfāl. He said, "It was revealed in connection with the Battle of Badr."

١٦٨ ـ حدّثنا محمّد بن عبد الرّحيم: حدّثنا سعيد بن سليمان: أخبرنا هشيم: أخبرنا أبو بشر، عن سعيد بن جبير قال: قلت لابن عبّاس رضي الله عنهما: سورة الأنفال؟ قال: نزلت في بدر. الشّوكة: الحدّ. مردفين: فوجا بعد فوج، ردفني وأردفني: جاء بعدي. ذوقوا: باشروا وجرّبوا، وليس هذا من ذوق الفم. فيركمه: يجمعه. شرّد: فرّق. وإن جنحوا: طلبوا السّلم والسّلم والسّلام واحد. يثخن: يغلب. وقال مجاهد: مكاء: إدخال أصابعهم في أفواههم. وتصدية: الصّفير. ليثبتوك: ليحبسوك.

(128) CHAPTER. 'Verily the worst of beasts in the sight of Allāh are the deaf and the dumb—those who understand not.' (8:22)

باب ـ إنّ شرّ الدّوابّ عند الله الصّمّ البكم الّذين لا يعقلون ـ.

169. Narrated Ibn 'Abbās regarding the Verse:–

١٦٩ ـ حدّثنا محمّد بن يوسف: حدّثنا ورقاء، عن ابن أبي نجيح، عن

> Verily! The worst of beasts in the Sight of Allāh are the deaf and the dumb — those who understand not.' (8:22)

(The people referred to here) were some persons from the tribe of Bani 'Abd-Ad-dār.

مُجاهد ، عَن ابن عبّاس - إنّ شرّ الدّوابّ عندَ الله الصمّ البُكمُ الّذينَ لايعقلُونَ - قالَ : هُم نفرٌ مِن بني عبدِ الدّار .

(129) CHAPTER. 'O you who believe! Answer the call of Allāh (by obeying Him) and His Messenger when He calls you to that which will give you life, and know that Allāh comes in between a man and his heart (i.e. He prevents the evil person to decide anything) and that it is He to Whom you shall (all) be gathered.' (8:24)

باب - يا أيُّها الّذينَ آمنُوا استجيبُوا لله وللرّسُولِ إذا دعاكُم لما يُحييكُم ، واعلَمُوا أنّ اللهَ يحُولُ بينَ المرءِ وقلبِهِ وأنّهُ إليهِ تُحشرُونَ . استجيبُوا: أجيبُوا . لِمَا يُحييكم : لِمَا يُصلِحُكم .

170. Narrated Abū Sa'īd bin Al-Mu'allā : While I was praying, Allāh's Messenger passed by and called me, but I did not go to him till I had finished the prayer. Then I went to him, and he said, "What prevented you from coming to me? Didn't Allāh say:—

> 'O you who believe! Answer the call of Allāh (by obeying Him) and His Messenger when He calls you'?"

He then said, "I will inform you of the greatest Sūra in the Qur'ān before I leave (the mosque)." When Allāh's Messenger got ready to leave (the mosque), I reminded him. He said, "It is:—

> 'Praise be to Allāh, the Lord of

١٧٠ - حدّثني إسحاقُ قالَ : أخبرَنا رَوحٌ : حدّثنا شُعبةُ ، عن خُبيبِ بنِ عبدِ الرّحمنِ ، سمِعتُ حفصَ بنَ عاصمٍ يُحدّثُ عن أبي سعيدِ بنِ المُعلّى رضيَ اللهُ عنهُ قالَ : كُنتُ أُصلّي فمرّ بي رسُولُ اللهِ صلى اللهُ عليهِ وسلّم فدعاني فلَم آتِهِ حتّى صلّيتُ ثُمّ أتيتُهُ فقالَ : ما منعكَ أن تأتيَ ؟ ألم يقُلِ اللهُ - يا أيُّها الّذينَ آمنُوا استجيبوا لله وللرّسُولِ إذا دعاكُم - ثُمّ قالَ : لأُعلّمنّكَ أعظمَ سُورةٍ في القرآنِ قبلَ أن أخرُجَ ، فذهبَ رسُولُ اللهِ صلى اللهُ عليهِ وسلّم ليخرُجَ فذكرتُ لهُ . وقالَ

the worlds.'

(i.e. Sūrat - al-Fātiḥa) ——As-sab'a Al-Mat̲h̲ānī (the seven repeatedly recited Verses)."

مُعاذٌ : حدَّثنا شُعْبَةُ ، عَنْ خُبَيْبِ بنِ عَبْدِ الرَّحْمٰنِ : سَمِعَ حَفْصًا : سَمِعَ أبا سَعِيدٍ رَجُلًا مِنْ أصحابِ النَّبِيِّ صلى اللهُ عليهِ وسلَّم بِهٰذا وَقالَ : هِيَ الحَمْدُ لِلّٰهِ رَبِّ العالَمِينَ . السَّبْعُ المَثانِي .

(130) CHAPTER. The Statement of Allāh :–

'And (remember) when they said, "O Allāh! If this (Qur'ān) is indeed the truth from You, then send on us a shower of stones.' " (8:32)

Ibn 'Uyaina said, Allāh did not use the word 'Maṭar' in the Qur'ān except when it means a shower of torture; and Arabs call the rain 'G̲h̲ait̲h̲' as occurs in the Statement of Allāh :–

'And it is He Who sends down the G̲h̲ait̲h̲ (rain) after they have given up all hope.' ——— (42:28)

بابُ قَوْلِهِ - وَإذْ قالُوا اللَّهُمَّ إنْ كانَ هٰذا هُوَ الحَقَّ مِنْ عِنْدِكَ فَأمْطِرْ - الآيَةَ . قالَ ابنُ عُيَيْنَةَ : ما سَمَّى اللهُ مَطَرًا في القُرآنِ إلَّا عَذابًا وتُسَمِّيهِ العَرَبُ الغَيْثَ وَهُوَ قَوْلُهُ تعالى - وَهُوَ الَّذي يُنَزِّلُ الغَيْثَ مِنْ بَعْدِ ما قَنَطُوا -.

171. Narrated Anas bin Mālik : Abū Jahl said, "O Allāh! If this (Qur'ān) is indeed the Truth from You, then rain down on us a shower of stones from the sky or bring on us a painful torment." So Allāh revealed:–

'But Allāh would not punish them while you were amongst them, nor He will punish them while they seek (Allāh's) forgiveness . . . (8:33)

١٧١ - حدَّثَني أحْمَدُ : حدَّثنا عُبَيْدُ اللهِ بنُ مُعاذٍ : حدَّثنا أبي : حدَّثنا شُعْبَةُ ، عَنْ عَبْدِ الحَميدِ صاحِبِ الزِّيادِيِّ : سَمِعَ أنَسَ بنَ مالِكٍ رَضِيَ اللهُ عَنْهُ قالَ أبو جَهْلٍ : اللَّهُمَّ إنْ كانَ هٰذا هُوَ الحَقَّ مِنْ عِنْدِكَ فَأمْطِرْ عَلَيْنا حِجارَةً مِنَ السَّماءِ أوِ ائْتِنا بِعَذابٍ ألِيمٍ .

And why Allāh should not punish them while they turn away (men) from Al-Masjid-al-Ḥarām (the Sacred Mosque of Mecca) . . . . . ' (8:33-34)

فنزلت - وما كان الله ليعذبهم وأنت فيهم وما كان الله معذبهم وهم يستغفرون وما لهم أن لا يعذبهم الله وهم يصدون عن المسجد الحرام - الآية

(131) CHAPTER. The Statement of Allāh تعالى :–

'And Allāh would not punish them while you (Muḥammad ﷺ) were amongst them; nor will He punish them while they seek (Allāh's) forgiveness.' (8:33)

باب قوله - وما كان الله ليعذبهم وأنت فيهم وما كان الله معذبهم وهم يستغفرون -.

172. Narrated Anas bin Mālik رضي الله عنه : Abū Jahl said, "O Allāh! If this (Qur'ān) is indeed the Truth (from You), then rain down on us a shower of stones from the sky or bring on us a painful punishment." So there was revealed:–

'But Allāh would not punish them while you (Muḥammad ﷺ) were amongst them, nor will He punish them while they seek (Allāh's) Forgiveness. And why Allāh should not punish them while they stop (men) from Al-Masjid-al-Ḥarām........'

(8:33-34)

١٧٢ - حدثنا محمد بن النضر: حدثنا عبيد الله بن معاذ: حدثنا أبي: حدثنا شعبة: عن عبد الحميد صاحب الزيادي: سمع أنس بن مالك. قال أبو جهل: اللهم إن كان هذا هو الحق من عندك فأمطر علينا حجارة من السماء أو ائتنا بعذاب أليم، فنزلت - وما كان الله ليعذبهم وأنت فيهم وما كان الله معذبهم وهم يستغفرون. وما لهم أن لا يعذبهم الله وهم يصدون عن المسجد الحرام - الآية.

(132) CHAPTER. 'And fight them until there is no more afflictions (i.e. worshipping others besides Allāh) and the religion (i.e. worship) will be all for Allāh (Alone) (in the whole of the world) .... (8:39)

بابٌ - وَقَاتِلُوهُمْ حَتَّى لا تَكُونَ فِتْنَةٌ وَيَكُونَ الدِّينُ كُلُّهُ لِلَّهِ..

173. Narrated Ibn 'Umar that a man came to him (while two groups of Muslims were fighting) and said, "O Abū 'Abdur Rahmān! Don't you hear what Allāh has mentioned in His Book:

'And if two groups of believers fight against each other......(49:9)

So what prevents you from fighting as Allāh has mentioned in His Book?'" Ibn 'Umar said, "O son of my brother! I would rather be blamed for not fighting because of this Verse than to be blamed because of another Verse where Allāh says:—

'And whoever kills a believer intentionally...' " (4:93)

Then that man said, "Allāh says:—

'And fight them until there is no more afflictions (worshipping other besides Allāh) and the religion (i.e. worship) will be all for Allāh (Alone),' " (8:39)

Ibn 'Umar said, "We did this during the lifetime of Allāh's Messenger when the number of Muslims was small, and a man was put to trial because of his religion; the pagans would either kill or chain him; but when the Muslims increased (and Islām spread), there was no persecution." When that man saw that

١٧٣ - حدَّثنا الحَسَنُ بنُ عَبْدِ العَزِيزِ: حدَّثنا عَبْدُ اللهِ بنُ يَحْيَى: حدَّثنا حَيْوَةُ، عَنْ بَكْرِ بنِ عَمْرٍو، عَنْ بُكَيْرٍ، عَنْ نافِعٍ، عَنِ ابنِ عُمَرَ رَضِيَ اللهُ عَنْهُما: أَنَّ رَجُلاً جاءَهُ فَقالَ: يا أَبا عَبْدِ الرَّحْمَنِ، أَلا تَسْمَعُ ما ذَكَرَ اللهُ في كِتابِهِ؟ وَإِنْ طائِفَتانِ مِنَ المُؤْمِنِينَ اقْتَتَلُوا - إلى آخِرِ الآيَةِ، فَما يَمْنَعُكَ أَنْ تُقاتِلَ كَما ذَكَرَ اللهُ في كِتابِهِ؟ فَقالَ: يا ابنَ أَخِي، أُعَيَّرُ بِهذِهِ الآيَةِ وَلا أُقاتِلُ أَحَبُّ إِلَيَّ مِنْ أَنْ أُعَيَّرَ بِهذِهِ الآيَةِ التي يَقُولُ اللهُ تَعالى - وَمَنْ يَقْتُلْ مُؤْمِنًا مُتَعَمِّدًا - إلى آخِرِها، قالَ: فَإِنَّ اللهَ يَقُولُ - وَقاتِلُوهُمْ حَتَّى لا تَكُونَ فِتْنَةٌ - قالَ ابنُ عُمَرَ: قَدْ فَعَلْنا عَلى عَهْدِ رَسُولِ اللهِ صلى اللهُ عليهِ وسلَّم إِذْ كانَ الإِسْلامُ قَلِيلاً فَكانَ الرَّجُلُ يُفْتَنُ في دِينِهِ إِمَّا يَقْتُلُوهُ وَإِمَّا يُوثِقُوهُ حَتَّى كَثُرَ الإِسْلامُ فَلَمْ تَكُنْ فِتْنَةٌ. فَلَمَّا رَأَى أَنَّهُ لا يُوافِقُهُ فِيما يُرِيدُ قالَ: فَما

Ibn 'Umar did not agree to his proposal, he said, "What is your opinion regarding 'Alī and 'Uthmān?" Ibn 'Umar said, "What is my opinion regarding 'Alī and 'Uthmān? As for 'Uthmān, Allāh forgave him and you disliked to forgive him, and 'Alī is the cousin and son-in-law of Allāh's Messenger ﷺ." Then he pointed out with his hand and said, "And that is his daughter's (house) which you can see."

قَوْلُكَ فى عَلِيٍّ وَعُثْمانَ ؟ قالَ ابنُ عُمَرَ : ما قَوْلى فى عَلِيٍّ وعُثْمانَ . أمّا عُثْمانُ فَكانَ اللهُ قَدْ عَفا عَنْهُ فَكَرِهْتُمْ أنْ تَعْفُوا عَنْهُ . وأمّا عَلِيٌّ فابنُ عَمِّ رَسُولِ اللهِ صلى اللهُ عليه وسلّم وخَتَنُهُ ، أشارَ بِيَدِهِ وَهذِهِ ابْنَتُهُ أوْ بِنْتُهُ حَيْثُ تَرَوْنَ .

174. Narrated Sa'id bin Jubair: Ibn 'Umar came to us and a man said (to him), "What do you think about 'Qitāl-al-Fitnah' (fighting caused by afflictions)." Ibn 'Umar said (to him), "And do you understand what an affliction is? Muḥammad ﷺ used to fight against the pagans, and his fighting with them was an affliction, (and his fighting was) not like your fighting which is carried on for the sake of ruling."

١٧٤ - حدَّثنا أحْمَدُ يُونُسَ : حدَّثنا زُهَيرٌ : حدَّثنا بَيانٌ : أنَّ وَبَرَةَ حدَّثَهُ قالَ حدَّثنى سَعيدُ بنُ جُبَيرٍ قال: خَرَجَ عَلَيْنا أوْ إلَيْنا ابنُ عُمَرَ فَقالَ رَجُلٌ : كَيْفَ تَرَى فى قِتالِ الفِتْنَةِ ؟ فَقالَ : وَهَلْ تَدْرى ما الفِتْنَةُ ؟ كانَ مُحَمَّدٌ صلى اللهُ عليه وسلَّم يُقاتِلُ المُشرِكينَ وكانَ الدُّخولُ عَلَيْهِم فِتْنَةً وَلَيْسَ كَقِتالِكُمْ عَلى المُلْكِ .

(133) CHAPTER. 'O Prophet (Muḥammad ﷺ)! Urge the believers to the fight............' (8:65)

بابُ - يا أيُّها النَّبىُّ حَرِّضِ المُؤمِنينَ عَلى القِتالِ - الآيَةَ .

175. Narrated Ibn 'Abbās (رضي الله عنهما):

١٧٥ - حدَّثنا عَلِيُّ بنُ عَبدِ اللهِ :

When the Verse:–

'If there are twenty steadfast amongst you, they will overcome two hundred.' (8:65)

was revealed, then it became obligatory for the Muslims that one (Muslim) should not flee from ten (non-Muslims). Sufyān (the sub-narrator) once said, "Twenty (Muslims) should not flee before two hundred (non Muslims)." Then there was revealed:

'But now Allāh has lightened your (task).......' (8:66)

So it became obligatory that one-hundred (Muslims) should not flee before two-hundred (non-muslims). (Once Sufyān said extra, "The Verse:

'Urge the believers to the fight. If there are twenty steadfast amongst you (Muslims) ....'

.........'

was revealed.) Sufyān said, "Ibn Shabrama said, "I see that this order is applicable to the obligation of enjoining good and forbidding evil."

حدثنا سفيان، عن عمرو، عن ابن عباس رضي الله عنهما: لما نزلت - إن يكن منكم عشرون صابرون يغلبوا مائتين - فكتب عليهم أن لا يفر واحد من عشرة. فقال سفيان غير مرة: أن لا يفر عشرون من مائتين، ثم نزلت - الآن خفف الله عنكم - الآية. فكتب أن لا يفر مائة من مائتين. وزاد سفيان مرة نزلت: حرض المؤمنين على القتال إن يكن منكم عشرون صابرون - قال سفيان: وقال ابن شبرمة: وأرى الأمر بالمعروف والنهي عن المنكر مثل هذا.

(134) CHAPTER. '(But) now Allāh has lightened your (task), for He knows that there is weakness in you . ...' (8:66)

باب - الآن خفف الله عنكم وعلم أن فيكم ضعفا - الآية.

176. Narrated Ibn 'Abbās :

When the Verse:–

'If there are twenty steadfast amongst you (Muslims), they

١٧٦ - حدثنا يحيى بن عبد الله السلمي: أخبرنا عبد الله بن المبارك: أخبرنا جرير بن حازم قال: أخبرني

will overcome two-hundred (non-Muslims).'

was revealed, it became hard on the Muslims when it became compulsory that one Muslim ought not to flee (in war) before ten (non-Muslims). So (Allāh) lightened the order by revealing:—

'(But)now Allāh has lightened your (task) for He knows that there is weakness in you. So if there are of you one-hundred steadfast, they will overcome (two-hundred (non-Muslims).' (8:66)

So when Allāh reduced the number of enemies which Muslims should withstand, their patience and perseverance against the enemy decreased as much as their task was lightened for them.

الزُّبَيرُ بنُ الخِرِّيتِ ، عَنْ عِكْرِمَةَ ، عَنِ ابنِ عبّاسٍ رَضِيَ اللهُ عَنْهُما قالَ : لمّا نَزَلَتْ - إنْ يَكُنْ مِنْكُم عِشْرُونَ صَابِرُونَ يَغْلِبُوا مائَتَيْنِ - شَقَّ ذَلكَ عَلَى المُسْلِمينَ حِينَ فُرِضَ عَلَيْهِم أنْ لا يَفِرَّ وَاحِدٌ مِن عَشَرَةٍ فَجاءَ التَّخْفيفُ فَقَالَ - الآنَ خَفَّفَ اللهُ عَنْكُم وَعَلِمَ أنَّ فِيكُم ضَعْفاً فإنْ يَكُنْ مِنْكُم مائَةٌ صَابِرَةٌ يَغْلِبُوا مائَتَيْنِ - قالَ : فَلَمّا خَفَّفَ اللهُ عَنْهُمْ مِنَ العِدَّةِ نَقَصَ مِنَ الصَّبْرِ بقَدْرِ ما خُفِّفَ عَنْهُمْ .

SŪRAT-AT-TAUBAH: "BARĀ'A" IX

In the Name of Allāh,
the Most Beneficent, the Most Merciful

سورة براءة

بِسْمِ اللهِ الرَّحْمَنِ الرَّحِيمِ

مَرْصَدٌ : طَرِيقٌ . إلاًّ : الإلُّ : القَرَابَةُ والذِّمَّةُ والعَهْدُ . وَلِيجَةٌ : كلُّ شَيْءٍ أدْخَلْتَهُ فى شَيْءٍ . الشُّقَّةُ : السَّفَرُ . الخَبالُ : الفَسادُ . والخَبالُ : المَوْتُ . وَلا تَفْتِنِي : لا تُوَبِّخْني . كَرْهاً وكُرْهاً وَاحِدٌ . مُدَّخَلاً : يَدْخُلونَ فيهِ . يَجْمَحُونَ : يُسْرِعونَ . والمُؤْتَفِكاتُ : ائْتَفَكَتْ : انْقَلَبَتْ بِهَا الأرْضُ أهْوَى :

أَلقاهُ في هُوَّةٍ. عَدْن: خُلْد. عَدَنْتُ
بأرضٍ: أيْ أقمْتُ، ومنهُ مَعْدِنٌ.
ويقالُ مَعْدِنِ صِدْقٍ: في مَنْبِتِ صِدْقٍ.
الخَوالِفُ الخالِفُ الّذي خَلَفَني فقَعَدَ
بَعْدي ومنهُ يَخْلُفُهُ في الغابِرِينَ.
ويَجوزُ أنْ يَكُونَ مِنَ النِّساءِ الخالِفَةِ،
وإنْ كانَ جمعَ الذُّكُورِ فإنَّهُ لمْ يُوجَدْ
عَلى تَقْديرِ جَمْعِهِ إلاَّ حَرْفانِ فارِس
وفَوارِس، وهالِكٌ وهَوالِكُ. الخَيْرَاتُ:
واحِدُها خَيْرَةٌ وهِيَ الفَواضِلُ.
مُرْجَوْنَ: مُؤَخَّرُونَ الشَّفا: الشَّفِيرِ وَهُوَ
حَدُّهُ. والجُرُفُ: ما تَجَرَّفَ مِنَ
السُّيُولِ والأوْدِيَةِ. هارٍ: هائِرٍ، يُقالُ
تَهَوَّرَتِ البِئْرُ إذا انهَدَمَتْ وانْهارَ
مِثْلُهُ. لأوّاهٌ: شَفَقًا وفَرَقًا، وقالَ
الشّاعِرُ:

إذا ما قُمْتُ أَرْحَلُها بِلَيْلٍ
تأوَّهُ آهَةَ الرَّجُلِ الحَزِينِ

(135) CHAPTER. "Freedom from (all) obligations from Allāh and His Messenger to those of the pagans with whom you made a treaty.' (9:1)

بابُ قَوْلِهِ بَراءَةٌ مِنَ اللهِ وَرَسُولِهِ إلى الّذينَ عاهَدْتُمْ مِنَ المُشْرِكينَ - أذانٌ: إعْلامٌ. وقالَ ابنُ عبّاسٍ: أُذُنٌ يُصَدِّقُ تُطَهِّرُهُمْ وتُزَكِّيهِمْ بِها ونَحْوُها كَثيرٌ. والزَّكاةُ: الطّاعَةُ والإخْلاصُ، لا يُؤْتُونَ الزَّكاةَ. لا يَشْهَدُونَ أنْ لا إلهَ إلاَّ اللهُ، يُضاهِئُونَ: يُشَبِّهُونَ.

177. Narrated Al-Barā' : The last Verse that was revealed was:–

'They ask you for a legal verdict: Say: Allāh directs (thus) about Al-Kalālah (those who leave no descendants or ascendants as heirs).'

And the last Sūra which was revealed was Barā'atun (IX).

١٧٧ ـ حدّثنا أبو الوليد: حدّثنا شعبة، عن أبي إسحاق قال: سمعت البراء رضي الله عنه يقول آخر آية نزلت ـ يستفتونك قل الله يفتيكم في الكلالة ـ وآخر سورة نزلت براءة.

(136) CHAPTER. The Statement of Allāh :–

'So, travel freely (O Pagans) for four months (as you will) throughout the land, but know that you cannot escape (from the punishment of Allāh), and Allāh will disgrace the disbelievers.' (9:2)

باب قوله ـ فسيحوا في الأرض أربعة أشهر واعلموا أنكم غير معجزي الله وأن الله مخزي الكافرين ـ فسيحوا: سيروا.

178. Narrated Ḥumaid bin 'Abdur-Raḥmān: Abū Huraira said, "During that Ḥajj (in which Abū Bakr was the chief of the pilgrims), Abū Bakr sent me along with announcers on the Day of Naḥr (10th of Dhul-Ḥijja) in Minā to announce: "No pagans shall perform, Ḥajj after this year, and none shall perform the Ṭawāf around the Ka'ba in a naked state." Ḥumaid bin 'Abdur-Raḥmān added: Then Allāh's Messenger sent 'Alī bin Abī Ṭālib (after Abū Bakr) and ordered him to recite aloud in public Sūrat-Barā'a. Abū Huraira added, "So 'Alī, along with us, recited Barā'a (loudly) before the people at Minā on the Day of Naḥr and announced; "No pagan shall perform Ḥajj after this year and none shall

١٧٨ ـ حدّثنا سعيد بن عفير قال: حدّثني الليث، عن عقيل، عن ابن شهاب: أخبرني حميد بن عبد الرحمن: أنّ أبا هريرة رضي الله عنه قال: قال: بعثني أبو بكر في تلك الحجة في مؤذنين بعثهم يوم النحر يؤذنون بمنى أن لا يحجّ بعد العام مشرك، ولا يطوف بالبيت عريان. قال حميد بن عبد الرحمن: ثمّ أردف رسول الله صلى الله عليه وسلّم بعلي ابن أبي طالب وأمره أن يؤذّن ببراءة. قال أبو هريرة: فأذّن معنا

perform the Ṭawāf around the Ka'ba in a naked state."

على يوم النحر في أهل منى ببراءة، وأن لا يحج بعد العام مشرك، ولا يطوف بالبيت عريان.

(137) CHAPTER. Allāh's Statement: 'And a proclamation from Allāh and His Messenger to mankind - on the 'greatest Day." (i.e. 10th Dhul-Ḥijja) (9:3)

باب قوله - وأذان من الله ورسوله - إلى قوله - المشركين - آذنهم: أعلمهم.

179. Narrated Ḥumaid bin 'Abdur-Raḥmān: Abū Huraira said, "Abū Bakr sent me in that Ḥajj in which he was the chief of the pilgrims along with the announcers whom he sent on the Day of Naḥr to announce at Minā: "No pagan shall perform Ḥajj after this year, and none shall perform the Ṭawāf around the Ka'ba in a naked state." Ḥumaid added: Then the Prophet sent 'Alī bin Abī Ṭālib (after Abū Bakr) and ordered him to recite aloud in public Sūrat-Barā'a. Abū Huraira added, "So 'Alī, along with us, recited Barā'a (loudly) before the people at Minā on the Day of Naḥr and announced "No pagan shall perform Ḥajj after this year and none shall perform the Ṭawāf around the Ka'ba in a naked state. .

.........Except those pagans with whom you (Muslims) have a treaty.' " (9:4)

١٧٩ - حدثنا عبد الله بن يوسف: حدثنا الليث قال: حدثني عقيل: قال ابن شهاب: فأخبرني حميد بن عبد الرحمن أن أبا هريرة قال: بعثني أبو بكر رضي الله عنه في تلك الحجة في المؤذنين، بعثهم يوم النحر يؤذنون بمنى: أن لا يحج بعد العام مشرك، ولا يطوف بالبيت عريان. قال حميد: ثم أردف النبي صلى الله عليه وسلم بعلي بن أبي طالب فأمره أن يؤذن ببراءة. قال أبو هريرة: فأذن معنا علي في أهل منى يوم النحر ببراءة. وأن لا يحج بعد العام مشرك ولا يطوف بالبيت عريان - إلا الذين عاهدتم من المشركين -.

180. Narrated Ḥumaid bin 'Abdur Raḥmān: Abū Huraira said that Abū Bakr sent him during the Ḥajj in which Abū Bakr was made the chief of the pilgrims by Allāh's Messenger before (the year of) Ḥajjat-al-Wadā'in a group (of announcers) to announce before the people; "No pagan shall perform the Ḥajj after this year, and none shall perform the Ṭawāf around the Ka'ba in a naked state. Ḥumaid used to say: The Day of Naḥr is the day of Al-Ḥajj Al-Akbar (the Greatest Day) because of the narration of Abū Huraira.

١٨٠ - حدَّثني إسحاقُ : حدَّثنا يعقوبُ بنُ إبراهيمَ : حدَّثنا أبي ، عن صالحٍ ، عن ابنِ شِهابٍ : أنَّ حُمَيْدَ بنَ عبدِ الرَّحمنِ أخبرَهُ : أنَّ أبا هُرَيرَةَ أخبرَهُ : أنَّ أبا بكرٍ رضيَ اللهُ عنهُ بعثَهُ في الحَجَّةِ التي أمَّرَهُ رسولُ اللهِ صلى اللهُ عليهِ وسلَّم عليها قبلَ حَجَّةِ الوَداعِ في رَهْطٍ يُؤذِّنُ في النَّاسِ أنْ لا يَحُجَّنَّ بعدَ العامِ مُشْرِكٌ ولا يَطوفَ بالبيتِ عُرْيانٌ . فكانَ حُمَيْدٌ يقولُ : يومُ النَّحرِ يومُ الحجِّ الأكبرِ من أجلِ حديثِ أبي هُرَيرَةَ .

(138) CHAPTER. The Statement of Allāh :–

'Fight you the leaders of disbelief. Verily! Their oaths are nothing to them.' (9:12)

باب قولِهِ تعالى - فقاتِلوا أئمَّةَ الكُفْرِ إنَّهُمْ لا أيمانَ لهُمْ - .

181. Narrated Zaid bin Wahb: We were with Ḥudhaifa and he said, "None remains of the people described by this Verse (9:12),

'Except three, and of the hyprocrites except four.'

A bedouin said, "You, the companions of Muḥammad! Tell us (things) and we do not know. What about those who break open our houses and steal our precious things?' " He (Ḥudhaifa) replied, "Those are Al-Fussāq (rebellious wrongdoers) (not disbelievers or hypo

١٨١ - حدَّثنا مُحمَّدُ بنُ المُثَنَّى : حدَّثنا يحيى : حدَّثنا إسماعيلُ : حدَّثنا زيدُ بنُ وهبٍ قالَ : كُنَّا عندَ حُذَيفَةَ فقالَ : ما بقيَ من أصحابِ هذهِ الآيةِ إلَّا ثلاثةٌ ، ولا منَ المُنافقينَ إلَّا أربعةٌ فقالَ أعرابيٌّ : إنَّكمْ أصحابَ مُحمَّدٍ صلى اللهُ عليهِ وسلَّم تُخبرونَنا فلا ندري فما بالُ هؤلاءِ الذينَ يَبقُرونَ بُيوتَنا

crites). Really, none remains of them (hypocrite) but four, one of whom is a very old man who, if he drinks water, does not feel its coldness." (1)

وَيَسْرِقُونَ أَعْلاقَنَا؟ قَالَ: أُولَئِكَ الفُسَّاقُ، أَجَلْ لَمْ يَبْقَ مِنْهُمْ إِلاَّ أَرْبَعَةٌ. أَحَدُهُمْ شَيْخٌ كَبِيرٌ لَوْ شَرِبَ المَاءَ البَارِدَ لَمَا وَجَدَ بَرْدَهُ.

(139) CHAPTER. The Statement of Allāh:

'They who hoard up gold and silver and spend them not in the way of Allāh: announce to them a painful torment.' (9:34)

بَابُ قَوْلِهِ - وَالَّذِينَ يَكْنِزُونَ الذَّهَبَ وَالفِضَّةَ وَلاَ يُنْفِقُونَهَا فِي سَبِيلِ اللهِ فَبَشِّرْهُمْ بِعَذَابٍ أَلِيمٍ -.

182. Narrated Abū Huraira: Allāh's Messenger said, "The Kanz (money, the Zakāt of which is not paid) of anyone of you will appear in the form of bald-headed poisonous male snake on the Day of Resurrection."

١٨٢ - حَدَّثَنَا الحَكَمُ بْنُ نَافِعٍ: أَخْبَرَنَا شُعَيْبٌ: حَدَّثَنَا أَبُو الزِّنَادِ أَنَّ عَبْدَ الرَّحْمَنِ الأَعْرَجَ حَدَّثَهُ أَنَّهُ قَالَ: حَدَّثَنِي أَبُو هُرَيْرَةَ رَضِيَ اللهُ عَنْهُ أَنَّهُ سَمِعَ رَسُولَ اللهِ صلى الله عليه وسلَّم يَقُولُ: يَكُونُ كَنْزُ أَحَدِكُمْ يَوْمَ القِيَامَةِ شُجَاعًا أَقْرَعَ.

183. Narrated Zaid bin Wahb: I passed by (visited) Abū Dhar at Ar-Rabadha and said to him, "What has brought you to this land?" He said, "We were at Shā'm and I recited the Verse:

١٨٣ - حَدَّثَنَا قُتَيْبَةُ بْنُ سَعِيدٍ: حَدَّثَنَا جَرِيرٌ، عَنْ حُصَيْنٍ، عَنْ زَيْدِ بْنِ وَهْبٍ قَالَ: مَرَرْتُ عَلَى أَبِي ذَرٍّ بِالرَّبَذَةِ فَقُلْتُ: مَا أَنْزَلَكَ بِهَذِهِ الأَرْضِ؟ قَالَ:

(1) i.e. Does not enjoy it because of Allāh's punishment he has incurred.

'They who hoard up gold and silver and spend them not in the way of Allāh; announce to them a painful torment, (9:34)

whereupon Mu'āwiya said, 'This Verse is not for us, but for the people of the Scripture.' Then I said, 'But it is both for us (Muslim) and for them.' "

كُنَّا بالشَّامِ فَقَرَأْتُ - وَالَّذِينَ يَكْنِزُونَ الذَّهَبَ وَالفِضَّةَ وَلا يُنْفِقُونَها فى سَبِيلِ اللهِ فَبَشِّرْهُمْ بِعَذابٍ أَلِيمٍ - قالَ مُعاوِيَةُ: ما هٰذِهِ فِينا، ما هٰذِهِ إلاَّ فى أَهْلِ الكِتابِ. قالَ: قُلْتُ: إنَّها لَفِينا وَفِيهِمْ.

(140) CHAPTER. The Statement of Allāh عزّوجلّ:–

'On the Day when that (hoarded up gold and silver) will be heated in the Fire of Hell, and with it will be branded their foreheads...' (9:35)

Narrated Khālid bin Aslam: We went out with 'Abdullāh bin 'Umar and he said, "This (Verse) was revealed before the prescription of Zakāt, and when Zakāt was prescribed, Allāh made it a means of purifying one's wealth."

بابُ قَوْلِهِ عَزَّ وَجَلَّ - يَوْمَ يُحْمَى عَلَيْها فى نارِ جَهَنَّمَ فَتُكْوَى بِها - الآيَةَ.

وَقالَ أَحْمَدُ ابنُ شَبِيبِ بنِ سَعِيدٍ: حَدَّثَنا أبى، عَنْ يُونُسَ، عَنِ ابنِ شِهابٍ، عَنْ خالِدِ بنِ أَسْلَمَ قالَ: خَرَجْنا مَعَ عَبْدِ اللهِ بنِ عُمَرَ فَقالَ: هٰذا قَبْلَ أَنْ تُنْزَلَ الزَّكاةُ، فَلَمَّا أُنْزِلَتْ جَعَلَها اللهُ طُهْرًا للأَمْوالِ.

(141) CHAPTER. The Statement of Allāh تعالى :-

'Verily, the number of months with Allāh is twelve months (in a year) ......So was it ordained by Him on the day when He created the Heavens and the Earth. Of them, four are sacred: (i.e. 1st. 7th, 11th, and 12th months of the Muslim calendar). That is the right religion; so do not wrong yourself therein.' (9:36)

بابُ قَوْلِهِ - إنَّ عِدَّةَ الشُّهُورِ عِنْدَ اللهِ اثْنا عَشَرَ شَهْرًا فى كِتابِ اللهِ يَوْمَ خَلَقَ السَّمٰوَاتِ وَالأَرْضَ مِنْها أَرْبَعَةٌ حُرُمٌ ذٰلِكَ الدِّينُ القَيِّمُ فَلا تَظْلِمُوا فِيهِنَّ أَنْفُسَكُمْ - القَيِّمُ: هُوَ القائِمُ.

184. Narrated Abū Bakr : The Prophet said, "Time has come back to its original state which it had when Allāh created the Heavens and the Earth; the year is twelve months, four of which are sacred. Three of them are in succession; Dhul-Qa'da, Dhul-Ḥijja and Al-Muḥarram, and (the fourth being) Rajab Muḍar (named after the tribe of Muḍar as they used to respect this month) which stands between Jumād (aththānī) and Sha'bān."

١٨٤ - حدثنا عبد الله بن عبد الوهاب : حدثنا حماد بن زيد ، عن أيوب ، عن محمد ، عن ابن أبي بكرة ، عن أبي بكرة ، عن النبي صلى الله عليه وسلم قال : إن الزمان قد استدار كهيئته يوم خلق الله السموات والأرض ، السنة اثنا عشر شهرا ، منها أربعة حرم ، ثلاث متواليات : ذو القعدة ، وذو الحجة ، والمحرم ، ورجب مضر الذى بين جمادى وشعبان

(142) CHAPTER. The Statement of Allāh :—

The second of two, when they (Muḥammad and Abū Bakr) were in the cave, and he said to his companion (Abū Bakr) "Be not sad (or afraid), surely Allāh is with us.' " (9:40)

باب قوله - ثاني اثنين إذ هما فى الغار إذ يقول لصاحبه لا تحزن إن الله معنا - ناصرنا . السكينة : فعيلة من السكون .

185. Narrated Abū Bakr : I was in the company of the Prophet in the cave, and on seeing the traces of the pagans, I said, "O Allāh's Messenger! If one of them (pagans) should lift up his foot, he will see us." He said, "What do you think of two, the third of whom is Allāh?"

١٨٥ - حدثنا عبد الله بن محمد : حدثنا حبان : حدثنا همام : حدثنا ثابت : حدثنا أنس قال : حدثني أبو بكر رضي الله عنه قال : كنت مع النبي صلى الله عليه وسلم فى الغار فرأيت آثار المشركين قلت : يا رسول الله ، لو أن أحدهم رفع قدمه رآنا ، قال : ما ظنك باثنين الله ثالثهما .

186. Narrated Ibn Abī Mulaika: When there happened the disagreement between Ibn Az-Zubair and Ibn 'Abbās , I said (to the latter), "(Why don't you take the oath of allegiance to him as) his father is Az-Zubair, and his mother is Asmā,' and his aunt is 'Āisha, and his maternal grandfather is Abū Bakr, and his grandmother is Ṣafiya?"

١٨٦ - حدثنا عبد الله بن محمد: حدثنا ابن عيينة، عن ابن جريج، عن ابن أبي مليكة، عن ابن عباس رضي الله عنهما أنه قال حين وقع بينه وبين ابن الزبير، قلت: أبوه الزبير، وأمه أسماء، وخالته عائشة، وجده أبو بكر، وجدته صفية. فقلت لسفيان: إسناده؟ فقال: حدثنا فشغله إنسان ولم يقل ابن جريج.

187. Narrated Ibn Abī Mulaika: There was a disagreement between them (i.e. Ibn 'Abbās and Ibn Az-Zubair) so I went to Ibn 'Abbās in the morning and said (to him), "Do you want to fight against Ibn Zubair and thus make lawful what Allāh has made unlawful (i.e. fighting in Mecca)?" Ibn 'Abbās said, "Allāh forbid! Allāh ordained that Ibn Zubair and Banī Umaiya would permit (fighting in Mecca), but by Allāh, I will never regard it as permissible." Ibn 'Abbās added. "The people asked me to take the oath of allegiance to Ibn Az-Zubair. I said, 'He is really entitled to assume authority for his father, Az-Zubair was the helper of the Prophet , his (maternal) grandfather, Abū Bakr was (the Prophet's) companion in the cave, his mother, Asmā' was 'Dhātun-Niṭāq', his aunt, 'Āisha was the mother of the Believers, his paternal aunt, Khadīja was the wife of the Prophet , and the paternal aunt of the Prophet was his grandmother. He himself is pious and chaste in Islām, wellversed in the knowle-

١٨٧ - حدثني عبد الله بن محمد قال: حدثني يحيى بن معين: حدثنا حجاج: قال ابن جريج، قال ابن أبي مليكة: وكان بينهما شيء فغدوت على ابن عباس فقلت: أتريد أن تقاتل ابن الزبير فتحل ما حرم الله، فقال: معاذ الله: إن الله كتب ابن الزبير وبني أمية محلين، وإني والله لا أحله أبدا، قال: قال الناس بايع لابن الزبير، فقلت وأين بهذا الأمر عنه؟ أما أبوه فحواري النبي صلى الله عليه وسلم يريد الزبير، وأما جده فصاحب الغار، يريد أبا بكر، وأما أمه فذات النطاق، يريد أسماء، وأما خالته فأم المؤمنين، يريد عائشة، وأما عمته،

dge of the Qur'ān. By Allāh! (Really, I left my relatives, Banī Umaiya for his sake though) they are my close relatives, and if they should be my rulers, they are equally apt to be so and are descended from a noble family.

فَزَوْجُ النَّبِيِّ صلى الله عليه وسلم، يُرِيدُ خَدِيجَةَ. وأمَّا عَمَّةُ النَّبِيِّ صلى الله عليه وسلم فَجَدَّتُهُ، يُرِيدُ صَفِيَّةَ، ثُمَّ عَفِيفٌ فِي الإِسْلامِ، قَارِئٌ لِلْقُرْآنِ. واللهِ إِنْ وَصَلُونِي وَصَلُونِي مِنْ قَرِيبٍ، وَإِنْ رَبُّونِي رَبُّونِي أَكْفَاءٌ كِرَامٌ. فَآثَرَ عَلَيَّ التُّوَيْتَاتِ والأُسَامَاتِ والحُمَيْدَاتِ. يُرِيدُ أَبْطُنًا مِنْ بَنِي أَسَدِ بْنِ تُوَيْتٍ، وَبَنِي أُسَامَةَ، وَبَنِي أَسَدٍ أَنَّ ابْنَ أَبِي العَاصِ بَرَزَ يَمْشِي القُدَمِيَّةَ، يَعْنِي عَبْدَ المَلِكِ بْنَ مَرْوَانَ، وَإِنَّهُ لَوَّى ذَنَبَهُ، يَعْنِي ابْنَ الزُّبَيْرِ.

188. Narrated Ibn Abī Mulaika: We entered upon Ibn 'Abbās and he said "Are you not astonished at Ibn Az-Zubair's assuming the caliphate?" I said (to myself), "I will support him and speak of his good traits as I did not do even for Abū Bakr and 'Umar though they were more entitled to receive all good than he was." I said "He (i.e. Ibn Az-Zubair) is the son of the aunt of the Prophet ﷺ and the son of Az-Zubair, and the grandson of Abū Bakr and the son of Khadīja's brother, and the son of 'Āisha's sister." Nevertheless, he considers himself to be superior to me and does not want me to be one of his friends. So I said, "I never expected that he would

١٨٨ ـ حَدَّثَنَا مُحَمَّدُ بْنُ عُبَيْدِ بْنِ مَيْمُونٍ: حَدَّثَنَا عِيسَى بْنُ يُونُسَ عَنْ عُمَرَ بْنِ سَعِيدٍ قَالَ: أَخْبَرَنِي ابْنُ أَبِي مُلَيْكَةَ: دَخَلْنَا عَلَى ابْنِ عَبَّاسٍ فَقَالَ: أَلا تَعْجَبُونَ لابْنِ الزُّبَيْرِ قَامَ فِي أَمْرِهِ هٰذَا؟ فَقُلْتُ: لأُحَاسِبَنَّ نَفْسِي لَهُ، مَا حَاسَبْتُهَا لأَبِي بَكْرٍ وَلا لِعُمَرَ، وَلَهُمَا كَانَا أَوْلَى بِكُلِّ خَيْرٍ مِنْهُ. وَقُلْتُ: ابْنُ عَمَّةِ النَّبِيِّ صلى الله عليه وسلم، وَابْنُ الزُّبَيْرِ، وَابْنُ أَبِي بَكْرٍ، وَابْنُ أَخِي خَدِيجَةَ، وَابْنُ أُخْتِ عَائِشَةَ، فَإِذَا هُوَ يَتَعَلَّى عَنِّي وَلا يُرِيدُ ذَلِكَ. فَقُلْتُ: مَا كُنْتُ أَظُنُّ أَنِّي أَعْرِضُ

refuse my offer to support him, and I don't think he intends to do me any good, therefore, if my cousins should inevitably be my rulers, it will be better for me to be ruled by them than by some others."

هذا من نفسي فبدعه وما أراه يريد خيرا وإن كان لا بد لأن يربني بنو عمي أحب إلي من أن يربني غيرهم .

(143) CHAPTER. The Statement of Allāh :

'(And for those) whose hearts have been inclined (towards Islām) and for to free the captives.. . . . . . .
(9:60)

Mujāhid said, "To attract their hearts by giving them gifts."

باب قوله - والمؤلفة قلوبهم وفي الرقاب - قال مجاهد : يتألفهم بالعطية .

189. Narrated Abū Sa'īd : Something was sent to the Prophet and he distributed it amongst four (men) and said, ""I want to attract their hearts, (to Islām thereby), " A man said (to the Prophet), "You have not done justice." Thereupon the Prophet said, "There will emerge from the offspring of this (man) some people who will renounce the religion."

١٨٩ - حدثنا محمد بن كثير : أخبرنا سفيان ، عن أبيه ، عن ابن أبي نعم ، عن أبي سعيد رضي الله عنه قال : بعث إلى النبي صلى الله عليه وسلم بشيء فقسمه بين أربعة وقال أتألفهم ، فقال رجل : ما عدلت ، فقال يخرج من ضئضئ هذا قوم يمرقون من الدين .

(144) CHAPTER. The Statement of Allāh :-

'Those who criticize such of the believers who give charity voluntarily.' (9:79)

باب قوله - الذين يلمزون المطوعين من المؤمنين في الصدقات - يلمزون : يعيبون . وجهدهم وجهدهم : طاقتهم .

190. Narrated Abū Mus'ūd: When we were ordered to give alms, we began to work as porters (to earn something we could give in charity). Abū 'Uqail came with one half of a Ṣā' (special measure for food grains) and another person brought more than he did. So the hypocrites said, "Allāh is not in need of the alms of this (i.e. 'Uqail); and this other person did not give alms but for showing off." Then Allāh revealed:—

> 'Those who criticize such of the Believers who give charity voluntarily and those who could not find to give in charity except what is available to them.' (9:79)

١٩٠ ـ حدثني بشر بن خالد أبو محمد : أخبرنا محمد بن جعفر ، عن شعبة عن سليمان ، عن أبي وائل ، عن أبي مسعود قال : لما أمرنا بالصدقة كنا نتحامل فجاء أبو عقيل بنصف صاع وجاء إنسان بأكثر منه فقال المنافقون إن الله لغني عن صدقة هذا وما فعل هذا الآخر ، إلا رياء فنزلت ـ الذين يلمزون المطوعين من المؤمنين في الصدقات والذين لا يجدون إلا جهدهم ـ الآية .

191. Narrated Shaqīq: Abū Mas'ūd Al-Anṣārī said, "Allāh's Messenger ﷺ used to order us to give alms. So one of us would exert himself to earn one Mud (special measure of wheat or dates, etc.,) to give in charity; while today one of us may have one hundred thousand." Shaqīq said: As if Abū Mas'ūd referred to himself.

١٩١ ـ حدثني إسحاق بن إبراهيم قال : قلت لأبي أسامة : أحدثكم زائدة عن سليمان عن شقيق عن أبي مسعود الأنصاري قال : كان رسول الله صلى الله عليه وسلم يأمر بالصدقة فيحتال أحدنا حتى يجيء بالمد وإن لأحدهم اليوم مائة ألف كأنه يعرض بنفسه .

(145) CHAPTER. The Statement of Allāh تعالى :—

> '(Whether you) (O Muḥammad) ask forgiveness for them or do not ask forgiveness for them; though you ask forgiveness for them seventy

باب قوله ـ استغفر لهم أو لا تستغفر لهم إن تستغفر لهم سبعين مرة فلن يغفر الله لهم ـ .

times, Allāh will not forgive them.'
(9:80)

192. Narrated Ibn 'Umar: When 'Abdullāh bin 'Ubai died, his son 'Abdullāh bin 'Abdullāh came to Allāh's Messenger ﷺ and asked him to give him his shirt in order to shroud his father in it. He gave it to him and then 'Abdullāh asked the Prophet ﷺ to offer the funeral prayer for him (his father). Allāh's Messenger ﷺ got up to offer the funeral prayer for him, but 'Umar got up too and got hold of the garment of Allāh's Messenger ﷺ and said, "O Allāh's Messenger! Will you offer the funeral prayer for him though your Lord has forbidden you to offer the prayer for him?" Allāh's Messenger ﷺ said, "But Allāh has given me the choice by saying:—

> '(Whether you) ask forgiveness for them, or do not ask forgiveness for them; even if you ask forgiveness for them seventy times.....'
> (9:80)

so I will ask more than seventy times." 'Umar said, "But he ('Abdullāh bin 'Ubai) is a hypocrite!" However, Allāh's Messenger ﷺ did offer the funeral prayer for him whereupon Allāh revealed:—

> 'And never (O Muḥammad) pray for anyone of them that dies, nor stand at his grave.' (9:84)

١٩٢ - حدَّثني عُبَيْدُ بنُ إسماعيلَ، عن أبي أُسامةَ، عن عُبَيْدِ اللهِ، عن نافعٍ، عن ابنِ عُمَرَ رضيَ اللهُ تعالى عنهُما قالَ: لمَّا تُوُفِّيَ عبدُ اللهِ بنُ أُبَيٍّ جاءَ ابنُهُ عبدُ اللهِ بنُ عبدِ اللهِ إلى رسولِ اللهِ صلى اللهُ عليهِ وسلَّم فسألَهُ أنْ يُعْطِيَهُ قميصَهُ يُكَفِّنُ فيهِ أباهُ، فأعطاهُ ثُمَّ سألَهُ أنْ يُصَلِّيَ عليهِ فقامَ رسولُ اللهِ صلى اللهُ عليهِ وسلَّم ليُصَلِّيَ عليهِ، فقامَ عُمَرُ فأخذَ بثوبِ رسولِ اللهِ صلى اللهُ عليهِ وسلَّم فقالَ: يا رسولَ اللهِ، أتُصَلِّي عليهِ وقد نهاكَ ربُّكَ أنْ تُصَلِّيَ عليهِ؟ فقالَ رسولُ اللهِ صلى اللهُ عليهِ وسلَّم إنَّما خيَّرني اللهُ فقالَ - استغفِرْ لهُم أوْ لا تستغفِرْ لهُم إنْ تستغفِرْ لهُم سبعينَ مرَّةً - وسأزيدُهُ على السبعينَ. قالَ: إنَّهُ منافقٌ، قالَ: فصلَّى رسولُ اللهِ صلى اللهُ عليهِ وسلَّم فأنزلَ اللهُ - ولا تُصَلِّ على أحدٍ منهُم ماتَ أبداً ولا تَقُمْ على قبرِهِ -.

193. Narrated 'Umar bin Al-Khaṭṭāb (رضي الله عنه): When 'Abdullāh bin Ubai bin Salūl died, Allāh's Messenger (ﷺ) was called in order to offer the funeral prayer for him. When Allāh's Messenger got up (to offer the prayer) I jumped towards him and said, "O Allāh's Messenger! Do you offer the prayer for Ibn Ubai although he said so-and-so on such-and-such a day?" I went on mentioning his sayings. Allāh's Messenger (ﷺ) smiled and said, "Keep away from me, O 'Umar!" But when I spoke too much to him, he said, "I have been given the choice, and I have chosen (this) ; and if I knew that if I asked forgiveness for him more than seventy times, he would be for given, I would ask it for more times than that." So Allāh's Messenger (ﷺ) offered the funeral prayer for him and then left, but he did not stay long before the two Verses of Sūrat-Barā'a were revealed, i.e. :–

> 'And never (O Muḥammad) pray for anyone of them that dies....
> and died in a state of rebellion.' (9:84)

Later I was astonished at my daring to speak like that to Allāh's Messenger (ﷺ): and Allāh and His Messenger (ﷺ) know best.

١٩٣ - حدَّثنا يحيى بنُ بُكير: حدَّثنا الليثُ، عن عُقيلٍ وقال غيرُه: حدَّثني الليثُ: حدَّثني عُقيلٌ، عن ابنِ شهابٍ قال: أخبرني عُبيدُ الله بنُ عبدِ الله، عن ابنِ عبّاسٍ، عن عُمرَ ابنِ الخطّابِ رضيَ اللهُ عنهُ أنهُ قال: لمّا ماتَ عبدُ الله بنُ أُبيٍّ ابنُ سلُولَ دُعيَ لهُ رسولُ الله صلى اللهُ عليهِ وسلَّم ليُصلّيَ عليهِ، فلمّا قامَ رسولُ الله صلى اللهُ عليهِ وسلَّم وثبتُ إليهِ فقلتُ: يا رسولَ الله، أتُصلّي على ابنِ أُبيٍّ وقد قالَ يومَ كذا كذا وكذا؟ قالَ أُعدِّدُ عليهِ قولَهُ، فتبسَّمَ رسولُ الله صلى اللهُ عليهِ وسلَّم وقال: أخِّرْ عنّي يا عُمرُ، فلمّا أكثرتُ عليهِ قالَ: إني خُيِّرتُ فاخترتُ، لو أعلمُ أني إنْ زدتُ على السبعينَ يُغفَرْ لهُ لزدتُ عليها. قالَ: فصلّى عليهِ رسولُ الله صلى اللهُ عليهِ وسلَّم ثمَّ انصرفَ فلم يمكُثْ إلّا يسيرًا حتّى نزلتِ الآيتانِ من براءةَ - ولا تُصلِّ على أحدٍ منهم ماتَ أبدًا - إلى قولهِ - وهم فاسقونَ - قال: فعجبتُ بعدُ من جُرأتي على رسولِ الله صلى اللهُ عليهِ وسلَّم، واللهُ ورسولُهُ أعلمُ.

(146) CHAPTER. The Statement of Allāh :—

'And never (O Muḥammad) pray (funeral prayer) for anyone of them that dies, nor stand at his grave.' (9:84)

باب قوله - ولا تصل على أحد منهم مات أبدا ولا تقم على قبره -.

194. Narrated Ibn 'Umar :

When Abdullāh bin Ubaī died, his son 'Abdullāh bin 'Abdullāh came to Allāh's Messenger who gave his shirt to him and ordered him to shroud his father in it. Then he stood up to offer the funeral prayer for the deceased, but 'Umar bin Al-Khaṭṭāb took hold of his garment and said, "Do you offer the funeral prayer for him though he was a hypocrite and Allāh has forbidden you to ask forgiveness for hypocrites?" The Prophet said, "Allāh has given me the choice (or Allāh has informed me) saying:—

> '(Whether you) (O Muḥammad) ask forgiveness for them, or do not ask forgiveness for them, even if you ask forgiveness for them seventy times, Allāh will not forgive them.' " (9:80)

Then he added, "I will (appeal to Allāh for his sake) more then seventy times." So Allāh's Messenger offered the funeral prayer for him and we too, offered the prayer along with him. Then Allāh revealed:—

> 'And never (O Muḥammad) pray (funeral prayer) for anyone of them that dies, nor stand at his

١٩٤ - حدثني إبراهيم بن المنذر: حدثنا أنس بن عياض، عن عبيد الله، عن نافع، عن ابن عمر رضي الله عنهما أنه قال: لما توفي عبد الله بن أبي جاء ابنه عبد الله بن عبد الله إلى رسول الله صلى الله عليه وسلم فأعطاه قميصه وأمره أن يكفنه فيه. ثم قام يصلي عليه فأخذ عمر بن الخطاب بثوبه فقال: تصلي عليه وهو منافق وقد نهاك الله أن تستغفر لهم؟ قال: إنما خيرني الله أو أخبرني الله فقال - استغفر لهم أو لا تستغفر لهم إن تستغفر لهم سبعين مرة فلن يغفر الله لهم - فقال: سأزيده على سبعين، قال: فصلى عليه رسول الله صلى الله عليه وسلم وصلينا معه ثم أنزل الله عليه - ولا تصل على أحد منهم مات أبدا ولا تقم على قبره إنهم كفروا بالله ورسوله وماتوا وهم فاسقون -.

grave. Certainly they disbelieved in Allāh and His Messenger and died in a state of rebellion.' (9:84)

(147) CHAPTER. The Statement of Allāh:— ﷻ 'They will swear by Allāh to you when you return to them that you may leave them alone. (9:95)

بابُ قوْلِهِ - سَيَحْلِفُونَ بِاللهِ لَكُمْ إذَا انْقَلَبْتُمْ إِلَيْهِمْ لِتُعْرِضُوا عَنْهُمْ - الآيَةَ.

195. Narrated 'Abdullāh bin Ka'b: I heard Ka'b bin Mālik at the time he remained behind and did not join (the battle of) Tabūk, saying, "By Allāh, no blessing has Allāh bestowed upon me, besides my guidance to Islām, better than that of helping me speak the truth to Allāh's Messenger ﷺ, otherwise I would have told the Prophet ﷺ a lie and would have been ruined like those who had told a lie when the Divine Inspiration was revealed:--

'They will swear by Allāh to you (Muslims) when you return to them.. ... the rebellious people.' (9:95-96)

١٩٥ - حدَّثَنا يَحْيَى: حدَّثَنا اللَّيْثُ، عَنْ عُقَيْلٍ، عَنْ ابنِ شِهابٍ، عَنْ عَبْدِ الرَّحْمٰنِ بنِ عَبْدِ اللهِ: أنَّ عَبْدَ اللهِ بنَ كَعْبٍ قالَ: سَمِعْتُ كَعْبَ ابنَ مالكٍ حِينَ تَخَلَّفَ عَنْ تَبُوكَ: واللهِ ما أنْعَمَ اللهُ عَلَيَّ مِنْ نِعْمَةٍ بَعْدَ إذْ هَدَانِي أعْظَمَ مِنْ صِدْقِي رَسُولَ اللهِ صلى اللهُ عليهِ وسلَّم أنْ لا أكُونَ كَذَبْتُهُ فأهْلِكَ كَمَا هَلَكَ الَّذِينَ كَذَبُوا حِينَ أُنْزِلَ الوَحْيُ - سَيَحْلِفُونَ بِاللهِ لَكُمْ إذَا انْقَلَبْتُمْ إلَيْهِمْ - إلى قَوْلِهِ - الفاسِقِينَ -.

(148) CHAPTER. (A) The Statement of Allāh ﷻ :—

'Others who have acknowledged their sins.... (9:102)

بابُ قوْلِهِ - يَحْلِفُونَ لَكُمْ لِتَرْضَوْا عَنْهُمْ فإنْ تَرْضَوْا عَنْهُمْ - إلى قَوْلِهِ - الفاسِقِينَ -.

(148) CHAPTER (B) The Statement of Allāh ﷺ:—

'They will swear by Allāh to you (Muslims) when you return to them

(9:95-96)

196. Narrated Samura bin Jundab: Allāh's Messenger ﷺ said, "Tonight two (visitors) came to me (in my dream) and took me to a town built with gold bricks and silver bricks. There we met men who, half of their bodies, look like the most-handsome human beings you have ever seen, and the other half, the ugliest human beings you have ever seen. Those two visitors said to those men, 'Go and dip yourselves in that river. So they dipped themselves therein and then came to us, their ugliness having disappeared and they were in the most-handsome shape. The visitors said, 'The first is the Garden of Eden and that is your dwelling place.' Then they added, 'As for those people who were half ugly and half handsome, they were those who mixed good deeds and bad deeds, but Allāh forgave them.'"

(149) CHAPTER. The Statement of Allāh ﷺ:—

باب قَوْلِهِ ـ وَآخَرُونَ اعْتَرَفُوا بِذُنُوبِهِمْ ـ الآيَةَ.

١٩٦ ـ حَدَّثَنِي مُؤَمَّلٌ: حَدَّثَنَا إِسْمَاعِيلُ بْنُ إِبْرَاهِيمَ: حَدَّثَنَا عَوْفٌ: حَدَّثَنَا أَبُو رَجَاءٍ: حَدَّثَنَا سَمُرَةُ بْنُ جُنْدَبٍ رَضِيَ اللَّهُ عَنْهُ قَالَ: قَالَ رَسُولُ اللَّهِ صلى الله عليه وسلم لَنَا: أَتَانِي اللَّيْلَةَ آتِيَانِ فَابْتَعَثَانِي فَانْتَهَيْنَا إِلَى مَدِينَةٍ مَبْنِيَّةٍ بِلَبِنِ ذَهَبٍ وَلَبِنِ فِضَّةٍ، فَتَلَقَّانَا رِجَالٌ، شَطْرٌ مِنْ خَلْقِهِمْ كَأَحْسَنِ مَا أَنْتَ رَاءٍ، وَشَطْرٌ كَأَقْبَحِ مَا أَنْتَ رَاءٍ، قَالَا لَهُمْ: اذْهَبُوا فَقَعُوا فِي ذَلِكَ النَّهْرِ فَوَقَعُوا فِيهِ ثُمَّ رَجَعُوا إِلَيْنَا قَدْ ذَهَبَ ذَلِكَ السُّوءُ عَنْهُمْ فَصَارُوا فِي أَحْسَنِ صُورَةٍ. فَالأُولَى هَذِهِ جَنَّةُ عَدْنٍ وَهَذَاكَ مَنْزِلُكَ. قَالَ: أَمَّا الْقَوْمُ الَّذِينَ كَانُوا شَطْرٌ مِنْهُمْ حَسَنٌ وَشَطْرٌ مِنْهُمْ قَبِيحٌ فَإِنَّهُمْ خَلَطُوا عَمَلاً صَالِحاً وَآخَرَ سَيِّئاً، تَجَاوَزَ اللَّهُ عَنْهُمْ.

باب قَوْلِهِ ـ مَا كَانَ لِلنَّبِيِّ وَالَّذِينَ آمَنُوا أَنْ يَسْتَغْفِرُوا لِلْمُشْرِكِينَ ـ.

'It is not fitting for the Prophet ﷺ and those who believe, that they should invoke (Allāh) for forgiveness for pagans.' (9:113)

197. Narrated Al-Musaiyab: When Abū Ṭālib's death approached, the Prophet ﷺ went to him while Abū Jahl and 'Abdullāh bin Abī Umaiya were present with him. The Prophet ﷺ said, "O uncle, say: None has the right to be worshipped except Allāh, so that I may argue for your case with it before Allāh." On that, Abū Jahl and 'Abdullāh bin Abī' Umaiya said, "O Abū Ṭālib! Do you want to renounce 'Abdul Muṭṭalib's religion?" Then the Prophet ﷺ said, "I will keep on asking (Allāh for) forgiveness for you unless I am forbidden to do so." Then there was revealed:—

> 'It is not fitting for the Prophet and those who believe that they should invoke (Allāh) for forgiveness for pagans even though they be of kin, after it has become clear to them that they are companions of the Fire.' (9:113)

١٩٧ - حدثنا إسحاقُ بنُ إبراهيمَ: حدثنا عبدُ الرزاقِ: أخبرنا معمرٌ، عن الزهريِّ، عن سعيدِ ابنِ المسيبِ، عن أبيهِ قال: لما حضرتْ أبا طالبٍ الوفاةُ دخلَ عليهِ النبيُّ صلى اللهُ عليه وسلم وعندَهُ أبو جهلٍ وعبدُ اللهِ بنُ أبي أميةَ فقالَ النبيُّ صلى الله عليه وسلم: أيْ عمِّ، قلْ لا إلهَ إلاَّ اللهُ أُحاجُّ لكَ بها عندَ اللهِ. فقالَ أبو جهلٍ وعبدُ اللهِ ابنُ أبي أميةَ: يا أبا طالبٍ أترغبُ عنْ ملةِ عبدِ المطلبِ؟ فقالَ النبيُّ صلى اللهُ عليه وسلم: لأستغفرنَّ لكَ ما لمْ أُنهَ عنكَ، فنزلتْ - ما كانَ للنبيِّ والذينَ آمنوا أنْ يستغفروا للمشركينَ ولوْ كانوا أُولي قربى منْ بعدِ ما تبيَّنَ لهمْ أنهمْ أصحابُ الجحيمِ -.

(150) CHAPTER. The Statement of Allāh تعالى :—

> Verily, Allāh has forgiven the Prophet, the Muhājirīn and the Anṣār....' (9:117)

بابُ قولهِ - لقدْ تابَ اللهُ على النبيِّ والمهاجرينَ والأنصارِ - الآيةَ.

198. Narrated 'Abdullāh bin Ka'b: I heard Ka'b bin Mālik talking about the Verse:—

'And to the three (He also forgave) who remained behind.' (9:118)

saying in the last portion of his talk, "(I said), 'As a part (sign) of my repentance, I would like to give up all my property in the cause of Allāh and His Messenger.' The Prophet ﷺ said to me, 'Keep some of your wealth as it is good for you." (To the three (He also forgave) who remained behind till for them the earth, vast as it is, was straitened.........
.. ..) (9:118)

١٩٨ - حدَّثنا أحمدُ بنُ صالحٍ قالَ: حدَّثني ابنُ وهبٍ قالَ: أخبرني يونُسُ: قالَ أحمدُ. وحدثنا عنبسةُ: حدَّثنا يونُسُ: عنِ ابنِ شهابٍ قالَ: أخبرني عبدُ الرحمنِ بنُ كعبٍ قالَ: أخبرني عبدُ اللهِ بنُ كعبٍ وكانَ قائدَ كعبٍ منْ بنيهِ حينَ عميَ قالَ: سمعتُ كعبَ بنَ مالكٍ في حديثهِ - وعلى الثلاثةِ الذينَ خُلِّفوا - قالَ في آخرِ حديثهِ: إنَّ منْ توبتي أنْ أنخلعَ منْ مالي صدقةً إلى اللهِ ورسولهِ، فقالَ النبيُّ صلى اللهُ عليهِ وسلَّم: أمسكْ بعضَ مالكَ فهوَ خيرٌ لكَ - وعلى الثلاثةِ الذينَ خُلِّفوا حتى إذا ضاقتْ عليهمُ الأرضُ بما رحُبتْ - الآيةَ.

199. Narrated 'Abdullāh bin Ka'b: I heard Ka'b bin Mālik who was one of the three who were forgiven, saying that he had never remained behind Allāh's Messenger ﷺ in any Ghazwa which he had fought except two Ghazwāt. Ghazwat-al-'Usra (Tabūk) and Ghazwat-Badr. He added. "I decided to tell the truth to Allāh's Messenger ﷺ in the forenoon, and scarcely did he return from a journey he made, except in the forenoon, he would go first to the mosque and offer a two-Rak-'āt prayer. The Prophet ﷺ forbade others to speak to me or

١٩٩ - حدَّثني محمَّدٌ: حدَّثنا أحمدُ ابنُ أبي شُعيبٍ: حدَّثنا موسى بنُ أعينَ: حدَّثنا إسحاقُ ابنُ راشدٍ: أنَّ الزُّهريَّ حدَّثهُ قالَ: أخبرني عبدُ الرحمنِ بنُ عبدِ اللهِ بنِ كعبِ بنِ مالكٍ عنْ أبيهِ قالَ: سمعتُ أبي كعبَ ابنَ مالكٍ وهوَ أحدُ الثلاثةِ الذينَ تِيبَ عليهمْ أنهُ لمْ يتخلَّفْ عنْ رسولِ اللهِ صلى اللهُ عليهِ وسلَّم في غزوةٍ غزاها قطُّ غيرَ غزوتينِ: غزوةِ.

to my two companions, but he did not prohibit speaking to any of those who had remained behind excepting us. So the people avoided speaking to us, and I stayed in that state till I could no longer bear it, and the only thing that worried me was that I might die and the Prophet ﷺ would not offer the funeral prayer for me, or Allāh's Messenger ﷺ might die and I would be left in that social status among the people that nobody would speak to me or offer the funeral prayer for me. But Allāh revealed His Forgiveness for us to the Prophet ﷺ in the last third of the night while Allāh's Messenger ﷺ was with Um Salama. Um Salama sympathized with me and helped me in my disaster. Allāh's Messenger ﷺ said, 'O Um Salama! Ka'b has been forgiven!' She said, 'Shall I send someone to him to give him the good tidings?' He said, 'If you did so, the people would not let you sleep the rest of the night.' So when the Prophet ﷺ had offered the Fajr prayer, he announced Allāh's Forgiveness for us. His face used to look as bright as a piece of the (full) moon whenever he was pleased. When Allāh revealed His Forgiveness for us, we were the three whose case had been deferred while the excuse presented by those who had apologised had been accepted. But when there were mentioned those who had told the Prophet ﷺ lies and remained behind (the battle of Tabūk) and had given false excuses, they were described with the worse description one may be described with. Allāh سُبْحَانَهُ said:–

> 'They will present their excuses to you(muslims) when you return to them. Say: Present no excuses; we

العُشْرَةِ، وَغَزْوَةِ بَدْرٍ . قالَ: فأجمعتُ صِدْقَ رَسُولِ اللهِ صلى اللهُ عليهِ وسلَّم ضُحًى وكانَ قَلَّما يَقْدَمُ مِنْ سَفَرٍ سافَرَهُ إلاَّ ضُحًى، وكانَ يَبْدَأُ بالمَسْجِدِ فيَرْكَعُ رَكْعَتَيْنِ ونَهَى النَّبِيُّ صلى اللهُ عليهِ وسلَّم عَنْ كَلامي وكَلامِ صاحِبَيَّ ولمْ يَنْهَ عَنْ كَلامِ أحَدٍ مِنَ المُتَخَلِّفِينَ غَيْرِنا. فاجْتَنَبَ النّاسُ كَلامَنا فلَبِثْتُ كَذَلكَ حتَّى طالَ عَلَيَّ الأمْرُ وَما مِنْ شَيْءٍ أهَمَّ إليَّ مِنْ أنْ أمُوتَ فَلا يُصَلِّي عَلَيَّ النَّبِيُّ صلى اللهُ عليهِ وسلَّم، أوْ يَمُوتَ رَسُولُ اللهِ صلى اللهُ عليهِ وسلَّم فأكُونُ مِنَ النّاسِ بِتِلْكَ المَنْزِلَةِ فَلا يُكَلِّمُني أحَدٌ مِنْهُمْ وَلا يُصَلِّي عَلَيَّ، فأنْزَلَ اللهُ تَوْبَتَنا عَلَى نَبِيِّهِ صلى اللهُ عليه وسلَّم حِينَ بَقِيَ الثُّلُثُ الآخِرُ مِنَ اللَّيْلِ وَرَسُولُ اللهِ صلى اللهُ عليهِ وسلَّم عِنْدَ أُمِّ سَلَمَةَ، وكانَتْ أُمُّ سَلَمَةَ مُحْسِنَةً في شأني، مَعْنِيَّةً في أمْرِي. فَقالَ رَسُولُ اللهِ صلى اللهُ عليهِ وسلَّم: يا أُمَّ سَلَمَةَ، تِيبَ عَلَى كَعْبٍ. قالَتْ: أفَلا أُرْسِلُ إلَيْهِ فأُبَشِّرَهُ؟ قالَ: إذًا يَحْطِمُكُمُ النّاسُ فَيَمْنَعُونَكُمُ النَّوْمَ سائِرَ اللَّيْلَةِ، حتَّى إذا صَلَّى رَسُولُ اللهِ صلى اللهُ عليهِ وسلَّم صَلاةَ الفَجْرِ آذَنَ بِتَوْبَةِ اللهِ عَلَيْنا، وكانَ إذا اسْتَبْشَرَ اسْتَنارَ وَجْهُهُ حتَّى كأنَّهُ قِطْعَةٌ مِنَ القَمَرِ، وكُنّا

shall not believe you. Allāh has already informed us of the true state of matters concerning you. Allāh and His Messenger will observe your actions.......'' (9:94)

أيها الثلاثة الذين خلفوا عن الأمر الذى قبل من هؤلاء الذين اعتذروا حين أنزل الله لنا التوبة. فلما ذكر الذين كذبوا رسول الله صلى الله عليه وسلم من المتخلفين فاعتذروا بالباطل ذكروا بشر ما ذكر به أحد، قال الله سبحانه - يعتذرون إليكم إذا رجعتم إليهم قل لا تعتذروا لن نؤمن لكم قد نبأنا الله من أخباركم وسيرى الله عملكم ورسوله - الآية.

(151) CHAPTER. 'O you who believe! Fear Allāh (obey Him) and be with those who are true (in words and deeds): (9:119)

باب - يا أيها الذين آمنوا اتقوا الله وكونوا مع الصادقين -.

200. Narrated 'Abdullāh bin Ka'b: I heard Ka'b bin Mālik talking about the story of the battle of Tabūk when he remained behind, "By Allāh, I do not know anyone whom Allāh has helped for telling the truth more than me. Since I mentioned that truth to Allāh's Messenger ﷺ till today, I have never intended to tell a lie. And Allāh عز وجل revealed to His Messenger:–

Verily! Allāh has forgiven the Prophet, the Muhājirīn............
and be with those who are true (in words and deeds).'
(9:117-119)

(See Hadīth No. 702 Vol 5).

٢٠٠ - حدثنا يحيى بن بكير: حدثنا الليث، عن عقيل، عن ابن شهاب، عن عبد الرحمن ابن عبد الله بن كعب بن مالك أن عبد الله ابن كعب بن مالك وكان قائد كعب بن مالك قال: سمعت كعب بن مالك يحدث حين تخلف عن قصة تبوك فوالله ما أعلم أحدا أبلاه الله فى صدق الحديث أحسن مما أبلانى، ما تعمدت منذ ذكرت ذلك لرسول الله صلى الله عليه وسلم إلى يومى هذا كذبا، وأنزل

اللهُ عزَّ وجلَّ على رسولِهِ صلى الله عليه وسلّم - لقد تابَ اللهُ على النبيِّ والمهاجرينَ - إلى قوله - وكونوا مع الصادقينَ - .

(152) CHAPTER. The Statement of Allāh :-

Verily there has come to you a Messenger (Muḥammad) from amongst yourselves. It grieves him that you should receive any injury or difficulty......' (9:128')

بابُ قولِهِ - لقد جاءَكم رسولٌ من أنفسِكم عزيزٌ عليهِ ما عنتُّم - الآيةَ . منَ الرأفةِ .

201. Narrated Zaid bin Thābit Al-Anṣārī who was one of those who used to write the Divine Revelation: Abū Bakr sent for me after the (heavy) casualties among the warriors (of the battle) of Yamāma (where a great number of Qurrā' were killed). 'Umar was present with Abū Bakr who said, 'Umar has come to me and said, "The people have suffered heavy casualties on the day of (the battle of) Yamāma, and I am afraid that there will be more casualties among the Qurrā' (those who know the Qur'ān by heart) at other battle-fields, whereby a large part of the Qur'ān may be lost, unless you collect it. And I am of the opinion that you should collect the Qur'ān. . " Abū Bakr added, "I said to 'Umar, 'How can I do something which Allāh's Messenger has not done?' 'Umar said (to me), 'By Allāh, it is (really) a good thing.' So 'Umar kept on pressing, trying to

٢٠١ - حدَّثنا أبو اليمانِ : أخبرَنا شعيبٌ ، عنِ الزُّهريِّ قالَ : أخبرَني ابنُ السَّبّاقِ : أنَّ زيدَ بنَ ثابتٍ الأنصاريَّ رضيَ اللهُ عنهُ وكانَ ممَّن يكتبُ الوحيَ قالَ : أرسلَ إليَّ أبو بكرٍ مقتلَ أهلِ اليمامةِ وعندَهُ عمرُ فقالَ أبو بكرٍ : إنَّ عمرَ أتاني فقالَ : إنَّ القتلَ قدِ استحرَّ يومَ اليمامةِ بالنّاسِ ، وإني أخشى أنْ يستحرَّ القتلُ بالقرّاءِ في المواطنِ فيذهبَ كثيرٌ منَ القرآنِ إلّا أنْ تجمعوهُ . وإني لأرى أنْ تجمعَ القرآنَ ، قالَ أبو بكرٍ : قلتُ لعمرَ : كيفَ أفعلُ شيئًا لم يفعلْهُ رسولُ اللهِ صلى اللهُ عليهِ وسلّمَ ؟

persuade me to accept his proposal, till Allāh opened my bosom for it and I had the same opinion as 'Umar." (Zaid bin Thābit added:) 'Umar was sitting with him (Abū Bakr) and was not speaking. Abū Bakr said (to me). "You are a wise young man and we do not suspect you (of telling lies or of forgetfulness): and you used to write the Divine Inspiration for Allāh's Messenger ﷺ. Therefore, look for the Qur'ān and collect it (in one manuscript). " By Allāh, if he (Abū Bakr) had ordered me to shift one of the mountains (from its place), it would not have been harder for me than what he had ordered me concerning the collection of the Qur'ān. I said to both of them, "How dare you do a thing which the Prophet ﷺ has not done?" Abū Bakr said, "By Allāh, it is (really) a good thing. So I kept on arguing with him about it till Allāh opened my bosom for that which He had opened the bosoms of Abū Bakr and 'Umar. So I started to search for the Qur'ānic material and to collect it from parchments, scapula, leaf-stalks of date palms and from the memories of men (who knew it by heart). I found with Khuzaima two Verses of Sūrat-at- Tauba which I had not found with anybody else, (and they were):—

> Verily there has come to you a Messenger (Muḥammad) from amongst yourselves. It grieves him that you should receive any injury or difficulty. He (Muḥammad ﷺ) is anxious over you (to be rightly guided.). (9:128)

The manuscript on which the Qur'ān was collected, remained with Abū Bakr till Allāh took him unto Him, and then with 'Umar till Allāh took him unto Him, and

فقال عمر: هو والله خير، فلم يزل عمر يراجعني فيه حتى شرح الله لذلك صدري ورأيت الذي رأى عمر. قال زيد بن ثابت: وعمر عنده جالس لا يتكلم، فقال أبو بكر: إنك رجل شاب عاقل ولا نتهمك، كنت تكتب الوحي لرسول الله صلى الله عليه وسلم فتتبع القرآن فاجمعه. فوالله لو كلفني نقل جبل من الجبال ما كان أثقل علي مما أمرني به من جمع القرآن. قلت: كيف تفعلان شيئا لم يفعله النبي صلى الله عليه وسلم؟ فقال أبو بكر: هو والله خير، فلم أزل أراجعه حتى شرح الله صدري للذي شرح الله له صدر أبي بكر وعمر. فقمت فتتبعت القرآن أجمعه من الرقاع والأكتاف والعسب وصدور الرجال حتى وجدت من سورة التوبة آيتين مع خزيمة الأنصاري لم أجدهما مع أحد غيره. لقد جاءكم رسول من أنفسكم عزيز عليه ما عنتم حريص عليكم - إلى آخرها. وكانت الصحف التي جمع فيها القرآن عند أبي بكر حتى توفاه الله، ثم عند عمر حتى توفاه الله، ثم عند حفصة بنت عمر. تابعه عثمان بن عمر، والليث

finally it remained with Hafṣa, 'Umar's daughter.

عَنْ يُونُسَ ، عَنِ ابْنِ شِهَابٍ . وَقَالَ اللَّيْثُ : حَدَّثَنِي عَبْدُ الرَّحْمَنِ بْنُ خَالِدٍ ، عَنِ ابْنِ شِهَابٍ وَقَالَ : مَعَ أَبِي خُزَيْمَةَ الأَنْصَارِيِّ ، وَقَالَ مُوسَى ، عَنْ إِبْرَاهِيمَ : حَدَّثَنَا ابْنُ شِهَابٍ مَعَ أَبِي خُزَيْمَةَ وَتَابَعَهُ يَعْقُوبُ بْنُ إِبْرَاهِيمَ عَنْ أَبِيهِ . وَقَالَ أَبُو ثَابِتٍ : حَدَّثَنَا إِبْرَاهِيمُ وَقَالَ مَعَ خُزَيْمَةَ أَوْ أَبِي خُزَيْمَةَ .

In the Name of Allāh,
the Most Beneficent, the Most Merciful

بِسْمِ اللهِ الرَّحْمَنِ الرَّحِيمِ :

SŪRAṬ-YŪNUS (JONAH No. X)

سورة يونس

وَقَالَ ابْنُ عَبَّاسٍ : فَاخْتَلَطَ : فَنَبَتَ بِالمَاءِ مِنْ كُلِّ لَوْنٍ . وَقَالُوا - اتَّخَذَ اللهُ وَلَدًا سُبْحَانَهُ هُوَ الغَنِيُّ - وَقَالَ زَيْدُ بْنُ أَسْلَمَ - أَنَّ لَهُمْ قَدَمَ صِدْقٍ - مُحَمَّدٌ صلى الله عليه وسلم . وَقَالَ مُجَاهِدٌ : خَيْرٌ ، يُقَالُ تِلْكَ آيَاتُ ، يَعْنِي هَذِهِ أَعْلَامُ القُرْآنِ . وَمِثْلُهُ - حَتَّى إِذَا كُنْتُمْ فِي الفُلْكِ وَجَرَيْنَ بِهِمْ - المَعْنَى بِكُمْ . دَعْوَاهُمْ : دُعَاؤُهُمْ . أُحِيطَ بِهِمْ : دَنَوْا مِنَ الهَلَكَةِ ، أَحَاطَتْ بِهِ خَطِيئَتُهُ . فَاتَّبَعَهُمْ وَأَتْبَعَهُمْ وَاحِدٌ . عَدْوًا : مِنَ العُدْوَانِ . وَقَالَ مُجَاهِدٌ :

يُعَجِّلُ اللهُ لِلنَّاسِ الشَّرَّ اسْتِعْجَالَهُمْ بِالْخَيْرِ. قَوْلُ الْإِنْسَانِ لِوَلَدِهِ وَمَالِهِ إِذَا غَضِبَ: اللَّهُمَّ لَا تُبَارِكْ فِيهِ وَالْعَنْهُ. ـ لَقُضِيَ إِلَيْهِمْ أَجَلُهُمْ ـ: لَأَهْلَكَ مَنْ دُعِيَ عَلَيْهِ وَلَأَمَاتَهُ ـ لِلَّذِينَ أَحْسَنُوا الحُسْنَى مِثْلُهَا ـ حُسْنَى. وَزِيَادَةٌ: مَغْفِرَةٌ وَرِضْوَانٌ. وَقَالَ غَيْرُهُ: النَّظَرُ إِلَى وَجْهِهِ. الْكِبْرِيَاءُ: المُلْكُ.

(153) CHAPTER. And We took the children of Isrāel across the sea, and Pharaoh and his hosts followed (chased) them in oppression and enmity till when the drowning overtook him, he said, "I believe that none has the right to be worshipped except Him, in Whom the children of Isrāel believe, and I am one of the Muslims. (those who surrender to Allāh)". (10:90)

بابٌ ـ وَجَاوَزْنَا بِبَنِي إِسْرَائِيلَ الْبَحْرَ فَأَتْبَعَهُمْ فِرْعَوْنُ وَجُنُودُهُ بَغْيًا وَعَدْوًا حَتَّى إِذَا أَدْرَكَهُ الْغَرَقُ قَالَ آمَنْتُ أَنَّهُ لَا إِلَهَ إِلَّا الَّذِي آمَنَتْ بِهِ بَنُو إِسْرَائِيلَ وَأَنَا مِنَ الْمُسْلِمِينَ ـ نُنَجِّيكَ: عَلَى نَجْوَةٍ مِنَ الْأَرْضِ، وَهُوَ النَّشَزُ، الْمَكَانُ الْمُرْتَفِعُ.

202. Narrated Ibn 'Abbās: When the Prophet ﷺ arrived at Medīna, the Jews were observing the fast on 'Āshūra' (10th of Muḥarram) and they said, "This is the day when Moses became victorious over Pharoah," On that, the Prophet ﷺ said to his companions, "You (Muslims) have more right to celebrate Moses' victory than they have, so observe the fast on this day."

٢٠٢ ـ حَدَّثَنِي مُحَمَّدُ بْنُ بَشَّارٍ: حَدَّثَنَا غُنْدَرٌ: حَدَّثَنَا شُعْبَةُ، عَنْ أَبِي بِشْرٍ، عَنْ سَعِيدِ بْنِ جُبَيْرٍ، عَنِ ابْنِ عَبَّاسٍ قَالَ: قَدِمَ النَّبِيُّ صَلَّى اللهُ عَلَيْهِ وَسَلَّمَ الْمَدِينَةَ وَالْيَهُودُ تَصُومُ عَاشُورَاءَ فَقَالُوا: هَذَا يَوْمٌ ظَهَرَ فِيهِ مُوسَى عَلَى فِرْعَوْنَ. فَقَالَ النَّبِيُّ صَلَّى اللهُ عَلَيْهِ وَسَلَّمَ لِأَصْحَابِهِ: أَنْتُمْ أَحَقُّ بِمُوسَى

مِنْهُمْ فَصُومُوا .

SŪRAH-HŪD (No. XI)

In the Name of Allāh, the Most Beneficent, the Most Merciful

سورة هود

بِسْمِ اللهِ الرَّحْمَنِ الرَّحِيمِ

قَالَ ابنُ عَبَّاسٍ : عَصِيبٌ : شَدِيدٌ . لا جَرَمَ : بَلَى . وَقَالَ غَيْرُهُ : وَحَاقَ : نَزَلَ : يَحِيقُ : يَنْزِلُ . يَئُوسٌ : فَعُولٌ مِنْ يَئِسْتُ . وَقَالَ مُجَاهِدٌ : تَبْتَئِسْ : تَحْزَنْ . يَثْنُونَ صُدُورَهُمْ : شَكٌّ وَامْتِرَاءٌ فِى الحَقِّ . لِيَسْتَخْفُوا مِنْهُ : مِنَ اللهِ إِنِ اسْتَطَاعُوا . وَقَالَ أَبُو مَيْسَرَةَ : الأَوَّاهُ : الرَّحِيمُ بِالحَبَشِيَّةِ . وَقَالَ ابنُ عَبَّاسٍ : بَادِيَ الرأيِ : مَا ظَهَرَ لَنَا . وَقَالَ مُجَاهِدٌ : الجُودِيُّ بِالجَزِيرَةِ . وَقَالَ الحَسَنُ - إِنَّكَ لأَنْتَ الحَلِيمُ - يَسْتَهْزِئُونَ بِهِ . وَقَالَ ابنُ عَبَّاسٍ : أَقْلِعِى : أَمْسِكِى . عَصِيبٌ : شَدِيدٌ . لا جَرَمَ : بَلَى . وَفَارَ التَّنُّورُ : نَبَعَ المَاءُ . وَقَالَ عِكْرِمَةُ : وَجْهُ الأَرْضِ .

(154) CHAPTER. No doubt! They fold up their breasts that they may hide from Him. Surely! Even when they cover themselves with their garments, He knows what they conceal, and what they reveal;

بَاب - أَلا إِنَّهُمْ يَثْنُونَ صُدُورَهُمْ لِيَسْتَخْفُوا مِنْهُ أَلا حِينَ يَسْتَغْشُونَ ثِيَابَهُمْ يَعْلَمُ مَا يُسِرُّونَ وَمَا يُعْلِنُونَ إِنَّهُ عَلِيمٌ بِذَاتِ الصُّدُورِ - وَقَالَ غَيْرُهُ :

Verily, He knows well the (innermost secrets) of the breasts." (11:5)

وَحاقَ: نَزَلَ. يَحِيقُ: يَنْزِلُ. يَئُوسٌ: فَعُولٌ مِنْ يَئِسْتُ. وَقَالَ مُجَاهِدٌ: تَبْتَئِسْ: تَحْزَنْ. يَثْنُونَ صُدُورَهُمْ: شَكٌّ وَامْتِرَاءٌ فِي الحَقِّ. لِيَسْتَخْفُوا مِنْهُ: مِنَ اللهِ إِنِ اسْتَطَاعُوا.

203. Narrated Muḥammad bin 'Abbād bin Ja'far that he heard Ibn 'Abbās reciting:—

> No doubt! They fold up their breasts." (11:5)

and asked him about its explanation. He said, "Some people used to hide themselves while answering the call of nature in an open space lest they be exposed to the sky, and also when they had sexual relation with their wives in an open space lest they be exposed to the sky, so the above revelation was sent down regarding them."

٢٠٣ - حدَّثنا الحَسَنُ بنُ مُحَمَّدِ ابنِ صَبَّاحٍ: حدَّثنا حَجَّاجٌ قالَ: قالَ ابنُ جُرَيْجٍ: أخبرَني مُحَمَّدُ بنُ عَبَّادِ بنِ جَعْفَرٍ: أنَّهُ سَمِعَ ابنَ عَبَّاسٍ يَقرأُ. ألا إنَّهُمْ يَثْنُونَ صُدُورَهُمْ - قالَ: سألتُهُ عَنْها فقالَ: أُنَاسٌ كانُوا يَسْتَخْفُونَ أنْ يَتَخَلَّوْا فَيُفْضُوا إلى السَّماءِ وأنْ يُجامِعُوا نِساءَهُمْ فَيُفْضُوا إلى السَّماءِ. فنَزَلَ ذَلكَ فيهِمْ.

204. Narrated Muḥammad bin 'Abbād bin Ja'far: Ibn 'Abbās recited.

> No doubt! They fold up their breasts.'

I said, "O Abal 'Abbās! What is meant by "They fold up their breasts?' " He said, "A man used to feel shy on having sexual relation with his wife or on answering the call of nature (in an open space) so this Verse was revealed:—

> No doubt! They fold up their breasts. ' "

٢٠٤ - حدَّثني إبْرَاهِيمُ بنُ مُوسَى: أخبرَنا هِشامٌ، عَنِ ابنِ جُرَيْجٍ. وأخبرَني مُحَمَّدُ بنُ عَبَّادِ ابنِ جَعْفَرٍ: أنَّ ابنَ عَبَّاسٍ قرأَ - ألا إنَّهُمْ يَثْنُونَ صُدُورَهُمْ - قُلْتُ: يا أبا العَبَّاسِ، ما يَثْنُونَ صُدُورَهُمْ؟ قالَ: كانَ الرَّجُلُ يُجامِعُ امرأتَهُ فيَسْتَحي أوْ يَتَخَلَّى فيَسْتَحي، فنَزَلَتْ - ألا إنَّهُمْ يَثْنُونَ صُدُورَهُمْ -.

205. Narrated 'Amr: Ibn 'Abbās recited:–

> No doubt! They fold up their breasts in order to hide from Him. Surely! Even when they cover themselves with their garments......' "
>
> (11:5)

٢٠٥ - حَدَّثَنَا الحُمَيْدِيُّ: حَدَّثَنَا سُفْيَانُ: حَدَّثَنَا عَمْرٌو قَالَ: قَرَأَ ابنُ عَبَّاسٍ - أَلا إِنَّهُمْ يَثْنُونَ صُدُورَهُمْ لِيَسْتَخْفُوا مِنْهُ أَلا حِينَ يَسْتَغْشُونَ ثِيَابَهُمْ - وَقَالَ غَيْرُهُ عَنِ ابنِ عَبَّاسٍ: يَسْتَغْشُونَ يُغَطُّونَ رُءُوسَهُمْ. سِيءَ بِهِمْ: سَاءَ ظَنُّهُ بِقَوْمِهِ، وَضَاقَ بِهِمْ بِأَضْيَافِهِ. بِقِطْعٍ مِنَ اللَّيْلِ: بِسَوَادٍ، إِلَيْهِ أُنِيبُ: أَرْجِعُ ..

(155) CHAPTER. The Statement of Allāh :–

> 'And His Throne was over the water.' (11:7)

بَابُ قَوْلِهِ - وَكَانَ عَرْشُهُ عَلَى المَاءِ -

206. Narrated Abū Huraira : Allāh's Messenger said, "Allāh said, 'Spend (O man), and I shall spend on you. ' " He also said, "Allāh's Hand is full, and (its fullness) is not affected by the continuous spending night and day." He also said, "Do you see what He has spent since He created the Heavens and the Earth? Nevertheless, what is in His Hand is not decreased, and His Throne was over the water; and in His Hand there is the balance (of justice) whereby He raises and lowers (people)."

٢٠٦ - حَدَّثَنَا أَبُو اليَمَانِ: أَخْبَرَنَا شُعَيْبٌ: حَدَّثَنَا أَبُو الزِّنَادِ، عَنِ الأَعْرَجِ، عَنْ أَبِي هُرَيْرَةَ رَضِيَ اللهُ عَنْهُ أَنَّ رَسُولَ اللهِ صلى الله عليه وسلم قَالَ: قَالَ اللهُ عَزَّ وَجَلَّ: أَنْفِقْ أُنْفِقْ عَلَيْكَ، وَقَالَ: يَدُ اللهِ مَلأَى لا تَغِيضُهَا نَفَقَةٌ سَحَّاءُ: اللَّيْلَ وَالنَّهَارَ. وَقَالَ: أَرَأَيْتُمْ مَا أَنْفَقَ مُنْذُ خَلَقَ السَّمَاءَ وَالأَرْضَ فَإِنَّهُ لَمْ يَغِضْ مَا فِي يَدِهِ وَكَانَ عَرْشُهُ عَلَى المَاءِ، وَبِيَدِهِ المِيزَانُ يَخْفِضُ وَيَرْفَعُ. اعْتَرَاكَ، افْتَعَلْتَ مِنْ عَرَوْتُهُ أَيْ أَصَبْتُهُ. وَمِنْهُ يَعْرُوهُ وَاعْتَرَانِي.

آخِذٌ بِناصِيَتِها أىْ فى مُلْكِهِ وسُلْطانِهِ. عَنِيدٌ وعَنُودٌ وعانِدٌ واحدٌ. هُوَ تأكِيدُ التَّجَبُّرِ، ويَقُولُ الأشْهادُ واحِدُهُ شاهِدٌ مِثْلُ صاحِبٍ وأصحَابٍ. اسْتَعْمَرَكُمْ: جَعَلَكُمْ عُمَّارًا، أعْمَرْتُهُ الدَّارَ فَهِىَ عُمْرَى: جَعَلْتُها لهُ. نَكِرَهُمْ وأنْكَرَهُمْ واسْتَنْكَرَهُمْ واحِدٌ. حَمِيدٌ مَجِيدٌ: كأنَّهُ فَعِيلٌ مِنْ ماجِدٍ. مَحْمُودٌ: مِنْ حَمِدَ. سِجِّيلٌ: الشَّدِيدُ الكَبِيرُ، سِجِّيلٌ وسِجِّينٌ واحِدٌ واللامُ والنُّونُ أُخْتانِ، وقالَ تَمِيمُ بنُ مُقْبِلٍ:

وَرَجْلَةٍ يَضْرِبُونَ البَيْضَ ضاحِيَةً

ضَرْبًا تَواصَى بهِ الأبْطالُ سِجِّينا

ـ وإلى مَدْيَنَ أخاهُمْ شُعَيْبا ـ أىْ إلى أهْلِ مَدْيَنَ لأنَّ مَدْيَنَ بَلَدٌ. ومِثْلُهُ ـ واسألِ القَرْيَةَ ـ واسألِ العِيرَ ـ يَعْنِى أهْلَ القَرْيَةِ والعِيرِ ـ ورَاءَكُمْ ظِهْرِيًّا ـ يَقُولُ لمْ تَلْتَفِتُوا إلَيْهِ، ويُقالُ إذا لمْ يَقْضِ الرَّجُلُ حاجَتَهُ ظَهَرْتَ لحاجَتِى وجَعَلْتَنِى ظِهْرِيًّا. والظِّهْرِىُّ هاهُنا: أنْ تأخُذَ مَعَكَ دابَّةً أوْ وِعاءً تَسْتَظْهِرُ بهِ. أرَاذِلُنا: سُقاطُنا. إجْرامِى: هُوَ مَصْدَرٌ مِنْ أجْرَمْتَ، وبَعْضُهُمْ يَقُولُ: جَرَمْتُ. الفُلْكُ والفَلَكُ واحِدٌ وهِىَ السَّفِينَةُ والسُّفُنُ. مَجْرَاها: مَدْفَعُها، وهُوَ مَصْدَرُ أجْرَيْتَ.

وأرسيت: حبست. ويقرأ مجراها
من جرت هي - ومرساها - من رست.
ومجريها ومرسيها - من فعل بها.
الراسيات: ثابتات

(156) CHAPTER. The Statement of Allāh تعالى :–

'The witnesses will say: These are the ones who lied against their Lord......' (11:18)

باب قوله - ويقول الأشهاد
هؤلاء الذين كذبوا - الآية. وواحد
الأشهاد شاهد - مثل صاحب
وأصحاب.

207. Narrated Ṣafwān bin Muḥriz: While Ibn 'Umar was performing the Ṭawāf (around the Ka'ba), a man came up to him and said, "O Abū 'Abdur-Raḥmān!" or said, "O Ibn 'Umar! Did you hear anything from the Prophet ﷺ about An-Najwa?" (1) Ibn 'Umar said, "I heard the Prophet ﷺ saying, 'The Believer will be brought near his Lord.' " (Hishām, a subnarrator said, reporting the Prophet's words), "The believer will come near (his Lord) till his Lord covers him with His screen and makes him confess his sins. (Allāh will ask him), 'Do you know (that you did) 'such-and-such sin?" He will say twice, 'Yes, I do.' Then Allāh will say, 'I concealed it in the world and I forgive it for you today.' Then the record of his good deeds will be folded up.(2) As for the others or the disbelievers, it will be announced

٢٠٧ - حدثنا مسدد: حدثنا
يزيد بن زريع: حدثنا سعيد وهشام
قالا: حدثنا قتادة، عن صفوان بن
محرز قال: بينا ابن عمر يطوف إذ
عرض رجل فقال: يا أبا عبد الرحمن،
أو قال يا ابن عمر، هل سمعت
النبي صلى الله عليه وسلم في النجوى؟
فقال: سمعت النبي صلى الله عليه وسلم
يقول: يدنى المؤمن من ربه. وقال
هشام: يدنو المؤمن حتى يضع عليه
كنفه فيقرره بذنوبه. تعرف ذنب
كذا؟ يقول: أعرف، مرتين.
فيقول سترتها في الدنيا وأغفرها لك

(1) See the glossary.
(2) See Ḥadith No. 621, Vol 3 (Then the Book of his good deeds will be given to him).

publicly before the witnesses: 'These are ones who lied against their Lord.' "

اليوم . ثم تطوى صحيفة حسناته . وأما الآخرون أو الكفار فينادى على رءوس الأشهاد : هؤلاء الذين كذبوا على ربهم . وقال شيبان عن قتادة : حدثنا صفوان .

(157) CHAPTER. The Statement of Allāh ﷻ :-

'Such is the seizure of your Lord when He seizes communities in the midst of their wrong: Painful indeed, and severe is His seizure.

(11:102)

باب قوله ـ وكذلك أخذ ربك إذا أخذ القرى وهى ظالمة إن أخذه أليم شديد ـ . الرفد المرفود : العون المعين ، رفدته : أعنته . تركنوا : تميلوا ـ فلولا كان ـ فهلا كان . أترفوا : أهلكوا . وقال ابن عباس : زفير وشهيق : شديد وصوت ضعيف .

208. Narrated Abū Mūsā (رضي الله عنه) : Allāh's Messenger ﷺ said, "Allāh gives respite to the oppressor, but when He takes him over, He never releases him." Then he recited:—

"Such is the seizure of your Lord when He seizes (population of) towns in the midst of their wrong: Painful indeed, and severe is His seizure.'

(11:102)

٢٠٨ ـ حدثنا صدقة بن الفضل : أخبرنا أبو معاوية : حدثنا بريد بن أبى بردة ، عن أبى بردة عن أبى موسى رضى الله عنه قال : قال رسول الله صلى الله عليه وسلم : إن الله ليملى للظالم حتى إذا أخذه لم يفلته ، قال : ثم قرأ ـ وكذلك أخذ ربك إذا أخذ القرى وهى ظالمة إن أخذه أليم شديد ـ .

(158) CHAPTER. The Statement of Allāh ﷻ :-

باب قوله ـ وأقم الصلاة طرفى النهار وزلفا من الليل إن الحسنات

'And offer prayers (1) perfectly at the two ends of the day and in some hours of the night; (i.e. five (5) compulsory prayers). Verily, the good deeds remove the evil deeds (Small Sins)...... (11:114)

يُذْهِبْنَ السَّيِّئَاتِ ـ الآيَةَ وزُلَفًا : سَاعَاتٍ بَعْدَ سَاعَاتٍ . وَمِنْهُ سُمِّيَتِ المُزْدَلِفَةُ . الزُّلَفُ : مَنْزِلَةٌ بَعْدَ مَنْزِلَةٍ . وأمَّا زُلْفَى فَمَصْدَرٌ مِنَ القُرْبَى . ازْدَلَفُوا : اجْتَمَعُوا . أزْلَفْنَا : جَمَعْنَا .

209. Narrated Ibn Mas'ūd : A man kissed a woman and then came to Allāh's Messenger and told him of that, so this Divine Inspiration was revealed to the Prophet :-

'And offer Prayers (1) perfectly
at the two ends of the day,
and in some hours of the night;
(i.e. (five) compulsory prayers).
Verily, the good deeds
remove the evil deeds (small sins)
That is a reminder for the mindful.'
(11:114)

The man said, "Is this instruction for me only ?" The Prophet said, "It is for all those of my followers who encounter a similar situation."

٢٠٩ ـ حَدَّثَنَا مُسَدَّدٌ : حَدَّثَنَا يَزِيدُ بنُ زُرَيْعٍ : حَدَّثَنَا سُلَيْمَانُ التَّيْمِيُّ ، عَنْ أبي عُثْمَانَ ، عَنِ ابنِ مَسْعُودٍ رَضِيَ اللهُ تَعَالَى عَنْهُ أنَّ رَجُلاً أصَابَ مِنَ امْرَأةٍ قُبْلَةً فَأتَى رَسُولَ اللهِ صلى اللهُ عليهِ وسلَّمَ فَذَكَرَ ذَلِكَ لَهُ فَأُنْزِلَتْ عَلَيْهِ ـ وأقِمِ الصَّلاةَ طَرَفَيِ النَّهَارِ وَزُلَفًا مِنَ اللَّيْلِ إنَّ الحَسَنَاتِ يُذْهِبْنَ السَّيِّئَاتِ ذَلِكَ ذِكْرَى لِلذَّاكِرِينَ ـ قَالَ الرَّجُلُ : ألِي هَذِهِ ؟ قَالَ : لِمَنْ عَمِلَ بِهَا مِنْ أُمَّتِي .

(1) See "Iqāmat-aṣ-ṣalāt" in the glossary.

SŪRAT YŪSUF (JOSEPH No. 12)

**In the Name of Allāh,
the Most Beneficent, the Most Merciful**

سورة يوسف

بِسْمِ اللهِ الرَّحْمَنِ الرَّحِيمِ

وَقَالَ فُضَيْلٌ، عَنْ حُصَيْنٍ، عَنْ
مُجَاهِدٍ: مُتَّكَأً: الأُتْرُجُّ بِالحَبَشِيَّةِ
مُتْكًا. وَقَالَ ابْنُ عُيَيْنَةَ، عَنْ رَجُلٍ،
عَنْ مُجَاهِدٍ: مُتْكًا: كُلُّ شَيْءٍ قُطِعَ
بِالسِّكِّينِ. وَقَالَ قَتَادَةُ: لَذُو عِلْمٍ:
عَامِلٌ بِمَا عَلِمَ. وَقَالَ سَعِيدُ بْنُ جُبَيْرٍ:
صُوَاعَ: مَكُّوكُ الفَارِسِيِّ الَّذِى يَلْتَقِى
طَرَفَاهُ، كَانَتْ تَشْرَبُ بِهِ الأَعَاجِمُ.
وَقَالَ ابْنُ عَبَّاسٍ: تُفَنِّدُونِ تُجَهِّلُونِ.
وَقَالَ غَيْرُهُ: غَيَابَةُ الجُبِّ: كُلُّ شَيْءٍ
غَيَّبَ عَنْكَ شَيْئًا فَهُوَ غَيَابَةٌ. وَالجُبُّ
الرَّكِيَّةُ الَّتِى لَمْ تُطْوَ. بِمُؤْمِنٍ لَنَا:
بِمُصَدِّقٍ. أَشُدَّهُ قَبْلَ أَنْ يَأْخُذَ فِى
النُّقْصَانِ يُقَالُ بَلَغَ أَشُدَّهُ وَبَلَغُوا
أَشُدَّهُمْ. وَقَالَ بَعْضُهُمْ: وَاحِدُهَا
شَدٌّ. وَالمُتَّكَأُ مَا اتَّكَأْتَ عَلَيْهِ لِشَرَابٍ
أَوْ لِحَدِيثٍ أَوْ لِطَعَامٍ، وَأَبْطَلَ الَّذِى
قَالَ الأُتْرُجُّ وَلَيْسَ فِى كَلَامِ العَرَبِ
الأُتْرُجُّ فَلَمَّا احْتَجَّ عَلَيْهِمْ بِأَنَّهُ
المُتَّكَأُ مِنْ نَمَارِقَ فَرُّوا إِلَى شَرٍّ مِنْهُ،
فَقَالُوا إِنَّمَا هُوَ المُتْكُ سَاكِنَةَ التَّاءِ،
وَإِنَّمَا المُتْكُ طَرَفُ البَظْرِ. وَمِنْ
ذَلِكَ قِيلَ لَهَا مُتَّكَأٌ وَأَيْنَ المُتَّكَأُ؟
فَإِنْ كَانَ ثَمَّ أُتْرُجٌّ فَإِنَّهُ بَعْدَ المُتَّكَا.

شَغَفَهَا: يُقَالُ بَلَغَ إلى شِغَافِهَا، وَهُوَ غِلَافُ قَلْبِهَا، وَأَمَّا شَغَفَهَا: فَمِنَ الْمَشْغُوفِ. أَصْبُ إِلَيْهِنَّ: أَمِيلُ إِلَيْهِنَّ حُبًّا. أَضْغَاثُ أَحْلَامٍ: مَالَا تَأْوِيلَ لَهُ. والضِّغْثُ مِلْءُ الْيَدِ مِنْ حَشِيشٍ وَمَا أَشْبَهَهُ وَمِنْهُ ـ وَخُذْ بِيَدِكَ ضِغْثًا ـ لَامِنْ قَوْلِهِ أَضْغَاثُ أَحْلَامٍ، وَاحِدُهَا ضِغْثٌ. نَمِيرُ مِنَ الْمِيرَةِ. وَنَزْدَادُ كَيْلَ بَعِيرٍ: مَا يَحْمِلُ بَعِيرٌ. أَوَى إِلَيْهِ: ضَمَّ إِلَيْهِ. السِّقَايَةُ: مِكْيَالٌ. اسْتَيْأَسُوا: يَئِسُوا. وَلَا تَيْأَسُوا مِنْ رَوْحِ اللَّهِ مَعْنَاهُ الرَّجَاءُ. خَلَصُوا نَجِيًّا: اعْتَزَلُوا نَجِيًّا، وَالْجَمْعُ أَنْجِيَةٌ، يَتَنَاجَوْنَ الْوَاحِدُ نَجِيٌّ وَالِاثْنَانِ وَالْجَمْعُ نَجِيٌّ وَأَنْجِيَةٌ. تَفْتَؤُ: لَا تَزَالُ. حَرَضًا: مُحْرَضًا: بُذِّبِكَ الْهَمُّ. تَحَسَّسُوا: تَخَبَّرُوا. مُزْجَاةٌ: قَلِيلَةٌ. غَاشِيَةٌ مِنْ عَذَابِ اللَّهِ: عَامَّةٌ مُجَلِّلَةٌ.

بَابُ قَوْلِهِ ـ وَيُتِمُّ نِعْمَتَهُ عَلَيْكَ وَعَلَى آلِ يَعْقُوبَ ـ الْآيَةَ.

(159) CHAPTER. The Statement of Allāh ﷻ :—
'And perfect His favour on you and on the offspring of Jacob......'
(12:6)

٢١٠ ـ حَدَّثَنَا عَبْدُ اللَّهِ بْنُ مُحَمَّدٍ: حَدَّثَنَا عَبْدُ الصَّمَدِ، عَنْ عَبْدِ الرَّحْمَنِ

210. Narrated 'Abdullāh bin 'Umar ؓ : The Prophet ﷺ said, "The honourable, the son of the honourable the son of the honourable, i.e. Joseph, the son of Jacob, the son of Isaac, the son of Abraham."

ابن عبد الله بن دينار، عن أبيه: عن عبد الله بن عمر رضي الله عنهما، عن النبي صلى الله عليه وسلم قال: الكريم ابن الكريم ابن الكريم ابن الكريم يوسف بن يعقوب بن إسحاق بن إبراهيم

(160) CHAPTER. The Statement of Allāh. :–

Verily, in Joseph and his brothers, there have been signs for those who ask. (12:7)

باب قوله - لقد كان في يوسف وإخوته آيات للسائلين -.

211. Narrated Abū Huraira : Allāh's Messenger was asked, "Who are the most honourable of the people?" The Prophet said, "The most honourable of them in Allāh's Sight are those who keep their duty to Allāh and fear Him. They said, "We do not ask you about that." He said, "Then the most honourable of the people is Joseph, Allāh's prophet, the son of Allāh's prophet, the son of Allāh's prophet, the son of Allāh's Khalīl (1) i.e. Abraham)." They said, "We do not ask you about that." The Prophet said, Do you ask about (the virtues of)the ancestry of the Arabs?" They said, "Yes," He said, "Those who were the best amongst you in the Pre-Islāmic Period are the

٢١١ - حدثني محمد: أخبرنا عبدة، عن عبيد الله، عن سعيد بن أبي سعيد، عن أبي هريرة رضي الله تعالى عنه قال: سئل رسول الله صلى الله عليه وسلم: أي الناس أكرم؟ قال: أكرمهم عند الله أتقاهم، قالوا: ليس عن هذا نسألك، قال: فأكرم الناس يوسف نبي الله ابن نبي الله ابن نبي الله ابن خليل الله. قالوا ليس عن هذا نسألك، قال فعن معادن العرب تسألوني؟ قالوا: نعم، قال:

(1) Khalīl: See the glossary.

best amongst you in Islām if they comprehend (the Islāmic Religion)."

فخيارُكم في الجاهلية خيارُكم في الإسلام إذا فقهوا. تابعه أبو أسامة، عن عبيد الله

(161) CHAPTER. The Statement of Allāh ﷻ :—

'He said, "Nay but your minds have made up a tale. So (for me), patience is most fitting. And it is Allāh (Alone) Whose help can be sought against that which you assert." . (12:18)

بابُ قوله - قالَ بلْ سوَّلتْ لكمْ أنفسكمْ أمرًا فصبرٌ جميلٌ - سوَّلتْ: زيَّنتْ.

212. Narrated Az-Zuhrī: 'Urwa bin Az-Zubair, Sa'īd bin Al-Musaiyab, 'Al-Qama bin Waqqāṣ and 'Ubaidullāh bin 'Abdullāh related the narration of 'Āisha, the wife the Prophet ﷺ, when the slanderers had said about her what they had said and Allāh later declared her innocence. Each of them related a part of the narration (wherein) the Prophet ﷺ said (to 'Āisha). "If you are innocent, then Allāh will declare your innocence: but if you have committed a sin, then ask for Allāh's Forgiveness and repent to him." 'Āisha said, "By Allāh, I find no example for my case except that of Joseph's father (when he said), 'So (for me) patience is most fitting.' " Then Allāh revealed the ten Verses:—
Verily! those who spread the slander are a gang amongst you.....'
(24:11)

٢١٢ - حدَّثنا عبدُ العزيزِ بنُ عبدِ الله: حدَّثنا إبراهيمُ بنُ سعدٍ، عنْ صالحٍ، عنِ ابنِ شهابٍ، قالَ: وحدَّثنا الحجَّاجُ: حدَّثنا عبدُ الله بنُ عمرَ النُّميريُّ: حدَّثنا يونسُ بنُ يزيدَ الأيليُّ قالَ: سمعتُ الزُّهريَّ: سمعتُ عروةَ بنَ الزُّبيرِ، وسعيدَ بنَ المسيَّبِ، وعلقمةَ بنَ وقَّاصٍ، وعبيدَ الله بنَ عبدِ الله، عنْ حديثِ عائشةَ زوجِ النَّبيِّ صلى اللهُ عليهِ وسلَّمَ حينَ قالَ لها أهلُ الإفكِ ما قالوا فبرَّأها اللهُ. كلٌّ حدَّثني طائفةً منَ الحديثِ. قالَ النَّبيُّ صلى اللهُ عليهِ وسلَّمَ: إنْ كنتِ بريئةً فسيبرِّئكِ اللهُ، وإنْ كنتِ ألممتِ بذنبٍ فاستغفري اللهَ وتوبي

إلَيْهِ . قُلْتُ : إنِّي وَاللهِ لا أجِدُ مَثَلاً إلاَّ أبا يُوسُفَ - فَصَبْرٌ جَمِيلٌ وَاللهُ المُسْتَعانُ عَلى ما تَصِفُونَ - وأنْزَلَ اللهُ - إنْ الَّذينَ جاءُوا بالإفْكِ عُصْبَةٌ مِنْكُمْ - العَشْرَ الآياتِ - .

213. Narrated Um Rūmān who was 'Āisha's mother: While I was with 'Āisha, 'Āisha got fever, whereupon the Prophet said, "Probably her fever is caused by the story related by the people (about her)." I said, "Yes." Then 'Āisha sat up and said, "My example and your example is similar to that of Jacob and his sons:—

> 'Nay, but your minds have made up a tale. So (for me) patience is most fitting. It is Allāh (alone) Whose help can be sought against that which you assert.'
>
> (12:18)

٢١٣ - حدَّثَنا مُوسَى : حدَّثَنا أبو عَوانَةَ ، عَنْ حُصَيْنٍ ، عَنْ أبي وَائِلٍ : حدَّثَني مَسْرُوقُ بنُ الأجْدَعِ قالَ : حَدَّثَتْني أُمُّ رُومانَ ، وَهِيَ أُمُّ عائِشَةَ قالَتْ : بَيْنا أنا وَعائِشَةُ أخَذَتْها الحُمَّى ، فَقالَ النَّبِيُّ صلى اللهُ عليهِ وسلَّم : لَعَلَّ في حَديثٍ تُحُدِّثَ ، قالَتْ : نَعَمْ ، وَقَعَدَتْ عائِشَةُ ، قالَتْ : مَثَلي وَمَثَلُكُمْ كَيَعْقُوبَ وَبَنِيهِ - بَلْ سَوَّلَتْ لَكُمْ أنْفُسُكُمْ أمْراً فَصَبْرٌ جَميلٌ وَاللهُ المُسْتَعانُ عَلى ما تَصِفُونَ - .

(162) CHAPTER. The Statement of Allāh :—

> 'But she in whose house he was, sought to seduce him (to do an evil act). She closed the doors and said, "Now come you?" ' (12:23)

بابُ قَوْلِهِ - وَرَاوَدَتْهُ الَّتي هُوَ في بَيْتِها عَنْ نَفْسِهِ وَغَلَّقَتِ الأبْوابَ وَقالَتْ هَيْتَ لكَ - وَقالَ عِكْرِمَةُ : هَيْتَ لَكَ بالحَوْرَانيةِ هَلُمَّ . وَقالَ ابنُ جُبَيْرٍ : تَعالَهْ .

214. Narrated Abū Wā'il: 'Abdullāh bin Mas'ūd recited "Haita laka (Come

٢١٤ - حدَّثَني أحْمَدُ بنُ سَعيدٍ : حدَّثَنا بِشْرُ بنُ عُمَرَ : حدَّثَنا شُعْبَةُ ،

you)," and added, "We recite it as we were taught it."

عَنْ سُلَيْمانَ ، عَنْ أبي وَائِلٍ ، عَنْ عَبْدِ اللهِ بنِ مَسْعُودٍ قالَ : هَيْتَ لَكَ ، قالَ : وإنَّما نَقْرَؤُها كَما عُلِّمْناها. مَثْواهُ : مُقامُهُ . وأَلْفَيا : وَجَدا ، أَلْفَوْا آباءَهُمْ وأَلْفَيْنا. وعَنِ ابنِ مَسْعُودٍ : بَلْ عَجِبْتَ وَيَسْخَرُونَ .

215. Narrated Abdullāh (bin Mas'ūd): When the Prophet ﷺ realized that the Quraish had delayed in embracing Islām, he said, "O Allāh! Protect me against their evil by afflicting them with seven (years of famine) like the seven years of (Prophet) Joseph." So they were struck with a year of famine that destroyed everything till they had to eat bones, and till a man would look towards the sky and see something like smoke between him and it. Allāh said:—

> 'Then watch you (O Muhammad) for the day when the sky will produce a kind of smoke plainly visible.' (44:10)

And Allāh further said:—

> "Verily! We shall withdraw the punishment a little, Verily you will return (to disbelief)." (44:15)

(Will Allāh relieve them from torture on the Day of Resurrection?) (The punishment of) the smoke had passed and Al-Batsha (the destruction of the pagans in the Badr battle) had passed too.

٢١٥ - حدَّثَنا الحُمَيْدِيُّ : حدَّثَنا سُفْيانُ ، عَنِ الأعْمَشِ ، عَنْ مُسْلِمٍ : عَنْ مَسْرُوقٍ ، عَنْ عَبْدِ اللهِ رَضِيَ اللهُ تَعالَى عَنْهُ أنَّ قُرَيْشاً لمَّا أبْطَئُوا عَنِ النَّبِيِّ صلَّى اللهُ عليه وسلَّم بالإسْلامِ قالَ : اللَّهُمَّ اكْفِنِيهِمْ بِسَبْعٍ كَسَبْعِ يُوسُفَ . فأصابَتْهُمْ سَنَةٌ حَصَّتْ كُلَّ شَيْءٍ حتَّى أكَلُوا العِظامَ حتَّى جَعَلَ الرَّجُلُ يَنْظُرُ إلى السَّماءِ فَيَرَى بَيْنَهُ وبَيْنَها مِثْلَ الدُّخانِ . قالَ اللهُ - فارْتَقِبْ يَوْمَ تأتِي السَّماءُ بِدُخانٍ مُبِينٍ - قالَ اللهُ - إنَّا كاشِفُوا العَذابِ قَلِيلاً إنَّكُمْ عائِدُونَ - أفَيُكْشَفُ عَنْهُمُ العَذابُ يَوْمَ القِيامَةِ - وقَدْ مَضَى الدُّخانُ ومَضَتِ البَطْشَةُ

(163) CHAPTER. The Statement of Allāh (تعالى) :–

'But when the messenger came to him, (Joseph) said, "Go back to your lord.....(The women said), "Allāh forbid." ' (12:50–51)

بابُ قَوْلِهِ ـ فَلَمَّا جاءَهُ الرَّسُولُ قالَ ارْجِعْ إلى رَبِّكَ ـ إلى قَوْلِهِ ـ قُلْنَ حاشَ لِلّهِ ـ حاشَ وحاشا تَنْزِيهٌ واسْتِثْناءٌ. حَصْحَصَ : وَضَحَ .

216. Narrated Abū Huraira (رضي الله عنه) : Allāh's Messenger (ﷺ) said, "May Allāh bestow His Mercy on (Prophet) Lot (عليه السلام). (When his nation troubled him) he wished if he could betake himself to some powerful support; and if I were to remain in prison for the period Joseph had remained, I would surely respond to the call; and we shall have more right (to be in doubt) than Abraham: When Allāh said to him, "Don't you believe?' Abraham said, 'Yes, (I do believe) but to be stronger in faith; (2:260)

٢١٦ ـ حدَّثَنا سَعِيدُ بنُ تَلِيدٍ : حدَّثَنا عَبْدُ الرَّحْمَنِ بنُ القاسِمِ ، عَنْ بَكْرِ بنِ مُضَرَ ، عَنْ عَمْرِو ابنِ الحارِثِ ، عَنْ يُونُسَ بنِ يَزِيدَ ، عَنِ ابنِ شِهابٍ ، عَنْ سَعِيدِ بنِ المُسَيَّبِ وأبي سَلَمَةَ بنِ عَبْدِ الرَّحْمَنِ ، عَنْ أبي هُرَيْرَةَ رَضِيَ اللهُ عَنْهُ قالَ : قالَ رَسُولُ اللهِ صلى اللهُ عليهِ وسلَّم : يَرْحَمُ اللهُ لُوطاً لَقَدْ كانَ يأوِي إلى رُكْنٍ شَدِيدٍ ولَوْ لَبِثْتُ في السِّجْنِ ما لَبِثَ يُوسُفُ لأجَبْتُ الدَّاعِيَ . ونَحْنُ أحَقُّ مِنْ إبْراهِيمَ إذْ قالَ لَهُ ـ أوَلَمْ تُؤْمِنْ قالَ بَلَى ولَكِنْ لِيَطْمَئِنَّ قَلْبِي ـ .

(164) CHAPTER. "Until when the Apostles gave up hope (of their people).' (12:110)

بابُ قَوْلِهِ ـ حَتَّى إذا اسْتَيْأسَ الرُّسُلُ .

217. Narrated 'Urwa bin Az-Zubair that when he asked 'Āisha about the statement of Allāh (تعالى) :–

٢١٧ ـ حدَّثَنا عَبْدُ العَزِيزِ بنُ عَبْدِ اللهِ : حدَّثَنا إبْراهِيمُ بنُ سَعْدٍ ، عَنْ صالِحٍ ، عَنِ ابنِ شِهابٍ قالَ :

"Until when the Messengers gave up hope (of their people)."

(12:110)

she told him (its meaning), 'Urwa added, "I said, 'Did they (Messengers) suspect that they were betrayed (by Allāh) or that they were treated as liars by (their people)?' 'Āisha said, '(They suspected) that they were treated as liars by (their people),' I said, 'But they were sure that their people treated them as liars and it was not a matter of suspicion.' She said, 'Yes, upon my life they were sure about it.' I said to her. 'So they (Messengers) suspected that they were betrayed (by Allāh).' She said, "Allāh forbid! The Messengers never suspected their Lord of such a thing.' I said, 'What about this Verse then?' She said, 'It is about the Messengers' followers who believed in their Lord and trusted their Messengers but the period of trials was prolonged and victory was delayed till the Messengers gave up all hope of converting those of the people who disbelieved them and the Messengers thought that their followers treated them as liars; thereupon Allāh's help came to them.

أخبرني عروة بن الزبير، عن عائشة رضي الله تعالى عنها قالت له وهو يسألها عن قول الله تعالى - حتى إذا استيأس الرسل - قال: قلت أكذبوا أم كذبوا؟ قالت عائشة: كذبوا. قلت: فقد استيقنوا أن قومهم كذبوهم فما هو بالظن قالت: أجل لعمري لقد استيقنوا بذلك، فقلت لها: وظنوا أنهم قد كذبوا، قالت: معاذ الله، لم تكن الرسل تظن ذلك بربها، قلت: فما هذه الآية؟ قالت: هم أتباع الرسل الذين آمنوا بربهم وصدقوهم فطال عليهم البلاء واستأخر عنهم النصر حتى إذا استيأس الرسل ممن كذبهم من قومهم، وظنت الرسل أن أتباعهم قد كذبوهم جاءهم نصر الله عند ذلك.

218. Narrated 'Urwa, "I told her ('Āisha): (Regarding the above narration), they (Messengers) were betrayed (by Allāh)." She said: Allāh forbid or said similarly.

٢١٨ - حدثنا أبو اليمان: أخبرنا شعيب، عن الزهري قال: أخبرني عروة، فقلت لعلها كذبوا مخففة، قالت: معاذ الله نحوه.

SŪRAT-AR-RA'D (THUNDER) XIII

In the Name of Allāh, the Most Beneficent, the Most Merciful

سورة الرعد

بِسْمِ اللهِ الرَّحْمَٰنِ الرَّحِيمِ

قالَ ابنُ عبّاسٍ ـ كَباسطِ كَفَّيْهِ ـ مَثَلُ
المُشْرِكِ الّذى عَبَدَ مَعَ اللهِ إلها غيرَهُ
كمَثَلِ العَطْشانِ الّذى ينْظُرُ إلى ظلّ
خيالِه فى المَاءِ مِنْ بعيدٍ وَهُوَ يُريدُ
أنْ يتَناوَلَهُ ولا يقْدِرُ. وقالَ غيرُهُ:
مُتَجاوِرَاتٌ: مُتَدانياتٌ. وقالَ غيرُهُ:
المَثُلاتُ واحِدُها مَثُلةٌ: وهيَ الأشْباهُ
والأمْثالُ. وقال إلاّ مِثْلَ أيّامِ الّذينَ
خَلَوْا. بمِقْدارٍ: بقَدَرٍ. يُقالُ
مُعَقِّباتٌ: مَلائكةٌ حَفَظَةٌ تُعَقِّبُ
الأُولى مِنْها الأُخْرَى. وَمِنْهُ قيلَ
العَقيبُ أيْ عَقَبْتُ فى أثَرِهِ. المِحالُ:
العُقُوبةُ. ـ كَباسِطِ كَفَّيْهِ إلى المَاءِ ـ
ليَقْبِضَ علَى المَاءِ. رَابِيا: مِنْ رَبا
يَرْبُو ـ أوْ مَتاعٍ زَبَدٌ مِثْلُهُ ـ المَتاعُ:
ما تَمَتَّعْتَ بهِ. جُفاءً: يُقالُ أجْفَأتِ
القِدْرُ: إذَا غَلَتْ فعَلاها الزَّبَدُ، ثُمّ
تَسْكُنُ فيَذْهَبُ الزَّبَدُ بلا مَنْفَعَةٍ
فكَذَلكَ يُمَيِّزُ الحَقُّ مِنَ الباطلِ.
المِهادُ: الفِراشُ. يَدْرَءُونَ: يَدْفَعُونَ.
دَرَأْتُهُ عنى: دَفَعْتُهُ سَلامٌ عَلَيْكُمْ:
أىْ يقُولُونَ سَلامٌ علَيْكُمْ، والمَتابُ
إلَيْهِ تَوْبَتِى. أفلَمْ ييأس: أفلَمْ
يَتَبَيَّنْ. قارِعَةٌ: داهيَةٌ. فأمْلَيْتُ:

أَمْلَتْ، مِنَ المَلَى وَالمِلاوَةِ وَمِنْهُ مَلِيًّا، وَيُقَالُ لِلْوَاسِعِ الطَّوِيلِ مِنَ الأَرْضِ: مَلَى مِنَ الأَرْضِ، مَلَى. أَشَقُّ: أَشَدُّ، مِنَ المَشَقَّةِ. مُعَقِّبٌ: مُغَيِّرٌ. وَقَالَ مُجَاهِدٌ: مُتَجَاوِرَاتٌ طَيِّبُهَا وَخَبِيثُهَا السِّبَاخُ. صِنْوَانٌ: النَّخْلَتَانِ أَوْ أَكْثَرُ فِي أَصْلٍ وَاحِدٍ. وَغَيْرُ صِنْوَانٍ: وَحْدَهَا بِمَاءٍ وَاحِدٍ، كَصَالِحِ بَنِي آدَمَ وَخَبِيثِهِمْ أَبُوهُمْ وَاحِدٌ. السَّحَابُ الثِّقَالُ: الَّذِي فِيهِ المَاءُ. كَبَاسِطِ كَفَّيْهِ إِلَى المَاءِ ـ يَدْعُو المَاءَ بِلِسَانِهِ وَيُشِيرُ إِلَيْهِ بِيَدِهِ، فَلَا يَأْتِيهِ أَبَدًا ـ فَسَالَتْ أَوْدِيَةٌ بِقَدَرِهَا ـ تَمْلَأُ بَطْنَ كُلِّ وَادٍ. زَبَدًا رَابِيًا: الزَّبَدُ السَّيْلُ. زَبَدٌ مِثْلُهُ خَبَثُ الحَدِيدِ وَالحِلْيَةِ.

(165) CHAPTER. The Statement of Allāh ﷻ :—

'Allāh does know what every female (womb) bears, and by how much the wombs fall short (of their time or number) or exceed.' (13:8)

بَابُ قَوْلِهِ ـ اللهُ يَعْلَمُ مَا تَحْمِلُ كُلُّ أُنْثَى وَمَا تَغِيضُ الأَرْحَامُ ـ غِيضَ: نُقِصَ.

219. Narrated Ibn 'Umar ؓ : Allāh's Messenger ﷺ said, "The keys of Unseen are five which none knows

٢١٩ ـ حَدَّثَنِي إِبْرَاهِيمُ بْنُ المُنْذِرِ: حَدَّثَنَا مَعْنٌ قَالَ: حَدَّثَنِي مَالِكٌ، عَنْ

عَبْدِ اللهِ بنِ دِينارٍ ، عَنِ ابنِ عُمَرَ رَضِيَ اللهُ تَعالى عَنْهُما : أنَّ رَسُولَ اللهِ صلى اللهُ عليهِ وسلَّم قالَ : مَفاتِيحُ الغَيْبِ خَمْسٌ لا يَعْلَمُها إلاَّ اللهُ : لا يَعْلَمُ ما فى غَدٍ إلاَّ اللهُ ، وَلا يَعْلَمُ ما تَغيضُ الأرْحامُ إلاَّ اللهُ ، وَلا يَعْلَمُ مَتى يأتِى المَطَرُ أحَدٌ إلاَّ اللهُ ، وَلا تَدْرِى نَفْسٌ بِأىِّ أرْضٍ تَمُوتُ ، وَلا يَعْلَمُ مَتى تَقُومُ السّاعَةُ إلاَّ اللهُ .

but Allāh: None knows what will happen tomorrow but Allāh; none knows what is in the wombs (a male child or a female) but Allāh; none knows when it will rain but Allāh; none knows at what place one will die; none knows when the Hour will be established but Allāh."

(See The Qur'ān, 31:34.")

سورة ابراهيم

بِسْمِ اللهِ الرَّحْمَنِ الرَّحِيمِ

وَقالَ ابنُ عَبّاسٍ : هادٍ : داعٍ . وَقالَ مُجاهِدٌ : صَدِيدٌ : قَيْحٌ وَدَمٌ . وَقالَ ابنُ عُيَيْنَةَ : - اذْكُرُوا نِعْمَةَ اللهِ عَلَيْكُمْ - أيادِىَ اللهِ عِنْدَكُمْ وأيّامَهُ . وَقالَ مُجاهِدٌ : مِنْ كُلِّ ما سألْتُمُوهُ : رَغِبْتُمْ إلَيْهِ فِيهِ . تَبْغُونَها عِوَجاً : تَلْتَمِسُونَ لَها عِوَجاً . وَإذْ تأذَّنَ رَبُّكُمْ : أعْلَمَكُمْ . آذَنَكُمْ . رَدُّوا أيْدِيَهُمْ فى أفْواهِهِمْ : هَذا مَثَلٌ ، كَفُّوا عَمّا أُمِرُوا بِهِ . مَقامِى : حَيْثُ يُقِيمُهُ اللهُ بَيْنَ يَدَيْهِ . مِنْ وَرائِهِ : قُدّامَهُ جَهَنَّمُ . لَكُمْ تَبَعاً : واحِدُها تابِعٌ مِثْلُ غَيَبٍ وغائِبٍ . بِمُصْرِخِكُمْ : اسْتَصْرَخَنِى

SŪRAT-ABRAHAM XIV

In the Name of Allāh, the Most Beneficent, the Most Merciful

اسْتَغَاثَنِي، يَسْتَصْرِخُهُ: مِنَ الصُّرَاخِ.
وَلَا خِلَالٌ: مَصْدَرُ خَالَلْتُهُ خِلَالًا،
وَيَجُوزُ أَيْضًا جَمْعُ خُلَّةٍ وَخِلَالٍ.
اجْتُثَّتْ: اسْتُؤْصِلَتْ.

(166) CHAPTER. The Statement of Allāh:–

"as a goodly tree whose root is firmly fixed.....' (14:24)

بَابُ قَوْلِهِ - كَشَجَرَةٍ طَيِّبَةٍ أَصْلُهَا ثَابِتٌ - الآيَةَ.

220. Narrated Ibn 'Umar : While we were with Allāh's Messenger , he said, "Tell me of a tree which resembles a Muslim man. Its leaves do not fall and it does not, and does not, and does not, (1) and it gives its fruits every now and then." It came to my mind that such a tree must be the date palm, but seeing Abū Bakr and 'Umar saying nothing, I disliked to speak. So when they did not say anything, Allāh's Messenger said, "It is the date-palm tree." When we got up (from that place), I said to 'Umar, "O my father! By Allāh, it came to my mind that it must be the datepalm tree." 'Umar said, "What prevented you from speaking" I replied, "I did not see you speaking, so I disliked to speak or say anything."

٢٢٠- حَدَّثَنِي عُبَيْدُ بْنُ إِسْمَاعِيلَ، عَنْ أَبِي أُسَامَةَ، عَنْ عُبَيْدِ اللهِ، عَنْ نَافِعٍ، عَنِ ابْنِ عُمَرَ رَضِيَ اللهُ عَنْهُمَا قَالَ: كُنَّا عِنْدَ رَسُولِ اللهِ صلى اللهُ عليه وسلَّم فَقَالَ: أَخْبِرُونِي بِشَجَرَةٍ تُشْبِهُ أَوْ كَالرَّجُلِ الْمُسْلِمِ لَا يَتَحَاتُّ وَرَقُهَا وَلَا وَلَا وَلَا، تُؤْتِي أُكُلَهَا كُلَّ حِينٍ، قَالَ ابْنُ عُمَرَ: فَوَقَعَ فِي نَفْسِي أَنَّهَا النَّخْلَةُ، ورأيْتُ أَبَا بَكْرٍ وَعُمَرَ لَا يَتَكَلَّمَانِ فَكَرِهْتُ أَنْ أَتَكَلَّمَ. فَلَمَّا لَمْ يَقُولُوا شَيْئًا قَالَ رَسُولُ اللهِ صلى اللهُ عليهِ وسلَّم: هِيَ النَّخْلَةُ. فَلَمَّا قُمْنَا

(1) The narrator seems to have forgotten what the Prophet said therefore he just repeats the expression 'does not' three times to indicate that the Prophet described the tree with three other qualities.

'Umar then said, "If you had said it, it would have been dearer to me than so-and-so."

قُلْتُ لِعُمَرَ : يا أَبَتاهُ ، وَاللهِ لَقَدْ كانَ وَقَعَ في نَفْسِي أَنَّها النَّخْلَةُ . فَقالَ : ما مَنَعَكَ أَنْ تَكَلَّمَ ؟ قالَ : لَمْ أَرَكُمْ تَكَلَّمُونَ فَكَرِهْتُ أَنْ أَتَكَلَّمَ أَوْ أَقُولَ شَيْئاً . قالَ عُمَرُ : لَأَنْ تَكُونَ قُلْتَها أَحَبُّ إِلَيَّ مِنْ كَذا وَكَذا .

(167) CHAPTER. The Statement of Allāh :–

> 'Allāh will keep firm those who believe with a Word that stands firm.' (14:27)

بابُ - يُثَبِّتُ اللهُ الَّذِينَ آمَنُوا بِالقَوْلِ الثّابِتِ - .

221. Narrated Al-Barā' bin 'Āzib: Allāh's Messenger said, "When a Muslim is questioned in his grave, he will testify that none has the right to be worshipped but Allāh and that Muḥammad is Allāh's Messenger, and that is what is meant by Allāh's Statement:–

> Allāh will keep firm those who believe with a Word that stands firm in this world and in the Hereafter.' (14:27)

٢٢١ - حَدَّثَنا أَبُو الوَلِيدِ : حَدَّثَنا شُعْبَةُ قالَ : أَخْبَرَنِي عَلْقَمَةُ بْنُ مَرْثَدٍ قالَ : سَمِعْتُ سَعْدَ بْنَ عُبَيْدَةَ ، عَنِ البَراءِ بْنِ عازِبٍ رَضِيَ اللهُ تَعالى عَنْهُ أَنَّ رَسُولَ اللهِ صلى اللهُ عليهِ وسلَّمَ قالَ : المُسْلِمُ إِذا سُئِلَ في القَبْرِ يَشْهَدُ أَنْ لا إِلٰهَ إِلَّا اللهُ ، وأَنَّ مُحَمَّداً رَسُولُ اللهِ ، فَذٰلِكَ قَوْلُهُ - يُثَبِّتُ اللهُ الَّذِينَ آمَنُوا بِالقَوْلِ الثّابِتِ في الحَياةِ الدُّنْيا وفي الآخِرَةِ . -

(168) CHAPTER. 'Have you not seen those who have changed the favour of Allāh into disbelief?' (14 ; 28)

بابٌ - أَلَمْ تَرَ إِلى الَّذِينَ بَدَّلُوا نِعْمَةَ اللهِ كُفْراً - أَلَمْ تَرَ : أَلَمْ تَعْلَمْ . كَقَوْلِهِ - أَلَمْ تَرَ إِلى الَّذِينَ خَرَجُوا -

البَوَارُ: الهَلاكُ. بارَ يَبُورُ بُورًا. قَوْمًا بُورًا: هالِكِينَ.

222. Narrated 'Aṭā': When Ibn 'Abbās heard:—

'Have you not seen those who have changed the favour of Allāh into disbelief?' (14: 28)

he said, "Those were the disbelieving pagans of Mecca."

٢٢٢ - حدَّثنا عَلِيُّ بنُ عَبْدِ اللهِ: حدَّثنا سُفْيانُ، عَنْ عَمْرٍو، عَنْ عَطاءٍ: سَمِعَ ابنَ عَبَّاسٍ - أَلَمْ تَرَ إِلى الَّذِينَ بَدَّلُوا نِعْمَةَ اللهِ كُفْرًا - قال: هُمْ كُفَّارُ أَهْلِ مَكَّةَ.

SŪRAT–AL–ḤIJR XV

In the Name of Allāh, the Most Beneficent, the Most Merciful

تفسير سورة الحجر

بِسْمِ اللهِ الرَّحْمَنِ الرَّحِيمِ

وَقالَ مُجاهِدٌ: صِراطٌ عَلَيَّ مُسْتَقِيمٌ: الحَقُّ يَرْجِعُ إِلى اللهِ، وَعَلَيْهِ طَرِيقُهُ. لَبِإِمامٍ مُبِينٍ: عَلَى الطَّرِيقِ. وَقالَ ابنُ عَبَّاسٍ: لَعَمْرُكَ: لَعَيْشُكَ. قَوْمٌ مُنْكَرُونَ: أَنْكَرَهُمْ لُوطٌ. كِتابٌ مَعْلُومٌ: أَجَلٌ. لَوْما: هَلاَّ تَأْتِينا. شِيَعٌ: أُمَمٌ وَلِلأَوْلِياءِ أَيْضًا شِيَعٌ. وَقالَ ابنُ عَبَّاسٍ: يُهْرَعُونَ: مُسْرِعِينَ. لِلْمُتَوَسِّمِينَ: لِلنَّاظِرِينَ. سُكِّرَتْ: غُشِّيَتْ. بُرُوجًا: مَنازِلَ لِلشَّمْسِ وَالقَمَرِ. لَوَاقِحَ: مَلاقِحَ مُلْقَحَةً. حَمَإٍ: جَماعَةُ حَمْأَةٍ، وَهُوَ الطِّينُ المُتَغَيِّرُ. وَالمَسْنُونُ: المَصْبُوبُ. تَوْجَلْ: تَخَفْ. دابِرَ: آخِرَ. لَبِإِمامٍ

مُبِينٍ : الإِمَامُ كُلُّ مَا ائْتَمَمْتَ وَاهْتَدَيْتَ بِهِ . الصَّيْحَةُ : الهَلَكَةُ .

(169) CHAPTER. The Statement of Allāh :–
'Except him (devil) that gain hearing by stealing, is pursued by a clear flaming fire.' (15:18)

بابُ قَوْلِهِ ـ إلاَّ مَنِ اسْتَرَقَ السَّمْعَ فَأَتْبَعَهُ شِهَابٌ مُبِينٌ ـ .

223. Narrated Abū Huraira : The Prophet said, "When Allāh has ordained some affair in the Heaven, the angels beat with their wings in obedience to His statement, which sounds like a chain dragged over a rock." ('Alī and other sub-narrators said, "The sound reaches them.") "Until when fear is banished from their (angel's) hearts, they (angels) say, 'What was it that your Lord said? They say, 'The truth; And He is the Most High, the Most Great.' (34:23) Then those who gain a hearing by stealing (i.e. devils) will hear Allāh's Statement:–

> 'Those who gain a hearing by stealing, (stand one over the other like this).

(Sufyān, to illustrate this, spread the fingers of his right hand and placed them one over the other horizontally.) A flame may overtake and burn the eavesdropper before conveying the news to the one below him; or it may not overtake him till he has conveyed it to the one below him, who in his turn, conveys it to the one below him, and so on till they convey the news to the earth. (Or probably Sufyān said, "Till the news reaches the

٢٢٣ ـ حدَّثنا عَلِيُّ بنُ عبدِ اللهِ : حدَّثنا سُفْيانُ ، عَنْ عَمْرٍو : عَنْ عِكْرِمَةَ ، عَنْ أبي هُرَيْرَةَ يَبْلُغُ بِهِ النَّبيَّ صلى اللهُ عليه وسلَّمَ قالَ : إذَا قَضَى اللهُ الأَمْرَ في السَّماءِ ضَرَبَتِ المَلائكةُ بأَجْنِحَتِها خُضْعاناً لقَوْلِهِ كالسِّلْسِلَةِ عَلَى صَفْوانٍ . قالَ عَلِيٌّ وقالَ غَيْرُهُ : صَفْوَانٍ يَنْفُذُهُمْ ، ذَلِكَ ـ فإذَا فُزِّعَ عَنْ قُلُوبِهِمْ قالُوا ماذَا قالَ رَبُّكُمْ قالوا للَّذي قالَ الحَقَّ وَهُوَ العَلِيُّ الكَبِيرُ ـ فيَسْمَعُها مُسْتَرِقُو السَّمْعِ هكَذَا وَاحِدٌ فَوْقَ آخَرَ . وَوَصَفَ سُفْيانُ بيَدِهِ وَفَرَّجَ بَيْنَ أصابِعِ يَدِهِ اليُمْنَى ، نَصَبَها بَعْضَها فَوْقَ بَعْضٍ فَرُبَّما أَدْرَكَ الشِّهابُ المُسْتَمِعَ قَبْلَ أنْ يَرْمِيَ بِها إلى صاحِبِهِ فيُحْرِقَهُ ، وَرُبَّما لَمْ يُدْرِكْهُ حتَّى يَرْمِيَ بِها إلى الَّذي يَلِيهِ إلى الَّذي هُوَ أَسْفَلَ

earth.") Then the news is inspired to a sorcerer who would add a hundred lies to it. His prophecy will prove true (as far as the heavenly news is concerned). The people will say. 'Didn't he tell us that on such-and-such a day, such-and such a thing will happen? We have found that that is true because of the true news heard from heaven."

مِنْهُ حتى يُلْقُوها إلى الأرْضِ. وَرُبَّما قال سُفْيانُ: حتى تَنْتَهِيَ إلى الأرْضِ، فَتُلْقَى على فَمِ السَّاحِرِ فَيَكْذِبُ مَعَها مِائَةَ كَذْبَةٍ فَيَصْدُقُ فَيَقُولُونَ: ألَمْ يُخْبِرْنا يَوْمَ كَذا وكَذا يَكُونُ كَذا وكَذا؟ فَوَجَدْنا حَقًّا لِلْكَلِمَةِ التي سُمِعَتْ مِنَ السَّماءِ.

224. Narrated Abū Huraira : (The same Ḥadīth above, starting: 'When Allāh has ordained some affair... ...') In this narration the word' foreteller' is added to the word' wizard'.

٢٢٤ ـ حدثنا عليُّ بنُ عبدِ الله: حدثنا سُفْيانُ: حدثنا عَمْرٌو، عَنْ عِكْرِمَةَ، عَنْ أبي هُرَيْرَةَ: إذا قَضَى اللهُ الأمْرَ، وزادَ: والكاهِن. وحدثنا سُفْيانُ فقالَ: قالَ عَمْرٌو: سَمِعْتُ عِكْرِمَةَ: حدثنا أبو هُرَيْرَةَ قالَ: إذا قَضَى اللهُ الأمْرَ وقالَ على فَمِ السَّاحِرِ، قُلْتُ لِسُفْيانَ: أنْتَ سَمِعْتَ عَمْرًا؟ قالَ: سَمِعْتُ عِكْرِمَةَ، قالَ: سَمِعْتُ أبا هُرَيْرَةَ؟ قالَ: نَعَمْ. قُلْتُ لِسُفْيانَ: إنَّ إنسانًا رَوَى عَنْكَ، عَنْ عَمْرٍو، عَنْ عِكْرِمَةَ، عَنْ أبي هُرَيْرَةَ وَيَرْفَعُهُ أنَّهُ قَرَأَ فُزِّعَ، قالَ سُفْيانُ: هكذا قَرَأَ عَمْرٌو فلا أدْري سَمِعَهُ هكذا أمْ لا؟ قالَ سُفْيانُ: وَهِيَ قِراءَتُنا.

(170) CHAPTER. The Statement of Allāh ﷻ :–
'Surely! The dwellers of Al-Ḥijr (Rocky Tract, i.e. Thamūd people) also rejected the Messengers.'
(15:80)

بابُ قولِهِ ـ وَلَقَدْ كَذَّبَ أَصْحَابُ الحِجْرِ المُرْسَلِينَ ـ.

225. Narrated 'Abdullāh bin 'Umar رضي الله عنهما : (While we were going for the Battle of Tabūk and when we reached the places of the dwellers of Al-Ḥijr), Allāh's Messenger ﷺ said about the dwellers of Al-Ḥijr (to us). "Do not enter (the dwelling places) of these people unless you enter weeping, but if you weep not, then do not enter upon them, lest you be afflicted with what they were afflicted with."

٢٢٥ ـ حدَّثَنا إبْرَاهِيمُ بنُ المُنْذِرِ: حدَّثَنا مَعْنٌ قالَ: حدَّثَني مالِكٌ، عَنْ عَبْدِ اللهِ بنِ دِينارٍ، عَنْ عَبْدِ اللهِ بنِ عُمَرَ رَضِيَ اللهُ تَعالى عَنْهُما: أنَّ رَسُولَ اللهِ صلى اللهُ عليهِ وسلَّمَ قال لأصْحابِ الحِجْرِ: لا تَدْخُلوا عَلَى هؤُلاءِ القَوْمِ إلاَّ أنْ تَكُونُوا باكِينَ، فإنْ لمْ تَكُونُوا باكِينَ فَلا تَدْخُلوا عَلَيْهِمْ أنْ يُصِيبَكُم مِثْلُ ما أصابَهُمْ.

(171) CHAPTER. The Statement of Allāh ﷻ :–

'And indeed We have bestowed upon you the seven Al-Mathānī (oft-repeated Verses) Sūra-al-Fātiḥah and the Grand Qur'ān.' (15:87)

بابُ قولِهِ ـ وَلَقَدْ آتَيْناكَ سَبْعاً مِنَ المَثانِي والقُرْآنِ العَظِيمِ ـ.

226. Narrated Abū Sa'īd Al-Muallā: While I was praying, the Prophet ﷺ passed by and called me, but I did not go to him till I had finished my prayer. When I went to him, he said, "What prevented you from coming?" I said, "I was praying." He said, "Didn't Allāh say.
'O you who believe! Give your

٢٢٦ ـ حدَّثَني مُحَمَّدُ بنُ بَشَّارٍ: حدَّثَنا غُنْدَرٌ: حدَّثَنا شُعْبَةُ، عَنْ خُبَيْبِ بنِ عَبْدِ الرَّحْمنِ، عَنْ حَفْصِ بنِ عاصِمٍ، عَنْ أبي سَعِيدِ بنِ المُعَلَّى قالَ: مَرَّ بِيَ النَّبِيُّ صلى اللهُ عليهِ وسلَّمَ وأنا أُصَلِّي فَدَعاني فَلَمْ آتِهِ حَتَّى

response to Allāh (by obeying Him) and to His Messenger." (8:24)
Then he added, "Shall I tell you the most superior Sūra in the Qur'ān before I go out of the mosque?". When the Prophet ﷺ intended to go out (of the Mosque), I reminded him and he said, "That is: "Alḥamdu-lilāhi Rabbil-'Ālamīn (Sūrat-al-Fātiḥa)' which is the seven oft-repeated verses (Al-Mathānī) and the Grand Qur'ān which has been given to me."

صليت. ثم أتيته فقال: ما منعك أن تأتي؟ فقلت: كنت أصلي، فقال: ألم يقل الله - يا أيها الذين آمنوا استجيبوا لله وللرسول - ثم قال: ألا أعلمك أعظم سورة في القرآن قبل أن أخرج من المسجد؟ فذهب النبي صلى الله عليه وسلم ليخرج فذكرته فقال: الحمد لله رب العالمين هي السبع المثاني والقرآن العظيم الذي أوتيته.

227. Narrated Abū Huraira ﵁: Allāh's Messenger ﷺ said, "The Um (substance) of the Qur'ān is the seven oft-repeated verses (Al-Mathānī) and is the Great Qur'ān (i.e. Sūrat-al-Fātiḥa)."

٢٢٧ - حدثنا آدم: حدثنا ابن أبي ذئب: حدثنا سعيد المقبري، عن أبي هريرة رضي الله عنه قال: قال رسول الله صلى الله عليه وسلم: أم القرآن هي السبع المثاني والقرآن العظيم.

(172) CHAPTER. The Statement of Allāh عز وجل:-

'Who (the Jews and the Christians) have made (their) Scripture into parts (i.e. believed in a part and disbelieved the other).' (15:91)

باب قوله عز وجل - الذين جعلوا القرآن عضين -

المقتسمين: الذين حلفوا ومنه لا أقسم: أي أقسم وتقرأ لأقسم - قاسمهما: حلف لهما ولم يحلفا له. وقال مجاهد تقاسموا: تحالفوا.

228. Narrated Ibn 'Abbās ﵄:

٢٢٨ - حدثنا يعقوب بن إبراهيم:

Those who have made their Scripture into parts are the people of the Scripture who divided it into portions and believed in a part of it and disbelieved the other.

حدثنا هشيم: أخبرنا أبو بشر، عن سعيد بن جبير، عن ابن عباس رضي الله تعالى عنهما - الذين جعلوا القرآن عضين - قال: هم أهل الكتاب جزءوه أجزاء فآمنوا ببعضه وكفروا ببعضه.

229. Narrated Ibn 'Abbās : concerning:—

'As We sent down (the Scripture) on those who are divided (Jews and Christians).' (15:90)

They believed in a part of it and disbelieved in the other, are the Jews and the Christians.

٢٢٩ - حدثني عبيد الله بن موسى، عن الأعمش، عن أبي ظبيان، عن ابن عباس رضي الله تعالى عنهما: كما أنزلنا على المقتسمين، قال: آمنوا ببعض وكفروا ببعض، اليهود والنصارى.

(173 CHAPTER. The Statement of Allāh :—

'And worship your Lord until there comes unto you the Hour that is certain (i.e. death). (15:99)

Sālim said: "That is certain", means the death."

باب قوله - واعبد ربك حتى يأتيك اليقين - قال سالم: اليقين: الموت.

SŪRAT AN—NAḤL. XVI

سورة النحل

**In the Name of Allāh,
the Most Beneficent, the Most Merciful**

بسم الله الرحمن الرحيم

روح القدس: جبريل. نزل به الروح الأمين. في ضيق: يقال أمر ضيق وضيق مثل هين وهين، ولين ولين، وميت وميت. قال ابن عباس:

تَنَفَيَّأُت ظِلالُه : تَنَهَيْنا . سُبُلَ رَبِّكِ
ذُلُلاً : لا يَتَوَعَّرُ عَلَيْها مَكانٌ سَلَكَتْهُ .
وَقَالَ ابنُ عَبَّاسٍ : فى تَقَلُّبِهِم :
اخْتِلافِهِم . وَقَالَ مُجاهِدٌ : تَمِيدُ :
تَكَفَّأُ . مُفْرَطُونَ : مَنْسِيُّونَ . وَقَالَ
غَيْرُهُ : فَإِذَا قَرَأْتَ القُرْآنَ فَاسْتَعِذْ بالله
مِنَ الشَّيْطَانِ الرَّجِيمِ ، هَذَا مُقَدَّمٌ وَ
مُؤَخَّرٌ، وَذَلِكَ أَنَّ الاسْتِعاذَةَ قَبْلَ القِراءَةِ
وَمَعْناها الاعْتِصامُ بالله . وَقَالَ ابنُ عَبَّاسٍ :
تُسِيمُونَ : تَرْعَوْنَ . شاكِلَتِهِ ناحِيَتِهِ . قَصْدُ
السَّبِيلِ : البَيَانُ . الدِّفْءُ : ما اسْتُدْفِئَ
بِهِ . تُرِيحُونَ : بِالعَشِيِّ . وَتَسْرَحُونَ :
بِالغَداةِ . بِشِقٍّ : يَعْنى المَشَقَّةَ . عَلَى
تَخَوُّفٍ : تَنَقُّصٍ . الأَنْعامُ لَعِبْرَةً ،
وَهِىَ تُؤَنَّثُ وَتُذَكَّرُ ، وَكَذَلِكَ
النَّعَمُ لِلأَنْعامِ جَماعَةَ النَّعَمِ . أَكْنانا :
واحِدُها كِنٌّ مِثْلُ حِمْلٍ وأَحْمالٍ .
سَرابِيلَ : قُمُصٌ تَقِيكُمُ الحَرَّ . وَأَمَّا
سَرابِيلَ تَقِيكُم بَأْسَكُم ، فَإِنَّها الدُّرُوعُ .
دَخَلاً بَيْنَكُم : كُلُّ شَىْءٍ لَمْ يَصِحَّ
فَهُوَ دَخَلٌ . قَالَ ابنُ عَبَّاسٍ : حَفَدَةٌ :
مَنْ وَلَدَ الرَّجُلُ . السَّكَرُ : ما حُرِّمَ
مِنْ ثَمَرَتِها ، والرِّزْقُ الحَسَنُ : ما
أَحَلَّ . وَقَالَ ابنُ عُيَيْنَةَ عَنْ صَدَقَةَ :
أَنْكاثًا : هِىَ خَرْقاءُ كانَتْ إِذَا أَبْرَمَتْ
غَزْلَها نَقَضَتْهُ . وَقَالَ ابنُ مَسْعُودٍ :

الأُمَّةُ مُعَلِّمُ الخَيْرِ، والقَانِتُ: المُطِيعُ.

(174) CHAPTER. The Statement of Allāh ﷻ :–
'And of you there are some who are sent back to senility.'
(16:70)

بابُ قَوْلِهِ تَعالى - وَمِنْكُمْ مَنْ يُرَدُّ إلى أَرْذَلِ العُمُرِ - .

230. Narrated Anas bin Mālik رضي الله عنه : Allāh's Messenger ﷺ used to invoke thus: "O Allāh! I seek refuge with You from miserliness, from laziness; from old geriatric age, from the punishment in the grave; from the affliction of Ad-Dajjal; and from the afflictions of life and death.

٢٣٠ - حدَّثَنا مُوسَى بنُ أسْماعِيلَ: حدَّثَنا هارُونُ بنُ مُوسَى أبو عَبْدِ اللهِ الأعْوَرُ، عَنْ شُعَيْبٍ، عَنْ أنَسِ ابنِ مالِكٍ رَضِيَ اللهُ تَعالى عَنْهُ أنَّ رَسُولَ اللهِ صلى اللهُ عليهِ وسلَّمَ كانَ يَدْعُو: أعُوذُ بِكَ مِنَ البُخْلِ والكَسَلِ، وأرْذَلِ العُمُرِ، وعَذابِ القَبْرِ، وَفِتْنَةِ الدَّجَّالِ وَفِتْنَةِ المَحْيا والمَماتِ.

SŪRAT BANĪ–ISRĀEL XVII
(Children of Isrāel) also called
"Sūrat-al-Isrā)"

**In the Name of Allāh,
the Most Beneficent, the Most Merciful**

231. Narrated Ibn Mas'ūd; Sūrat Banī Isrāel and Al-Kahf and Mary are among my first old property.

سورة بنى اسرائيل

بِسْمِ اللهِ الرَّحْمَنِ الرَّحِيمِ

٢٣١ - حدَّثنا آدَمُ : حدَّثنا شُعْبَةُ ، عَن أبي إسحاقَ قالَ : سَمِعْتُ عَبْدَ الرَّحْمَنِ بنَ يَزِيدَ قالَ : سَمِعْتُ ابنَ مَسْعُودٍ رَضِيَ اللهُ عَنْهُ قالَ في بَنى إسْرائيلَ والكَهْفِ وَمَرْيَمَ إنَّهُنَّ مِنَ العِتاقِ الأُوَلِ . وَهُنَّ مِنْ تلادى . فَسَيُنْغِضُونَ إلَيْكَ رُءُوسَهُمْ ، قالَ ابنُ عَبَّاسٍ : يَهُزُّونَ . وَقالَ غَيْرُهُ : نَغَضَتْ سِنُّكَ أَىْ تَحَرَّكَتْ . وَقَضَيْنا إلى بَنى إسرائيلَ أخبرْناهُمْ أنَّهُمْ سَيُفْسِدونَ . والقَضاءُ عَلى وُجُوهٍ . وَقَضَى رَبُّكَ : أمَرَ رَبُّكَ وَمِنْهُ الحُكْمُ . إنَّ رَبَّكَ يَقْضِي بَيْنَهُمْ . وَمِنْهُ الخَلْقُ . فَقَضاهُنَّ سَبْعَ سَمَوَاتٍ . خَلَقَهُنَّ . نَفيرًا مَنْ يَنْفِرُ مَعَهُ . مَيْسُورًا : لَيِّنا . وليُتَبِّرُوا : يُدَمِّرُوا ما عَلَوْا . حَصِيرًا : مَحْبِسا ، مَحْصَرًا . حَقَّ : وَجَبَ . مَيْسُورًا : لَيِّنا . خِطْأً : إثما ، وَهُوَ اسْمٌ مِنْ خَطِئْتُ . والخَطَأُ

مَفْتوحٌ مَصْدَرُهُ مِنَ الإِثْمِ. خَطِئْتُ بِمَعْنَى أَخْطَأْتُ. تَخْرِقَ: تَقْطَعَ. وَإِذْ هُمْ نَجْوَى: مَصْدَرٌ مِنْ نَاجَيْتُ فَوَصَفَهُمْ بِهَا، وَالمَعْنَى يَتَنَاجَوْنَ. رُفَاتًا: حُطَامًا. وَاسْتَفْزِزْ: اسْتَخِفَّ بِخَيْلِكَ الفُرْسَانِ. وَالرَّجْلُ وَالرِّجَالُ وَالرَّجَّالَةُ وَاحِدُهَا رَاجِلٌ مِثْلُ صَاحِبٍ وَصَحْبٍ وَتَاجِرٍ وَتَجْرٍ. حَاصِبًا: الرِّيحُ العَاصِفُ، وَالحَاصِبُ أَيْضًا مَا تَرْمِي بِهِ الرِّيحُ. وَمِنْهُ حَصَبُ جَهَنَّمَ. يُرْمَى بِهِ فى جَهَنَّمَ وَهُمْ حَصَبُهَا، وَيُقَالُ حَصَبَ فى الأَرْضِ ذَهَبَ. وَالحَصَبُ مُشْتَقٌّ مِنَ الحَصْبَاءِ وَالحِجَارَةِ. تَارَةً: مَرَّةً، وَجَمَاعَتُهُ تِيَرٌ وَتَارَاتٌ لأَحْتَنِكَنَّ: لأَسْتَأْصِلَنَّهُمْ. يُقَالُ: احْتَنَكَ فُلانٌ مَا عِنْدَ فُلانٍ مِنْ عِلْمٍ: اسْتَقْصَاهُ. طَائِرَهُ: حَظَّهُ. قَالَ ابْنُ عَبَّاسٍ: كُلُّ سُلْطَانٍ فى القُرْآنِ فَهُوَ حُجَّةٌ. وَلِيٌّ مِنَ الذُّلِّ: لَمْ يُحَالِفْ أَحَدًا.

بَابُ قَوْلِهِ ـ أَسْرَى بِعَبْدِهِ لَيْلًا مِنَ المَسْجِدِ الحَرَامِ ـ.

(175) CHAPTER. The Statement of Allāh ﷻ :-

'Glorified be He (Allāh), Who did take His Slave (Muḥammad ﷺ) for a journey by night from Al-Masjid-al-Ḥarām (Mecca).' . . . .(17:1)

232. Narrated Abū Huraira ﷺ: Allāh's Messenger ﷺ was presented with two cups one containing wine and the other milk on the night of his night journey at Jerusalem. He looked at it and took the milk. Gabriel said, "Thanks to Allāh Who guided you to the Fiṭra (i.e. Islām); if you had taken the wine, your followers would have gone astray.

٢٣٢ - حدَّثنا عبدانُ: حدَّثنا عبدُ الله: أخبرَنا يونسُ ح. وحدَّثنا أحمدُ بنُ صالحٍ: حدَّثنا عنبسةُ: حدَّثنا يونسُ، عن ابنِ شهابٍ: قالَ ابنُ المسيِّبِ: قالَ أبو هريرةَ: أُتيَ رسولُ اللهِ صلى اللهُ عليهِ وسلَّم ليلةَ أُسريَ بهِ بإيلياءَ بقدحينِ من خمرٍ ولبنٍ. فنظرَ إليهما فأخذَ اللبنَ، قالَ جبريلُ: الحمدُ للهِ الذي هداكَ للفطرةِ. لو أخذتَ الخمرَ غوتْ أُمتُكَ.

233. Narrated Jābir bin 'Abdullāh ﷺ: The Prophet ﷺ said, "When the Quraish disbelieved me (concerning my night journey), I stood up in Al-Ḥijr (the unroofed portion of the Ka'ba) and Allāh displayed Bait-ul-Maqdis before me, and I started to inform them (Quraish) about its signs while looking at it."

٢٣٣ - حدَّثنا أحمدُ بنُ صالحٍ: حدَّثنا ابنُ وهبٍ قالَ: أخبرَني يونسُ، عن ابنِ شهابٍ قالَ أبو سلمةَ: سمعتُ جابرَ بنَ عبدِ اللهِ رضيَ اللهُ تعالى عنهُما قالَ: سمعتُ النبيَّ صلى اللهُ عليهِ وسلَّم يقولُ: لمَّا كذَّبتني قريشٌ قمتُ في الحجرِ فجلَّى اللهُ لي بيتَ المقدسِ فطفقتُ أُخبرُهم عن آياتهِ وأنا أنظرُ إليهِ. زادَ يعقوبُ بنُ إبراهيمَ: حدَّثنا ابنُ أخي ابنِ شهابٍ، عن عمِّهِ: لمَّا كذَّبتني قريشٌ حينَ أُسريَ بي إلى بيتِ المقدسِ، نحوَهُ. قاصفاً: ريحٌ تقصفُ كلَّ شيءٍ.

(176) CHAPTER. The Statement of

بابُ قولهِ تعالى - ولقدْ كرَّمنا

Allāh :-
"And indeed, We have honoured the offspring of Adam.' (17:70)

بَنِى آدَمَ - كَرَّمْنا : وأَكْرَمْنا وَاحِدٌ ، ضِعْفَ الحَيَاةِ وَضِعْفَ المَمَاتِ : عَذَابَ الحَيَاةِ وَعَذَابَ المَمَاتِ . خِلافَكَ وَخَلْفَكَ سَوَاءٌ . وَنَأى : تَبَاعَدَ . شاكِلَتِه . نَاحِيَتِهِ . وَهِىَ مِنْ شَكْلَتِهِ . صَرَّفْنا : وَجَّهْنا . قَبِيلاً : مُعَايَنَةً وَمُقَابَلَةً . وَقِيلَ القَابِلَةُ لأَنَّها مُقَابِلَتُها ، وَتَقْبَلُ وَلَدَها . خَشْيَةَ الإِنْفاقِ ، يُقالُ أَنْفَقَ الرَّجُلُ أَمْلَقَ . وَنَفِقَ الشَّىْءُ ذَهَبَ : قَتُوراً : مُقَتِّراً . لِلأَذْقانِ : مُجْتَمَعُ اللَّحْيَيْنِ ، الوَاحِدُ ذَقَنٌ . وَقالَ مُجاهِدٌ : مَوْفُوراً : وَافِراً . تَبِيعاً : ثَائِراً ، وقالَ ابْنُ عَبَّاسٍ : نَصِيراً . خَبَتْ : طَفِئَتْ . وَقالَ ابْنُ عَبَّاسٍ : لاتُبَذِّرْ : لاتُنْفِقْ فى البَاطِلِ . ابْتِغاءَ رَحْمَةٍ . رِزْقٍ . مَثْبُوراً : مَلْعُوناً . لاتَقْفُ : لاتَقُلْ . فَجاسُوا : تَيَمَّمُوا . يُزْجِى الفُلْكَ : يُجْرِى الفُلْكَ . يَخِرُّونَ لِلأَذْقانِ : لِلوُجُوهِ .

(177) CHAPTER . When We decide to destroy a population We (first) send a definite Order (to obey Allāh) to those among them who are given the good thing of this life.' (17:16)

بابٌ - وَإِذا أَرَدْنا أَنْ نُهْلِكَ قَرْيَةً أَمَرْنا مُتْرَفِيها - الآيَةَ .

234. Narrated 'Abdullāh : During the Pre-Islāmic period of ignor-

٢٣٤ - حَدَّثَنا عَلِىُّ بنُ عَبْدِ اللهِ : حَدَّثَنا سُفْيانُ : أَخْبَرَنا مَنْصُورٌ ، عَنْ أَبى

وَائِلٍ ، عَنْ عَبْدِ اللهِ قَالَ : كُنَّا نَقُولُ لِلحَيِّ إِذَا كَثُرُوا فِى الجَاهِلِيَّةِ ، أَمِرَ بَنُو فُلَانٍ .

ance if any tribe became great in number, we used to say, "Amira the children of so-and-so." (1)

٢٣٥ - حَدَّثَنَا الحُمَيْدِيُّ : حَدَّثَنَا سُفْيَانُ وَقَالَ أَمِرَ .

235: Narrated Al-Humaidī: Sufyān narrated to us something and used the word 'Amira'.

باب ذُرِّيَّةَ مَنْ حَمَلْنَا مَعَ نُوحٍ إِنَّهُ كَانَ عَبْدًا شَكُورًا .

(178) CHAPTER. 'O offspring of those whom We carried (in the ship) with Noah. Verily, he was a grateful slave.' (17:3)

٢٣٦ - حَدَّثَنَا مُحَمَّدُ بنُ مُقَاتِلٍ : أَخْبَرَنَا عَبْدُ اللهِ : أَخْبَرَنَا أَبُو حَيَّانَ التَّيْمِيُّ ، عَنْ أَبِى زُرْعَةَ ابنِ عَمْرِو بنِ جَرِيرٍ ، عَنْ أَبِى هُرَيْرَةَ رَضِيَ اللهُ عَنْهُ قَالَ : أُتِيَ رَسُولُ اللهِ صلى الله عليه وسلم بِلَحْمٍ فَرُفِعَ إِلَيْهِ الذِّرَاعُ وَكَانَتْ تُعْجِبُهُ ، فَنَهَسَ مِنْهَا نَهْسَةً ثُمَّ قَالَ : أَنَا سَيِّدُ النَّاسِ يَوْمَ القِيَامَةِ ، وَهَلْ تَدْرُونَ مِمَّ ذَلِكَ ؟ يَجْمَعُ اللهُ النَّاسَ الأَوَّلِينَ وَالآخِرِينَ فِى صَعِيدٍ

236. Narrated Abū Huraira ﷺ: Some (cooked) meat was brought to Allāh's Messenger ﷺ and the meat of a forearm was presented to him as he used to like it. He ate a morsel of it and said, "I will be the chief of all the people on the Day of Resurrection. Do you know the reason for it? Allāh will gather all the human being of early generations as well as late generation on one plain so that the announcer will be able to make them all-hear his voice and the watcher will be able to see all of them. The sun will come so close to the people that they will suffer such distress and trouble as they will not be able to bear

(1) In narration No. 234 and 235 the word 'Amira' means increase in number. The same word occurs in the Verse above (17:16), if we apply the same meaning to the word, then the translation of the Verse will be: We (first) increase in number those of its population who are given the luxury of this life.(17:16)

or stand. Then the people will say, 'Don't you see to what state you have reached? Won't you look for someone who can intercede for you with your Lord?' Some people will say to some others, 'Go to Adam.' So they will go to Adam and say to him. 'You are the father of mankind; Allāh created you with His Own Hand, and breathed into you of His Spirit (meaning the spirit which he created for you); and ordered the angels to prostrate before you; so (please) intercede for us with your Lord. Don't you see in what state we are? Don't you see what condition we have reached?' Adam will say, 'Today my Lord has become angry as He has never become before, nor will ever become thereafter. He forbade me (to eat of the fruit of) the tree, but I disobeyed Him. Myself! Myself! Myself! (has more need for intercession). Go to someone else; go to Noah.' So they will go to Noah and say (to him), 'O Noah! You are the first (of Allāh's Messengers) to the people of the earth, and Allāh has named you a thankful slave; please intercede for us with your Lord. Don't you see in what state we are?' He will say.' Today my Lord has become angry as He has never become nor will ever become thereafter. I had (in the world) the right to make one definitely accepted invocation, and I made it against my nation. Myself! Myself! Myself! Go to someone else; go to Abraham.' They will go to Abraham and say, 'O Abraham! You are Allāh's Messenger and His Khalīl (1) from among the people of the earth; so please intercede for us with your Lord. Don't you see in what state we are?' He will

(1) See the Glossary.

وَاحِدٍ، يُسْمِعُهُمُ الدَّاعِي وَيَنْفُذُهُمُ البَصَرُ، وَتَدْنُو الشَّمْسُ فَيَبْلُغُ النَّاسُ مِنَ الغَمِّ وَالكَرْبِ مَا لا يُطِيقُونَ وَلا يَحْتَمِلُونَ. فَيَقُولُ النَّاسُ: أَلا تَرَوْنَ مَا قَدْ بَلَغَكُمْ؟ أَلا تَنْظُرُونَ مَنْ يَشْفَعُ لَكُمْ إِلَى رَبِّكُمْ؟ فَيَقُولُ بَعْضُ النَّاسِ لِبَعْضٍ: عَلَيْكُمْ بِآدَمَ، فَيَأْتُونَ آدَمَ عَلَيْهِ السَّلامُ فَيَقُولُونَ لَهُ: أَنْتَ أَبُو البَشَرِ، خَلَقَكَ اللهُ بِيَدِهِ وَنَفَخَ فِيكَ مِنْ رُوحِهِ، وَأَمَرَ المَلائِكَةَ فَسَجَدُوا لَكَ، اشْفَعْ لَنَا إِلَى رَبِّكَ، أَلا تَرَى إِلَى مَا نَحْنُ فِيهِ؟ أَلا تَرَى إِلَى مَا قَدْ بَلَغَنَا؟ فَيَقُولُ آدَمُ: إِنَّ رَبِّي قَدْ غَضِبَ اليَوْمَ غَضَبًا لَمْ يَغْضَبْ قَبْلَهُ مِثْلَهُ وَلَنْ يَغْضَبَ بَعْدَهُ مِثْلَهُ، وَإِنَّهُ نَهَانِي عَنِ الشَّجَرَةِ فَعَصَيْتُهُ، نَفْسِي نَفْسِي نَفْسِي، اذْهَبُوا إِلَى غَيْرِي، اذْهَبُوا إِلَى نُوحٍ. فَيَأْتُونَ نُوحًا فَيَقُولُونَ: يَا نُوحُ إِنَّكَ أَنْتَ أَوَّلُ الرُّسُلِ إِلَى أَهْلِ الأَرْضِ، وَقَدْ سَمَّاكَ اللهُ عَبْدًا شَكُورًا، اشْفَعْ لَنَا إِلَى رَبِّكَ، أَلا تَرَى إِلَى مَا نَحْنُ فِيهِ؟ فَيَقُولُ: إِنَّ رَبِّي عَزَّ وَجَلَّ قَدْ غَضِبَ اليَوْمَ غَضَبًا لَمْ يَغْضَبْ قَبْلَهُ مِثْلَهُ وَلَنْ يَغْضَبَ بَعْدَهُ مِثْلَهُ، وَإِنَّهُ قَدْ كَانَتْ لِي دَعْوَةٌ دَعَوْتُهَا عَلَى قَوْمِي، نَفْسِي نَفْسِي نَفْسِي، اذْهَبُوا إِلَى غَيْرِي، اذْهَبُوا إِلَى إِبْرَاهِيمَ. فَيَأْتُونَ

say to them, 'My Lord has today become angry as He has never become before, nor will ever become thereafter. I had told three lies [Abū Ḥaiyān (the sub-narrator) mentioned them in the Ḥadīth] Myself! Myself! Myself! Go to someone else; go to Moses.' The people will then go to Moses and say, 'O Moses! You are Allāh's Messenger and Allāh gave you superiority above the others with this message and with His direct Talk to you; (please) intercede for us with your Lord Don't you see in what state we are?' Moses will say, 'My Lord has today become angry as He has never become before, nor will become thereafter, I killed a person whom I had not been ordered to kill. Myself! Myself! Myself! Go to someone else; go to Jesus.' So they will go to Jesus and say, 'O Jesus! You are Allāh's Messenger and His Word which He sent to Mary, and a superior soul created by Him, (2) and you talked to the people while still young in the cradle. Please intercede for us with your Lord. Don't you see in what state we are?' Jesus will say. 'My Lord has today become angry as He has never become before nor will ever become thereafter. Jesus will not mention any sin, but will say, 'Myself! Myself! Myself! Go to someone else; go to Muḥammad.' So they will come to me and say, 'O Muḥammad! You are Allāh's Messenger and the last of the prophets, and Allāh forgave your early and late sins. (Please) intercede for us

إبْرَاهِيمَ فَيَقُولُونَ : يَا إبْرَاهِيمُ ، أنْتَ نَبِيُّ اللهِ وَخَلِيلُهُ مِنْ الأرْضِ ، اشْفَعْ لَنَا إلى رَبِّكَ . ألا تَرَى إلى مَا نَحْنُ فِيهِ ؟ فَيَقُولُ لَهُمْ : إنَّ رَبِّي قَدْ غَضِبَ اليَوْمَ غَضَبًا لَمْ يَغْضَبْ قَبْلَهُ مِثْلَهُ وَلَنْ يَغْضَبَ بَعْدَهُ مِثْلَهُ . وَإنِّي قَدْ كُنْتُ كَذَبْتُ ثَلاثَ كَذَبَاتٍ ، فَذَكَرَهُنَّ أبُو حَيَّانَ في الحَدِيثِ : نَفْسِي نَفْسِي نَفْسِي ، اذْهَبُوا إلى غَيْرِي ، اذْهَبُوا إلى مُوسَى . فَيَأتُونَ مُوسَى . فَيَقُولُونَ : يَا مُوسَى ، أنْتَ رَسُولُ اللهِ ، فَضَّلَكَ اللهُ بِرِسَالَتِهِ وَبِكَلامِهِ عَلَى النَّاسِ ، اشْفَعْ لَنَا إلى رَبِّكَ ، ألا تَرَى إلى مَا نَحْنُ فِيهِ ؟ فَيَقُولُ : إنَّ رَبِّي قَدْ غَضِبَ اليَوْمَ غَضَبًا لَمْ يَغْضَبْ قَبْلَهُ مِثْلَهُ وَلَنْ يَغْضَبَ بَعْدَهُ مِثْلَهُ ، وَإنِّي قَدْ قَتَلْتُ نَفْسًا لَمْ أُومَرْ بِقَتْلِهَا ، نَفْسِي نَفْسِي نَفْسِي ، اذْهَبُوا إلى عِيسَى . فَيَأتُونَ عِيسَى فَيَقُولُونَ : يَا عِيسَى ، أنْتَ رَسُولُ اللهِ وَكَلِمَتُهُ ألْقَاهَا إلى مَرْيَمَ وَرُوحٌ مِنْهُ ، وَكَلَّمْتَ النَّاسَ في المَهْدِ صَبِيًّا ، اشْفَعْ لَنَا ، ألا تَرَى إلى مَا نَحْنُ فِيهِ ؟

(2) "Rouḥ-ullāh": See in the glossary.

with your Lord. Don't you see in what state we are?" ' The Prophet ﷺ added, "Then I will go beneath Allāh's Throne and fall in prostration before my Lord. And then Allāh تعالى will guide me to such praises and glorifications to Him as He has never guided anybody else before me. Then it will be said, 'O Muḥammad! Raise your head. Ask, and it will be granted. Intercede! It (your intercession) will be accepted.' So I will raise my head and say, 'My followers, O my Lord! My followers, O my Lord'. It will be said, 'O Muḥammad! Let those of your followers who have no accounts, enter through such a gate of the gates of Paradise as lies on the right; and they will share the other gates with the people.'" The Prophet ﷺ further said, "By Him in Whose Hand my soul is, the distance between every two gate-posts of Paradise is like the distance between Mecca and Buṣra (in Shā'm)."

٢٠١

فَيَقُولُ عِيسَى إِنَّ رَبِّي قَدْ غَضِبَ الْيَوْمَ غَضَبًا لَمْ يَغْضَبْ قَبْلَهُ مِثْلَهُ وَلَنْ يَغْضَبَ بَعْدَهُ مِثْلَهُ ؟ وَلَمْ يَذْكُرْ ذَنْبًا . نَفْسِي نَفْسِي نَفْسِي ، اذْهَبُوا إِلَى غَيْرِي ، اذْهَبُوا إِلَى مُحَمَّدٍ صلى اللهُ عليه وسلَّمَ . فَيَأْتُونَ مُحَمَّدًا صلى اللهُ عليه وسلَّمَ فَيَقُولُونَ : يَا مُحَمَّدُ ، أَنْتَ رَسُولُ اللهِ وَخَاتَمُ الْأَنْبِيَاءِ ، وَقَدْ غَفَرَ اللهُ لَكَ مَا تَقَدَّمَ مِنْ ذَنْبِكَ وَمَا تَأَخَّرَ ، اشْفَعْ لَنَا إِلَى رَبِّكَ ، أَلَا تَرَى إِلَى مَا نَحْنُ فِيهِ ؟ فَأَنْطَلِقُ فَآتِي تَحْتَ الْعَرْشِ ، فَأَقَعُ سَاجِدًا لِرَبِّي عَزَّ وَجَلَّ . ثُمَّ يَفْتَحُ اللهُ عَلَيَّ مِنْ مَحَامِدِهِ وَحُسْنِ الثَّنَاءِ عَلَيْهِ شَيْئًا لَمْ يَفْتَحْهُ عَلَى أَحَدٍ قَبْلِي ، ثُمَّ يُقَالُ : يَا مُحَمَّدُ : ارْفَعْ رَأْسَكَ ، سَلْ تُعْطَهْ ، وَاشْفَعْ تُشَفَّعْ . فَأَرْفَعُ رَأْسِي فَأَقُولُ : أُمَّتِي يَا رَبِّ ، أُمَّتِي يَا رَبِّ . فَيُقَالُ : يَا مُحَمَّدُ ، أَدْخِلْ مِنْ أُمَّتِكَ مَنْ لَا حِسَابَ عَلَيْهِمْ مِنَ الْبَابِ الْأَيْمَنِ مِنْ أَبْوَابِ الْجَنَّةِ ، وَهُمْ شُرَكَاءُ النَّاسِ فِيمَا سِوَى ذَلِكَ مِنَ الْأَبْوَابِ . ثُمَّ قَالَ : وَالَّذِي نَفْسِي بِيَدِهِ إِنَّ مَا بَيْنَ الْمِصْرَاعَيْنِ مِنْ مَصَارِيعِ الْجَنَّةِ كَمَا بَيْنَ مَكَّةَ وَحِمْيَرَ ، أَوْ كَمَا بَيْنَ مَكَّةَ وَبُصْرَى .

(179) CHAPTER. The Statement of Allāh :–

'And to David We gave the Psalms.'
(17 : 55)

بابُ قولِهِ ـ وآتينا داودَ زَبُورًا ـ.

237. Narrated Abū Huraira : The Prophet said, "The recitation of Psalms (David's Qur'ān) was made light and easy for David that he used to have his riding animal be saddled while he would finish the recitation before the servant had saddled it."

٢٣٧ ـ حدَّثنا إسحاقُ بنُ نصرٍ: حدَّثنا عبدُ الرَّزَّاقِ، عنْ معمرٍ، عنْ همَّامِ بنِ مُنبِّهٍ، عنْ أبي هُريرةَ رَضِيَ اللهُ عنهُ، عنِ النبيِّ صلى اللهُ عليهِ وسلَّمَ قالَ: خُفِّفَ على داودَ القُرآنُ فكانَ يأمُرُ دابَّتَهُ لِتُسْرَجَ، فكانَ يقرأُ قبلَ أنْ يفرُغَ، يعني القُرآنَ.

(180) CHAPTER. 'Say (O Muḥammad) :Call unto those besides Him whom you assume (to be gods)......'
(17:56)

باب ـ قُلِ ادعُوا الَّذينَ زَعَمتُمْ مِنْ دُونِهِ ـ الآيةَ.

238. Narrated 'Abdullāh regarding the explanation of the Verse:–

'Those whom they call upon (worship) (like Jesus the Son of Mary, angels etc.) desire (for themselves) means of access to their Lord (Allāh) as to which of them should be the nearer and they hope for His Mercy and fear His torment.'
(17: 57)

They themselves (e.g. Angels, saints, Messengers, Jesus, etc.,) worshipped Allāh,

٢٣٨ ـ حدَّثني عمرُو بنُ عليٍّ: حدَّثنا يحيى: حدَّثنا سُفيانُ: حدَّثني سُليمانُ، عنْ إبراهيمَ، عنْ أبي معمرٍ، عنْ عبدِ اللهِ ـ إلى ربِّهِمُ الوسيلةَ ـ قالَ: كانَ ناسٌ منَ الإنسِ يعبُدُونَ ناسًا منَ الجنِّ، فأسلمَ الجنُّ وتمسَّكَ هؤلاءِ بدينِهِم. زادَ الأشجعيُّ، عنْ سُفيانَ عنِ الأعمشِ ـ قُلِ ادعُوا الَّذينَ زَعَمتُمْ ـ.

Those Jinns who were worshipped by some Arabs became Muslims (embraced Islām), but those human beings stuck to their (old) religion. Al-A'mash said extra:—

'Say, (O Muḥammad): Call unto those besides Him whom you assume (to be gods).' (17:56)

(181) CHAPTER. The Statement of Allāh ﷻ :—

'Those whom they call upon (worship) (like Jesus the son of Mary or angels etc.) desire (for themselves) means of access......' (17 : 57)

بَابُ قَوْلِهِ - أُولَئِكَ الَّذِينَ يَدْعُونَ يَبْتَغُونَ إِلَى رَبِّهِمُ الوَسِيلَةَ - الآيَةَ .

239. Narrated 'Abdullāh رضي الله عنه regarding the Verse:—

'Those whom they call upon (worship) (like Jesus the Son of Mary or angels etc.) desire (for themselves) means of access, to their Lord....' (17 : 57)

(It was revealed regarding) some Jinns who used to be worshipped (by human beings). They later embraced Islam (while those people kept on worshipping them).

٢٣٩ - حدَّثَنَا بِشْرُ بنُ خَالِدٍ : أخبرَنا مُحَمَّدُ بنُ جَعْفَرٍ ، عَنْ شُعْبَةَ ، عَنْ سُلَيْمَانَ ، عَنْ إِبْرَاهِيمَ ، عَنْ أَبِي مَعْمَرٍ ، عَنْ عَبْدِ اللهِ رَضِيَ اللهُ عَنْهُ فِي هَذِهِ الآيَةِ - الَّذِينَ يَدْعُونَ يَبْتَغُونَ إِلَى رَبِّهِمُ الوَسِيلَةَ - قَالَ : نَاسٌ مِنَ الجِنِّ يُعْبَدُونَ فَأَسْلَمُوا .

(182) CHAPTER. 'And We granted the vision (Ascension to the Heavens "Mi'rāj") which We showed you (O'

بَابُ - وَمَا جَعَلْنَا الرُّؤْيَا الَّتِي أَرَيْنَاكَ إِلَّا فِتْنَةً لِلنَّاسِ .

Muhammad, as an actual eye-witness), but as a trial for mankind........(17-60)

240. Narrated Ibn 'Abbās : Regarding:–

> 'And We granted the vision (Ascension to the Heaven "Mi'raj") which We showed you (O, Muhammad as an actual eye witness) but as a trial for mankind.' (17:60)

It was an actual eye-witness which was shown to Allāh's Messenger during the night he was taken on a journey (through the heavens). And the cursed tree is the tree of Az-Zaqqūm (a bitter pungent tree which grows at the bottom of Hell).

٢٤٠ ـ حدَّثنا عليُّ بنُ عبدِ اللهِ :
حدَّثنا سُفيانُ ، عنْ عمْرٍو ، عنْ
عِكْرِمَةَ ، عنِ ابنِ عبَّاسٍ رَضِيَ اللهُ
عنهُما ـ وَما جعَلْنا الرُّؤْيا التي أرَيْناكَ
إلاَّ فِتْنَةً للنّاسِ ـ قالَ : هيَ رُؤْيا عيْنٍ
أُرِيَها رَسُولُ اللهِ صلى اللهُ عليهِ وسلَّم ليْلَةَ
أُسْرِيَ بِهِ ، والشَّجَرَةَ المَلْعُونَةَ
شَجَرَةُ الزَّقُّومِ .

(183) CHAPTER. Verily! The recitation of the Qur'an in the early dawn is ever witnessed. (attended by the angels in-charge of mankind of the day and the night). (17:78)

Mujāhid said: (Qur'ān at dawn) means the Fajr (morning compulsory congregational) prayer.

باب قولِهِ ـ إنَّ قُرآنَ الفجْرِ
كانَ مَشْهُوداً ـ قالَ مُجاهِدٌ : صَلاةَ
الفَجْرِ .

241. Narrated Ibn Al-Musaiyab: Abū Huraira said, "The Prophet said, 'A prayer performed in congregation is twenty-five times more superior in reward to a prayer performed by a single person. The angels of the night and the angels of the day are assembled at the time of the Fajr (Morning) prayer." ' Abū Huraira added, "If you wish, you can recite:–

> Verily! The recitation of the Qur'ān in the early dawn (Morning prayer) is

٢٤١ ـ حدَّثني عبْدُ اللهِ بنُ مُحمَّدٍ :
حدَّثنا عبْدُ الرَّزّاقِ : أخبرَنا معْمَرٌ ،
عنِ الزُّهْرِيِّ ، عنْ أبي سلَمةَ وابنِ
المُسيَّبِ ، عنْ أبي هُريْرَةَ رَضِيَ اللهُ
عنْهُ ، عنِ النبيِّ صلى اللهُ عليهِ وسلَّم قالَ :
فَضْلُ صَلاةِ الجميعِ علَى صَلاةِ الواحدِ
خمْسٌ وعِشْرُونَ درَجَةً ، وتجْتمعُ
ملائكَةُ اللَّيْلِ وملائكَةُ النَّهارِ في

ever witnessed (attended by the angels in-charge of mankind of the day and the night). (17:78)

صَلاةِ الصُّبْحِ . يَقُولُ أَبُو هُرَيْرَةَ : اقْرَءُوا إِنْ شِئْتُمْ ـ وَقُرْآنَ الْفَجْرِ إِنَّ قُرْآنَ الْفَجْرِ كَانَ مَشْهُودًا ـ .

(184) CHAPTER. The Statement of Allāh :–

'It may be that your Lord will raise you to a station of praise and glory.' (17:79)

بابُ قَوْلِهِ ـ عَسَى أَنْ يَبْعَثَكَ رَبُّكَ مَقَامًا مَحْمُودًا ـ .

242. Narrated Ibn 'Umar : On the Day of Resurrection the people will fall on their knees and every nation will follow their prophet and they will say, "O so-and-so! Intercede (for us with Allāh), "till (the right) intercession will be given to the Prophet (Muḥammad) and that will be the day when Allāh will raise him to a station of praise and glory (i.e. Al-Maqām-al-Maḥmūd).

٢٤٢ ـ حَدَّثَنَا إِسْمَاعِيلُ بْنُ أَبَانَ : حَدَّثَنَا أَبُو الأَحْوَصِ ، عَنْ آدَمَ بْنِ عَلِيٍّ قَالَ : سَمِعْتُ ابْنَ عُمَرَ رَضِيَ اللهُ عَنْهُمَا يَقُولُ : إِنَّ النَّاسَ يَصِيرُونَ يَوْمَ الْقِيَامَةِ جُثًا ، كُلُّ أُمَّةٍ تَتْبَعُ نَبِيَّهَا ، يَقُولُونَ : يَا فُلانُ اشْفَعْ حَتَّى تَنْتَهِيَ الشَّفَاعَةُ إِلَى النَّبِيِّ صَلَّى اللهُ عَلَيْهِ وَسَلَّمَ فَذَلِكَ يَوْمَ يَبْعَثُهُ اللهُ الْمَقَامَ الْمَحْمُودَ .

243. Narrated Jabir bin 'Abdullāh : Allāh's Messenger said, "Whoever, after listening to the Ādhān (for the prayer) says, 'O Allāh, the Lord of this complete call and of this prayer, which is going to be established! Give Muḥammad Al-Waṣila and Al-

٢٤٣ ـ حَدَّثَنَا عَلِيُّ بْنُ عَيَّاشٍ : حَدَّثَنَا شُعَيْبُ بْنُ أَبِي حَمْزَةَ ، عَنْ مُحَمَّدِ ابْنِ الْمُنْكَدِرِ ، عَنْ جَابِرِ بْنِ عَبْدِ اللهِ رَضِيَ اللهُ عَنْهُمَا : أَنَّ رَسُولَ اللهِ صَلَّى اللهُ عَلَيْهِ وَسَلَّمَ قَالَ : مَنْ قَالَ حِينَ يَسْمَعُ

Fadīla (1) and raise him to Al-Maqām-al-Maḥmūd which You have promised him,' will be granted my intercession for him on the Day of Resurrection."

النداء اللهم رب هذه الدعوة التامة والصلاة القائمة، آت محمدا الوسيلة والفضيلة، وابعثه مقاما محمودا الذي وعدته، حلت له شفاعتي يوم القيامة، رواه حمزة بن عبد الله، عن أبيه، عن النبي صلى الله عليه وسلم.

(185) CHAPTER. And say: Truth (i.e. Islām) has come and falsehood (disbelief) vanished... ......' (17:81)

باب - وقل جاء الحق وزهق الباطل - الآية. يزهق: يهلك.

244. Narrated 'Abdullāh bin Mas'ūd رضي الله عنه : Allāh's Messenger ﷺ entered Mecca (in the year of the Conquest) and there were three-hundred and sixty idols around the Ka'ba. He then started hitting them with a stick in his hand and say:—

> 'Truth (i.e. Islām) has come and falsehood (disbelief) vanished. Truly falsehood (disbelief) is ever bound to vanish.' (17:81)
>
> 'Truth (The Qur'ān and Allāh's Inspiration) has come and falsehood (Iblīs) cannot create anything, nor resurrect anything.' (34:49)

٢٤٤ - حدثنا الحميدي: حدثنا سفيان، عن ابن أبي نجيح، عن مجاهد، عن أبي معمر، عن عبد الله ابن مسعود رضي الله عنه قال: دخل رسول الله صلى الله عليه وسلم مكة وحول البيت ستون وثلثمائة نصب فجعل يطعنها بعود في يده ويقول: جاء الحق وزهق الباطل إن الباطل كان زهوقا. جاء الحق وما يبدئ الباطل وما يعيد.

(1) Al-Waṣīla is the highest position in Paradise which is granted to the Prophet ﷺ particularly; Al-Faḍīla is the extra degree of honour which is bestowed on him above all creation.

(186) CHAPTER. 'They ask you (O. Muhammad) concerning the spirit.' (17:85)

بابٌ ـ وَيَسْأَلُونَكَ عَنِ الرُّوحِ ـ.

245: Narrated 'Abdullāh (رضي الله عنه): While I was in the company of the Prophet ﷺ on a farm and he was reclining on a palm leave stalk, some Jews passed by. Some of them said to the others. "Ask him (the Prophet ﷺ) about the spirit." Some of them said, "What urges you to ask him about it?" Others said, "(Don't) lest he should give you a reply which you dislike." But they said, "Ask him." So they asked him about the Spirit. The Prophet ﷺ kept quiet and did not give them any answer. I knew that he was being divinely inspired so I stayed at my place. When the divine inspiration had been revealed, the Prophet ﷺ said,

> " 'They ask you (O, Muhammad) concerning the Spirit, Say: "The spirit," its knowledge is with my Lord; and of knowledge you (mankind) have been given only a Little." (17:85)

(See Hadith No. 400, Vol 9)

٢٤٥ ـ حدَّثنا عُمَرُ بنُ حَفْصِ بنِ غياثٍ: حدَّثنا أبي: حدَّثنا الأعْمَشُ قالَ: حدَّثني إبْرَاهِيمُ عَنْ عَلْقَمَةَ، عَنْ عَبْدِ اللهِ رَضِيَ اللهُ عَنْهُ قالَ: بَيْنا أنا مَعَ النَّبِيِّ صلى اللهُ عليهِ وسلَّم في حَرْثٍ وهُوَ يَتَّكِئُ على عَسِيبٍ إذْ مَرَّ اليَهُودُ فَقالَ بَعْضُهُمْ لِبَعْضٍ: سَلُوهُ عَنِ الرُّوحِ، فَقالَ: ما رَابَكُمْ إلَيْهِ، وقالَ بَعْضُهُمْ لا يَسْتَقْبِلُكُمْ بِشَيْءٍ تَكْرَهُونَهُ، فَقالُوا سَلُوهُ فَسَألُوهُ عَنِ الرُّوحِ، فَأمْسَكَ النَّبِيُّ صلى اللهُ عليهِ وسلَّم فَلَمْ يَرُدَّ عَلَيْهِمْ شَيْئاً، فعلِمْتُ أنَّهُ يُوحَى إلَيْهِ. فَقُمْتُ مَقامي، فَلَمَّا نَزَلَ الوَحْيُ قالَ ـ وَيَسْألُونَكَ عَنِ الرُّوحِ قُلِ الرُّوحُ مِنْ أمْرِ رَبِّي وَما أُوتِيتُمْ مِنَ العِلْمِ إلاَّ قَلِيلاً ـ

(187) CHAPTER. Neither say your prayer aloud, nor say it in a low tone.' - - - - - - - - - - - - - - (17 : 110)

بابٌ ـ ولا تَجْهَرْ بِصَلاتِكَ وَلا تُخافِتْ بِها ـ.

246. Narrated Ibn 'Abbās : (regarding):—

> Neither say your, prayer aloud, nor say it in a low tone.'
>
> (17 : 110)

This Verse was revealed while Allāh's Messenger was hiding himself in Mecca. When he prayed with his companions, he used to raise his voice with the recitation of the Qur'ān, and if the pagans happened to hear him, they would abuse the Qur'ān, the One who revealed it and the one who brought it. Therefore Allāh said to His Prophet :

> 'Neither say your prayer aloud.'
>
> (17:110)

i. e. your recitation of the Qur'ān lest the pagans should hear you, and abuse the Qur'ān, nor say it in a low tone from your companions, so that they should not hear you, but follow a way between.

٢٤٦ - حدثنا يعقوب بن إبراهيم: حدثنا هشيم: حدثنا أبو بشر، عن سعيد بن جبير، عن ابن عباس رضي الله عنهما في قوله تعالى - ولا تجهر بصلاتك ولا تخافت بها - قال: نزلت ورسول الله صلى الله عليه وسلم مختف بمكة، كان إذا صلى بأصحابه رفع صوته بالقرآن فإذا سمع المشركون سبوا القرآن ومن أنزله ومن جاء به، فقال الله تعالى لنبيه صلى الله عليه وسلم - ولا تجهر بصلاتك - أي بقراءتك فيسمع المشركون فيسبوا القرآن - ولا تخافت بها - عن أصحابك فلا تسمعهم - وابتغ بين ذلك سبيلا - .

247. Narrated 'Āisha : The (above) verse was revealed in connection with the invocations.

٢٤٧ - حدثنا طلق بن غنام: حدثنا زائدة، عن هشام، عن أبيه، عن عائشة رضي الله عنها قالت: أنزل ذلك في الدعاء.

SŪRAT-AL-KAHF (The cave) XVIII

سورة الكهف

In the Name of Allāh, the Most Beneficent, the Most Merciful

بسم الله الرحمن الرحيم

وقال مجاهد: تقرضهم: تتركهم. وكان له ثمر - ذهب وفضة. قال

غَيْرُهُ: جماعةُ الثَّمَرِ. باخِعٌ: مُهْلِكٌ،
أسفًا: نَدَمًا. الكَهْفُ: الفَتْحُ في الجَبَلِ.
والرَّقِيمُ: الكِتابُ. مَرْقُومٌ: مَكْتُوبٌ
مِنَ الرَّقْمِ. رَبَطْنا على قُلُوبِهِمْ:
أَلْهَمْناهُمْ صَبْرًا. لَوْلا أنْ رَبَطْنا على
قَلْبِها. شَطَطًا: إفْراطًا. الوَصِيدُ: الفِناءُ،
جَمْعُهُ وَصائِدُ وَوُصُدٌ. وَيُقالُ الوَصِيدُ
البابُ. مُؤْصَدَةٌ مُطْبَقَةٌ، آصَدَ البابَ
وأَوْصَدَ. بَعَثْناهُمْ: أَحْيَيْناهُمْ. أَزْكَى:
أَكْثَرُ، وَيُقالُ أَحَلُّ، وَيُقالُ
أَكْثَرُ رَيْعًا. قالَ ابنُ عَبّاسٍ: أُكُلَها،
ولَمْ تَظْلِمْ: لَمْ تَنْقُصْ. وَقالَ سَعِيدٌ،
عَنِ ابنِ عَبّاسٍ: الرَّقِيمُ: اللَّوْحُ
مِنْ رَصاصٍ. كَتَبَ عامِلُهُمْ أَسْماءَ
هُمْ ثُمَّ طَرَحَهُ في خِزانَتِهِ، فَضَرَبَ
اللهُ عَلَى آذانِهِمْ فَنامُوا. وَقالَ غَيْرُهُ:
وأَلَتْ تَئِلُ: تَنْجُو. وَقالَ مُجاهِدٌ:
مَوْئِلًا: مَحْرِزًا. لا يَسْتَطِيعُونَ سَمْعًا:
لا يَعْقِلُونَ.

(188) CHAPTER. The Statement of Allāh :–
'But man is more quarrelsome than anything.' (18 : 54)

باب - وَكانَ الإنسانُ أكْثَرَ شَيْءٍ جَدَلًا -.

248. Narrated 'Alī that one night Allāh's Messenger came to him and Fāṭima and said, "Don't you (both)

٢٤٨ - حَدَّثَنا عَلِيُّ بنُ عَبْدِ اللهِ:
حَدَّثَنا يَعْقُوبُ بنُ إبْراهِيمَ بنِ سَعْدٍ:.

offer the (Tahajjud) prayer?" (1) 'Alī said, "When Allāh wishes us to get up, we get up." The Prophet ﷺ then recited:—

> 'But man is more quarrelsome than anything.' (18 : 54)

(See Ḥadīth No. 227,Vol. II)

حدثنا أبي، عن صالح، عن ابن شهاب
قال: أخبرني علي بن حسين أن حسين
بن علي أخبره عن علي رضي الله عنه:
أن رسول الله صلى الله عليه وسلم طرقه
وفاطمة، قال: ألا تصليان؟ رجما
بالغيب: لم يستبن، يقال فرطا:
ندما. سرادقها مثل السرادق،
والحجرة التي تطيف بالفساطيط.
يحاوره من المحاورة ـ لكنا هو الله
ربي ـ أي لكن أنا هو الله ربي، ثم
حذف الألف وأدغم إحدى النونين
في الأخرى ـ وفجرنا خلالهما نهرا ـ
تقول بينهما نهرا. زلقا: لا يثبت
فيه قدم ـ هنالك الولاية ـ ولي الولي
ولاء. عقبا: عاقبة، وعقبى وعقبة
واحد وهي الآخرة. قبلا وقبلا:
استئنافا. ليدحضوا: ليزيلوا،
الدحض: الزلق.

(189) CHAPTER. The Statement of Allāh تعالى :— ·

"And (remember) when Moses said to his boy-servant: I will not give up (travelling) until I reach the junction of the two seas or

باب قوله ـ وإذ قال موسى
لفتاه لا أبرح حتى أبلغ مجمع
البحرين أو أمضي حقبا ـ زمانا
جمعه أحقاب.

(1) The Prophet ﷺ blamed himself for awakening them and then recited.

(until) I spend years and years in travelling) (18:60)

249. Narrated Sa'id bin Jubair: I said to Ibn 'Abbās, "Nauf Al-Bikālī claims that Moses, the companion of Al-Khaḍir was not the Moses of the children of Israel." Ibn 'Abbās said, "The enemy of Allāh (Nauf) told a lie." Narrated Ubaī bin Ka'b that he heard Allāh's Messenger ﷺ saying, "Moses got up to deliver a speech before the children of Israel and he was asked, 'Who is the most learned person among the people?' Moses replied, 'I (am the most learned).' Allāh admonished him for he did not ascribe knowledge to Allāh alone. So Allāh revealed to him:

> 'At the junction of the two seas there is a slave of Ours who is more learned than you.'

Moses asked, 'O my Lord, how can I meet him?' Allāh said, 'Take a fish and put it in a basket (and set out), and where you, will lose the fish, you will find him.' So Moses (took a fish and put it in a basket and) set out, along with his boy-servant Yūsha' bin Nūn, till they reached a rock (on which) they both lay their heads and slept. The fish moved vigorously in the basket and got out of it and fell into the sea and there it took its way through the sea (straight) as in a tunnel). (18:61) Allāh stopped the current of water on both sides of the way created by the fish, and so that way was like a tunnel. When Moses got up, his companion forgot to tell him about the fish, and so they carried on their journey during the rest of the day and the whole night. The

٢٤٩ - حدثنا الحميدي : حدثنا سفيان ، حدثنا عمرو بن دينار قال : أخبرني سعيد بن جبير قال : قلت لابن عباس : إن نوفا البكالي يزعم أن موسى صاحب الخضر ليس هو موسى صاحب بني إسرائيل ، فقال ابن عباس : كذب عدو الله ، حدثني أبي بن كعب أنه سمع رسول الله صلى الله عليه وسلم يقول : إن موسى قام خطيبا في بني إسرائيل ، فسئل : أي الناس أعلم ؟ فقال : أنا ، فعتب الله عليه إذ لم يرد العلم إليه . فأوحى الله إليه إن لي عبدا بمجمع البحرين هو أعلم منك . قال موسى : يا رب فكيف لي به ؟ قال : تأخذ معك حوتا فتجعله في مكتل ثم انطلق وانطلق معه بفتاه يوشع بن نون حتى إذا أتيا الصخرة وضعا رؤوسهما فناما ، واضطرب الحوت في المكتل فخرج منه فسقط في البحر - فاتخذ سبيله في البحر سربا - وأمسك الله عن الحوت جرية الماء فصار عليه مثل الطاق . فلما استيقظ نسي صاحبه أن يخبره بالحوت فانطلقا

next morning Moses asked his boy-servant 'Bring us our early meal; no doubt, we have suffered much fatigue in this journey of ours.' (18:62)

Moses did not get tired till he had passed the place which Allāh had ordered him to seek after. His boy-servant then said to him,' 'Do you remember when we be-took ourselves to the rock I indeed forgot the fish, none but Satan made me forget to remember it. It took its course into the sea in a marvellous way.' (18:63)

There was a tunnel for the fish and for Moses and his boy-servant there was astonishment. Moses said, 'That is what we have been seeking'. So they went back retracing their footsteps. (18:64) They both returned, retracing their steps till they reached the rock. Behold! There they found a man covered with a garment. Moses greeted him. Al-Khadir said astonishingly. 'Is there such a greeting in your land?' Moses said, 'I am Moses.' He said, 'Are you the Moses of the children of Isrāel?' Moses said: Yes, and added, I have come to you so that you may teach me of what you have been taught.

Al-Khadir said, 'You will not be able to have patience with me. (18:66)
O Moses! I have some of Allāh's knowledge which He has bestowed upon me but you do not know it; and you too, have some of Allāh's knowledge which He has bestowed upon you, but I do not know it." Moses said, "Allāh willing, you will find me patient, and I will not disobey you in anything.' (18:69)
Al-Khadir said to him. 'If you then follow me, do not ask me about anything until

بقيةَ يومِهما وليلتِهما حتى إذا كانَ
منَ الغدِ قالَ موسى لفتاهُ ـ آتنا غداءنا
لقدْ لقينا منْ سفرِنا هذا نصبا ـ قالَ:
ولمْ يجدْ موسى النصبَ حتى جاوزَ
المكانَ الذى أمرَ اللهُ بهِ. فقالَ لهُ
فتاهُ ـ أرأيتَ إذْ أوينا إلى الصخرةِ
فإنى نسيتُ الحوتَ وما أنسانيهِ إلاَّ
الشيطانُ أنْ أذكرَهُ واتخذَ سبيلَهُ فى
البحرِ عجبا ـ قالَ: فكانَ للحوتِ
سربا ولموسى ولفتاهُ عجبا. فقالَ
موسى ـ ذلكَ ما كنا نبغى. فارتدا
على آثارِهما قصصا ـ قالَ: رجعا
يقصانِ آثارَهما حتى انتهيا إلى الصخرةِ
فإذا رجلٌ مسجى ثوبا، فسلمَ عليهِ
موسى فقالَ الخضرُ: وأنى بأرضكَ
السلامُ. قالَ: أنا موسى، قالَ: موسى بنى
إسرائيلَ؟ قالَ: نعمْ أتيتُكَ لتعلمنى
مما علمتَ رشدا ـ قالَ إنكَ لنْ
تستطيعَ معىَ صبرا ـ يا موسى إنى على
علمٍ منْ علمِ اللهِ علمنيهِ لا تعلمُهُ
أنتَ، وأنتَ على علمٍ منْ علمِ اللهِ
علمكَ اللهُ لا أعلمُهُ، فقالَ موسى ـ
ستجدُنى إنْ شاءَ اللهُ صابرا ولا أعصى
لكَ أمرا ـ فقالَ لهُ الخضرُ: فإنِ

I myself speak to you concerning it.' (18:70), After that both of them proceeded along the sea coast, till a boat passed by and they requested the crew to let them go on board. The crew recognized Al-Khadir and allowed them to get on board free of charge. When they got on board, suddenly Moses saw that Al-Khadir had pulled out one of the planks of the boat with an adze. Moses said to him.' These people gave us a free lift, yet you have scuttled their boat so as to drown its people! Truly, you have done a dreadful thing.' (18:71)

Al-Khadir said, 'Didn't I say that you can have no patience with me ?' (18:72) Moses said, 'Call me not to account for what I forgot and be not hard upon me for my affair (with you.)" (18:73)

Allāh's Messenger ﷺ said, "The first excuse given by Moses, was that he had forgotten. Then a sparrow came and sat over the edge of the boat and dipped its beak once in the sea. Al-Khadir said to Moses, 'My knowledge and your knowledge, compared to Allāh's knowledge is like what this sparrow has taken out of the sea.' Then they both got out of the boat, and while they were walking on the sea shore, Al-Khadir saw a boy playing with other boys. Al-Khadir got hold of the head of that boy and pulled it out with his hands and killed him. Moses said, 'Have you killed an innocent soul who has killed nobody! Truly, you have done an illegal thing.' (18:74) He said, "Didn't I tell you that you can have no patience with me?' (18:75) (The subnarrator said, 'The second blame was stronger than the first one.) Moses said, 'If I ask you about anything after this, keep me not in your

اتَّبَعْتَنِي فَلَا تَسْأَلْنِي عَنْ شَيْءٍ حَتَّى أُحْدِثَ لَكَ مِنْهُ ذِكْرًا. فَانْطَلَقَا يَمْشِيَانِ عَلَى سَاحِلِ الْبَحْرِ. فَمَرَّتْ سَفِينَةٌ فَكَلَّمُوهُمْ أَنْ يَحْمِلُوهُمْ فَعَرَفُوا الْخَضِرَ فَحَمَلُوهُ بِغَيْرِ نَوْلٍ، فَلَمَّا رَكِبَا فِي السَّفِينَةِ لَمْ يَفْجَأْ إِلَّا وَالْخَضِرُ قَدْ قَلَعَ لَوْحًا مِنْ أَلْوَاحِ السَّفِينَةِ بِالْقَدُومِ. فَقَالَ لَهُ مُوسَى: قَوْمٌ حَمَلُونَا بِغَيْرِ نَوْلٍ عَمَدْتَ إِلَى سَفِينَتِهِمْ فَخَرَقْتَهَا لِتُغْرِقَ أَهْلَهَا لَقَدْ جِئْتَ شَيْئًا إِمْرًا. قَالَ أَلَمْ أَقُلْ لَكَ إِنَّكَ لَنْ تَسْتَطِيعَ مَعِيَ صَبْرًا. قَالَ: لَا تُؤَاخِذْنِي بِمَا نَسِيتُ وَلَا تُرْهِقْنِي مِنْ أَمْرِي عُسْرًا. قَالَ: وَقَالَ رَسُولُ اللهِ صلى الله عليه وسلم: وَكَانَتِ الْأُولَى مِنْ مُوسَى نِسْيَانًا: قَالَ: وَجَاءَ عُصْفُورٌ فَوَقَعَ عَلَى حَرْفِ السَّفِينَةِ فَنَقَرَ فِي الْبَحْرِ نَقْرَةً. فَقَالَ لَهُ الْخَضِرُ: مَا عِلْمِي وَعِلْمُكَ مِنْ عِلْمِ اللهِ إِلَّا مِثْلُ مَا نَقَصَ هَذَا الْعُصْفُورُ مِنْ هَذَا الْبَحْرِ، ثُمَّ خَرَجَا مِنَ السَّفِينَةِ. فَبَيْنَا هُمَا يَمْشِيَانِ عَلَى السَّاحِلِ إِذْ أَبْصَرَ الْخَضِرُ غُلَامًا يَلْعَبُ مَعَ الْغِلْمَانِ، فَأَخَذَ الْخَضِرُ رَأْسَهُ بِيَدِهِ فَاقْتَلَعَهُ بِيَدِهِ فَقَتَلَهُ فَقَالَ لَهُ مُوسَى - أَقَتَلْتَ نَفْسًا زَكِيَّةً بِغَيْرِ نَفْسٍ لَقَدْ جِئْتَ شَيْئًا نُكْرًا - قَالَ أَلَمْ أَقُلْ لَكَ إِنَّكَ لَنْ تَسْتَطِيعَ

company, you have received an excuse from me.' (18:76)

Then they both proceeded until they came to the inhabitants of a town. They asked them food but they refused to entertain them. (In that town) they found there a wall on the point of falling down. (18:77)

Al-Khadir set it up straight with his own hands. Moses said, 'These are people to whom we came, but they neither fed us nor received us as guests. If you had wished, you could surely have exacted some recompense for it. Al-Khadir said, 'This is the parting between me and you ...that is the interpretation of (those things) over which you were unable to hold patience.' (18:78-82)

Allāh's Messenger ﷺ said, "We wished that Moses could have been more patient so that Allāh might have described to us more about their story."

مَعِيَ صَبْرًا - قَالَ: وهَذَا أَشَدُّ مِنَ الأُولَى - قَالَ إِنْ سَأَلْتُكَ عَنْ شَيْءٍ بَعْدَهَا فَلَا تُصَاحِبْنِي قَدْ بَلَغْتَ مِنْ لَدُنِّي عُذْرًا - فَانْطَلَقَا حَتَّى إِذَا أَتَيَا أَهْلَ قَرْيَةٍ اسْتَطْعَمَا أَهْلَهَا فَأَبَوْا أَنْ يُضَيِّفُوهُمَا فَوَجَدَا فِيهَا جِدَارًا يُرِيدُ أَنْ يَنْقَضَّ - قَالَ: مَائِلٌ. فَقَامَ الخَضِرُ فَأَقَامَهُ بِيَدِهِ، فَقَالَ مُوسَى: قَوْمٌ أَتَيْنَاهُمْ فَلَمْ يُطْعِمُونَا ولَمْ يُضَيِّفُونَا - لَوْ شِئْتَ لَاتَّخَذْتَ عَلَيْهِ أَجْرًا - قَالَ هَذَا فِرَاقُ بَيْنِي وَبَيْنِكَ - إِلَى قَوْلِهِ - ذَلِكَ تَأْوِيلُ مَا لَمْ تَسْتَطِعْ عَلَيْهِ صَبْرًا - فَقَالَ رَسُولُ اللهِ صلى اللهُ عليهِ وسلَّم: وَدِدْنَا أَنَّ مُوسَى كَانَ صَبَرَ حَتَّى يَقُصَّ اللهُ عَلَيْنَا مِنْ خَبَرِهِمَا. قَالَ سَعِيدُ بنُ جُبَيْرٍ: فَكَانَ ابنُ عَبَّاسٍ يَقْرَأُ - وكَانَ أَمَامَهُمْ مَلِكٌ يَأْخُذُ كُلَّ سَفِينَةٍ صَالِحَةٍ غَصْبًا وكَانَ يَقْرَأُ - وأَمَّا الغُلَامُ فَكَانَ كَافِرًا وكَانَ أَبَوَاهُ مُؤْمِنَيْنِ -.

(190) CHAPTER. The Statement of Allāh تعالى :–

'But when they reached the junction of the two Seas they forgot (about) their fish, and it took its course through the sea (straight) as in a tunnel.' (18:61)

باب قوله - فلما بلغا مجمع بينهما نسيا حوتهما فاتخذ سبيله في البحر سربا - مذهبا، يسرب: يسلك، ومنه - وسارب بالنهار -.

250. Narrated Ibn Juraij: Ya'lā bin Muslim and 'Amr bin Dīnār and some others narrated the narration of Sa'īd bin Jubair.

Narrated Sa'īd: While we were at the house of Ibn 'Abbās, Ibn 'Abbās said, "Ask me (any question)." I said, "O Abū 'Abbās! May Allāh let me be sacrificed for you! There is a man at Kūfa who is a story-teller called Nauf; who claims that he (Al-Khadir's companion) is not Moses of Banī Isrāel." As for 'Amr, he said to me, "Ibn 'Abbās said, "(Nauf) the enemy of Allāh told a lie." But Ya'lā said to me, "Ibn 'Abbās said, Ubai bin Ka'b said, Allāh's Messenger ﷺ said, 'Once Moses, Allāh's Messenger ﷺ, preached to the people till their eyes shed tears and their hearts became tender, whereupon he finished his sermon. Then a man came to Moses and asked, 'O Allāh's Messenger! Is there anyone on the earth who is more learned than you?' Moses replied, 'No.' So Allāh

٢٥٠ - حدثنا إبراهيم بن موسى: أخبرنا هشام بن يوسف: أن ابن جريج أخبرهم قال: أخبرني يعلى ابن مسلم وعمرو بن دينار، عن سعيد ابن جبير، يزيد أحدهما على صاحبه وغيرهما قد سمعته يحدثه عن سعيد قال: إنا لعند ابن عباس في بيته. إذ قال: سلوني، قلت: أي أبا عباس جعلني الله فداءك: إن بالكوفة رجلا قاصا يقال له نوف يزعم أنه ليس بموسى بني إسرائيل، أما عمرو فقال لي قال قد كذب عدو الله وأما يعلى فقال لي: قال ابن عباس: حدثني أبي ابن كعب قال: قال رسول الله صلى الله عليه وسلم موسى رسول الله صلى الله عليه وسلم، قال: ذكر الناس يوما حتى إذا

admonished him (Moses), for he did not ascribe all knowledge to Allāh. It was said, (on behalf of Allāh), 'Yes, (there is a slave of Ours who knows more than you).' Moses said, 'O my Lord! Where is he?' Allāh said, 'At the junction of the two seas.' Moses said, 'O my Lord! Tell me of a sign whereby I will recognize the place.' " 'Amr said to me, Allāh said, "That place will be where the fish will leave you." Ya'lā said to me, "Allāh said (to Moses), 'Take a dead fish (and your goal will be) the place where it will become alive.' " So Moses took a fish and put it in a basket and said to his boy-servant "I don't want to trouble you, except that you should inform me as soon as this fish leaves you." He said (to Moses)." You have not demanded too much." And that is as mentioned by Allāh:

'And (remember) when Moses said to his attendant . . . . ' (18:60 Yūsha' bin Nūn. (Sa'īd did not state that). The Prophet said, "While the attendant was in the shade of the rock at a wet place, the fish slipped out (alive) while Moses was sleeping. His attendant said (to himself), "I will not wake him,' but when he woke up, he forgot to tell him. The fish slipped out and entered the sea. Allāh stopped the flow of the sea where the fish was, so that its trace looked as if it was made on a rock. 'Amr, forming a hole with his two thumbs and index fingers, said to me, "Like this, as if its trace was made on a rock." Moses said, 'We have suffered much fatigue on this journey of ours." (This was not narrated by Sa'īd). Then they returned back

فاضت العيون ورقت القلوب، ولى فادركه رجل فقال: أى رسول الله، هل فى الارض أحد أعلم منك؟ قال: لا، فعتب عليه إذ لم يرد العلم إلى الله. قيل: بلى، قال: أى رب، فأين؟ قال: بمجمع البحرين قال: أى رب اجعل لى علما أعلم ذلك منه، فقال لى عمرو، قال حيث يفارقك الحوت، وقال لى يعلى: قال خذ حوتا ميتا حيث ينفخ فيه الروح، فأخذ حوتا فجعله فى مكتل فقال لفتاه: لا أكلفك إلا أن تخبرنى بحيث يفارقك الحوت، قال ما كلفت كثيرا. فذلك قوله جل ذكره - وإذ قال موسى لفتاه - يوشع بن نون ليست عن سعيد، قال: فبينما هو فى ظل صخرة فى مكان ثريان إذ تضرب الحوت وموسى نائم، فقال فتاه لا أوقظه حتى إذا استيقظ فنسى أن يخبره وتضرب الحوت حتى دخل البحر فأمسك الله عنه جرية البحر حتى كأن أثره فى حجر. قال لى عمرو، هكذا كأن أثره فى حجر وحلق بين إبهاميه واللتين تليانهما - لقد لقينا من سفرنا هذا نصبا - قال: قد قطع الله عنك النصب، ليست هذه عن سعيد، أخبره فرجعا فوجدا

and found Al-Khaḍir. 'Uthmān bin Abī Sulaimān said to me, (they found him) on a green carpet in the middle of the sea. Al-Khaḍir was covered with his garment with one end under his feet and the other end under his head. When Moses greeted, he uncovered his face and said astonishingly, 'Is there such a greeting in my land? Who are you?' Moses said, 'I am Moses.' Al-Khaḍir said, 'Are you the Moses of Banī Isrāel?' Moses said, 'Yes.' Al-Khaḍir said, "What do you want?' Moses said, 'I came to you so that you may teach me of the truth which you were taught.' Al-Khaḍir said, 'Is it not sufficient for you that the Torah is in your hands and the Divine Inspiration comes to you, O Moses? Verily, I have a knowledge that you ought not learn, and you have a knowledge which I ought not learn.' At that time a bird took with its beak (some water) from the sea: Al-Khaḍir then said, 'By Allāh, my knowledge and your knowledge besides Allāh's Knowledge is like what this bird has taken with its beak from the sea.' Until, when they went on board the boat (18:71), they found a small boat which used to carry the people from this sea-side to the other sea-side. The crew recognised Al-Khaḍir and said, 'The pious slave of Allāh.' (We said to Sa'īd: "Was that Khaḍir?" He said, "Yes.") The boat men said, 'We will not get him on board with fare.' Al-Khaḍir scuttled the boat and

خضيرًا، قال لي عثمان بن أبي سليمان: على طنفسة خضراء على كبد البحر. قال سعيد بن جبير: مسجى بثوبه: قد جعل طرفه تحت رجليه وطرفه تحت رأسه فسلم عليه موسى فكشف عن وجهه وقال: هل بأرضي من سلام؟ من أنت؟ قال: أنا موسى، قال: موسى بني إسرائيل؟ قال: نعم، قال: فما شأنك؟ قال: جئت لتعلمني مما علمت رشدًا، قال: أما يكفيك أن التوراة بيديك وأن الوحي يأتيك يا موسى؟ إن لي علمًا لا ينبغي لك أن تعلمه وإن لك علمًا لا ينبغي لي أن أعلمه. فأخذ طائر بمنقاره من البحر، وقال: والله ما علمي وما علمك في جنب علم الله إلا كما أخذ هذا الطائر بمنقاره من البحر حتى إذا ركبا في السفينة وجدا معابر صغارًا تحمل أهل هذا الساحل إلى أهل هذا الساحل الآخر عرفوه، فقالوا عبد الله الصالح، قال: قلنا لسعيد: خضر؟ قال: نعم، لا نحمله بأجر فخرقها ووتد فيها وتدًا، قال موسى - أخرقتها لتغرق أهلها لقد جئت شيئًا إمرًا - قال مجاهد: منكرًا. قال ألم أقل إنك لن تستطيع معي صبرًا - كانت الأولى نسيانا، والوسطى

then plugged the hole with a piece of wood. Moses said, 'Have you scuttled it in order to drown these people; surely, you have done a dreadful thing.' (18:71) (Mujāhid said. "Moses said so protestingly.") Al-Khaḍir said, 'Didn't I say that you can have no patience with me?' (18:72) The first inquiry of Moses was done because of forgetfulness, the second caused him to be bound with a stipulation, and the third was done intentionally. Moses said, 'Call me not to account for what I forgot and be not hard upon me for my affair (with you).' (18:73)

(Then) they found a boy and Al-Khaḍir killed him. Ya'lā said: Sa'īd said, 'They found boys playing and Al-Khaḍir got hold of a handsome infidel boy, laid him down and then slew him with a knife. Moses said, 'Have you killed an innocent soul who has killed nobody?' (18:74). Then they proceeded and found a wall which was on the point of falling down, and Al-Khaḍir set it up straight. Sa'īd moved his hand thus and said, 'Al-Khaḍir raised his hand and the wall became straight. Ya'lā said, 'I think Sa'īd said, 'Al-Khaḍir touched the wall with his hand and it became straight! (Moses said to Al-Khaḍir), 'If you had wished, you could have taken wages for it." Sa'īd said, 'Wages that we might have eaten.' And there was a king in front (ahead) of them"' (18:79) And there was in front of them. Ibn 'Abbās recited: 'In front of them (was) a king.'

شَرْطًا، وَالثَّالِثَةُ عَمْدًا - قَالَ لَا تُؤَاخِذْنِي
بِمَا نَسِيتُ وَلَا تُرْهِقْنِي مِنْ أَمْرِي
عُسْرًا - لَقِيَا غُلَامًا فَقَتَلَهُ : قَالَ يَعْلَى :
قَالَ سَعِيدٌ : وَجَدَ غِلْمَانًا يَلْعَبُونَ فَأَخَذَ
غُلَامًا كَافِرًا ظَرِيفًا فَأَضْجَعَهُ ثُمَّ ذَبَحَهُ
بِالسِّكِّينِ - قَالَ أَقَتَلْتَ نَفْسًا زَكِيَّةً
بِغَيْرِ نَفْسٍ - لَمْ تَعْمَلْ بِالْحِنْثِ وَابْنُ
عَبَّاسٍ قَرَأَهَا زَكِيَّةً زَاكِيَةً زَاكِيَةً
مُسْلِمَةً كَقَوْلِكَ غُلَامًا زَاكِيًا - فَانْطَلَقَا
فَوَجَدَا جِدَارًا يُرِيدُ أَنْ يَنْقَضَّ فَأَقَامَهُ -
قَالَ سَعِيدٌ بِيَدِهِ هَكَذَا، وَرَفَعَ يَدَهُ
فَاسْتَقَامَ، قَالَ يَعْلَى : حَسِبْتُ أَنَّ
سَعِيدًا قَالَ : فَمَسَحَهُ بِيَدِهِ فَاسْتَقَامَ -
لَوْ شِئْتَ لَاتَّخَذْتَ عَلَيْهِ أَجْرًا - قَالَ
سَعِيدٌ : أَجْرًا نَأْكُلُهُ - وَكَانَ وَرَاءَهُمْ
مَلِكٌ - وَكَانَ أَمَامَهُمْ، قَرَأَهَا ابْنُ عَبَّاسٍ :
أَمَامَهُمْ مَلِكٌ. يَزْعُمُونَ عَنْ غَيْرِ
سَعِيدٍ أَنَّهُ هُدَدُ بْنُ بُدَدٍ، الْغُلَامُ
الْمَقْتُولُ : يَزْعُمُونَ اسْمُهُ حَيْسُورٌ -
مَلِكٌ يَأْخُذُ كُلَّ سَفِينَةٍ غَصْبًا - فَأَرَدْتُ
إِذَا هِيَ مَرَّتْ بِهِ أَنْ يَدَعَهَا لِعَيْبِهَا .
فَإِذَا جَاوَزُوا أَصْلَحُوهَا فَانْتَفَعُوا بِهَا
وَمِنْهُمْ مَنْ يَقُولُ سَدُّوهَا بِقَارُورَةٍ ،
وَمِنْهُمْ مَنْ يَقُولُ بِالْقَارِ . كَانَ أَبَوَاهُ
مُؤْمِنَيْنِ وَكَانَ كَافِرًا - فَخَشِينَا أَنْ
يُرْهِقَهُمَا طُغْيَانًا وَكُفْرًا - أَنْ يَحْمِلَهُمَا
حُبُّهُ عَلَى أَنْ يُتَابِعَاهُ عَلَى دِينِهِ - فَأَرَدْنَا

It is said on the authority of somebody other than Sa'īd that the king was Hudad bin Budad. They say that the boy was called Ḥaisūr. 'A king who seized every ship by force. (18:79) So I wished that if that boat passed by him, he would leave it because of its defect and when they have passed they would repair it and get benefit from it. Some people said that they closed that hole with a bottle, and some said with tar. 'His parents were believers, and he (the boy) was a non-believer and we (Khaḍir) feared lest he would oppress them by obstinate rebellion and disbelief.' (18:80) (i.e. that their love for him would urge them to follow him in his religion, 'so we (Khaḍir) desired that their Lord should change him for them for one better in righteousness and near to mercy' (18:81). This was in reply to Moses' saying: Have you killed an innocent soul.'?(18:74). 'Near to mercy" means they will be more merciful to him than they were to the former whom Khaḍir had killed. Other than Sa'īd said that they were compensated with a girl. Dāwūd bin Abī 'Āṣim said on the authority of more than one that this next child was a girl.

أنْ يُبْدِلَهُما رَبُّهُما خَيْراً مِنْهُ زَكاةً وأقْرَبَ رُحْماً ـ لقَوْلِهِ ـ أقَتَلْتَ نَفْساً زَكِيَّةً ـ وأقْرَبَ رُحْماً : هُمَا بِهِ أرْحَمُ مِنْهُما بالأوَّلِ الَّذِى قَتَلَ ، خَضِرٌ . وزَعَمَ غيرُ سَعِيدٍ أنَّهُما أُبْدِلا جارِيَةً . وأمّا دَاوُدُ بنُ أبي عاصِمٍ فقالَ عَنْ غَيْرِ واحِدٍ إنَّها جارِيَةٌ .

(191) CHAPTER. The Statement of Allāh (تعالى) :–

So, when they had passed on further, Moses said to his boy-servant, Bring us our early meal: Truly we have suffered much fatigue in this journey of ours......following the path they had come.' (18:62-64)

بَابٌ قَوْلُهُ - فَلَمَّا جَاوَزَا قَالَ لِفَتَاهُ آتِنَا غَدَاءَنَا لَقَدْ لَقِينَا مِنْ سَفَرِنَا هَذَا نَصَبًا - إِلَى قَوْلِهِ قَصَصًا - صُنْعًا: عَمَلاً. حِوَلاً: تَحَوُّلاً - قَالَ ذَلِكَ مَا كُنَّا نَبْغِ فَارْتَدَّا عَلَى آثَارِهِمَا قَصَصًا - نُكْرًا: دَاهِيَةً. يَنْقَضَّ: يَنْقَاضُ كَمَا يَنْقَاضُ السِّنُّ. لَتَخِذْتَ وَاتَّخَذْتَ وَاحِدٌ. رُحْمًا مِنَ الرُّحْمِ وَهِيَ أَشَدُّ مُبَالَغَةً مِنَ الرَّحْمَةِ وَيُظَنُّ أَنَّهُ مِنَ الرَّحِيمِ. وَتُدْعَى مَكَّةُ أُمَّ رُحْمٍ أَيِ الرَّحْمَةُ تَنْزِلُ بِهَا.

(192) CHAPTER. The Statement of Allāh (تعالى) :–

'He said: Do you remember (what happened) when we betook ourselves to the rock......' (18:63)

بَابُ قَوْلِهِ تَعَالَى - قَالَ أَرَأَيْتَ إِذْ أَوَيْنَا إِلَى الصَّخْرَةِ - إِلَى آخِرِهِ.

251. Narrated Sa'īd bin Jubair: I said to Ibn 'Abbās, "Nauf-al-Bakālī" claims that Moses of Banī Isrāel was not Moses, the companion of Al-Khaḍir." Ibn 'Abbās said, "Allāh's enemy tells a lie! Ubaī

٢٥١ - حَدَّثَنِي قُتَيْبَةُ بْنُ سَعِيدٍ: حَدَّثَنِي سُفْيَانُ بْنُ عُيَيْنَةَ، عَنْ عَمْرِو ابْنِ دِينَارٍ، عَنْ سَعِيدِ بْنِ جُبَيْرٍ قَالَ: قُلْتُ لِابْنِ عَبَّاسٍ: إِنَّ نَوْفًا الْبَكَالِيَّ

bin Ka'b narrated to us that Allāh's Messenger ﷺ said, 'Moses got up to deliver a sermon before Banī Israel and he was asked, 'Who is the most learned person among the people?' Moses replied, 'I (am the most learned).' Allāh then admonished Moses for he did not ascribe all knowledge to Allāh only. (Then) came the Divine Inspiration:—

'Yes, one of Our slaves at the junction of the two seas is more learned than you.'

Moses said, 'O my Lord! How can I meet him?' Allāh said, 'Take a fish in a basket and wherever the fish is lost, follow it (you will find him at that place). So Moses set out along with his attendant Yūsha' bin Nūn, and they carried with them a fish till they reached a rock and rested there. Moses put his head down and slept. (Sufyān, a sub-narrator said that somebody other than 'Amr said) 'At the rock there was a water spring called 'Al-Ḥayāt' and none came in touch with its water but became alive. So some of the water of that spring fell over that fish, so it moved and slipped out of the basket and entered the sea. When Moses woke up, he asked his attendant, 'Bring our early meal......... (18:62)'. The narrator added: Moses did not suffer from fatigue except after he had passed the place he had been ordered to observe. His attendant Yūsha' bin Nūn said to him, 'Do you remember (what happened) when we betook our

يزعم أنّ موسى بني إسرائيل لبس بموسى الخضر، فقال: كذب عدوّ الله، حدّثنا أُبيّ بن كعب، عن رسول الله صلى الله عليه وسلّم قال: قام موسى خطيبا في بني إسرائيل فقيل له: أيّ الناس أعلم؟ قال: أنا، فعتب الله عليه إذ لم يردّ العلم إليه وأوحى إليه: بلى عبد من عبادي بمجمع البحرين هو أعلم منك. قال: أيّ ربّ، كيف السبيل إليه؟ قال: تأخذ حوتا في مكتل فحيثما فقدت الحوت فاتبعه. قال: فخرج موسى ومعه فتاه يوشع بن نون ومعهما الحوت حتى انتهيا إلى الصخرة فنزلا عندها. قال: فوضع موسى رأسه فنام. قال سفيان: وفي حديث غير عمرو قال: وفي أصل الصخرة عين يقال لها الحياة لا يصيب من مائها شيء إلا حيي. فأصاب الحوت من ماء تلك العين، قال: فتحرّك وانسلّ من المكتل فدخل البحر فلمّا استيقظ موسى ـ قال لفتاه آتنا غداءنا الآية. قال: ولم يجد النصب حتى جاوز ما أمر به. قال له فتاه يوشع بن نون ـ أرأيت إذ أوينا إلى الصخرة فإنّي نسيت الحوت ـ الآية، قال: فرجعا يقصّان في آثارهما فوجدا في البحر

selves to the rock? I did indeed forget (about) the fish . . . .'(18:63) The narrator added: So they came back, retracing their steps and then they found in the sea, the way of the fish looking like a tunnel. So there was an astonishing event for his attendant, and there was tunnel for the fish. When they reached the rock, they found a man covered with a garment. Moses greeted him. The man said astonishingly, 'Is there any such greeting in your land?' Moses said, 'I am Moses.' The man said, 'Moses of Banī Israel?' Moses said, 'Yes,' and added, 'may I follow you so that you teach me something of the Knowledge which you have been taught?' (18:66). Al-Khaḍir said to him, 'O Moses! You have something of Allāh's knowledge which Allāh has taught you and which I do not know; and I have something of Allāh's know ledge which Allāh has taught me and which you do not know.' Moses said, 'But I will follow you.' Al-Khaḍir said, 'Then if you follow me, ask me no question about anything until I myself speak to you concerning it.' (18:70). After that both of them proceeded along the seashore. There passed by them a boat whose crew recognized Al-Khaḍir and received them on board free of charge. So they both got on board. A sparrow came and sat on the edge of the boat and dipped its beak into the sea. Al-Khaḍir said to Moses. 'My knowledge and your knowledge and all the creation's knowledge compared to Allāh's

كالطاق ممر الحوت . فكان لفتاه عجبا وللحوت سربا ، قال : فلما انتهيا إلى الصخرة إذا هما برجل مسجى بثوب فسلم عليه موسى ، قال : وأنى بأرضك السلام . فقال : أنا موسى ، قال : موسى بنى إسرائيل ؟ قال : نعم . قال : هل أتبعك على أن تعلمني مما علمت رشدا ؟ قال له الخضر : يا موسى إنك على علم من علم الله علمكه الله لا أعلمه ، وأنا على علم من علم الله علمنيه الله لا تعلمه . قال : بل أتبعك ، قال : فإن اتبعتني فلا تسألني عن شيء حتى أحدث لك منه ذكرا . فانطلقا يمشيان على الساحل فمرت بهما سفينة فعرف الخضر فحملوهم فى سفينتهم بغير نول ، يقول بغير أجر : فركبا السفينة . قال : ووقع عصفور على حرف السفينة فغمس منقاره فى البحر فقال الخضر لموسى : ما علمك وعلمى وعلم الخلائق فى علم الله إلا مقدار ما غمس هذا العصفور منقاره . قال : فلم يفجأ موسى إذ عمد الخضر إلى قدوم فخرق السفينة ، فقال له موسى : قوم حملونا بغير نول عمدت إلى سفينتهم فخرقتها لتغرق أهلها لقد جئت ، الآية . فانطلقا إذا

knowledge is not more than the water taken by this sparrow's beak.' Then Moses was startled by Al-Khaḏir's action of taking an adze and scuttling the boat with it. Moses said to him, 'These people gave us a free lift, but you intentionally scuttled their boat so as to drown them. Surely you have. . . . . (18:71)

Then they both proceeded and found a boy playing with other boys. Al-Khaḏir took hold of him by the head and cut it off. Moses said to him, 'Have you killed an innocent soul who has killed nobody? Surely you have done an illegal thing!' (18:74)

He said, "Didn't I tell you that you will not be able to have patient with me up to ...but they refused to entertain them as their guests. There they found a wall therein at the point of collapsing.' (18:75-77)

Al-Khaḏir moved his hand thus and set it upright (repaired it). Moses said to him, 'When we entered this town, they neither gave us hospitality nor fed us; if you had wished, you could have taken wages for it,' Al-Khaḏir said, 'This is the parting between you and me. I will tell you the interpretation of (those things) about which you were unable to hold patience.'. . . . .(18:78)

Allāh's Messenger ﷺ said, 'We wished that Moses could have been more patient so that He (Allāh) could have described to us more about their story.'

Ibn 'Abbās used to recite:—

'And in front (ahead) of them there

هُمَا بِغُلامٍ يَلْعَبُ مَعَ الغِلْمانِ . فأخَذَ
الخَضِرُ بِرَأسِهِ فقَطَعَهُ . قالَ لَهُ مُوسَى -
أقَتَلْتَ نَفْسًا زَكِيَّةً بِغَيْرِ نَفْسٍ لَقَدْ
جِئْتَ شَيْئًا نُكْرًا . قالَ أَلَمْ أَقُلْ لَكَ
إنَّكَ لَنْ تَسْتَطِيعَ مَعِيَ صَبْرًا - إلى قَوْلِهِ -
فأبَوْا أنْ يُضَيِّفُوهُما فَوَجَدَا فِيها
جِدَارًا يُرِيدُ أنْ يَنْقَضَّ - فقالَ بِيَدِهِ
هَكَذا فأقامَهُ . فقالَ لَهُ مُوسَى : إنَّا
دَخَلْنا هَذِهِ القَرْيَةَ فَلَمْ يُضَيِّفُونا
ولَمْ يُطْعِمُونا - لَوْ شِئْتَ لاتَّخَذْتَ
عَلَيْهِ أجْرًا ، قالَ هَذا فِراقُ بَيْنِي
وَبَيْنِكَ سَأُنَبِّئُكَ بِتَأْوِيلِ ما لَمْ تَسْتَطِعْ عَلَيْهِ
صَبْرًا - فقالَ رَسُولُ اللهِ صلى اللهُ عليه
وسلَّمَ : وَدِدْنا أنَّ مُوسَى صَبَرَ حَتَّى
يَقُصَّ عَلَيْنا مِنْ أمْرِهِما . قالَ : وكانَ
ابنُ عَبَّاسٍ يَقْرَأُ - وكانَ أمامَهُمْ مَلِكٌ
يأخُذُ كُلَّ سَفِينَةٍ - صالِحَةٍ - غَصْبًا -
وأمَّا الغُلامُ فكانَ كافِرًا .

was a king who used to seize every (serviceable) boat by force. (18:79) .... And as for the boy he was a disbeliever."

(193) CHAPTER. The Statement of Allāh تعالى :–

'Say: (O, Muḥammad) Shall We tell you the greatest losers in respect of their deeds?' (18:103)

باب قوله - قل هل ننبئكم بالأخسرين أعمالا -

252. Narrated Muṣ'ab: I asked my father, "Was the Verse:–

'Say: (O Muḥammad) Shall We tell you the greatest losers in respect of their deeds?' (18:103)

revealed regarding 'Al-Ḥarūriyya?" He said, "No, but regarding the Jews and the Christians, for the Jews disbelieved Muḥammad ﷺ and the Christians disbelieved in Paradise and say that there are neither meals nor drinks therein. Al-Ḥarūriyya are those people who break their pledge to Allāh after they have confirmed that they will fulfill it, and Sa'd used to call them 'Al Fāsiqīn (evil-doers who foresake Allāh's obedience).

٢٥٢ - حدثني محمد بن بشار: حدثنا محمد بن جعفر: حدثنا شعبة، عن عمرو، عن مصعب: سألت أبي - قل هل ننبئكم بالأخسرين أعمالا - هم الحرورية؟ قال: لا، هم اليهود والنصارى. أما اليهود فكذبوا محمدا صلى الله عليه وسلم، وأما النصارى كفروا بالجنة وقالوا لا طعام فيها ولا شراب. والحرورية الذين ينقضون عهد الله من بعد ميثاقه، وكان سعد يسميهم الفاسقين.

(194) CHAPTER. 'They are those

باب أولئك الذين كفروا

who deny in the Signs of their Lord and the meeting with Him (in the Hereafter); so (all of) their deeds are in vain.' (18:105)

253: Narrated Abū Huraira : Allāh's Messenger ﷺ said, "On the Day of Resurrection, a huge fat man will come who will not weigh, the weight of the wing of a mosquito in Allāh's Sight." and then the Prophet ﷺ added, 'We shall not give them any weight on the Day of Resurrection.' (18:105)

In the Name of Allāh, the Most Beneficent, the Most Merciful
SŪRAT KĀF ḤĀ YĀ 'AIN ṢĀD XIX

بِآيَاتِ رَبِّهِمْ وَلِقَائِهِ فَحَبِطَتْ أَعْمَالُهُمْ ـ الْآيَةَ.

٢٥٣ ـ حَدَّثَنَا مُحَمَّدُ بْنُ عَبْدِ اللهِ: حَدَّثَنَا سَعِيدُ بْنُ أَبِي مَرْيَمَ: أَخْبَرَنَا الْمُغِيرَةُ بْنُ عَبْدِ الرَّحْمَنِ: حَدَّثَنِي أَبُو الزِّنَادِ، عَنِ الْأَعْرَجِ، عَنْ أَبِي هُرَيْرَةَ رَضِيَ اللهُ عَنْهُ، عَنْ رَسُولِ اللهِ صَلَّى اللهُ عَلَيْهِ وَسَلَّمَ قَالَ: إِنَّهُ لَيَأْتِي الرَّجُلُ الْعَظِيمُ السَّمِينُ يَوْمَ الْقِيَامَةِ لَا يَزِنُ عِنْدَ اللهِ جَنَاحَ بَعُوضَةٍ. وَقَالَ اقْرَءُوا ـ فَلَا نُقِيمُ لَهُمْ يَوْمَ الْقِيَامَةِ وَزْنًا ـ وَعَنْ يَحْيَى بْنِ بُكَيْرٍ، عَنِ الْمُغِيرَةِ بْنِ عَبْدِ الرَّحْمَنِ، عَنْ أَبِي الزِّنَادِ مِثْلُهُ.

بِسْمِ اللهِ الرَّحْمَنِ الرَّحِيمِ
سُورَةُ كهيعص

وَقَالَ ابْنُ عَبَّاسٍ ـ أَسْمِعْ بِهِمْ وَأَبْصِرْ ـ اللهُ يَقُولُهُ وَهُمُ الْيَوْمَ لَا يَسْمَعُونَ وَلَا يُبْصِرُونَ فِي ضَلَالٍ مُبِينٍ: يَعْنِي قَوْلَهُ ـ أَسْمِعْ بِهِمْ وَأَبْصِرْ ـ الْكُفَّارُ يَوْمَئِذٍ أَسْمَعُ شَيْءٍ وَأَبْصَرُهُ..

لأَرْجُمَنَّكَ : لأَشْتُمَنَّكَ . وَرِئْيا : مَنْظَرًا. وَقالَ أبو وائِلٍ : عَلِمَتْ مَرْيَمُ أنَّ التَّقِيَّ ذُو نُهْيَةٍ حتَّى قالَتْ - إنِّي أعُوذُ بالرَّحْمَنِ مِنْكَ إنْ كُنْتَ تَقِيًّا - وَقالَ ابنُ عُيَيْنَةَ : تَؤُزُّهُمْ أزًّا : تُزْعِجُهُمْ إلى المَعاصِي إزْعاجا. وَقالَ مُجاهِدٌ : إدًّا : عِوَجا. وَقالَ ابنُ عَبَّاسٍ : وِرْدًا : عِطاشا. أثاثا : مالا. إدًّا : قَوْلاً عَظِيما. رِكْزًا : صَوْتا. وَقالَ غَيْرُهُ : غَيًّا : خُسْرانا. بُكِيًّا : جَماعَةُ باكٍ. صِلِيًّا : صَلِيَ يَصْلَى. نَدِيًّا والنَّادي واحِدٌ : مَجْلِسا.

(195) CHAPTER. The Statement of Allāh ﷻ :–

'And warn them of the day of distress (regrets).' (19:39)

بابُ قَوْلِهِ عَزَّ وَجَلَّ - وأنْذِرْهُمْ يَوْمَ الحَسْرَةِ -.

254. Narrated Abū Sa'īd Al-Khudrī ؓ : Allāh's Messenger ﷺ said, "On the Day of Resurrection Death will be brought forward in the shape of a black and white ram. Then a callmaker will call, 'O people of Paradise!' Thereupon they will stretch their necks and look carefully. The caller will say, 'Do you know this?' They will say, 'Yes, this is Death.' By then all of them will have seen it. Then it will be announced again, 'O people of Hell!' They will stretch their necks and look carefully. The

٢٥٤ - حدَّثَنا عُمَرُ بنُ حَفْصِ ابنِ غِياثٍ : حدَّثَنا أبي! حدَّثَنا الأعْمَشُ : حدَّثَنا أبو صالِحٍ ، عَنْ أبي سَعيدٍ الخُدْرِيِّ رَضِيَ اللهُ عَنْهُ قالَ : قالَ رَسُولُ اللهِ صلى اللهُ عليه وسلَّم: يُؤْتَى بالمَوْتِ كَهَيْئَةِ كَبْشٍ أمْلَحَ فَيُنادي مُنادٍ يا أهْلَ الجَنَّةِ فَيَشْرَئِبُّونَ وَيَنْظُرُونَ فَيَقُولُ : هَلْ تَعْرِفُونَ هذا؟ فَيَقُولُونَ : نَعَمْ ، هذا المَوْتُ ، وكُلُّهُمْ قَدْ رآهُ . ثُمَّ يُنادي :

caller will say, 'Do you know this?' They will say, 'Yes, this is Death.' And by then all of them will have seen it. Then it (that ram) will be slaughtered and the caller will say, 'O people of Paradise! Eternity for you and no death. O people of Hell! Eternity for you and no death.''' Then the Prophet ﷺ recited:–

> 'And warn them of the Day of distress when the case has been decided, while (now) they are in a state of carelessness (i.e. the people of the world) and they do not believe.' (19:39)

يا أهل النار ، فيشرئبون وينظرون فيقول: هل تعرفون هذا ؟ فيقولون: نعم ، هذا الموت ، وكلهم قد رآه فيذبح . ثم يقول : يا أهل الجنة خلود فلا موت . ويا أهل النار خلود فلا موت ، ثم قرأ - وأنذرهم يوم الحسرة إذ قضي الأمر وهم في غفلة :وهؤلاء في غفلة أهل الدنيا- وهم لا يؤمنون -.

(196) CHAPTER. The Statement of Allāh تعالى :–

> "And we (angels) descend not, but by the command of your Lord. To Him belongs what is before us and what is behind and what is between, these two. . . . .(19:64)

باب قوله - وما نتنزل إلا بأمر ربك له ما بين أيدينا وما خلفنا وما بين ذلك -.

255. Narrated Ibn 'Abbās رضي الله عنهما : The Prophet ﷺ said to Gabriel, "What prevents you from visiting us more often than you visit us now?" So there was revealed:–

> 'And we (angels) descend not but by the command of your Lord. To Him belongs what is before us and what is behind us. . . . .(19:64)

٢٥٥ - حدثنا أبو نعيم : حدثنا عمر بن ذر قال : سمعت أبي ، عن سعيد بن جبير ، عن ابن عباس رضي الله تعالى عنهما :قال النبي صلى الله عليه وسلم لجبريل : ما يمنعك أن تزورنا أكثر مما تزورنا ؟ فنزلت - وما نتنزل إلا بأمر ربك له ما بين أيدينا وما خلفنا -.

(197) CHAPTER. The Statement of Allāh تعالى :—

'Have you then seen him who disbelieved in Our Signs and (yet) says: I shall certainly be given wealth and children?' (19:77)

بابٌ قوْله ـ أفرأيتَ الذى كفَرَ بآياتِنا وقالَ لأُوتينَّ مالاً وولدًا ـ.

256. Narrated Khabbāb: I came to Al-'Āṣī bin Wā'il As-Sahmī and demanded something which he owed me. He said, "I will not give you (your money) till you disbelieve in Muḥammad." I said, "No, I shall not disbelieve in Muḥammad till you die and then be resurrected." He said, "Will I die and then be resurrected?" I said, 'Yes'. He said', "Then I will have wealth and children there, and I will pay you (there)." So this Verse was revealed:—

'Have you then seen him who disbelieved in Our Signs and (yet) says: I shall certainly be given wealth and children?' ....(19:77)

٢٥٦ ـ حدثنا الحُمَيْدِيُّ: حدثنا سُفيانُ، عنِ الأعْمَشِ، عنْ أبي الضُّحى، عنْ مَسْروقٍ قالَ: سمعْتُ خبّابًا قالَ: جِئتُ العاصيَ بنَ وائلٍ السَّهْميَّ أتقاضاهُ حقًّا لى عِنْدَهُ فقالَ: لا أُعطيكَ حتّى تَكفُرَ بمُحمّدٍ صلى الله عليه وسلَّم، فقلْتُ: لا حتّى تموتَ ثمَّ تُبعثَ، قالَ: وإني لمَيِّتٌ ثمَّ مَبعوثٌ؟ قلْتُ: نعَمْ، قالَ: إنَّ لى هُناكَ مالاً وولدًا فأقضيكَ، فنزلَتْ هذهِ الآيةُ ـ أفرأيتَ الذى كفَرَ بآياتِنا وقالَ لأُوتينَّ مالا وولدًا ـ رواهُ الثوريُّ وشُعْبةُ وحفصٌ وأبو مُعاويةَ ووكيعٌ، عنِ الأعْمَشِ.

(198) CHAPTER. 'Has he known the unseen, or has he taken a convenant from (Allāh) the Beneficent?' (19:78)

بابٌ أطّلعَ الغيْبَ أمِ اتّخذَ عِندَ الرَّحمنِ عهدًا ـ قالَ: موْثقا.

257. Narrated Khabbāb: I was a

٢٥٧ ـ حدثنا مُحمّدُ بنُ كَثيرٍ:

blacksmith in Mecca. Once I made a sword for Al-'Āṣī bin Wā'il As-Sahmī. When I went to demand its price, he said, "I will not give it to you till you disbelieve in Muḥammad." I said, "I shall not disbelieve in Muḥammad till Allāh make you die and then bring you to life again." He said, "If Allāh should make me die and then resurrect me and I would have wealth and children." So Allāh revealed:—

> 'Have you seen him who disbelieved in Our Signs, and (yet) says: I shall certainly be given wealth and children? Has he known the unseen or has he taken a covenant from (Allāh) the Beneficent?'
> (19:77-78)

أخبرنا سفيان، عن الأعمش، عن أبى الضحى، عن مسروق عن خباب قال: كنت قينا بمكة فعملت للعاصى بن وائل السهمى سيفا فجئت أتقاضاه فقال: لا أعطيك حتى تكفر بمحمد، قلت: لا أكفر بمحمد صلى الله عليه وسلم حتى يميتك الله ثم يحييك، قال: إذا أماتنى الله ثم بعثنى ولى مال وولد فأنزل الله - أفرأيت الذى كفر بآياتنا وقال لأوتين مالا وولدا أطلع الغيب أم اتخذ عند الرحمن عهدا - قال: موثقا. لم يقل الأشجعى، عن سفيان سيفا ولا موثقا.

(199) CHAPTER. 'Nay! We shall record what he says, and We shall add and add to his Punishment.' (19:79)

باب كلا سنكتب ما يقول ونمد له من العذاب مدا.

258. Narrated Masrūq: Khabbāb said, "During the pre-Islāmic period, I was a blacksmith and Al-'Āṣī bin Wā'il owed me a debt." So Khabbāb went to him to demand the debt. He said, "I will not give you (your due) till you disbelieve in Muḥammad." Khabbāb said, "By Allāh, I shall not disbelieve in Muḥammad till Allāh makes you die and then resurrects you." Al-'Āṣī said, "So leave me till I die and then be resurrected, for I will be given wealth and children whereupon I will pay you your debt." So this Verse was revealed:—

٢٥٨ - حدثنا بشر بن خالد: حدثنا محمد بن جعفر، عن شعبة، عن سليمان: سمعت أبا الضحى يحدث عن مسروق عن خباب قال: كنت قينا فى الجاهلية وكان لى دين على العاصى بن وائل، قال: فأتاه يتقاضاه فقال: لا أعطيك حتى تكفر بمحمد صلى الله عليه وسلم فقال: والله لا أكفر حتى يميتك الله ثم تبعث،

> 'Have you seen him who disbelieved in Our Signs and, (yet) says: I shall certainly be given wealth and children.' (19:77)

قالَ: فذَرْني حتّى أموتَ ثمّ أبعثَ فسوفَ أُوتى مالا وولدًا فأقضيكَ فنزلتْ هذهِ الآيةُ - أفرأيتَ الّذى كفرَ بآياتِنا وقالَ لأُوتينَّ مالاً وولدًا.

(200) CHAPTER. And We shall inherit from him all that he talks of, and he shall appear before Us alone (without his wealth and children).' (19:80)

بابٌ ونرثُهُ ما يقولُ ويأتينا فردًا - وقالَ ابنُ عبّاسٍ: الجبالُ هدًّا: هدمًا.

259. Narrated Khabbāb: I was a blacksmith and Al-Āṣi Bin Wā'il owed me a debt, so I went to him to demand it. He said to me. "I will not pay you your debt till you disbelieve in Muḥammad." I said, "I will not disbelieve in Muḥammad till you die and then be resurrected." He said, "Will I be resurrected after my death? If so, I shall pay you (there) if I should find wealth and children." So there was revealed:—

> Have you seen him who disbelieved in Our Signs, and yet says: I shall certainly be given wealth and children? Has he, known to the unseen or has he taken a covenant from (Allāh) the Beneficent? Nay! We shall record what he says, and we shall add and add to his punishment. And We shall inherit from him all that he talks of, and he shall appear before Us alone.'
>
> (19:77:80)

٢٥٩ - حدّثنا يحيى: حدّثنا وكيعٌ، عنِ الأعمشِ، عن أبي الضُّحى، عن مسروقٍ، عن خبّابٍ قالَ: كنتُ رجلاً قينًا وكانَ لى على العاصى بنِ وائلٍ دَينٌ فأتيتُهُ أتقاضاهُ، فقالَ لى: لا أقضيكَ حتّى تكفرَ بمحمّدٍ. قالَ: قلتُ لنْ أكفرَ بهِ حتّى تموتَ ثمّ تُبعثَ، قالَ: وإنّى لمبعوثٌ مِن بعدِ الموتِ؟ فسوفَ أقضيكَ إذا رجعتُ إلى مالٍ وولدٍ، قالَ: فنزلتْ - أفرأيتَ الّذى كفرَ بآياتِنا وقالَ لأُوتينَّ مالاً وولدًا أطّلعَ الغيبَ أمِ اتّخذَ عندَ الرّحمنِ عهدًا كلاّ سنكتبُ ما يقولُ ونمدُّ لهُ منَ العذابِ مدًّا ونرثُهُ ما يقولُ ويأتينا فردًا -

In the Name of Allāh,
the Most Beneficent, the Most Merciful

SŪRAT ṬĀHĀ: XX

بِسْمِ اللهِ الرَّحْمَنِ الرَّحِيمِ

سورة طٰـهٰ

قَالَ عِكْرِمَةُ وَالضَّحَّاكُ بِالنَّبَطِيَّةِ . أَيْ طَهَ : يَا رَجُلُ وَقَالَ مُجَاهِدٌ : أَلْقَى : صَنَعَ . أَزْرِى : ظَهْرِى ، فَيُسْحِتَكُمْ : يُهْلِكَكُم . المُثْلَى : تَأنِيثُ الأَمْثَلِ يَقُولُ بِدِينِكُمْ . يُقَالُ خُذِ المُثْلَى خُذِ الأَمْثَلَ . ثُمَّ ائْتُوا صَفًّا . يُقَالُ هَلْ أَتَيْتَ الصَّفَّ اليَوْمَ ؟ يَعنى المُصَلَّى الَّذى الَّذى يُصَلَّى فيه . فَأَوْجَسَ : أَضْمَرَ خَوْفًا فَذَهَبَتِ الوَاوُ مِنْ خِيفَةً لِكَسْرَةِ الخاءِ . فى جُذُوعِ : أىْ عَلَى جُذُوعِ النَّخْلِ . خَطْبُكَ : بَالُكَ . مِسَاسَ : مَصْدَرُ ماسه مِسَاسا . لَنَنْسِفَنَّه : لَنَذْرِيَنَّه . قاعا : يَعْلُوه المَاءُ . والصَّفْصَفُ : المُسْتَوِى مِنَ الأَرْضِ . وَقَالَ مُجَاهِدٌ : أَوْزَارً : أثقالاً . مِنْ زِينَةِ القَوْمِ : الحَلْىِ الَّذى اسْتَعَارُوا . مِنْ آلِ فِرعَوْنَ : فَقَذَفْنُهَا فَأَلْقَيْتُهَا . أَلْقَى : صَنَعَ فَنَسِيَ مُوسَاهُمْ : يَقُولُونَه أخطأ الرَّبَّ . لا يَرْجِعُ إِلَيْهِمْ قَوْلاً : العِجْلُ . هَمْسا : حِسُّ الأَقْدَامِ . حَشَرْتَنِى أَعْمَى عَنْ حُجَّتِى وَقَدْ كُنْتُ بَصِيرًا فى الدُّنْيا . قالَ ابن عَبَّاسٍ : بِقَبَسٍ : ضَلُّوا الطَّرِيقَ وكانُوا شاتِينَ فَقَالَ : إِنْ لَمْ أَجِدْ عَلَيْهَا مَنْ يَهْدِى الطَّرِيقَ آتِكُمْ بِنَارٍ تُوقِدونَ . وَقَالَ ابن عُيَيْنَةَ : أَمْثَلُهُمْ طَرِيقَةً :

أعدلهم. وقال ابن عباس: هضما: لا يظلم فيهضم من حسناته. عوجا: واديا. ولا أمتا: رابية. سيرتها: حالتها الأولى. النهى: التقى. ضنكا: الشقاء. هوى: شقي. بالواد المقدس: المبارك. طوى: اسم الوادي. بملكنا: بأمرنا. مكانا سوى: منصف بينهم. يبسا: يابسا. على قدر: موعد. لاتنيا: لا تضعفا. يفرط: عقوبة.

(201) CHAPTER. The Statement of Allāh :–

'And I have chosen you for Myself.' (20:41)

باب قوله - واصطنعتك لنفسي -.

260. Narrated Abū Ḥuraira : Allāh's Messenger said, "Adam and Moses met, and Moses said to Adam "You are the one who made people miserable and turned them out of Paradise". Adam said to him, "You are the one whom Allāh selected for His message and whom He selected for Himself and upon whom He revealed the Torah." Moses said, 'Yes.' Adam said, "Did you find that written in my fate before my creation?' Moses said, 'Yes.' So Adam overcame Moses with this argument."

٢٦٠ - حدثنا الصلت بن محمد: حدثنا مهدي بن ميمون: حدثنا محمد ابن سيرين، عن أبي هريرة، عن رسول الله صلى الله عليه وسلم قال: التقى آدم وموسى فقال موسى لآدم: أنت الذي أشقيت الناس وأخرجتهم من الجنة؟ قال له آدم: أنت الذي اصطفاك الله برسالته، واصطفاك لنفسه، وأنزل عليك التوراة؟ قال: نعم، قال: فوجدتها كتب علي قبل أن يخلقني؟ قال: نعم، فحج آدم موسى. اليم: البحر.

(202) CHAPTER. 'And indeed We inspired Moses: (Saying) "Travel by night with My slaves and strike a dry path for them in the sea, fearing neither to be overtaken (by Pharaoh), nor, being afraid (from drowning in the Sea). Then Pharaoh pursued them with his forces, but the Sea-water completely overwhelmed them and covered them up; Pharaoh led his people astray and he did not guide them.' (20:77–79)

باب ـ وَلَقَدْ أَوْحَيْنا إلى مُوسَى أَنْ أَسْرِ بعبادى فاضْرِبْ لَهُمْ طَرِيقا فى البَحْرِ يَبَسا لا تَخافُ دَرَكا وَلا تخْشَى فاتْبَعَهُمْ فِرْعَوْنُ بِجُنُودِهِ فَغَشِيَهُمْ مِنَ اليَمِّ ما غَشِيَهُمْ وأَضَلَّ فِرْعَوْنُ قَوْمَهُ وَما هَدَى ـ.

261. Narrated Ibn 'Abbās ﷺ: When Allāh's Messenger ﷺ arrived at Medīna, he found the Jews observing the fast on the day of 'Āshūrā' (10th of Muharram). The Prophet ﷺ asked them (about it) and they replied, "This is the day when Moses became victorious over Pharaoh." The Prophet ﷺ said (to the Muslims), "We are nearer to Moses than they, so fast on this day."

٢٦١ ـ حدَّثني يَعْقُوبُ بنُ إبْراهيمَ: حدَّثنا رَوْحٌ: حدَّثنا شُعْبَةُ: حدَّثنا أبو بِشْرٍ، عَنْ سَعيدِ بنِ جُبَيْرٍ، عَنِ ابنِ عَبّاسٍ رَضِيَ اللهُ عَنْهُما قالَ: لمّا قَدِمَ رَسُولُ اللهِ صلى اللهُ عليهِ وسلَّم المَدينَةَ واليَهُودُ تَصُومُ عاشُوراءَ فَسَأَلَهُمْ فَقالُوا: هذا اليَوْمُ الَّذى ظَهَرَ فيهِ مُوسَى عَلى فِرْعَوْنَ، فَقالَ النَّبِيُّ صلى اللهُ عليهِ وسلَّم: نَحْنُ أَوْلَى بِمُوسَى مِنْهُمْ فَصُومُوهُ.

(203) CHAPTER. The Statement of Allāh ﷻ :–

'So let him not get you both out of the Garden, so that you come to toil.' (20:117)

بابُ قَوْلِهِ فَلا يُخْرِجَنَّكُما مِنَ الجَنَّةِ فَتَشْقَى ـ.

262. Narrated Abū Huraira ﷺ:
The Prophet ﷺ said, "Moses argued with Adam and said to him (Adam), 'You are the one who got the people out of Paradise by your sin, and thus made them miserable.' Adam replied, 'O Moses! You are the one whom Allāh selected for His Message and for His direct talk. Yet you blame me for a thing which Allāh had ordained for me before He created me? ." Allāh's Messenger ﷺ further said, "So Adam overcame Moses by this Argument."

٢٦٢ - حدَّثنا قُتَيْبَةُ بنُ سَعِيدٍ: حدَّثنا أيُّوبُ بنُ النَّجارِ، عَنْ يَحْيَى ابنِ أبي كَثِيرٍ، عَنْ أبي سَلَمَةَ ابنِ عَبْدِ الرَّحْمَنِ، عَنْ أبي هُرَيْرَةَ رَضِيَ اللهُ عَنْهُ، عَنِ النَّبِيِّ صلى اللهُ عليه وسلَّم قالَ: حاجَّ مُوسَى آدَمَ فَقالَ لَهُ: أنْتَ الَّذي أخْرَجْتَ النَّاسَ مِنَ الجَنَّةِ بِذَنْبِكَ فأشْقَيْتَهُمْ؟ قالَ: قالَ آدَمُ: يا مُوسَى أنْتَ الَّذي اصْطَفاكَ اللهُ بِرِسالَتِهِ وبِكَلامِهِ، أتَلُومُنِي عَلى أمْرٍ كَتَبَهُ اللهُ عَلَيَّ قَبْلَ أنْ يَخْلُقَنِي؟ أوْ قَدَّرَهُ عَلَيَّ قَبْلَ أنْ يَخْلُقَنِي؟ قالَ رَسُولُ اللهِ صلى اللهُ عليه وسلَّم: فَحَجَّ آدَمُ مُوسَى.

In the Name of Allāh, the Most Beneficent, the Most Merciful

بِسْمِ اللهِ الرَّحْمَنِ الرَّحِيمِ

SŪRAT-AL-ANBIYĀ' XXI
(The Prophets):

سورة الأنبياء

263. Narrated 'Abdullāh ﷺ:
The Sūras of Banī Israel, Al-Kahf, Mariyam, Ṭāhā and Al-Anbiyā' are from the very old Sūras which I learnt by heart, and they are my first property.

٢٦٣ - حدَّثنا مُحَمَّدُ بنُ بَشَّارٍ: حدَّثنا غُنْدَرٌ: حدَّثنا شُعْبَةُ، عَنْ أبي إسحاقَ قالَ: سَمِعْتُ عَبْدَ الرَّحْمَنِ بنَ يَزِيدَ، عَنْ عَبْدِ اللهِ قالَ: بَنِي إسْرائيلَ، والكَهْفُ، ومَرْيَمُ، وطَهَ، والأنْبِياءُ، هُنَّ مِنَ العِتاقِ الأُوَلِ، وهُنَّ مِنْ تِلادي. وقالَ قَتادَةُ: جُذاذًا:

قَطَّعَهُنَّ : وَقَالَ الحَسَنُ : فِي فَلَكٍ مِثْلِ فِلْكَةِ المِغْزَلِ . يَسْبَحُونَ : يَدُورُونَ . قَالَ ابنُ عَبَّاسٍ : نَفَشَتْ : رَعَتْ لَيْلاً . يُصْحَبُونَ : يُمْنَعُونَ . أُمَّتُكُمْ أُمَّةً وَاحِدَةً قَالَ : دِينُكُمْ دِينٌ وَاحِدٌ . قَالَ عِكْرِمَةُ : حَصَبُ جَهَنَّمَ : حَطَبُ بِالحَبَشِيَّةِ . وَقَالَ غَيْرُهُ : أَحَسُّوا : تَوَقَّعُوا ، مِنْ أَحْسَسْتُ . خَامِدِينَ : هَامِدِينَ ، والحَصِيدُ : مُسْتَأْصَلٌ يَقَعُ عَلَى الوَاحِدِ وَالاثْنَيْنِ والجَمِيعِ لا يَسْتَحْسِرُونَ : لا يُعْيُونَ ، وَمِنْهُ حَسِيرٌ وَحَسَرْتُ بَعِيرِي . عَمِيقٌ : بَعِيدٌ ، نُكِسُوا : رُدُّوا . صَنْعَةَ لَبُوسٍ : الدُّرُوعُ . تَقَطَّعُوا أَمْرَهُمْ : اخْتَلَفُوا . الحَسِيسُ والحِسُّ والجَرْسُ والهَمْسُ وَاحِدٌ وَهُوَ مِنَ الصَّوْتِ الخَفِيِّ . آذَنَّاكَ : أَعْلَمْنَاكَ . آذَنْتُكُمْ إِذَا أَعْلَمْتَهُ فَأَنْتَ وَهُوَ عَلَى سَوَاءٍ لَمْ تَغْدِرْ . وَقَالَ مُجَاهِدٌ : لَعَلَّكُمْ تُسْئَلُونَ : تُفْهَمُونَ . ارْتَضَى : رَضِيَ . التَّمَاثِيلُ : الأَصْنَامُ . السِّجِلُّ الصَّحِيفَةُ .

(204) CHAPTER 'As We began the first creation, We shall repeat it, (It is a promise,We have undertaken . (21: 104)

باب : كَمَا بَدَأْنَا أَوَّلَ خَلْقٍ نُعِيدُهُ وَعْدًا عَلَيْنَا .

264. Narrated Ibn 'Abbās ﷺ: The Prophet ﷺ delivered a sermon and said, "You (people) will be gathered before Allāh(on the Day of Resurrection) bare-footed, naked and uncircumcised." (The Prophet ﷺ then recited):–

'As We began the first creation, We shall repeat it. (It is) a promise We have undertaken and truly We shall do it.'

and added, "The first man who will be dressed on the Day of Resurrection, will be Abraham. Lo! Some men from my followers will be brought and taken towards the left side, whereupon I will say, 'O Lord, (these are) my companions!' It will be said, 'You do not know what new things they introduced (into the religion) after you.' I will then say as the righteous pious slave, Jesus, said, 'I was a witness over them while I dwelt among them...(to His Statement)...and You are the Witness to all things.' (5:117) Then it will be said, '(O Muḥammad) These people never stopped to apostate since you left them.' "

٢٦٤ - حدَّثنا سُليمانُ بنُ حَرْبٍ: حدَّثنا شُعْبَةُ، عن المغيرةِ ابنِ النُّعمانِ شيخٍ من النَّخَعِ، عن سعيدِ بنِ جُبيرٍ، عن ابنِ عبّاسٍ رضي اللهُ عنهما قالَ: خَطَبَ النبيُّ صلى اللهُ عليهِ وسلَّمَ فقالَ: إنكم مَحشورونَ إلى اللهِ حُفاةً عُراةً غُرْلاً - كما بَدأنا أوَّلَ خلْقٍ نُعيدُهُ وَعْداً علينا إنّا كُنّا فاعِلينَ - ثمَّ إنَّ أوَّلَ مَنْ يُكْسى يومَ القيامةِ إبراهيمُ، ألا إنهُ يُجاءُ برجالٍ من أُمَّتي فيُؤخَذُ بهم ذاتَ الشِّمالِ فأقولُ: يا ربِّ أصحابي، فيُقالُ: لا تدري ما أحدَثوا بعدَكَ. فأقولُ كما قالَ العبدُ الصالحُ - وكُنْتُ عليهم شهيداً ما دُمْتُ فيهم - إلى قولِه - شهيدٌ - فيُقالُ: إنَّ هؤلاءِ لم يزالوا مُرتدِّينَ على أعقابِهم مُنذُ فارقتَهم.

In the Name of Allāh,
the Most Beneficent, the Most Merciful

SŪRAT-AL-ḤAJJ:XXII

بسمِ اللهِ الرَّحمنِ الرَّحيمِ

سورة الحج

وقالَ ابنُ عُيَيْنَةَ: المُخْبِتينَ: المُطْمَئِنّينَ. وقالَ ابنُ عبّاسٍ في -

إِذَا تَمَنَّى أَلْقَى الشَّيْطَانُ فِى أُمْنِيَّتِهِ ـ إِذَا حَدَّثَ أَلْقَى الشَّيْطَانُ فِى حَدِيثِهِ فَيُبْطِلُ اللهُ مَا يُلْقِى الشَّيْطَانُ وَ يُحْكِمُ آيَاتِهِ . وَيُقَالُ أُمْنِيَّتُهُ : قِرَاءَتُهُ . إِلاَّ أَمَانِيَّ : يَقْرَءُونَ وَلاَ يَكْتُبُونَ . وَقَالَ مُجَاهِدٌ : مَشِيدٌ بِالْقَصَّةِ جِصٍّ . وَقَالَ غَيْرُهُ : يَسْطُونَ يَفْرُطُونَ مِنَ السَّطْوَةِ ، وَيُقَالُ يَسْطُونَ : يَبْطِشُونَ . وَهُدُوا إِلَى الطَّيِّبِ مِنَ الْقَوْلِ : أُلْهِمُوا إِلَى الْقُرْآنِ ، وَهُدُوا إِلَى صِرَاطِ الْحَمِيدِ : الإِسْلاَمِ . وَقَالَ ابْنُ عَبَّاسٍ : بِسَبَبٍ : بِحَبْلٍ إِلَى سَقْفِ الْبَيْتِ . ثَانِىَ عِطْفِهِ : مُسْتَكْبِرٌ . تَذْهَلُ : تُشْغَلُ .

(205) CHAPTER. The Statement of Allāh ﷻ :–

'And you shall see mankind as in a drunken state. (22:2)

بَابُ قَوْلِهِ ـ وَتَرَى النَّاسَ سُكَارَى ـ .

265. Narrated Abū Sa'īd Al-Khudrī ؓ : The Prophet ﷺ said, "On the Day of Resurrection Allāh ﷻ will say, 'O Adam!' Adam will reply, 'Labbaik our Lord, and Sa'daik ' Then there will be a loud call (saying), Allāh orders you to take from among your offspring a mission for the (Hell) Fire.' Adam will say, 'O Lord! Who are the mission for the (Hell) Fire?' Allāh will say, 'Out of each thousand, take out 999.' At that time every pregnant female shall drop her load (have a miscarriage) and a child will have grey hair. And you shall see mankind as in

٢٦٥ ـ حَدَّثَنَا عُمَرُ بْنُ حَفْصٍ : حَدَّثَنَا أَبِى : حَدَّثَنَا الأَعْمَشُ : حَدَّثَنَا أَبُو صَالِحٍ ، عَنْ أَبِى سَعِيدٍ الْخُدْرِىِّ قَالَ : قَالَ النَّبِيُّ صلى الله عليه وسلَّم : يَقُولُ اللهُ عَزَّ وَجَلَّ يَوْمَ الْقِيَامَةِ : يَا آدَمُ ، فَيَقُولُ : لَبَّيْكَ رَبَّنَا وَسَعْدَيْكَ . فَيُنَادَى بِصَوْتٍ : إِنَّ اللهَ يَأْمُرُكَ أَنْ تُخْرِجَ مِنْ ذُرِّيَّتِكَ بَعْثًا إِلَى النَّارِ . قَالَ : يَا رَبِّ وَمَا بَعْثُ النَّارِ ؟ قَالَ :

a drunken state, yet not drunk, but severe will be the torment of Allāh." (22:2) (When the Prophet ﷺ mentioned this), the people were so distressed (and afraid) that their faces got changed (in colour) whereupon the Prophet ﷺ said, "From Gog and Magog nine-hundred-ninety-nine will be taken out and one from you. You Muslims (compared to the large number of other people) will be like a black hair on the side of a white ox, or a white hair on the side of a black ox, and I hope that you will be one-fourth of the people of Paradise." On that, we said, "Allāhu-Akbar!" Then he said, "I hope that you will be) one-third of the people of Paradise." We again said, "Allāhu-Akbar!" Then he said, "(I hope that you will be) one-half of the people of Paradise." So we said, Allāhu Akbar."

مِنْ كُلِّ أَلْفٍ أُرَاهُ قَالَ تِسْعَمِائَةٍ وَتِسْعَةً وَتِسْعِينَ، فَحِينَئِذٍ تَضَعُ الْحَامِلُ حَمْلَهَا وَيَشِيبُ الْوَلِيدُ - وَتَرَى النَّاسَ سُكَارَى وَمَا هُمْ بِسُكَارَى وَلَكِنَّ عَذَابَ اللهِ شَدِيدٌ - فَشَقَّ ذَلِكَ عَلَى النَّاسِ حَتَّى تَغَيَّرَتْ وُجُوهُهُمْ. فَقَالَ النَّبِيُّ صلى الله عليه وسلم: مِنْ يَأْجُوجَ وَمَأْجُوجَ تِسْعَمِائَةٍ وَتِسْعَةً وَتِسْعِينَ وَمِنْكُمْ وَاحِدٌ. ثُمَّ أَنْتُمْ فِى النَّاسِ كَالشَّعْرَةِ السَّوْدَاءِ فِى جَنْبِ الثَّوْرِ الأَبْيَضِ أَوْ كَالشَّعْرَةِ الْبَيْضَاءِ فِى جَنْبِ الثَّوْرِ الأَسْوَدِ. وَإِنِّى لأَرْجُو (١) أَنْ تَكُونُوا رُبُعَ أَهْلِ الْجَنَّةِ فَكَبَّرْنَا. ثُمَّ قَالَ ثُلُثَ أَهْلِ الْجَنَّةِ فَكَبَّرْنَا. ثُمَّ قَالَ شَطْرَ أَهْلِ الْجَنَّةِ فَكَبَّرْنَا. وَقَالَ أَبُو أُسَامَةَ، عَنِ الأَعْمَشِ - تَرَى النَّاسَ سُكَارَى وَمَا هُمْ بِسُكَارَى - قَالَ: مِنْ كُلِّ أَلْفٍ تِسْعَمِائَةٍ وَتِسْعَةً وَتِسْعِينَ. وَقَالَ جَرِيرٌ وَعِيسَى بْنُ يُونُسَ وَأَبُو مُعَاوِيَةَ: سَكْرَى وَمَا هُمْ بِسَكْرَى.

(206) CHAPTER. "And among men is he who worships Allāh as it were upon the very edge.' (22:11) (i.e. not deep in the religion).

بَابُ - وَمِنَ النَّاسِ مَنْ يَعْبُدُ اللهَ عَلَى حَرْفٍ - شَكٍّ. أَتْرَفْنَاهُمْ: وَسَّعْنَاهُمْ.

266. Narrated Ibn 'Abbās (رضي الله عنهما) :

٢٦٦ - حَدَّثَنِى إِبْرَاهِيمُ بْنُ الْمُنْذِرِ:

Regarding the Verse:—

'And among men is he who worships Allāh as it were on the very edge —— (22:11)

A man used to come to Medīna and if his wife brought a son and his mares produced offspring. He would say, "This religion (Islām) is good," but if his wife did not give birth to a child and his mares produced no offspring, he would say, "This religion is bad."

حَدَّثَنَا يَحْيَى بْنُ أَبِي بُكَيْرٍ : حَدَّثَنَا إِسْرَائِيلُ ، عَنْ أَبِي حُصَيْنٍ ، عَنْ سَعِيدِ ابْنِ جُبَيْرٍ ، عَنِ ابْنِ عَبَّاسٍ رَضِيَ اللّٰهُ عَنْهُمَا قَالَ - وَمِنَ النَّاسِ مَنْ يَعْبُدُ اللّٰهَ عَلَى حَرْفٍ - قَالَ : كَانَ الرَّجُلُ يَقْدَمُ الْمَدِينَةَ ، فَإِنْ وَلَدَتِ امْرَأَتُهُ غُلَامًا وَنُتِجَتْ خَيْلُهُ قَالَ هَذَا دِينٌ صَالِحٌ ، وَإِنْ لَمْ تَلِدِ امْرَأَتُهُ وَلَمْ تُنْتَجْ خَيْلُهُ قَالَ : هَذَا دِينُ سُوءٍ .

(207) CHAPTER. The Statement of Allāh تعالى :—

'These two opponents (believers and disbelievers) dispute with each other about their Lord,' (22:19)

بَابُ قَوْلِهِ - هَذَانِ خَصْمَانِ اخْتَصَمُوا فِى رَبِّهِمْ - .

267. Narrated Qais bin 'Ubād: Abū Dharr رضى الله عنه used to take an oath confirming that the Verse,

'These two opponents (believers, and disbelievers) dispute with each other about their Lord.' (22:19)

was revealed in connection with Ḥamza and his two companions and 'Utbah and his two companions on the day when they came out to combat on the Day of the battle of Badr. (1)

٢٦٧ - حَدَّثَنَا حَجَّاجُ بْنُ مِنْهَالٍ : حَدَّثَنَا هُشَيْمٌ : أَخْبَرَنَا أَبُو هَاشِمٍ ، عَنْ أَبِي مِجْلَزٍ ، عَنْ قَيْسِ ابْنِ عُبَادٍ ، عَنْ أَبِي ذَرٍّ رَضِيَ اللّٰهُ عَنْهُ أَنَّهُ كَانَ يُقْسِمُ قَسَمًا إِنَّ هَذِهِ الْآيَةَ - هَذَانِ خَصْمَانِ اخْتَصَمُوا فِى رَبِّهِمْ - نَزَلَتْ فِى حَمْزَةَ وَصَاحِبَيْهِ ، وَعُتْبَةَ وَصَاحِبَيْهِ يَوْمَ بَرَزُوا فِى يَوْمِ بَدْرٍ .

(1) Ḥamza and his companions were Muslims while the others were pagans.

رَوَاهُ سُفْيانُ عَنْ أبى هاشِمٍ . وَقَالَ عُثْمانُ ، عَنْ جَرِيرٍ ، عَنْ مَنْصُورٍ ، عَنْ أبى هاشِمٍ ، عَنْ أبى مِجْلَزٍ قَوْلَهُ .

268. Narrated Qais bin 'Ubād: 'Alī said, "I will be the first to kneel before the Benificent on the Day of Resurrection because of the dispute." Qais said; This Verse:

> 'These two opponents (believers and disbelievers) dispute with each other about their Lord,' (22:19)

was revealed in connection with those who came out for the Battle of Badr, i.e. 'Alī, Ḥamza, 'Ubaida, Shaiba bin Rabī'a, 'Utbā bin Rabī'a and Al-Walīd bin 'Utba.

٢٦٨ - حدَّثَنا حَجَّاجُ بنُ مِنْهالٍ : حدَّثَنا مُعْتَمِرُ بنُ سُلَيْمانَ قالَ : سَمِعْتُ أبى قالَ : حدَّثَنا أبو مِجْلَزٍ ، عَنْ قَيْسِ بنِ عُبادٍ عَنْ عَلِىٍّ رَضِىَ اللهُ عَنْهُ قالَ : أنا أوَّلُ مَنْ يَجْثُو بَيْنَ يَدَىِ الرَّحْمَنِ لِلْخُصُومَةِ يَوْمَ القِيامَةِ . قالَ قَيْسٌ : وَفِيهِمْ نَزَلَتْ - هٰذَانِ خَصْمانِ اخْتَصَمُوا فى رَبِّهِمْ - قالَ : هُمُ الَّذِينَ بارَزُوا يَوْمَ بَدْرٍ : عَلِىٌّ ، وحَمْزَةَ ، وعُبَيْدَةُ ، وَشَيْبَةُ بنُ رَبِيعَةَ ، وعُتْبَةُ بنُ رَبِيعَةَ ، والوَلِيدُ بنُ عُتْبَةَ .

SŪRAT-AL-MU'MINŪN
(The Believers) XXIII

In the Name of Allāh,
the Most Beneficent, the Most Merciful

No. Ḥadīth is mentioned here.

سورة المؤمنون

بِسْمِ اللهِ الرَّحْمَنِ الرَّحِيمِ

قالَ ابنُ عُيَيْنَةَ : سَبْعَ طَرائِقَ : سَبْعَ سَمَوَاتٍ . لها سابِقونَ : سَبَقَتْ لَهُمُ السَّعادَةُ . قُلُوبُهُمْ وَجِلَةٌ : خائِفِينَ . وَقالَ ابنُ عَبَّاسٍ : هَيْهاتَ هَيْهاتَ : بَعِيدٌ بَعِيدٌ . فاسأَلِ العادِّينَ المَلائِكَةَ . لَناكِبُونَ : لَعادِلونَ . كالِحُونَ : عابِسُونَ . وَقالَ غَيرُهُ : مِنْ سُلالَةٍ : الوَلَدُ

٢٤١

والنُّطْفَةُ السُّلالَةُ . والجِنَّةُ والجُنُونُ واحِدٌ . والغُثاءُ : الزَّبَدُ وَما ارْتَفَعَ عَنِ الماءِ وَما لا يُنْتَفَعُ بِهِ . يَجْأَرُونَ : يَرْفَعُونَ أَصْواتَهُمْ كَما تَجْأَرُ البَقَرَةُ . عَلَى أَعْقابِكُمْ : رَجَعَ عَلَى عَقِبَيْهِ . سامِرًا مِنَ السَّمَرِ والجَمِيعُ السُّمَّارُ ، والسّامِرُ هاهُنا فى مَوْضِعِ الجَمْعِ . تُسْحَرُونَ : تَعْمَوْنَ مِنَ السِّحْرِ .

SŪRAT AN-NŪR (Light) XXIV.

In the Name of Allāh,
the Most Beneficent, the Most Merciful

سورة النور

بِسْمِ اللهِ الرَّحْمَنِ الرَّحِيمِ

مِنْ خِلالِهِ : مِنْ بَيْنَ أَضْعافِ السَّحابِ . سَنا بَرْقِهِ وَهُوَ الضِّياءُ . مُذْعِنِينَ ، يُقالُ لِلْمُسْتَخْذِى مُذْعِنٌ . أَشْتاتًا وَشَتَّى وَشَتاتٌ وَشَتٌّ وَاحِدٌ . وَقالَ ابنُ عَبّاسٍ ـ سُورَةٌ أَنْزَلْناها ـ بَيَّنّاها . وَقالَ غَيْرُهُ : سُمِّيَ القُرْآنُ لِجَماعَةِ السُّوَرِ وسُمِّيَتِ السُّورَةُ لأَنَّها مَقْطُوعَةٌ مِنَ الأُخْرَى . فَلَمّا قُرِنَ بَعْضُها إلى بَعْضٍ سُمِّيَ قُرْآنًا . وَقالَ سَعْدُ بنُ عِياضٍ الثُّمالِىُّ : المِشْكاةُ : الكُوَّةُ بِلِسانِ الحَبَشَةِ . وَقَوْلُهُ تَعالَى ـ إِنَّ عَلَيْنا جَمْعَهُ وَقُرْآنَهُ ـ تَأْلِيفَ بَعْضِهِ إلى بَعْضٍ ـ فَإِذا قَرَأْناهُ فاتَّبِعْ قُرْآنَهُ ـ فَإِذا جَمَعْناهُ وأَلَّفْناهُ فاتَّبِعْ قُرْآنَهُ ، أَىْ ما جُمِعَ فِيهِ

فاعمَلْ بِما أمرَكَ وانْتهِ عمّا نهاكَ. ويُقال لبِئسَ لشِعْرِه قُرآنٌ أىْ تأليفٌ، وسمّىَ الفُرْقانُ لأنّه يُفرّقُ بينَ الحقّ والباطِلِ. ويُقال للمرأةِ ما قرأتْ بِسلًا قطُّ أىْ لمْ تجمَعْ فى بطْنِها ولَدًا. وقالَ - فرَضْناها - أنزَلْنا فيها فرائِضَ مختلِفةً. ومَنْ قرأ فرَضْناها يقُول فرَضْنا عليْكم وعلى منْ بعْدَكم. قالَ مجاهِدٌ: أوِ الطّفْلِ الّذينَ لمْ يظْهَروا: لمْ يدْروا لمَا بِهِمْ مِنَ الصِّغَرِ. وقالَ الشّعْبِىُّ - أولى الإرْبَةِ - منْ ليْسَ لَه أرَبٌ. وقالَ مجاهِدٌ: لايُهِمّهُ إلاّ بَطْنُه ولا يَخافُ علَى النِّساءِ. وقالَ طاوسٌ: هُوَ الأحْمَقُ الّذى لا حاجةَ لَه فى النِّساءِ.

(208) CHAPTER. The Statement of Allāh عَزَّوَجَلَّ :-

'As for those who accuse their wives but have no witnesses except themselves......' (24: 6)

باب قوْلِه عزّوجلّ - والّذينَ يرْمُونَ أزْواجَهُمْ ولمْ يكُنْ لهُمْ شُهَداءُ - الآيَةَ.

269. Narrated Sahl bin Sa'd: 'Uwaimir came to 'Āṣim bin 'Adī who was the chief of Banī 'Ajlān and said, "What do you say about a man who has found another man with his wife? Should he kill him whereupon you would kill him (i.e. the husband), or what should he do? Please ask Allāh's Messenger

٢٦٩ - حدّثنا إسحاقُ: حدّثنا مُحمّدُ بنِ يُوسُفَ الفِرْيابى: حدّثنا الأوْزاعىُّ قالَ: حدّثنِى الزُّهْرِىّ عنْ سَهْلِ بنِ سعْدٍ، أنّ عُوَيْمِرًا أتَى عاصِمَ ابنَ عدِىٍّ وكانَ سيّدَ بنِى عجْلانَ فقالَ:

ﷺ about this matter on my behalf." 'Āṣim then went to the Prophet ﷺ and said, "O Allāh's Messenger! (And asked him that question) but Allāh's Messenger ﷺ disliked the question," When 'Uwaimir asked 'Āṣim (about the Prophet's answer) 'Āṣim replied that Allāh's Messenger ﷺ disliked such questions and considered it shameful. "Uwaimir then said, "By Allāh, I will not give up asking unless I ask Allāh's Messenger ﷺ about it." 'Uwaimir came (to the Prophet ﷺ) and said, "O Allāh's Messenger! A man has found another man with his wife! Should he kill him whereupon you would kill him (the husband, in Qiṣāṣ) (1) or what should he do?" Allāh's Messenger ﷺ said, "Allāh has revealed regarding you and your wife's case in the Qur'ān "So Allāh's Messenger ﷺ ordered them to perform the measures of Mulā'ana (2) according to what Allāh had mentioned in His Book. So 'Uwaimir did Mulā'ana with her and said, "O Allāh's Messenger! If I kept her I would oppress her." So 'Uwaimir divorced her and so divorce became a tradition after them for those who happened to be involved in a case of Mulā'ana. Allāh's Messenger ﷺ then said, "Look! If she (Uwaimir's wife) delivers a black child with deep black large eyes, big hips and fat legs, then I will be of the opinion that 'Uwaimir has spoken the truth; but if she delivers a red child looking like a Waḥra (3) then we will consider that 'Uwaimir has

كَيْفَ تَقُولُونَ فِى رَجُلٍ وَجَدَ مَعَ
امْرَأَتِهِ رَجُلاً؟ أَيَقْتُلُهُ فَتَقْتُلُونَهُ؟ أَمْ
كَيْفَ يَصْنَعُ؟ سَلْ لِى رَسُولَ اللهِ صلى
اللهُ عليه وسلَّم عَنْ ذَلِكَ. فَأَتَى عَاصِمٌ
النَّبِيَّ صلى اللهُ عليه وسلَّم فَقَالَ: يَا
رَسُولَ اللهِ، فَكَرِهَ رَسُولُ اللهِ صلى اللهُ
عليه وسلَّم المَسَائِلَ فَسَأَلَهُ عُوَيْمِرٌ فَقَالَ:
إِنَّ رَسُولَ اللهِ صلى اللهُ عليه وسلَّم كَرِهَ
المَسَائِلَ وَعَابَهَا. قَالَ عُوَيْمِرٌ: وَاللهِ
لا أَنْتَهِى حَتَّى أَسْأَلَ رَسُولَ اللهِ صلى اللهُ
عليه وسلَّم عَنْ ذَلِكَ، فَجَاءَ عُوَيْمِرٌ
فَقَالَ: يَا رَسُولَ اللهِ، رَجُلٌ وَجَدَ مَعَ
امْرَأَتِهِ رَجُلاً أَيَقْتُلُهُ فَتَقْتُلُونَهُ؟ أَمْ
كَيْفَ يَصْنَعُ؟ فَقَالَ رَسُولُ اللهِ صلى الله
عليه وسلَّم: قَدْ أَنْزَلَ اللهُ القُرْآنَ فِيكَ
وَفِى صَاحِبَتِكَ. فَأَمَرَهُمَا رَسُولُ اللهِ صلى
اللهُ عليه وسلَّم بِالمُلاعَنَةِ بِمَا سَمَّى اللهُ فِى
كِتَابِهِ فَلاعَنَهَا ثُمَّ قَالَ: يَا رَسُولَ اللهِ،
إِنْ حَبَسْتُهَا فَقَدْ ظَلَمْتُهَا فَطَلَّقَهَا
فَكَانَتْ سُنَّةً لِمَنْ كَانَ بَعْدَهُمَا فِى
المُتَلاعِنَيْنِ. ثُمَّ قَالَ رَسُولُ اللهِ صلى اللهُ
عليه وسلَّم: انْظُرُوا فَإِنْ جَاءَتْ بِهِ
أَسْحَمَ أَدْعَجَ العَيْنَيْنِ، عَظِيمَ الأَلْيَتَيْنِ،

(1) Qiṣāṣ: (Retaliation – equality in punishment)

(2) See the word "Li'ān" in the glossary.

(3) A short red animal.

told a lie against her." Later on she delivered a child carrying the qualities which Allāh's Messenger ﷺ had mentioned as a proof for 'Uwaimir's claim; therefore the child was ascribed to its mother henceforth.

خدلج الساقين، فلا أحسب عويمرا إلا قد صدق عليها وإن جاءت به أحيمر كأنه وحرة فلا أحسب عويمرا إلا قد كذب عليها. فجاءت به على النعت الذي نعت به رسول الله صلى الله عليه وسلم من تصديق عويمر، فكان بعد ينسب إلى أمه.

(209) CHAPTER. And the fifth testimony (should be) the invoking of the curse of Allāh on him if he is of those who tell a lie (against her).' (24:7)

باب - والخامسة أن لعنة الله عليه إن كان من الكاذبين -.

270. Narrated Sahl bin Sa'd: A man came to Allāh's Messenger ﷺ and said, "O Allāh's Messenger! Suppose a man saw another man with his wife, should he kill him whereupon you might kill him (i.e. the killer) (in Qiṣāṣ)or what should he do?" So Allāh revealed concerning their case what is mentioned of the order of Mulā'ana. Allāh's Messenger ﷺ said to the man, "The matter between you and your wife has been decided." So they did Mulā'ana in the pre-

٢٧٠ - حدثني سليمان بن داود أبو الربيع: حدثنا فليح، عن الزهري، عن سهل بن سعد أن رجلا أتى رسول الله صلى الله عليه وسلم فقال: يا رسول الله، أرأيت رجلا رأى مع امرأته رجلا، أيقتله فتقتلونه؟ أم كيف يفعل؟ فأنزل الله فيهما ما ذكر في القرآن من التلاعن، فقال له رسول

sence of Allāh's Messenger ﷺ and I was present there, and then the man divorced his wife. So it became a tradition to dissolve the marriage of those spouses who were involved in a case of Mulā'ana. The woman was pregnant and the husband denied that he was the cause of her pregnancy, so the son was (later) ascribed to her. Then it became a tradition that such a son would be the heir of his mother, and she would inherit of him what Allāh prescribed for her.

اللهِ صلى اللهُ عليهِ وسلَّم : قَدْ قُضِيَ فيكَ وفى امْرأتِكَ ، قالَ : فتَلاعَنا وأنا شاهِدٌ عِنْدَ رَسُولِ اللهِ صلى اللهُ عليهِ وسلَّم ففارَقَها فكانَتْ سُنَّةً أنْ يُفَرَّقَ بينَ المُتَلاعِنَيْنِ ، وكانَتْ حامِلاً فأنكَرَ حَمْلَها وكانَ ابنُها يُدْعَى إليْها . ثُمَّ جَرَتِ السُّنَّةُ فى المِيراثِ أنْ يَرِثَها وتَرِثَ مِنْهُ ما فَرَضَ اللهُ لها .

(210) CHAPTER. 'But it shall avert the punishment from her (the wife)...' (24:8)

بابٌ - وَيَدْرأُ عَنْها العَذابَ - الآيَةَ .

271. Narrated Ibn 'Abbās رضي الله عنهما Hilāl bin Umaiya accused his wife of committing illegal sexual intercourse with Sharīk bin Saḥmā' and filed the case before the Prophet ﷺ. The Prophet ﷺ said (to Hilāl), "Either you bring forth a proof (four witnesses) or you will receive the legal punishment (lashes) on your back." Hilāl said, "O Allāh's Messenger! If anyone of us saw a man over his wife, would he go to seek after witnesses?" The Prophet ﷺ kept on saying, "Either you bring forth the witnesses or you will receive the legal punishment (lashes) on your back." Hilāl then said, "By Him Who sent you with the Truth, I am telling the truth and Allāh will reveal to you what will save my back from legal punishment."

٢٧١ - حدَّثَنِي مُحَمَّدُ بنُ بَشّارٍ : حدَّثنا ابنُ أبي عَدِيّ ، عَنْ هِشامِ بنِ حَسّانَ : حدَّثنا عِكْرِمَةُ عَنِ ابنِ عَبّاسٍ : أنَّ هِلالَ بنَ أُمَيَّةَ قَذَفَ امْرأتَهُ عِنْدَ النَّبِيِّ صلى اللهُ عليهِ وسلَّم بِشَرِيكِ بنِ سَحْماءَ ، فَقالَ النَّبِيُّ صلى اللهُ عليهِ وسلَّم : البَيِّنَةُ أوْ حَدٌّ فى ظَهْرِكَ ، فَقالَ : يا رَسُولَ اللهِ ، إذا رأى أحَدُنا على امْرأتِهِ رَجُلاً يَنْطَلِقُ يَلْتَمِسُ البَيِّنَةَ ؟ فَجَعَلَ النَّبِيُّ صلى اللهُ عليهِ وسلَّم يَقُولُ : البَيِّنَةَ وإلاّ حَدٌّ فى ظَهْرِكَ . فَقالَ هِلالٌ : والّذى بَعَثَكَ بالحَقِّ إنّى لَصادِقٌ

Then Gabriel came down and revealed to him:—

> 'As for those who accuse their wives...' (24:6-9)

The Prophet ﷺ recited it till he reached: '... (her accuser) is telling the truth.' Then the Prophet ﷺ left and sent for the woman, and Hilāl went (and brought) her and then took the oaths (confirming the claim). The Prophet ﷺ was saying, "Allāh knows that one of you is a liar, so will any of you repent?" Then the woman got up and took the oaths and when she was going to take the fifth one, the people stopped her and said, "It (the fifth oath) will definitely bring Allāh's curse on you (if you are guilty)." So she hesitated and recoiled (from taking the oath) so much that we thought that she would withdraw her denial. But then she said, "I will not dishonour my family all through these days," and carried on (the process of taking oaths). The Prophet ﷺ then said, "Watch her; if she delivers a black-eyed child with big hips and fat shins then it is Sharīk bin Saḥmā's child." Later she delivered a child of that description. So the Prophet ﷺ said, "If the case was not settled by Allāh's Law, I would punish her severely."

وَلَيُنْزِلَنَّ اللهُ مَا يُبَرِّئُ ظَهْرِي مِنَ الحَدِّ. فَنَزَلَ جِبْرِيلُ وأَنْزَلَ عَلَيْهِ - وَالَّذِينَ يَرْمُونَ أَزْوَاجَهُمْ - فَقَرَأَ حَتَّى بَلَغَ - إِنْ كَانَ مِنَ الصَّادِقِينَ - فَانْصَرَفَ النَّبِيُّ صلى اللهُ عليهِ وسلَّم فأَرْسَلَ إِلَيْهَا فَجَاءَ هِلَالٌ فَشَهِدَ والنَّبِيُّ صلى اللهُ عليهِ وسلَّم يَقُولُ: إِنَّ اللهَ يَعْلَمُ أَنَّ أَحَدَكُمَا كَاذِبٌ، فَهَلْ مِنْكُمَا تَائِبٌ؟ ثُمَّ قَامَتْ فَشَهِدَتْ، فَلَمَّا كَانَتْ عِنْدَ الخَامِسَةِ وَقَّفُوهَا وَقَالُوا إِنَّهَا مُوجِبَةٌ. قَالَ ابنُ عَبَّاسٍ: فَتَلَكَّأَتْ وَنَكَصَتْ حَتَّى ظَنَنَّا أَنَّهَا تَرْجِعُ ثُمَّ قَالَتْ: لا أَفْضَحُ قَوْمِي سَائِرَ اليَوْمِ فَمَضَتْ، فَقَالَ النَّبِيُّ صلى اللهُ عليهِ وسلَّم: أَبْصِرُوهَا، فَإِنْ جَاءَتْ بِهِ أَكْحَلَ العَيْنَيْنِ، سَابِغَ الأَلْيَتَيْنِ، خَدَلَّجَ السَّاقَيْنِ، فَهُوَ لِشَرِيكِ بنِ سَحْمَاءَ. فَجَاءَتْ بِهِ كَذَلِكَ. فَقَالَ النَّبِيُّ صلى اللهُ عليهِ وسلَّم: لَوْلَا مَا مَضَى مِنْ كِتَابِ اللهِ لَكَانَ لِي وَلَهَا شَأْنٌ.

(211) CHAPTER. The Statement of Allāh :–

'And the fifth (testimony) should be that the wrath of Allāh be upon her if he (her husband) speaks the truth.' (24:9)

باب قوله - والخامسة أن غضب الله عليها إن كان من الصادقين - .

272. Narrated Ibn' Umar : A man accused his wife of illegal sexual intercourse and denied his paternity to her (conceived) child during the lifetime of Allāh's Messenger . Allāh's Messenger ordered them both to do Mula'ana (1) as Allāh decreed and then gave his decision that the child would be for the mother, and a divorce decree was issued for the couple involved in a case of Mulā'ana.

٢٧٢ - حدثني مقدم بن محمد ابن يحيى: حدثنا عمي القاسم بن يحيى، عن عبيد الله وقد سمع منه، عن نافع، عن ابن عمر رضي الله عنهما: أن رجلا رمى امرأته فانتفى من ولدها في زمان رسول الله صلى الله عليه وسلم فأمر بهما رسول الله صلى الله عليه وسلم فتلاعنا كما قال الله ثم قضى بالولد للمرأة وفرق بين المتلاعنين .

(212) CHAPTER. The Statement of Allāh :–

'Verily! Those who spread the slander are a gang among you.' (24:11)

باب قوله - إن الذين جاءوا بالإفك عصبة منكم - أفاك: كذاب

273. Narrated 'Āisha : And as for him among them who had the greater share...' (24:11) was 'Abdullāh bin Ubai bin Salūl.

٢٧٣ - حدثنا أبو نعيم: حدثنا سفيان، عن معمر، عن الزهري، عن عروة، عن عائشة رضي الله عنها - والذي تولى كبره - قالت:

(1) See the word "Li'ān" in the glossary.

عَبْدُ اللهِ بنُ أُبَىٍّ بنِ سَلُولَ .

(213) CHAPTER. 'Why did not the believers — men and women — when you heard it (the slander) think good of their own people and say: This (charge) is an obvious lie......lie.' (24: 12-13)

بابٌ - لَوْلا إِذْ سَمِعْتُمُوهُ ظَنَّ المُؤْمِنُونَ وَالمُؤْمِنَاتُ بِأَنْفُسِهِمْ خَيْرًا - إلى قَوْلِهِ - الكَاذِبُونَ -

274. Narrated 'Āisha (رضي الله عنها), the wife of the Prophet ﷺ: Whenever Allāh's Messenger ﷺ intended to go on a journey, he used to draw lots among his wives and would take with him the one on whom the lot had fallen. Once he drew lots when he wanted to carry out a Ghazwa, and the lot came upon me. So I proceeded with Allāh's Messenger ﷺ after Allāh's order of veiling (the women) had been revealed and thus I was carried in my howdah (on a camel) and dismounted while still in it. We carried on our journey, and when Allāh's Messenger ﷺ had finished his Ghazwa and returned and we approached Medīna, Allāh's Messenger ﷺ ordered to proceed at night. When the army was ordered to resume the homeward journey, I got up and walked on till I left the army (camp) behind. When I had answered the call of nature, I went towards my howdah, but behold ! A necklace of mine made of Jaz' Azfār (a kind of black bead) was broken and I looked for it and my search for it detained me. The group of people who used to carry me, came and carried my howdah on to the back of my camel on which I was riding, considering that I was therein. At that time women were light in weight and

٢٧٤ - حدَّثنا يَحْيَى بنُ بُكَيْرٍ : حدَّثنا اللَّيْثُ ، عَنْ يُونُسَ ، عَنِ ابنِ شِهابٍ قالَ : أَخْبَرَنِى عُرْوَةُ بنُ الزُّبَيْرِ ، وَسَعِيدُ بنُ المُسَيَّبِ ، وَعَلْقَمَةُ بنُ وَقّاصٍ ، وَعُبَيْدُ اللهِ بنُ عَبْدِ اللهِ بنِ عُتْبَةَ بنِ مَسْعُودٍ ، عَنْ حَدِيثِ عائشةَ رَضِيَ اللهُ عَنْها زَوْجِ النَّبِيِّ صلى الله عليه وسلَّم حِينَ قالَ لَها أَهْلُ الإفْكِ ما قالُوا ، فَبَرَّأَها اللهُ مِمَّا قالُوا ، وكُلٌّ حدَّثَنِى طائِفَةً مِنَ الحَدِيثِ . وبَعْضُ حَدِيثِهِمْ يُصَدِّقُ بَعْضًا ، وإنْ كانَ بَعْضُهُمْ أَوْعَى لَهُ مِنْ بَعْضٍ . الَّذِى حدَّثَنِى عُرْوَةُ عَنْ عائشةَ رَضِيَ اللهُ عَنْها : أَنَّ عائشةَ رَضِيَ اللهُ عَنْها زَوْجَ النَّبِيِّ صلى الله عليه وسلَّم قالَتْ : كانَ رَسُولُ اللهِ صلى الله عليه وسلَّم إذا أَرادَ أَنْ يَخْرُجَ أَقْرَعَ بَيْنَ أَزْواجِهِ فَأَيَّتُهُنَّ خَرَجَ سَهْمُها خَرَجَ بِها رَسُولُ اللهِ صلى الله عليه وسلَّم مَعَهُ . قالَتْ عائشةُ : فَأَقْرَعَ

were not fleshy for they used to eat little (food), so those people did not feel the lightness of the howdah while raising it up, and I was still a young lady.[1] They drove away the camel and proceeded. Then I found my necklace after the army had gone. I came to their camp but found nobody therein so I went to the place where I used to stay, thinking that they would miss me and come back in my search. While I was sitting at my place, I felt sleepy and slept. Ṣafwān bin Al-Mu'aṭṭil As-Sulamī Adh-Dhakwānī was behind the army. He had started in the last part of the night and reached my stationing place in the morning and saw the figure of a sleeping person. He came to me and recognized me on seeing me for he used to see me before veiling. I got up because of his saying: "Innā Lillāhi wa innā ilaihi rāji'ūn,"[2] which he uttered on recognizing me. I covered my face with my garment, and by Allāh, he did not say to me a single word except, "Innā Lillāhi wa innā ilaihi rāji'ūn," till he made his she-camel kneel down whereupon he trod on its forelegs and I mounted it. Then Ṣafwān set out, leading the she-camel that was carrying me, till we met the army while they were resting during the hot midday. Then whoever was meant for destruction, fell in destruction, and the leader of the Ifk (forged statement) was 'Abdullāh bin Ubaī bin Salūl. After this we arrived at Medīna and I became ill for one month while the people were spreading

بينما في غزوة غزاها فخرج سهمي،
فخرجت مع رسول الله صلى الله عليه
وسلم بعد ما نزل الحجاب فأنا أحمل
في هودجي وأنزل فيه. فسرنا حتى
إذا فرغ رسول الله صلى الله عليه وسلم
من غزوته تلك وقفل ودنونا من
المدينة قافلين، آذن ليلة بالرحيل
فقمت حين آذنوا بالرحيل فمشيت
حتى إذا جاوزت الجيش فلما قضيت
شأني أقبلت إلى رحلي فإذا عقد لي
من جزع أظفار قد انقطع فالتمست
عقدي وحبسني ابتغاؤه. وأقبل الرهط
الذين كانوا يرحلون لي فاحتملوا
هودجي فرحلوه على بعيري الذي
كنت ركبت وهم يحسبون أني فيه،
وكان النساء إذ ذاك خفافا لم يثقلهن
اللحم إنما يأكلن العلقة من الطعام
فلم يستنكر القوم خفة الهودج
حين رفعوه، وكنت جارية حديثة
السن، فبعثوا الجمل وساروا، فوجدت
عقدي بعد ما استمر الجيش فجئت
منازلهم وليس بها داع ولا مجيب
فأممت منزلي الذي كنت به وظننت
أنهم سيفقدونني فيرجعون إلي. فبينا

(1) Less than fifteen years old.

(2) That means: Truly to Allāh we belong and truly to Him we shall return. (2: 156).

the forged statements of the people of the Ifk, and I was not aware of anything thereof. But what aroused my doubt while I was sick, was that I was no longer receiving from Allāh's Messenger ﷺ the same kindness as I used to receive when I fell sick. Allāh's Messenger ﷺ would enter upon me, say a greeting and add, "How is that (lady)?" and then depart. That aroused my suspicion but I was not aware of the propogated evil till I recovered from my ailment. I went out with Um Misṭaḥ to answer the call of nature towards Al-Mạnāṣi', the place where we used to relieve ourselves, and used not to go out for this purpose except from night to night, and that was before we had lavatories close to our houses. And this habit of ours was similar to the habit of the old 'Arabs (in the deserts or in the tents) concerning the evacuation of the bowels, for we considered it troublesome and harmful to take lavatories in the houses. So I went out with Um Misṭaḥ who was the daughter of Abī Ruhm bin 'Abd Manāf, and her mother was daughter of Ṣakhr bin 'Āmir who was the aunt of Abī Bakr Aṣ-Ṣiddīq, and her son was Misṭaḥ bin Uthātha. When we had finished our affair, Um Misṭaḥ and I came back towards my house. Um Misṭaḥ stumbled over her robe whereupon she said, "Let Misṭaḥ be ruined!" I said to her, "What a bad word you have said! Do you abuse a man who has taken part in the Battle of Badr?' She said, "O you there! Didn't you hear what he has said?" I said, "And what did he say?" She then told me the statement of the people of the Ifk (forged statement) which added to my ailment. When I returned home, Allāh's

أنا جالسةٌ فى مَنزلى غلبتنى عينى
فنمت وكانَ صفوانُ بنُ المعطّلِ
السُّلَمى ثُمَّ الذَّكوانىُّ مِنْ وَراءِ
الجيشِ فادَّلجَ فأصبحَ عِندَ منزلى
فرأى سوادَ إنسانٍ نائمٍ ، فأتانى فعرفنى
حينَ رآنى ، وكانَ يَرانى قبلَ الحِجابِ ،
فاستيقظتُ باسترجاعِهِ حينَ عرفنى
فخمّرتُ وَجهى بجلبابى ، وَاللهِ ما
كلّمنى كلمةً ولا سمعتُ مِنهُ كلمةً
غيرَ استرجاعِهِ ، حتّى أناخَ راحلتَهُ
فوَطِئَ عَلى يدَيها فركِبتُها ، فانطلَقَ
يقودُ بى الراحلةَ حتّى أتينا الجيشَ
بعدَ ما نزلوا مُوغِرينَ فى نحرِ
الظهيرةِ ، فهلكَ مَنْ هلكَ . وكانَ
الّذى تَوَلّى الإفكَ عبدُ اللهِ بنُ أُبىٍّ
ابنِ سلولَ ، فقدِمنا المدينةَ فاشتكيتُ
حينَ قدِمتُ شهرًا والنّاسُ يُفيضونَ
فى قولِ أصحابِ الإفكِ وَلا أشعرُ
بشىءٍ مِنْ ذلكَ وَهوَ يُريبُنى فى
وَجَعى أنّنى لاأعرفُ مِنْ رَسولِ اللهِ
صلى اللهُ عليهِ وسلّم اللُّطفَ الّذى كُنتُ
أرى مِنهُ حينَ أشتكى ، إنّما يدخُلُ
علَىَّ رَسولُ اللهِ صلى اللهُ عليهِ وسلّم فيُسلِّمُ
ثُمّ يقولُ : كيفَ تيكُم ؟ ثُمّ ينصرِفُ
فذاكَ الّذى يَريبُنى وَلا أشعرُ بالشّرِّ
حتّى خرجتُ بعدَما نقِهتُ فخرجتُ
معَ أُمِّ مِسطحٍ قِبَلَ المناصعِ وَهوَ

Messenger ﷺ came to me, and after greeting, he said, "How is that (lady)?" I said, "Will you allow me to go to my parents?" At that time I intended to be sure of the news through them. Allāh's Messenger ﷺ allowed me and I went to my parents and asked my mother, "O my mother! What are the people talking about?" My mother said, "O my daughter! Take it easy, for by Allāh, there is no charming lady who is loved by her husband who has other wives as well, but that those wives would find fault with her." I said, "Subhān Allāh! Did the people really talk about that?" That night I kept on weeping the whole night till the morning. My tears never stopped, nor did I sleep, and morning broke while I was still weeping, Allāh's Messenger ﷺ called 'Alī bin Abī Ṭālib and Usāma bin Zaid when the Divine Inspiration delayed, in order to consult them as to the idea of divorcing his wife. Usāma bin Zaid told Allāh's Messenger ﷺ of what he knew about the innocence of his wife and of his affection he kept for her. He said, "O Allāh's Messenger! She is your wife, and we do not know anything about her except good." But 'Alī bin Abī Ṭālib said, "O Allāh's Messenger! Allāh does not impose restrictions on you; and there are plenty of women other than her. If you however, ask (her) slave girl, she will tell you the truth." 'Āisha added: So Allāh's Messenger ﷺ called for Barīra and said, "O Barīra! Did you ever see anything which might have aroused your suspicion? (as regards 'Āisha). Barīra said, "By Allāh Who has sent you with the truth, I have never seen anything regarding 'Āisha which I would blame her for except that she is

متبرزنا وكنا لا نخرج إلا ليلاً إلى ليل وذلك قبل أن نتخذ الكنف قريبا من بيوتنا، وأمرنا أمر العرب الأول في التبرز قبل الغائط، فكنا نتأذى بالكنف أن نتخذها عند بيوتنا، فانطلقت أنا وأم مسطح، وهي ابنة أبي رهم ابن عبد مناف، وأمها بنت صخر بن عامر خالة أبي بكر الصديق، وابنها مسطح بن أثاثة. فأقبلت أنا وأم مسطح قبل بيتي وقد فرغنا من شأننا فعثرت أم مسطح في مرطها فقالت: تعس مسطح، فقلت لها: بئس ما قلت: أتسبين رجلا شهد بدرا؟ قالت: أي هنتاه، أولم تسمعي ما قال؟ قالت: قلت وما قال؟ قالت: فأخبرتني بقول أهل الإفك فازددت مرضا على مرضي، قالت: فلما رجعت إلى بيتي ودخل علي رسول الله صلى الله عليه وسلم تعني سلم ثم قال: كيف تيكم؟ فقلت: أتأذن لي أن آتي أبوي؟ قالت: وأنا حينئذ أريد أستيقن الخبر من قبلهما، قالت: فأذن لي رسول الله صلى الله عليه وسلم فجئت أبوي فقلت لأمي: يا أمتاه، ما يتحدث الناس؟ قالت: يا بنية هوني عليك، فوالله لقلما كانت امرأة قط وضيئة عند

a girl of immature age who sometimes sleeps and leaves the dough of her family unprotected so that the domestic goats come and eat it." So Allāh's Messenger ﷺ got up (and addressed) the people and asked for somebody who would take revenge on 'Abdullāh bin Ubaī bin Salūl then. Allāh's Messenger ﷺ, while on the pulpit, said, "O Muslims! Who will help me against a man who has hurt me by slandering my family? By Allāh, I know nothing except good about my family, and people have blamed a man of whom I know nothing except good, and he never used to visit my family except with me," Sa'd bin Mu'ādh Al-Anṣārī got up and said, "O Allāh's Messenger! By Allāh, I will relieve you from him. If he be from the tribe of (Banī) Al-Aus, then I will chop his head off; and if he be from our brethern, the Khazraj, then you give us your order and we will obey it." On that, Sa'd bin 'Ubāda got up, and he was the chief of the Khazraj, and before this incident he had been a pious man but he was incited by his zeal for his tribe. He said to Sa'd (bin Mu'ādh), "By Allāh the Eternal, you have told a lie! You shall not kill him and you will never be able to kill him!" On that, Usaid bin Ḥuḍair, the cousin of Sa'd (bin Mu'ādh) got up and said to Sa'd bin 'Ubāda, "You are a liar! By Allāh the Eternal, we will surely kill him; and you are a hypocrite defending the hypocrites!" So the two tribes of Al-Aus and Al-Khazraj got excited till they were on the point of fighting with each other while Allāh's Messenger ﷺ was standing on the pulpit. Allāh's Messenger ﷺ continued quietening them till they became silent whereupon he became silent too. On that day I kept on

رَجُلٍ يُحِبُّهَا وَلَهَا ضَرَائِرُ إِلَّا أَكْثَرْنَ عَلَيْهَا قَالَتْ: فَقُلْتُ: سُبْحَانَ اللهِ: أَوَ لَقَدْ تَحَدَّثَ النَّاسُ بِهَذَا؟ قَالَتْ: فَبَكَيْتُ تِلْكَ اللَّيْلَةَ حَتَّى أَصْبَحْتُ لَا يَرْقَأُ لِي دَمْعٌ وَلَا أَكْتَحِلُ بِنَوْمٍ حَتَّى أَصْبَحْتُ أَبْكِي. فَدَعَا رَسُولُ اللهِ صلى اللهُ عليه وسلم عَلِيَّ بْنَ أَبِي طَالِبٍ وَأُسَامَةَ بْنَ زَيْدٍ رَضِيَ اللهُ عَنْهُمَا حِينَ اسْتَلْبَثَ الْوَحْيُ يَسْتَأْمِرُهُمَا فِي فِرَاقِ أَهْلِهِ. قَالَتْ: فَأَمَّا أُسَامَةُ بْنُ زَيْدٍ فَأَشَارَ عَلَى رَسُولِ اللهِ صلى اللهُ عليه وسلم بِالَّذِي يَعْلَمُ مِنْ بَرَاءَةِ أَهْلِهِ، وَبِالَّذِي يَعْلَمُ لَهُمْ فِي نَفْسِهِ مِنَ الْوُدِّ، فَقَالَ: يَا رَسُولَ اللهِ، أَهْلَكَ وَمَا نَعْلَمُ إِلَّا خَيْرًا. وَأَمَّا عَلِيُّ بْنُ أَبِي طَالِبٍ فَقَالَ: يَا رَسُولَ اللهِ، لَمْ يُضَيِّقِ اللهُ عَلَيْكَ وَالنِّسَاءُ سِوَاهَا كَثِيرٌ، وَإِنْ تَسْأَلِ الْجَارِيَةَ تَصْدُقْكَ. قَالَتْ: فَدَعَا رَسُولُ اللهِ صلى اللهُ عليه وسلم بَرِيرَةَ فَقَالَ: أَيْ بَرِيرَةُ هَلْ رَأَيْتِ مِنْ شَيْءٍ يَرِيبُكِ؟ قَالَتْ بَرِيرَةُ: لَا وَالَّذِي بَعَثَكَ بِالْحَقِّ، إِنْ رَأَيْتُ عَلَيْهَا أَمْرًا أَغْمِصُهُ عَلَيْهَا أَكْثَرَ مِنْ أَنَّهَا جَارِيَةٌ حَدِيثَةُ السِّنِّ تَنَامُ عَنْ عَجِينِ أَهْلِهَا فَتَأْتِي الدَّاجِنُ فَتَأْكُلُهُ. فَقَامَ رَسُولُ اللهِ صلى اللهُ عليه وسلم فَاسْتَعْذَرَ يَوْمَئِذٍ مِنْ عَبْدِ اللهِ بْنِ أُبَيٍّ ابْنِ

weeping so much that neither did my tears stop, nor could I sleep. In the morning my parents were with me, and I had wept for two nights and a day without sleeping and with incessant tears till they thought that my liver would burst with weeping. While they were with me and I was weeping, an Anṣārī woman asked permission to see me. I admitted her and she sat and started weeping with me. While I was in that state, Allāh's Messenger ﷺ came to us, greeted, and sat down,. He had never sat with me since the day what was said, was said. He had stayed a month without receiving any Divine Inspiration concerning my case. Allāh's Messenger ﷺ recited the Tashahhud (1) after he had sat down, and then said, "Thereafter, O'Āisha! I have been informed such and-such a thing about you, ; and if you are innocent, Allāh will reveal your innocence, and if you have committed a sin, then ask for Allāh's forgiveness and repent to Him, for when a slave confesses his sin and then repents to Allāh, Allāh accepts his repentance." When Allāh's Messenger ﷺ had finished his speech, my tears ceased completely so that I no longer felt even a drop thereof. Then I said to my father, "Reply to Allāh's Messenger ﷺ on my behalf as to what he said." He said, "By Allāh, I do not know what to say to Allāh's Messenger ﷺ." Then I said to my mother, "Reply to Allāh's Apostle ﷺ." She said, "I do not know what to say to Allāh's Messenger ﷺ." Still a young girl as I was and though I had little knowledge of Qur'ān, I said, "By Allāh, I know that you heard this story (of the Ifk) so much so that it has been planted in your minds and you have believed it. So now, if I tell you that I am

سلول. قالت: فقال رسول الله صلى الله عليه وسلم وهو على المنبر: يا معشر المسلمين، من يعذرني من رجل قد بلغني أذاه في أهل بيتي؟ فوالله ما علمت على أهلي إلا خيرا، ولقد ذكروا رجلا ما علمت عليه إلا خيرا، وما كان يدخل على أهلي إلا معي. فقام سعد بن معاذ الأنصاري فقال: يا رسول الله أنا أعذرك منه، إن كان من الأوس ضربت عنقه. وإن كان من إخواننا من الخزرج أمرتنا ففعلنا أمرك. قالت: فقام سعد ابن عبادة وهو سيد الخزرج، وكان قبل ذلك رجلا صالحا ولكن احتملته الحمية فقال لسعد: كذبت، لعمر الله لا تقتله ولا تقدر على قتله. فقام أسيد بن حضير وهو ابن عم سعد فقال لسعد بن عبادة: كذبت لعمر الله لنقتلنه فإنك منافق تجادل عن المنافقين. فتثاور الحيان الأوس والخزرج حتى هموا أن يقتتلوا ورسول الله صلى الله عليه وسلم قائم على المنبر. فلم يزل رسول الله صلى الله عليه وسلم يخفضهم حتى سكتوا وسكت. قالت: فمكثت يومي ذلك لا يرقأ لي دمع ولا أكتحل بنوم. قالت: فأصبح أبواي عندي وقد بكيت ليلتين ويوما، لا أكتحل

(1) I testify that none has the right to be worshipped but Allāh, and that Muḥammad is His Messenger.

innocent — and Allāh knows that I am innocent — you will not believe me; and if I confess something — and Allāh knows that I am innocent of it — you will believe me. By Allāh, I cannot find of you an example except that of Joseph's father: "So (for me) patience is most fitting against that which you assert and it is Allāh (Alone) Whose help can be sought. Then I turned away and lay on my bed, and at that time I knew that I was innocent and that Allāh would reveal my innocence. But by Allāh, I never thought that Allāh would sent down about my affair, Divine Inspiration that would be recited (forever), as I considered myself too unworthy to be talked of by Allāh with something that was to be recited: but I hoped that Allāh's Messenger ﷺ might have a vision in which Allāh would prove my innocence. By Allāh, Allāh's Messenger had not left his seat and nobody had left the house when the Divine Inspiration came to Allāh's Messenger ﷺ. So there overtook him the same hard condition which used to overtake him (when he was Divinely Inspired) so that the drops of his sweat were running down, like pearls, though it was a (cold) winter day, and that was because of the heaviness of the Statement which was revealed to him. When that state of Allāh's Messenger ﷺ was over — and he was smiling when he was relieved — the first word he said was, "'Āisha, Allāh عَزَّوَجَلَّ has declared your innocence." My mother said to me, "Get up and go to him." I

بِنَوْمٍ وَلَا أُرْقَا لِى دَمْعٌ، يَظُنَّانِ أَنَّ الْبُكَاءَ فَالِقٌ كَبِدِى. قَالَتْ: فَبَيْنَا هُمَا جَالِسَانِ عِنْدِى وَأَنَا أَبْكِى فَاسْتَأْذَنَتْ عَلَيَّ امْرَأَةٌ مِنَ الْأَنْصَارِ، فَأَذِنْتُ لَهَا فَجَلَسَتْ تَبْكِى مَعِى، قَالَتْ: فَبَيْنَا نَحْنُ عَلَى ذَلِكَ دَخَلَ عَلَيْنَا رَسُولُ اللَّهِ صَلَّى اللَّهُ عَلَيْهِ وَسَلَّمَ فَسَلَّمَ ثُمَّ جَلَسَ. قَالَتْ: وَلَمْ يَجْلِسْ عِنْدِى مُنْذُ مَا قِيلَ قَبْلَهَا. وَقَدْ لَبِثَ شَهْرًا لَا يُوحَى إِلَيْهِ فِى شَأْنِنَا، قَالَتْ: فَتَشَهَّدَ رَسُولُ اللَّهِ صَلَّى اللَّهُ عَلَيْهِ وَسَلَّمَ حِينَ جَلَسَ، ثُمَّ قَالَ: أَمَّا بَعْدُ، يَا عَائِشَةُ فَإِنَّهُ قَدْ بَلَغَنِى عَنْكِ كَذَا وَكَذَا، فَإِنْ كُنْتِ بَرِيئَةً فَسَيُبَرِّئُكِ اللَّهُ. وَإِنْ كُنْتِ أَلْمَمْتِ بِذَنْبٍ فَاسْتَغْفِرِى اللَّهَ وَتُوبِى إِلَيْهِ. فَإِنَّ الْعَبْدَ إِذَا اعْتَرَفَ بِذَنْبِهِ ثُمَّ تَابَ إِلَى اللَّهِ تَابَ اللَّهُ عَلَيْهِ. قَالَتْ: فَلَمَّا قَضَى مَقَالَتَهُ قَلَصَ دَمْعِى حَتَّى مَا أُحِسُّ مِنْهُ قَطْرَةً، فَقُلْتُ لِأَبِى: أَجِبْ رَسُولَ اللَّهِ صَلَّى اللَّهُ عَلَيْهِ وَسَلَّمَ فِيمَا قَالَ. قَالَ: وَاللَّهِ مَا أَدْرِى مَا أَقُولُ لِرَسُولِ اللَّهِ صَلَّى اللَّهُ عَلَيْهِ وَسَلَّمَ، فَقُلْتُ لِأُمِّى: أَجِيبِى رَسُولَ اللَّهِ صَلَّى اللَّهُ عَلَيْهِ وَسَلَّمَ، قَالَتْ: مَا أَدْرِى مَا أَقُولُ لِرَسُولِ

said, "By Allāh, I will not go to him and I will not thank anybody but Allāh عزّوجلّ." So Allāh عزّوجلّ revealed:—

> Verily! They who spread the Slander are a gang among you. Think it not bad....... ' (24: 11-20)

When Allāh revealed this to confirm my innocence, Abū Bakr Aṣ-Ṣiddīq who used to provide for Misṭaḥ bin Uthātha because of the latter's kinship to him and his poverty, said, "By Allāh, I will never provide for Misṭaḥ anything after what he has said about Āisha". So Allāh revealed:—

> 'Let not those among you who are good and are wealthy swear not to give (help) to their kinsmen, those in need, and those who have left their homes for Allāh's Cause. Let them pardon and forgive (i.e. do not punish them). Do you not love that Allāh should forgive you? And Allāh is Oft-for-giving. Most Merciful.' (24:22)

Abū Bakr said, "Yes, by Allāh, I wish that Allāh should forgive me." So he resumed giving Misṭaḥ the aid he used to give him before and said, "By Allāh, I will never withold it from him at all." 'Āisha further said: Allāh's Messenger ﷺ also asked Zainab bint Jaḥsh about my case. He said, "O Zainab! What have you learnt and what have you seen?" She replied, "O Allāh's Messenger! I protect my hearing and my sight (by refraining from telling lies). I know nothing but good (about 'Āisha)." Of all the wives of Allāh's Messenger ﷺ, it was Zainab who aspired to receive from him the same favour as I used to receive, yet, Allāh saved her (from telling lies)

الله صلى الله عليه وسلم، قالت: قلت وأنا جارية حديثة السن لا أقرأ كثيرا من القرآن: إني والله لقد علمت لقد سمعتم هذا الحديث حتى استقر في أنفسكم وصدقتم به، فلئن قلت لكم إني بريئة والله يعلم أني منه بريئة لا تصدقوني بذلك. ولئن اعترفت لكم بأمر والله يعلم أني منه بريئة لتصدقني. والله ما أجد لكم مثلا إلا قول أبي يوسف قال - فصبر جميل والله المستعان على ما تصفون - قالت: ثم تحولت فاضطجعت على فراشي. قالت: وأنا حينئذ أعلم أني بريئة، وأن الله مبرئي ببراءتي. ولكن والله ما كنت أظن أن الله منزل في شأني وحيا يتلى، ولشأني في نفسي كان أحقر من أن يتكلم الله في بأمر يتلى، ولكن كنت أرجو أن يرى رسول الله صلى الله عليه وسلم في النوم رؤيا يبرئني الله بها قالت: فوالله ما رام رسول الله صلى الله عليه وسلم ولا خرج أحد من أهل البيت حتى أنزل عليه فأخذه ما كان يأخذه من البرحاء، حتى إنه ليتحدر منه مثل الجمان من العرق، وهو في يوم شات، من ثقل القول الذي

because of her piety. But her sister, Ḥamna, kept on fighting on her behalf, so she was destroyed as were those who invented and spread the slander.

يُنْزَلُ عَلَيْهِ. قالَتْ: فَلَمّا سُرِّيَ عَنْ رَسُولِ اللهِ صلى الله عليه وسلم سُرِّيَ عَنْهُ وَهُوَ يَضْحَكُ، فَكانَ أَوَّلُ كَلِمَةٍ تَكَلَّمَ بِها: يا عائِشَةُ، أَمَّا اللهُ عَزَّ وَجَلَّ فَقَدْ بَرَّأَكِ. فَقالَتْ أُمِّي: قُومي إِلَيْهِ، قالَتْ: فَقُلْتُ: وَاللهِ لا أَقُومُ إِلَيْهِ وَلا أَحْمَدُ إِلّا اللهَ عَزَّ وَجَلَّ. وَأَنْزَلَ اللهُ عَزَّ وَجَلَّ - إِنَّ الَّذينَ جاءُوا بِالإِفْكِ عُصْبَةٌ مِنْكُمْ لا تَحْسَبُوهُ - العَشْرَ الآياتِ كُلَّها، فَلَمّا أَنْزَلَ اللهُ هَذا في بَراءَتي قالَ أَبو بَكْرٍ الصِّدِّيقُ رَضِيَ اللهُ عَنْهُ وَكانَ يُنْفِقُ عَلى مِسْطَحِ بْنِ أُثاثَةَ لِقَرابَتِهِ مِنْهُ وَفَقْرِهِ: وَاللهِ لا أُنْفِقُ عَلى مِسْطَحٍ شَيْئًا أَبَدًا بَعْدَ الَّذي قالَ لِعائِشَةَ ما قالَ. فَأَنْزَلَ اللهُ - وَلا يَأْتَلِ أُولُو الفَضْلِ مِنْكُمْ وَالسَّعَةِ أَنْ يُؤْتُوا أُولِي القُرْبى وَالمَساكينَ وَالمُهاجِرينَ في سَبيلِ اللهِ وَلْيَعْفُوا وَلْيَصْفَحُوا أَلا تُحِبُّونَ أَنْ يَغْفِرَ اللهُ لَكُمْ وَاللهُ غَفُورٌ رَحيمٌ - قالَ أَبو بَكْرٍ: بَلى وَاللهِ إِنِّي أُحِبُّ أَنْ يَغْفِرَ اللهُ لي، فَرَجَعَ إِلى مِسْطَحٍ النَّفَقَةَ الَّتي كانَ يُنْفِقُ عَلَيْهِ. وَقالَ: وَاللهِ لا أَنْزِعُها عَنْهُ مِنْهُ أَبَدًا. قالَتْ عائِشَةُ: وَكانَ رَسُولُ اللهِ صلى الله عليه وسلم يَسْأَلُ زَيْنَبَ ابْنَةَ جَحْشٍ عَنْ أَمْري، فَقالَ: يا زَيْنَبُ ماذا عَلِمْتِ أَوْ رَأَيْتِ؟

فَقَالَتْ : يَا رَسُولَ اللهِ ، أَحْمِي سَمْعِي وَبَصَرِي ، مَا عَلِمْتُ إِلَّا خَيْرًا . قَالَتْ : وَهِيَ الَّتِي كَانَتْ تُسَامِينِي مِنْ أَزْوَاجِ رَسُولِ اللهِ صلى اللهُ عليهِ وسلَّم فَعَصَمَهَا اللهُ بِالْوَرَعِ . وَطَفِقَتْ أُخْتُهَا حَمْنَةُ تُحَارِبُ لَهَا فَهَلَكَتْ فِيمَنْ هَلَكَ مِنْ أَصْحَابِ الْإِفْكِ .

(214) CHAPTER. The Statement of Allāh ﷻ :–

'Had it not been for the grace of Allāh and His mercy unto you in this world and the Hereafter, a great torment had touched you for that whereof you have spoken." (24:14)

بَابُ قَوْلِهِ ـ وَلَوْلَا فَضْلُ اللهِ عَلَيْكُمْ وَرَحْمَتُهُ فِي الدُّنْيَا وَالْآخِرَةِ لَمَسَّكُمْ فِيمَا أَفَضْتُمْ فِيهِ عَذَابٌ عَظِيمٌ ـ وَقَالَ مُجَاهِدٌ : تَلَقَّوْنَهُ : يَرْوِيهِ بَعْضُكُمْ عَنْ بَعْضٍ . تُفِيضُونَ تَقُولُونَ .

٢٧٥ - حَدَّثَنَا مُحَمَّدُ بنُ كَثِيرٍ : حَدَّثَنَا سُلَيْمَانُ ، عَنْ حُصَيْنٍ ، عَنْ أَبِي وَائِلٍ ، عَنْ مَسْرُوقٍ ، عَنْ أُمِّ رُومَانَ أُمِّ عَائِشَةَ : أَنَّهَا قَالَتْ : لَمَّا رُمِيَتْ عَائِشَةُ خَرَّتْ مَغْشِيًّا عَلَيْهَا .

275. Narrated Um Rumān, 'Āisha's mother, When 'Āisha was accused, she fell down unconscious.

بابٌ - إِذْ تَلَقَّوْنَهُ بِأَلْسِنَتِكُمْ وَتَقُولُونَ بِأَفْوَاهِكُمْ مَا لَيْسَ لَكُمْ بِهِ عِلْمٌ - الآيَةَ .

(215) CHAPTER. The Statement of Allāh ﷻ :–

"When you welcomed it with your tongues, and uttered with your mouths that whereof you had no knowledge..........' (24:15)

٢٧٦ - حَدَّثَنَا إِبْرَاهِيمُ بنُ مُوسَى : حَدَّثَنَا هِشَامٌ : أَنَّ ابْنَ جُرَيْجٍ أَخْبَرَهُمْ : قَالَ ابْنُ أَبِي مُلَيْكَةَ : سَمِعْتُ عَائِشَةَ تَقْرَأُ - إِذْ تَلِقُونَهُ بِأَلْسِنَتِكُمْ - .

276: Narrated Ibn Abī Mulaika: I heard 'Āisha reciting:–

'When you invented a lie (and carry it) on your tongues.' (24: 15) (1)

بابٌ - وَلَوْلا إِذْ سَمِعْتُمُوهُ قُلْتُمْ مَا يَكُونُ لَنَا أَنْ نَتَكَلَّمَ بِهَذَا - الآيَةَ .

(216) CHAPTER. And why did you not, when you heard it, say: It is not right for us to speak of this?' (24:16)

٢٧٧ - حَدَّثَنَا مُحَمَّدُ بنُ المُثَنَّى :

277. Narrated Ibn Abū Mulaika:

(1) The difference in the translation of this Verse comes from the way one word is read, i.e. 'Talquanahū' (you welcomed it) or, 'Taliquanaha' (you invented a lie). The popular recitation is 'Talquanaha' while 'Āisha recited it: 'Taliqūanaha.'

Ibn 'Abbās asked permission to visit 'Āisha before her death, and at that time she was in a state of agony. She then said. "I am afraid that he will praise me too much." And then it was said to her, "He is the cousin of Allāh's Messenger ﷺ and one of the prominent Muslims." Then she said, "Allow him to enter." (When he entered) he said, "How are you?" She replied, "I am alright if I fear (Allāh)." Ibn Abbās said, "Allāh willing, you are alright as you are the wife of Allāh's Messenger ﷺ and he did not marry any virgin except you and proof of your innocence was revealed from the Heaven." Later on Ibn Az-Zubair entered after him and 'Āisha said to him, "Ibn 'Abbās came to me and praised me greatly, but I wish that I was a thing forgotten and out of sight."

حدَّثنا يحيى، عن عُمرَ بنِ سعيد بن أبي حُسين قالَ: حدَّثني ابنُ أبي مُليكةَ قالَ: استأذنَ ابنُ عبّاس قبلَ موتها على عائشةَ وهيَ مغلوبةٌ قالتْ: أخشى أنْ يُثنيَ عليَّ فقيلَ ابنُ عمِّ رسولِ الله صلى اللهُ عليه وسلّم ومِنْ وُجوهِ المُسلمينَ، قالتْ ائذنوا لهُ، فقالَ: كيفَ تجدينكِ؟ قالتْ: بخيرٍ إنِ اتّقيتُ، قالَ: فأنتِ بخيرٍ إنْ شاءَ اللهُ تعالى، زوجةُ رسولِ الله صلى اللهُ عليه وسلّم ولم ينكحْ بِكرًا غيرَكِ، ونزلَ عُذرُكِ مِنَ السَّماء. ودخلَ ابنُ الزُّبيرِ خلافَهُ فقالتْ: دخلَ ابنُ عبّاسٍ فأثنى عليَّ ووددتُ أني كنتُ نِسيًا منسيًّا.

278. Narrated Al-Qāsim: Ibn 'Abbās asked 'Āisha's permission to enter. Al-Qāsim then narrated the whole Ḥadīth (as in 277) but did not mention: "Would that I had been forgotten and out of sight."

٢٧٨ - حدَّثنا مُحمّدُ بنُ المُثنّى: حدَّثنا عبدُ الوهّابِ بنُ عبدِ المَجيد: حدَّثنا ابنُ عونٍ، عنِ القاسمِ: أنَّ ابنَ عبّاسٍ رضيَ اللهُ عنهُ استأذنَ على عائشةَ نحوَهُ، ولم يذكرْ: نِسيًا منسيًّا.

(217) CHAPTER. The Statement of Allāh :–

'Allāh admonishes you that you repeat not the like of it if you are believers.' (24:17)

بابُ قولِهِ - يَعِظُكُمُ اللهُ أنْ تعودوا لمثلِهِ أبدًا - الآيةَ.

279. Narrated Masrūq: 'Āisha said that Ḥassān bin Thābit came and asked permission to visit her. I said, "How do you permit such a person?" She said, "Hasn't he received a severely penalty?" (Sufyān, the subnarrator, said: She meant the loss of his sight.) Thereupon Ḥassān said the following poetic verse:

'A chaste pious woman who arouses no suspicion. She never talks about chaste heedless women behind their backs.' On that she said, "But you are not so."

٢٧٩ ـ حدَّثنا مُحَمَّدُ بنُ يُوسُفَ: حدَّثنا سُفْيانُ، عَنِ الأعْمَشِ، عَنْ أبي الضُّحَى، عَنْ مَسْرُوقٍ، عَنْ عائشةَ رَضِيَ اللهُ عَنْها قالَتْ: جاءَ حَسَّانُ بنُ ثابِتٍ يَستأذِنُ عَلَيْها، قُلْتُ: أتأذَنينَ لِهذا؟ قالَتْ: أوَ لَيْسَ قَدْ أصابَهُ عَذابٌ عَظيمٌ؟ قالَ سُفْيانُ: تَعني ذَهابَ بَصَرِهِ، فقالَ:

حَصانٌ رَزانٌ ما تُزَنُّ بِريبةٍ
وتُصْبِحُ غَرْثَى مِن لُحُومِ الغَوافِلِ

قالَتْ: لَكِنْ أنتَ.

(218) CHAPTER. The Statement of Allāh :–

'And Allāh makes the signs plain to you. And Allāh is All-Knowing, All-Wise.' (24:18)

باب قَوْلِهِ ـ وَيُبَيِّنُ اللهُ لَكُمُ الآياتِ واللهُ عَليمٌ حَكيمٌ ـ.

280. Narrated Masrūq: Ḥassān came to 'Āisha and said the following poetic Verse: 'A chaste pious woman who arouses no suspicion. She never talks against chaste heedless women behind their backs.' 'Āisha said, "But you are not," I said (to 'Āisha), "Why do you allow such a person to enter upon you after Allāh has revealed:

'...and as for him among them who had the greater share therein'?" (24:11)

٢٨٠ ـ حدَّثنا مُحَمَّدُ بنُ بَشَّارٍ: حدَّثنا ابنُ أبي عَدِيٍّ: أنبأنا شُعْبَةُ، عَنِ الأعْمَشِ، عَنْ أبي الضُّحَى، عَنْ مَسْرُوقٍ قالَ: دَخَلَ حَسَّانُ بنُ ثابِتٍ عَلى عائشةَ فَشَبَّبَ وقالَ:

She said, "What punishment is worse than blindness?" She added, "And he used to defend Allāh's Messenger ﷺ against the pagans (in his poetry).

حَصَانٌ رَزَانٌ مَا تُزَنُّ بِرِيبَةٍ
وَتُصْبِحُ غَرْثَى مِنْ لُحُومِ الْغَوَافِلِ
قَالَتْ عَائِشَةُ: لَسْتَ كَذَاكَ، قُلْتُ:
تَدَعِينَ مِثْلَ هَذَا يَدْخُلُ عَلَيْكِ وَقَدْ
أَنْزَلَ اللَّهُ - وَالَّذِي تَوَلَّى كِبْرَهُ مِنْهُمْ -
فَقَالَتْ: وَأَيُّ عَذَابٍ أَشَدُّ مِنَ الْعَمَى،
وَقَالَتْ: وَقَدْ كَانَ يَرُدُّ عَنْ رَسُولِ
اللَّهِ صلى اللهُ عليهِ وسلَّم.

(219) CHAPTER. The Statement of Allāh تعالى :–

> Verily, those who like that (the crime of) illegal sexual intervourse should be propagated about those who Believe......and that Allāh is Full of pity, Most Merciful.'
>
> (24: 19-20)

> 'Let not those among you who are good and are wealthy, swear not to give (any sort of help) to their kinsmen, those in need ....and Allāh is Oft-Forgiving, Most Merciful '
>
> (24: 22)

بَابٌ - إِنَّ الَّذِينَ يُحِبُّونَ أَنْ
تَشِيعَ الْفَاحِشَةُ فِي الَّذِينَ آمَنُوا - الآيَة
إِلَى قَوْلِهِ - رَءُوفٌ رَحِيمٌ - تَشِيعُ:
تَظْهَرُ - وَلَا يَأْتَلِ أُولُو الْفَضْلِ مِنْكُمْ
وَالسَّعَةِ أَنْ يُؤْتُوا أُولِي الْقُرْبَى
وَالْمَسَاكِينَ إِلَى قَوْلِهِ - وَاللَّهُ غَفُورٌ
رَحِيمٌ -

281. Narrated 'Āisha رضي الله عنها : When there was said about me what was said which I myself was unaware of, Allāh's Messenger ﷺ got up and addressed the people. He recited Tashāh-hud, (1) and after glorifying and praising Allāh as He

٢٨١ - وَقَالَ أَبُو أُسَامَةَ، عَنْ هِشَامِ بْنِ
عُرْوَةَ قَالَ: أَخْبَرَنِي أَبِي، عَنْ عَائِشَةَ
قَالَتْ: لَمَّا ذُكِرَ مِنْ شَأْنِي الَّذِي ذُكِرَ
وَمَا عَلِمْتُ بِهِ قَامَ رَسُولُ اللَّهِ صلى الله

(1) "Tashah-hud" See footnote of page 253.

deserved, he said, "To proceed: O people! Give me your opinion regarding those people who made a forged story against my wife. By Allāh, I do not know anything bad about her. By Allāh, they accused her of being with a man about whom I have never known anything bad, and he never entered my house unless I was present there, and whenever I went on a journey, he went with me." Sa'd bin Mu'ādh got up and said, "O Allāh's Messenger! Allow me to chop their heads off!" Then a man from the Al-Khazraj (Sa'd bin 'Ubāda) to whom the mother of (the poet) Ḥassān bin Thābit was a relative, got up and said (to Sa'd bin Mu'ādh), "You have told a lie! By Allāh, if those persons were from the Aus Tribe, you would not like to chop their heads off." It was probable that some evil would take place between the Aus and the Khazraj in the mosque, and I was unaware of all that. In the evening of that day, I went out for some of my needs (i.e. to relieve myself), and Um Misṭaḥ was accompanying me. On our return, Um Misṭaḥ stumbled and said, "Let Misṭaḥ be ruined!" I said to her, "O mother! Why do you abuse your son?" On that Um Misṭaḥ became silent for a while, and stumbling again, she said, "Let Misṭaḥ be ruined!" I said to her, "Why do you abuse your son?" She stumbled for the third time and said, "Let Misṭaḥ be ruined!" whereupon I rebuked her for that. She said, "By Allāh, I do not abuse him except because of you." I asked her, "Concerning what of my affairs?" So she disclosed the whole story to me. I said, "Has this really happened?" She

عليه وسلَّم فِي خَطِيبًا فَتَشَهَّدَ فَحَمِدَ اللهَ
وأَثْنَى عَلَيْهِ بِما هُوَ أَهْلُهُ ثُمَّ قالَ : أَمَّا
بَعْدُ ، أَشِيرُوا عَلَيَّ فِي أُناسٍ أَبَنُوا أَهْلِي .
وأَيْمُ اللهِ ما عَلِمْتُ عَلَى أَهْلِي مِنْ سُوءٍ ،
وأَبَنُوهُمْ بِمَنْ وَاللهِ ما عَلِمْتُ عَلَيْهِ
مِنْ سُوءٍ قَطُّ . وَلا يَدْخُلُ بَيْتِي قَطُّ
إِلاَّ وأنا حاضِرٌ ، وَلا غِبْتُ فِي سَفَرٍ إِلاَّ
غابَ مَعِي . فَقامَ سَعْدُ بْنُ مُعاذٍ فَقالَ :
ائْذَنْ لِي يا رَسُولَ اللهِ أَنْ نَضْرِبَ
أَعْناقَهُمْ . وَقامَ رَجُلٌ مِنْ بَنِي الخَزْرَجِ
وكانَتْ أُمُّ حَسَّانَ بْنِ ثابِتٍ مِنْ رَهْطِ
ذَلِكَ الرَّجُلِ فَقالَ : كَذَبْتَ ، أَما وَاللهِ
أَنْ لَوْ كانُوا مِنَ الأَوْسِ ما أَحْبَبْتَ أَنْ
تُضْرَبَ أَعْناقُهُمْ ، حَتَّى كادَ أَنْ يَكُونَ
بَيْنَ الأَوْسِ والخَزْرَجِ شَرٌّ فِي المَسْجِدِ
وَما عَلِمْتُ . فَلَمَّا كانَ مَساءَ ذَلِكَ
اليَوْمِ خَرَجْتُ لِبَعْضِ حاجَتِي وَمَعِي
أُمُّ مِسْطَحٍ فَعَثَرَتْ وَقالَتْ : تَعِسَ
مِسْطَحٌ . فَقُلْتُ : أَيْ أُمُّ ، تَسُبِّينَ
ابْنَكِ ؟ وسَكَتَتْ ثُمَّ عَثَرَتِ الثَّانِيَةَ
فَقالَتْ تَعِسَ مِسْطَحٌ ، فَقُلْتُ لَها :
تَسُبِّينَ ابْنَكِ ؟ ثُمَّ عَثَرَتِ الثَّالِثَةَ
فَقالَتْ : تَعِسَ مِسْطَحٌ ، فانْتَهَرْتُها ،
فَقالَتْ : وَاللهِ ما أَسُبُّهُ إِلاَّ فِيكِ . فَقُلْتُ :
فِي أَيِّ شَأْنِي ؟ قالَتْ : فَبَقَرَتْ لِي الحَدِيثَ ،
فَقُلْتُ : وَقَدْ كانَ هَذا ؟ قالَتْ : نَعَمْ ،
وَاللهِ . فَرَجَعْتُ إِلى بَيْتِي كَأَنَّ الَّذِي

replied, "Yes, by Allāh." I returned to my house, astonished (and distressed) that I did not know for what purpose I had gone out. Then I became sick (fever) and said to Allāh's Messenger ﷺ "Send me to my father's house." So he sent a slave with me, and when I entered the house, I found Um Rumān (my mother) downstairs while (my father) Abū Bakr was reciting something upstairs. My mother asked, "What has brought you, O (my) daughter?" I informed her and mentioned to her the whole story, but she did not feel it as I did. She said, "O my daughter! Take it easy, for there is never a charming lady loved by her husband who has other wives but that they feel jealous of her and speak badly of her." But she did not feel the news as I did. I asked (her), "Does my father know about it?" She said, "yes" I asked, Does Allāh's Messenger ﷺ know about it too?" She said, "Yes, Allāh's Messenger does too." So the tears filled my eyes and I wept. Abū Bakr, who was reading upstairs heard my voice and came down and asked my mother, "What is the matter with her? " She said, "She has heard what has been said about her (as regards the story of Al-Ifk)." On that Abū Bakr wept and said, "I beseech you by Allāh, O my daughter, to go back to your home." I went back to my home and Allāh's Messenger ﷺ had come to my house and asked my maid-servant about me (my character). The maid-servant said, "By Allāh, I do not know of any defect in her character except that she sleeps and let the sheep enter (her house) and eat her dough." On that, some of the Prophet's companions spoke harshly to her and said, "Tell the truth to Allāh's Messenger ﷺ." Finally they

خرجتُ له لا أجدُ منهُ قليلاً ولا كثيراً. ووعكتُ فقلتُ لرسول الله صلى الله عليه وسلم أرسلني إلى بيتِ أبي فأرسل معي الغلام فدخلتُ الدار فوجدتُ أمَّ رومان في السُّفل وأبا بكر فوق البيت يقرأ. فقالت أمي: ما جاء بكِ يا بُنيّة؟ فأخبرتُها وذكرتُ لها الحديث وإذا هو لم يبلغ منها مثل ما بلغ مني. فقالت: يا بُنيّة، خففي عليكِ الشأن فإنه والله لقلما كانت امرأة قط حسناء عند رجل يحبها لها ضرائر إلا حسدنها وقيل فيها. وإذا لم يبلغ منها ما بلغ مني. قلتُ: وقد علم به أبي؟ قالت: نعم. قلتُ: ورسولُ الله صلى الله عليه وسلم؟ قالت: نعم، ورسولُ الله صلى الله عليه وسلم. واستعبرتُ وبكيتُ فسمع أبو بكر صوتي وهو فوق البيت يقرأ فنزل فقال لأمي: ما شأنها؟ قالت: بلغها الذي ذُكر من شأنها ففاضت عيناه. قال: أقسمتُ عليكِ أي بُنيّة إلا رجعتِ إلى بيتكِ فرجعتُ ولقد جاء رسولُ الله صلى الله عليه وسلم بيتي فسأل عني خادمتي فقالت: لا والله ما علمتُ عليها عيباً إلا أنها كانت ترقد حتى تدخل الشاة فتأكل خميرها أو عجينها. وانتهرها بعضُ أصحابه فقال: اصدقي

told her of the affair (of the slander). She said, "Subḥān Allāh! By Allāh, I know nothing against her except what goldsmith knows about a piece of pure gold." Then this news reached the man who was accused, and he said, "Subḥān Allāh! By Allāh, I have never uncovered the private parts of any woman." Later that man was martyred in Allāh's Cause. Next morning my parents came to pay me a visit and they stayed with me till Allāh's Messenger ﷺ came to me after he had offered the 'Aṣr prayer. He came to me while my parents were sitting around me on my right and my left. He praised and glorified Allāh and said, "Now then O 'Āisha! If you have committed a bad deed or you have wronged (yourself), then repent to Allāh as Allāh accepts the repentance from his slaves." An Al-Anṣārī woman had come and was sitting near the gate. I said (to the Prophet ﷺ). "Isn't it improper that you speak in such a way in the presence of this lady? Allāh's Messenger ﷺ then gave a piece of advice and I turned to my father and requested him to answer him (on my behalf). My father said, "What should I say?" Then I turned to my mother and asked her to answer him. She said, "What should I say?" When my parents did not give a reply to the Prophet ﷺ, I said, "I testify that none has the right to be worshipped except Allāh, and that Muḥammad ﷺ is His Messenger!" And after praising and glorifying Allāh as He deserves, I said, "Now then, by Allāh, if I were to tell you that I have not done (this evil action) and Allāh عزّ وجلّ is a witness that I am telling the truth, that would not be of any use to me on your part because you (people)

رَسُولَ اللهِ صلى اللهُ عليهِ وسلَّمَ حتَّى أسقطوا لها بهِ. فقالَتْ: سُبْحانَ اللهِ، واللهِ ما علِمْتُ عليها إلاَّ ما يعلمُ الصائغُ على تبرِ الذهبِ الأحمرِ. وبلغَ الأمرُ إلى ذلكَ الرجلِ الذي قيلَ لهُ، فقالَ: سُبْحانَ اللهِ، واللهِ ما كشفتُ كنفَ أُنثى قطُّ. قالتْ عائشةُ: فقُتِلَ شهيدًا في سبيلِ اللهِ، قالتْ: وأصبحَ أبوايَ عندي فلمْ يزالا حتَّى دخلَ عليَّ رسولُ اللهِ صلى اللهُ عليهِ وسلَّمَ وقدْ صلَّى العصرَ. ثُمَّ دخلَ وقدْ اكتنفني أبوايَ عنْ يميني وعنْ شمالي. فحمدَ اللهَ وأثنى عليهِ، ثُمَّ قالَ: أمَّا بعدُ، يا عائشةُ إنْ كُنْتِ قارفْتِ سوءًا أوْ ظلمْتِ فتوبي إلى اللهِ فإنَّ اللهَ يقبلُ التوبةَ منْ عبادِهِ. قالتْ: وقدْ جاءتْ امرأةٌ منَ الأنصارِ فهيَ جالسةٌ بالبابِ. فقلتُ: ألا تستحي منْ هذهِ المرأةِ أنْ تذكرَ شيئًا؟ فوعظَ رسولُ اللهِ صلى اللهُ عليهِ وسلَّمَ فالتفتُّ إلى أبي فقلتُ: أجبهُ، قالَ: فماذا أقولُ؟ فالتفتُّ إلى أُمِّي فقلتُ أجيبيهِ، فقالتْ: أقولُ ماذا؟ فلمَّا لمْ تجيباهُ تشهَّدتُ فحمدتُ اللهَ وأثنيتُ عليهِ بما هوَ أهلُهُ. قلتُ: أمَّا بعدُ. فواللهِ لئنْ قلتُ لكمْ إني لمْ أفعلْ. واللهُ عزَّ وجلَّ يشهدُ إني لصادقةٌ، ما ذاكَ بنافعي

have spoken about it and your hearts have absorbed it; and if I were to tell you that I have done this sin and Allāh knows that I have not done it, then you will say, 'She has confessed herself guilty." By Allāh, 'I do not see a suitable example for me and you but the example of (I tried to remember Jacob's name but couldn't) Joseph's father when he said; So (for me) "Patience is most fitting against that which you assert. It is Allāh (alone) whose help can be sought.' At that very hour the Divine Inspiration came to Allāh's Messenger ﷺ and we remained silent. Then the inspiration was over and I noticed the signs of happiness on his face while he was removing (the sweat) from his forehead and saying, "Have the good tidings O ' "Āisha! Allāh has revealed your innocence." At that time I was extremely angry. My parents said to me. "Get up and go to him." I said, "By Allāh, I will not do it and will not thank him nor thank either of you, but I will thank Allāh Who has revealed my innocence. You have heard this story but neither did not deny it nor change it (to defend me)," (Āisha used to say:) "But as regards Zainab bint Jahsh, (the Prophet's wife), Allāh protected her because of her piety, so she did not say anything except good (about me), but her sister, Ḥamna, was ruined among those who were ruined. Those who used to speak evil about me were Mistah, Ḥassān bin Thābit, and the hypocrite, ' 'Abdullāh bin Ubai, who used to spread that news and tempt others to speak of it, and it was he and Ḥamna who had the greater share therein. Abū Bakr took an oath that he

عِنْدَكُم، لَقَدْ تَكَلَّمْتُمْ بِهِ وَأُشْرِبَتْهُ قُلُوبُكُمْ. وَإِنْ قُلْتُ إِنِّى فَعَلْتُ وَاللهُ يَعْلَمُ أَنِّى لَمْ أَفْعَلْ لَتَقُولُنَّ قَدْ بَاءَتْ بِهِ عَلَى نَفْسِهَا، وَإِنِّى وَاللهِ مَا أَجِدُ لِى وَلَكُمْ مَثَلاً. وَالْتَمَسْتُ اسْمَ يَعْقُوبَ فَلَمْ أَقْدِرْ عَلَيْهِ، إِلاَّ أَبَا يُوسُفَ حِينَ قَالَ - فَصَبْرٌ جَمِيلٌ وَاللهُ الْمُسْتَعَانُ عَلَى مَا تَصِفُونَ - وَأُنْزِلَ عَلَى رَسُولِ اللهِ صلى الله عليه وسلم مِنْ سَاعَتِهِ فَسَكَتْنَا فَرُفِعَ عَنْهُ وَإِنِّى لأَتَبَيَّنُ السُّرُورَ فِى وَجْهِهِ وَهُوَ يَمْسَحُ جَبِينَهُ وَيَقُولُ: أَبْشِرِى يَا عَائِشَةُ، فَقَدْ أَنْزَلَ اللهُ بَرَاءَتَكِ. قَالَتْ: وَكُنْتُ أَشَدَّ مَا كُنْتُ غَضَبًا، فَقَالَ لِى أَبَوَاىَ: قُومِى إِلَيْهِ، فَقُلْتُ وَاللهِ لاَ أَقُومُ إِلَيْهِ وَلاَ أَحْمَدُهُ وَلاَ أَحْمَدُكُمَا، وَلَكِنْ أَحْمَدُ اللهَ الَّذِى أَنْزَلَ بَرَاءَتِى. لَقَدْ سَمِعْتُمُوهُ فَمَا أَنْكَرْتُمُوهُ وَلاَ غَيَّرْتُمُوهُ. وَكَانَتْ عَائِشَةُ تَقُولُ: أَمَّا زَيْنَبُ ابْنَةُ جَحْشٍ فَعَصَمَهَا اللهُ بِدِينِهَا فَلَمْ تَقُلْ إِلاَّ خَيْرًا، وَأَمَّا أُخْتُهَا حَمْنَةُ فَهَلَكَتْ فِيمَنْ هَلَكَ. وَكَانَ الَّذِى يَتَكَلَّمُ فِيهِ مِسْطَحٌ وَحَسَّانُ بْنُ ثَابِتٍ وَالْمُنَافِقُ عَبْدُ اللهِ بْنُ أُبَىٍّ وَهُوَ الَّذِى كَانَ يَسْتَوْشِيهِ وَيَجْمَعُهُ وَهُوَ الَّذِى تَوَلَّى كِبْرَهُ مِنْهُمْ هُوَ وَحَمْنَةُ. قَالَتْ: فَحَلَفَ أَبُو بَكْرٍ أَنْ لاَ يَنْفَعَ مِسْطَحًا

would never do any favour to Misṭaḥ at all. Then Allāh عَزَّوَجَلَّ revealed the Divine Verse:–

> 'Let not those among you who are good and wealthy (i.e. Abū Bakr) swear not to give (any sort of help) to their kinsmen, and those in need (i.e. Misṭaḥ) .....Do you not love that Allāh should forgive you? And Allāh if Oft-Forgiving, Most Merciful.'
>
> (24:22)

On that, Abū Bakr said, "Yes, by Allāh, O our Lord! We wish that You should forgive us." So Abū Bakr again started giving to Misṭaḥ the expenditure which he used to give him before.

بِنَافِعَةٍ أَبَدًا، فَأَنْزَلَ اللهُ عَزَّ وَجَلَّ - وَلَا يَأْتَلِ أُولُو الْفَضْلِ مِنْكُمْ - إِلَى آخِرِ الآيَةِ، يَعْنِي أَبَا بَكْرٍ - وَالسَّعَةِ أَنْ يُؤْتُوا أُولِي الْقُرْبَى وَالْمَسَاكِينَ - يَعْنِي مِسْطَحًا. إِلَى قَوْلِهِ - أَلَا تُحِبُّونَ أَنْ يَغْفِرَ اللهُ لَكُمْ وَاللهُ غَفُورٌ رَحِيمٌ - حَتَّى قَالَ أَبُو بَكْرٍ: بَلَى وَاللهِ يَا رَبَّنَا إِنَّا لَنُحِبُّ أَنْ تَغْفِرَ لَنَا، وَعَادَ لَهُ بِمَا كَانَ يَصْنَعُ.

(220) CHAPTER. 'They should cover (draw their veils over) their necks and bosoms not to reveal their beauty.' (24:31)

Narrated 'Āisha: May Allāh bestow His Mercy on the early emigrant women. When Allāh revealed:

> 'They should draw their veils over their necks and bosoms,

they tore their aprons and covered their faces with it.'

بابٌ - ولْيَضْرِبْنَ بِخُمُرِهِنَّ عَلَى جُيُوبِهِنَّ - وقالَ أحمَدُ بنُ شَبِيبٍ: حدَّثَنا أبي، عَنْ يُونُسَ: قالَ ابنُ شِهابٍ، عَنْ عُرْوَةَ، عَنْ عائِشَةَ رَضِيَ اللهُ عَنْها قالَتْ: يَرْحَمُ اللهُ نِساءَ المُهاجِراتِ الأُوَلَ، لمَّا أنزَلَ اللهُ - ولْيَضْرِبْنَ بِخُمُرِهِنَّ عَلَى جُيُوبِهِنَّ شَقَقْنَ مُرُوطَهُنَّ فاخْتَمَرْنَ بِهِ.

282. Narrated Ṣafiya bint Shaiba: 'Āisha used to say: "When (the Verse):

> 'They should draw their veils over their necks and bosoms,'

was revealed, (the ladies) cut their waist sheets at the edges and covered their faces with the cut pieces."

٢٨٢ - حدَّثَنا أبو نُعَيْمٍ: حدَّثَنا إبْراهِيمُ بنُ نافِعٍ، عَنْ ابنِ مُسْلِمٍ، عَنْ صَفِيَّةَ بِنْتِ شَيْبَةَ: أنَّ عائِشَةَ رَضِيَ اللهُ عَنْها كانَتْ تَقُولُ لمَّا نَزَلَتْ هَذِهِ الآيَةُ - ولْيَضْرِبْنَ بِخُمُرِهِنَّ عَلَى جُيُوبِهِنَّ - أخَذْنَ أُزْرَهُنَّ فَشَقَقْنَها مِنْ قِبَلِ الحَواشِي فاخْتَمَرْنَ بِها.

SŪRAT AL-FURQĀN XXV

سورة الفرقان

**In the Name of Allāh,
the Most Beneficent, the Most Merciful**

بِسْمِ اللهِ الرَّحْمَنِ الرَّحِيمِ

قَالَ ابْنُ عَبَّاسٍ : هَبَاءً مَنْثُورًا : مَا تَسْفِي بِهِ الرِّيحُ . مَدَّ الظِّلَّ : مَا بَيْنَ طُلُوعِ الْفَجْرِ إِلَى طُلُوعِ الشَّمْسِ . سَاكِنًا : دَائِمًا . عَلَيْهِ دَلِيلاً : طُلُوعُ الشَّمْسِ . خِلْفَةً : مَنْ فَاتَهُ مِنَ اللَّيْلِ عَمَلٌ أَدْرَكَهُ بِالنَّهَارِ ، أَوْ فَاتَهُ بِالنَّهَارِ أَدْرَكَهُ بِاللَّيْلِ . وَقَالَ الْحَسَنُ : هَبْ لَنَا مِنْ أَزْوَاجِنَا وَذُرِّيَّاتِنَا قُرَّةَ أَعْيُنٍ : فِي طَاعَةِ اللهِ ، وَمَا شَيْءٌ أَقَرَّ لِعَيْنِ الْمُؤْمِنِ مِنْ أَنْ يَرَى حَبِيبَهُ فِي طَاعَةِ اللهِ ، وَقَالَ ابْنُ عَبَّاسٍ : ثُبُورًا : وَيْلاً . وَقَالَ غَيْرُهُ : السَّعِيرُ مُذَكَّرٌ . وَالتَّسَعُّرُ وَالاضْطِرَامُ : التَّوَقُّدُ الشَّدِيدُ - تُمْلَى عَلَيْهِ - تُقْرَأُ عَلَيْهِ ، مِنْ أَمْلَيْتُ وَأَمْلَلْتُ . الرَّسُّ : الْمَعْدِنُ ، جَمْعُهُ رِسَاسٌ . مَا يَعْبَأُ يُقَالُ مَا عَبَأْتُ بِهِ شَيْئًا ، لا يُعْتَدُّ بِهِ . غَرَامًا : هَلاكًا . وَقَالَ مُجَاهِدٌ : وَعَتَوْا : طَغَوْا . وَقَالَ ابْنُ عُيَيْنَةَ : عَاتِيَةٍ : عَتَتْ عَلَى الْخُزَّانِ .

(221) CHAPTER. The Statement of Allāh ﷻ :—
'Those who will be gathered to Hell on their faces......' (25:34)

بَابُ قَوْلِهِ - الَّذِينَ يُحْشَرُونَ عَلَى وُجُوهِهِمْ إِلَى جَهَنَّمَ - الآيَةَ .

283. Narrated Anas bin Mālik : A man said, "O Allāh's Prophet! Will Allāh gather the non-believers on their faces on the Day of Resurrection?" He said, "Will not the One Who made him walk on his feet in this world, be able to make him walk on his face on the Day of Resurrection?" (Qatāda, a sub-narrator, said: Yes, By the Power of Our Lord!)

٢٨٣ - حدثنا عبد الله بن محمد: حدثنا يونس بن محمد البغدادى: حدثنا شيبان، عن قتادة: حدثنا أنس بن مالك رضى الله عنه: أن رجلا قال: يا نبى الله، يحشر الكافر على وجهه يوم القيامة؟ قال: أليس الذى أمشاه على الرجلين فى الدنيا قادرا على أن يمشيه على وجهه يوم القيامة؟ قال قتادة: بلى وعزة ربنا.

(222) CHAPTER. The Statement of Allāh :–

'Those who invoke not with Allāh any other god, not kill such life as Allāh has forbidden..........'

(25:68)

باب قوله - والذين لا يدعون مع الله إلها آخر ولا يقتلون النفس - الآية. يلق أثاما: العقوبة.

284. Narrated 'Abdullāh :I, or somebody, asked Allāh's Messenger ," Which is the biggest sin in the Sight of Allāh?" He said, "That you set up a rival (in worship) to Allāh though He Alone created you." I asked, "What is next?" He said, "Then, that you kill your son, being afraid that he may share your meals with you." I asked, "What is next?" He said, "That you commit illegal sexual intercourse with the wife of your neighbour."

Then the following Verse was revealed:

٢٨٤ - حدثنا مسدد: حدثنا يحيى، عن سفيان قال: حدثنى منصور وسليمان، عن أبى وائل، عن أبى ميسرة، عن عبد الله. قال: وحدثنى واصل، عن أبى وائل، عن عبد الله رضى الله عنه قال: سألت أو سئل رسول الله صلى الله عليه وسلم: أى الذنب عند الله أكبر؟ قال: أن تجعل لله ندا وهو خلقك. قلت:

to confirm the statement of Allāh's Messenger ﷺ :—

'Those who invoke not with Allāh, any other god, nor kill life as Allāh has forbidden except for just cause, nor commit illegal sexual intercourse." (25:68)

ثم أي؟ قال: ثم أن تقتل ولدك خشية أن يطعم معك. قلت: ثم أي؟ قال: أن تزاني بحليلة جارك. قال: ونزلت هذه الآية تصديقا لقول رسول الله صلى الله عليه وسلم - والذين لا يدعون مع الله إلها آخر ولا يقتلون النفس التي حرم الله إلا بالحق ولا يزنون -.

285. Narrated Al-Qāsim bin Abī Bazza that he asked Sa'īd bin Jubair, "Is there any repentance for the one who has murdered a believer intentionally?" Then I recited to him:—

'Nor kill such life as Allāh has forbidden except for a just cause.'

Sa'īd said, "I recited this very Verse before Ibn 'Abbās as you have recited it before me. Ibn 'Abbās said, 'This Verse was revealed in Mecca and it has been abrogated by a Verse in Sūrat-An-Nisā' which was later revealed in Medīna.' " (1)

٢٨٥ - حدثنا إبراهيم بن موسى: أخبرنا هشام بن يوسف: أن ابن جريج أخبرهم قال: أخبرني القاسم ابن أبي بزة أنه سأل سعيد بن جبير: هل لمن قتل مؤمنا متعمدا من توبة؟ فقرأت عليه - ولا يقتلون النفس التي حرم الله إلا بالحق - فقال سعيد: قرأتها على ابن عباس كما قرأتها علي، فقال هذه مكية نسختها آية مدنية التي في سورة النساء.

(1) In Sūrat-Al-Furqān, Allāh gives the chance to one who has murdered a believer to repent: 'Unless he repents, believes, and works righteous deeds, for Allāh will change the evil of such persons into good, and Allāh is Oft-For-giving, Most Merciful,' (25:70) while in Sūrat-An-Nisā', Allāh says: If a man kills a believer intentionally, his recompense in Hell, to abide therein (forever); and the wrath and curse of Allāh are upon him and a great torment is prepared for him.' (4:93) Ibn 'Abbās thinks that the latter Verse has abrogated the former. In Ḥadīth 287, he says that the former Verse was applicable only to the pagans before embracing Islām. The latter Verse is concerned with those who have embraced Islām. See Ḥadīth No. 287, 288, 289.

286. Narrated Sa'īd bin Jubair: The people of Kūfa differed as regards the killing of a believer so I entered upon Ibn 'Abbās (and asked him) about that. Ibn 'Abbās said, "The Verse (in Sūrat-An-Nisā', 4:93) was the last thing revealed in this respect and nothing cancelled its validity."

٢٨٦ - حدثنى محمد بن بشار: حدثنا غندر: حدثنا شعبة، عن المغيرة بن النعمان، عن سعيد بن جبير قال: اختلف أهل الكوفة فى قتل المؤمن، فدخلت فيه إلى ابن عباس فقال: نزلت آخر ما نزل ولم ينسخها شىء.

287. Narrated Sa'īd bin Jubair: I asked Ibn 'Abbās about Allāh's saying:—

'...his reward is Hell Fire.' (4:93)

He said, "No repentance is accepted from him (i.e. the muderer of a believer)." I asked him regarding the saying of Allāh :—

'Those who invoke not with Allāh any other god.' ....(25:68)

He said, "This Verse was revealed concerning the pagans of the pre-Islamic period." (1)

٢٨٧ - حدثنا آدم: حدثنا شعبة حدثنا منصور، عن سعيد بن جبير: سألت ابن عباس رضى الله عنهما عن قوله تعالى - فجزاؤه جهنم - قال. لا توبة له وعن قوله جل ذكره - لا يدعون مع الله إلها آخر - قال: كانت هذه فى الجاهلية.

(223) CHAPTER. The Statement of Allāh :—

'The torment will be doubled to him, on the Day of Resurrection and he will abide therein in disgrace.' (25:69)

باب قوله - يضاعف له العذاب يوم القيامة ويخلد فيه مهانا -.

(1) See the previous footnote and Ḥadīth No. 288.

288. Narrated Sa'īd bin Jubair: Ibn Abzā said to me, "Ask Ibn 'Abbās regarding the Statement of Allāh ﷻ: 'And whoever murders a believer intentionally, his recompense is Hell.' (4:69)

And also His Statement:—

> ...'nor kill such life as Allāh has forbidden, except for a just cause ......except those who repent, believe, and do good deeds.' " (25: 68—70)

So I asked Ibn 'Abbās and he said, "When this (25:68-69) was revealed, the people of Mecca said, "We have invoked other gods with Allāh, and we have murdered such lives which Allāh has made sacred, and we have committed illegal sexual intercourse."
So Allāh revealed:—

> 'Except those who repent, believe, and do good deeds.......and Allāh is Oft-Forgiving, Most Merciful.' (25:70)

٢٨٨ - حدثنا سعد بن حفص : حدثنا شيبان ، عن منصور ، عن سعيد ابن جبير قال : قال ابن أبزى : سئل ابن عباس عن قوله تعالى - ومن يقتل مؤمنا متعمدا فجزاؤه جهنم - وقوله - ولا يقتلون النفس التى حرم الله إلا بالحق - حتى بلغ - إلا من تاب وآمن - فسألته فقال : لما نزلت قال أهل مكة : فقد عدلنا بالله وقتلنا النفس التى حرم الله إلا بالحق وأتينا الفواحش ، فأنزل الله - إلا من تاب وآمن وعمل عملا صالحا - إلى قوله - غفورا رحيما -

(224) CHAPTER. 'Except those who repent, believe, and do good deeds. For those Allāh will change their sins into good, and Allāh is Oft-Forgiving, Most Merciful." (25:70)

باب - إلا من تاب وآمن وعمل عملا صالحا فأولئك يبدل الله سيئاتهم حسنات وكان الله غفورا رحيما -

289. Narrated Sa'īd bin Jubair: 'Abdur-Raḥmān bin Abzā ordered me to ask Ibn 'Abbās regarding the two Verses (the first of which was):—

'And whosoever murders a believer intentionally." (4:93)

So I asked him, and he said, "Nothing has abrogated this Verse." About (the other Verse):—

'And those who invoke not with Allāh any other god.'

he said, "It was revealed concerning the pagans,' (1)

٢٨٩ - حَدَّثَنَا عَبْدَانُ: أَخْبَرَنَا أَبِي، عَنْ شُعْبَةَ، عَنْ مَنْصُورٍ، عَنْ سَعِيدِ بْنِ جُبَيْرٍ قَالَ: أَمَرَنِي عَبْدُ الرَّحْمَنِ بْنُ أَبْزَى أَنْ أَسْأَلَ ابْنَ عَبَّاسٍ عَنْ هَاتَيْنِ الآيَتَيْنِ - وَمَنْ يَقْتُلْ مُؤْمِنًا مُتَعَمِّدًا - فَسَأَلْتُهُ فَقَالَ: لَمْ يَنْسَخْهَا شَيْءٌ، وَعَنْ - وَالَّذِينَ لَا يَدْعُونَ مَعَ اللهِ إِلَهًا آخَرَ - قَالَ: نَزَلَتْ فِي أَهْلِ الشِّرْكِ.

(225) CHAPTER. 'So the torment will be yours forever.'

بَابُ فَسَوْفَ يَكُونُ لِزَامًا - هَلَكَةً.

290. Narrated 'Abdullāh (رضي الله عنه);
Five (great events) (2) have passed: the Smoke, the Moon, the Romans, the Mighty grasp and the constant Punishment which occurs in:—

'So the torment will be yours forever.' (25 : 77)

٢٩٠ - حَدَّثَنَا عُمَرُ بْنُ حَفْصِ ابْنِ غِيَاثٍ: حَدَّثَنَا أَبِي: حَدَّثَنَا الأَعْمَشُ: حَدَّثَنَا مُسْلِمٌ، عَنْ مَسْرُوقٍ قَالَ: قَالَ عَبْدُ اللهِ: خَمْسٌ قَدْ مَضَيْنَ: الدُّخَانُ، وَالْقَمَرُ، وَالرُّومُ، وَالْبَطْشَةُ، وَاللِّزَامُ فَسَوْفَ يَكُونُ لِزَامًا.

(1) See Ḥadīth No. 288.

(2) The events referred to here are all mentioned in the Holy Qur'ān.

(a) The Smoke here means what the pagans of Mecca imagined to see in the sky because of their severe hunger when Allāh afflicted them with famine. See (44:10).

(b) The event of the splitting of the Moon which took place in the lifetime of

SŪRAT ASH-SHU'ARĀ'

سورة الشعراء

(The Poets) XXVI

In the Name of Allāh,
the Most Beneficent, the Most Merciful

بِسْمِ اللهِ الرَّحْمَنِ الرَّحِيمِ

وَقَالَ مُجَاهِدٌ: تَعْبَثُونَ: تَبْنُونَ. هَضِيمٌ: يَتَفَتَّتُ إِذَا مُسَّ. مُسَحَّرِينَ: مَسْحُورِينَ. اللَّيْكَةُ وَالأَيْكَةُ: جَمْعُ أَيْكَةٍ وَهِيَ جَمْعُ الشَّجَرِ. يَوْمِ الظُّلَّةِ: إِظْلالُ العَذَابِ إِيَّاهُمْ. مَوْزُونٍ: مَعْلُومٍ. كَالطَّوْدِ: كَالجَبَلِ. الشِّرْذِمَةُ: طَائِفَةٌ قَلِيلَةٌ. السَّاجِدِينَ: المُصَلِّينَ. قَالَ ابْنُ عَبَّاسٍ: لَعَلَّكُمْ تَخْلُدُونَ - كَأَنَّكُمْ، الرِّيعُ: الأَيْفَاعُ مِنَ الأَرْضِ وَجَمْعُهُ رِيَعَةٌ وَأَرْيَاعٌ، وَاحِدُهُ الرِّيعَةُ. مَصَانِعُ: كُلُّ بِنَاءٍ فَهُوَ مَصْنَعَةٌ. فَرِهِينَ: مَرِحِينَ، فَارِهِينَ بِمَعْنَاهُ، وَيُقَالُ فَارِهِينَ: حَاذِقِينَ. تَعْثَوْا: هُوَ

the Prophet ﷺ and was witnessed by the pagans, his companions and some believers (See (54–1) : one of the Miracles of the Prophet ﷺ

(c) The Romans were defeated by the Persian pagans whereupon the Quraish pagans of Mecca rejoiced. See (30:1)

(d) The Mighty grasp is that which Allāh sent upon the pagans of Quraish in the Badr Battle. See (74: 16)

(e) The constant Punishment will definitely be inflicted upon those who rejected faith. 'Abdullāh regards this future inevitable event as definite as any past event, therefore he includes it in the four other events.

(f) Please see the Miracles of the Prophet ﷺ

أشد الفساد ، وعاث يعيث عيثا ، الجبلة : الخلق . جبل : خلق ، ومنه جبلا وجبلا وجبلا يعني الخلق ، قاله ابن عباس .

(226) CHAPTER. 'And let me not be in disgrace on the Day when people will be resurrected." (26:87)

باب - ولا تخزني يوم يبعثون -

291. Narrated Abū Huraira: The Prophet said, "On the Day of Resurrection Abraham will see his father covered with Qatara and Ghabara. (i.e. having a dark face)."

٢٩١ - وقال إبراهيم بن طهمان ، عن ابن أبي ذئب ، عن سعيد بن أبي سعيد المقبري ، عن أبيه ، عن أبي هريرة رضي الله عنه ، عن النبي صلى الله عليه وسلم قال : إن إبراهيم عليه الصلاة والسلام يرى أباه يوم القيامة عليه الغبرة والقترة . الغبرة : هي القترة .

292. Narrated Abū Huraira: The Prophet said, "Abraham will meet his father (on the Day of Recurrection) and will say, 'O my Lord! You promised me that You would not let me in disgrace on the Day when people will be resurrected.' Allāh will say, 'I have forbidden Paradise to the non-believers.' "

٢٩٢ - حدثنا إسماعيل : حدثنا أخي ، عن ابن أبي ذئب ، عن سعيد المقبري ، عن أبي هريرة رضي الله عنه ، عن النبي صلى الله عليه وسلم قال : يلقى إبراهيم أباه فيقول : يا رب إنك وعدتني أن لا تخزني يوم يبعثون ، فيقول الله : إني حرمت الجنة على الكافرين .

(227) CHAPTER. 'And warn your tribe

باب - وأنذر عشيرتك

of near kindred, and be kind and humble) to the believers who followed you.'
(26: 214-215)

293. Narrated Ibn 'Abbās ؓ :
When the Verse:—
'And warn your tribe of near-kindred, was revealed, the Prophet ﷺ ascended the Ṣafā (mountain) and started calling, "O Banī Fihr! O Banī 'Adī!" addressing various tribes of Quraish till they were assembled. Those who could not come themselves, sent their messengers to see what was there. Abū Lahab and other people from Quraish came, and the Prophet ﷺ then said, "Suppose I told you that there is an (enemy) cavalry in the valley intending to attack you, would you believe me?" They said, "Yes, for we have not found you telling anything other than the truth." He then said, "I am a warner to you in face of a terrific punishment." Abū Lahab said (to the Prophet ﷺ). "May your hands perish all this day. Is it for this purpose you have gathered us?" Then it was revealed:—

> 'Perish the hands of Abū Lahab (one of the Prophet's uncle), and perish he! His wealth and his children will not profit him....(111:1-5)

الأقربين واخفض جناحك: ألن جانبك.

٢٩٣ - حدثنا عمر بن حفص ابن غياث: حدثنا أبي: حدثنا الأعمش قال: حدثني عمرو ابن مرة، عن سعيد بن جبير، عن ابن عباس رضي الله عنهما قال: لما نزلت - وأنذر عشيرتك الأقربين - صعد النبي صلى الله عليه وسلم على الصفا فجعل ينادي: يا بني فهر، يا بني عدي، لبطون قريش حتى اجتمعوا فجعل الرجل إذا لم يستطع أن يخرج أرسل رسولا لينظر ما هو، فجاء أبو لهب وقريش فقال: أرأيتكم لو أخبرتكم أن خيلا بالوادي تريد تغير عليكم أكنتم مصدقي؟ قالوا: نعم، ما جربنا عليك إلا صدقا. قال: إني نذير لكم بين يدي عذاب شديد، فقال أبو لهب: تبا لك سائر اليوم، ألهذا جمعتنا؟ فنزلت - تبت يدا أبي لهب وتب ما أغنى عنه ماله وما كسب -.

294. Narrated Abū Huraira : Allāh's Messenger got up when the Verse:—

'And warn your tribe of near-kindred. .... (26:214)

was revealed and said, "O Quraish people! (or he said a similar word) Buy your-selves! I cannot save you from Allāh (if you disobey Him) O Banī 'Abd Manāf! I cannot save you from Allāh (if you disobey Him). O 'Abbās! The son of 'Abdul Muṭṭalib! I cannot save you from Allāh (if you disobey Him) O Ṣafiya, (the aunt of Allāh's Apostle) I cannot save you from Allāh (if you disobey Him). O Fāṭima, the daughter of Muḥammad! Ask what you wish from my property, but I cannot save you from Allāh (if you disobey Him)."

٢٩٤ - حدثنا أبو اليمان: أخبرنا شعيب، عن الزهري قال: أخبرني سعيد بن المسيب وأبو سلمة بن عبد الرحمن: أن أبا هريرة قال: قام رسول الله صلى الله عليه وسلم حين أنزل الله - وأنذر عشيرتك الأقربين - قال: يا معشر قريش أو كلمة نحوها، اشتروا أنفسكم، لا أغني عنكم من الله شيئا. يا بني عبد مناف، لا أغني عنكم من الله شيئا. يا عباس بن عبد المطلب: لا أغني عنك من الله شيئا. ويا صفية عمة رسول الله: لا أغني عنك من الله شيئا. ويا فاطمة بنت محمد صلى الله عليه وسلم: سليني ما شئت من مالي، لا أغني عنك من الله شيئا. تابعه أصبغ، عن ابن وهب، عن يونس، عن ابن شهاب.

SŪRAT AN-NAML
(The Ants): XXVII

In the Name of Allāh, the Most Beneficent, the Most Merciful

سورة النمل

بسم الله الرحمن الرحيم

والخبء: ما خبأت. لاقبل: لا طاقة. الصرح: كل ملاط اتخذ من القوارير: والصرح: القصر، وجماعته صروح. وقال ابن عباس: ولها عرش: سرير

كَرِيمٌ، حُسْنُ الصَّنْعَةِ وَغَلاءُ الثَّمَنِ. يأْتُونِي مُسْلِمِينَ: طائِعِينَ. رَدِفَ: اقْتَرَبَ. جامِدَةً: قائِمَةً. أوْزِعْنِي: اجْعَلْنِي وَقالَ مُجاهِدٌ: نَكِّرُوا: غَيِّرُوا. وأُوتِينا العِلْمَ: يَقُولُهُ سُلَيْمانُ. الصَّرْحُ: بِرْكَةُ ماءٍ ضَرَبَ عَلَيْها سُلَيْمانُ قَوارِيرَ وَألْبَسَها إيّاهُ.

SŪRAT AL-QAṢAṢ
(The Narration) XXVIII

In the Name of Allāh, the Most Beneficent, the Most Merciful

سورة القصص

بِسْمِ اللهِ الرَّحْمَنِ الرَّحِيمِ

'Everything (that exists) will perish save His countenance.' (28 : 88)

- كُلُّ شَيْءٍ هالِكٌ إلاَّ وَجْهَهُ - إلاَّ مُلْكَهُ، ويُقالُ إلاَّ ما أُرِيدَ بِهِ وَجْهُ اللهِ. وَقالَ مُجاهِدٌ: الأنْباءُ: الحُجَجُ.

(228) CHAPTER. The Statement of Allāh ﷻ :–

'Verily! You (O Muḥammad) guide not whom you like, but Allāh guides whom He will.' (28:56)

بابُ قَوْلِهِ - إنَّكَ لا تَهْدِي مَنْ أحْبَبْتَ وَلَكِنَّ اللهَ يَهْدِي مَنْ يَشاءُ -.

295. Narrated Al-Musaiyab: When Abū Ṭālib was on his death bed, Allāh's Messenger ﷺ came to him and found with him, Abū Jahl and 'Abdullāh bin

٢٩٥ - حَدَّثَنا أبُو اليَمانِ: أخْبَرَنا شُعَيْبٌ، عَنِ الزُّهْرِيِّ قالَ: أخْبَرَنِي سَعِيدُ بْنُ المُسَيَّبِ، عَنْ أبِيهِ قالَ: لَمّا

Abī Umaiya bin Al-Mughīra. Allāh's Messenger ﷺ said, "O uncle! Say: None has the right to be worshipped except Allāh, a sentence with which I will defend you before Allāh." On that Abū Jahl and 'Abdullāh bin Abī Umaiya said to Abū Ṭālib, "Will you now leave the religion of 'Abdul Muṭṭalib?" Allāh's Messenger ﷺ kept on inviting him to say that sentence while the other two kept on repeating their sentence before him till Abū Ṭālib said as the last thing he said to them, "I am on the religion of 'Abdul Muṭṭalib," and refused to say: None has the right to be worshipped except Allāh. On that Allāh's Messenger ﷺ said, "By Allāh, I will keep on asking Allāh's forgiveness for you unless I am forbidden (by Allāh) to do so." So Allāh revealed:—

> 'It is not fitting for the Prophet and those who believe that they should invoke (Allāh) for forgiveness for pagans.' (9:113)

And then Allāh revealed especially about Abū Ṭālib:—

> 'Verily! You (O, Muḥammad) guide not whom you like, but Allāh guides whom He will.'
>
> (28:56)

حَضَرَتْ أبا طالِبٍ الوَفاةُ جاءَهُ رَسُولُ اللهِ صلى اللهُ عليه وسلَّم فوَجَدَ عِنْدَهُ أبا جَهْلٍ وَعَبْدَ اللهِ بنَ أبي أُمَيَّةَ بنِ المُغِيرَةِ . فقالَ : أيْ عَمِّ قُلْ لا إلَهَ إلاَّ اللهُ ، كَلِمَةً أُحاجُّ لَكَ بِها عِنْدَ اللهِ . فقالَ أبو جَهْلٍ وَعَبْدُ اللهِ بنُ أبي أُمَيَّةَ : أتَرْغَبُ عَنْ مِلَّةِ عَبْدِ المُطَّلِبِ ؟ فلَمْ يَزَلْ رَسُولُ اللهِ صلى اللهُ عليه وسلَّم يَعْرِضُها عَلَيْهِ وَيُعِيدانِهِ بِتِلْكَ المَقالَةِ حتَّى قالَ أبو طالِبٍ آخِرَ ما كَلَّمَهُمْ : عَلى مِلَّةِ عَبْدِ المُطَّلِبِ ، وأبَى أنْ يَقُولَ لا إلَهَ إلاَّ اللهُ . قالَ : قالَ رَسُولُ اللهِ صلى اللهُ عليه وسلَّم : وَاللهِ لأسْتَغْفِرَنَّ لكَ ما لَمْ أُنْهَ عَنْكَ ، فأنْزَلَ اللهُ - ما كانَ للنَّبِيِّ وَالَّذِينَ آمَنُوا أنْ يَسْتَغْفِرُوا لِلْمُشْرِكِينَ - وأنْزَلَ اللهُ في أبي طالِبٍ فقالَ لِرَسُولِ اللهِ صلى اللهُ عليه وسلَّم - إنَّكَ لا تَهْدِي مَنْ أحْبَبْتَ وَلَكِنَّ اللهَ يَهْدِي مَنْ يَشاءُ - . قالَ ابنُ عَبَّاسٍ : أُولي القُوَّةِ : لا يَرْفَعُها العُصْبَةُ مِنَ الرِّجالِ . لَتَنُوءُ : لَتُثْقِلُ . فارِغاً إلاَّ مِنْ ذِكْرِ مُوسَى . الفَرِحِينَ : المَرِحِينَ . قُصِّيهِ : اتَّبِعِي أثَرَهُ . وَقَدْ يَكُونُ أنْ يَقُصَّ الكَلامَ - نَحْنُ نَقُصُّ عَلَيْكَ - عَنْ جُنُبٍ : عَنْ بُعْدٍ ، وَعَنْ جَنابَةٍ وَاحِدٌ ، وَعَنِ اجْتِنابٍ أيْضاً . نَبْطِشُ

وَنَبْطُشُ . يَأْتَمِرُونَ : يَتَشَاوَرُونَ .
الْعُدْوَانُ وَالْعَدَاءُ وَالتَّعَدِّي وَاحِدٌ .
آنَسَ : أَبْصَرَ . الْجِذْوَةُ : قِطْعَةٌ
غَلِيظَةٌ مِنَ الْخَشَبِ لَيْسَ فِيهَا لَهَبٌ .
وَالشِّهَابُ فِيهِ لَهَبٌ . وَالْحَيَّاتُ : أَجْنَاسٌ :
الْجَانُّ . وَالْأَفَاعِي ، وَالْأَسَاوِدُ . رِدْءًا :
مُعِينًا . قَالَ ابْنُ عَبَّاسٍ : يُصَدِّقُنِي .
وَقَالَ غَيْرُهُ سَنَشُدُّ : سَنُعِينُكَ . كُلَّمَا
عَزَّزْتَ شَيْئًا فَقَدْ جَعَلْتَ لَهُ عَضُدًا .
مَقْبُوحِينَ : مُهْلَكِينَ . وَصَّلْنَا : بَيَّنَّاهُ
وَأَتْمَمْنَاهُ . يُجْبَى : يُجْلَبُ . بَطِرَتْ :
أَشِرَتْ . فِي أُمِّهَا رَسُولًا . أُمُّ الْقُرَى :
مَكَّةُ وَمَا حَوْلَهَا . تُكِنُّ : تُخْفِي ،
أَكْنَنْتُ الشَّيْءَ أَخْفَيْتُهُ . وَكَنَنْتُهُ :
أَخْفَيْتُهُ وَأَظْهَرْتُهُ . وَيْكَأَنَّ اللَّهَ : مِثْلُ
أَلَمْ تَرَ أَنَّ اللَّهَ يَبْسُطُ الرِّزْقَ لِمَنْ
يَشَاءُ وَيَقْدِرُ - يُوَسِّعُ عَلَيْهِ وَيُضَيِّقُ
عَلَيْهِ .

(229) CHAPTER. 'Verily, He Who has revealed to you (O Muḥammad) the Qur'ān will certainly bring you home (to Mecca) again.

(28:85)

بَابُ - إِنَّ الَّذِي فَرَضَ عَلَيْكَ الْقُرْآنَ - .

296. Narrated Ibn 'Abbās : ....will bring you home ' means to Mecca.

٢٩٦ - حَدَّثَنَا مُحَمَّدُ بْنُ مُقَاتِلٍ :
أَخْبَرَنَا يَعْلَى : حَدَّثَنَا سُفْيَانُ الْعُصْفُرِيُّ ،
عَنْ عِكْرِمَةَ ، عَنِ ابْنِ عَبَّاسٍ - لَرَادُّكَ

إلى مَعاذٍ ـ قالَ : إلى مَكَّةَ .

SŪRAT AL–'ANKABŪT

(The Spider) XXIX

No. Ḥadiths are mentioned here.

In the Name of Allāh, the Most Beneficent, the Most Merciful

سورة العنكبوت

بِسْمِ اللهِ الرَّحْمَنِ الرَّحِيمِ

قالَ مُجاهِدٌ : مُسْتَبْصِرِينَ : ضَلَلَةً . وَقالَ غَيْرُهُ : الحَيَوانُ والحَيُّ واحِدٌ . فَلَيَعْلَمَنَّ اللهُ : عَلِمَ اللهُ ذَلِكَ إِنَّما هِيَ بِمَنْزِلَةِ فَلِيَمِيزَ اللهُ كَقَوْلِهِ ـ لِيَمِيزَ اللهُ الخَبِيثَ ـ أَثْقالاً مَعَ أَثْقالِهِمْ ـ أَوْزاراً مَعَ أَوْزارِهِمْ .

SŪRAT-AR-RŪM

(The Roman Empire) XXX

In the Name of Allāh, the Most Beneficent, the Most Merciful

سورة الروم

بِسْمِ اللهِ الرَّحْمَنِ الرَّحِيمِ

فَلا يَرْبُو مَنْ أَعْطَى يَبْتَغِي أَفْضَلَ فَلا أَجْرَ لَهُ فِيها ـ قالَ مُجاهِدٌ : يُحْبَرُونَ : يُنَعَّمُونَ . يَمْهَدُونَ : يُسَوُّونَ المَضاجِعَ . الوَدْقُ : المَطَرُ . قالَ ابن عبَّاس ـ هَلْ لَكُمْ مِمّا مَلَكَتْ أَيْمانُكُمْ ـ فِي الآلِهَةِ . وفيهِ : تَخافُونَهُمْ : أَنْ يَرِثُوكُمْ كَما يَرِثُ بَعْضُكُمْ بَعْضاً . يَصَّدَّعُونَ : يَتَفَرَّقُونَ . فاصْدَعْ . وَقالَ غَيْرُهُ : ضُعْفٌ وَضَعْفٌ لُغَتانِ . وَقالَ مُجاهِدٌ: السُّوأَى الإِساءَةُ ، جَزاءُ

297. Narrated Masrūq: While a man was delivering a speech in the tribe of Kinda, he said, "Smoke will prevail on the Day of Resurrection and will deprive the hypocrites their faculties of hearing and seeing. The believers will be afflicted with something like cold only thereof." That news scared us, so I went to ('Abdullāh) Ibn Mas'ūd while he was reclining (and told him the story) whereupon he became angry, sat up and said, "He who knows a thing can say, it, but if he does not know, he should say, 'Allāh knows best,' for it is an aspect of knowledge to say, 'I do not know,' if you do not know a certain thing. Allāh said to His prophet.

> 'Say (O Muḥammad): No wage do I ask of you for this (Qur'ān), nor I am one of the pretenders (a person who pretends things which do not exist.)
>
> (38:86)

The Qur'aish delayed in embracing Islām for a period, so the Prophet ﷺ invoked evil on them, saying, 'O Allāh! Help me against them by sending seven years of (famine) like those of Joseph.' So they were afflicted with such a severe year of famine that they were destroyed therein and ate dead animals and bones. They started seeing something like smoke between the sky and the earth (because of severe hunger). Abū Sufyān then came (to the prophet ﷺ) and said, "O Muḥammad! You came to order us for to keep good relations with kith and kin, and your kinsmen are perished, so

المُسيئِينَ .

٢٩٧ ـ حدَّثنا مُحمَّدُ بنُ كثِيرٍ : حدَّثنا سُفيانُ : حدَّثنا منصُورٌ والأعمَشُ ، عنْ أبي الضُّحَى ، عنْ مسْرُوقٍ قالَ : بيْنَما رجُلٌ يُحدِّثُ في كِنْدَةَ فقالَ : يجِيءُ دُخانٌ يوْمَ القِيامَةِ فيأخُذُ بأسْماعِ المُنافِقِينَ وأبْصارِهِمْ . يأخُذُ المُؤْمِنَ كهيْئةِ الزُّكامِ ، ففزِعْنا فأتيْتُ ابنَ مسْعُودٍ وكانَ مُتَّكِئاً فغضِبَ ، فجلَسَ فقالَ : منْ علِمَ فلْيقُلْ ومنْ لمْ يعْلَمْ فلْيقُلِ اللهُ أعْلَمُ ، فإنَّ منَ العِلْمِ أنْ يقُولَ لما لا يعْلَمُ لا أعْلَمُ . فإنَّ اللهَ قالَ لِنبِيِّهِ صلى اللهُ عليه وسلَّمَ ـ قُلْ ما أسألُكُمْ عليْهِ منْ أجْرٍ وما أنا منَ المُتكلِّفِينَ ـ وإنَّ قُريْشاً أبْطئُوا عنِ الإسْلامِ فدَعا عليْهِمُ النبيُّ صلى اللهُ عليه وسلَّمَ فقالَ : اللهُمَّ أعِنِّي عليْهِمْ بسبْعٍ كسبْعِ يُوسُفَ ، فأخذَتْهُمْ سنَةٌ حتَّى هلَكُوا فيها وأكلُوا الميْتَةَ والعِظامَ ، ويرَى الرَّجُلُ ما بيْنَ السَّماءِ والأرْضِ كهيْئةِ الدُّخانِ ، فجاءَهُ أبو سُفْيانَ فقالَ : يا مُحمَّدُ جِئْتَ تأمُرُنا بصِلةِ الرَّحِمِ وإنَّ قوْمَكَ قدْ هلَكُوا فادْعُ اللهَ . فقرأ ـ فارْتقِبْ يوْمَ تأتِي السَّماءُ بدُخانٍ مُبِينٍ ـ إلى قوْلِهِ ـ عائِدُونَ ـ أفيُكْشَفُ عنْهُمْ عذابُ الآخِرَةِ إذا

please invoke Allāh (to relieve them).' Then Ibn Mas'ūd recited:–

'Then watch you for the day that sky will bring forth a kind of smoke plainly visible..........but truly you will return! (to disbelief) (44:10-15)

Ibn Mas'ūd added, 'Then the punishment was stopped, but truly, they reverted to heathenism (their old way). So Allāh تعالى (threatened them thus):–

On the day when we shall seize you with a mighty grasp.' (44:16)

And that was the day of the Battle of Badr. Allāh's saying:– "Lizāma" (the punishment).'

refers to the day of Badr. Allāh's Statement:–

'Alif-Lām-Mīm, the Romans have been defeated...and they, after their defeat, will be victorious,' (30:1–3)

(This verse): Indicates that the defeat of Byzantines has already passed.

جاءَ ثُمَّ عادُوا إلى كُفْرِهِمْ ؟ فَذَلِكَ قَوْلُهُ تَعالى - يَوْمَ نَبْطِشُ البَطْشَةَ الكُبْرَى - يَوْمَ بَدْرٍ . وَلِزاماً يَوْمَ بَدْرٍ . - ألم غُلِبَتِ الرُّومُ - إلى - سَيَغْلِبُونَ - والرُّومُ قَدْ مَضَى .

(230) CHAPTER. Allāh's Statement: 'Let, there be no change in the Religion of Allāh (i.e. joining

بابُ قَوْلِهِ - لا تَبْدِيلَ لِخَلْقِ اللهِ - لِدِينِ اللهِ . خَلْقُ الأَوَّلِينَ : دِينُ

none in Allāh's worship).'
(30:30)

الأولين، والفطرة: الإسلام.

298. Narrated Abū Huraira ﷺ: Allāh's Messenger ﷺ said, "No child is born except on Al-Fiṭra (Islām) and then his parents make him Jewish, Christian or Magian, as an animal produces a perfect young animal: do you see any part of its body amputated?" Then he recited:–

'The religion of pure Islāmic Faith (Ḥanīfa),(i.e. to worship none but Allāh) , The pure Allāh's Islāmic nature with which He (Allāh) has created mankind. Let There be no change in Allāh's religion (i.e. to join none in Allāh's worship). That is the straight religion; but most of men know not. . . . .(30:30)

٢٩٨ - حدثنا عبدان: أخبرنا عبد الله: أخبرنا يونس، عن الزهري قال: أخبرني أبو سلمة بن عبد الرحمن: أن أبا هريرة رضي الله عنه قال: قال رسول الله صلى الله عليه وسلم: ما من مولود إلا يولد على الفطرة فأبواه يهودانه أو ينصرانه أو يمجسانه: كما تنتج البهيمة بهيمة جمعاء هل تحسون فيها من جدعاء؟ ثم يقول - فطرة الله التي فطر الناس عليها لا تبديل لخلق الله ذلك الدين القيم -.

SŪRAT LUQMĀN XXXI

In the Name of Allāh,
the Most Beneficent, the Most Merciful

سورة لقمان

بسم الله الرحمن الرحيم

(231) CHAPTER. 'O my son! join not in Worship others with Allāh. Verily! Joining others in worship with Allāh,

- لا تشرك بالله إن الشرك لظلم عظيم -.

is a great wrong indeed.'

(31:13)

299. Narrated 'Abdullāh :
When there was revealed:—

'It is those who believe and confuse not their beliefs with wrong.' (6:82)

It was very hard for the companions of Allāh's Messenger ﷺ, so they said, "Which of us has not confused his belief with wrong?" Allāh's Messenger ﷺ said, "The Verse does not mean this. Don't you hear Luqmān's statement to his son: Verily! Joining others in worship, with Allāh is a great wrong indeed. (31:13)

٢٩٩ ـ حدثنا قتيبة بن سعيد: حدثنا جرير، عن الأعمش، عن إبراهيم، عن علقمة، عن عبد الله رضي الله عنه قال: لما نزلت هذه الآية ـ الذين آمنوا ولم يلبسوا إيمانهم بظلم ـ شق ذلك على أصحاب رسول الله صلى الله عليه وسلم وقالوا: أينا لم يلبس إيمانه بظلم؟ فقال رسول الله صلى الله عليه وسلم: إنه ليس بذاك، ألا تسمع إلى قول لقمان لابنه ـ إن الشرك لظلم عظيم ـ.

(232) CHAPTER. The Statement of Allāh :—

'Verily, the knowledge of the Hour is with Allāh (alone).'

(31:34)

باب قوله ـ إن الله عنده علم الساعة ـ.

300. Narrated Abū Huraira :
One day while Allāh's Messenger ﷺ was sitting with the people, a man came to him walking and said, "O Allāh's Messenger! What is Belief?" The Prophet ﷺ.

٣٠٠ ـ حدثني إسحاق، عن جرير، عن أبي حيان، عن أبي زرعة، عن أبي هريرة رضي الله عنه: أن رسول الله صلى الله عليه وسلم كان يوما بارزا للناس

said, "Belief is to believe in Allāh, His Angels, His Books, His Messengers, and the meeting with Him, and to believe in the Resurrection." The man asked, "O Allāh's Messenger! What is Islām?" The Prophet ﷺ replied, "Islām is to worship Allāh and not worship anything besides Him, to offer prayers (1) perfectly, to pay the (compulsory) charity i.e. Zakāt and to fast the month of Ramaḍān." The man again asked, "O Allāh's Messenger! What is Iḥsān (i.e. perfection or Benevolence)?" The Prophet ﷺ said, "Iḥsān is to worship Allāh as if you see Him, and if you do not achieve this state of devotion, then (take it for granted that) Allāh sees you." The man further asked, "O Allāh's Messenger! When will the Hour be established?" The Prophet ﷺ replied, "The one who is asked about it does not know more than the questioner does, but I will describe to you its portents. When the lady slave gives birth to her mistress, that will be of its portents; when the

إذْ أتاهُ رَجُلٌ يَمْشِي فقالَ : يا رَسُولَ
اللهِ ، ما الإيمانُ ؟ قالَ : الإيمانُ أنْ
تُؤمِنَ باللهِ ومَلائكتِهِ وكُتُبِهِ ورُسُلِهِ
ولِقائِهِ وتُؤْمِنَ بالبَعْثِ الآخِرِ .
قالَ : يا رَسُولَ اللهِ ، ما الإسْلامُ ؟ قالَ :
الإسْلامُ أنْ تَعْبُدَ اللهَ ولا تُشْرِكَ بِهِ
شَيْئًا ، وتُقِيمَ الصَّلاةَ ، وتُؤْتِيَ الزَّكاةَ
المَفْرُوضَةَ ، وتَصُومَ رَمَضانَ . قالَ :
يا رَسُولَ اللهِ ما الإحْسانُ ؟ قالَ :
الإحْسانُ أنْ تَعْبُدَ اللهَ كأنَّكَ تَراهُ
فإنْ لَمْ تَكُنْ تَراهُ فإنَّهُ يَراكَ . قالَ : يا
رَسُولَ اللهِ ، مَتى تَقُومُ السَّاعَةُ ؟ قالَ : ما
المَسْئُولُ عَنْها بأعْلَمَ مِنَ السَّائِلِ ، ولَكِنْ
سأُحَدِّثُكَ عَنْ أشْراطِها . إذا وَلَدَتِ
المَرْأةُ رَبَّتَها فَذَلِكَ مِنْ أشْراطِها .
وإذا كانَ الحُفاةُ العُراةُ رُءُوسَ النَّاسِ

(1) 'Iqāmat-aṣ-Ṣalāt' i.e. The offering of prayers; is not understood by many of our Muslims. It means (a): All members of a family or group, etc. of a town or a village must offer the prayers; all the mature males in the mosque for all five congregational prayers and all females in their houses, both young and old (and no member of the family is to be excused) at the five fixed stated hours for the five compulsory congregational prayers, and if any member intentionally did not offer the prayer, then even if the others prayed, they did not offer the prayer (dutifully and perfectly). Each chief (of the town, village, family, etc), is responsible for it before Allāh (b) To offer the prayer in a way just as the Prophet ﷺ offered it with all its rules and regulations. Please see Ḥadith No. 785, 786, 788, in the 1st Volume in order to know the Prophet's way of praying.

bare-footed naked people become the chiefs of the people, that will be of its portents. The Hour is one of five things which nobody knows except Allāh. Verily, the knowledge of the Hour is with Allāh (alone). He sends down the rain, and knows that which is in the wombs." (31:34)
Then the man left. The Prophet ﷺ said, "Call him back to me." They went to call him back but could not see him. The Prophet ﷺ said, "That was Gabriel who came to teach the people their religion."
(See Ḥadīth No. 47 Vol I)

فَذَاكَ مِنْ أَشْرَاطِهَا ، فِى خَمْسٍ لَا يَعْلَمُهُنَّ إِلَّا اللهُ - إِنَّ اللهَ عِنْدَهُ عِلْمُ السَّاعَةِ وَيُنَزِّلُ الغَيْثَ وَيَعْلَمُ مَا فِى الأَرْحَامِ - ثُمَّ انْصَرَفَ الرَّجُلُ فَقَالَ : رُدُّوا عَلَىَّ ، فَأَخَذُوا لِيَرُدُّوا فَلَمْ يَرَوْا شَيْئًا . فَقَالَ : هَذَا جِبْرِيلُ جَاءَ لِيُعَلِّمَ النَّاسَ دِينَهُمْ .

301. Narrated 'Abdullāh bin 'Umar رضي الله عنهما: The Prophet ﷺ said, "The keys of the Unseen are five." And then he recited:—
'Verily, the knowledge of the Hour is with Allāh (alone).'......(31:34)

٣٠١ - حَدَّثَنَا يَحْيَى بْنُ سُلَيْمَانَ قَالَ : حَدَّثَنَا ابْنُ وَهْبٍ قَالَ : حَدَّثَنِى عُمَرُ بْنُ مُحَمَّدِ بْنِ زَائِدَةَ بْنِ عَبْدِ اللهِ ابْنِ عُمَرَ : أَنَّ أَبَاهُ حَدَّثَهُ أَنَّ عَبْدَ اللهِ ابْنَ عُمَرَ رَضِىَ اللهُ عَنْهُمَا قَالَ : قَالَ النَّبِىُّ صلى الله عليه وسلم : مَفَاتِيحُ الغَيْبِ خَمْسٌ ، ثُمَّ قَرَأَ - إِنَّ اللهَ عِنْدَهُ عِلْمُ السَّاعَةِ - .

SŪRAT-AS-SAJDA: XXXII

In the Name of Allāh, the Most Beneficent, the Most Merciful

سورة السجدة

بِسْمِ اللهِ الرَّحْمَنِ الرَّحِيمِ

وَقَالَ مُجَاهِدٌ : مَهِينٍ : ضَعِيفٍ . نُطْفَةُ الرَّجُلِ . ضَلَلْنَا : هَلَكْنَا . وَقَالَ ابْنُ عَبَّاسٍ : الْجُرُزُ الَّتِي لاَ تُمْطَرُ إِلاَّ مَطَرًا لاَ يُغْنِي عَنْهَا شَيْئًا . يَهْدِ : يُبَيِّنْ .

(233) CHAPTER. The Statement of Allāh ﷻ :–

'No soul knows what is kept hidden (in reserve) for them of joy.' (32: 17)

بَابُ قَوْلِهِ ـ فَلاَ تَعْلَمُ نَفْسٌ مَا أُخْفِيَ لَهُمْ ـ .

302. Narrated Abū Huraira رضي الله عنه : Allāh's Messenger ﷺ said, "Allāh said, 'I have prepared for my pious worshippers such things as no eye has ever seen, no ear has ever heard of, and nobody has ever thought of, ' " Abū Huraira added: If you wish you can read:–

'No soul knows what is kept hidden (in reserve) for them of joy as a reward for what they used to do.' (32:17)

٣٠٢ ـ حَدَّثَنَا عَلِيُّ بْنُ عَبْدِ اللهِ : حَدَّثَنَا سُفْيَانُ ، عَنِ الزِّنَادِ ، عَنِ الأَعْرَجِ ، عَنْ أَبِي هُرَيْرَةَ رَضِيَ اللهُ عَنْهُ ، عَنْ رَسُولِ اللهِ صلى اللهُ عليه وسلَّمَ قَالَ : قَالَ اللهُ تَبَارَكَ وَتَعَالَى : أَعْدَدْتُ لِعِبَادِي الصَّالِحِينَ مَا لاَ عَيْنٌ رَأَتْ ، وَلاَ أُذُنٌ سَمِعَتْ ، وَلاَ خَطَرَ عَلَى قَلْبِ بَشَرٍ . قَالَ أَبُو هُرَيْرَةَ : اقْرَءُوا إِنْ شِئْتُمْ ـ فَلاَ تَعْلَمُ نَفْسٌ مَا أُخْفِيَ لَهُمْ مِنْ قُرَّةِ أَعْيُنٍ ـ . وَحَدَّثَنَا سُفْيَانُ : حَدَّثَنَا أَبُو الزِّنَادِ ، عَنِ الأَعْرَجِ ، عَنْ أَبِي هُرَيْرَةَ قَالَ : قَالَ اللهُ مِثْلَهُ : قِيلَ لِسُفْيَانَ : رِوَايَةً ؟ قَالَ : فَأَيُّ شَيْءٍ ؟ .

وَقالَ أبو مُعاوِيَةَ ، عَنْ أبي صالِحٍ ، قَرَأَ أبو هُرَيْرَةَ : قُرّاتِ أعْيُنٍ .

303. Narrated Abu Huraira : The Prophet said, "Allāh said, 'I have prepared for My pious worshippers such things as no eye has ever seen, no ear has ever heard of, and nobody has ever thought of. All that is reserved, besides which, all that you have seen, is nothing.'" Then he recited :–

> 'No soul knows what is kept hidden (in reserve) for them of joy as a reward for what they used to do.' (32:17)

٣٠٣ ـ حَدَّثَني إسحاقُ بنُ نَصْرٍ : حدَّثنا أبو أُسامَةَ ، عَنِ الأعْمَشِ : حدَّثنا أبو صالِحٍ ، عَنْ أبي هُرَيْرَةَ رَضِيَ اللهُ عَنْهُ ، عَنِ النَّبِيِّ صلى الله عليه وسلَّمَ : يَقُولُ اللهُ تَعالى . أعْدَدْتُ لِعِبادي الصّالِحينَ ما لا عَيْنٌ رَأَتْ ، وَلا أُذُنٌ سَمِعَتْ ، وَلا خَطَرَ عَلى قَلْبِ بَشَرٍ . ذُخْرًا مِنْ بَلْهِ ما أُطْلِعْتُمْ عَلَيْهِ . ثُمَّ قَرَأَ ـ فَلا تَعْلَمُ نَفْسٌ ما أُخْفِيَ لَهُمْ مِنْ قُرَّةِ أعْيُنٍ جَزاءً بِما كانُوا يَعْمَلُونَ ـ .

SŪRAT-AL-AḤZĀB XXXIII
(The Clans)
In the Name of Allāh, the Most Beneficent, the Most Merciful

سورة الأحزاب

بِسْمِ اللهِ الرَّحْمَنِ الرَّحيمِ

(234) CHAPTER. 'The Prophet is closer to the believers than their own selves." . . . . (33:6)

وَقالَ مُجاهِدٌ : صَياصِيهِمْ : قُصُورِهِمْ مَعْرُوفًا في الكِتابِ . ـ النَّبِيُّ أوْلى بِالمُؤْمِنينَ مِنْ أنْفُسِهِمْ ـ .

304. Narrated Abū Huraira : The Prophet said, "There is no

٣٠٤ ـ حَدَّثَني إبْراهيمُ بنُ المُنْذِرِ : حدَّثنا مُحَمَّدُ بنُ فُلَيْحٍ :

believer but I, of all the people, I am the closest to him both in this world and in the Hereafter. Recite if you wish:

> 'The Prophet is closer to the believers than their own selves.'
>
> (33:6)

so if a believer (dies) leaves some property then his relatives will inherit that property; but if he is in debt or he leaves poor children, let those (creditors and children) come to me (that I may pay the debt and provide for the children), for then I am his sponsor (surely).

حدَّثنا أبي، عَنْ هِلالِ بنِ عَلِيٍّ ، عَنْ عَبْدِ الرَّحمٰنِ بنِ أبي عَمْرَةَ رَضِيَ اللهُ عَنْهُ ، عَنِ النَّبِيِّ صلى اللهُ عليهِ وسلَّمَ قالَ : ما مِنْ مُؤْمِنٍ إلاَّ و أنا أوْلى النَّاسِ بِهِ في الدُّنيا والآخِرةِ ، اقْرَءُوا إنْ شِئْتُمْ ـ النَّبِيُّ أوْلى بالمُؤْمِنِينَ مِنْ أنْفُسِهِمْ ـ فأيُّما مُؤْمِنٍ تَرَكَ مالاً فَلْيَرِثْهُ عَصَبَتُهُ مَنْ كانُوا ، فإنْ تَرَكَ دَيْناً أوْ ضَياعاً فَلْيَأْتِني و أنا مَوْلاهُ .

(235) CHAPTER. "Call them (adopted sons) by (the names of) their fathers: That is more just in the Sight of Allāh.'

(33: 5)

بابٌ ـ ادْعُوهُمْ لِآبائِهِمْ هُوَ أقْسَطُ عِنْدَ اللهِ ـ .

305. Narrated 'Abdullāh bin 'Umar (رضي الله عنه) : We used not to call Zaid bin Hāritha, the freed slave of Allāh's Messenger ﷺ except Zaid bin Muhammad ﷺ till the Qur'ānic Verse was revealed 'Call them (adopted sons) by (the names of) their fathers. That is more just in the Sight of Allāh."

(33:5)

٣٠٥ ـ حدَّثنا مُعَلَّى بنُ أسَدٍ : حدَّثنا عَبْدُ العَزِيزِ بنُ المُخْتارِ : حدَّثنا مُوسَى بنُ عُقْبَةَ قالَ : حدَّثني سالِمٌ ، عَنْ عَبْدِ اللهِ بنِ عُمَرَ رَضِيَ اللهُ عَنْهُما : أنَّ زَيْدَ بنَ حارِثَةَ مَوْلَى رَسُولِ اللهِ صلى اللهُ عليهِ وسلَّمَ ما كُنَّا نَدْعُوهُ إلاَّ زَيْدَ بنَ مُحَمَّدٍ حتى نَزَلَ القُرْآنُ ، ـ ادْعُوهُمْ لِآبائِهِمْ هُوَ أقْسَطُ عِنْدَ اللهِ ـ .

(236) CHAPTER. '(Among the believers are men who have been true to their

بابٌ ـ فَمِنْهُمْ مَنْ قَضَى نَحْبَهُ وَمِنْهُمْ مَنْ يَنْتَظِرُ وَما بَدَّلُوا تَبْدِيلاً .

their covenant with Allāh) Of them, some have fulfilled their obligations (met their death) and some still wait, but they have never changed (their determination) in the least.' (33:23)

نحبه : عهده . أقطارها : جوانبها .
الفتنة لآتوها : لأعطوها .

306. Narrated Anas : We think that the Verse:—

> 'Among the believers are men who have been true to their covenant with Allāh.'

was revealed in favour of Anas bin An-Naḍir.

٣٠٦ ـ حدثنا محمد بن بشار : حدثنا محمد بن عبد الله الأنصاري قال : حدثني أبي ، عن ثمامة ، عن أنس رضي الله عنه قال : نرى هذه الآية نزلت في أنس بن النضر ـ من المؤمنين رجال صدقوا ما عاهدوا الله عليه ـ .

307. Narrated Zaid bin Thābit: When we collected the fragramentary manuscripts of the Qur'ān into copies, I missed one of the Verses of Sūrat al-Aḥzāb which I used to hear Allāh's Messenger reading. Finally I did not find it with anybody except Khuzaima Al-Anṣārī, whose witness was considered by Allāh's Messenger equal to the witness of two men. (And that Verse was:)

> 'Among the believers are men who have been true to their covenant with Allāh.'

٣٠٧ ـ حدثنا أبو اليمان : أخبرنا شعيب ، عن الزهري قال : أخبرني خارجة بن زيد بن ثابت ، أن زيد بن ثابت قال : لما نسخنا الصحف في المصاحف فقدت آية من سورة الأحزاب كنت أسمع رسول الله صلى الله عليه وسلم يقرؤها لم أجدها مع أحد إلا مع خزيمة الأنصاري الذي جعل رسول الله صلى الله عليه وسلم شهادته شهادة رجلين ـ من المؤمنين رجال صدقوا ما عاهدوا الله عليه ـ .

(237) CHAPTER. The Statement of Allāh :—

باب قوله ـ يا أيها النبي قل لأزواجك إن كنتن تردن الحياة

'O Prophet! (Muhammad ﷺ) Say to your wives, 'If you desire the life of this world and its glitter then come! I will make a provision for you and set you free in a handsome manner (divorce).'

الدنيا وزينتها فتعالين أمتعكن
وأسرحكن سراحا جميلا - وقال
معمر: التبرج: أن تخرج محاسنها.
سنة الله: استنها: جعلها.

308. Narrated 'Āisha (رضي الله عنها), the wife of the Prophet ﷺ : Allāh's Messenger ﷺ came to me when Allāh ordered him to give option to his wives. So Allāh's Messenger ﷺ started with me, saying, "I am going to mention to you something but you should not hasten (to give your reply) unless you consult your parents.' He knew that my parents would not order me to leave him. Then he said, "Allah says:—

'O Prophet! Say to your wives
.... (33:28-29)

On that I said to him, "Then why should I consult my parents? Verily, I seek Allah, His Messenger and the Home of the Hereafter."

٣٠٨ - حدثنا أبو اليمان: أخبرنا
شعيب، عن الزهري قال: أخبرني
أبو سلمة بن عبد الرحمن: أن عائشة
رضي الله عنها زوج النبي صلى الله
عليه وسلم أخبرته: أن رسول الله صلى
الله عليه وسلم جاءها حين أمره الله أن
يخير أزواجه فبدأبي رسول الله صلى الله
عليه وسلم فقال: إني ذاكر لك أمرا فلا
عليك أن تستعجلي حتى تستأمري أبويك
وقد علم أن أبوي لم يكونا يأمراني
بفراقه. قالت: ثم قال: إن الله قال -
يا أيها النبي قل لأزواجك - إلى تمام
الآيتين. فقلت له: ففي أي هذا
أستأمر أبوي؟ فإني أريد الله ورسوله
والدار الآخرة.

(238) CHAPTER. The Statement of Allāh (تعالى) :

'But if you desire Allāh, His Messenger, and the Home of the Hereafter, then verily, Allāh has

باب قوله - وإن كنتن تردن
الله ورسوله والدار الآخرة فإن الله
أعد للمحسنات منكن أجرا عظيما -
وقال قتادة: واذكرن ما يتلى في

prepared for the good doers among you, a great reward.' [(33:29)

Regarding the Verse :—

'And remember that which is recited in your homes of the verses of Allāh and Wisdom.' (33:34)

Qatāda said: That means the Qur'ān and the Sunna (Prophet's tradition).

بُيُوتِكُنَّ مِنْ آيَاتِ اللهِ وَالحِكْمَةِ : القُرآن والسُّنَّةِ .

309. Narrated 'Āisha, the wife of the Prophet ﷺ :When Allāh's Messenger ﷺ was ordered to give option to his wives, he started with me, saying, "I am going to mention to you something, but you shall not hasten (to give your reply) unless you consult your parents." The Prophet ﷺ knew that my parents would not order me to leave him. Then he said, "Allāh تعالى says:—

'O Prophet (Muḥammad ﷺ)! Say to your wives: If you desire the life of this world and its glitter .... a great reward.' " (33:28-29)

I said, "Then why I consult my parents? Verily, I seek Allāh, His Messenger and the Home of the Hereafter." Then all the other wives of the Prophet did the same as I did.

٣٠٩ ـ وَقَالَ اللَّيْثُ : حَدَّثَنِي يُونُسُ ، عَنْ ابنِ شِهَابٍ قَالَ : أَخْبَرَنِي أبو سَلَمَةَ بنَ عَبْدِ الرَّحْمَنِ : أَنَّ عائشةَ زَوْجَ النَّبِيِّ صلى اللهُ عليهِ وسلَّمَ قَالَتْ : لمَّا أُمِرَ رَسُولُ اللهِ صلى اللهُ عليه وسلَّم بتَخْيِيرِ أَزْوَاجِهِ بدأ بي فَقَالَ : إنِّي ذَاكِرٌ لَكِ أمْرًا فَلا عَلَيْكِ أَنْ لا تَعْجَلِي حتَّى تَسْتَأمِري أبَوَيْكِ . قالَتْ : وَقَدْ عَلِمَ أنَّ أبَوَيَّ لم يَكُونا يأْمُرانِي بفِراقِهِ . قالَتْ ثم قال : إنَّ اللهَ جَلَّ ثَنَاؤُهُ قالَ ـ يا أيُّها النَّبِيُّ قُلْ لأزْوَاجِكَ إنْ كُنْتُنَّ تُرِدْنَ الحَيَاةَ الدُّنْيا وَزِينَتَها ـ إلى ـ أجْرًا عَظِيما ـ قالَتْ : فَقُلْتُ : فَفِي أيِّ هَذَا اسْتَأمِرُ أبَوَيَّ ؟ فإنِّي أُرِيدُ اللهَ وَرَسُولَهُ والدَّارَ الآخِرَةَ . قالَتْ : ثُمَّ فَعَلَ أزْوَاجُ النَّبِيِّ صلى اللهُ عليهِ وسلَّم مِثْلَ ما فَعَلْتُ . تابَعَهُ مُوسَى بنُ أعْيَنَ ، عَنْ مَعْمَرٍ ، عَنِ الزُّهْرِيِّ ، قال: أخْبَرَنِي أبو سَلَمَةَ . وَقالَ عَبْدُ الرَّزَّاق

وأبو سُفْيانَ المَعْمَرِيُّ، عَنْ مَعْمَرٍ، عَنِ الزُّهْرِيِّ عَنْ عُرْوَةَ، عَنْ عائِشَةَ.

(239) CHAPTER. The Statement of Allāh :–

But you did hide in your mind that which Allāh was about to make manifest. You did fear mankind, whereas Allāh had a better right that you should fear him.' (33:37)

بابُ قَوْلِهِ ـ وتُخْفِي في نَفْسِكَ ما اللهُ مُبْدِيهِ وتَخْشَى النّاسَ واللهُ أحَقُّ أنْ تَخْشاهُ ـ.

310. Narrated Anas bin Mālik :

The Verse:–

But you did hide in your mind that which Allāh was about to make manifest.' (33:37)

was revealed concerning Zainab bint Jaḥsh and Zaid bin Ḥāritha.

٣١٠ـ حدَّثَنا مُحَمَّدُ بنُ عَبْدِ الرَّحِيمِ: حدَّثَنا مُعَلّى بنُ مَنْصُورٍ، عَنْ حَمّادِ ابنِ زَيْدٍ: حدَّثَنا ثابِتٌ، عَنْ أنَسِ بنِ مالِكٍ رَضِيَ اللهُ عَنْهُ: أنَّ هذِهِ الآيَةَ ـ وتُخْفِي في نَفْسِكَ ما اللهُ مُبْدِيهِ ـ نَزَلَتْ في شأنِ زَيْنَبَ ابْنَةِ جَحْشٍ وزَيْدِ بنِ حارِثَةَ.

(240) CHAPTER. The Statement of Allāh :–

"You (O Muḥammad) can postpone (the turn of) whom you will of them (your wives) and you may receive whom you will, and there is no blame on you

بابُ قَوْلِهِ ـ تُرْجِي مَنْ تَشاءُ مِنْهُنَّ وتُؤْوِي إلَيْكَ مَنْ تَشاءُ ومَنِ ابْتَغَيْتَ مِمَّنْ عَزَلْتَ فَلا جُناحَ عَلَيْكَ ـ. قالَ ابنُ عَبّاسٍ: تُرْجِي: تُؤَخِّرُ، أرْجِهِ: أخِّرْهُ.

if you invite one whose (turn) you have set aside (temporarily).'
(33:51)

311. Narrated 'Āisha ﷺ: I used to look down upon those ladies who had given themselves to Allāh's Messenger ﷺ and I used to say, "Can a lady give herself (to a man)?" But when Allāh revealed:—

"You (O Muḥammad ﷺ) can postpone (the turn of) whom you will of them (your wives), and you may receive any of them whom you will; and there is no blame on you if you invite one whose turn you have set aside (temporarily).' (33:51)

I said (to the Prophet ﷺ), "I feel that your Lord hastens in fulfilling your wishes and desires."

312. Narrated Mu'ādha: 'Āisha ﷺ said, "Allāh's Messenger ﷺ used to take the permission of that wife with whom he was supposed to stay overnight if he wanted to go to one other than her, after this Verse was revealed:—

"You (O Muḥammad ﷺ) can postpone (the turn of) whom you will of them (your wives), and you may receive any (of them) whom you will; and there is no blame on you if you invite one

٣١١ ـ حدَّثَنا زَكَرِيَّا بنُ يَحْيَى: حدَّثَنا أَبو أُسامَةَ، قالَ هِشامٌ: حدَّثَنا عَنْ أَبِيهِ، عَنْ عَائِشَةَ رَضِيَ اللهُ عَنْها قالَتْ: كُنْتُ أُغارُ عَلى اللَّاتِي وَهَبْنَ أَنْفُسَهُنَّ لِرَسُولِ اللهِ صلى الله عليه وسلّم وَأَقُولُ: أَتَهَبُ المَرْأَةُ نَفْسَها؟ فَلَمَّا أَنْزَلَ اللهُ تَعالى ـ تُرْجِي مِنْ تَشاءُ مِنْهُنَّ وَتُؤْوِي إِلَيْكَ مَنْ تَشاءُ وَمَنِ ابْتَغَيْتَ مِمَّنْ عَزَلْتَ فَلا جُناحَ عَلَيْكَ ـ قُلْتُ. ما أَرى رَبَّكَ إِلاَّ يُسارِعُ فِي هَوَاكَ.

٣١٢ ـ حدَّثَنا حِبَّانُ بنُ مُوسَى: أَخْبَرَنا عَبْدُ اللهِ: أَخْبَرَنا عاصِمٌ الأَحْوَلُ، عَنْ مُعَاذَةَ، عَنْ عائِشَةَ رَضِيَ اللهُ عَنْها: أَنَّ رَسُولَ اللهِ صلى الله عليه وسلّم كانَ يَسْتَأْذِنُ فِي يَوْمِ المَرْأَةِ مِنَّا بَعْدَ أَنْ أُنْزِلَتْ هَذِهِ الآيَةُ ـ تُرْجِي مِنْ تَشاءُ مِنْهُنَّ وَتُؤْوي إِلَيْكَ مَنْ تَشاءُ وَمَنِ ابْتَغَيْتَ مِمَّنْ عَزَلْتَ فَلا جُناحَ عَلَيْكَ ـ فَقُلْتُ لَها: ما كُنْتِ تَقُولِينَ؟ قالَتْ: كُنْتُ أَقُولُ لَهُ: إِنْ كانَ ذَاكَ

whose turn you have set aside (temporarily). (33:51)

I asked 'Āisha, "What did you use to say (in this case)?" She said, "I used to say to him, "If I could deny you the permission (to go to your other wives) I would not allow your favour to be bestowed on any other person."

إليَّ فإني لا أريدُ يا رسولَ اللهِ أنْ أوثِرَ عليكَ أحدًا. تابعَهُ عبادُ بنُ عبادٍ: سمعَ عاصمًا.

(241) CHAPTER. The Statement of Allāh :–

'Enter not the Prophet's houses
until leave is given to you
for a meal
truly, such a thing is in
Allāh's Sight an enormity. (33:53-54)

بابُ قولِهِ ـ لا تدخلُوا بيوتَ النبيِّ إلاَّ أنْ يُؤْذَنَ لكمْ إلى طعامٍ ـ إلى قولِهِ ـ إنَّ ذلِكمْ كانَ عندَ اللهِ عظيمًا ـ يُقالُ: إناهُ: إدراكُهُ، أنى يأني أناةً فهوَ آنٍ. ـ لعلَّ الساعةَ تكونُ قريبًا ـ إذا وصفتَ صفةَ المؤنثِ قلتَ قريبةً، وإذا جعلتَهُ ظرفًا وبدلًا، ولمْ تُرِدِ الصفةَ نزعتَ الهاءَ منَ المؤنثِ. وكذلكَ لفظُها في الواحدِ والاثنينِ والجمعِ للذكرِ والأنثى.

313. Narrated 'Umar : I said, "O Allāh's Messenger! Good and bad persons enter upon you, so I suggest that you order the mothers of the Believers (i.e. your wives) to observe veils." Then Allāh revealed the Verses of Al-

٣١٣ ـ حدثنا مُسدَّدٌ، عنْ يحيى، عنْ حُميدٍ، عنْ أنسٍ قالَ: قالَ عمرُ رضيَ اللهُ عنهُ: قلتُ: يا رسولَ اللهِ، يدخلُ عليكَ البرُّ والفاجرُ، فلوْ أمرتَ أمهاتِ المؤمنينَ بالحجابِ،

Hijāb. (1)

فأنزل الله آية الحجاب .

314. Narrated Anas bin Mālik: When Allāh's Messenger married Zainab bint Jahsh, he invited the people to a meal. They took the meal and remained sitting and talking. Then the Prophet (showed them) as if he is ready to get up, yet they did not get up. When he noticed that (there was no response to his movement), he got up, and the others too, got up except three persons who kept on sitting. The Prophet came back in order to enter his house, but he found those people still sitting (so he went away again). Then they left, whereupon I set out and went to the Prophet to tell him that they had departed, so he came and entered his house. I wanted to enter along with him, but he put a screen between me and him. Then Allah revealed :—

> 'O you who believe ! Do not enter the houses of the Prophet.......' (33:53)

٣١٤ - حدثنا محمد بن عبد الله الرقاشي : حدثنا معتمر بن سليمان قال : سمعت أبي يقول : حدثنا أبو مجلز ، عن أنس بن مالك رضي الله عنه قال : لما تزوج رسول الله صلى الله وسلم زينب ابنة جحش دعا القوم فطعموا ثم جلسوا يتحدثون . وإذا هو كأنه يتهيأ للقيام فلم يقوموا فلما رأى ذلك قام فلما قام من قام وقعد ثلاثة نفر ، فجاء النبي صلى الله عليه وسلم ليدخل فإذا القوم جلوس ، ثم إنهم قاموا . فانطلقت فجئت فأخبرت النبي صلى الله عليه وسلم أنهم قد انطلقوا فجاء حتى دخل . فذهبت أدخل فألقى الحجاب بيني وبينه ، فأنزل الله - يا أيها الذين آمنوا لا تدخلوا بيوت النبي - الآية .

315. Narrated Anas bin Mālik: I of all the people know best this verse

٣١٥ - حدثنا سليمان بن حرب : حدثنا حماد بن زيد ، عن أيوب .

(1) i.e. The observing of veils (a complete body cover excluding the eyes) by the muslim women. Please see chapter No. 220 and Hadith No. 282.

of Al-Ḥijāb. When Allāh's Messenger ﷺ married Zainab bint Jaḥsh رضي الله عنها, she was with him in the house and he prepared a meal and invited the people (to it). They sat down (after finishing their meal) and started chatting. So the Prophet ﷺ went out and then returned several times while they were still sitting and talking. So Allāh revealed the Verse:—

> 'O you who believe! Enter not the Prophet's houses until leave is given to you for a meal, (and then) not (so early as) to wait for its preparation . . . . .ask them from behind a screen.' (33:53)

So the screen was set up and the people went away.

عَنْ أبي قِلابَةَ : قالَ أنَسُ بنُ مالِكٍ : أنا أعْلَمُ النّاسِ بِهَذِهِ الآيَةِ الحِجابِ ، لَمّا أُهْدِيَتْ زَيْنَبُ بِنْتُ جَحْشٍ رَضِيَ اللهُ عَنْها إلى رَسُولِ اللهِ صلى اللهُ عليه وسلَّم كانَتْ مَعَهُ في البَيْتِ صَنَعَ طَعاماً ، وَدَعا القَوْمَ فَقَعَدُوا يَتَحَدَّثُونَ فَجَعَلَ النَّبِيُّ صلى الله عليه وسلَّم يَخْرُجُ ثُمَّ يَرْجِعُ وَهُمْ قُعُودٌ يَتَحَدَّثُونَ فَأنْزَلَ اللهُ تَعالى - يا أيُّها الَّذِينَ آمَنُوا لا تَدْخُلُوا بُيُوتَ النَّبِيِّ إلاّ أنْ يُؤْذَنَ لَكُمْ إلى طَعامٍ غَيْرَ ناظِرِينَ إناهُ - إلى قَوْلِهِ - مِنْ وَرَاءِ حِجابٍ - فَضُرِبَ الحِجابُ وقامَ القَوْمُ .

316. Narrated Anas رضي الله عنه : A banquet of bread and meat was held on the occasion of the marriage of the Prophet ﷺ to Zainab bint Jaḥsh. I was sent to invite the people (to the banquet), and so the people started coming (in groups); They would eat and then leave. Another batch would come, eat and leave. So I kept on inviting the people till I found nobody to invite. Then I said, "O Allāh's Prophet! I do not find anybody to invite." He said, "Carry away the remaining food." Then a batch of three persons stayed in the house chatting. The Prophet ﷺ left and went towards the dwelling place of 'Āisha and said, "Peace and Allāh's Mercy be on you, O the people of the

٣١٦ - حَدَّثَنا أبو مَعْمَرٍ : حَدَّثَنا عَبْدُ الوارِثِ : حَدَّثَنا عَبْدُ العَزِيزِ بنُ صُهَيْبٍ ، عَنْ أنَسٍ رَضِيَ اللهُ عَنْهُ قالَ : بُنِيَ عَلَى النَّبِيِّ صلى اللهُ عليه وسلَّم بِزَيْنَبَ ابْنَةِ جَحْشٍ بِخُبْزٍ ولَحْمٍ . فَأُرْسِلْتُ عَلَى الطَّعامِ داعِياً فَيَجِيءُ قَوْمٌ فَيَأْكُلُونَ ويَخْرُجُونَ ، ثُمَّ يَجِيءُ قَوْمٌ فَيَأْكُلُونَ ويَخْرُجُونَ فَدَعَوْتُ حَتّى ما أجِدُ أحَداً أدْعُو . فَقُلْتُ : يا نَبِيَّ اللهِ ما أجِدُ أحَداً أدْعُوهُ ، قالَ : ارْفَعُوا طَعامَكُمْ وبَقِيَ ثَلاثَةُ رَهْطٍ

house!" She replied, "Peace and the mercy of Allāh be on you too. How did you find your wife? May Allāh bless you. Then he went to the dwelling places of all his other wives and said to them the same as he said to 'Āisha and they said to him the same as 'Āisha had said to him. Then the Prophet ﷺ returned and found a group of three persons still in the house chatting. The Prophet ﷺ was a very shy person, so he went out (for the second time) and went towards the dwelling place of 'Āisha. I do not remember whether I informed him that the people have gone away. So he returned and as soon as he entered the gate, he drew the curtain between me and him, and then the Verse of Al-Ḥijāb (1) was revealed.

يتحدثون في البيت. فخرج النبي صلى الله عليه وسلم فانطلق إلى حجرة عائشة، فقال: السلام عليكم أهل البيت ورحمة الله، فقالت: وعليك السلام ورحمة الله، كيف وجدت أهلك؟ بارك الله لك. فتقرى حجر نسائه كلهن يقول لهن كما يقول لعائشة ويقلن له كما قالت عائشة. ثم رجع النبي صلى الله عليه وسلم فإذا ثلاثة من رهط في البيت يتحدثون، وكان النبي صلى الله عليه وسلم شديد الحياء فخرج منطلقا نحو حجرة عائشة، فما أدري آخبرته أو أخبر أن القوم خرجوا، فرجع حتى إذا وضع رجله في أسكفة الباب داخلة وأخرى خارجة أرخى الستر بيني وبينه، وأنزلت آية الحجاب.

317. Narrated Anas رضي الله عنه : When Allāh's Messenger ﷺ married Zainab bint Jaḥsh, he made the people eat meat and bread to their fill (by giving a Walīma banquet). Then he went out to the dwelling places of the mothers of the believers (his wives), as he used to do in the morning of his marriage. He would greet them and invoke good on them, and they (too) would return his greeting and invoke good on him. When he returned to

٣١٧ - حدثنا إسحاق بن منصور: أخبرنا عبد الله بن بكر السهمي: حدثنا حميد، عن أنس رضي الله عنه قال: أولم رسول الله صلى الله عليه وسلم حين بنى بزينب ابنة جحش فأشبع الناس خبزا ولحما. ثم خرج إلى حجر أمهات المؤمنين

(1) See the Foot-note of Ḥadīth No. 313.

his house, he found two men talking to each other; and when he saw them, he went out of his house again. When those two men saw Allāh's Messenger ﷺ going out of his house, they quickly got up (and departed). I do not remember whether I informed him of their departure, or he was informed (by somebody else). So he returned, and when he entered the house, he lowered the curtain between me and him. Then the Verse of Al-Ḥijāb was revealed.

كما كان يصنع صبيحة بنائه فيسلم
عليهن ويدعو لهن ويسلمن عليه
ويدعون له . فلما رجع إلى بيته رأى
رجلين جرى بهما الحديث فلما
رآهما رجع عن بيته فلما رأى
الرجلان نبي الله صلى الله عليه وسلم
رجع عن بيته وثبا مسرعين ، فما
أدري أنا أخبرته بخروجهما أم أخبر
فرجع حتى دخل البيت وأرخى الستر
بيني وبينه وأنزلت آية الحجاب .
وقال ابن أبي مريم : أخبرنا يحيى :
حدثني حميد : سمع أنسا ، عن النبي
صلى الله عليه وسلم .

318. Narrated 'Āisha ﵂: Sauda (the wife of the Prophet ﷺ) went out to answer the call of nature after it was made obligatory (for all the Muslims ladies) to observe the veil. She was a fat huge lady, and everybody who knew her before could recognize her. So 'Umar bin Al-Khaṭṭāb saw her and said, "O Sauda! By Allāh, you cannot hide yourself from us, so think of a way by which you should not be recognized on going out. Sauda returned while Allāh's Messenger ﷺ was in my house taking his supper and a bone covered with meat was in his hand. She entered and said, "O Allāh's Messenger! I went out to answer the call of nature and 'Umar said to me so-and-so." Then Allāh inspired him (the Prophet ﷺ) and when the state of inspiration was

٣١٨ - حدثني زكريا بن يحيى :
حدثنا أبو أسامة ، عن هشام ، عن أبيه ،
عن عائشة رضي الله عنها قالت :
خرجت سودة بعد ما ضرب الحجاب
لحاجتها وكانت امرأة جسيمة لا تخفى
على من يعرفها . فرآها عمر بن
الخطاب فقال : يا سودة ، أما والله ما
تخفين علينا فانظري كيف تخرجين ؟
قالت : فانكفأت راجعة ورسول الله
صلى الله عليه وسلم في بيتي وإنه ليتعشى
وفي يده عرق ، فدخلت فقالت : يا
رسول الله ، إني خرجت لبعض

over and the bone was still in his hand as he had not put in down, he said (to Sauda), "You (women) have been allowed to go out for your needs."

حاجتي فقال لي عمر كذا وكذا، قالت: فأوحى الله إليه، ثم رفع عنه وإن العرق في يده ما وضعه فقال: إنه قد أذن لكن أن تخرجن لحاجتكن.

(242) CHAPTER. The Statement of Allāh تعالى :-

'Whether you reveal anything, or conceal it, verily, Allāh is Knower of all things......Verily Allāh is Witness over all things.'

(33:54-55)

باب قوله - إن تبدوا شيئا أو تخفوه فإن الله كان - إلى قوله - شهيدا -.

319. Narrated 'Āisha رضي الله عنها : Aflaḥ, the brother of Abī Al-Qu'ais, asked permission to visit me after the order of Al-Ḥijāb was revealed. I said, "I will not permit him unless I take permission of the Prophet ﷺ about him for it was not the brother of Abī Al-Qu'ais but the wife of Abī Al-Qu'ais that nursed me." The Prophet ﷺ entered upon me, and I said to him, "O Allāh's Messenger! Aflaḥ, the brother of Abī Al-Qu'ais asked permission to visit me but I refused to permit him unless I took your permission." The Prophet ﷺ said, "What stopped you from permitting him? He is your uncle." I said, "O Allāh's Messenger! The man was not the person who had nursed me, but the woman, the wife of Abī Al-Qu'ais had nursed me." He said, "Admit him, for

٣١٩ - حدثنا أبو اليمان: أخبرنا شعيب، عن الزهري: حدثني عروة ابن الزبير، أن عائشة رضي الله عنها قالت: استأذن علي أفلح أخو أبي القعيس بعد ما أنزل الحجاب فقلت: لا آذن له حتى أستأذن فيه النبي صلى الله عليه وسلم فإن أخاه أبا القعيس ليس هو أرضعني ولكن أرضعتني امرأة أبي القعيس. فدخل علي النبي صلى الله عليه وسلم فقلت له: يا رسول الله، إن أفلح أخا أبي القعيس استأذن فأبيت أن آذن حتى أستأذنك. فقال النبي صلى الله عليه

he is your uncle. Taribat Yamīnuki (may your right hand be saved)" 'Urwa, the sub-narrator added: For that 'Āisha used to say, "Consider those things which are illegal because of blood relations as illegal because of the corresponding foster relations."

وسلم: وما منعك أن تأذنين؟ عمك. قلت: يا رسول الله إن الرجل ليس هو أرضعتني ولكن أرضعتني امرأة أبي القعيس. فقال: ائذني له فإنه عمك، تربت يمينك. قال عروة: فلذلك كانت عائشة تقول: حرموا من الرضاعة ما تحرمون من النسب.

(243) CHAPTER. The Statement of Allāh تعالى :—

> 'Allāh sends His blessings and mercy on the Prophet ﷺ and His angels ask Allāh to bless and forgive him . . . . . . (33:56)

Abū 'Al-'Āliya said, "Allāh's blessings (in this Verse) means His compliments to him before the Angels, and the blessings of Angels means their invocations,"

باب قوله - إن الله وملائكته يصلون على النبي - الآية قال أبو العالية: صلاة الله ثناؤه عليه عند الملائكة. وصلاة الملائكة الدعاء. وقال ابن عباس: يصلون: يبركون. لنغرينك: لنسلطنك.

320. Narrated Ka'b bin 'Ujra: It was said, "O Allāh's Messenger! We know how to greet you, but how to invoke Allāh for you?" The Prophet ﷺ said, "Say: Allāhumma ṣalli 'alā Muḥammadin wa'alā Āli Muḥammaddin, kamā ṣallaita 'alā āli Ebrāhīm, innaka

٣٢٠ - حدثني سعيد بن يحيى: حدثنا أبي: حدثنا مسعر، عن الحكم، عن ابن أبي ليلى عن كعب بن عجرة رضي الله عنه، قيل: يا رسول الله أما السلام عليك فقد عرفناه، فكيف الصلاة عليك؟ قال: قولوا: اللهم

صَلِّ عَلَى مُحَمَّدٍ وَعَلَى آلِ مُحَمَّدٍ ، كَمَا صَلَّيْتَ عَلَى آلِ إِبْرَاهِيمَ إِنَّكَ حَمِيدٌ مَجِيدٌ ، اللَّهُمَّ بَارِكْ عَلَى مُحَمَّدٍ ، وَعَلَى آلِ مُحَمَّدٍ ، كَمَا بَارَكْتَ عَلَى آلِ إِبْرَاهِيمَ إِنَّكَ حَمِيدٌ مَجِيدٌ .

Ḥamīdun Majīd." (1)

٣٢١ - حَدَّثَنَا عَبْدُ اللهِ بنُ يُوسُفَ : حَدَّثَنَا اللَّيْثُ قَالَ : حَدَّثَنِي ابنُ الهَادِ ، عَنْ عَبْدِ اللهِ بنِ خَبَّابٍ ، عَنْ أَبِي سَعِيدٍ الخُدْرِيِّ قَالَ : قُلْنَا يَا رَسُولَ اللهِ ، هٰذَا التَّسْلِيمُ فَكَيْفَ نُصَلِّي عَلَيْكَ ؟ قَالَ : قُولُوا : اللَّهُمَّ صَلِّ عَلَى مُحَمَّدٍ عَبْدِكَ وَرَسُولِكَ كَمَا صَلَّيْتَ عَلَى آلِ إِبْرَاهِيمَ ، وَبَارِكْ عَلَى مُحَمَّدٍ وَعَلَى آلِ مُحَمَّدٍ كَمَا بَارَكْتَ عَلَى إِبْرَاهِيمَ . قَالَ أَبُو صَالِحٍ ، عَنِ اللَّيْثِ : عَلَى مُحَمَّدٍ وَعَلَى آلِ مُحَمَّدٍ كَمَا بَارَكْتَ عَلَى آلِ إِبْرَاهِيمَ .

321. Narrated Abū Sa'īd Al-Khudrī: We said, "O Allāh's Messenger! (We know) this greeting (to you) but how shall we invoke Allāh for you?" He said, "Say! Allāhumma ṣalli 'alā Muḥammadin 'Abdika wa rasūlika kamā ṣallaita 'alā āli Ebrāhīm wa bārik 'alā Muḥammadin wa'alā āli Muḥammadin kamā bārakta 'alā āli Ebrāhīm.' (2) Al-Laith said: 'Alā Muḥammadin wa 'alā ali Muḥammadin kamā bārakta 'alā āli Ebrāhīm.

٣٢٢ - حَدَّثَنَا إِبْرَاهِيمُ بنُ حَمْزَةَ :

322. Narrated Ibn Abī Ḥāzim and

(1) O Allāh! Send Your Ṣalāt (Blessings and Mercy) on Muḥammad and his family as You sent Your Ṣalāt (Blessing and Mercy) on Abraham's family. O Allāh! Send Your Blessings on Muhammad and his family as you sent Your Blessings on Abraham's family. You are Praiseworthy, Most Gracious. See Ḥadīth No. 368, 369 in the 8th Volume for details.

(2) Send Your Ṣalāt upon Muḥammad, Your Slave and Your Messenger, as You sent Your Ṣalāt on Abraham's family, and send Your Blessings upon Muhammad and his family as You sent Your Blessings upon Abraham.

Ad-Darāwardi: Yazīd said, "Kamā ṣallaita 'alā Ebrāhīma wa bārik'alā Muḥammadin wa āli Muḥammadin kamā bārakta 'alā Ebrāhīma wa āli Ebrāhīm." (1)

حدَّثنا ابن أبي حازِم والدَّرَاوَرْدي عَنْ
يَزِيدَ . وقالَ : كما صلَّيْتَ على إبراهيمَ .
وبارِكْ على محمَّدٍ وآلِ محمَّدٍ كما
باركْتَ على إبْرَاهيمَ وآلِ إبْرَاهيمَ .

(244) CHAPTER. 'Be you not like those who annoyed Moses.'

(33-69)

باب - لا تكونُوا كالذينَ آذَوْا
موسَى -

323. Narrated Abū Huraira : Allāh's Messenger said, "Moses was a shy man, and that is what the Statement of Allāh means:—

'O you who believe! Be not like those who annoyed Moses, but Allāh proved his innocence of that which they alleged and he was honourable in Allāh's Sight.'

(33:69)

٣٢٣ - حدَّثنا إسحاقُ بنُ إبْرَاهيمَ :
أخبرَنا رَوْحُ بنُ عُبادَةَ : حدَّثنا عوفٌ ،
عن الحسَنِ ومحمَّدٍ وخِلاسٍ ، عنْ أبي
هُرَيرَةَ رَضِيَ اللهُ عنْهُ قالَ : قالَ
رَسُولُ اللهِ صلى اللهُ عليهِ وسلَّم : إنَّ مُوسَى
كانَ رَجُلاً حَيِيّاً ، وذَلكَ قوْلُه تعالى -
يا أيُّها الذينَ آمنُوا لا تكُونُوا كالذينَ
آذَوْا مُوسَى فبرَّأهُ اللهُ مِمّا قالُوا وكانَ
عِنْدَ اللهِ وَجِيهاً - .

SŪRAT SABĀ (The City of Sabā) XXXIV

In the Name of Allāh, the Most Beneficent, the Most Merciful

سورة سبأ

بِسْمِ اللهِ الرَّحْمَنِ الرَّحِيمِ

يُقالُ مُعاجِزِينَ : مُسابِقِينَ . بِمُعْجِزِينَ :

(1) The same invocation as in 320 and 321 with a little modification in form.

Note: "Ṣalāt" from Allāh means (here) His graces and honours, (upon Muḥammad)

بفائتينَ . مُعاجِزِينَ : مُعاجِزِىَّ ، مُسابِقِىَّ . سَبَقُوا ، فاتُوا . لا يُعْجِزُونَ : لا يَفُوتُونَ . يَسْبِقُونا : يُعْجِزُونا . قَوْلُهُ بِمُعْجِزِينَ : بفائتينَ ، وَمَعْنَى مُعاجِزِينَ مُغالِبِينَ . يُرِيدُ كُلُّ وَاحِدٍ مِنْهُما أنْ يُظْهِرَ عَجْزَ صَاحِبِهِ . مِعشارُ : عُشْرٌ الأُكُلُ : الثَمَرُ . باعِدْ وَبَعِّدْ واحِدٌ . وَقالَ مُجاهِدٌ : لا يَعْزُبُ لا يَغِيبُ . سَيْلُ العَرِمِ : السُّدُّ ماءٌ أحْمَرُ أرْسَلَهُ اللهُ فى السُّدِّ فَشَقَّهُ وَهَدَمَهُ وَحَفَرَ الوَادى فارتَفَعَتا عَنِ الجَنْبَتَيْنِ وَغابَ عَنْهُما المَاءُ فَيَبِسَتا وَلَمْ يَكُنِ المَاءُ الأحْمَرُ مِنَ السُّدِّ وَلَكِنْ كانَ عَذَابا أرْسَلَهُ اللهُ عَلَيْهِمْ مِنْ حَيْثُ شاءَ . وَقالَ عَمْرُو بنُ شُرَحْبِيلَ : العَرِمُ : المُسَنَّاةُ بلَحْنِ أهْلِ اليَمَنِ . وَقالَ غَيْرُهُ : العَرِمُ : الوَادى . السَّابِغاتُ : الدُّرُوعُ . وَقالَ مُجاهِدٌ : يُجازَى : يُعاقَبُ . أعِظُكُمْ بِوَاحِدَةٍ : بطاعَةِ اللهِ . مَثْنَى وَفُرَادَى : وَاحِدٌ وَاثْنَيْنِ . التَناوُشُ : الرَّدُّ مِنَ الآخِرَةِ إلى الدُّنْيا . وَبَيْنَ ما يَشْتَهُونَ : مِنْ مالٍ أوْ وَلَدٍ أوْ زَهْرَةٍ . بأشْياعِهِمْ : بأمْثالِهِمْ . وَقالَ ابنُ عَبّاسٍ : كالجوابى : كالجَوْبَةِ مِنَ الأرْضِ . الخَمْطُ الأرَاكُ . والأثْلُ : الطَرْفاءُ . العَرِمُ : الشَّدِيدُ .

(245) CHAPTER, Until when fear is banished from their (angels) hearts, they say: What is it that your Lord said? They say: The Truth, and He is the Most High, the Most Great.'

324. Narrated Abū Huraira ﷺ: Allāh's Prophet ﷺ said, "When Allāh decrees some order in the heaven, the angels flutter their wings indicating complete surrender to His saying which sounds like chains being dragged on rock. And when the (state of) fear is banished from their hearts they say, "What is that your Lord said? They say that He has said that which is true and just, and He is the Most High, the Most Great." (34:23) Then the stealthy listeners (devil) hear this order, and these stealthy listeners are like this, one over the other, (Sufyān, a sub-narrator demonstrated that by holding his hand upright and separating the fingers. A stealthy listener hears a word which he will convey to that which is below him and the second will convey it to that who is below him till the last of them will convey it to the wizard or foreteller. Sometimes a flame (fire) may strike the devil before he can convey it, and sometimes he may convey it before the flame (fire) strikes him whereupon the wizard adds to that word a hundred lies. The people will then say, "Didn't he (i.e. magician) tell such-and-such a thing on such-and-such date?' So that magician is said to have told the truth because of the Statement which has been heard from the heavens."

باب - حَتَّى إِذَا فُزِّعَ عَنْ قُلُوبِهِمْ قَالُوا مَاذَا قَالَ رَبُّكُمْ قَالُوا الحَقَّ وَهُوَ العَلِيُّ الكَبِيرُ -

٣٢٤ - حدَّثنا الحُمَيْدِيُّ: حدَّثنا سُفْيَانُ: حدَّثنا عَمْرٌو قالَ، سَمِعْتُ عِكْرِمَةَ يَقُولُ سَمِعْتُ أبا هُرَيْرَةَ يَقُولُ: إنَّ نَبِيَّ اللهِ صلى اللهُ عليهِ وسلَّم قالَ: إذَا قَضَى اللهُ الأمْرَ فِي السَّمَاءِ ضَرَبَتِ المَلَائِكَةُ بِأَجْنِحَتِها خُضْعَانًا لِقَوْلِهِ كَأَنَّهُ سِلْسِلَةٌ عَلَى صَفْوَانٍ فإِذَا فُزِّعَ عَنْ قُلُوبِهِمْ قَالُوا مَاذَا قَالَ رَبُّكُمْ، قَالُوا: الَّذِي قَالَ الحَقُّ. وَهُوَ العَلِيُّ الكَبِيرُ فَيَسْمَعُهَا مُسْتَرِقُ السَّمْعِ وَمُسْتَرِقُوا السَّمْعِ هَكَذَا بَعْضُهُ فَوْقَ بَعْضٍ. وَصَفَهُ سُفْيَانُ بِكَفِّهِ فَحَرَّفَهَا وَبَدَّدَ بَيْنَ أَصَابِعِهِ. فَيَسْمَعُ الكَلِمَةَ فَيُلْقِيهَا إلى مَنْ تَحْتَهُ ثُمَّ يُلْقِيهَا الآخَرُ إلى مَنْ تَحْتَهُ حَتَّى يُلْقِيهَا عَلَى لِسَانِ السَّاحِرِ أَوِ الكَاهِنِ. فَرُبَّمَا أَدْرَكَ الشِّهَابُ قَبْلَ أَنْ يُلْقِيَهَا. وربما أَلْقَاهَا قَبْلَ أَنْ يُدْرِكَهُ فَيَكْذِبُ مَعَهَا مِائَةَ كَذْبَةٍ فَيُقَالُ: أَلَيْسَ قَدْ قَالَ لَنَا يَوْمَ كَذَا وَكَذَا كَذَا وَكَذَا؟ فَيُصَدَّقُ بِتِلْكَ الكَلِمَةِ الَّتِي سُمِعَتْ مِنَ السَّمَاءِ.

(246) CHAPTER. 'He is only a warner to you in face of a severe torment.'

(34:46)

باب - إن هو إلا نذير لكم بين يدى عذاب شديد -.

325. Narrated Ibn 'Abbās : One day the Prophet ascended Ṣafā mountain and said, "Oh Ṣabāḥāh! " (1) All the Quraish gathered round him and said, "What is the matter?" He said, Look, if I told you that an enemy is going to attack you in the morning or in the evening, would you not believe me?" They said, "Yes, we will believe you." He said, "I am a warner to you in face of a terrible punishment." On that Abū Lahab said, "May you perish! Is it for this thing that you have gathered us?" So Allāh revealed:

'Perish the hands of Abū Lahab!
......

(111:1)

٣٢٥ - حدثنا على بن عبد الله: حدثنا محمد بن حازم: حدثنا الأعمش: عن عمرو بن مرة، عن سعيد بن جبير، عن ابن عباس رضى الله عنهما قال: صعد النبى صلى الله عليه وسلم الصفا ذات يوم فقال: يا صباحاه، فاجتمعت إليه قريش قالوا: مالك؟ قال أرأيتم لو أخبرتكم أن العدو يصبحكم أو يمسيكم أما كنتم تصدقونى؟ قالوا: بلى. قال: فإنى نذير لكم بين يدى عذاب شديد. فقال أبو لهب: تبا لك، ألهذا جمعتنا؟ فأنزل الله - تبت يدا أبى لهب -.

SŪRAT-AL-MALĀ'IKA XXXV
(The Angels)
(also called Sūrat-Fāṭir)
The Originator of Creation

سورة الملائكة

In the Name of Allāh, the Most Beneficent, the Most Merciful

بسم الله الرحمن الرحيم

القطمير: لفافة النواة. مثقلة: مثقلة. وقال غيره: الحرور بالنهار

(1) An expression used for calling to assemble because of an emergency.

(No Ḥadīṯhs are mentioned here)

مَعَ الشَّمْسِ. وَقَالَ ابْنُ عَبَّاسٍ: الحَرُورُ بِاللَّيْلِ. وَالسَّمُومُ بِالنَّهَارِ. وَغَرَابِيبُ سُودٌ: أَشَدُّ سَوَادًا. الغِرْبِيبُ.

SŪRAT YĀSĪN XXXVI

سورة يٰس

In the Name of Allāh, the Most Beneficent, the Most Merciful

بِسْمِ اللهِ الرَّحْمَنِ الرَّحِيمِ

وَقَالَ مُجَاهِدٌ: فَعَزَّزْنَا: شَدَّدْنَا. يَا حَسْرَةً عَلَى العِبَادِ: كَانَ حَسْرَةً عَلَيْهِمْ اسْتِهْزَاؤُهُمْ بِالرُّسُلِ - أَنْ تُدْرِكَ القَمَرَ. لَا يَسْتُرُ ضَوْءُ أَحَدِهِمَا ضَوْءَ الآخَرِ، وَلَا يَنْبَغِي لَهُمَا ذَلِكَ. سَابِقُ النَّهَارِ: يَتَطَالَبَانِ حَثِيثَيْنِ نَسْلَخُ: نُخْرِجُ أَحَدَهُمَا مِنَ الآخَرِ وَيَجْرِي كُلُّ وَاحِدٍ مِنْهُمَا مِنْ مِثْلِهِ مِنَ الأَنْعَامِ. فَكِهُونَ: مُعْجَبُونَ. جُنْدٌ مُحْضَرُونَ عِنْدَ الحِسَابِ. وَيُذْكَرُ عَنْ عِكْرِمَةَ: المَشْحُونِ: المُوقَرُ.

وَقَالَ ابنُ عَبَّاسٍ: طَائِرُكُمْ: مَصَائِبُكُمْ. يَنْسِلُونَ: يَخْرُجُونَ. مَرْقَدِنَا: مَخْرَجِنَا. أَحْصَيْنَاهُ: حَفِظْنَاهُ. مَكَانَتِهِمْ وَمَكَانِهِمْ وَاحِدٌ.

(247) CHAPTER. Allāh's Statement: 'And the Sun runs on its fixed course

بَابُ قَوْلِهِ - وَالشَّمْسُ تَجْرِي لِمُسْتَقَرٍّ لَهَا ذَلِكَ تَقْدِيرُ العَزِيزِ

for a term (decreed). That is the decree of the All-Mighty, the All-Knowing.' (36:38)

العَلِيمِ ـ .

326. Narrated Abū Dharr: Once I was with the Prophet ﷺ in the mosque at the time of sunset. The Prophet ﷺ said, "O Abū Dharr! Do you know where the sun sets?" I replied, "Allāh and His Messenger know best." He said, "It goes and prostrates (1) underneath (Allāh's) Throne; and that is Allāh's Statement:—

'And the sun runs on its fixed course for a term (decreed). And that is the decree of All-Mighty, the All-Knowing...........(36:38)

٣٢٦ ـ حدَّثنا أبو نُعَيْمٍ : حدَّثنا الأعْمَشُ ، عَنْ إبْراهيمَ التَّيْمِيِّ ، عَنْ أبيهِ ، عَنْ أبي ذَرٍّ رَضِيَ اللهُ عَنْهُ قالَ : كُنْتُ مَعَ النَّبِيِّ صلى اللهُ عليهِ وسلَّمَ فى المَسْجِدِ عِنْدَ غُرُوبِ الشَّمْسِ فَقالَ : يا أبا ذَرٍّ ، أتَدْرِي أيْنَ تَغْربُ الشَّمْسُ ؟ قُلْتُ : اللهُ ورَسُولُهُ أعْلَمُ ، قالَ : فإنَّها تَذْهَبُ حتَّى تَسْجُدَ تَحْتَ العَرْشِ ، فَذَلكَ قَوْلُهُ تعالىٰ ـ والشَّمْسُ تَجْرِي لِمُسْتَقَرٍّ لهَا ذَلكَ تَقْدِيرُ العَزِيزِ العَلِيمِ ـ .

327. Narrated Abū Dharr: I asked the Prophet ﷺ about the Statement of Allāh:—

'And the sun runs on fixed course for a term (decreed), (36:38)

He said, "Its course is underneath "Allāh's Throne." (Prostration of Sun trees, stars. mentioned in Qur'ān and Ḥadīth does not mean like our prostration but it means that these objects are

٣٢٧ ـ حدَّثنا الحُمَيْدِيُّ : حدَّثنا وكيعٌ : حدَّثنا الأعْمَشُ ، عَنْ إبْراهيمَ التَّيْمِيِّ ، عَنْ أبيهِ ، عَنْ أبي ذَرٍّ قالَ : سألْتُ النَّبِيَّ صلى اللهُ عليهِ وسلَّمَ عَنْ قَوْلِهِ تعالى ـ والشَّمْسُ تَجْرِي لِمُسْتَقَرٍّ لهَا ـ قالَ : مُسْتَقَرُّها تَحْتَ العَرْشِ .

(1) According to the statement of religious scholars "prostration" here means "obedience" (i.e. it obeys Allāh's orders). And in our limited knowledge of geography, it is well known that the Sun is going round the Earth Continuously on its fixed course without stopping, as fixed by Almighty (Allāh) its Creator and that is under His Throne. The Verse. (36:40) They all swim, each in an orbit.

obedient to their Creator (Allāh عز وجل) and they obey for what they have been created for).

SŪRAT-AṢ-ṢAFFĀT XXXVII
(Those ranged in ranks)

**In the Name of Allāh,
the Most Beneficent, the Most Merciful**

سورة الصافات

بِسْمِ اللهِ الرَّحْمَنِ الرَّحِيمِ

وَقَالَ مُجَاهِدٌ - وَيَقْذِفُونَ بِالغَيْبِ مِنْ مَكَانٍ بَعِيدٍ - مِنْ كُلِّ مَكَانٍ - وَيُقْذَفُونَ مِنْ كُلِّ جَانِبٍ دُحُورًا - يُرْمَوْنَ. وَاصِبٌ: دَائِمٌ. لَازِبٌ: لَازِمٌ. تَأْتُونَنَا عَنِ اليَمِينِ: يَعْنِي الحَقَّ، الكُفَّارُ تَقُولُهُ لِلشَّيَاطِينِ. غَوْلٌ: وَجَعُ بَطْنٍ. يُنْزَفُونَ: لَا تَذْهَبُ عُقُولُهُمْ. قَرِينٌ: شَيْطَانٌ. يُهْرَعُونَ: كَهَيْئَةِ الهَرْوَلَةِ. يَزِفُّونَ: النَّسَلَانُ فِي المَشْيِ. وَبَيْنَ الجِنَّةِ نَسَبًا: قَالَ كُفَّارُ قُرَيْشٍ: المَلَائِكَةُ بَنَاتُ اللهِ، وَأُمَّهَاتُهُمْ بَنَاتُ سَرَوَاتِ الجِنِّ. وَقَالَ اللهُ تَعَالَى - وَلَقَدْ عَلِمَتِ الجِنَّةُ إِنَّهُمْ لَمُحْضَرُونَ - سَتُحْضَرُ لِلْحِسَابِ. وَقَالَ ابْنُ عَبَّاسٍ: لَنَحْنُ الصَّافُّونَ: المَلَائِكَةُ. صِرَاطِ الجَحِيمِ: سَوَاءِ الجَحِيمِ وَوَسَطِ الجَحِيمِ. لَشَوْبًا: يُخْلَطُ طَعَامُهُمْ، وَيُسَاطُ بِالحَمِيمِ. مَدْحُورًا: مَطْرُودًا.

بَيْضٌ مَكْنُونٌ: اللُّؤْلُؤُ المَكْنُونُ.-
وَتَرَكْنَا عَلَيْهِ فِي الآخِرِينَ- يُذْكَرُ
بِخَيْرٍ. يَسْتَسْخِرُونَ: يَسْخَرُونَ.
بَعْلاً: رَبًّا. الأَسْبَابُ: السَّمَاءُ.

(248) CHAPTER. The Statement of Allāh ﷻ :–

'Verily! Jonah was one of the Apostles.' (37:139)

بابُ قَوْلِهِ - وَإِنَّ يُونُسَ لَمِنَ المُرْسَلِينَ -.

328. Narrated 'Abdullāh رضي الله عنه : Allāh's Messenger ﷺ said, "Nobody has the right to be better than (Jonah) bin Matta."

٣٢٨ - حدَّثنا قُتَيْبَةُ بنُ سَعِيدٍ: حدَّثنا جَرِيرٌ، عَنِ الأَعْمَشِ، عَنْ أَبِي وَائِلٍ، عَنْ عَبْدِ اللهِ رَضِيَ اللهُ عَنْهُ قالَ: قالَ رَسُولُ اللهِ صلى اللهُ عليهِ وسلَّم: ما يَنْبَغِي لأَحَدٍ أَنْ يَكُونَ خَيْرًا مِنِ ابنِ مَتَّى.

329. Narrated Abū Huraira رضي الله عنه : The Prophet ﷺ said, "He who says that I am better than Jonah bin Matta, tells a lie.'

٣٢٩- حدَّثني إبْرَاهيمُ بنُ المُنْذِرِ: حدَّثنا مُحَمَّدُ بنُ فُلَيْحٍ: حدَّثني أَبي، عَنْ هِلالِ بنِ عَلِيٍّ مِنْ بَنِي عامِرِ بنِ لُؤَيٍّ، عَنْ عَطاءِ بنِ يَسارٍ، عَنْ أَبي هُرَيْرَةَ رَضِيَ اللهُ عَنْهُ، عَنِ النَّبِيِّ صلى اللهُ عليهِ وسلَّم قالَ: مَنْ قالَ أَنا خَيْرٌ مِنْ يُونُسَ بنِ مَتَّى فَقَدْ كَذَبَ.

SŪRAT-ṢĀD XXXVIII

سورة ص

In the Name of Allāh,
the Most Beneficent, the Most Merciful

بِسْمِ اللهِ الرَّحْمَنِ الرَّحِيمِ

330. Narrated Al-Awwām: I asked Muhājid regarding the prostration in Sūrat Ṣād. He said, "Ibn 'Abbās was asked the same question and he said, 'Those are they (the prophets) whom Allāh had Guided.

So follow their guidance."

(6:90)

Ibn 'Abbās used to perform a prostration (on reading this Sūra).

٣٣٠ - حدَّثَنَا مُحَمَّدُ بنُ بَشَّارٍ: حدَّثنا غُنْدَرٌ: حدَّثنا شُعْبَةُ، عَنِ العَوَّامِ قَالَ: سَأَلْتُ مُجَاهِدًا عَنِ السَّجْدَةِ فِى صَ قَالَ: سُئِلَ ابنُ عَبَّاسٍ فَقَالَ - أُولَئِكَ الَّذِينَ هَدَى اللهُ فَبِهُدَاهُمُ اقْتَدِهِ - وكَانَ ابنُ عَبَّاسٍ يَسْجُدُ فِيهَا.

331. Narrated Al-'Awwām: I asked Mujāhid regarding the prostration in Sūrat Ṣād. He said, "I asked Ibn 'Abbās, 'What evidence makes you prostrate?' He said, "Don't you recite:—

'And among his progeny, David and Solomon..... (6:84). Those are they whom Allāh had guided. So follow their guidance.' (6:90)

So David was the one of those prophets whom Prophet (Muḥammad ﷺ) was ordered to follow. David (عليه السلام) prostrated, so Allāh's Messenger (Muḥammad ﷺ) performed this prostration too.'

٣٣١ - حدَّثَنِى مُحَمَّدُ بنُ عَبْدِ اللهِ: حدَّثنا مُحَمَّدُ بنُ عُبَيْدٍ الطَّنَافِسِيُّ، عَنِ العَوَّامِ قَالَ: سَأَلْتُ مُجَاهِدًا عَنْ سَجْدَةِ صَ فَقَالَ: سَأَلْتُ ابنَ عَبَّاسٍ: مِنْ أَيْنَ سَجَدْتَ؟ فَقَالَ: أَوَ مَا تَقْرَأُ: - وَمِنْ ذُرِّيَّتِهِ دَاوُدَ وَسُلَيْمَانَ - أُولَئِكَ الَّذِينَ هَدَى اللهُ فَبِهُدَاهُمُ اقْتَدِهْ - فَكَانَ دَاوُدُ مِمَّنْ أُمِرَ نَبِيُّكُمْ صلى اللهُ عليهِ وسلَّمَ أَنْ يَقْتَدِيَ بِهِ. فَسَجَدَهَا دَاوُدُ عَلَيْهِ السَّلامُ فَسَجَدَهَا رَسُولُ اللهِ صلى اللهُ عليهِ وسلَّمَ. عُجَابٌ: عَجِيبٌ. القِطُّ: الصَّحِيفَةُ. هُوَ هَاهُنَا صَحِيفَةُ الحَسَنَاتِ وَقَالَ مُجَاهِدٌ: فِى عِزَّةٍ: مُعَازِّينَ. المِلَّةُ: الآخِرَةُ: مِلَّةُ قُرَيْشٍ. الاخْتِلاقُ: الكَذِبُ. الأَسْبَابُ:

طُرُقُ السَّمَاءِ فى أبْوَابِهَا. جُنْدٌ مَا هُنَالِكَ مَهْزُومٌ: يعنى قُرَيْشًا. أُولَئِكَ الأَحْزَابُ: القُرُونُ المَاضِيَةُ. فَوَاقٍ: رُجُوعٍ. قِطَّنَا عَذَابَنَا. الصَّافَّاتُ: صُفِنَّ الفَرَسُ. أَتَّخَذْنَاهُمْ سُخْرِيًّا: أَحَطْنَا بِهِمْ. أَتْرَابٌ: أَمْثَالٌ. وَقَالَ ابْنُ عَبَّاسٍ: الأَيْدُ: القُوَّةُ فى العِبَادَةِ. الأَبْصَارُ: البَصَرُ فى أمْرِ اللهِ. حُبَّ الخَيْرِ عَنْ ذِكْرِ رَبِّى: مِنْ ذِكْرِ. طَفِقَ مَسْحًا: يَمْسَحُ أعْرَافَ الخَيْلِ وَعَرَاقِيبَهَا. الأَصْفَادُ: الوَثَاقِ.

(249) CHAPTER. The Statement of Allāh ﷺ :— He said:
'My Lord! Forgive me and bestow on me a kingdom such as shall not belong to any other after me. Verily. You are the Bestower.' (38:35)

بابُ قَوْلِهِ ـ هَبْ لِى مُلْكًا لا يَنْبَغِى لأحَدٍ مِنْ بَعْدِى إنَّكَ أَنْتَ الوَهَّابُ ـ.

(332) Narrated Abū Huraira ﷺ :
The Prophet ﷺ said, "Last night a demon from the Jinns came to me (or the Prophet ﷺ said, a similar sentence) to disturb my prayer, but Allāh gave me the power to overcome him. I intended to tie him to one of the pillars of the mosque till the morning so that all of you could see him, but then I remembered the Statement of my brother Solomon:—
'My Lord! Forgive me and bestow on

٣٣٢ ـ حدَّثَنَا إسْحَاقُ بْنُ إبْرَاهِيمَ: حدَّثَنَا رَوْحٌ وَمُحَمَّدُ بْنُ جَعْفَرٍ، عَنْ شُعْبَةَ، عَنْ مُحَمَّدِ بْنِ زِيَادٍ، عَنْ أَبِى هُرَيْرَةَ، عَنِ النَّبِىِّ صلى الله عليه وسلم قَالَ: إنَّ عِفْرِيتًا مِنَ الجِنِّ تَفَلَّتَ عَلَىَّ البَارِحَةَ، أَوْ كَلِمَةً نَحْوَهَا، لِيَقْطَعَ عَلَىَّ الصَّلَاةَ فَأَمْكَنَنِى اللهُ مِنْهُ

me a kingdom such as shall not belong to any other after me.' (38:35)
The narrator added: Then he (the Prophet ﷺ) dismissed him, rejected.

وأردت أن أربطه إلى سارية من سواري المسجد حتى تصبحوا وتنظروا إليه كلكم فذكرت قول أخي سليمان - رب هب لي ملكا لا ينبغي لأحد من بعدي - قال روح: فرده خاسئا.

(250) CHAPTER. The Statement of Allāh تعالیٰ :–
'Nor am I one of the pretenders (a person who pretends things which do not exist).
(38:86)

باب قوله - وما أنا من المتكلفين -.

333. Narrated Masrūq: We came upon 'Abdullāh bin Mas'ūd and he said "O people! If somebody knows something, he can say it, but if he does not know it, he should say, "Allāh knows better,' for it is a sign of having knowledge to say about something which one does not know, 'Allāh knows better.' Allāh عزّوجلّ said to His Prophet ﷺ :
'Say (O Muḥammad!) No wage do I ask of you for this (Qu'rān) nor am I one of the pretenders (a person who pretends things which do not exist).'
(38:86)
Now I will tell you about Ad-Dukhān (the smoke), Allāh's Messenger ﷺ invited the Quraish to embrace Islam, but they delayed their response. So he said, "O Allāh! Help me against them by sending on them seven years of famine

٣٣٣ - حدثنا قتيبة بن سعيد: حدثنا جرير، عن الأعمش، عن أبي الضحى، عن مسروق قال: دخلنا على عبد الله بن مسعود قال: يا أيها الناس من علم شيئا فليقل به، ومن لم يعلم فليقل الله أعلم، فإن من العلم أن يقول لما لا يعلم: الله أعلم، قال الله عز وجل لنبيه صلى الله عليه وسلم - قل ما أسألكم عليه من أجر وما أنا من المتكلفين - وسأحدثكم عن الدخان. إن رسول الله صلى الله عليه وسلم دعا قريشا إلى الإسلام فأبطئوا عليه فقال: اللهم أعني عليهم بسبع

similar to the seven years of famine of Joseph." So the famine year overtook them and everything was destroyed till they ate dead animals and skins. People started imagining to see smoke between them and the sky because of severe hunger. Allāh عَزَّوَجَلَّ said,

> 'Then watch you for the Day that the sky will bring forth a kind of smoke plainly visible, covering the people. . . This is painful torment.'
>
> (44:10-11)

(So they invoked Allāh) "Our Lord! Remove the punishment from us really we are believers." How can there be an (effectual) reminder for them when a Messenger explaining things clearly, has already come to them? Then they had turned away from him and said: 'One taught (by a human being), a madman?'

> 'We shall indeed remove punishment for a while, but truly, you will revert (to disbelief).'
>
> (44:12-15)

Will the punishment be removed on the Day of Resurrection?" 'Abdullāh added, "The punishment was removed from them for a while but they reverted to disbelief, so Allāh destroyed them on the Day of Badr. Allāh تَعَالَى said:—

> 'The day We shall seize you with a mighty grasp. We will indeed (then) exact retribution "'
>
> (44:16)

كَسَبْعِ يُوسُفَ ، فَأَخَذَتْهُمْ سَنَةٌ فَحَصَّتْ كُلَّ شَيْءٍ حَتَّى أَكَلُوا الْمَيْتَةَ وَالْجُلُودَ حَتَّى جَعَلَ الرَّجُلُ يَرَى بَيْنَهُ وَبَيْنَ السَّمَاءِ دُخَانًا مِنَ الْجُوعِ . قَالَ اللهُ عَزَّ وَجَلَّ ـ فَارْتَقِبْ يَوْمَ تَأْتِي السَّمَاءُ بِدُخَانٍ مُبِينٍ . يَغْشَى النَّاسَ هَذَا عَذَابٌ أَلِيمٌ ـ قَالَ فَدَعَوْا ـ رَبَّنَا اكْشِفْ عَنَّا الْعَذَابَ إِنَّا مُؤْمِنُونَ أَنَّى لَهُمُ الذِّكْرَى وَقَدْ جَاءَهُمْ رَسُولٌ مُبِينٌ . ثُمَّ تَوَلَّوْا عَنْهُ وَقَالُوا مُعَلَّمٌ مَجْنُونٌ . إِنَّا كَاشِفُو الْعَذَابِ قَلِيلاً إِنَّكُمْ عَائِدُونَ ـ أَفَيُكْشَفُ الْعَذَابُ يَوْمَ الْقِيَامَةِ ؟ قَالَ فَكُشِفَ ثُمَّ عَادُوا فِي كُفْرِهِمْ فَأَخَذَهُمُ اللهُ يَوْمَ بَدْرٍ ، قَالَ اللهُ تَعَالَى ـ يَوْمَ نَبْطِشُ الْبَطْشَةَ الْكُبْرَى إِنَّا مُنْتَقِمُونَ ـ .

SŪRAT AZ-ZUMAR XXXIX
(The Crowds)

**In the Name of Allāh,
the Most Beneficent, the Most Merciful**

سورة الزمر

بِسْمِ اللهِ الرَّحْمَنِ الرَّحِيمِ

وَقَالَ مُجَاهِدٌ: ـ أفمَنْ يَتقى بوَجْهِهِ ـ: يجرُّ على وَجْهِهِ فى النَّارِ وَهُوَ قوْلُهُ تعالى ـ أفمَنْ يُلْقَى فى النَّارِ خيرٌ أمْ منْ يأتى آمِنًا يوْمَ القيامَةِ ـ ذى عوَجٍ ـ لَبْسٍ. وَرَجُلاً سَلَما لرَجُلٍ صَالِحا. ويخوِّفُونَكَ بالذينَ منْ دونِهِ: بالأوْثانِ، خوَّلْنا: أعْطَيْنا. وَالذى جاءَ بالصِّدْقِ القُرآن وَصَدَّقَ بهِ المُؤْمن يجئ يوْمَ القيامَةِ، وَقالَ غيرُهُ: مُتَشاكِسُونَ، الرَّجُلُ الشَّكِسُ: العَسِر لا يرْضَى بالإنْصافِ. وَرَجُلاً سِلْما. وَيُقالُ سالما: صَالِحا. اشْمأزَّتْ: نفرَتْ. بِمَفازَتِهِمْ منَ الفوْزِ. حافِّينَ: أطافُوا بهِ، مُطِيفِينَ بِحِفافَيْهِ: بجوَانِبِهِ. مُتَشابِها ليْسَ منَ الاشْتِباهِ وَلَكِنْ يُشْبِهُ بَعْضُهُ بَعْضا فى التَّصْدِيقِ.

(251) CHAPTER. The Statement of Allāh ﷻ :—
'O My slaves who have trangressed against their souls! Despair not of the Mercy of Allāh.'
(39:53)

باب قوْلِهِ ـ يا عِبادِىَ الذينَ أسْرَفُوا على أنْفُسِهِمْ لا تقْنَطُوا منْ رَحْمَةِ اللهِ ـ الآيَة.

334. Narrated Ibn 'Abbās رضي الله عنهما : Some pagans who committed murders in great number and committed illegal

٣٣٤ ـ حدَّثنى إبْراهِيمُ بن مُوسَى: أخبرَنا هِشام بن يوسُفَ: أنَّ ابنَ جُرَيْجٍ

sexual intercourse excessively, came to Muhammad ﷺ and said, "O Muhammad! Whatever you say and invite people to, is good: but we wish if you could inform us whether we can make an expi-ation for our (past evil) deeds."
So the Divine Verses came:—

> Those who invoke not with Allāh any other god, not kill such life as Allāh has forbidden except for just cause, nor commit illegal sexual intercourse.' (25:68)

And there was also revealed:—

> 'Say: O My slaves who have transgressed against their souls! Despair not of the Mercy of Allāh.' (39:53)

أخبرهم: قال يعلى: إن سعيد بن
جبير أخبره عن ابن عباس رضي الله
عنهما: أن أناسا من أهل الشرك كانوا
قد قتلوا وأكثروا، وزنوا وأكثروا
فأتوا محمدا صلى الله عليه وسلم فقالوا
إن الذى تقول وتدعو إليه لحسن
لو تخبرنا أن لما عملنا كفارة
فنزل - والذين لا يدعون مع الله إلها
آخر ولا يقتلون النفس التى حرم الله
إلا بالحق ولا يزنون - ونزل - قل يا
عبادي الذين أسرفوا على أنفسهم
لا تقنطوا من رحمة الله -.

(255) CHAPTER. The Statement of Allāh تعالى :—

> 'No just estimate have they made of Allāh such as due to Him.' (39:67)

باب قوله - وما قدروا الله حق قدره -.

335. Narrated 'Abdullāh رضي الله عنه : A (Jewish) Rabbi came to Allāh's Messenger ﷺ and he said, "O Muhammad! We learn that Allāh will put all the heavens on one finger, and the earths on one finger, and the trees on one finger, and the water and the dust on one finger, and all the other created beings on one finger. Then He will say, 'I am the King.'" Thereupon the Prophet ﷺ smiled so that his pre-molar teeth became visible, and that was the confirmation of the

٣٣٥ - حدثنا آدم: حدثنا شيبان،
عن منصور، عن إبراهيم، عن
عبيدة، عن عبد الله رضي الله عنه
قال: جاء حبر من الأحبار إلى رسول
الله صلى الله عليه وسلم فقال: يا محمد،
إنا نجد أن الله يجعل السموات على
إصبع، والأرضين على إصبع، والشجر
على إصبع، والماء والثرى على

Rabbi. Then Allāh's Messenger ﷺ recited:–

> No just estimate have they made of Allāh such as due to Him. And on the day of Resurrection the whole of the Earth wil be grasped by His Hand, and the Heavens will be rolled up in His Right Hand. Glorified be He, and High is He above all that they associate as partners with Him.' (39 : 67)

صبع ، وسائر الخلائق على إصبع ، فيقول : أنا الملك . فضحك النبي صلى الله عليه وسلم حتى بدت نواجذه تصديقا لقول الحبر . ثم قرأ رسول الله صلى الله عليه وسلم - وما قدروا الله حق قدره - .

(253) CHAPTER. His Statement:–

'On the Day of Resurrection, the whole of the earth will be grasped by His Hand and the heavens will be rolled up in His Right Hand.' (39:67)

باب قوله - والأرض جميعا قبضته يوم القيامة والسموات مطويات بيمينه -

336. Narrated Abū Huraira رضي الله عنه : I heard Allāh's Messenger ﷺ saying, "Allāh will hold the whole earth, and roll all the heavens up in His Right Hand, and then He will say, 'I am the King; where are the kings of the earth?'"

٣٣٦ - حدثنا سعيد بن عفير قال : حدثني الليث قال : حدثني عبد الرحمن بن خالد بن مسافر ، عن ابن شهاب ، عن أبي سلمة : أن أبا هريرة قال : سمعت رسول الله صلى الله عليه وسلم يقول : يقبض الله الأرض ويطوي السموات بيمينه ثم يقول : أنا الملك ، أين ملوك الأرض ؟ .

(254) CHAPTER. The Statement of Allāh تعالى :–

'And the trumpet will be blown; and all who are in the heavens, and all who are on earth will swoon away except him whom Allāh wills.....' (39:68)

باب قوله - ونفخ في الصور فصعق من في السموات ومن في الأرض إلا من شاء الله - الآية .

337. Narrated Abū Huraira رضي الله عنه : The Prophet ﷺ said, "I will be the first to raise my head after the second blowing of the trumpet and will see Moses clinging to the Throne, and I will not know whether he had been in that state all the time or after the blowing of the trumpet."

٣٣٧ - حدَّثني الحسَنُ : حدَّثنا إسماعيلُ بنُ خَليلٍ : أخبرَنا عبدُ الرَّحيمِ ، عَنْ زكَرِيَّاءَ بنِ أبي زائدةَ ، عَنْ عامرٍ ، عَنْ أبي هُرَيرةَ رَضيَ اللهُ عنهُ ، عَنِ النَّبيِّ صلى اللهُ عليه وسلَّم قالَ : إني مِنْ أوَّلِ مَنْ يرفَعُ رأسَهُ بعدَ النفخَةِ الآخِرَةِ ، فإذا أنا بِموسَى مُتعلِّقٌ بالعرشِ فلا أدري أكَذلكَ كانَ أمْ بعدَ النفخَةِ ؟.

338. Narrated Abū Huraira رضي الله عنه : The Prophet ﷺ said, "Between the two blowings of the trumpet there will be forty." The people said, "O Abū Huraira! Forty days?" I refused to reply. They said, "Forty years?" I refused to reply and added: Everything of the human body will decay except the coccyx bone (of the tail) and from that bone Allāh will reconstruct the whole body.

٣٣٨ - حدَّثنا عُمَرُ بنُ حفْصٍ : حدَّثنا أبي: حدَّثنا الأعمَشُ قالَ : سَمِعتُ أبا صالحٍ قالَ : سَمِعتُ أبا هُرَيرةَ عَنِ النَّبيِّ صلى اللهُ عليه وسلَّم قالَ : ما بَينَ النفخَتَينِ أربَعونَ . قالُوا : يا أبا هُرَيرَةَ ، أربَعونَ يوماً ؟ قالَ : أبَيتُ ، قالَ : أربَعونَ سَنَةً ؟ قالَ : أبَيتُ : قالَ : أربَعونَ شهراً ؟ قالَ : أبَيتُ . ويَبلَى كلُّ شيءٍ منَ الإنسانِ إلاَّ عَجْبَ ذَنَبِهِ فيهِ يُركَّبُ الخَلْقُ .

SŪRAT-AL-MU'MIN
(The Believer) XL

سورة المؤمن

In the Name of Allāh, the Most Beneficent, the Most Merciful

بِسْمِ اللهِ الرحمٰنِ الرَّحيمِ

قالَ مُجاهِدٌ : مَجازُها مَجازُ أوائلِ

السُّوَرِ : وَيُقالُ بَلْ هُوَ اسْمٌ لِقَوْلِ
شُرَيْحِ بنِ أبي أوْفى العَبْسِيِّ :
يُذَكِّرُني حاميمَ والرُّمْحُ شاجِرٌ
فَهَلاَّ تَلا حاميمَ قَبْلَ التَّقَدُّمِ ؟
الطَّوْلُ : التَّفَضُّلُ ، داخِرينَ :
خاضِعينَ . وَقالَ مُجاهِدٌ : إلى النَّجاةِ :
الإيمانِ . لَيْسَ لَهُ دَعْوَةٌ : يَعْني الوَثَنَ .
يُسْجَرُونَ : تُوقَدُ بِهِمُ النّارُ .
تَمْرَحُونَ : تَبْطَرُونَ . وَكانَ العَلاءُ بنُ
زِيادٍ يُذَكِّرُ النّارَ ، فَقالَ رَجُلٌ : لِمَ
تُقَنِّطُ النّاسَ ؟ قالَ : وأنا أقْدِرُ أنْ أُقَنِّطَ
النّاسَ ، وَاللهُ عَزَّ وَجَلَّ يَقُولُ - يا
عِبادِيَ الَّذينَ أسْرَفُوا عَلى أنْفُسِهِمْ لا
تَقْنَطُوا مِنْ رَحْمَةِ اللهِ - وَيَقُولُ : وإنَّ
المُسْرِفينَ هُمْ أصْحابُ النّارِ -
وَلٰكِنَّكُمْ تُحِبُّونَ أنْ تُبَشَّرُوا بالجَنَّةِ
عَلى مَساوِئِ أعْمالِكُمْ ، وإنَّما بَعَثَ
مُحَمَّدًا صلى اللهُ عليهِ وسلَّمَ مُبَشِّرًا بالجَنَّةِ
لِمَنْ أطاعَهُ ، وَمُنْذِرًا بالنّارِ لِمَنْ
عَصاهُ .

339. Narrated 'Urwa bin Az-Zubair: I asked 'Abdullāh bin 'Amr bin Al-'Āṣ to inform me of the worst thing the pagans had done to Allāh's Messenger ﷺ. He said: "While Allāh's Messenger ﷺ was praying in the courtyard of the Ka'ba, 'Uqba bin Abī Mu'aiṭ came and seized Allāh's Messenger ﷺ by the shoulder

٣٣٩ - حَدَّثَنا عَلِيُّ بنُ عَبْدِ اللهِ :
حَدَّثَنا الوَليدُ بنُ مُسْلِمٍ : حَدَّثَنا الأوْزاعيُّ
قالَ : حَدَّثَني يَحْيى بنُ أبي كَثيرٍ قالَ :
حَدَّثَني مُحَمَّدُ بنُ إبْراهيمَ التَّيْميُّ :
حَدَّثَني عُرْوَةُ بنُ الزُّبَيْرِ قالَ : قُلْتُ

and twisted his garment round his neck and throttled him severely. Abū Bakr came and seized 'Uqba's shoulder and threw him away from Allāh's Messenger ﷺ and said, "Would you kill a man because he says: 'My Lord is Allāh,' and has come to you with clear Signs from your Lord?' " (40:28)

لِعَبْدِ اللهِ بنِ عَمْرِو بنِ العاصِ : أَخْبِرْنِى بِأَشَدِّ ما صَنَعَ المُشْرِكُونَ بِرَسُولِ اللهِ صلى اللهُ عليه وسلَّم ، قالَ : بَيْنا رَسُولُ اللهِ صلى اللهُ عليه وسلَّم يُصَلِّى بِفِناءِ الكَعْبَةِ إِذْ أَقْبَلَ عُقْبَةُ بنُ أَبِى مُعَيْطٍ فأَخَذَ بِمَنْكِبِ رَسُولِ اللهِ صلى اللهُ عليه وسلَّم وَلَوَى ثَوْبَهُ فى عُنُقِهِ فَخَنَقَهُ خَنْقًا شَدِيدًا . فأَقْبَلَ أبو بَكْرٍ . فأَخَذَ بِمَنْكِبِهِ وَدَفَعَ عَنْ رَسُولِ اللهِ صلى اللهُ عليه وسلَّم وَقالَ ـ أَتَقْتُلُونَ رَجُلًا أَنْ يَقُولَ رَبِّىَ اللهُ وَقَدْ جاءَكُمْ بالبَيِّناتِ مِنْ رَبِّكُمْ .

SŪRAT ḤĀ MĪM (The Prostration) OR SURAT-FUṢṢILAT XLI

سورة حم السجدة

In the Name of Allāh, the Most Beneficent, the Most Merciful

بِسْمِ اللهِ الرَّحْمَنِ الرَّحِيمِ

وَقالَ طاوُسٌ عَنِ ابنِ عَبَّاسٍ ـ ائْتِيا طَوْعًا أَوْ كَرْهًا ـ أَعْطِيا ـ قالَتا أَتَيْنا طائِعِينَ ـ أَعْطَيْنا .

(255) CHAPTER. Sa'īd said: A man said to Ibn 'Abbās, "I find in the Qur'ān certain things which seem to me contradictory, for example Allāh says:—

> 'There will be no Kinship between them that Day, nor will they ask of one another.' (23: 101)

(yet He says:)

> 'And they will turn to one another and question one another.'
>
> (37: 27)

وَقالَ المِنْهالُ : عَنْ سَعِيدٍ قالَ : قالَ رَجُلٌ لابنِ عَبَّاسٍ : إِنِّى أَجِدُ فى القُرْآنِ أَشْياءَ تَخْتَلِفُ عَلَىَّ ، قالَ ـ فَلا أَنْسابَ بَيْنَهُمْ يَوْمَئِذٍ وَلا يَتَساءَلُونَ ـ وأَقْبَلَ بَعْضُهُمْ عَلَى بَعْضٍ يَتَساءَلُونَ ـ وَلا يَكْتُمُونَ اللهَ حَدِيثًا ـ رَبَّنا ما كُنّا مُشْرِكِينَ ـ فَقَدْ

Allāh says:—

> 'But they will never be able to hide a single fact from Allāh.' (4:42)

(Yet He reports what the pagans will say:)

> '(By Allāh) our Lord, we were not those who joined others in worship with Allāh.' (6:23)

According to this Verse, they will hide some facts. Allāh says:—

> 'Are you the more difficult to create, or is the heaven that He constructed? .... And after that He spreaded the earth.' (79:27&30)

In this Verse He mentions the creation of the heavens before the creation of the earth. Then He says: "Say (O Muḥammad) :—

> 'Do you verily disbelieve in Him Who created the earth in two days (periods) .... obedient." (41:9-11)

So He mentions in this Verse the creation of the earth before the sky. And He says:

> 'And Allāh is Oft-Forgiving, Most Merciful.' (4:23)
>
> '(Allāh) is All-Mighty, All-Wise.' (4:56)
>
> 'Allāh is All Hearer, All-Seer.' (4:58)

This seems to be something that was and has passed." Then Ibn 'Abbās answered, "There will be no relationship between them.' that is on the first blowing of the Trumpet. So the Trumpet will be blown whereupon all that are in the Heavens and on the earth will swoon, except those whom Allāh will exempt" (39:68) Then 'there will be no relationship between them, and at that time one will not ask another. Then, when the Trumpet will be

كَتَمُوا فى هَذِهِ الآيَةِ ، وَقَالَ - أَمِ السَّمَاءُ
بَنَاهَا - إِلَى قَوْلِهِ - دَحَاهَا - فَذَكَرَ خَلْقَ
السَّمَاءِ قَبْلَ خَلْقِ الأَرْضِ ، ثُمَّ قَالَ -
إِنَّكُمْ لَتَكْفُرُونَ بِالَّذِى خَلَقَ الأَرْضَ
فى يَوْمَيْنِ إِلَى - طَائِعِينَ - فَذَكَرَ فى هَذِهِ
خَلْقَ الأَرْضِ قَبْلَ السَّمَاءِ . وَقَالَ -
وَكَانَ اللهُ غَفُورًا رَحِيمًا - عَزِيزًا حَكِيمًا -
سَمِيعًا بَصِيرًا - فَكَأَنَّهُ كَانَ ثُمَّ مَضَى .
فَقَالَ - فَلا أَنْسَابَ بَيْنَهُمْ - فى النَّفْخَةِ
الأُولَى ، ثُمَّ يُنْفَخُ فى الصُّورِ - فَصَعِقَ
مَنْ فى السَّمَوَاتِ وَمَنْ فى الأَرْضِ إِلاَّ
مَنْ شَاءَ اللهُ فَلا أَنْسَابَ بَيْنَهُمْ - عِنْدَ
ذَلِكَ وَلا يَتَسَاءَلُونَ . ثُمَّ فى النَّفْخَةِ
الآخِرَةِ - أَقْبَلَ بَعْضُهُمْ عَلَى بَعْضٍ
يَتَسَاءَلُونَ - وَأَمَّا قَوْلُهُ - مَا كُنَّا
مُشْرِكِينَ - وَلا يَكْتُمُونَ اللهَ - فَإِنَّ
اللهَ يَغْفِرُ لأَهْلِ الإِخْلاصِ ذُنُوبَهُمْ .
وَقَالَ الْمُشْرِكُونَ تَعَالَوْا نَقُولُ لَمْ
نَكُنْ مُشْرِكِينَ فَخَتَمَ عَلَى أَفْوَاهِهِمْ
فَتَنْطِقُ أَيْدِيهِمْ ، فَعِنْدَ ذَلِكَ عَرَفَ
أَنَّ اللهَ لا يُكْتَمُ حَدِيثًا ، وَعِنْدَهُ - يَوَدُّ
الَّذِينَ كَفَرُوا - الآيَةَ . وَخَلَقَ الأَرْضَ
فى يَوْمَيْنِ ثُمَّ خَلَقَ السَّمَاءَ ، ثُمَّ اسْتَوَى
إِلَى السَّمَاءِ فَسَوَّاهُنَّ فى يَوْمَيْنِ آخَرَيْنِ .
ثُمَّ دَحَا الأَرْضَ . وَدَحْوُهَا أَنْ أَخْرَجَ
مِنْهَا الْمَاءَ وَالْمَرْعَى . وَخَلَقَ الْجِبَالَ
وَالْجِمَالَ وَالآكَامَ وَمَا بَيْنَهُمَا فى يَوْمَيْنِ

blown for the second time.' they will turn to one another and question one another.' As for His Statement: 'We never worshipped others besides Allāh," 'But they will not be able to hide a single fact from Allāh,' Allāh will forgive the sins of those who were sincere in their worship, whereupon the pagans will say (to each other), 'Come let's say we never worshipped others besides Allāh.' But their mouths will be sealed and their hands will speak (the truth). At that time it will be evident that no speech can be concealed from Allāh, and those who disbelieved (and disobeyed the Messenger ﷺ) will wish (that they were level with the ground, but they will never be able to hide a single fact from Allāh). (4:42). Allāh created the earth in two days and then created the heavens, then He turned towards the Heavens and gave it perfection in two (other) days. Then he spread the earth, and its spreading means the bringing of water and pasture out of it. He then created the mountains, the camels and the hillocks and whatever is inbetween them (the earth and the heaven) in two (other) days. That is the meaning of Allāh's saying: 'He spread it,' And His Saying: And He created the earth in two days.' So the earth and whatever is on it, was created in four days; and the heavens were created in two days. (Concerning His Saying:) And Allāh was Oft-Forgiving.' He named Himself like that (so the naming has passed) but the contents of His saying is still valid, for if Allāh ever wants to do something. He surely fulfils what He wants. So you should not see contradiction in the Qur'ān, for all of it is from Allāh."

آخَرَيْنِ ، فَذَلِكَ قَوْلُهُ دَحَاهَا . وَقَوْلُهُ
خَلَقَ الأَرْضَ فِي يَوْمَيْنِ فَجُعِلَتِ
الأَرْضُ وَمَا فِيهَا مِنْ شَيْءٍ فِي أَرْبَعَةِ
أَيَّامٍ . وَخُلِقَتِ السَّمَوَاتُ فِي يَوْمَيْنِ .
وَكَانَ اللهُ غَفُورًا . سَمَّى نَفْسَهُ ذَلِكَ ،
وَذَلِكَ قَوْلُهُ ، أَيْ لَمْ يَزَلْ كَذَلِكَ فَإِنَّ اللهَ
لَمْ يُرِدْ شَيْئًا إِلَّا أَصَابَ بِهِ الَّذِي أَرَادَ ،
فَلَا يَخْتَلِفْ عَلَيْكَ الْقُرْآنُ ، فَإِنَّ كُلًّا
مِنْ عِنْدِ اللهِ . حَدَّثَنِيهِ يُوسُفُ بْنُ
عَدِيٍّ : حَدَّثَنَا عُبَيْدُ اللهِ بْنُ عَمْرٍو ،
عَنْ زَيْدِ بْنِ أَبِي أُنَيْسَةَ . عَنِ الْمِنْهَالِ
بِهَذَا . وَقَالَ مُجَاهِدٌ - لَهُمْ أَجْرٌ غَيْرُ
مَمْنُونٍ - مَحْسُوبٍ . أَقْوَاتَهَا : أَرْزَاقَهَا .
فِي كُلِّ سَمَاءٍ أَمْرَهَا مِمَّا أُمِرَ بِهِ . نَحِسَاتٍ :
مَشَايِيمَ . وَقَيَّضْنَا لَهُمْ قُرَنَاءَ تَتَنَزَّلُ
عَلَيْهِمُ الْمَلَائِكَةُ عِنْدَ الْمَوْتِ . اهْتَزَّتْ
بِالنَّبَاتِ وَرَبَتْ : ارْتَفَعَتْ . وَقَالَ
غَيْرُهُ : مِنْ أَكْمَامِهَا حِينَ تَطْلُعُ
لَيَقُولَنَّ هَذَا لِي : أَيْ بِعِلْمِي أَنَا مَحْقُوقٌ
بِهَذَا . وَقَالَ غَيْرُهُ - سَوَاءً لِلسَّائِلِينَ -
قَدَّرَهَا سَوَاءً - فَهَدَيْنَاهُمْ - دَلَلْنَاهُمْ
عَلَى الْخَيْرِ وَالشَّرِّ ، كَقَوْلِهِ - وَهَدَيْنَاهُ
النَّجْدَيْنِ - وَكَقَوْلِهِ - هَدَيْنَاهُ السَّبِيلَ -
وَالْهُدَى الَّذِي هُوَ الْإِرْشَادُ بِمَنْزِلَةِ
أَسْعَدْنَاهُ ، مِنْ ذَلِكَ قَوْلُهُ - أُولَئِكَ
الَّذِينَ هَدَى اللهُ فَبِهُدَاهُمُ اقْتَدِهْ -
يُوزَعُونَ : يُكَفُّونَ . مِنْ أَكْمَامِهَا :

قِشْرُ الكُفُرَّى الكُمُّ . وَقَالَ غَيْرُهُ : وَيُقَالُ لِلعِنَبِ إِذَا خَرَجَ أَيْضًا كَافُورٌ وَكُفُرَّى . وَلِيٌّ حَمِيمٌ : القَرِيبُ . مِنْ مَحِيصٍ : حَاصَ عَنْهُ : حَادَ عَنْهُ . مِرْيَةٌ وَمُرْيَةٌ وَاحِدٌ : أَيِ امْتِرَاءٌ . وَقَالَ مُجَاهِدٌ . اعْمَلُوا مَا شِئْتُمْ : الوَعِيدُ . وَقَالَ ابنُ عَبَّاسٍ - بِالَّتِي هِيَ أَحْسَنُ - الصَّبْرُ عِنْدَ الغَضَبِ وَالعَفْوُ عِنْدَ الإِسَاءَةِ فَإِذَا فَعَلُوهُ عَصَمَهُمُ اللهُ وَخَضَعَ لَهُمْ عَدُوُّهُمْ - كَأَنَّهُ وَلِيٌّ حَمِيمٌ - .

(256) CHAPTER. The Statement of Allāh تعالى :–

'And you have not been screening against yourself, lest your ears, and your eyes, and your skins should testify against you. (41:22)

بَابُ قَوْلِهِ - وَمَا كُنْتُمْ تَسْتَتِرُونَ أَنْ يَشْهَدَ عَلَيْكُمْ سَمْعُكُمْ وَلَا أَبْصَارُكُمْ - الآيَةَ .

340. Narrated Ibn Mas'ūd (regarding) the Verse:–

'And you have not been screening against yourself lest your ears, and your eyes and your skins should testify against you.........' (41: 22)

While two persons from Quraish and their brother-in-law from Thaqif (or two

٣٤٠ - حَدَّثَنَا الصَّلْتُ بنُ مُحَمَّدٍ : حَدَّثَنَا يَزِيدُ بنُ زُرَيْعٍ ، عَنْ رَوْحِ بنِ القَاسِمِ عَنْ مَنْصُورٍ ، عَنْ مُجَاهِدٍ ، عَنْ أَبِي مَعْمَرٍ ، عَنِ ابنِ مَسْعُودٍ - وَمَا كُنْتُمْ تَسْتَتِرُونَ أَنْ يَشْهَدَ عَلَيْكُمْ سَمْعُكُمْ - الآيَةَ ، كَانَ رَجُلَانِ مِنْ

persons from Thaqīf and their brother-in-law from Quraish) were in a house, they said to each other, "Do you think that Allāh hears our talks?" Some said, "He hears a portion thereof" Others said, "If He can hear a portion of it, He can hear all of it." Then the following Verse was revealed:—

> 'And you have not been screeening against yourself lest your ears, and your eyes and your skins should testify against you....... (41:22)

قُرَيْشٍ وَخَتَنٌ لَهُما مِنْ ثَقِيفٍ . أَوْ رَجُلانِ مِنْ ثَقِيفٍ وَخَتَنٌ لَهُما مِنْ قُرَيْشٍ فِي بَيْتٍ ، فَقالَ بَعْضُهُمْ لِبَعْضٍ : أَتَرَوْنَ أَنَّ اللهَ يَسْمَعُ حَدِيثَنا؟ قالَ بَعْضُهُمْ : يَسْمَعُ بَعْضَهُ ، وَقالَ بَعْضُهُمْ : لَئِنْ كانَ يَسْمَعُ بَعْضَهُ لَقَدْ يَسْمَعُ كُلَّهُ ، فَأُنْزِلَتْ ـ وَما كُنْتُمْ تَسْتَتِرُونَ أَنْ يَشْهَدَ عَلَيْكُمْ سَمْعُكُمْ وَلا أَبْصارُكُمْ ـ الآيَةَ .

(257) CHAPTER. The Statement of Allāh :—

> 'And that thought of yours which you thought about your Lord, has brought you to destruction, and you have become (this Day) of those utterly lost.' (41:23)

بابٌ قَوْلُهُ ـ وَذَلِكُمْ ظَنُّكُمُ الَّذِي ظَنَنْتُمْ بِرَبِّكُمْ أَرْداكُمْ فَأَصْبَحْتُمْ مِنَ الخاسِرِينَ ـ

341. Narrated 'Abdullāh : There gathered near the House (i.e. the Ka'ba) two Quraishī persons and a person from Thaqīf (or two persons from Thaqīf and one from Quraish), and all of them with very fat bellies but very little intelligence. One of them said, "Do you think that Allāh hears what we say?" Another said, "He hears us when we talk in a loud voice, but He doesn't hear us when we talk in a low tone." The third said, "If He can hear when we talk in a loud tone, then He can also hear when we speak in a low tone." Then

٣٤١ ـ حَدَّثَنا الحُمَيْدِيُّ : حَدَّثَنا سُفْيانُ : حَدَّثَنا مَنْصُورٌ ، عَنْ مُجاهِدٍ ، عَنْ أَبِي مَعْمَرٍ ، عَنْ عَبْدِ اللهِ رَضِيَ اللهُ عَنْهُ قالَ : اجْتَمَعَ عِنْدَ البَيْتِ قُرَشِيّانِ وَثَقَفِيٌّ ، أَوْ ثَقَفِيّانِ وَقُرَشِيٌّ كَثِيرَةٌ شَحْمُ بُطُونِهِمْ . قَلِيلَةٌ فِقْهُ قُلُوبِهِمْ . فَقالَ أَحَدُهُمْ : أَتَرَوْنَ أَنَّ اللهَ يَسْمَعُ ما نَقُولُ؟ قالَ الآخَرُ : يَسْمَعُ إِنْ جَهَرْنا وَلا يَسْمَعُ إِنْ أَخْفَيْنا . وَقالَ الآخَرُ :

Allāh, the Honourable, the Majestic revealed:—

> 'And you have not been screening against yourself lest your ears, and your eyes and your skins should testify against you......'
> (41:22-23)

إنْ كانَ يَسْمَعُ إذا جَهَرْنا فإنَّهُ يَسْمَعُ إذا أخفَيْنا . فأنزلَ اللهُ عزَّ وجلَّ ـ وما كُنْتُمْ تَسْتَتِرُونَ أنْ يَشْهَدَ عَلَيْكُمْ سَمْعُكُمْ ولا أبْصارُكُمْ ولا جُلُودُكُمْ ـ الآيَةَ ، وكانَ سُفْيانُ يُحَدِّثُنا بِهذا فيَقُولُ : حدَّثَنا منصُورٌ أو ابنُ أبي نَجيحٍ أو حُمَيْدٌ أحَدُهُمْ أو اثنانِ منهُمْ ثُمَّ ثَبَتَ على منصُورٍ وتَرَكَ ذلكَ مِراراً غيرَ واحِدَةٍ .

(258) CHAPTER. The Statement of Allāh تعالى :—

> 'Then if they have patience, yet the Fire will be a Home for them. ....'
> (41:24)

باب قَوْلُهُ ـ فإنْ يَصْبِرُوا فالنَّارُ مَثْوًى لَهُمْ ـ الآيَة .

342. Narrated 'Abdullāh (bin Mas'ūd): (As above, Ḥadīth No. 341).

٣٤٢ ـ حدَّثَنا عَمْرُو بنُ عَلِيّ : حدَّثَنا يَحْيَى : حدَّثَنا سُفْيانُ قالَ : حدَّثَني منصُورٌ ، عنْ مُجاهِدٍ ، عنْ أبي مَعْمَرٍ ، عنْ عَبْدِ اللهِ بنَحْوِهِ .

SŪRAT-ASH-SHŪRĀ
SŪRAT-ḤĀ MĪM 'AIN SĪN, QĀF (XLII)

In the Name of Allāh, the Most Beneficent, the Most Merciful.

سورة حم عسق

بِسْمِ اللهِ الرَّحْمَنِ الرَّحِيمِ

ويُذْكَرُ عنِ ابنِ عبَّاسٍ : عَقِيماً : التي لا تَلِدُ . رُوحاً مِنْ أمْرِنا : القُرآنُ . وقالَ مُجاهِدٌ : يَذْرَؤُكُمْ فيهِ : نَسْلٌ

بَعْدَ نَسْلٍ. لا حُجة بَيْنَنَا: لا خُصُومَةَ بَيْنَنَا وَبَيْنَكُمْ. مِنْ طَرْفٍ خَفِيٍّ: ذَلِيلٍ. وَقَالَ غَيْرُهُ: فَيَظْلَلْنَ رَوَاكِدَ عَلَى ظَهْرِهِ: يَتَحَرَّكْنَ وَلَا يَجْرِينَ فِي الْبَحْرِ. شَرَعُوا: ابْتَدَعُوا.

(259) CHAPTER. The Statement of Allāh ﷻ :–

بابُ قَوْلِهِ - إِلَّا الْمَوَدَّةَ فِي الْقُرْبَى -.

"Except to be kind to me for my Kin-ship with you.' (42:23)

343 Narrated Ibn 'Abbās ﵄ that he was asked (regarding):–

"Except to be kind to me for my Kinship with you.' (42: 23) Sa'īd bin Zubair (who was present then) said, "It means here (to show what is due for) the relatives of Muḥammad ﷺ." On that Ibn 'Abbās said: you have hurried in giving the answer! There was no branch of the tribe of Quraish but the Prophet ﷺ had relatives therein. The Prophet ﷺ said, "I do not want anything from (you) except to be Kind to me for my Kinship with you."

٣٤٣ - حَدَّثَنَا مُحَمَّدُ بْنُ بَشَّارٍ: حَدَّثَنَا مُحَمَّدُ بْنُ جَعْفَرٍ: حَدَّثَنَا شُعْبَةُ، عَنْ عَبْدِ الْمَلِكِ بْنِ مَيْسَرَةَ قَالَ: سَمِعْتُ طَاوُسًا، عَنِ ابْنِ عَبَّاسٍ رَضِيَ اللهُ عَنْهُمَا: أَنَّهُ سُئِلَ عَنْ قَوْلِهِ إِلَّا الْمَوَدَّةَ فِي الْقُرْبَى - فَقَالَ سَعِيدُ بْنُ جُبَيْرٍ: قُرْبَى آلِ مُحَمَّدٍ صلى اللهُ عليهِ وسلَّم. فَقَالَ ابْنُ عَبَّاسٍ: عَجِلْتَ، إِنَّ النَّبِيَّ صلى اللهُ عليهِ وسلَّم لَمْ يَكُنْ بَطْنٌ مِنْ قُرَيْشٍ إِلَّا كَانَ لَهُ فِيهِمْ قَرَابَةٌ، فَقَالَ: إِلَّا أَنْ تَصِلُوا مَا بَيْنِي وَبَيْنَكُمْ مِنَ الْقَرَابَةِ.

SŪRAT ḤĀ MĪM XXXXIII
Az-Zukhruf (Good Adornments)

In the Name of Allāh, the Most Beneficent, the Most Merciful

سورة حم الزخرف

بِسْمِ اللَّهِ الرَّحْمَنِ الرَّحِيمِ

وَقَالَ مُجَاهِدٌ: عَلَى أُمَّةٍ: عَلَى إِمَامٍ
وَقِيلَهُ يَا رَبِّ، تَفْسِيرُهُ: أَيَحْسِبُونَ أَنَّا
لاَ نَسْمَعُ سِرَّهُمْ وَنَجْوَاهُمْ وَلاَ نَسْمَعُ
قِيلَهُمْ. وَقَالَ ابْنُ عَبَّاسٍ: وَلَوْلاَ أَنْ
يَكُونَ النَّاسُ أُمَّةً وَاحِدَةً: لَوْلاَ أَنْ
جَعَلَ النَّاسَ كُلَّهُمْ كُفَّارًا لَجَعَلْتُ
لِبُيُوتِ الْكُفَّارِ سُقُفًا مِنْ فِضَّةٍ
وَمَعَارِجَ مِنْ فِضَّةٍ وَهْيَ دَرَجٌ وَسُرُرُ
فِضَّةٍ. مُقْرِنِينَ: مُطِيقِينَ: آسَفُونَا:
أَسْخَطُونَا. يَعْشُ: يَعْمَى. وَقَالَ مُجَاهِدٌ
- أَفَنَضْرِبُ عَنْكُمُ الذِّكْرَ - أَيْ
تُكَذِّبُونَ بِالْقُرْآنِ ثُمَّ لاَ تُعَاقَبُونَ عَلَيْهِ -
وَمَضَى مَثَلُ الأَوَّلِينَ - سُنَّةُ الأَوَّلِينَ.
مُقْرِنِينَ: يَعْنِي الإِبِلَ وَالْخَيْلَ وَالْبِغَالَ
وَالْحَمِيرَ. يَنْشَأُ فِي الْحِلْيَةِ: الْجَوَارِي
جَعَلْتُمُوهُنَّ لِلرَّحْمَنِ وَلَدًا، فَكَيْفَ
تَحْكُمُونَ؟ لَوْ شَاءَ الرَّحْمَنُ مَا
عَبَدْنَاهُمْ: يَعْنُونَ الأَوْثَانَ، يَقُولُ اللَّهُ
تَعَالَى - مَا لَهُمْ بِذَلِكَ مِنْ عِلْمٍ - الأَوْثَانُ
إِنَّهُمْ لاَ يَعْلَمُونَ. فِي عَقِبِهِ: وَلَدِهِ.
مُقْتَرِنِينَ: يَمْشُونَ مَعًا. سَلَفًا: قَوْمُ
فِرْعَوْنَ سَلَفًا لِكُفَّارِ أُمَّةِ مُحَمَّدٍ صلى
الله عليه وسلم. وَمَثَلاً: عِبْرَةً. يَصِدُّونَ:
يَضِجُّونَ. مُبْرِمُونَ: مُجْمِعُونَ. أَوَّلُ
الْعَابِدِينَ: أَوَّلُ الْمُؤْمِنِينَ. وَقَالَ غَيْرُهُ:

إنني براءٌ ممّا تعبدون: العرب تقول نحن منك البراء والخلاء والواحدُ والاثنان والجميعُ من المذكّر والمؤنث، يقال فيه براءٌ لأنه مصدرٌ. ولو قال بريءٌ لقيل في الاثنين بريئان وفي الجميع بريئون. وقرأ عبد الله إنني بريٌ بالياء. والزخرف: الذهب. ملائكة يخلفون: يخلف بعضهم بعضًا.

(260) CHAPTER. The Statement of Allāh ﷻ:—

"They will cry, 'O Mālik (Keeper of Hell)! Let your Lord make an end of us?' He will say, 'Nay but you shall abide." (43:77)

باب قوله ـ ونادَوْا يا مالكُ ليقضِ علينا ربُّك قال إنَّكم ما كِثون ـ.

344. Narrated Ya'lā: I heard the Prophet ﷺ reciting when on the pulpit:

'They will cry, "O Mālik (Keeper of Hell) Let your Lord make an end of us.' (43:77)

٣٤٤ ـ حدَّثنا حجَّاجُ بن مِنهال: حدَّثنا سفيانُ بن عُيينة، عن عَمْرو، عن عطاء، عن صفوان بن يعلى، عن أبيه قال: سمعتُ النبيَّ صلى الله عليه وسلَّم يقرأُ على المنبر ـ ونادَوا يا مالك ليقضِ علينا ربُّك ـ. وقال قتادةُ: مَثَلًا للآخرين: عِظةً لمن بعدهم. وقال غيرُه: مُقْرنين: ضابطين، يقال فلان مُقْرنٌ لفلان: ضابطٌ له. والأكوابُ: الأباريق التي لا خراطيم

لهَا ، وَقَالَ قَتَادَةُ : فى أُمِّ الكِتَابِ :
جُمْلَةِ الكِتَابِ ، أَصْلِ الكِتَابِ . أَوَّلُ
العَابِدِينَ : أَيْ مَا كَانَ فَأَنَا أَوَّلُ الآنِفِينَ
وَهُمَا لُغَتَانِ ، رَجُلٌ عَابِدٌ وَعَبِدٌ .
وَقَرَأَ عَبْدُ اللهِ : وَقَالَ الرَّسُولُ يَارَبِّ ، وَيُقَالُ
أَوَّلُ العَابِدِينَ الجَاحِدِينَ مَنْ عَبِدَ يَعْبُدُ ـ
أَفَنَضْرِبُ عَنْكُمُ الذِّكْرَ صَفْحًا إِنْ
كُنْتُمْ قَوْمًا مُسْرِفِينَ ـ مُسْرِفِينَ ، وَاللهِ
لَوْ أَنَّ هَذَا القُرْآنَ رُفِعَ حَيْثُ رَدَّهُ
أَوَائِلُ هَذِهِ الأُمَّةِ لَهَلَكُوا ، فَأَهْلَكْنَا
أَشَدَّ مِنْهُمْ بَطْشًا وَمَضَى مَثَلُ الأَوَّلِينَ :
عُقُوبَةُ الأَوَّلِينَ : جُزْءًا : عِدْلًا .

SŪRA ḤĀ MĪM AL-DUKHĀN
(the smoke) XXXXIV

In the Name of Allāh,
the Most Beneficent, the Most Merciful

سورة حمَ الدخان

بِسْمِ اللهِ الرَّحْمَنِ الرَّحِيمِ

وَقَالَ مُجَاهِدٌ : رَهْوًا طَرِيقًا يَابِسًا ،
وَيُقَالُ رَهْوًا سَاكِنًا . عَلَى عِلْمٍ عَلَى العَالَمِينَ ،
عَلَى مَنْ بَيْنَ ظَهْرَيْهِ . فَاعْتُلُوهُ : ادْفَعُوهُ ـ
وَزَوَّجْنَاهُمْ بِحُورٍ عِينٍ ـ أَنْكَحْنَاهُمْ
حُورًا عِينًا يَحَارُ فِيهَا الطَّرْفُ . وَيُقَالُ
أَنْ تَرْجُمُونِ : القَتْلَ . وَرَهْوًا : سَاكِنًا .
وَقَالَ ابْنُ عَبَّاسٍ : كَالمُهْلِ : أَسْوَدُ
كَمُهْلِ الزَّيْتِ . وَقَالَ غَيْرُهُ : تُبَّعٍ :
مُلُوكُ اليَمَنِ ، كُلُّ وَاحِدٍ مِنْهُمْ

يُسَمَّى تُبَّعًا لأَنَّهُ يَتْبَعُ صَاحِبَهُ. وَالظِّلُّ يُسَمَّى تُبَّعًا لأَنَّهُ يَتْبَعُ الشَّمْسَ.

(261) CHAPTER. The Statement of Allāh ﷻ :–

'Then watch you for the Day that the sky will bring forth a kind of smoke plainly visible.'

(44:10)

بَابٌ - فَارْتَقِبْ يَوْمَ تَأْتِي السَّمَاءُ بِدُخَانٍ مُبِينٍ - فَارْتَقِبْ: فَانْتَظِرْ.

345: Narrated 'Abdullāh (رضي الله عنه): Five things have passed, i.e. the smoke, the defeat of the Romans, the splitting of the moon, Al-Baṭsha (the defeat of the infidels in the battle of Badr) and Al-Lizām (the punishment)' (1)

٣٤٥ - حَدَّثَنَا عَبْدَانُ، عَنْ أَبِي حَمْزَةَ، عَنِ الأَعْمَشِ، عَنْ مُسْلِمٍ، عَنْ مَسْرُوقٍ، عَنْ عَبْدِ اللهِ قَالَ: مَضَى خَمْسٌ: الدُّخَانُ، وَالرُّومُ، وَالْقَمَرُ، وَالْبَطْشَةُ، وَاللِّزَامُ -

(262) CHAPTER. 'Covering the people; this is a painful torment.'

(44:11)

بَابٌ - يَغْشَى النَّاسَ هَذَا عَذَابٌ أَلِيمٌ -.

346. Narrated 'Abdullāh (رضي الله عنه): It (i.e., the imagined smoke) was because, when the Quraish refused to obey the Prophet ﷺ, he asked Allāh to afflict them with years of drought (famine) similar to those of (Prophet) Joseph.,

٣٤٦ - حَدَّثَنَا يَحْيَى: حَدَّثَنَا أَبُو مُعَاوِيَةَ، عَنِ الأَعْمَشِ، عَنْ مُسْلِمٍ، عَنْ مَسْرُوقٍ قَالَ: قَالَ عَبْدُ اللهِ: إِنَّمَا كَانَ هَذَا لأَنَّ قُرَيْشًا لَمَّا اسْتَعْصَوْا

(1) See Ḥadīth No. 290 & No. 297.

and so they were stricken with drought (famine) and fatigue, so much so that they ate even bones. A man would look towards the sky and imagine seeing something like smoke between him and the sky because of extreme fatigue. So Allāh تعالى revealed:–

> Then watch you for the Day that the sky will bring forth a kind of smoke plainly visible, covering the people; this is a painful torment.' (44:10-11)

Then someone (Abū Sufyān) came to Allāh's Messenger ﷺ and said, "O Allāh's Messenger! ﷺ Invoke Allāh to send rain for the tribes of Mudar for they are on the verge of destruction." On that the Prophet ﷺ said (astonishingly) "Shall I invoke Allāh) for the tribes of Mudar? Verily, you are a brave man!" But the Prophet ﷺ prayed for rain and it rained for them. Then the Verse was revealed.

> But truly you will return (to disbelief). (44:15)

(When the famine was over and) they restored prosperity and welfare, they reverted to their ways (of heatheism) whereupon Allāh تعالى revealed:–

> 'On the Day when We shall seize you with a Mighty Grasp. We will indeed (then) exact retribution, (44:16)

The narrator said, "That was the day of the Battle of Badr."

عَلَى النَّبِيِّ صلى الله عليه وسلّم دَعَا عَلَيْهِمْ بِسِنِينَ كَسِنِي يُوسُفَ، فَأَصَابَتْهُمْ قَحْطٌ وَجَهْدٌ حَتَّى أَكَلُوا الْعِظَامَ فَجَعَلَ الرَّجُلُ يَنْظُرُ إِلَى السَّمَاءِ فَيَرَى مَا بَيْنَهُ وَبَيْنَهَا كَهَيْئَةِ الدُّخَانِ مِنَ الْجَهْدِ. فَأَنْزَلَ اللهُ تَعَالَى ـ فَارْتَقِبْ يَوْمَ تَأْتِي السَّمَاءُ بِدُخَانٍ مُبِينٍ ـ يَغْشَى النَّاسَ هَذَا عَذَابٌ أَلِيمٌ ـ قَالَ: فَأُتِيَ رَسُولُ اللهِ صلى الله عليه وسلّم فَقِيلَ: يَا رَسُولَ اللهِ، اسْتَسْقِ اللهَ لِمُضَرَ فَإِنَّهَا قَدْ هَلَكَتْ، قَالَ: لِمُضَرَ؟ إِنَّكَ لَجَرِيءٌ فَاسْتَسْقَى فَسُقُوا. فَنَزَلَتْ ـ إِنَّكُمْ عَائِدُونَ ـ فَلَمَّا أَصَابَتْهُمُ الرَّفَاهِيَةُ عَادُوا إِلَى حَالِهِمْ حِينَ أَصَابَتْهُمُ الرَّفَاهِيَةُ فَأَنْزَلَ اللهُ عَزَّ وَجَلَّ ـ يَوْمَ نَبْطِشُ الْبَطْشَةَ الْكُبْرَى إِنَّا مُنْتَقِمُونَ ـ قَالَ: يَعْنِي يَوْمَ بَدْرٍ.

(260) CHAPTER. The Statement of Allāh تعالى :—

"(They will say) Our Lord! Remove the torment from us, really we are believers." (44:12)

بَابُ قَوْلِهِ تَعَالَى ـ رَبَّنَا اكْشِفْ عَنَّا الْعَذَابَ إِنَّا مُؤْمِنُونَ ـ.

347. Narrated 'Abdullāh: It is a sign of having knowledge that, when you do not know something, you say: 'Allāh knows better.' Allāh said to his Prophet ﷺ :—

'Say: No wage do I ask of you for this (Qur'ān), nor am I one of the pretenders (a person who pretends things which do not exist) (38:86)

When the Quraish troubled and stood against the Prophet ﷺ he said, "O Allāh! Help me against them by afflicting them with seven years of famine like the seven years of Joseph." So they were stricken with a year of famine during which they ate bones and dead animals because of too much suffering, and one of them would see something like smoke between him and the sky because of hunger. Then they said:

Our Lord! Remove the torment from us, really we are believers. (44:12)

And then it was said to the Prophet ﷺ (by Allāh), "If we remove it from them. they will revert to their ways (of heathenism)." So the Prophet ﷺ invoked his Lord, who removed the punishment from them, but later they reverted (to heathenism), whereupon Allāh punished them on the day of the Battle of Badr, and that is what Allāh's Statement indicates:-

٣٤٧ ـ حَدَّثَنَا يَحْيَى : حَدَّثَنَا وَكِيعٌ ، عَنِ الأَعْمَشِ ، عَنْ أَبِي الضُّحَى ، عَنْ مَسْرُوقٍ قَالَ : دَخَلْتُ عَلَى عَبْدِ اللهِ فَقَالَ : إِنَّ مِنَ العِلْمِ أَنْ تَقُولَ لِمَا لا تَعْلَمُ : اللهُ أَعْلَمُ ، إِنَّ اللهَ قَالَ لِنَبِيِّهِ صَلَّى اللهُ عليه وسلَّمَ ـ قُلْ مَا أَسْأَلُكُمْ عَلَيْهِ مِنْ أَجْرٍ وَمَا أَنَا مِنَ الْمُتَكَلِّفِينَ ـ إِنَّ قُرَيْشًا لَمَّا غَلَبُوا النَّبِيَّ صَلَّى اللهُ عليه وسلَّمَ وَاسْتَعْصَوْا عَلَيْهِ قَالَ : اللَّهُمَّ أَعِنِّي عَلَيْهِمْ بِسَبْعٍ كَسَبْعِ يُوسُفَ ، فَأَخَذَتْهُمْ سَنَةٌ أَكَلُوا فِيهَا العِظَامَ وَالمَيْتَةَ مِنَ الجَهْدِ حَتَّى جَعَلَ أَحَدُهُمْ يَرَى مَا بَيْنَهُ وَبَيْنَ السَّمَاءِ كَهَيْئَةِ الدُّخَانِ مِنَ الجُوعِ . قَالُوا رَبَّنَا اكْشِفْ عَنَّا العَذَابَ إِنَّا مُؤْمِنُونَ . فَقِيلَ لَهُ إِنْ كَشَفْنَا عَنْهُمْ عَادُوا ، فَدَعَا رَبَّهُ فَكَشَفَ عَنْهُمْ فَعَادُوا فَانْتَقَمَ اللهُ مِنْهُمْ يَوْمَ بَدْرٍ . فَذَلِكَ قَوْلُهُ ـ يَوْمَ تَأْتِي السَّمَاءُ بِدُخَانٍ مُبِينٍ ـ إِلَى قَوْلِهِ جَلَّ ذِكْرُهُ إِنَّا مُنْتَقِمُونَ ـ.

'Then watch for the day that the sky will being forth a kind of smoke plainly visible........... We will indeed (then) exact retribution.'

(44:10)

(264) CHAPTER. How can there be for them an (effuctual) Reminder when an Apostle, explainings things clearly, has already come to them?' (44:13)

بابٌ - أنَّى لَهُمُ الذِّكْرَى وَقَدْ جاءَهُمْ رَسُولٌ مُبِينٌ - الذِّكْرُ والذِّكْرَى واحِدٌ .

348. Narrated Masrūq: I came upon 'Abdullāh and he said, "When Allāh's Messenger ﷺ invited Quraish (to Islām), they disbelieved him and stood against him. So he (the Prophet ﷺ) said, "O Allāh! Help me against them by afflicting them with seven years of famine similar to the seven years of Joseph.' So they were stricken with a year of drought that destroyed everything, and they started eating dead animals, and if one of them got up he would see something like smoke between him and the sky from the severe fatigue and hunger." 'Abdullāh then recited:–

'Then watch you for the Day

٣٤٨ - حَدَّثنا سُلَيْمانُ بنُ حَرْبٍ: حَدَّثنا جَرِيرُ بنُ حازِمٍ، عَنِ الأعْمَشِ، عَنْ أبِي الضُّحَى، عَنْ مَسْرُوقٍ قالَ: دَخَلْتُ عَلَى عَبْدِ اللهِ ثُمَّ قالَ: إنَّ رَسُولَ اللهِ صَلَّى اللهُ عليهِ وسلَّمَ لَمَّا دَعا قُرَيْشا كَذَّبُوهُ واسْتَعْصَوْا عَلَيْهِ: فَقالَ: اللَّهُمْ بِسَبْعٍ كَسَبْعِ يُوسُفَ، فَأصابَتْهُمْ سَنَةٌ حَصَّتْ يَعْنِي كُلَّ شَيْءٍ حَتَّى كانُوا يَأْكُلُونَ المَيْتَةَ فَكانَ يَقُومُ أحَدُهُمْ فَكانَ يَرَى بَيْنَهُ وَبَيْنَ السَّماءِ مِثْلَ الدُّخانِ مِنَ الجَهْدِ والجُوعِ، ثُمَّ

that the sky will bring forth a kind of smoke plainly visible, covering the people. This is a painful torment... (till he reached) .... We shall indeed remove the punishment for a while, but truly you will revert (to heathenism): (44:10-15)

'Abdullāh added: "Will the punishment be removed from them on the Day of Resurrection?" He added," The severe grasp" was the Day of the Battle of Badr."

قُرأ - فارْتَقِبْ يَوْمَ تَأْتِي السَّماءُ بِدُخانٍ مُبِينٍ يَغْشَى النَّاسَ هَذَا عَذَابٌ أَلِيمٌ - حتى بَلَغَ - إنَّا كاشِفُوا العَذابِ قَلِيلاً إنَّكُم عائِدُونَ - قالَ عَبْدُ اللهِ : أفَيُكْشَفُ عَنْهُمُ العَذابُ يَوْمَ القِيامَةِ ؟ قالَ : والبَطْشَةُ الكُبْرَى : يَوْمَ بَدْرٍ.

(265) CHAPTER. Then they had turned away from him (Messenger Muhammad ﷺ) and said: He (Muhammad ﷺ) is taught (by a human being), a madman.! (44:14)

بابٌ - ثُمَّ تَوَلَّوا عَنْهُ وَقالُوا مُعَلَّمٌ مَجْنُونٌ -.

349. Narrated 'Abdullāh رضي الله عنه : Allāh sent (the Prophet) Muhammad ﷺ and said:—

'Say, No wage do I ask of you for this (Qur'ān) nor am I one of the pretenders (i.e. a person who pretends things which do not exist). (38:68)

When Allāh's Messenger ﷺ saw Quraish standing against him, he said,"O Allāh! Help me against them by afflicting them with seven years of famine similar to the seven years (of famine) of Joseph. So they were afflicted with a year of drought that

٣٤٩ - حَدَّثَنا بِشْرُ بنُ خالِدٍ : أخبَرَنا مُحمدٌ ، عَنْ شُعْبَةَ ، عَنْ سُلَيْمانَ ، وَمَنْصُورٍ ، عَنْ أبي الضُّحَى ، عَنْ مَسْرُوقٍ قالَ : قالَ عَبْدُ اللهِ : إنَّ اللهَ بَعَثَ مُحَمَّداً صلى الله عليه وسلَّم وَقالَ - قُلْ ما أسألُكُمْ عَلَيْهِ مِنْ أجْرٍ وَما أنا مِنَ المُتَكَلِّفِينَ - فإنَّ رَسُولَ اللهِ صلى الله عليه وسلَّم لَمَّا رَأى قُرَيْشاً اسْتَعْصَوا عَلَيْهِ فَقالَ : اللَّهُمَّ أعِنِّي عَلَيْهِمْ بِسَبْعٍ كَسَبْعِ يُوسُفَ فَأخَذَتْهُمُ السَّنَةُ التي

destroyed everything, and they ate bones and hides. (One of them said), "And they ate hides and dead animals, and (it seemed to them that) something like smoke was coming out of the earth. So Abū Sufyān came to the Prophet ﷺ and said, "O Muḥammad! Your people are on the verge of destruction! Please invoke Allāh to relieve them." So the Prophet ﷺ invoked Allāh for them (and the famine disappeared). He said to them. "You will revert (to heathenism) after that." 'Abdullāh then recited:—

> Then watch you for the Day that the sky will bring forth a kind of smoke plainly visible ....but truly you will revert (to disbelief).'

He added, "Will the punishment be removed from them in the Hereafter? The smoke and the grasp and the Al-Lizām have all passed." One of the sub-narrater said, "The splitting of the moon." And another said, "The defeat of the Romans (has passed)."

حصت كل شيء حتى أكلوا العظام والجلود. فقال أحدهم: حتى أكلوا الجلود والميتة وجعل يخرج من الأرض كهيئة الدخان. فأتاه أبو سفيان فقال: أي محمد، إن قومك قد هلكوا فادع الله أن يكشف عنهم، فدعا ثم قال: تعودوا بعد هذا. في حديث منصور. ثم قرأ - فارتقب يوم تأتي السماء بدخان مبين - إلى - عائدون - أيكشف عذاب الآخرة؟ فقد مضى الدخان والبطشة واللزام، وقال أحدهم: القمر. وقال الآخر: الروم -

(266) CHAPTER. On the Day when We shall seize you with the Mighty Grasp.......We shall exact retribution.' (44:16)

يوم نبطش البطشة الكبرى إنا منتقمون -.

350. Narrated 'Abdullāh ﷺ : Five

٣٥٠ حدثنا يحيى وحدثنا

things have passed: Al-Lizām, the defeat of the Romans, the mighty grasp, the splitting of the moon, and the smoke.

وَكِيعٌ، عَنِ الأَعْمَشِ، عَنْ مُسْلِمٍ، عَنْ مَسْرُوقٍ، عَنْ عَبْدِ اللهِ قَالَ: خَمْسٌ قَدْ مَضَيْنَ: اللِّزَامُ، وَالرُّومُ، وَالبَطْشَةُ، القَمَرُ، وَالدُّخَانُ.

SŪRAT ḤĀ MĪM AL-JĀTHIYA: XLV

سورة حم الجاثية

In the Name of Allāh, the Most Beneficent, the Most Merciful

بِسْمِ اللهِ الرَّحْمَٰنِ الرَّحِيمِ

جَاثِيَةً: مُسْتَوْفِزِينَ عَلَى الرُّكَبِ. وَقَالَ مُجَاهِدٌ: نَسْتَنْسِخُ: نَكْتُبُ. نَنْسَاكُمْ: نَتْرُكُكُمْ.

(267) CHAPTER. 'And nothing destroys us but Time. (45:24)

بَابٌ وَمَا يُهْلِكُنَا إِلاَّ الدَّهْرُ - الآيَةَ.

351. Narrated Abū Huraira: Allāh's Messenger said, "Allāh said, 'The son of Adam hurts me for he abuses Time though I am Time: in My Hands are all things, and I cause the revolution of day and night.' "

٣٥١ - حَدَّثَنَا الحُمَيْدِيُّ: حَدَّثَنَا سُفْيَانُ: حَدَّثَنَا الزُّهْرِيُّ، عَنْ سَعِيدِ ابْنِ المُسَيَّبِ، عَنْ أَبِي هُرَيْرَةَ رَضِيَ اللهُ عَنْهُ قَالَ: قَالَ رَسُولُ اللهِ صلى الله عليه وسلم: قَالَ اللهُ عَزَّ وَجَلَّ: يُؤْذِينِي ابْنُ آدَمَ، يَسُبُّ الدَّهْرَ وَأَنَا الدَّهْرُ بِيَدِي الأَمْرُ أُقَلِّبُ اللَّيْلَ وَالنَّهَارَ

SŪRAT AL-AḤQĀF (Winding sand-tract) XLVI

سورة الأحقاف

In the Name of Allāh, the Most Beneficent, the Most Merciful

بِسْمِ اللهِ الرَّحْمَٰنِ الرَّحِيمِ

وَقَالَ مُجَاهِدٌ : تُفِيضُونَ : تَقُولُونَ . وَقَالَ بَعْضُهُمْ : أَثَرَةٍ وَأَثْرَةٍ وَأَثَارَةٍ : بَقِيَّةٌ مِنْ عِلْمٍ . وَقَالَ ابْنُ عَبَّاسٍ : بِدْعًا مِنَ الرُّسُلِ : مَا كُنْتُ بِأَوَّلِ الرُّسُلِ . وَقَالَ غَيْرُهُ : أَرَأَيْتُمْ هَذِهِ الأَلِفَ ؟ إِنَّمَا هِيَ تَوَعُّدٌ إِنْ صَحَّ مَا تَدَّعُونَ لَا يَسْتَحِقُّ أَنْ يُعْبَدَ ، وَلَيْسَ قَوْلُهُ أَرَأَيْتُمْ بِرُؤْيَةِ العَيْنِ ، إِنَّمَا هُوَ : أَتَعْلَمُونَ : أَبَلَغَكُمْ أَنَّ مَا تَدْعُونَ مِنْ دُونِ اللهِ خَلَقُوا شَيْئًا .

(268) CHAPTER. 'But he who says to his parents: 'Fie on you both! Do you hold out the promise to me that I shall be raised up (again)..........this is nothing but the tales of the ancient.' (46:17)

بَابٌ - وَالَّذِي قَالَ لِوَالِدَيْهِ أُفٍّ لَكُمَا أَتَعِدَانِنِي أَنْ أُخْرَجَ - إِلَى قَوْلِهِ - أَسَاطِيرُ الأَوَّلِينَ - .

352. Narrated Yūsuf bin Mā'hak: Marwān had been appointed as the governor of Hijāz by Mu'āwiya. He delivered a sermon and mentioned Yazīd bin Mu'āwiya so that the people might take the oath of allegiance to him as the successor of his father (Mu-'awiya). Then 'Abdur Rahmān bin Abū Bakr told him something whereupon Marwān ordered that he be arrested. But 'Abdur-Rahmān entered 'Aisha's house and they could not arrest him. Marwān said, "It is he ('Abdur-Rahmān) about whom Allāh revealed

٣٥٢ - حَدَّثَنَا مُوسَى بْنُ إِسْمَاعِيلَ : حَدَّثَنَا أَبُو عَوَانَةَ ، عَنْ أَبِي بِشْرٍ ، عَنْ يُوسُفَ بْنِ مَاهَكَ قَالَ : كَانَ مَرْوَانُ عَلَى الحِجَازِ اسْتَعْمَلَهُ مُعَاوِيَةُ فَخَطَبَ فَجَعَلَ يَذْكُرُ يَزِيدَ بْنَ مُعَاوِيَةَ لِكَيْ يُبَايَعَ لَهُ بَعْدَ أَبِيهِ . فَقَالَ لَهُ عَبْدُ الرَّحْمَنِ بْنُ أَبِي بَكْرٍ شَيْئًا ، فَقَالَ : خُذُوهُ . فَدَخَلَ بَيْتَ عَائِشَةَ فَلَمْ يَقْدِرُوا عَلَيْهِ ، فَقَالَ مَرْوَانُ : إِنَّ هَذَا

this Verse:–

'And the one who says to his parents: 'Fie on you! Do you hold out the promise to me......?' "

On that, 'Āisha said from behind a screen, "Allāh did not reveal anything from the Qur'ān about us except what was connected with the declaration of my innocence (of the slander)."

الَّذِى أَنْزَلَ اللهُ فِيهِ - وَالَّذِى قَالَ لِوَالِدَيْهِ أُفٍّ لَكُمَا أَتَعِدَانِنِى - فَقَالَتْ عَائِشَةُ مِنْ وَرَاءِ الحِجَابِ : مَا أَنْزَلَ اللهُ فِينَا شَيْئًا مِنَ القُرْآنِ إِلاَّ أَنَّ اللهَ أَنْزَلَ عُذْرِى .

(269) CHAPTER. The Statement of Allāh (تعالى) :–

'Then when they saw it as a dense cloud coming towards their valleys ....'(46:24)

بَابُ قَوْلِهِ - فَلَمَّا رَأَوْهُ عَارِضًا مُسْتَقْبِلَ أَوْدِيَتِهِمْ - الآيَةَ . قَالَ ابْنُ عَبَّاسٍ : عَارِضٌ : السَّحَابُ .

353. Narrated 'Āisha (رضي الله عنها) the wife of the Prophet (ﷺ) : I never saw Allāh's Messenger (ﷺ) laughing loudly enough to enable me to see his uvula, but he used to smile only. And whenever he saw clouds or winds, signs of deep concern would appear on his face. I said, "O Allāh's Messenger! When people see clouds they usually feel happy, hoping that it would rain, while I see that when you see clouds, one could notice signs of dissatisfaction on your face." He said, "O 'Āisha! What is the guarantee for me that there will be no punishment in it, since some people were punished with a wind? Verily, some people saw (received) the punishment, but (while seeing the cloud) they said, 'This cloud will give us rain.' "

٣٥٣ - حَدَّثَنَا أَحْمَدُ : حَدَّثَنَا ابْنُ وَهْبٍ : أَخْبَرَنَا عَمْرٌو أَنَّ أَبَا النَّضْرِ حَدَّثَهُ ، عَنْ سُلَيْمَانَ بْنِ يَسَارٍ ، عَنْ عَائِشَةَ رَضِيَ اللهُ عَنْهَا زَوْجِ النَّبِيِّ صلى اللهُ عليهِ وسلَّم قَالَتْ : مَا رَأَيْتُ رَسُولَ اللهِ صلى اللهُ عليهِ وسلَّم ضَاحِكًا حَتَّى أَرَى مِنْهُ لَهَوَاتِهِ ، إِنَّمَا كَانَ يَتَبَسَّمُ . قَالَتْ : وَكَانَ إِذَا رَأَى غَيْمًا أَوْ رِيحًا عُرِفَ فِى وَجْهِهِ . قَالَتْ : يَا رَسُولَ اللهِ ، إِنَّ النَّاسَ إِذَا رَأَوُا الغَيْمَ فَرِحُوا رَجَاءَ أَنْ يَكُونَ فِيهِ المَطَرُ ، وَأَرَاكَ إِذَا رَأَيْتَهُ عُرِفَ فِى وَجْهِكَ الكَرَاهِيَةُ ، فَقَالَ : يَا عَائِشَةُ ، مَا يُؤْمِنِّى

أنْ يكُونَ فِيهِ عذَابٌ ، عُذِّبَ قومٌ
بالرِّيح . وَقدْ رأى قومٌ العذَابَ فقالوا
هذَا عارِضٌ مُمْطِرُنا ـ .

SŪRAT MUHAMMAD (ﷺ) LXVII

سورة محمد

**In the Name of Allāh,
the Most Beneficent, the Most Merciful**

بِسْمِ اللهِ الرحمٰنِ الرَّحيمِ

أوْزَارَها : آثامَها. حتَّى لا يَبْقَى إلاَّ
مُسْلِمٌ . عرَّفَها : بيَّنَها . وقالَ مُجَاهِدٌ :
مَوْلَى الَّذينَ آمَنُوا : وَلِيُّهُمْ . فإذَا
عزَمَ الأمْرُ : أي جَدَّ الأمْرُ . فَلا تَهِنُوا :
لا تَضْعُفُوا. وقالَ ابنُ عبَّاسٍ : أضْغانَهُمْ :
حَسَدَهُمْ . آسِنٍ : مُتَغَيِّرٍ .

(270) CHAPTER. 'And sever your ties of kinship. (47:22)

بابٌ ـ وتُقَطِّعُوا أرْحامَكُمْ ـ .

354. Narrated Abū Huraira ﷺ: The Prophet ﷺ said, "Allāh created His creation, and when He had finished it, the womb, got up and caught hold of Allāh whereupon Allāh said, "What is the matter?' On that, it said, 'I seek refuge with you from those who sever the ties of kith and kin.' On that Allāh said, 'Will you be satisfied if I bestow My favours on him who keeps your ties, and withhold My favours from him who severs your

٣٥٤ ـ حدَّثنا خالدُ بنُ مَخْلَد :
حدَّثنا سُلَيْمانُ : حدَّثني مُعاوِيةُ بنُ أبي
مُزَرِّد ، عَنْ سَعيدِ بنِ يسارٍ ، عَنْ أبي
هُرَيْرَةَ رَضِيَ اللهُ عَنْهُ ، عَنِ النَّبيِّ
صلى اللهُ عليه وسلَّم قالَ : خلَقَ اللهُ الخَلْقَ
فلمَّا فرَغَ مِنْهُ قامَتِ الرَّحِمُ فأخَذَتْ ،
فقالَ لَهُ : مَهْ . قالَتْ : هذَا مَقامُ العائِذِ
بِكَ مِنَ القَطِيعَةِ . قالَ : ألا تَرْضَيْنَ أنْ

ties?' On that it said, 'Yes, O my Lord!' Then Allāh said, 'That is for you.' " Abū Huraira added: If you wish, you can recite: "Would you then if you were given the authority. do mischief in the land and sever your ties of kinship. (47:22)

أَصِلَ مَنْ وَصَلَكِ ، وأَقْطَعَ مَنْ قَطَعَكِ ؟ قَالَتْ : بَلَى يَا رَبِّ . قَالَ : فَذَاكِ . قَالَ أَبُو هُرَيْرَةَ : اقْرَءُوا إِنْ شِئْتُمْ - فَهَلْ عَسَيْتُمْ إِنْ تَوَلَّيْتُمْ أَنْ تُفْسِدُوا فِي الأَرْضِ وَتُقَطِّعُوا أَرْحَامَكُمْ - .

355. Narrated Abū Huraira: (As above, No. 354, but added) Then Allāh's Messenger ﷺ said, "Recite if you wish: "Would you then.' " ......(47:22)

٣٥٥ - حَدَّثَنَا إِبْرَاهِيمُ بْنُ حَمْزَةَ : حَدَّثَنَا حَاتِمٌ ، عَنْ مُعَاوِيَةَ قَالَ : حَدَّثَنِي عَمِّي أَبُو الحُبَابِ سَعِيدُ بْنُ يَسَارٍ ، عَنْ أَبِي هُرَيْرَةَ بِهَذَا . ثُمَّ قَالَ رَسُولُ اللهِ صلى اللهُ عليه وسلَّم : اقْرَءُوا إِنْ شِئْتُمْ - فَهَلْ عَسَيْتُمْ - .

356. Narrated Mu'āwiya bin Abī Al-Muzarrad: Allāh's Messenger ﷺ said, "Recite if you wish: Would you then if you were given the authority.......... (47:22)

٣٥٦ - حَدَّثَنَا بِشْرُ بْنُ مُحَمَّدٍ : أَخْبَرَنَا عَبْدُ اللهِ : أَخْبَرَنَا مُعَاوِيَةُ بْنُ أَبِي المُزَرِّدِ بِهَذَا . قَالَ رَسُولُ اللهِ صلى اللهُ عليه وسلَّم : وَاقْرَءُوا إِنْ شِئْتُمْ - فَهَلْ عَسَيْتُمْ - آسِنٍ : مُتَغَيِّرٌ .

SŪRAT AL-FATḤ (The Victory): XLVIII

سورة الفتح

In the Name of Allāh, the Most Beneficent, the Most Merciful

بِسْمِ اللهِ الرَّحْمَنِ الرَّحِيمِ

قال مجاهد: بورا: هالكين. وقال مجاهد: سيماهم في وجوههم: السحنة. وقال منصور، عن مجاهد: التواضع. شطأه: فراخه. فاستغلظ: غلظ. سوقه: الساق حاملة الشجرة ويقال دائرة السوء كقولك رجل السوء: ودائرة السوء: العذاب. يعزروه: ينصروه. شطأه: شطء السنبل تنبت الحبة عشرا أو ثمانيا وسبعا فيقوى بعضه ببعض، فذاك قوله تعالى: فآزره - قواه. ولو كانت واحدة لم تقم على ساق: وهو مثل ضربه الله للنبي صلى الله عليه وسلم إذ خرج وحده ثم قواه بأصحابه كما قوى الحبة بما ينبت منها.

(271) CHAPTER. The Statement of Allāh تعالى :–

'Verily, We have given you (O, Muḥammad) a manifest victory.' (48:1)

باب قوله - إنا فتحنا لك فتحا مبينا -.

357. Narrated Aslam: While Allāh's Messenger ﷺ was proceeding at night during one of his journeys and 'Umar bin Al-Khaṭṭāb was travelling beside him, 'Umar asked him about something but Allāh's Messenger ﷺ did not reply. He asked again, but he did not reply,

٣٥٧ - حدثنا عبد الله بن مسلمة: عن مالك، عن زيد بن أسلم، عن أبيه: أن رسول الله صلى الله عليه وسلم كان يسير في بعض أسفاره وعمر بن الخطاب يسير معه ليلا فسأله عمر

and then he asked (for the third time) but he did not reply. On that, 'Umar bin Al-Khaṭṭāb said to himself, "Thakilat Ummu 'Umar (May 'Umar's mother lose her son)! I asked Allāh's Messenger ﷺ three times but he did not reply." 'Umar then said, "I made my camel run faster and went ahead of the people, and I was afraid that some Qur'ānic Verses might be revealed about me. But before getting involved in any other matter. I heard somebody calling me. I said to myself, 'I fear that some Qur'ānic Verses have been revealed about me,' and so I went to Allāh's Messenger ﷺ and greeted him.

He (Allāh's Messenger ﷺ) said, 'Tonight a Sūra has been revealed to me, and it is dearer to me than that on which the sun rises (i.e., the world)' Then he recited: Verily, We have given you a manifest victory.' "

(48:1)

ابنُ الخطَّابِ عنْ شيْءٍ فلَمْ يُجِبْهُ رَسُولُ اللهِ صلى الله عليه وسلَّم، ثُمَّ سألَهُ فلَمْ يُجِبْهُ. ثُمَّ سألَهُ فلَمْ يُجِبْهُ فقالَ عُمَرُ بنُ الخطَّابِ: ثَكِلَتْ أُمُّ عُمَرَ، نزَرْتَ رَسُولَ اللهِ صلى الله عليه وسلَّم ثلاثَ مرَّاتٍ كلُّ ذلكَ لا يُجيبُكَ. قالَ عُمَرُ: فحرَّكْتُ بعيري ثُمَّ تقدَّمْتُ أمامَ النَّاسِ وخَشِيتُ أنْ يُنزَلَ فيَّ القُرآنُ فمَا نَشِبْتُ أنْ سَمِعْتُ صارِخًا يَصْرُخُ بي، فقُلْتُ لقَدْ خَشِيتُ أنْ يكُونَ نزَلَ فيَّ قُرآنٌ، فجِئْتُ رَسُولَ اللهِ صلى الله عليه وسلَّم فسلَّمْتُ علَيْهِ فقالَ: لقَدْ أُنزِلَتْ علَيَّ اللَّيْلَةَ سُورَةٌ لَهِيَ أحَبُّ إليَّ مِمَّا طلَعَتْ علَيْهِ الشَّمْسُ. ثُمَّ قرَأَ - إنَّا فتَحْنا لكَ فتْحًا مُبِينًا -.

358. Narrated Anas رضي الله عنه :Verily, We have given you (O Muḥammad ﷺ) a manifest victory,' refers to Al-Ḥudaibiya (peace treaty).

٣٥٨ - حدَّثَنا مُحمَّدُ بنُ بشَّارٍ: حدَّثَنا غُنْدَرٌ: حدَّثَنا شُعْبَةُ قالَ: سَمِعْتُ قَتادَةَ، عنْ أنسٍ رَضِيَ اللهُ عنْهُ - إنَّا فتَحْنا لكَ فتْحًا مُبِينًا - قالَ: الحُدَيْبِيَةُ.

359. Narrated 'Abdullāh bin

٣٥٩ - حدَّثَنا مُسْلِمُ بنُ إبْرَاهِيمَ:

Mughaffal: On the Day of the Conquest of Mecca, the Prophet ﷺ recited Sūrat Al-Fatḥ in a vibrating and pleasant voice. (Mu'āwaiya, the sub-narrator said, "If I could immitate the recitation of the Prophet ﷺ I would do so.")

حدثنا شعبة: حدثنا معاوية بن قرة،
عن عبد الله بن مغفل قال: قرأ
النبي صلى الله عليه وسلم يوم فتح
مكة سورة الفتح فرجع فيها، قال
معاوية: لو شئت أن أحكي لكم
قراءة النبي صلى الله عليه وسلم
لفعلت.

(273) CHAPTER. The Statement of Allāh تعالى :
'That Allāh may forgive you your faults of the past and those to follow, and complete His favours on you and guide you on the straight way.' (48:2)

باب قوله - ليغفر لك الله ما
تقدم من ذنبك وما تأخر ويتم
نعمته عليك ويهديك صراطا
مستقيما -

360. Narrated Al-Mughīra: The Prophet ﷺ used to offer night prayers till his feet became swollen. Somebody said, to him," "Allāh has forgiven you, your faults of the past and those to follow." On that, he said, "Shouldn't I be a thankful slave of Allāh)?"

٣٦٠ - حدثنا صدقة بن الفضل:
أخبرنا ابن عيينة: حدثنا زياد: أنه
سمع المغيرة يقول: قام النبي صلى
الله عليه وسلم حتى تورمت قدماه
فقيل له: غفر الله لك ما تقدم من
ذنبك وما تأخر، قال: أفلا أكون
عبدا شكورا؟

361. Narrated 'Āisha رضي الله عنها : The Prophet ﷺ, used to offer prayer at night (for such a long time) that his feet used to crack. I said, "O Allāh' Messenger! Why do you do it

٣٦١ - حدثنا الحسن بن
عبد العزيز: حدثنا عبد الله بن يحيى:
أخبرنا حيوة، عن أبي الأسود: سمع
عروة، عن عائشة رضي الله عنها

since Allāh has forgiven you your faults of the past and those to follow?" He said, "Shouldn't I love to be a thankful slave (of Allāh)?' When he became old, he prayed while sitting, but if he wanted to perform a bowing, he would get up, recite (some other verses) and then perform the bowing.

أنَّ نبيَّ اللهِ صلى الله عليه وسلم كانَ
يقومُ منَ الليلِ حتى تتفطرَ قدماهُ،
فقالتْ عائشةُ: لِمَ تصنعُ هذا يا
رسولَ اللهِ وقدْ غفرَ اللهُ لكَ ما تقدمَ
من ذنبكَ وما تأخرَ؟ قالَ: أفلا
أحبُّ أنْ أكونَ عبدًا شكورًا؟ فلما
كثرَ لحمُهُ صلى جالسًا فإذا أرادَ أنْ
يركعَ قامَ فقرأَ ثمَّ ركعَ.

(273) CHAPTER. Verily, 'We have sent you (O Muḥammad) as a witness, as a bringer of glad tidings, and as a warner.' (48:8)

باب - إنا أرسلناكَ شاهدًا ومبشرًا ونذيرًا -.

362. Narrated 'Abdullāh bin 'Amr bin Al-'Āṣ رضي الله عنهما : This Verse:–

> Verily We have sent you (O Muḥammad ﷺ) as a witness, as a bringer of glad tidings and as a warner.' (48:8)

Which is in the Qur'ān, appears in the Torah thus:–

> 'Verily We have sent you (O Muḥammad ﷺ) as a witness, as a bringer of glad tidings and as a warner, and as a protector for the illiterates (i.e., the Arabs.) You are my slave and My Messenger, and I have named you Al-Mutawakkil (one who depends upon Allāh). You are neither hard-hearted nor of fierce character, nor one who shouts in the markets. You do not return evil for evil, but

٣٦٢ - حدثنا عبدُ اللهِ بنُ مسلمةَ:
حدثنا عبدُ العزيزِ بنُ أبي سلمةَ، عنْ
هلالِ بنِ أبي هلالٍ عنْ عطاءِ بنِ يسارٍ،
عنْ عبدِ اللهِ بنِ عمرِو بنِ العاصِ
رضيَ اللهُ عنهما: أنَّ هذهِ الآيةَ
التي في القرآنِ - يا أيها النبيُّ إنا
أرسلناكَ شاهدًا ومبشرًا ونذيرًا -
قالَ: في التوراةِ: يا أيها النبيُّ إنا
أرسلناكَ شاهدًا ومبشرًا ونذيرًا
وحرزًا للأميينَ: أنتَ عبدي ورسولي،
سميتُكَ المتوكلَ، ليسَ بفظٍّ ولا
غليظٍ ولا سخابٍ بالأسواقِ، ولا
يدفعُ السيئةَ بالسيئةِ، ولكنْ يعفو
ويصفحُ، ولنْ يقبضَهُ اللهُ حتى يقيمَ

excuse and forgive. Allāh will not take you unto Him till He guides through you a crocked (curved) nation on the right path by causing them to say: "None has the right to be worshipped but Allāh." With such a statement He will cause to open blind eyes, deaf ears and hardened hearts.'

به المِلَّةَ العَوْجاءَ بأنْ يَقُولُوا لا إلهَ إلاَّ اللهُ، فيَفْتَحُ بها أعيُنًا عُمْيًا، وآذانًا صُمًّا، وقُلُوبًا غُلْفًا.

(274) CHAPTER. He is Who sent down tranquillity (calmness) into the hearts of believers.' (48:4)

باب - هُوَ الَّذِي أنزَلَ السَّكِينَةَ فِي قُلُوبِ المُؤْمِنِينَ -.

363. Narrated Al-Barā ﵁ : While a man from the companions of the Prophet ﷺ was reciting (Qur'ān) and his horse was tied in the house, the horse got startled and started jumping. The man came out, looked around but could not find anything, yet the horse went on jumping. The next morning he mentioned that to the Prophet ﷺ. The Prophet ﷺ said, "That was the tranquillity (calmness) which descended because of the recitation of the Qur'ān."

٣٦٣ - حدَّثنا عُبَيْدُ اللهِ بنُ مُوسَى، عَنْ إسْرائيلَ، عَنْ أبي إسحاقَ، عَنِ البَراءِ رَضِيَ اللهُ عَنْهُ قالَ: بَيْنَما رَجُلٌ مِنْ أصحابِ النَّبِيِّ صَلَّى اللهُ عليهِ وسلَّمَ يقرأُ وفَرَسٌ لَهُ مَرْبُوطٌ في الدَّارِ فَجَعَلَ يَنْفِرُ، فخَرَجَ الرَّجُلُ فَنَظَرَ فَلَمْ يَرَ شَيْئًا؟ وجَعَلَ يَنْفِرُ فَلَمَّا أصْبَحَ ذَكَرَ ذَلِكَ للنَّبِيِّ صلى الله عليه وسلَّم فقالَ: تِلْكَ السَّكِينَةُ تَنَزَّلَتْ بالقُرآنِ.

(275) CHAPTER. The Statement of Allāh ﷻ :-

باب قَوْلِه - إذْ يُبايِعُونَكَ تَحْتَ الشَّجَرَةِ -.

'When they swore allegiance to you (O, Muḥammad) under the tree.' (48:18)

364. Narrated Jābir: We were one thousand and four hundred on the Day of Al-Ḥudaibiya.

٣٦٤ ـ حدثنا قتيبة بن سعيد : حدثنا سفيان ، عن عمرو ، عن جابر قال : كنا يوم الحديبية ألفا وأربعمائة .

365. Narrated Uqba bin Ṣahbān; 'Abdullāh bin Mughaffal Al-Muzanī who was one of those who witnessed (the event of) the tree, said, "The Prophet ﷺ forbade the throwing of small stones (with two fingers)." 'Abdullāh bin Al-Mughaffal Al-Muzanī also said, "The Prophet ﷺ also forbade urinating at the place where one takes a bath."

٣٦٥ ـ حدثنا علي بن عبد الله : حدثنا شبابة : حدثنا شعبة ، عن قتادة قال : سمعت عقبة بن صهبان ، عن عبد الله بن مغفل المزني ممن شهد الشجرة : نهى النبي صلى الله عليه وسلم عن الخذف . وعقبة بن صهبان قال : سمعت عبد الله بن المغفل المزني في البول في المغتسل .

366. Narrated Thābit bin Ad-Daḥḥāk رضي الله عنه who was one of the companions of the tree (those who swore allegiance to the Prophet ﷺ beneath the tree at Al-Ḥudaibiya):

٣٦٦ ـ حدثنا محمد بن الوليد : حدثنا محمد بن جعفر : حدثنا شعبة ، عن خالد ، عن أبي قلابة ، عن ثابت ابن الضحاك رضي الله عنه وكان من أصحاب الشجرة .

367. Narrated Ḥabīb bin Abī Thābit: I went to Abū Wā'il to ask him (about those who had rebelled against 'Alī). On that Abū Wā'il said, "We were at

٣٦٧ ـ حدثنا أحمد بن إسحاق السلمي : حدثنا يعلى : حدثنا عبد العزيز ابن سياه ، عن حبيب ابن أبي ثابت

Ṣiffīn (a city on the bank of the Euphrates, the place where the battle took place between 'Alī and Mu'āwiya). A man said, "Will you be on the side of those who are called to consult Allāh's Book (to settle the dispute)?" 'Alī said, 'Yes (I agree that we should settle the matter in the light of the Qur'ān)." ' Some people objected to 'Alī's agreement and wanted to fight. On that Sahl bin Ḥunaif said, 'Blame yourselves! I remember how, on the day of Al-Ḥudaibiya (i.e. the peace treaty between the Prophet ﷺ and the (Quraish) pagans), if we had been allowed to choose fighting, we would have fought (the pagans). At that time 'Umar came (to the Prophet ﷺ) and said, "Aren't we on the right (path) and they (pagans) in the wrong? Won't our killed persons go to Paradise, and theirs in the Fire?" The Prophet replied, "Yes." 'Umar further said, "Then why should we let our religion be degraded and return before Allāh has settled the matter between us?" The Prophet ﷺ said, "O the son of Al-Khaṭṭāb! No doubt, I am Allāh's Messenger, and Allāh will never neglect me." So 'Umar left the place angrily and he was so impatient that he went to Abū Bakr and said, "O Abū Bakr! Aren't we on the right (path) and they (pagans) on the wrong?"' Abū Bakr said, "O the son of Al-Khaṭṭāb! He is Allāh's Messenger, and Allāh will never neglect him." Then Sūra Al-Fatḥ (The Victory) was revealed." '

قال: أتيت أبا وائل أسأله فقال: كنا بصفين، فقال رجل: ألم تر إلى الذين يدعون إلى كتاب الله تعالى؟ فقال علي: نعم، فقال سهل بن حنيف: اتهموا أنفسكم، فلقد رأيتنا يوم الحديبية، يعني الصلح الذي كان بين النبي صلى الله عليه وسلم والمشركين، ولو نرى قتالاً لقاتلنا، فجاء عمر فقال: ألسنا على الحق، وهم على الباطل؟ أليس قتلانا فى الجنة وقتلاهم فى النار؟ قال: بلى، قال: ففيم أعطي الدنية فى ديننا ونرجع، ولما يحكم الله بيننا؟ فقال: يا ابن الخطاب، إني رسول الله ولن يضيعني الله أبداً، فرجع متغيظاً فلم يصبر حتى جاء أبا بكر فقال: يا أبا بكر، ألسنا على الحق وهم على الباطل؟ قال: يا ابن الخطاب، إنه رسول الله صلى الله عليه وسلم ولن يضيعه الله أبداً، فنزلت سورة الفتح.

SŪRT Al-ḤUJURĀT
(The Inner Apartment)
XLIX

In the Name of Allāh,
the Most Beneficent, the Most Merciful

سورة الحجرات

بِسْمِ اللهِ الرَّحْمَنِ الرَّحِيمِ
وَقَالَ مُجَاهِدٌ: لاتُقَدِّمُوا: لاتَفْتَاتُوا عَلَى رَسُولِ اللهِ صلى اللهُ عليهِ وسلَّم حتَّى يَقْضِيَ اللهُ عَلَى لِسَانِهِ. امْتَحَنَ: أَخْلَصَ. تَنَابَزُوا: يُدْعَى بِالكُفْرِ بَعْدَ الإِسْلامِ. يَلِتْكُمْ: يَنْقُصْكُم. أَلَتْنَا: نَقَصْنَا.

(276) CHAPTER. 'Raise not your voices above the voice of the Prophet............' (49:2)

باب ـ لاتَرْفَعُوا أَصْوَاتَكُمْ فَوْقَ صَوْتِ النَّبِيِّ ـ الآيَة. تَشْعُرُونَ: تَعْلَمُونَ، وَمِنْهُ الشَّاعِرُ.

368. Narrated Ibn Abī Mulaika: The two righteous persons were about to be ruined. They were Abū Bakr and 'Umar who raised their voices in the presence of the Prophet ﷺ when a mission from Banī Tamīm came to him. One of the two recommended Al-Aqra' bin Ḥābis, the brother of Banī Mujāshi' (to be their governor) while the other recommended somebody else. (Nāfi', the sub-narrator said, I do not remember his name). Abū Bakr said to 'Umar, "You

٣٦٨ ـ حدَّثنا يَسَرَةُ بنُ صَفْوَانَ ابنِ جَمِيلٍ اللَّخْمِيُّ: حدَّثنا نافِعُ بنُ عُمَرَ، عَنِ ابنِ أَبِي مُلَيْكَةَ قالَ: كادَ الخَيِّرَانِ أَنْ يَهْلِكَا: أَبَا بَكْرٍ وعُمَرَ رَضِيَ اللهُ عَنْهُما، رَفَعَا أَصْوَاتَهُمَا عِنْدَ النَّبِيِّ صلى اللهُ عليهِ وسلَّم حِينَ قَدِمَ عَلَيْهِ رَكْبُ بَنِي تَمِيمٍ. فأَشَارَ أَحَدُهُمَا بِالأَقْرَعِ بنِ حَابِسٍ أَخِي بَنِي مُجَاشِعٍ.

٣٥٠

wanted nothing but to oppose me!" 'Umar said, "I did not intend to oppose you." Their voices grew loud in that argument, so Allāh revealed:

> 'O you who believe! Raise not your voices above the voice of the Prophet.' (49:2)

Ibn Az-Zubair said, "Since the revelation of this Verse, 'Umar used to speak in such a low tone that the Prophet ﷺ had to ask him to repeat his statements." But Ibn Az-Zubair did not mention the same about his (maternal) grandfather (i.e. Abū Bakr).

وأشارَ الآخرُ برجلٍ آخرَ ، قالَ نافعٌ : لا أحفظُ اسمَهُ ، فقالَ أبو بكرٍ لعمرَ : ما أردْتَ إلاَّ خلافي ، قالَ : ما أردْتُ خلافَكَ ، فارْتفعَتْ أصواتُهما في ذلكَ ، فأنزلَ اللهُ - يا أيُّها الذينَ آمنُوا لا ترْفعُوا أصواتَكمْ - الآيةَ . قالَ ابنُ الزُّبيرِ : فما كانَ عمرُ يُسْمعُ رسولَ اللهِ صلى اللهُ عليهِ وسلَّم بعْدَ هذهِ الآيةِ حتَّى يستفهِمَهُ ، ولمْ يذْكرْ ذلكَ عنْ أبيهِ ، يعْني أبا بكرٍ .

369. Narrated Anas bin Mālik: The Prophet ﷺ missed Thābit bin Qais for a period (So he inquired about him). A man said. "O Allāh's Apostle! I will bring you his news." So he went to Thābit and found him sitting in his house and bowing his head. The man said to Thābit, " 'What is the matter with you?" Thābit replied that it was an evil affair, for he used to raise his voice above the voice of the Prophet ﷺ and so all his good deeds had been annulled, and he considered himself as one of the people of the Fire. Then the man returned to the Prophet ﷺ and told him that Thābit had said, so-and-so. (Mūsā (bin Anas) said: The man returned to Thābit with great glad tidings). The Prophet ﷺ said to the man. "Go back to him and say to him: "You

٣٦٩ - حدَّثنا عليُّ بنُ عبْدِ اللهِ : حدَّثنا أزْهرُ بنُ سعْدٍ : أخبرَنا ابنُ عوْنٍ قالَ : أنبأني موسَى ابنُ أنسٍ ، عنْ أنسِ بنِ مالكٍ رضيَ اللهُ عنْهُ : أنَّ النبيَّ صلى اللهُ عليهِ وسلَّم افتقدَ ثابتَ بنَ قيْسٍ فقالَ رجلٌ : يا رسُولَ اللهِ ، أنا أعلَمُ لكَ علْمَهُ ، فأتاهُ فوجدَهُ جالِسًا في بيْتِهِ منكِّسًا رأسَهُ . فقالَ لهُ ما شأْنُكَ ؟ فقالَ : شرٌّ ، كانَ يرْفعُ صوْتَهُ فوْقَ صوْتِ النبيِّ صلى اللهُ عليهِ وسلَّم فقدْ حبِطَ عمَلُهُ وهُوَ منْ أهْلِ النارِ . فأتى الرَّجلُ النبيَّ صلى اللهُ عليهِ وسلَّم فأخبرَهُ أنَّهُ قالَ كذا وكذا ،

are not from the people of the Hell-Fire, but from the people of Paradise."'

فَقالَ مُوسَى: فَرَجَعَ إِلَيْهِ المَرَّةَ الآخِرَةَ بِبِشارَةٍ عَظِيمَةٍ، فَقالَ اذْهَبْ إِلَيْهِ فَقُلْ لَهُ إِنَّكَ لَسْتَ مِنْ أَهْلِ النّارِ، وَلَكِنَّكَ مِنْ أَهْلِ الجَنَّةِ.

(277) CHAPTER Verily! Those who call you from behind the dwellings most of them have no sense' (49:4)

باب - إِنَّ الَّذِينَ يُنادُونَكَ مِنْ وَراءِ الحُجُراتِ أَكْثَرُهُمْ لا يَعْقِلُونَ -.

370. Narrated 'Abdullāh bin Az-Zubair: A group of Banī Tamīm came to the Prophet ﷺ (and requested him to appoint a governor for them).

Abū Bakr said, "Appoint Al-Qa'qā' bin Ma'bad." 'Umar said, "Appoint Al-Aqra' bin Ḥābis." On that Abū Bakr said (to 'Umar). "You did not want but to oppose me!" 'Umar replied, "I did not intend to oppose you!" So both of them argued till their voices grew loud. So the following Verse was revealed:

'O you who believe! Be not forward................' (49:1)

٣٧٠ - حَدَّثَنا الحَسَنُ بنُ مُحَمَّدٍ: حَدَّثَنا حَجّاجٌ، عَنِ ابنِ جُرَيْجٍ قالَ: أَخْبَرَنِي ابنُ أَبِي مُلَيْكَةَ أَنَّ عَبْدَ اللهِ ابنَ الزُّبَيْرِ أَخْبَرَهُمْ أَنَّهُ قَدِمَ رَكْبٌ مِنْ بَنِي تَمِيمٍ عَلَى النَّبِيِّ صلى اللهُ عليهِ وسلَّم فَقالَ أَبُو بَكْرٍ: أَمِّرِ القَعْقاعَ بنَ مَعْبَدٍ. وَقالَ عُمَرُ: أَمِّرِ الأَقْرَعَ بنَ حابِسٍ. فَقالَ أَبُو بَكْرٍ: ما أَرَدْتَ إِلَى أَوْ إِلاّ خِلافِي، فَقالَ عُمَرُ: ما أَرَدْتُ خِلافَكَ. فَتَمارَيا حَتَّى ارْتَفَعَتْ أَصْواتُهُما، فَنَزَلَ فِي ذَلِكَ - يا أَيُّها الَّذِينَ آمَنُوا لا تُقَدِّمُوا بَيْنَ يَدَيِ اللهِ وَرَسُولِهِ - حَتَّى انْقَضَتِ الآيَةُ.

(278) CHAPTER. The statement of Allāh ﷻ :–
And if they had patience till you could come out to them, it would have been better for them.'
(49:5)

SURAT QĀF: L.

In the Name of Allāh, the Most Beneficent, the Most Merciful

باب قوله - ولو أنهم صبروا
حتى تخرج إليهم لكان خيرا لهم -.

سورة ق

بسم الله الرحمن الرحيم

رجع بعيد: رد. فروج: فتوق،
واحدها فرج. من حبل الوريد:
وريداه فى حلقه، والحبل العاتق.
وقال مجاهد: ما تنقص الأرض من
عظامهم. تبصرة بصيرة. حب
الحصيد: الحنطة. باسقات: الطوال.
أفعيينا: أفأعيا علينا. وقال قرينه:
الشيطان الذى قيض له. فنقبوا:
ضربوا. أو ألقى السمع: لا يحدث
نفسه بغيره حين أنشأكم وأنشأ
خلقكم. رقيب: عتيد. رصد:
سائق وشهيد: الملكان. كاتب وشهيد:
شهيد شاهد بالغيب. لغوب: النصب.
وقال غيره: نضيد: الكفرى ما دام
فى أكمامه ومعناه منضود بعضه على
بعض، فإذا خرج من أكمامه فليس
بنضيد. فى أدبار النجوم وأدبار
السجود كان عاصم يفتح التى فى ق

وَيَكْسِرُ الَّتِى فِى الطُّورِ، وَيُكْسَرَانِ جَمِيعًا وَيُنْصَبَانِ. وَقَالَ ابْنُ عَبَّاسٍ يَوْمَ الخُرُوجِ: يَوْمَ يَخْرُجُونَ إِلَى البَعْثِ مِنَ القُبُورِ.

(279) CHAPTER Allāh's Statement:

'It (Hell) will say: "Are there any more (to come)?" ' (50:30)

باب قَوْلِهِ . وَتَقُولُ هَلْ مِنْ مَزِيدٍ..

371. Narrated Anas: : The Prophet said, "The people will be thrown into the (Hell) Fire and it will say: "Are there any more (to come)?' (50:30) till Allāh will put His Foot over it and it will say, 'Qaṭi ! Qaṭi ! (Enough ! Enough !)' "

٣٧١ - حَدَّثَنَا عَبْدُ اللهِ بنُ أَبِى الأَسْوَدِ: حَدَّثَنَا حَرَمِىُّ بنُ عُمَارَةَ: حَدَّثَنَا شُعْبَةُ، عَنْ قَتَادَةَ، عَنْ أَنَسٍ رَضِىَ اللهُ عَنْهُ، عَنِ النَّبِىِّ صلى الله عليه وسلَّم قالَ: يُلْقَى فِى النَّارِ وَتَقُولُ هَلْ مِنْ مَزِيدٍ حَتَّى يَضَعَ قَدَمَهُ فَتَقُولُ قَطِ قَطِ.

372. Narrated Abū Huarira (that the Prophet said): "It will be said to the Hell, 'Are you filled?' It will say, 'Are there any more (to come)?' On that Allāh will put His Foot on it, and it will say 'Qaṭi! Qaṭi! (Enough! Enough!).' "

٣٧٢ - حَدَّثَنَا مُحَمَّدُ بنُ مُوسَى القَطَّانُ: حَدَّثَنَا أَبُو سُفْيَانَ الحِمْيَرِىُّ سَعِيدُ بنُ يَحْيَى بنِ مَهْدِىٍّ: حَدَّثَنَا عَوْفٌ، عَنْ مُحَمَّدٍ، عَنْ أَبِى هُرَيْرَةَ رَفَعَهُ، وَأَكْثَرُ مَا كَانَ يُوقِفُهُ أَبُو سُفْيَانَ، يُقَالُ لِجَهَنَّمَ هَلِ امْتَلأْتِ، وَتَقُولُ هَلْ مِنْ مَزِيدٍ؟ فَيَضَعُ الرَّبُّ تَبَارَكَ وَتَعَالَى قَدَمَهُ عَلَيْهَا فَتَقُولُ قَطْ قَطْ.

373. Narrated Abū Huraira : The Prophet said, "Paradise and the Fire (Hell) argued, and the Fire (Hell) said, "I have been given the privilege of receiving the arrogants and the tyrants.' Paradise said, 'What is the matter with me? Why do only the weak and the humble among the people enter me?' On that, Allāh said to Paradise. 'You are My Mercy which I bestow on whoever I wish of my slaves Then Allāh said to the (Hell) Fire, 'You are my (means of) punishment by which I punish whoever I wish of my slaves. And each of you will have its fill.' As for the Fire (Hell), it will not be filled till Allāh will put His Foot over it whereupon it will say, 'Qaṭi ! Qaṭi !' (1) at that time it will be filled, and its different parts will come closer to each other; and Allāh عزوجل will not wrong any of His created beings. As regards Paradise, Allāh will create a new creation to fill it with."

٣٧٣ ـ حدثنا عبد الله بن محمد : حدثنا عبد الرزاق : أخبرنا معمر ، عن همام ، عن أبي هريرة رضي الله عنه قال : قال النبي صلى الله عليه وسلم : تحاجت الجنة والنار ، فقالت النار : أوثرت بالمتكبرين والمتجبرين ، وقالت الجنة : مالي لا يدخلني إلا ضعفاء الناس وسقطهم ؟ قال الله تبارك وتعالى للجنة : أنت رحمتي أرحم بك من أشاء من عبادي ، وقال للنار : إنما أنت عذاب أعذب بك من أشاء من عبادي ، ولكل واحدة منهما ملؤها ، فأما النار فلا تمتلىء حتى يضع رجله فتقول قط قط ، فهنالك تمتلىء ويزوى بعضها إلى بعض ، ولا يظلم الله عز وجل من خلقه أحدا . وأما الجنة فإن الله عز وجل ينشىء لها خلقا .

(289) CHAPTER. The Statement of Allāh :–

> And celebrate the praises of your Lord before the rising of the sun and before (its) setting.' (i.e. the morning, Ẓuhr and 'Aṣr prayers) . . . . (50:39)

باب قوله ـ فسبح بحمد ربك قبل طلوع الشمس وقبل الغروب ـ .

(1) Enough, Enough

374. Narrated Jarir bin 'Abdullāh: We were in the company of the Prophet ﷺ on a fourteenth night (of the lunar month), and he looked at the (full) moon and said, "You will see your Lord as you see this moon, and you will have no trouble in looking at Him. So, whoever can, should not miss the offering of prayers before sunrise (Fajr prayer) and before sunset ('Aṣr prayer)." Then the Prophet ﷺ recited:

> 'And celebrate the praises of your Lord before the rising of the sun and before (its) setting.' (50:39)

٣٧٤ - حَدَّثَنَا إِسْحَاقُ بْنُ إِبْرَاهِيمَ، عَنْ جَرِيرٍ، عَنْ إِسْمَاعِيلَ، عَنْ قَيْسِ بْنِ أَبِى حَازِمٍ، عَنْ جَرِيرِ بْنِ عَبْدِ اللهِ قَالَ: كُنَّا جُلُوسًا لَيْلَةً مَعَ النَّبِىِّ صَلَّى اللهُ عَلَيْهِ وَسَلَّمَ فَنَظَرَ إِلَى الْقَمَرِ لَيْلَةَ أَرْبَعَ عَشْرَةَ فَقَالَ: إِنَّكُمْ سَتَرَوْنَ رَبَّكُمْ كَمَا تَرَوْنَ هَذَا، لَا تُضَامُونَ فِى رُؤْيَتِهِ، فَإِنِ اسْتَطَعْتُمْ أَنْ لَا تُغْلَبُوا عَلَى صَلَاةٍ قَبْلَ طُلُوعِ الشَّمْسِ، وَقَبْلَ غُرُوبِهَا فَافْعَلُوا. ثُمَّ قَرَأَ - وَسَبِّحْ بِحَمْدِ رَبِّكَ قَبْلَ طُلُوعِ الشَّمْسِ وَقَبْلَ الْغُرُوبِ -.

375. Narrated Mujāhid: Ibn 'Abbās said, "Allāh ordered His Prophet ﷺ to celebrate Allāh's praises after all prayers." He refers to His Statement: 'After the prayers.' (50:40)

(See Ḥadīth No. 804, Vol I)

٣٧٥ - حَدَّثَنَا آدَمُ: حَدَّثَنَا وَرْقَاءُ، عَنِ ابْنِ أَبِى نَجِيحٍ، عَنْ مُجَاهِدٍ قَالَ: قَالَ ابْنُ عَبَّاسٍ: أَمَرَهُ أَنْ يُسَبِّحَ فِى أَدْبَارِ الصَّلَوَاتِ كُلِّهَا، يَعْنِى قَوْلَهُ - وَأَدْبَارَ السُّجُودِ -.

SŪRAT ADH-DHĀRIYĀT LI
(The winds that scatter)

سورة والذاريات

In the Name of Allāh, the Most Beneficent, the Most Merciful

(No Ḥadīths were mentioned here)

بِسْمِ اللهِ الرَّحْمَنِ الرَّحِيمِ

قَالَ عَلِىٌّ عَلَيْهِ السَّلَامُ: الذَّارِيَاتُ: الرِّيَاحُ. وَقَالَ غَيْرُهُ: تَذْرُوهُ: تُفَرِّقُهُ - وَفِى أَنْفُسِكُمْ أَفَلَا تُبْصِرُونَ -

تَـأكُلُ وَتَشْرَبُ فى مَدْخَلٍ وَاحِدٍ
وَيَخْرُجُ مِنْ مَوْضِعَيْنِ. فَرَاغَ: فَرَجَعَ.
فَصَكَّتْ: فَجَمَعَتْ أصَابِعَهَا. فَضَرَبَتْ
بِهِ جَبْهَتَهَا. وَالرَّمِيمُ: نَبَاتُ الأرْضِ إذَا
يَبِسَ وَدِيسَ. لَمُوسِعُونَ: أىْ لَذُو سَعَةٍ،
وَكَذَلِكَ. عَلَى الْمُوسِعِ قَدَرُهُ. يَعْنى الْقَوِىَّ.
زَوْجَيْنِ: الذَّكَرَ وَالأُنْثَى، وَاخْتِلافُ
الألْوَانِ، حُلْوٌ وَحَامِضٌ، فَهُمَا زَوْجَانِ.
فَفِرُّوا إلى اللهِ. مِنَ اللهِ إلَيْهِ. إلاَّ لِيَعْبُدُونِ.
مَا خَلَقْتُ أهْلَ السَّعَادَةِ مِنْ أهْلِ
الْفَرِيقَيْنِ إلاَّ لِيُوَحِّدُونِ. وَقَالَ بَعْضُهُمْ:
خَلَقَهُمْ لِيَفْعَلُوا، فَفَعَلَ بَعْضٌ وَتَرَكَ
بَعْضٌ وَلَيْسَ فِيهِ حُجَّةٌ لأهْلِ الْقَدَرِ،
وَالذَّنُوبُ: الدَّلْوُ الْعَظِيمُ. وَقَالَ مُجَاهِدٌ:
ذَنُوبًا: سَبِيلاً. صَرَّةٍ: صَيْحَةٍ. الْعَقِيمُ:
الَّتِى لا تَلِدُ. وَقَالَ ابْنُ عَبَّاسٍ: وَالْحُبُكُ:
اسْتِوَاؤُهَا وَحُسْنُهَا. فى غَمْرَةٍ: فى
ضَلالَتِهِمْ يَتَمَادَوْنَ. وَقَالَ غَيْرُهُ:
تَوَاصَوْا: تَوَاطَئُوا. وَقَالَ مُسَوَّمَةً:
مُعَلَّمَةً مِنَ السِّيمَا. قُتِلَ الإنْسَانُ:
لُعِنَ.

سورة الطور

SŪRAT AṬ-ṬŪR (The Mount): LII

بِسْمِ اللهِ الرَّحْمَنِ الرَّحِيمِ

In the Name of Allāh, the Most Beneficent, the Most Merciful

وَقَالَ قَتَادَةُ: مَسْطُورٍ: مَكْتُوبٍ

وَقَالَ مُجَاهِدٌ : الطُّورُ : الجَبَلُ بالسُّرْيَانِيَّةِ . رَقٍّ مَنْشُورٍ : صَحِيفَةٍ . والسَّقْفِ المَرْفُوعِ : سَمَاءٌ . المَسْجُورِ : المُوقَدِ . وَقَالَ الحَسَنُ : تُسْجَرُ حَتَّى يَذْهَبَ مَاؤُهَا فَلَا يَبْقَى فِيهَا قَطْرَةٌ . وقال مُجَاهِدٌ : أَلَتْنَاهُمْ : نَقَصْنَاهُمْ . وقال غيرُهُ : تَمُورُ تَدُورُ . أَحْلَامُهُمْ : العُقُولُ . وَقَالَ ابنُ عَبَّاسٍ : البَرُّ : اللَّطِيفُ . المَنُونُ : المَوْتُ ، وَقَالَ غَيْرُهُ : يَتَنَازَعُونَ : يَتَعَاطَوْنَ .

376. Narrated Um Salama: I complained to Allāh's Messenger ﷺ that I was sick, so he said, "Perform the Ṭawāf (of Ka'ba at Mecca) while riding behind the people (who are performing the Ṭawāf on foot)." So I performed the Ṭawāf while Allāh's Messenger ﷺ was offering the prayer by the side of the Ka'ba and was reciting:

> 'By the Mount (Saini) and by the Book (of Eternal Decrees) Inscribed.' (52)

٣٧٦ ـ حَدَّثَنَا عَبْدُ اللهِ بنُ يُوسُفَ : أَخْبَرَنَا مَالِكٌ ، عَنْ مُحَمَّدِ بنِ عَبْدِ الرَّحْمَنِ بنِ نَوْفَلٍ ، عَنْ عُرْوَةَ ، عَنْ زَيْنَبَ ابْنَةِ أبي سَلَمَةَ ، عَنْ أُمِّ سَلَمَةَ قالت : شَكَوْتُ إلى رَسُولِ اللهِ صَلَّى اللهُ عليهِ وسلَّمَ أَنِّي أَشْتَكِي ، فَقَالَ : طُوفِي مِنْ وَرَاءِ النَّاسِ وأنتِ رَاكِبَةٌ ، فَطُفْتُ وَرَسُولُ اللهِ صَلَّى اللهُ عليهِ وسلَّمَ يُصَلِّي إلى جَنْبِ البَيْتِ يَقْرَأُ بالطُّورِ وكِتَابٍ مَسْطُورٍ .

377. Narrated Jubair bin Muṭ'im (رضي الله عنه): I heard the Prophet ﷺ reciting Sūrat Aṭ-Ṭūr in the Maghrib prayer, and when he reached the Verse:

'Were they created by nothing,
Or were they themselves the
  creators,
Or did they create the Heavens

٣٧٧ ـ حَدَّثَنَا الحُمَيْدِيُّ : حَدَّثَنَا سُفْيَانُ قَالَ : حَدَّثُونِي عَنِ الزُّهْرِيِّ ، عَنْ مُحَمَّدِ بنِ جُبَيْرِ بنِ مُطْعِمٍ ، عَنْ أبيهِ رَضِيَ اللهُ عَنْهُ قَالَ : سَمِعْتُ النَّبِيَّ صَلَّى اللهُ عليهِ وسلَّمَ يَقْرَأُ فِي المَغْرِبِ بالطُّورِ ، فَلَمَّا بَلَغَ هَذِهِ الآيَةَ ـ أَمْ

and the Earth?
Nay, but they have no firm belief
Or do they own the treasures of Your Lord? Or have they been given the authority to do as they like
. . . . (52:35–37)

my heart was about to fly (when I realised this firm argument).

خلقوا من غير شيء أم هم الخالقون ، أم خلقوا السموات والأرض بل لا يوقنون . أم عندهم خزائن ربك أم هم المسيطرون . كاد قلبي أن يطير . قال سفيان : فأما أنا فإنما سمعت الزهري يحدث عن محمد بن جبير بن مطعم عن أبيه : سمعت النبي صلى الله عليه وسلم يقرأ في المغرب بالطور ، لم أسمعه زاد الذي قالوا لي .

SURAT AN-NAJM (The star) LIII

In the Name of Allāh,
the Most Beneficent, the Most Merciful

سورة النجم

بسم الله الرحمن الرحيم

وقال مجاهد : ذو مرة : ذو قوة . قاب قوسين : حيث الوتر من القوس . ضيزى : عوجاء . وأكدى : قطع عطاءه . رب الشعرى : هو مرزم الجوزاء . الذي وفى : وفى ما فرض عليه . أزفت الآزفة : اقتربت الساعة . سامدون : البرطمة . وقال عكرمة : يتغنون بالحميرية . وقال إبراهيم : أفتمارونه : أفتجادلونه . ومن قرأ أفتمرونه : يعني أفتجحدونه . ما زاغ البصر : بصر محمد صلى الله عليه وسلم . وما طغى : وما جاوز ما رأى . فتماروا : كذبوا . وقال الحسن : إذا

378. Narrated Masrūq: I said to 'Āisha (رضي الله عنها) "O Mother! Did Prophet Muḥammad ﷺ see his Lord?" 'Āisha said, "What you have said makes my hair stand on end! Know that if somebody tells you one of the following three things, he is a liar: Whoever tells you that Muḥammad ﷺ saw his Lord, is a liar." Then 'Āisha recited the Verse:

> 'No vision can grasp Him, but His grasp is over all vision. He is the Most Courteous Well-Acquainted with all things.' (6:103)
>
> 'It is not fitting for a human being that Allāh should speak to him except by inspiration or from behind a veil.' (42:51)

'Āisha further said, "And whoever tells you that the Prophet ﷺ knows what is going to happen tomorrow, is a liar." She then recited:—

> 'No soul can know what it will earn tomorrow.' (31:34)

She added: "And whoever tell you that he concealed (some of Allāh's orders), is a liar." Then she recited:

> 'O Messenger! Proclaim (the Message) which has been sent down to you from your Lord........' (5:67)

'Āisha added. "But the Prophet ﷺ saw Gabriel in his true form twice."

هَوَى : غابَ . وقالَ ابنُ عبَّاسٍ : أَغْنَى وأَقْنَى : أَعْطَى فأَرْضَى .

٣٧٨ ـ حَدَّثنا يَحْيى : حَدَّثنا وَكيع ، عَنْ إسْماعِيلَ بنِ أبى خالِدٍ ، عَنْ عامِرٍ ، عَنْ مَسْرُوقٍ قالَ : قُلْتُ لِعائِشَةَ رضِىَ اللهُ عَنْها : يا أُمَّتاهُ ، هَلْ رأى مُحَمَّدٌ صَلَّى اللهُ عليهِ وسلَّمَ رَبَّهُ ؟ فَقالَتْ : لَقَدْ قَفَّ شَعَرِى مِمَّا قُلْتَ ، أيْنَ أنْتَ مِنْ ثَلاثٍ مَنْ حَدَّثَكَهُنَّ فَقَدْ كَذَبَ ؟ مَنْ حَدَّثَكَ أنَّ مُحَمَّدًا صَلَّى اللهُ عليهِ وسلَّمَ رأى رَبَّهُ فَقَدْ كَذَبَ . ثُمَّ قَرأَتْ لا تُدْرِكُهُ الأبْصارُ وَهُوَ يُدْرِكُ الأبْصارَ وَهُوَ اللَّطِيفُ الخَبِيرُ ـ وَما كانَ لِبَشَرٍ أنْ يُكَلِّمَهُ اللهُ إلاَّ وَحْيًا أوْ مِنْ وَراءِ حِجابٍ ـ وَمَنْ حَدَّثَكَ أنَّهُ يَعْلَمُ ما فى غَدٍ فَقَدْ كَذَبَ . ثُمَّ قَرأَتْ ـ وَما تَدْرِى نَفْسٌ ماذا تَكْسِبُ غَدًا ـ وَمَنْ حَدَّثَكَ أنَّهُ كَتَمَ فَقَدْ كَذَبَ ، ثُمَّ قَرأَتْ ـ يا أيُّها الرَّسُولُ بَلِّغْ ما أُنْزِلَ إلَيْكَ مِنْ رَبِّكَ ـ الآيَةَ . وَلَكِنْ رأى جِبْرِيلَ عَلَيْهِ السَّلامُ فى صُورَتِهِ مَرَّتَيْنِ .

(281) CHAPTER. 'And was at a distance of but two bow-lengths or (even) nearer.' (53-9)

بابٌ - فَكانَ قابَ قَوْسَيْنِ أَوْ أَدْنَى - حَيْثُ الوَتَرُ مِنَ القَوْسِ.

379. Narrated 'Abdullāh regarding the Verses:

'And was at a distance of but two bow-lengths or (even) nearer; So did (Allāh) convey the Inspiration to His slave (Gabriel) and then he Gabriel), conveyed (that to Muḥammad) (53:9:10):'

Ibn Mas'ūd narrated to us that the Prophet had seen Gabriel with six hundred wings.

٣٧٩ - حدَّثنا أبو النُّعمانِ: حدَّثنا عبدُ الواحدِ: حدَّثنا الشَّيْبانيُّ قالَ: سمِعتُ زِرًّا، عن عبدِ اللهِ - فكان قابَ قَوْسَيْنِ أو أدنى فأوحى إلى عبدِهِ ما أوحى - قال: حدَّثنا ابنُ مسعودٍ أنَّهُ رأى جبريلَ لهُ سِتُّمائةِ جَناحٍ.

(282) CHAPTER. The Statement of Allāh :

'So did (Allāh) convey the Inspiration to His slave (Gabriel) then he (Gabriel) conveyed (that to Muḥammad)' (53:10)

بابٌ قَوْلِهِ - فأوحى إلى عبدِهِ ما أوحى -.

380. Narrated Ash-Shaibānī: I asked Zirr about the Statement of Allāh :

'And was at a distance of but two bow-lengths or (even) nearer.

So did Allāh convey the Inspiration to His slave (Gabriel) and

٣٨٠ - حدَّثنا طَلْقُ بنُ غَنّامٍ: حدَّثنا زائدةُ، عنِ الشَّيْبانيِّ قال: سألتُ زِرًّا عن قولِهِ تعالى - فكان قابَ قَوْسَيْنِ أو أدنى فأوحى إلى عبدِهِ ما

then he (Gabriel) conveyed that to Muhammad ﷺ) (53:10)
He said, "Abdullāh (bin Mas'ūd) informed us that Muhammad ﷺ had seen Gabriel with six hundred wings."

أَوْحَى - قالَ: أَخْبَرَنا عَبْدُ اللهِ أَنَّ مُحَمَّدًا صلى اللهُ عليهِ وسلَّم رأى جِبْرِيلَ لَهُ سِتُّمائَةِ جَناحٍ.

(283) CHAPTER. Truly he (Muhammad ﷺ) did see of the signs of his Lord, the Greatest.' (53:18)

بابٌ - لَقَدْ رَأَى مِنْ آياتِ رَبِّهِ الكُبْرَى..

381. Narrated 'Abdullāh رضي الله عنه (regarding the revelation): Truly he (Muhammad ﷺ) did see of the signs of his Lord; the Greatest!' (53:18)

The Prophet ﷺ saw a green screen covering the horizon.

٣٨١ - حدَّثَنا قَبِيصَةُ: حدَّثَنا سُفْيانُ، عَنِ الأَعْمَشِ، عَنْ إِبْراهِيمَ، عَنْ عَلْقَمَةَ. عَنْ عَبْدِ اللهِ رَضِيَ اللهُ عَنْهُ - لَقَدْ رَأَى مِنْ آياتِ رَبِّهِ الكُبْرَى - قالَ: رَأَى رَفْرَفًا أَخْضَرَ قَدْ سَدَّ الأُفُقَ.

(284) CHAPTER. Have you seen the Lāt and the 'Uzza?' (1) (53:19)

بابٌ - أَفَرَأَيْتُمُ اللاتَ والعُزَّى..

382. Narrated Ibn 'Abbās رضي الله عنهما (regarding His Statement about the Lāt and the 'Uzza: Lat was originally a man

٣٨٢ - حدَّثَنا مُسْلِمُ بنُ إِبْراهِيمَ: حدَّثَنا أَبو الأَشْهَبِ: حدَّثَنا أَبو الجَوْزاءِ،

(1) Lāt and 'Uzza were two idols worshipped by the pagan Arabs during the Pre-Islāmic period of ignorance.

who used to mix Sawīq (1) for the pilgrims.

عن ابن عباس رضي الله عنهما في قوله. اللات والعزى. كان اللات رجلا يلت سويق الحاج.

383. Narrated Abū Huraira ﷺ: Allāh's Messenger ﷺ said, "Whoever takes an oath in which he mentions Lāt and 'Uzza (forgetfully), should say: None has the right to be worshipped but Allāh, and whoever says to his companion. 'Come along, let us gamble,' must give alms (as an expiation)."

٣٨٣ - حدثنا عبد الله بن محمد: أخبرنا هشام بن يوسف: أخبرنا معمر، عن الزهري، عن حميد بن عبد الرحمن، عن أبي هريرة رضي الله عنه قال: قال رسول الله صلى الله عليه وسلم: من حلف فقال في حلفه واللات والعزى، فليقل لا إله إلا الله. ومن قال لصاحبه تعال أقامرك فليتصدق.

(285) CHAPTER. And Manāt (another idol of the pagan Arabs) the third the other. (53:20)

باب - ومناة الثالثة الأخرى -.

384. Narrated 'Urwa: I asked 'Āisha ﷺ (regarding the Sa'ī between As-Ṣafā and Al-Marwa). She said, "Out of reverence to the idol Manāt which was placed in Al-Mushallal, those (pagans) who used to assume Iḥrām in its name, used not to perform Sa'ī between Aṣ-Ṣafā and Al-Marwa, (2) so Allāh revealed :

'Verily! The Aṣ-Ṣafā and Al-Marwa

٣٨٤ - حدثنا الحميدي: حدثنا سفيان: حدثنا الزهري: سمعت عروة: قلت لعائشة رضي الله عنها: فقالت إنما كان من أهل لمناة الطاغية التي بالمشلل لا يطوفون بين الصفا والمروة فأنزل الله تعالى - إن الصفا

(1) See the glossary.

(2) Because there were two other idols between Aṣ-Ṣafā and Al-Marwa which did not belong to them.

(two mountains at Mecca) are among the symbols of Allāh.' (2:158)

Thereupon, Allāh's Messenger ﷺ and the Muslims used to perform Sa'ī (between them)." Sufyān said: The (idol) Manāt was at Al-Mushallal in Qudaid. 'Āisha added, "The Verse was revealed in connection with the Anṣār. They and (the tribe of) Ghassān used to assume Iḥrām in the name of Manāt before they embraced Islām." 'Āisha added, "There were men from the Anṣār who used to assume Iḥrām in the name of Manāt which was an idol between Mecca and Medīna. They said, "O Allāh's Messenger! We used not to perform the Ṭawāf (Sa'ī) between Aṣ-Ṣafā and Al-Marwa out of reverence to Manāt.' "

والمَرْوَةَ مِنْ شَعَائِرِ اللهِ - فَطَافَ
رَسُولُ اللهِ صلى الله عليه وسلم والمُسْلِمُونَ.
قالَ سُفْيانُ: مَنَاةُ بالمُشَلَّلِ مِنْ قُدَيْدٍ.
وَقالَ عَبْدُ الرَّحْمَنِ بنُ خالِدٍ، عَنِ
ابنِ شِهابٍ: قالَ عُرْوَةُ: قالَتْ عائِشَةُ:
نَزَلَتْ في الأنْصارِ، كانُوا هُمْ وَغَسَّانُ
قَبْلَ أنْ يُسْلِمُوا يُهِلُّونَ لِمَناةَ
مِثْلَهُ. وَقالَ مَعْمَرٌ، عَنِ الزُّهْرِيِّ،
عَنْ عُرْوَةَ، عَنْ عائِشَةَ: كانَ رِجالٌ
مِنَ الأنْصارِ مِمَّنْ كانَ يُهِلُّ لِمَناةَ،
وَمَناةُ صَنَمٌ بَيْنَ مَكَّةَ والمَدِينَةِ.
قالُوا: يا نَبِيَّ اللهِ، كُنَّا لا نَطُوفُ بَيْنَ
الصَّفا والمَرْوَةِ تَعْظِيمًا لِمَناةَ. نَحْوَهُ.

(286) CHAPTER. So fall you down in prostration to Allāh and worship (Him alone.) (53:62)

بابٌ - فاسْجُدُوا لِلهِ وَاعْبُدُوا -

385. Narrated Ibn 'Abbās رضي الله عنهما: The Prophet ﷺ performed a prostration when he finished reciting Sūrat-an-Najm, and all the Muslims and pagans and Jinns and human beings prostrated along with him.

٣٨٥ - حَدَّثَنا أبُو مَعْمَرٍ: حَدَّثَنا
عَبْدُ الوَارِثِ: حَدَّثَنا أيُّوبُ، عَنْ
عِكْرِمَةَ، عَنِ ابنِ عَبَّاسٍ رَضِيَ اللهُ
عَنْهُما قالَ: سَجَدَ النَّبِيُّ صلى الله عليه
وسلم بالنَّجْمِ وَسَجَدَ مَعَهُ المُسْلِمُونَ
والمُشْرِكُونَ والجِنُّ والإنْسُ. تابَعَهُ
ابنُ طَهْمانَ، عَنْ أيُّوبَ. وَلَمْ يَذْكُرِ
ابنُ عُلَيَّةَ ابنَ عَبَّاسٍ.

386. Narrated 'Abdullāh ﷺ: The first Sūra in which a prostration was mentioned, was Sūra An-Najm (The Star). Allāh's Messenger ﷺ prostrated (while reciting it), and everybody behind him prostrated except a man whom I saw taking a hand-full of dust in his hand and prostrated on it. Later I saw that man killed as an infidel, and he was Umaiya bin Khalaf.

٣٨٦ - حَدَّثَنَا نَصْرُ بْنُ عَلِيٍّ أَخْبَرَنِي أَبُو أَحْمَدَ قَالَ حَدَّثَنَا إِسْرَائِيلُ عَنْ أَبِي إِسْحَاقَ عَنِ الأَسْوَدِ بْنِ يَزِيدَ عَنْ عَبْدِ اللهِ قَالَ أَوَّلُ سُورَةٍ أُنْزِلَتْ فِيهَا سَجْدَةٌ النَّجْمِ - قَالَ فَسَجَدَ رَسُولُ اللهِ صلى اللهُ عليهِ وسَلَّم وسَجَدَ مَنْ خَلْفَهُ إِلاَّ رَجُلٌ رَأَيْتُهُ أَخَذَ كَفًّا مِنْ تُرَابٍ فَسَجَدَ عَلَيْهِ فَرَأَيْتُ بَعْدَ ذَلِكَ قُتِلَ كَافِرًا وَهُوَ أُمَيَّةُ بْنُ خَلَفٍ .

SŪRAT-UL-QAMAR: LIV
The Sūra starting with, THE HOUR DREW NIGH

سورة اقتربت الساعة

In the Name of Allāh, the Most Beneficent, the Most Merciful

بِسْمِ اللهِ الرَّحْمَنِ الرَّحِيمِ

قَالَ مُجَاهِدٌ : مُسْتَمِرٌّ : ذَاهِبٌ . مُزْدَجَرٌ : مُتَنَاهٍ . وَازْدُجِرَ : فَاسْتُطِيرَ جُنُونًا . دُسُرٍ : أَضْلاَعُ السَّفِينَةِ . لِمَنْ كَانَ كُفِرَ - يَقُولُ كُفِرَ لَهُ جَزَاءً مِنَ اللهِ . مُحْتَضَرٌ : يَحْضُرُونَ المَاءَ . وَقَالَ ابْنُ جُبَيْرٍ : مُهْطِعِينَ : النَّسَلاَنُ . الخَبَبُ : السِّرَاعُ . وَقَالَ غَيْرُهُ : فَتَعَاطَى : فَعَاطَهَا بِيَدِهِ فَعَقَرَهَا . المُحْتَظِرِ : كَحِظَارٍ مِنَ الشَّجَرِ مُحْتَرِقٍ ازْدُجِرَ : افْتُعِلَ مِنْ زَجَرْتُ . كُفِرَ : فَعَلْنَا بِهِ وَبِهِمْ مَا فَعَلْنَا جَزَاءً لِمَا صُنِعَ بِنُوحٍ وَأَصْحَابِهِ . مُسْتَقِرٌّ : عَذَابٌ

حَقٌّ . يُقَالُ الأشَرُ : المَرَحُ وَالتَّجَبُّرُ .

(287) CHAPTER. 'And the moon is cleft asunder, but if they see a sign, they turn away.' (54:1-2)

بابٌ ـ وَانْشَقَّ القَمَرُ وَإِنْ يَرَوْا آيَةً يُعْرِضُوا ـ

387 Narrated Ibn Mas'ūd: During the lifetime of Allāh's Messenger ﷺ the moon was split into two parts; one part remained over the mountain, and the other part went beyond the mountain. On that, Allāh's Messenger ﷺ said, "Witness (this miracle.") (1)

٣٨٧ ـ حَدَّثَنَا مُسَدَّدٌ : حَدَّثَنَا يَحْيَى ، عَنْ شُعْبَةَ ، وَسُفْيَانَ عَنِ الأعْمَشِ ، عَنْ إِبْرَاهِيمَ ، عَنْ أَبِي مَعْمَرٍ ، عَنِ ابنِ مَسْعُودٍ قَالَ : انْشَقَّ القَمَرُ عَلَى عَهْدِ رَسُولِ اللهِ صَلَّى اللهُ عليهِ وسلَّمَ فِرْقَتَيْنِ : فِرْقَةٌ فَوْقَ الجَبَلِ ، وَفِرْقَةٌ دُونَهُ . فَقَالَ رَسُولُ اللهِ صلى اللهُ عليهِ وسلَّم ـ اشْهَدُوا .

388. Narrated 'Abdullāh: The moon was cleft asunder while we were in the company of the Prophet ﷺ, and it became two parts. The Prophet ﷺ said, Witness, witness (this miracle)."

٣٨٨ ـ حَدَّثَنا عَلِيُّ بنُ عَبْدِ اللهِ : حَدَّثَنا سُفْيَانُ : أَخْبَرَنا ابنُ أبي نَجِيحٍ ، عَنْ مُجَاهِدٍ ، عَنْ أبي مَعْمَرٍ ، عَنْ عَبْدِ اللهِ قَالَ : انْشَقَّ القَمَرُ وَنَحْنُ مَعَ النَّبِيِّ صَلَّى اللهُ عَلَيْهِ وسلَّمَ فَصَارَ فِرْقَتَيْنِ ، فقالَ لَنَا : اشْهَدُوا ، اشْهَدُوا .

389. Narrated Ibn 'Abbās: The moon was cleft asunder during the lifetime of the Prophet ﷺ

٣٨٩ ـ حدَّثَنَا يَحْيَى بنُ بُكَيْرٍ ، قَالَ : حدَّثَنِي بَكْرٌ ، عَنْ جَعْفَرٍ ،

(1) See the Miracle of the Prophet ﷺ :

عَنْ عِرَاكِ بْنِ مَالِكٍ عَنْ عُبَيْدِ اللهِ بْنِ عَبْدِ اللهِ بْنِ عُتْبَةَ بْنِ مَسْعُودٍ. عَنِ ابْنِ عَبَّاسٍ رَضِيَ اللهُ عَنْهُمَا قَالَ: انْشَقَّ القَمَرُ فِي زَمَانِ النَّبِيِّ صَلَّى اللهُ عَلَيْهِ وَسَلَّمَ.

390. Narrated Anas ﷺ : The people of Mecca asked the Prophet ﷺ to show them a sign (miracle). So he showed them (the miracle) of the cleaving of the moon.

٣٩٠ - حَدَّثَنَا عَبْدُ اللهِ بْنُ مُحَمَّدٍ: حَدَّثَنَا يُونُسُ بْنُ مُحَمَّدٍ: حَدَّثَنَا شَيْبَانُ، عَنْ قَتَادَةَ، عَنْ أَنَسٍ رَضِيَ اللهُ عَنْهُ قَالَ: سَأَلَ أَهْلُ مَكَّةَ أَنْ يُرِيَهُمْ آيَةً فَأَرَاهُمُ انْشِقَاقَ القَمَرِ.

391. Narrated Anas: The moon was cleft asunder into two parts.

٣٩١ - حَدَّثَنَا مُسَدَّدٌ: حَدَّثَنَا يَحْيَى، عَنْ شُعْبَةَ، عَنْ قَتَادَةَ، عَنْ أَنَسٍ قَالَ: انْشَقَّ القَمَرُ فِرْقَتَيْنِ.

(288) CHAPTER. The Statement of Allāh ﷻ :

(Noah's Ark) floating under Our Eyes (and care): a recompense for him who had been rejected. And indeed, We have left this as a sign; Then is there; any that will receive admonition? (54:14-15)

Qatāda said, "Allāh preserved Noah's Ark till the early converts of this nation saw it."

بَابٌ - تَجْرِي بِأَعْيُنِنَا جَزَاءً لِمَنْ كَانَ كُفِرَ، وَلَقَدْ تَرَكْنَاهَا آيَةً فَهَلْ مِنْ مُدَّكِرٍ - قَالَ قَتَادَةُ: أَبْقَى اللهُ سَفِينَةَ نُوحٍ حَتَّى أَدْرَكَهَا أَوَائِلُ هَذِهِ الأُمَّةِ.

392. Narrated 'Adullāh bin Mas'ūd:

٣٩٢ - حَدَّثَنَا حَفْصُ بْنُ عُمَرَ:

The Prophet ﷺ used to recite:
'Fahal-min-Maddakir' (then is there any that will receive admonition.?)

حدَّثنا شعبةُ، عن أبي إسحاقَ، عن الأسودِ، عن عبدِ الله قال: كانَ النبيُّ صلى الله عليه وسلَّم يقرأ - فهل من مُدَّكرٍ -.

(289) CHAPTER. The Statement of Allāh تعالى :

'And we have indeed made the Qur'ān easy to understand and remember; then is there any that will receive admonition?'

(54:17)

باب - ولقد يسَّرنا القرآنَ للذِّكر فهل من مُدَّكِرٍ - قال مجاهد: يسَّرنا: هوَّنا قراءتَه.

393. Narrated 'Abdullāh رضي الله عنه The Prophet ﷺ used to recite: Is there any that remember?' and a furious wind (plucking out men). As if they were uprooted stems of palm trees, then how terrible was My punishment and My warnings!

(54:20-21)

٣٩٣ - حدَّثنا مسدَّدٌ، عن يحيى، عن شعبةَ، عن أبي إسحاقَ، عن الأسودِ، عن عبدِ الله رضيَ اللهُ عنه، عن النبيِّ صلى الله عليه وسلَّم أنه كانَ يقرأ - فهل من مُدَّكرٍ؟ أعجازُ نخلٍ مُنقعرٍ فكيفَ كانَ عذابي ونُذُرِ -.

394. Narrated Abū Isḥāq: A man asked Al-Aswad, 'is It 'Fahal-min-Muddakir' or'......Mudhdhakir?" Al-Aswad replied, 'I have heard 'Abdullāh bin Mas'ūd reciting it, 'Fahal-min Muddakir'; I too, heard the Prophet ﷺ reciting it 'Fahal-min-Muddakir' with 'd'.

٣٩٤ - حدَّثنا أبو نُعيمٍ: حدَّثنا زُهيرٌ، عن أبي إسحاقَ أنه سمعَ رجلاً سألَ الأسودَ: فهل من مُدَّكرٍ أو مُذَّكرٍ. فقال: سمعتُ عبدَ الله يقرؤها - فهل من مُدَّكرٍ - قال: وسمعتُ النبيَّ صلى الله عليه وسلَّم يقرؤها - فهل من مُدَّكرٍ - دالاً -.

(290) CHAPTER. 'And they became like the dry stubble used by one who pens cattle. And We have indeed made the Qur'ān easy to understand and remember; then is there any that will receive admonition. (54:31-32)

فكانوا كهشيم المحتظر ـ ولقد يسرنا القرآن للذكر فهل من مدكر ـ.

395. Narrated 'Abdullāh: The Prophet recited: 'Fahal-min-Muddakir' "And Verily an abiding torment seized them early in the morning So, taste you My torment and My warnings' (54:38:39)

٣٩٥ ـ حدثنا عبدان : أخبرنا أبي، عن شعبة، عن أبي إسحاق، عن الأسود، عن عبد الله رضي الله عنه، عن النبي صلى الله عليه وسلم قرأ ـ فهل من مدكر ـ الآية ـ ولقد صبحهم بكرة عذاب مستقر فذوقوا عذابي ونذر.

396. Narrated 'Abdullāh: The Prophet recited: 'Fahal-min-Muddakir':

'And verily, We have destroyed nations like unto you; then is there any that will receive admonition? (54:51)

٣٩٦ ـ حدثنا محمد: حدثنا غندر: حدثنا شعبة، عن أبي إسحاق، عن الأسود، عن عبد الله، عن النبي صلى الله عليه وسلم قرأ ـ فهل من مدكر ـ ولقد أهلكنا أشياعكم فهل من مدكر ـ.

397. Narrated 'Abdullāh: I recited before the Prophet: 'Fahal-min-Mudhdhakir'. The Prophet said, "(It is) 'Fahal-min-Muddakir'."

٣٩٧ ـ حدثنا يحيى : حدثنا وكيع، عن إسرائيل، عن أبي إسحاق، عن الأسود بن يزيد، عن عبد الله قال : قرأت على النبي صلى الله عليه وسلم ـ فهل من مدكر ـ فقال النبي صلى الله عليه وسلم ـ فهل من مدكر ـ.

(291) CHAPTER. The Statement of Allāh :

> Their multitude will be put to flight, and they will show their backs.' (54:45)

باب قوله - سيهزم الجمع ويولون الدبر -.

398. Narrated 'Abbās : Allāh's Messenger while in a tent on the day of the Battle of Badr, said, "O Allāh! I request you (to fulfil) Your promise and contract! O Allāh! If You wish that you will not be worshipped henceforth................." On that Abū Bakr held the Prophet by the hand and said, "That is enough, O Allāh's Messenger! You have appealed to your Lord too pressingly," while the Prophet was putting on his armour. So Allāh's Messenger went out, reciting

> Their multitude will be put to flight, and they will show their backs.' (54:45)

٣٩٨ - حدثنا محمد بن عبد الله ابن حوشب: حدثنا خالد، عن عكرمة، عن ابن عباس ح. وحدثني محمد: حدثنا عفان بن مسلم، عن وهيب: حدثنا خالد، عن عكرمة عن ابن عباس رضي الله عنهما: أن رسول الله صلى الله عليه وسلم قال وهو في قبة يوم بدر: اللهم إني أنشدك عهدك ووعدك، اللهم إن تشأ لا تعبد بعد اليوم، فأخذ أبو بكر بيده فقال: حسبك يا رسول الله، ألححت على ربك، وهو يثب في الدرع، فخرج وهو يقول - سيهزم الجمع ويولون الدبر -.

(292) CHAPTER. The Statement of Allāh :

> 'Nay but the Hour is their appointed time (for their full recompense), and the Hour will be more grevious and most bitter.' (54:46)

باب قوله - بل الساعة موعدهم والساعة أدهى وأمر - يعني من المرارة.

399. Narrated Yūsuf bin Māhik:

٣٩٩ - حدثنا إبراهيم بن موسى:

فَلَيْسَ بِمُنْشَأَةٍ . وَقَالَ مُجَاهِدٌ : كَمَا يُصْنَعُ الفَخَّارُ . الشُّوَاظُ : لَهَبٌ مِنْ نَارٍ . وَقَالَ مُجَاهِدٌ : وَنُحَاسٌ : النحاسُ الصُّفْرُ يُصَبُّ عَلَى رُءُوسِهِمْ . يُعَذَّبُونَ بِهِ . خَافَ مَقَامَ رَبِّهِ : يَهُمُّ بِالمَعْصِيَةِ فَيَذْكُرُ اللهَ عَزَّ وَجَلَّ فَيَتْرُكُهَا . مُدْهَامَّتَانِ : سَوْدَاوَانِ مِنَ الرِّيِّ . صَلْصَالٍ : طِينٍ خُلِطَ بِرَمْلٍ فَصَلْصَلَ كَمَا يُصَلْصِلُ الفَخَّارُ : وَيُقَالُ مُنْتِنٌ يُرِيدُونَ بِهِ صَلَّ ، يُقَالُ صَلْصَالٌ كَمَا يُقَالُ صَرَّ البَابُ عِنْدَ الإِغْلَاقِ ، وَصَرْصَرَ مِثْلُ كَبْكَبْتُهُ ، يَعْنِي كَبَبْتُهُ . ـ فَاكِهَةٌ وَنَخْلٌ وَرُمَّانٌ ـ قَالَ بَعْضُهُمْ : لَيْسَ الرُّمَّانُ وَالنَّخْلُ بِالفَاكِهَةِ . وَأَمَّا العَرَبُ فَإِنَّهَا تَعُدُّهَا فَاكِهَةً كَقَوْلِهِ عَزَّ وَجَلَّ ـ حَافِظُوا عَلَى الصَّلَوَاتِ وَالصَّلَاةِ الوُسْطَى ـ فَأَمَرَهُمْ بِالمُحَافَظَةِ عَلَى كُلِّ الصَّلَوَاتِ ، ثُمَّ أَعَادَ العَصْرَ تَشْدِيدًا لَهَا كَمَا أُعِيدَ النَّخْلُ وَالرُّمَّانُ ، وَمِثْلُهَا ـ أَلَمْ تَرَ أَنَّ اللهَ يَسْجُدُ لَهُ مَنْ فِي السَّمَوَاتِ وَمَنْ فِي الأَرْضِ ـ ثُمَّ قَالَ ـ وَكَثِيرٌ مِنَ النَّاسِ وَكَثِيرٌ حَقَّ عَلَيْهِ العَذَابُ ـ وَقَدْ ذَكَرَهُمْ فِي أَوَّلِ قَوْلِهِ ـ مَنْ فِي السَّمَوَاتِ وَمَنْ فِي الأَرْضِ ـ وَقَالَ غَيْرُهُ : أَفْنَانٍ : أَغْصَانٍ . وَجَنَى الجَنَّتَيْنِ دَانٍ : مَا يُجْتَنَى قَرِيبٌ . وَقَالَ الحَسَنُ ـ

فَبِأَيِّ آلاءِ - نِعَمِهِ، وَقَالَ قَتَادَةُ - رَبُّكُمَا تُكَذِّبَانِ - يَعْنِي الجِنَّ وَالإِنْسَ. وَقَالَ أَبُو الدَّرْدَاءِ - كُلَّ يَوْمٍ هُوَ فِي شَأْنٍ - يَغْفِرُ ذَنْبًا وَيَكْشِفُ كَرْبًا. وَيَرْفَعُ قَوْمًا وَيَضَعُ آخَرِينَ. وَقَالَ ابْنُ عَبَّاسٍ: بَرْزَخٌ: حَاجِزٌ. الأَنَامُ: الخَلْقُ. نَضَّاخَتَانِ: فَيَّاضَتَانِ. ذُو الجَلَالِ: العَظَمَةِ. وَقَالَ غَيْرُهُ: مَارِجٌ: خَالِصٌ مِنَ النَّارِ، يُقَالُ مَرَجَ الأَمِيرُ رَعِيَّتَهُ إِذَا خَلَّاهُمْ يَعْدُو بَعْضُهُمْ عَلَى بَعْضٍ. مَرَجَ أَمْرُ النَّاسِ. مَرِيجٍ مُلْتَبِسٍ. مَرَجَ: اخْتَلَطَ مِنْ مَرَجْتَ دَابَّتَكَ تَرَكْتَهَا. سَنَفْرُغُ لَكُمْ - سَنُحَاسِبُكُمْ، لَا يَشْغَلُهُ شَيْءٌ عَنْ شَيْءٍ، وَهُوَ مَعْرُوفٌ فِي كَلَامِ العَرَبِ. يُقَالُ: لَا تَفْرُغَنَّ لَكَ، وَمَا بِهِ شُغْلٌ يَقُولُ لَآخُذَنَّكَ عَلَى غِرَّتِكَ.

(293) CHAPTER. The Statement of Allāh ﷻ:

بَابُ قَوْلِهِ - وَمِنْ دُونِهِمَا جَنَّتَانِ -

'And besides these two, there are two other gardens.' (55:62)

401. Narrated 'Abdullāh bin Qais: Allāh's Messenger ﷺ said, "Two gardens, the utensils and the contents of which are of silver, and two other gardens, the utensils and

٤٠١ - حَدَّثَنَا عَبْدُ اللَّهِ بْنُ الأَسْوَدِ: حَدَّثَنَا عَبْدُ العَزِيزِ بْنُ عَبْدِ الصَّمَدِ العَمِّيُّ: حَدَّثَنَا أَبُو عِمْرَانَ

contents of which are of gold. And nothing will prevent the people who will be in the Garden of Eden from seeing their Lord except the curtain of Majesty over His Face."

الجَوْنِيُّ، عَنْ أَبِي بَكْرِ بْنِ عَبْدِ اللهِ بْنِ قَيْسٍ، عَنْ أَبِيهِ: أَنَّ رَسُولَ اللهِ صلى الله عليه وسلَّم قَالَ: جَنَّتَانِ مِنْ فِضَّةٍ آنِيَتُهُمَا وَمَا فِيهِمَا، وَجَنَّتَانِ مِنْ ذَهَبٍ آنِيَتُهُمَا وَمَا فِيهِمَا، وَمَا بَيْنَ القَوْمِ وَبَيْنَ أَنْ يَنْظُرُوا إِلَى رَبِّهِمْ إِلاَّ رِدَاءُ الكِبْرِ عَلَى وَجْهِهِ فِي جَنَّةِ عَدْنٍ.

(294) CHAPTER. The Statement of Allāh تعالى :—

Beautiful fair females restrained in pavilions. (55:72)

بَابٌ - حُورٌ مَقْصُورَاتٌ فِي الخِيَامِ - وَقَالَ ابْنُ عَبَّاسٍ: حُورٌ: سُودُ الحَدَقِ. وَقَالَ مُجَاهِدٌ: مَقْصُورَاتٌ: مَحْبُوسَاتٌ، قُصِرَ طَرْفُهُنَّ وَأَنْفُسُهُنَّ عَلَى أَزْوَاجِهِنَّ.

402. Narrated 'Abdullāh bin Qais: Allāh's Messenger ﷺ said, "In Paradise there is a pavilion made of a single hollow pearl sixty miles wide, in each corner of which there are wives who will not see those in the other corners; and the believers will visit and enjoy them. And there are two gardens, the utensils and contents of which are made of silver; and two other gardens, the utensils and contents of which are made of so-and-so (i.e. gold) and nothing will prevent the people staying in the Garden of Eden from seeing their Lord except the curtain of Majesty over His Face."

٤٠٢ - حَدَّثَنَا مُحَمَّدُ بْنُ المُثَنَّى: حَدَّثَنَا عَبْدُ العَزِيزِ بْنُ عَبْدِ الصَّمَدِ: حَدَّثَنَا أَبُو عِمْرَانَ الجَوْنِيُّ عَنْ أَبِي بَكْرِ ابْنِ عَبْدِ اللهِ بْنِ قَيْسٍ، عَنْ أَبِيهِ: أَنَّ رَسُولَ اللهِ صلى الله عليه وسلَّم قَالَ: إِنَّ فِي الجَنَّةِ خَيْمَةً مِنْ لُؤْلُؤَةٍ مُجَوَّفَةٍ عَرْضُهَا سِتُّونَ مِيلاً فِي كُلِّ زَاوِيَةٍ مِنْهَا أَهْلٌ مَا يَرَوْنَ الآخَرِينَ، يَطُوفُ المُؤْمِنُونَ. وَجَنَّتَانِ مِنْ فِضَّةٍ آنِيَتُهُمَا وَمَا فِيهِمَا، وَجَنَّتَانِ مِنْ كَذَا آنِيَتُهُمَا وَمَا فِيهِمَا. وَمَا بَيْنَ القَوْمِ وَبَيْنَ أَنْ

يَنْظُرُوا إلى رَبِّهِم إلاَّ رِدَاءُ الكِبْرِ عَلَى
وَجْهِهِ فِي جَنَّةِ عَدْنٍ.

SŪRAT AL-WĀQI'A LVI
(The Inevitable Event)

In the Name of Allāh, the Most Beneficent, the Most Merciful

سورة الواقعة

بِسْمِ اللهِ الرَّحْمَنِ الرَّحِيمِ

وَقَالَ مُجَاهِدٌ: رُجَّتْ: زُلْزِلَتْ: بُسَّتْ: فُتَّتْ، لُتَّتْ كَمَا يُلَتُّ السَّوِيقُ. المَخْضُودُ: لاشَوْكَ لَهُ. مَنْضُودٍ: المَوْزُ، والعُرُبُ: المُحَبَّبَاتُ إلى أزْوَاجِهِنَّ. ثُلَّةٌ: أُمَّةٌ. يَحْمُومٌ: دُخَانٌ أسْوَدُ. يُصِرُّونَ: يُدِيمُونَ. الهِيمُ: الإبِلُ الظِّمَاءُ. لَمُغْرَمُونَ: لَمُلْزَمُونَ مدينين محاسبين. رَوْحٌ: جَنَّةٌ وَرَخَاءٌ. وَرَيحانٌ: الرِّزْقُ. وَنُنْشِئَكُمْ فِيما لا تَعْلَمُونَ: أيْ فِي أيِّ خَلْقٍ نَشاءُ. وَقالَ غَيْرُهُ: تَفَكَّهُونَ: تَعْجَبُونَ. عُرُبا مُثْقَلَةً واحِدُها عَرُوبٌ مِثْلُ صَبُورٍ وَصُبُرٍ، يَسَمِّيها أهْلُ مَكَّةَ العَرِبَةَ، وأهْلُ المَدِينَةِ الغَنِجَةَ، وأهْلُ العِرَاقِ الشَّكِلَةَ، وقال في: خافِضَةٌ لِقَوْمٍ إلى النَّارِ، وَرَافِعَةٌ إلى الجَنَّةِ. مَوْضُونَةٍ: مَنْسُوجَةٍ، وَمِنْهُ وَضِينُ النَّاقَةِ. والكُوبُ: لا آذانَ لَهُ ولا عُرْوَةَ. والأبارِيقُ: ذَوَاتُ الآذانِ والعُرَى.

مَسْكُوبٍ : جارٍ . وفُرُشٍ مَرْفُوعَةٍ : بَعْضُها فَوْقَ بَعْضٍ . مُتْرَفِينَ : مُتَمَتِّعِينَ . مَدِينِينَ : مُحَاسَبِينَ ما تُمْنُونَ : هِيَ النُّطْفَةُ فِى أَرْحَامِ النِّساءِ . لِلْمُقْوِينَ: لِلْمُسافِرِينَ ،والقِيّ : القَفْرُ . بِمَوَاقِعِ النُّجُومِ : بِمُحْكَمِ القُرْآنِ ، ويُقال بِمَسْقِطِ النُّجُومِ إذَا سَقَطْنَ ، ومَوَاقِعُ ومَوْقِعٌ وَاحِدٌ . مُدْهِنُونَ : مُكَذِّبونَ ، مِثْلُ - لَوْ تُدْهِنُ فَيُدْهِنُونَ - . فَسَلامٌ لَكَ - أَىْ مُسَلَّمٌ لَكَ - إنَّكَ مِنْ أصحابِ اليَمِينِ - وأُلْغِيَتْ إنَّ وَهُوَ مَعْنَاها كمَا تَقُولُ : أنتَ مُصَدَّقٌ مُسافِرٌ عَنْ قَلِيلٍ . إذَا كانَ قَدْ قالَ إنِّى مُسافِرٌ عَنْ قَلِيلٍ ، وَقَدْ يَكُونُ كالدُّعاءِ لَهُ كَقَوْلِكَ فَسَقْيًا مِنَ الرِّجالِ ، إنْ رَفَعْتَ السَّلامُ فَهُوَ مِنَ الدُّعاءِ . تُورُونَ : تَسْتَخْرِجُونَ ، أَوْرَيْتُ : أَوْقَدْتُ . لَغْوًا : باطِلاً . تأثِيما : كَذِبا .

(295) CHAPTER. The Statement of Allāh ﷻ :

'In shade long extended.' (56:30)

بابُ قَوْلِهِ - وَظِلٍّ مَمْدُودٍ - .

403. Narrated Abū Huraira رضي الله عنه : The Prophet ﷺ said, "In Paradise there is a tree which is so big that a rider can travel in its shade for one hundred years without crossing it; and if you wish, you can recite :

٤٠٣ - حدَّثنا عَلِيُّ بنُ عَبْدِ اللهِ : حدَّثنا سُفْيانُ ، عَنْ أبِى الزِّنادِ ، عَنِ الأعْرَجِ ، عَنْ أبِى هُرَيْرَةَ رَضِىَ اللهُ عَنْهُ يَبْلُغُ بِهِ النَّبِىَّ صلى اللهُ عليه وسلَّم

'In shade long extended.' "
(56:30)

قالَ: إنَّ في الجنّةِ شَجَرَةً يَسيرُ الرَّاكِبُ في ظِلِّها مائةَ عامٍ لا يَقْطَعُها، وَاقْرَءُوا إنْ شِئْتُمْ - وَظِلٍّ مَمْدُودٍ

SŪRAT AL-ḤADĪD (Iron) LVII

. سورة الحديد والمجادلة

In the Name of Allāh, the Most Beneficent, the Most Merciful

بِسْمِ اللهِ الرَّحْمَنِ الرَّحِيمِ

(No Ḥadīths were mentioned here)

قالَ مُجاهِدٌ: جَعَلَكُمْ مُسْتَخْلَفِينَ: مُعَمَّرِينَ فيهِ - مِنَ الظُّلُماتِ إلى النُّورِ: مِنَ الضَّلالَةِ إلى الهُدَى. فيهِ بأسٌ شَديدٌ وَمَنافِعُ للنّاسِ: جُنَّةٌ وَسِلاحٌ. مَوْلاكُمْ: أَوْلَى بِكُمْ لِئَلاَّ يَعْلَمَ أَهْلُ الكِتابِ: لِيَعْلَمَ أَهْلُ الكِتابِ، يُقالُ الظّاهِرُ عَلَى كُلِّ شَيْءٍ عِلْماً، والباطِنُ عَلَى كُلِّ شَيْءٍ عِلْماً، أَنْظِرُونا: انْتَظِرُونا.

SŪRAT-AL-MUJĀDALA: LVIII

سورة المجادلة

In the Name of Allāh, the Most Beneficent, the Most Merciful

بِسْمِ اللهِ الرَّحْمَنِ الرَّحِيمِ

(No Ḥadīths were mentioned here)

وقال مجاهد: يحادون: يشاقون الله - كبتوا: أُخزُوا من الخزي. استحوذ: غلب.

SŪRAT AL-ḤASHR LIX (The Gathering)

سورة الحشر

In the Name of Allāh, the Most Beneficent, the Most Merciful

بِسْمِ اللهِ الرَّحْمَنِ الرَّحِيمِ

الجلاءَ: الإِخْرَاجُ مِنْ أَرْضٍ إلى أَرْضٍ.

404. Narrated Sa'īd bin Jubair: I asked Ibn 'Abbās about Sūrat Al-Tauba, and he said, "Sūrat Al-Tauba? It is

٤٠٤ - حدَّثنا مُحَمَّدُ بنُ عَبدِ الرَّحيمِ: حدَّثنا سَعيدُ بنُ سُلَيْمانَ: حَدَّثَنا

the exposure (of all the evils of the infidels and the hypocrites). And it continued revealing (the oft-repeated expression): '............and of them .... and of them.' till they started thinking that none would be left unmentioned therein." I said, "What about) Sūrat Al-Anfāl?" He replied, "Sūrat Al-Anfāl was revealed in connection with the Badr Battle." I said, "(What about) Sūrat Al-Ḥashr?" He replied, "It was revealed in connection with Banī an-Naḍīr." (1)

هُشَيْمٌ: أَخْبَرَنَا أَبُو بِشْرٍ، عَنْ سَعِيدِ بْنِ جُبَيْرٍ قَالَ: قُلْتُ لِابْنِ عَبَّاسٍ: سُورَةُ التَّوْبَةِ؟ قَالَ التَّوْبَةُ هِيَ الْفَاضِحَةُ مَازَالَتْ تَنْزِلُ، وَمِنْهُمْ وَمِنْهُمْ حَتَّى ظَنُّوا أَنَّهَا لَمْ تُبْقِ أَحَدًا مِنْهُمْ إِلَّا ذُكِرَ فِيهَا. قَالَ: قُلْتُ سُورَةُ الْأَنْفَالِ؟ قَالَ: نَزَلَتْ فِي بَدْرٍ. قَالَ: قُلْتُ سُورَةُ الْحَشْرِ؟ قَالَ: نَزَلَتْ فِي بَنِي النَّضِيرِ.

405. Narrated Sa'īd: I asked Ibn 'Abbās about Sūrat Al-Ḥashr. He replied, "Say Sūrat An-Naḍīr."

٤٠٥ - حَدَّثَنَا الْحَسَنُ بْنُ مُدْرِكٍ: حَدَّثَنَا يَحْيَى بْنُ حَمَّادٍ: أَخْبَرَنَا أَبُو عَوَانَةَ، عَنْ أَبِي بِشْرٍ، عَنْ سَعِيدٍ قَالَ: قُلْتُ لِابْنِ عَبَّاسٍ رَضِيَ اللَّهُ عَنْهُمَا: سُورَةُ الْحَشْرِ؟ قَالَ: قُلْ سُورَةُ النَّضِيرِ.

(296) CHAPTER. The Statement of Allāh :—

What you (O Muslims) cut down of the palm tree (of the enemy) or .... (59:5)

بَابُ قَوْلِهِ - مَا قَطَعْتُمْ مِنْ لِينَةٍ - نَخْلَةٍ مَا لَمْ تَكُنْ عَجْوَةً أَوْ بَرْنِيَّةً.

406. Narrated Ibn 'Umar: 'Allāh's Messenger burnt and cut down the palm trees of Banī An-Naḍīr which

٤٠٦ - حَدَّثَنَا قُتَيْبَةُ: حَدَّثَنَا لَيْثٌ، عَنِ ابْنِ عُمَرَ رَضِيَ اللَّهُ عَنْهُمَا: أَنَّ رَسُولَ اللَّهِ صلى اللهُ عليه وسلَّم حَرَّقَ

(1) Banī An-Naḍīr was a Jewish tribe in Medīna.

were at Al-Buwair (a place near Medīna). There upon Allāh revealed:

> 'What you (O Muslims) cut down of the palm trees (of the enemy) or you left them standing on their stems, it was by the leave of Allāh, so that He might cover with shame the rebellious.' (59:5)

نخل بني النضير وقطع وهي البويرة، فأنزل الله تعالى - ما قطعتم من لينة أو تركتموها قائمة على أصولها فبإذن الله وليخزي الفاسقين - .

(297) CHAPTER. The statement of Allāh :–

> 'What Allāh gave as (Fai) booty to His Messenger ..... '(59:7)

باب قوله - ما أفاء الله على رسوله - .

407. Narrated Umar : The properties of Banī An-Naḍīr were among the booty that Allāh gave to His Messenger : such Booty were not obtained by any expedition on the part of Muslims, neither with cavalry, nor with camelry. So those properties were for Allāh's Messenger only, and he used to provide thereof the yearly expenditure for his wives, and dedicate the rest of its revenues for purchasing arms and horses as war material to be used in Allāh's Cause.

٤٠٧ - حدثنا علي بن عبد الله: حدثنا سفيان غير مرة، عن عمرو، عن الزهري، عن مالك بن أوس بن الحدثان، عن عمر رضي الله عنه قال: كانت أموال بني النضير مما أفاء الله على رسوله صلى الله عليه وسلم مما لم يوجف المسلمون عليه بخيل ولا ركاب، فكانت لرسول الله صلى الله عليه وسلم خاصة. ينفق على أهله منها نفقة سنته. ثم يجعل ما بقي في السلاح والكراع عدة في سبيل الله .

(298) CHAPTER. 'And whatsoever, the Messenger gives you take it.' (59:7)

باب وما آتاكم الرسول فخذوه - .

408. Narrated 'Alqama: 'Abdullāh (bin Mas'ūd) said. "Allāh curses those ladies who practise tatooing and those who get themselves tatooed, and those ladies who remove the hair from their faces and those who make artificial spaces between their teeth in order to look more beautiful whereby they change Allāh's creation." His saying reached a lady frome Banī Asd called Um Ya'qūb who came (to 'Abdullāh) and said, "I have come to know that you have cursed such-and-such (ladies)?" He replied, "Why should I not curse these whom Allāh's Messenger ﷺ has cursed and who are (cursed) in Allāh's Book!" Um Ya'qūb said, "I have read the whole Qur'ān, but I did not find in it what you say." He said, "Verily, if you have read it (i.e. the Qur'ān), you have found it. Didn't you read:

> 'And whatsoever the Apostle gives you take it and whatsoever he forbids you, you abstain (from it). (59:7)

She replied "Yes, I did," He said, "Verily, Allāh's Messenger ﷺ forbade such things." "She said, "But I see your wife doing these things?" He said, "Go and watch her." She went and watched her but could not see anything in support of her statement. On that he said, "If my wife was as you thought, I would not keep her in my company." (1)

٤٠٨ ـ حدثنا محمد بن يوسف: حدثنا سفيان، عن منصور، عن إبراهيم، عن علقمة، عن عبد الله قال: لعن الله الواشمات والموتشمات، والمتنمصات والمتفلجات للحسن، المغيرات خلق الله. فبلغ ذلك امرأة من بني أسد يقال لها أم يعقوب فجاءت فقالت: إنه بلغني أنك لعنت كيت وكيت. فقال: وما لي لا ألعن من لعن رسول الله صلى الله عليه وسلم ومن هو في كتاب الله؟ فقالت: لقد قرأت ما بين اللوحين فما وجدت فيه ما تقول. قال: لئن كنت قرأتيه لقد وجدتيه، أما قرأت ـ وما آتاكم الرسول فخذوه وما نهاكم عنه فانتهوا ـ قالت: بلى، قال فإنه قد نهى عنه. قالت: فإني أرى أهلك يفعلونه، قال: فاذهبي فانظري. فذهبت فنظرت فلم تر من حاجتها شيئا. فقال: لو كانت كذلك ما جامعتها.

(1) i.e. I would divorce her.

409. Narrated 'Abdullāh (bin Mus'ūd) ﷺ: Allāh's Messenger ﷺ has cursed the lady who uses false hair.

٤٠٩ ـ حَدَّثَنَا عَلِيٌّ: حَدَّثَنَا عَبْدُ الرَّحْمَنِ، عَنْ سُفْيَانَ قَالَ: ذَكَرْتُ لِعَبْدِ الرَّحْمَنِ بْنِ عَابِسٍ حَدِيثَ مَنْصُورٍ، عَنْ إِبْرَاهِيمَ، عَنْ عَلْقَمَةَ، عَنْ عَبْدِ اللهِ رَضِيَ اللهُ عَنْهُ قَالَ: لَعَنَ رَسُولُ اللهِ صلى اللهُ عليه وسلَّم الوَاصِلَةَ فَقَالَ: سَمِعْتُهُ مِنِ امْرَأَةٍ يُقَالُ لَهَا أُمُّ يَعْقُوبَ، عَنْ عَبْدِ اللهِ مِثْلَ حَدِيثِ مَنْصُورٍ.

(299) CHAPTER. 'But those who, before them, had homes (in Medīna) and had adopted the Faith.' (59:9)

بابٌ ـ وَالَّذِينَ تَبَوَّءُوا الدَّارَ وَالإِيمَانَ ـ .

410. Narrated 'Umar ﷺ: I recommend that my successor should take care of and secure the rights of the early emigrants; and I also advise my successor to be kind to the Anṣār who had homes (in Medīna) and had adopted the Faith, before the Prophet ﷺ migrated to them, and to accept the good from their good ones and excuse their wrong doers.

٤١٠ ـ حَدَّثَنَا أَحْمَدُ بنُ يُونُسَ: حَدَّثَنَا أَبُو بَكْرٍ، يَعْنِي ابنَ عَيَّاشٍ، عَنْ حُصَيْنٍ، عَنْ عَمْرِو ابنِ مَيْمُونٍ قَالَ: قَالَ عُمَرُ رَضِيَ اللهُ عَنْهُ: أُوصِي الخَلِيفَةَ بِالمُهَاجِرِينَ الأَوَّلِينَ أَنْ يَعْرِفَ لَهُمْ حَقَّهُمْ، وَأُوصِي الخَلِيفَةَ بِالأَنْصَارِ الَّذِينَ تَبَوَّءُوا الدَّارَ وَالإِيمَانَ مِنْ قَبْلِ أَنْ يُهَاجِرَ النَّبِيُّ صلى اللهُ عليه

وسلَّم أنْ يَقْبَلَ مِنْ مُحْسِنِهِمْ وَيَعْفُوَ عَنْ مُسِيئِهِمْ .

(300) CHAPTER. The Statement of Allāh تعالى :–

'But give them (emigrants) preference over themselves.' (59:9)

بابُ قَوْلِهِ - وَيُؤْثِرُونَ عَلَى أنفُسِهِمْ - الآيَةَ . الخَصَاصَةُ : فاقَةٌ . المُفْلِحُونَ : الفائِزُونَ بالخُلُودِ . والفلاحُ : البَقاءُ . حَيَّ عَلَى الفَلاحِ : عَجِّلْ . وَقالَ الحَسَنُ : حاجَةً : حَسَدًا .

411. Narrated Abū Huraira رضي الله عنه :

A man came to Allāh's Messenger ﷺ and said, "O Allāh's Messenger! I am suffering from fatigue and hunger." The Prophet ﷺ sent (somebody) to his wives (to get something), but the messenger found nothing with them. Then Allāh's Messenger ﷺ said (to his companions). "Isn't there anybody who can entertain this man tonight so that Allāh may be merciful to him?" An Anṣari man got up and said, "I (will, entertain him), O Allāh's Messenger!" So he went to his wife and said to her, "This is the guest of Allāh's Messenger, so do not keep anything away from him." She said. "By Allāh, I have nothing but the children's food." He said, "When the children ask for their dinner, put them to bed and put out the light; we shall not take our meals tonight," She did so. In the morning the Anṣari man went to Allāh's Messenger ﷺ who said, "Allāh عزوجل was pleased with (or He bestowed His Mercy) on so-and-so and his wife (because of their good deed)." Then Allāh تعالى revealed:

٤١١ - حدَّثنا يَعْقُوبُ بنُ إبْراهِيمَ ابنِ كَثِيرٍ : حدَّثنا أبُو أُسامَةَ : حدَّثنا فُضَيلُ بنُ غَزْوانَ : حدَّثنا أبُو حازِمٍ الأشْجَعِيُّ ، عَنْ أبي هُرَيْرَةَ رَضِيَ اللهُ عَنْهُ قالَ : أتَى رَجُلٌ رَسُولَ اللهِ صلى اللهُ عليهِ وسلَّم فَقالَ : يا رَسُولَ اللهِ أصابَنِي الجَهْدُ : فأرْسَلَ إلى نِسائِهِ فَلَمْ يَجِدْ عِنْدَهُنَّ شَيْئًا ، فَقالَ رَسُولُ اللهِ صلى اللهُ عليهِ وسلَّم : ألا رَجُلٌ يُضَيِّفُهُ هذِهِ اللَّيْلَةَ يَرْحَمُهُ اللهُ ؟ فَقامَ رَجُلٌ مِنَ الأنْصارِ فَقالَ : أنا يا رَسُولَ اللهِ ، فَذَهَبَ إلى أهْلِهِ فَقالَ لامْرأتِهِ : ضَيْفُ رَسُولِ اللهِ صلى اللهُ عليهِ وسلَّم لا تَدَّخِرِيهِ شَيْئًا . قالَتْ : وَاللهِ ما عِنْدِي إلاَّ قُوتُ الصِّبْيَةِ ، قالَ : فإذا أرادَ الصِّبْيَةُ العَشاءَ فَنَوِّمِيهِمْ وَتَعالَيْ فأطْفِئِي السِّراجَ . وَنَطْوِي بُطُونَنا اللَّيْلَةَ فَفَعَلَتْ ، ثُمَّ غَدا الرَّجُلُ عَلَى رَسُولِ اللهِ صلى اللهُ عليهِ وسلَّم فَقالَ :

‘But give them preference over themselves even though they were in need of that. (59:9)

لَقَدْ عَجِبَ اللهُ عَزَّ وَجَلَّ، أَوْ ضَحِكَ مِنْ فُلانٍ وَفُلانَةَ، فَأَنْزَلَ اللهُ عَزَّ وَجَلَّ - وَيُؤْثِرُونَ عَلَى أَنْفُسِهِمْ وَلَوْ كَانَ بِهِمْ خَصَاصَةٌ -.

SŪRAT-AL-MUMTAḤINA (The Women to be examined) LX

In the Name of Allāh, the Most Beneficent, the Most Merciful

سورة الممتحنة

بِسْمِ اللهِ الرَّحْمَنِ الرَّحِيمِ

وَقَالَ مُجَاهِدٌ: لا تَجْعَلْنَا فِتْنَةً: لا تُعَذِّبْنَا بِأَيْدِيهِمْ فَيَقُولُونَ لَوْ كَانَ هَؤُلاءِ عَلَى الحَقِّ مَا أَصَابَهُمْ هَذَا. بِعِصَمِ الكَوَافِرِ: أُمِرَ أَصْحَابُ النَّبِيِّ صلى اللهُ عليه وسلَّم بِفِرَاقِ نِسَائِهِمْ كُنَّ كَوَافِرَ بِمَكَّةَ.

(301) CHAPTER. ‘(O you who believe!) Take not My enemies and your enemies as friends.’ (60:1)

بَابٌ - لا تَتَّخِذُوا عَدُوِّي وَعَدُوَّكُمْ أَوْلِيَاءَ -.

412. Narrated ‘Alī : Allāh's Messenger sent me along with Az-Zubair and Al-Miqdād and said, "Proceed till you reach a place called Rauḍat-Khākh where there is a lady travelling in a howda on a camel. She has a letter. Take the letter from

٤١٢ - حَدَّثَنَا الحُمَيْدِيُّ: حَدَّثَنَا سُفْيَانُ: حَدَّثَنَا عَمْرُو بْنُ دِينَارٍ قَالَ: حَدَّثَنِي الحَسَنُ بْنُ مُحَمَّدِ بْنِ عَلِيٍّ: أَنَّهُ سَمِعَ عُبَيْدَ اللهِ بْنَ أَبِي رَافِعٍ كَاتِبَ

her." So we set out, and our horses ran at full pace till we reached Rauḍat-Khākh, and behold, we saw the lady and said (to her), "Take out the letter!" She said, "I have no letter with me." We said, "Either you take out the letter or we will strip you of your clothes." So she took the letter out of her hair braid. We brought the letter to the Prophet ﷺ, and behold, it was addressed by Ḥātib bin Abī Balta'a to some pagans at Mecca, informing them of some of the affairs of the Prophet ﷺ. The Prophet ﷺ said, "What is this, O Ḥātib?" Ḥātib replied, "Do not be hasty with me, O Allāh's Messenger! I am an Anṣārī man and do not belong to them (Quraish infidels) while the emigrants who were with you had their relatives who used to protect their families and properties at Mecca. So, to compensate for not having blood relation with them.' I intended to do them some favour so that they might protect my relatives (at Mecca), and I did not do this out of disbelief or an inclination to desert my religion." The Prophet ﷺ then said (to his companions), "He (Ḥātib) has told you the truth." 'Umar said, "O Allāh's Messenger! Allow me to chop his head off?" The Prophet ﷺ said, "He is one of those who witnessed (fought in) the Battle of Badr, and what do you know, perhaps Allāh looked upon the people of Badr (Badr warriors) and said, 'Do what you want as I have forgiven you.' " (A'mr, a sub-narrator, said,: This Verse was revealed about him (Ḥātib):

> 'O you who believe! Take not My enemies and your enemies as friends or protectors.') (60:1)

عَلِيٍّ يَقُولُ: سَمِعْتُ عَلِيًّا رَضِيَ اللهُ عَنْهُ يَقُولُ: بَعَثَنِي رَسُولُ اللهِ صَلَّى اللهُ عَلَيْهِ وَسَلَّمَ أَنَا وَالزُّبَيْرَ وَالْمِقْدَادَ وَقَالَ: انْطَلِقُوا حَتَّى تَأْتُوا رَوْضَةَ خَاخٍ، فَإِنَّ بِهَا ظَعِينَةً مَعَهَا كِتَابٌ فَخُذُوهُ مِنْهَا. فَذَهَبْنَا تَعَادَى بِنَا خَيْلُنَا حَتَّى أَتَيْنَا الرَّوْضَةَ فَإِذَا نَحْنُ بِالظَّعِينَةِ فَقُلْنَا: أَخْرِجِي الْكِتَابَ، فَقَالَتْ: مَا مَعِي مِنْ كِتَابٍ، فَقُلْنَا: لَتُخْرِجِنَّ الْكِتَابَ أَوْ لَنُلْقِيَنَّ الثِّيَابَ. فَأَخْرَجَتْهُ مِنْ عِقَاصِهَا، فَأَتَيْنَا بِهِ النَّبِيَّ صَلَّى اللهُ عَلَيْهِ وَسَلَّمَ فَإِذَا فِيهِ: مِنْ حَاطِبِ بْنِ أَبِي بَلْتَعَةَ إِلَى أُنَاسٍ مِنَ الْمُشْرِكِينَ مِمَّنْ بِمَكَّةَ يُخْبِرُهُمْ بِبَعْضِ أَمْرِ النَّبِيِّ صَلَّى اللهُ عَلَيْهِ وَسَلَّمَ. فَقَالَ النَّبِيُّ صَلَّى اللهُ عَلَيْهِ وَسَلَّمَ. مَا هَذَا يَا حَاطِبُ؟ قَالَ: لَا تَعْجَلْ عَلَيَّ يَا رَسُولَ اللهِ، إِنِّي كُنْتُ امْرَأً مِنَ الْأَنْصَارِ وَلَمْ أَكُنْ مِنْ أَنْفُسِهِمْ، وَكَانَ مَنْ مَعَكَ مِنَ الْمُهَاجِرِينَ لَهُمْ قَرَابَاتٌ يَحْمُونَ بِهَا أَهْلِيهِمْ وَأَمْوَالَهُمْ بِمَكَّةَ. فَأَحْبَبْتُ إِذْ فَاتَنِي مِنَ النَّسَبِ فِيهِمْ أَنْ أَصْطَنِعَ إِلَيْهِمْ يَدًا يَحْمُونَ قَرَابَتِي. وَمَا فَعَلْتُ ذَلِكَ كُفْرًا وَلَا ارْتِدَادًا عَنْ دِينِي. فَقَالَ النَّبِيُّ صَلَّى اللهُ عَلَيْهِ وَسَلَّمَ: إِنَّهُ قَدْ صَدَقَكُمْ، فَقَالَ عُمَرُ: دَعْنِي يَا رَسُولَ اللهِ فَأَضْرِبَ عُنُقَهُ، فَقَالَ: إِنَّهُ

شهد بدرا ، وما يدريك لعل الله اطلع على أهل بدر فقال : اعملوا ما شئتم فقد غفرت لكم . قال عمرو : ونزلت فيه - يا أيها الذين آمنوا لا تتخذوا عدوي وعدوكم أولياء - قال : لا أدري الآية في الحديث ، أو قول عمرو .

413. Narrated 'Alī: Sufyān was asked whether (the Verse),

'Take not My enemies and your enemies....................

was revealed in connection with Ḥāṭib. Sufyān replied, "This occurs only in the narration of the people. I memorized the Ḥadīth from 'Amr, not overlooking even a single letter thereof, and I do not know of anybody who remembered it by heart other than myself."

٤١٣ - حدثنا علي قال : قيل لسفيان في هذا ، فنزلت - لا تتخذوا عدوي وعدوكم - الآية . قال سفيان : هذا في حديث الناس حفظته من عمرو ، ما تركت منه حرفا وما أرى أحدا حفظه غيري .

(302) CHAPTER. The Statement of Allāh :-

'When there come to you believing women as emigrants.' (60:10)

باب - إذا جاءكم المؤمنات مهاجرات - .

414. Narrated 'Urwa: 'Āisha the wife of the Prophet ﷺ, said, "Allāh's Messenger ﷺ used to examine the believing women who migrated to him in accordance with this Verse:-

'O Prophet! When believing

٤١٤ - حدثنا إسحاق : حدثنا يعقوب بن إبراهيم : حدثنا ابن أخي ابن شهاب ، عن عمه : أخبرني عروة : أن عائشة رضي الله عنها

women come to you to take the oath of allegiance to you..........
Verily! Allāh is Oft-Forgiving. Most Merciful.' (60:12)

'Aisha said, "And if any of the believing women accepted the condition (assigned in the above-mentioned Verse), Allāh's Messenger ﷺ would say to her. "I have accepted your pledge of allegiance." "He would only say that, for, by Allāh, his hand never touched, any lady during that pledge of allegiance. He did not receive their pledge except by saying, "I have accepted your pledge of allegiance for that."

زَوْجَ النَّبِيِّ صلى اللهُ عليه وسلَّم أخبرَتْهُ أنَّ رَسُولَ اللهِ صلى اللهُ عليهِ وسلَّم كانَ يَمْتَحِنُ مَنْ هاجَرَ إليْهِ مِنَ المُؤْمِنات بهذه الآيَةِ ، بِقَوْلِ اللهِ - يا أيُّها النَّبِيُّ إذَا جاءَكَ المُؤْمِناتُ يُبايِعْنَكَ - إلى قَوْلِهِ - غَفُورٌ رَحِيمٌ - قالَ عُرْوَةُ ، قالَتْ عائِشَةُ : فَمَنْ أقرَّ بِهذَا الشَّرْطِ مِنَ المُؤْمِناتِ قالَ لَها رَسُولُ اللهِ صلى اللهُ عليهِ وسلَّم قَدْ بايَعْتُكِ كَلاماً . وَالا وَاللهِ ما مَسَّتْ يَدُهُ يَدَ امْرأةٍ قَطُّ في المُبايَعَةِ . ما يُبايِعُهُنَّ إلاَّ بقَوْلِهِ : قَدْ بايَعْتُكِ عَلى ذَلِكِ . تابَعَهُ يُونُسُ ، وَمَعْمَرٌ ، وَعَبْدُ الرَّحْمَنِ بنُ إسحاقَ ، عَنِ الزُّهْرِيِّ . وَقالَ إسحاقُ بنُ راشِدٍ ، عَنِ الزُّهْرِيِّ ، عَنْ عُرْوَةَ وعَمْرَةَ .

(303) CHAPTER. 'O Prophet! When believing women come to you to take the oath of allegiance.' (60:12)

بابٌ - إذَا جاءَكَ المُؤْمِناتُ يُبايِعْنَكَ -.

415. Narrated Um 'Aṭiya رضي الله عنها : We took the oath of allegiance to Allāh's Messenger ﷺ and he recited to us:—

'They will not associate anything in worship with Allāh,' and forbade us to bewail the dead. Thereupon a lady withdrew her hand (refrained from taking

٤١٥ - حدَّثَنا أبُو مَعْمَرٍ : حدَّثَنا عَبْدُ الوَارِثِ : حدَّثَنا أيُّوبُ ، عَنْ حَفْصَةَ بِنْتِ سِيرِينَ ، عَنْ أُمِّ عَطِيَّةَ رَضِيَ اللهُ عَنْها قالَتْ : بايَعْنا رَسُولَ اللهِ صلى اللهُ عليهِ وسلَّم فَقَرَأ عَلَيْنا أنْ لا يُشْرِكْنَ باللهِ شَيْئاً وَنَهانا عَنِ النِّياحَةِ .

the oath of allegiance), and said, "But such-and-such lady lamented over one of my relatives, so I must reward (do the same over the dead relatives of) hers." The Prophet ﷺ did not object to that, so she went (there) and returned to the Prophet ﷺ so he accepted her pledge of allegiance.

فقبضت امرأة يدها فقالت: أسعدتني فلانة، أريد أن أجزيها، فما قال لها النبي صلى الله عليه وسلم شيئا، فانطلقت ورجعت فبايعها.

416. Narrated Ibn 'Abbās regarding the saying of Allāh :

'And they will not disobey you in any just matter.' (60:12)

That was one of the conditions which Allāh imposed on (the believing) women (who came to take the oath of allegiance to the Prophet ﷺ).

٤١٦ - حدثنا عبد الله بن محمد: حدثنا وهب بن جرير: قال: حدثنا أبي قال: سمعت الزبير عن عكرمة، عن ابن عباس في قوله تعالى - ولا يعصينك في معروف قال: إنما هو شرط شرطه الله للنساء.

417. Narrated 'Ubāda bin Aṣ-Ṣāmit : While we were with the Prophet, he said, "Will you swear to me the pledge of allegiance that you will not worship any thing besides Allāh , will not commit illegal sexual intercourse, and will not steal?" Then he recited the Verse concerning the women. (Sufyān, the sub-narrator, often said that the Prophet ﷺ added, "Whoever among you fulfills his pledge, will receive his reward from Allāh , and whoever commits any of those sins and receives the legal punishment (in this life), his punishment will be an expiation for that sin; and whoever commits any of those sins and Allāh screens him, then it is up to Allāh

٤١٧ - حدثنا علي بن عبد الله: حدثنا سفيان قال: الزهري حدثناه قال: حدثني أبو إدريس: سمع عبادة ابن الصامت رضي الله عنه قال: كنا عند النبي صلى الله عليه وسلم فقال: أتبايعوني على أن لا تشركوا بالله شيئا ولا تزنوا ولا تسرقوا؟ وقرأ آية النساء، وأكثر لفظ سفيان قرأ الآية - فمن وفى منكم فأجره على الله - ومن أصاب من ذلك شيئا فعوقب فهو كفارة له - ومن

to punish or forgive them."

أَصَابَ مِنْهَا شَيْئًا مِنْ ذَلِكَ فَسَتَرَهُ اللهُ فَهُوَ إِلَى اللهِ إِنْ شَاءَ عَذَّبَهُ وَإِنْ شَاءَ غَفَرَ لَهُ. تَابَعَهُ عَبْدُ الرَّزَّاقِ، عَنْ مَعْمَرٍ فِى الآيَةِ.

418. Narrated Ibn 'Abbās:
I witnessed the 'Īd-al-Fiṭr prayer with Allāh's Messenger, Abū-Bakr, 'Umar and 'Uthmān; and all of them offered it before delivering the sermon............... and then delivered the sermon. Once the Prophet, (after completing the prayer and the sermon) came down ....as if I am now looking at him waving at the men with his hand to sit down .... and walked through them till he, along with Bilāl, reached (the rows of) the women. Then he recited:

> 'O Prophet! When believing women come to you to take the oath of allegiance that they will not worship anything other than Allāh, will not steal, will not commit illegal sexual intercourse will not kill their children, and will not utter slander, intentionally forging falsehood (by making illegal children belonging to their husbands) . . . .(60:12)

Having finished, he said, 'Do you agree to that?" One lady, other than whom none replied the Prophet said, "Yes, O Allāh's Messenger!" (The, sub-narrator, Al-Ḥasan did not know who the lady was.) Then the Prophet said to them: "Will you give alms?" Thereupon Bilāl spread out his garment and the women started throwing big

٤١٨ - حَدَّثَنَا مُحَمَّدُ بْنُ عَبْدِ الرَّحِيمِ: حَدَّثَنَا هَارُونُ بْنُ مَعْرُوفٍ: حَدَّثَنَا عَبْدُ اللهِ بْنُ وَهْبٍ قَالَ: وَأَخْبَرَنِى ابْنُ جُرَيْجٍ: أَنَّ الحَسَنَ بْنَ مُسْلِمٍ أَخْبَرَهُ عَنْ طَاوُسٍ، عَنِ ابْنِ عَبَّاسٍ رَضِىَ اللهُ عَنْهُمَا قَالَ: شَهِدْتُ الصَّلَاةَ يَوْمَ الفِطْرِ مَعَ رَسُولِ اللهِ صلى اللهُ عليهِ وسلَّم وَأَبِى بَكْرٍ وَعُمَرَ وَعُثْمَانَ، فَكُلُّهُمْ يُصَلِّيهَا قَبْلَ الخُطْبَةِ، ثُمَّ يَخْطُبُ بَعْدُ. فَنَزَلَ نَبِىُّ اللهِ صلى اللهُ عليهِ وسلَّم فَكَأَنِّى أَنْظُرُ إِلَيْهِ حِينَ يُجَلِّسُ الرِّجَالَ بِيَدِهِ، ثُمَّ أَقْبَلَ يَشُقُّهُمْ حَتَّى أَتَى النِّسَاءَ مَعَ بِلَالٍ فَقَالَ - يَا أَيُّهَا النَّبِىُّ إِذَا جَاءَكَ المُؤْمِنَاتُ يُبَايِعْنَكَ عَلَى أَنْ لَا يُشْرِكْنَ بِاللهِ شَيْئًا وَلَا يَسْرِقْنَ وَلَا يَزْنِينَ وَلَا يَقْتُلْنَ أَوْلَادَهُنَّ وَلَا يَأْتِينَ بِبُهْتَانٍ يَفْتَرِينَهُ بَيْنَ أَيْدِيهِنَّ وَأَرْجُلِهِنَّ - حَتَّى فَرَغَ مِنَ الآيَةِ كُلِّهَا. ثُمَّ قَالَ حِينَ فَرَغَ: أَنْتُنَّ عَلَى ذَلِكَ؟ وَقَالَتِ امْرَأَةٌ وَاحِدَةٌ لَمْ يُجِبْهُ غَيْرُهَا: نَعَمْ يَا رَسُولَ اللهِ، لَا يَدْرِى

rings and small rings into Bilāl's garment. (See Ḥadīth No 95,Vol 2)

الحسن من هي ؟ قال : فتصدقن وبسط بلال ثوبه فجعلن يلقين الفتخ والخواتيم في ثوب بلال .

SŪRAT AṢ-ṢAFF (Battle Array) LXI

سورة الصف

In the Name of Allāh, the Most Beneficent, the Most Merciful

بسم الله الرحمن الرحيم

وقال مجاهد : من أنصاري إلى الله : من يتبعني إلى الله . وقال ابن عباس : مرصوص : ملصق بعضه إلى بعض . وقال يحيى بالرصاص . من بعدي اسمه أحمد .

419. Narrated Jubair bin Muṭ'im : I heard Allāh's Messenger saying , 'I have several names: I am Muḥammad and I am Aḥmad, and I am Al-Māḥī with whom Allāh obliterates Kufr (disbelief), and I am Al-Ḥāshir (gatherer) at whose feet (i.e. behind whom) the people will be gathered (on the Day of Resurrection), and I am Al-'Āqib (i.e. who succeeds the other prophets in bringing about good)."

٤١٩ ـ حدثنا أبو اليمان : أخبرنا شعيب ، عن الزهري قال : أخبرني محمد بن جبير بن مطعم ، عن أبيه رضي الله عنه قال : سمعت رسول الله صلى الله عليه وسلم يقول : إن لي أسماء : أنا محمد ، وأنا أحمد ، وأنا الماحي الذي يمحو الله بي الكفر ، وأنا الحاشر الذي يحشر الناس على قدمي ، وأنا العاقب .

SŪRAT AL–JUMU'A LXII

In the Name of Allāh, the Most Beneficent, the Most Merciful

سورة الجمعة

بسم الله الرحمن الرحيم

(304) CHAPTER. The Statement of Allāh :– "And He has sent him Muḥammad also to other (Muslims) who have not yet joined them' .... (62:3)

باب قوله. وآخرين منهم لما يلحقوا بهم. وقرأ عمر: فامضوا إلى ذكر الله.

420. Narrated Abū Huraira : While we were sitting with the Prophet , Sūrat Al-Jumu'a was revealed to him, and when the Verse, "And He (Allāh) has sent him (Muḥammad) also to other (Muslims)..... (62:3)

was recited by the Prophet , I said, "Who are they, O Allāh's Messenger?" The Prophet did not reply till I repeated my question thrice. At that time, Salmān Al-Fārisī was with us. So Allāh's Messenger put his hand on Salmān, saying, "If Faith were at (the place of) Ath-Thuraiyā (pleiades, the highest star), even then (some men or man from these people (i.e. Salmān's folk) would attain it."

٤٢٠ - حدثنا عبد العزيز بن عبد الله قال: حدثنا سليمان بن بلال، عن ثور، عن أبي الغيث، عن أبي هريرة رضي الله عنه قال: كنا جلوسا عند النبي صلى الله عليه وسلم فأنزلت عليه سورة الجمعة. وآخرين منهم لما يلحقوا بهم. قال: قلت: من هم يا رسول الله؟ فلم يراجعه حتى سأل ثلاثا وفينا سلمان الفارسي، وضع رسول الله صلى الله عليه وسلم يده على سلمان، ثم قال: لو كان الإيمان عند الثريا لناله رجال أو رجل من هؤلاء.

421. Narrated Abū Huraira :

٤٢١ - حدثنا عبد الله بن

The Prophet ﷺ said.' Then some men from these people would attain it." (See Ḥadīth No. 420)

عَبْدِ الوَهَّابِ: حَدَّثَنَا عَبْدُ العَزِيزِ: أَخْبَرَنِي ثَوْرٌ، عَنْ أَبِي الغَيْثِ، عَنْ أَبِي هُرَيْرَةَ، عَنِ النَّبِيِّ صلى الله عليه وسلم لَنَالَهُ رِجَالٌ مِنْ هَؤُلَاءِ

(305) CHAPTER. 'But when they see some bargain or some amusement. (62:11)

بَابٌ - وَإِذَا رَأَوْا تِجَارَةً أَوْ لَهْوًا..

422\. Narrated Jābir bin 'Abdullāh (رضي الله عنه): A caravan of merchandise arrived at Medīna on a Friday while we were with the Prophet ﷺ All the people left (the Prophet ﷺ, and headed for the caravan) except twelve persons. Then Allāh revealed:—

> 'But when they see some bargain or some amusement they disperse headlong to it.' . . . .(62:11)

٤٢٢ - حَدَّثَنِي حَفْصُ بْنُ عُمَرَ: حَدَّثَنَا خَالِدُ بْنُ عَبْدِ اللهِ: حَدَّثَنَا حُصَيْنٌ، عَنْ سَالِمِ بْنِ أَبِي الجَعْدِ، وَعَنْ أَبِي سُفْيَانَ، عَنْ جَابِرِ بْنِ عَبْدِ اللهِ رَضِيَ اللهُ عَنْهُمَا قَالَ: أَقْبَلَتْ عِيرٌ يَوْمَ الجُمُعَةِ وَنَحْنُ مَعَ النَّبِيِّ صلى الله عليه وسلم فَثَارَ النَّاسُ إِلَّا اثْنَا عَشَرَ رَجُلًا فَأَنْزَلَ اللهُ - وَإِذَا رَأَوْا تِجَارَةً أَوْ لَهْوًا انْفَضُّوا إِلَيْهَا -.

SŪRAT AL—MUNĀFIQŪN (The Hypocrites) LXIII

سورة المنافقين

In the Name of Allāh, the Most Beneficent, the Most Merciful

بِسْمِ اللهِ الرَّحْمَنِ الرَّحِيمِ.

(306) CHAPTER. The Statement of

بَابٌ قَوْلِهِ - إِذَا جَاءَكَ المُنَافِقُونَ

Allāh ﷻ :–

'When the hypocrites come to you (O Muḥammad ﷺ) they say: We bear witness that you are indeed the Messenger of Allāh. . ...'

(63:1)

قالوا نشهد إنك لرسول الله - الآية .

423. Narrated Zaid bin Arqam: While I was taking part in a Ghazwa. (1) I heard 'Abdullāh bin Ubaī (bin Abī-Salūl) saying. "Don't spend on those who are with Allāh's Messenger ﷺ that they may disperse and go away from him. If we return (to Medīna), surely, the more honourable will expel the meaner amongst them." I reported that (saying) to my uncle or to 'Umar who, in his turn, informed the Prophet ﷺ of it. The Prophet ﷺ called me and I narrated to him the whole story. Then Allāh's Messenger ﷺ sent for 'Abdullāh bin Ubai and his companions, and they took an oath that they did not say that. So Allāh's Messenger ﷺ disbelieved my saying and believed his. I was distressed as I never was before. I stayed at home and my uncle said to me. "You just wanted Allāh's Messenger ﷺ to disbelieve your statement and hate you." So Allāh ﷻ revealed (the Sūra beginning with)

'When the hypocrites come to you.'

(63:1)

The Prophet ﷺ then sent for me and recited it and said, "O Zaid! Allāh confirmed your statement."

٤٢٣ - حدثنا عبد الله بن رجاء : حدثنا إسرائيل ، عن أبي إسحاق ، عن زيد بن أرقم قال : كنت في غزاة فسمعت عبد الله بن أبي يقول : لا تنفقوا على من عند رسول الله صلى الله عليه وسلم حتى ينفضوا من حوله ، ولئن رجعنا من عنده ليخرجن الأعز منها الأذل . فذكرت ذلك لعمي أو لعمر فذكره للنبي صلى الله عليه وسلم فدعاني فحدثته . فأرسل رسول الله صلى الله عليه وسلم إلى عبد الله ابن أبي وأصحابه فحلفوا ما قالوا . فكذبني رسول الله صلى الله عليه وسلم وصدقه ، فأصابني هم لم يصبني مثله قط . فجلست في البيت فقال لي عمي : ما أردت إلى أن كذبك رسول الله صلى الله عليه وسلم ومقتك ، فأنزل الله تعالى - إذا جاءك المنافقون - فبعث إلى النبي صلى الله عليه وسلم

(1) See the glossary.

فقرأ فقال: إن الله قد صدقك يا زيد.

(307) CHAPTER. 'They have made their oaths a screen (for their hypocrisy).'

باب - اتخذوا أيمانهم جنة - يجتنون بها.

(63:1-2)

424. Narrated Zaid bin Arqam ﷺ: I was with my uncle and I heard 'Abdullāh bin Ubai bin Salūl, saying, "Don't spend on those who are with Allāh's Messenger ﷺ that they may disperse and go away from him." He also said, "If we return to Medīna, surely, the more honourable will expel the meaner." So I informed my uncle of that and then my uncle informed Allāh's Messenger ﷺ thereof. Allāh's Messenger ﷺ sent for 'Abdullāh bin Ubai and his companions. They swore that they did not say anything of that sort Allāh's Messenger ﷺ deemed their statement true and rejected mine. Thereof I became as distressed as I have never been before, and stayed at home. Then Allāh ﷻ revealed (Sūrat Al-Munāfiqīn):—

'When the hypocrites come to you ....(63:1)

They are the ones who say: Spend nothing on those who are with Allāh's Messenger ......(63:7)

Verily the more honourable will

٤٢٤ - حدثنا آدم بن إياس: حدثنا إسرائيل، عن أبي إسحاق، عن زيد بن أرقم رضي الله عنه قال: كنت مع عمي فسمعت عبد الله بن أبي ابن سلول يقول: لا تنفقوا على من عند رسول الله حتى ينفضوا. وقال أيضا: لئن رجعنا إلى المدينة ليخرجن الأعز منها الأذل. فذكرت ذلك لعمي، فذكر عمي لرسول الله صلى الله عليه وسلم فأرسل رسول الله صلى الله عليه وسلم إلى عبد الله ابن أبي وأصحابه فحلفوا ما قالوا فصدقهم رسول الله صلى الله عليه وسلم وكذبني. فأصابني هم لم يصبني مثله فجلست في بيتي. فأنزل الله عز وجل - إذا جاءك المنافقون - إلى قوله - هم الذين يقولون لا تنفقوا

expel therefrom the meaner.' (63:7-8)

على مَنْ عِنْدَ رَسُولِ اللهِ - إلى قَوْلِهِ - لَيُخْرِجَنَّ الأَعَزُّ مِنْهَا الأَذَلَّ - فأرْسَلَ إلى رَسُولُ اللهِ صلى اللهُ عليهِ وسلَّم فَقَرَأها عَلَيَّ ثُمَّ قالَ: إنَّ اللهَ قَدْ صَدَّقَكَ.

Allāh's Messenger ﷺ sent for me and recited that Sūra for me and said, "Allāh has confirmed your statement."

(308) CHAPTER. The Statement of Allāh ﷻ :–

'That is because they believed, then disbelieved, so a seal was set on their hearts, therefore they understand not.' (63:3)

بابُ قَوْلِهِ - ذَلِكَ بِأَنَّهُمْ آمَنُوا ثُمَّ كَفَرُوا فَطُبِعَ عَلَى قُلُوبِهِمْ فَهُمْ لا يَفْقَهُونَ - .

425. Narrated Zaid bin Arqam رضي الله عنه : When 'Abdullāh bin Ubai said, "Do not spend on those who are with Allāh's Messenger," and also said, "If we return to Medina," I informed the Prophet ﷺ of his saying. The Anṣār blamed me for that, and 'Abdullāh bin Ubai swore that he did not say. I returned to my house and slept. Allāh's Messenger ﷺ then called me and I went to him. He said, "Allāh has confirmed your statement." The Verse:–

"They are the one who say: Spend nothing . . . .(63:7)
was revealed.

٤٢٥ - حدَّثنا آدَمُ: حدَّثنا شُعْبَةُ، عَنِ الحَكَمِ قالَ: سَمِعْتُ مُحَمَّدَ بنَ كَعْبٍ القُرَظِيَّ قالَ: سَمِعْتُ زَيْدَ بنَ أرْقَمَ رَضِيَ اللهُ عَنْهُ قالَ: لَمَّا قالَ عَبْدُ اللهِ بنُ أُبَيٍّ: لا تُنْفِقُوا عَلَى مَنْ عِنْدَ رَسُولِ اللهِ، وَقالَ أيْضًا: لَئِنْ رَجَعْنَا إلى المَدِينَةِ، أخْبَرْتُ بِهِ النَّبِيَّ صلى اللهُ عليهِ وسلَّم فَلامَنِي الأنْصَارُ، وَحَلَفَ عَبْدُ اللهِ بنُ أُبَيٍّ ما قالَ ذَلِكَ. فَرَجَعْتُ إلى المَنْزِلِ فَنِمْتُ، فَدَعانِي رَسُولُ اللهِ صلى اللهُ عليهِ وسلَّم فَأتَيْتُهُ، فَقالَ: إنَّ اللهَ قَدْ صَدَّقَكَ وَنَزَلَ -

هم الذين يقولون لا تنفقوا - الآية.
وقال ابن أبي زائدة، عن الأعمش،
عن عمرو، عن ابن أبي ليلى، عن
زيد، عن النبي صلى الله عليه وسلم.

(309) CHAPTER. 'When you look at them, their bodies please you, and when they speak, you listen to their words. They are as (worthless as hollow) blocks of wood propped up. They think that every cry is against them. They are the enemies. So beware of them. May Allāh curse them! How are they deluded (away from the Truth) (63:4)

باب - وإذا رأيتهم تعجبك أجسامهم وإن يقولوا تسمع لقولهم - الآية - كأنهم خشب مسندة يحسبون كل صيحة عليهم هم العدو فاحذرهم قاتلهم الله أنى يؤفكون -.

426. Narrated Zaid bin Arqam: We went out with the Prophet ﷺ on a journey and the people suffered from lack of provisions. So 'Abdullāh bin Ubai said to his companions, "Don't spend on those who are with Allāh's Messenger, that they may disperse and go away from him." He also said, "If we return to Medīna, surely, the more honourable will expel therefrom the meaner. So I went to the Prophet ﷺ and informed him of that. He sent for 'Abdullāh bin Ubai and asked him, but 'Abdullāh bin Ubai swore that he did not say so. The people said, "Zaid told a lie to 'Allāh's Messenger." What they said distressed me very much. Later Allāh revealed the confirmation of my statement in his saying:–
"(When the hypocrites come to

٤٢٦ - حدثنا عمرو بن خالد: حدثنا زهير بن معاوية: حدثنا أبو إسحاق قال: سمعت زيد بن أرقم قال: خرجنا مع النبي صلى الله عليه وسلم في سفر أصاب الناس فيه شدة، فقال عبد الله بن أبي لأصحابه، لا تنفقوا على من عند رسول الله حتى ينفضوا من حوله. وقال: لئن رجعنا إلى المدينة ليخرجن الأعز منها الأذل. فأتيت النبي صلى الله عليه وسلم فأخبرته فأرسل إلى عبد الله ابن أبي فسأله، فاجتهد يمينه ما فعل. قالوا: كذب زيد رسول الله

٣٩٦

you.) (63:1)
So the Prophet ﷺ called them that they might ask Allāh to forgive them, but they turned their heads aside. (Concerning Allāh's saying: 'Pieces of wood propped up,' Zaid said; They were the most handsome men.)

صلى اللهُ عليه وسلَّم ، فوقعَ في نفسي مما قالوا شدةٌ ، فأنزلَ اللهُ عزَّ وجلَّ تصديقي في - إذا جاءكَ المنافقونَ - فدعاهمُ النبيُّ صلى اللهُ عليه وسلَّم ليستغفرَ لهُم فلَوَّوْا رُءُوسَهُمْ - وقولُهُ خُشُبٌ مُسَنَّدَةٌ ، قالَ : كانَ رجالاً أجملَ شيءٍ .

(310) CHAPTER. The Statement of Allāh تعالى :-

> 'And when it is said to them: "Come, Allāh's Messenger will ask forgiveness (from Allāh) for you," they turn aside their heads and you would see them turning away their faces in pride.' (63:5)

بابُ قولِهِ - وإذا قيلَ لهُمْ تعالَوْا يستغفرْ لكُمْ رسولُ اللهِ لوَّوْا رُءُوسَهُمْ - إلى قولِهِ - مُستكبِرُونَ -

ورأيتهُمْ يصدُّونَ وهُمْ مُستكبِرُونَ - حرَّكوا : استهزءوا بالنبيِّ صلى اللهُ عليه وسلَّم ، ويُقرأُ بالتخفيفِ مِنْ لَوَيْتُ .

427. Narrated Zaid bin Arqam: While I was with my uncle, I heard 'Abdullāh bin Ubaī bin Salūl saying, "Do not spend on those who are with Allāh's Messenger, that they may disperse and go away (from him). And if we return to Medīna, surely, the more honourable will expel therefrom the meaner." I mentioned that to my uncle who, in turn, mentioned it to the Prophet ﷺ. The Prophet ﷺ, called me and I told him about that. Then he sent for 'Abdullāh bin Ubaī and his companions, and they swore that they did not say so. The Prophet ﷺ disbelieved my statement and believed theirs. I was distressed

٤٢٧ - حدَّثنا عُبيدُ اللهِ بنُ مُوسَى ، عَنْ إسرائيلَ ، عَنْ أبي إسحاقَ ، عَنْ زيدِ بنِ أرقمَ قالَ : كُنتُ معَ عمِّي ، فسمعتُ عبدَ اللهِ بنَ أُبَيٍّ ابنَ سلولَ يقولُ : لا تُنفِقُوا عَلَى مَنْ عِندَ رسولِ اللهِ حتَّى ينفضُّوا ، ولَئِنْ رجعنا إلى المدينةِ ليُخرِجنَّ الأعزُّ منها الأذلَّ . فذكرتُ ذلكَ لعمِّي ، فذكرَ عمِّي للنبيِّ صلى اللهُ عليه وسلَّم فدعاني فحدَّثتُهُ ، فأرسلَ إلى عبدِ اللهِ ابنِ أُبَيٍّ وأصحابِهِ ،

as I have never been before, and I remained in my house. My uncle said to me, "You just wanted the Prophet ﷺ to consider you a liar and hate you." Then Allāh revealed:—

> 'When the hypocrites come to you, they say: 'We bear witness that you are indeed the Messenger of Allāh." (63:1)

So the Prophet ﷺ sent for me and recited it and said, "Allāh has confirmed your statement."

فحلفوا ما قالوا وكذبني النبي صلى الله عليه وسلم وصدقهم ، فأصابني هم لم يصبني مثله قط ، فجلست في بيتي ، وقال عمي : ما أردت إلى أن كذبك النبي صلى الله عليه وسلم ومقتك ، فأنزل الله تعالى - إذا جاءك المنافقون قالوا نشهد إنك لرسول الله - وأرسل إلي النبي صلى الله عليه وسلم فقرأها وقال : إن الله قد صدقك .

(311) CHAPTER. The Statement of Allāh تعالى :—

> 'It is equal to them whether you ask for their forgiveness or ask not forgiveness for them. . . . .(63:6)

باب قوله - سواء عليهم أستغفرت لهم - الآية .

428. Narrated Jābir bin 'Abdullāh رضي الله عنه : We were in a Ghazwa (Sufyān once said, in an army) and a man from the emigrants kicked an Anṣāri man (on the buttocks with his foot). The Anṣāri man said, "O the Anṣār! (Help!)" and the emigrant said. "O the emigrants! (Help!) Allāh's Messenger ﷺ heard that and said, "What is this call for, which is characteristic of the period of ignorance?" They said, "O Allāh's Messenger! A man from the emigrants kicked one of the Anṣār (on the buttocks with his foot)." Allāh's Messenger

٤٢٨ - حدثنا علي : حدثنا سفيان : قال عمرو : سمعت جابر بن عبد الله رضي الله عنهما قال : كنا في غزاة ، قال سفيان مرة في جيش . فكسع رجل من المهاجرين رجلا من الأنصار ، فقال الأنصاري : يا للأنصار ، وقال المهاجري : يا للمهاجرين ، فسمع ذلك رسول الله صلى الله عليه وسلم فقال : ما بال دعوى جاهلية ؟

ﷺ said, "Leave it (that call) as it is a detestable thing." 'Abdullāh bin Ubaī heard that and said, 'Have they (the emigrants) done so? By Allāh, if we return Medīna, surely, the more honourable will expel therefrom the meaner." When this statement reached the Prophet ﷺ. 'Umar got up and said, "O Allāh's Messenger! Let me chop off the head of this hypocrite ('Abdullāh bin Ubaī)!" The Prophet ﷺ said, "Leave him, lest the people say that Muḥammad kills his companions." The Anṣār were then more in number than the emigrants when the latter came to Medīna, but later on the emigrants increased.

قَالُوا: يَا رَسُولَ اللهِ، كَسَعَ رَجُلٌ مِنَ الْمُهَاجِرِينَ رَجُلاً مِنَ الأَنْصَارِ، فَقَالَ: دَعُوهَا فَإِنَّهَا مُنْتِنَةٌ. فَسَمِعَ بِذَلِكَ عَبْدُ اللهِ بْنُ أُبَيٍّ فَقَالَ: فَعَلُوهَا؟ أَمَا وَاللهِ لَئِنْ رَجَعْنَا إِلَى الْمَدِينَةِ لَيُخْرِجَنَّ الأَعَزُّ مِنْهَا الأَذَلَّ. فَبَلَغَ النَّبِيَّ صلى اللهُ عليه وسلَّم، فَقَامَ عُمَرُ فَقَالَ: يَا رَسُولَ اللهِ، دَعْنِي أَضْرِبْ عُنُقَ هَذَا الْمُنَافِقِ. فَقَالَ النَّبِيُّ صلى اللهُ عليه وسلَّم: دَعْهُ، لا يَتَحَدَّثُ النَّاسُ أَنَّ مُحَمَّدًا يَقْتُلُ أَصْحَابَهُ. وَكَانَتِ الأَنْصَارُ أَكْثَرَ مِنَ الْمُهَاجِرِينَ حِينَ قَدِمُوا الْمَدِينَةَ. ثُمَّ إِنَّ الْمُهَاجِرِينَ كَثُرُوا بَعْدُ. قَالَ سُفْيَانُ: فَحَفِظْتُهُ مِنْ عَمْرٍو، قَالَ عَمْرٌو: سَمِعْتُ جَابِرًا: كُنَّا مَعَ النَّبِيِّ صلى اللهُ عليه وسلَّم.

(312) CHAPTER. Allāh's (تعالى) Statement:—

'They are the ones who say: Spend nothing on those who are with Allāh's Messenger, until they disperse (from him).' (63:7)

بَاب قَوْلِهِ ـ هُمُ الَّذِينَ يَقُولُونَ لا تُنْفِقُوا عَلَى مَنْ عِنْدَ رَسُولِ اللهِ حَتَّى يَنْفَضُّوا ـ يَنْفَضُّوا: يَتَفَرَّقُوا.

429. Narrated Mūsā bin 'Uqba: 'Abdullāh bin Al-Faḍl told me that Anas bin Mālik said, "I was much grieved over those who had been killed in the Battle of Al-Ḥarra. When Zaid bin Arqam heard of my intense grief (over the

٤٢٩ ـ حَدَّثَنَا إِسْمَاعِيلُ بْنُ عَبْدِ اللهِ قَالَ: حَدَّثَنِي إِسْمَاعِيلُ بْنُ إِبْرَاهِيمَ بْنِ عُقْبَةَ، عَنْ مُوسَى بْنِ عُقْبَةَ قَالَ: حَدَّثَنِي عَبْدُ اللهِ بْنُ الْفَضْلِ:

killed Anṣār), he wrote a letter to me saying that he heard Allāh's Messenger ﷺ saying, O Allāh! Forgive the Anṣār and the Anṣār children. The sub-narrator, Ibn Al-Faḍl, is not sure whether the Prophet ﷺ also said, And their grand-children." Some of those who were present, asked Anas (about Zaid). He said, "He (Zaid) is the one about whom Allāh's Messenger ﷺ said, 'He is the one whose sound hearing Allāh testified.' "

أنهُ سمعَ أنسَ بنَ مالكٍ يقولُ: حزنتُ علَى مَنْ أُصيبَ بالحرّةِ. فكتبَ إلىَّ زيدُ بنُ أرقمَ وبلغهُ شدّةُ حزني يذكرُ أنهُ سمعَ رسولَ اللهِ صلى اللهُ عليهِ وسلّم يقولُ: اللهمَّ اغفرْ للأنصارِ ولأبناءِ الأنصارِ، وشكَّ ابنُ الفضلِ في أبناءِ أبناءِ الأنصارِ، فسألَ أنساً بعضُ مَنْ كانَ عندهُ فقالَ: هوَ الذي يقولُ رسولُ اللهِ صلى اللهُ عليهِ وسلّم، هذا الذي أوفَى اللهُ لهُ بأذنِهِ.

(313) CHAPTER. The Statement of Allāh (تعالى) :–

'They say: "If we return to Medīna, surely' the more honourable will expel therefrom the meaner.!"

(63:8)

باب قولهُ - يقولونَ لئنْ رجعنا إلى المدينةِ ليُخرجنَّ الأعزُّ منها الأذلَّ - الآيةَ.

430. Narrated Jābir bin 'Abdullāh (رضي الله عنهما) :

We were in a Ghazwa (1) and a man from the emigrants kicked an Anṣārī (on the buttocks with his foot). The Anṣārī man said, "O the Anṣārs! (Help!)" The emigrant said, "O the emigrants! (Help)." When Allāh's Messenger ﷺ heard that, he said, "What is that?" They said, "A man from the emigrants kicked a man from the Anṣār (on the buttocks

٤٣٠ - حدّثنا الحُميديُّ: حدّثنا سُفيانُ قالَ: حفظناهُ مِنْ عمرِو بنِ دينارٍ قالَ: سمعتُ جابرَ بنَ عبدِ اللهِ رضيَ اللهُ عنهُما يقولُ: كنّا في غزاةٍ فكسعَ رجلٌ منَ المهاجرينَ رجلاً منَ الأنصارِ، فقالَ الأنصاريُّ: يا للأنصارِ، وقالَ المهاجريُّ: يا

(1) See the glossary.

with his foot). On that the Anṣār said, 'O the Anṣār!' and the emigrant said, 'O the emigrants!" The Prophet ﷺ said' "Leave it (that call) for it is a detestable thing." The number of Anṣār was larger (than that of the emigrants) at the time when the Prophet ﷺ came to Medīna, but later the number of emigrants increased. 'Abdullāh bin Ubai said, "Have they, (the emigrants) done so? By Allāh, if we return to Medīna, surely, the more honourable will expel therefrom the meaner," 'Umar bin Al-Khaṭṭāb said, "O Allāh's Messenger! Let me chop off the head of this hypocrite!" The prophet ﷺ said, "Leave him, lest the people say Muhammad kills his companions:"

للمهاجرين ، فسمعها الله رسوله صلى الله عليه وسلم ، قال : ما هذا ؟ فقالوا : كسع رجل من المهاجرين رجلاً من الأنصار فقال الأنصاري : يالَلأنصار ، وقال المهاجري : يا للمهاجرين . فقال النبي صلى الله عليه وسلم : دعوها فإنها منتنة . قال جابر : وكانت الأنصار حين قدم النبي صلى الله عليه وسلم أكثر ، ثم كثر المهاجرون بعد . فقال عبد الله بن أبي : أو قد فعلوا ؟ والله لئن رجعنا إلى المدينة ليخرجن الأعز منها الأذل . فقال عمر بن الخطاب رضي الله عنه : دعني يا رسول الله أضرب عنق هذا المنافق . قال النبي صلى الله عليه وسلم : دعه ، لا يتحدث الناس أن محمداً يقتل أصحابه .

SŪRAT AT–TAGHĀBUN (Mutual Loss and Gain) LXIV)

سورة التغابن

In the Name of Allāh,
the Most Beneficent, the Most Merciful

(No Ḥadīths were mentioned here)

بسم الله الرحمن الرحيم

وقال علقمة عن عبد الله ـ ومن يؤمن بالله يهد قلبه ـ هو الذي إذا أصابته مصيبة رضي وعرف أنها من الله . وقال مجاهد : التغابن : غبن أهل الجنة أهل النار . إن ارتبتم : إن لم تعلموا أتحيض أم

لا تحيضُ . فاللائى قعَدْنَ عَنِ المَحيضِ وَاللائى لَمْ يَحِضْنَ بَعْدُ فَعِدَّتُهُنَّ ثلاثةُ أشهرٍ .

SŪRAT AṬ-ṬALĀQ (The Divorce)
LXV

In the Name of Allāh, the Most Beneficent, the Most Merciful

سورة الطلاق

بِسْمِ اللهِ الرَّحْمَنِ الرَّحِيمِ .

وَقَالَ مُجَاهِدٌ : وبالَ أمْرِها : جزَاءَ أمْرِها .

431. Narrated Sālim that 'Abdullāh bin 'Umar told him that he had divorced his wife while she was in her menses, so 'Umar informed Allāh's Messenger ﷺ of that. Allāh's Messenger ﷺ became very angry at that and said, "(Ibn 'Umar must return her to his house and keep her as his wife till she becomes clean and then menstruates and becomes clean again, whereupon, if he wishes to divorce her, he may do so while she is still clean and before having any sexual relations with her, for that is the legally prescribed period for divorce as Allāh has ordered."

٤٣١ ـ حدَّثنا يَحْيَى بنُ بُكَيرٍ : حدَّثنا اللَّيْثُ قالَ : حدَّثني عُقَيْلٌ ، عَنِ ابنِ شِهابٍ قالَ : أخبرَني سالِمٌ : أنَّ عبْدَ اللهِ بنَ عُمَرَ رَضِيَ اللهُ عنهُما أخبرَهُ أنَّهُ طَلَّقَ امْرأتَهُ وَهِيَ حائِضٌ ، فَذَكَرَ عُمَرُ لِرَسُولِ اللهِ صلى اللهُ عليه وسلَّم فتَغَيَّظَ فيهِ رَسُولُ اللهِ صلى اللهُ عليه وسلَّم ثُمَّ قالَ : لِيُراجِعْها ثُمَّ يُمْسِكْها حتَّى تَطْهُرَ ، ثُمَّ تَحيضَ فتَطْهُرَ ، فإنْ بَدَا لَهُ أنْ يُطَلِّقَها فَلْيُطَلِّقْها طاهِراً قَبْلَ أنْ يَمَسَّها ، فتِلكَ العِدَّةُ كما أمَرَهُ اللهُ .

(314) CHAPTER. The Statement of Allāh تعالى :–

'For those who are pregnant (whether they are divorced or their husbands are dead) their prescribed period is until they deliver (their burdens), and whoever keeps his duty to Allāh. He will make his path easy.' (65:4)

وَأُولاتُ الأَحْمالِ أَجَلُهُنَّ أَنْ يَضَعْنَ حَمْلَهُنَّ وَمَنْ يَتَّقِ اللهَ يَجْعَلْ لَهُ مِنْ أَمْرِهِ يُسْرًا ـ وأُولاتِ الأَحْمالِ: وَاحِدُها ذاتُ حَمْلٍ.

432. Narrated Abū Salama: A man came to Ibn 'Abbās while Abū Huraira was sitting with him and said, "Give me your verdict regarding a lady who delivered a baby forty days after the death of her husband." Ibn 'Abbās said, "This indicates the end of one of the two prescribed periods." I said "For those who are pregnant, their prescribed period is until they deliver their burdens." Abū Huraira said, I agree with my cousin (Abū Salama)." Then Ibn 'Abbās sent his slave, Kuraib to Um Salama to ask her (regarding this matter). She replied. "The husband of Subai 'a al-Aslamiya was killed while she was pregnant, and she delivered a baby forty days after his death. Then her hand was asked in marriage and Allāh's Messenger ﷺ married her (to somebody). Abū As-Sanābil was one of those who asked for her hand in marriage".

٤٣٢ ـ حَدَّثَنا سَعْدُ بنُ حَفْصٍ: حَدَّثَنا شَيْبانُ، عَنْ يَحْيَى قالَ: أَخْبَرَني أَبُو سَلَمَةَ قالَ جاءَ رَجُلٌ إِلى ابنِ عَبّاسٍ وأَبُو هُرَيْرَةَ جالِسٌ عِنْدَهُ فَقالَ: أَفْتِني في امْرَأَةٍ وَلَدَتْ بَعْدَ زَوْجِها بِأَرْبَعِينَ لَيْلَةً. فَقالَ ابنُ عَبّاسٍ: آخِرُ الأَجَلَيْنِ. قُلْتُ أَنا ـ وأُولاتُ الأَحْمالِ أَجَلُهُنَّ أَنْ يَضَعْنَ حَمْلَهُنَّ ـ قالَ أَبُو هُرَيْرَةَ: أَنا مَعَ ابنِ أَخِي، يَعْنِي أَبا سَلَمَةَ. فَأَرْسَلَ ابنُ عَبّاسٍ غُلامَهُ كُرَيْبًا إِلى أُمِّ سَلَمَةَ يَسْأَلُها فَقالَتْ: قُتِلَ زَوْجُ سُبَيْعَةَ الأَسْلَمِيَّةِ وَهِيَ حُبْلَى فَوَضَعَتْ بَعْدَ مَوْتِهِ بِأَرْبَعِينَ لَيْلَةً، فَخُطِبَتْ فَأَنْكَحَها رَسُولُ اللهِ صلى اللهُ عليهِ وسلَّمَ وكانَ أَبُو السَّنابِلِ فِيمَنْ خَطَبَها. وَقالَ سُلَيْمانُ

ابنُ حَرْبٍ وأبو النُّعْمان : حدَّثنا حَمّادُ ابنُ زَيْدٍ ، عَنْ أيُّوبَ ، عَنْ مُحَمَّدٍ قالَ : كُنْتُ فى حَلْقَةٍ فيها عَبْدُ الرَّحْمَٰنِ بنُ أبى لَيْلَى وكانَ أصحابُهُ يُعَظِّمُونَهُ . فَذَكَرَ آخِرَ الأجَلَيْنِ فَحَدَّثْتُ بِحَدِيثِ سُبَيْعَةَ بِنتِ الحارِثِ ، عَنْ عَبْدِ اللهِ بنِ عُتْبَةَ ، قالَ : فَضَمَّزَ لى بَعْضُ أصحابِهِ قالَ مُحَمَّدٌ : فَفَطِنْتُ لَهُ فَقُلْتُ إنِّى إذًا لجَرِىءٌ إنْ كَذَبْتُ عَلَى عَبْدِ اللهِ بنِ عُتْبَةَ وَهُوَ فى ناحِيَةِ الكُوفَةِ ، فاسْتَحْيا وَقالَ : لكِنْ عَمُّهُ لَمْ يَقُلْ ذَاكَ . فَلَقِيتُ أبا عَطِيَّةَ مالكَ بنَ عامِرٍ فَسألْتُهُ فَذَهَبَ يُحَدِّثُنِى حَدِيثَ سُبَيْعَةَ ، فَقُلْتُ : هَلْ سَمِعْتَ عَنْ عَبْدِ اللهِ فيها شَيْئًا ؟ فَقالَ : كُنّا عِنْدَ عَبْدِ اللهِ فَقالَ : أتَجْعَلُونَ عَلَيْها التَّغْلِيظَ وَلا تَجْعَلُونَ عَلَيْها الرُّخْصَةَ ؟ لَنَزَلَتْ سُورَةُ النِّساءِ القُصْرَى بَعْدَ الطُّولَى ـ وأُولاتُ الأحْمالِ أجَلُهُنَّ أنْ يَضَعْنَ حَمْلَهُنَّ ـ .

سورة التحريم

SŪRAT AT–TAḤRĪM (Banning "something") LXVI

بِسْمِ اللهِ الرَّحْمَٰنِ الرَّحِيمِ

In the Name of Allāh, the Most Beneficent, the Most Merciful

بابٌ ـ يا أيُّها النَّبِىُّ لِمَ تُحَرِّمُ

(315) CHAPTER. The Statement of

Allāh :–

'O Prophet! Why do you ban that which Allāh has made lawful for you?' (66:1)

ما أحَلَّ اللهُ لكَ - الآيَة .

433. Narrated Ibn 'Abbās : If someone says to his wife, "You are unlawful to me." he must make an expiation (for his oath). (1) Ibn 'Abbās added: There is for you in Allāh's Messenger , an excellent example to follow.

٤٣٣ - حدَّثَنا مُعاذُ بنُ فُضالَةَ : حدَّثَنا هِشامٌ ، عَنْ يَحْيَى ، عَنْ ابنِ حَكيمٍ ، عَنْ سَعيدِ بنِ جُبَيرٍ : أنَّ ابنَ عَبّاسٍ رَضِيَ اللهُ عَنْهُما قالَ : في الحَرامِ يُكَفِّرُ . وقالَ ابنُ عَبّاسٍ - لَقَدْ كانَ لَكُمْ في رَسُولِ اللهِ أُسْوَةٌ حَسَنَةٌ - .

434. Narrated 'Āisha : Allāh's Messenger used to drink honey in the house of Zainab, the daughter of Jaḥsh, and would stay there with her. So Ḥafṣa and I agreed secretly that, if he come to either of us, she would say to him. "It seems you have eaten Maghāfīr (a kind of bad-smelling resin), for I smell in you the smell of Maghāfīr," (We did so) and he replied. "No, but I was drinking honey in the house of Zainab, the daughter of Jaḥsh, and I shall never take it again. I have taken an oath as to that, and you should not tell anybody about it."

٤٣٤ - حدَّثَنا إبْراهيمُ بنُ مُوسَى أخبرَنا هِشامُ بنُ يُوسُفَ ، عَنِ ابنِ جُرَيجٍ ، عَنْ عَطاءٍ ، عَنْ عُبَيدِ بنِ عُمَيرٍ ، عَنْ عائِشَةَ رَضِيَ اللهُ عَنْها قالَتْ : كانَ رَسُولُ اللهِ صلى اللهُ عليه وسلَّم يَشْرَبُ عَسَلاً عِنْدَ زَيْنَبَ ابْنَةِ جَحْشٍ وَيَمْكُثُ عِنْدَها ، فَواطَأْتُ أنا وحَفْصَةُ عَنْ أيَّتُنا دَخَلَ عَلَيْها فَلْتَقُلْ لَهُ : أكَلْتَ مَغافيرَ ، إني أجِدُ مِنْكَ رِيحَ مَغافيرَ . قالَ : لا ، وَلَكِنِّي كُنْتُ أشْرَبُ عَسَلاً عِنْدَ زَيْنَبَ ابْنَةِ جَحْشٍ فَلَنْ أعُودَ لَهُ . وَقَدْ حَلَفْتُ

(1) His saying will not mean a decision to divorce her.

لا تخبري بذلك أحدا .

(316) CHAPTER. Seeking to please your wives ....(66:1)

Allāh has already ordained for you (O men), the dissolution of your oaths.' (66:2)

باب . تبتغي مرضاة أزواجك

قد فرض الله لكم تحلة أيمانكم . .

435. Narrated Ibn 'Abbās ﷺ: For the whole year I had the desire to ask 'Umar bin Al-Khaṭṭāb regarding the explanation of a Verse (in Sūrat Al-Taḥrīm), but I could not ask him because I respected him very much. When he went to perform the Ḥajj, I too went along with him. On our return, while we were still on the way home. 'Umar went aside to answer the call of nature by the Arāk trees. I waited till he finished and then I proceeded with him and asked him. "O chief of the Believers! Who were the two wives of the Prophet ﷺ who aided one another against him?" He said, "They were Ḥafṣa and 'Āisha." Then I said to him, "By Allāh, I wanted to ask you about this a year ago, but I could not do so owing to my respect for you." 'Umar said, "Do not refrain from asking me. If you think that I have knowledge (about a certain matter), ask me; and if I know (something about it), I will tell you." Then 'Umar added, "By Allāh, in the Pre-Islāmic Period of Ignorance we did not pay attention to women until Allāh revealed regarding them what He revealed regarding them and assigned for

٤٣٥ - حدثنا عبد العزيز بن عبد الله : حدثنا سليمان بن بلال ، عن يحيى ، عن عبيد بن حنين : أنه سمع ابن عباس رضي الله عنهما يحدث أنه قال : مكثت سنة أريد أن أسأل عمر بن الخطاب عن آية فما أستطيع أن أسأله هيبة له حتى خرج حاجا فخرجت معه . فلما رجعت وكنا ببعض الطريق عدل إلى الأراك لحاجة له . قال : فوقفت له حتى فرغ ، ثم سرت معه فقلت : يا أمير المؤمنين ، من اللتان تظاهرتا على النبي صلى الله عليه وسلم من أزواجه ؟ فقال : تلك حفصة وعائشة . قال فقلت : والله إن كنت لأريد أن أسألك عن هذا منذ سنة فما أستطيع هيبة لك ، قال : فلا تفعل ، ما ظننت أن عندي من علم فاسألني ، فإن كان لي علم خبرتك به . قال : ثم قال

them what He has assigned. Once while I was thinking over a certain matter, my wife said, "I recommend that you do so-and-so." I said to her, "What have you got to do with this matter? Why do you poke your nose in a matter which I want to see fulfilled.?" She said, How strange you are, O son of Al-Khaṭṭāb! You don't want to be argued with whereas your daughter, Ḥafṣa surely, argues with Allāh's Messenger ﷺ so much that he remains angry for a full day!" 'Umar then reported; how he at once put on his outer garment and went to Ḥafṣa and said to her, "O my daughter! Do you argue with Allāh's Messenger so that he remains angry the whole day?" Ḥafṣa said, "By Allāh, we argue with him." 'Umar said, "Know that I warn you of Allāh's punishment and the anger of Allāh's Messenger ﷺ . . . O my daughter! Don't be betrayed by the one who is proud of her beauty because of the love of Allāh's Messenger ﷺ for her (i.e. 'Āisha)." 'Umar added, "Then I went out to Um Salama's house who was one of my relatives, and I talked to her. She said, O son of Al-Khaṭṭāb! It is rather astonishing that you interfere in everything; you even want to interfere between Allāh's Messenger and his wives!' By Allāh, by her talk she influenced me so much that I lost some of my anger. I left her (and went home). At that time I had a friend from the Anṣār who used to bring news (from the Prophet ﷺ) in case of my absence, and I used to bring him the news if he was absent. In those days we were afraid of one of the kings of Ghassān tribe. We heard that he intended to move and attack us,

عُمَرُ: وَاللهِ إنْ كُنّا في الجاهليةِ ما نَعُدُّ للنساءِ أمْرًا حتى أنزلَ اللهُ فيهنّ ما أنزلَ، وقسَمَ لهنّ ما قسَمَ، قالَ: فبينا أنا في أمرٍ أتأمّرُهُ إذْ قالتِ امرأتي لو صنعتَ كذا وكذا، قالَ: فقلتُ لها مالكِ ولِما هاهُنا؟ فيما تكلُّفكِ في أمرٍ أُريدُهُ؟ فقالتْ: عجبًا لكَ يا ابنَ الخطّابِ، ما تُريدُ أنْ تُراجَعَ أنتَ، وإنّ ابنتَكَ لتُراجِعُ رسولَ اللهِ صلى اللهُ عليهِ وسلّم حتى يظَلَّ يومَهُ غضبانَ. فقامَ عُمرُ فأخذَ رِداءَهُ مكانَهُ حتى دخلَ على حفصةَ فقالَ لها يا بُنيّةُ، إنّكِ لتُراجعينَ رسولَ اللهِ صلى اللهُ عليهِ وسلّم حتى يظلّ يومَهُ غضبانَ؟ فقالتْ حفصةُ: واللهِ إنّا لنُراجعُهُ. فقلتُ: تعلمينَ أنّي أُحذّرُكِ عقوبةَ اللهِ وغضبَ رسولِهِ صلى اللهُ عليهِ وسلّم، يا بُنيّةُ لا يغُرّنّكِ هذهِ التي أعجبَها حُسنُها حُبُّ رسولِ اللهِ صلى اللهُ عليهِ وسلّم إيّاها، يُريدُ عائشةَ. قالَ: ثُمّ خرجتُ حتى دخلتُ على أُمِّ سلمةَ لقرابتي منها فكلّمتُها، فقالتْ أُمُّ سلمةَ: عجبًا لكَ يا ابنَ الخطّابِ، دخلتَ في كُلِّ شيءٍ حتى

so fear filled our hearts because of that. (One day) my Anṣārī friend unexpectedly knocked at my door, and said, "Open Open!' I said, 'Has the king of Ghassān come?' He said, 'No, but something worse; Allāh's Messenger has isolated himself from his wives.' I said, 'Let the nose of 'Āisha and Ḥafṣa be stuck to dust (i.e. humiliated)!' Then I put on my clothes and went to Allāh's Messenger's residence, and behold, he was staying in an upper room of his to which he ascended by a ladder, and a black slave of Allāh's Messenger ﷺ was (sitting) at the first ladder-step. I said to him, 'Say (to the Prophet ﷺ) 'Umar bin Al-Khaṭṭāb is here.' Then the Prophet ﷺ admitted me and I narrated the story to Allāh's Messenger ﷺ. When I reached the story of Um Salama, Allāh's Messenger ﷺ smiled while he was lying on a mat made of palm tree leaves with nothing between him and the mat. Underneath his head there was a leather pillow stuffed with palm fibres, and leaves of a saut tree were piled at his feet, and above his head hung a few waterskins. On seeing the marks of the mat imprinted on his side, I wept. He said.' 'Why are you weeping?' I replied, "O Allāh's Messenger! Caesar and Khosrau are leading the life (i.e. luxurious life) while you, Allāh's Messenger ﷺ though you are (is living in destitute)". The Prophet ﷺ then replied. 'Won't you be satisfied that they enjoy this world and we the Hereafter?' "

تَبْتَغِي أَنْ تَدْخُلَ بَيْنَ رَسُولِ اللهِ صلى اللهُ عليه وسلّم وأَزْوَاجِهِ ! فأَخَذَتْنِي وَاللهِ أَخْذًا كَسَرَتْنِي عَنْ بَعْضِ مَا كُنْتُ أَجِدُ . فَخَرَجْتُ مِنْ عِنْدِهَا وكَانَ لي صَاحِبٌ مِنَ الأَنْصَارِ إِذَا غِبْتُ أَتَانِي بالخَبَرِ . وإذَا غَابَ كُنْتُ أنا آتِيهِ بالخَبَرِ ، ونَحْنُ نَتَخَوَّفُ مَلِكًا مِنْ مُلُوكِ غَسَّانَ ذُكِرَ لنَا أَنَّهُ يُرِيدُ أَنْ يَسِيرَ إِلَيْنَا فَقَدِ امْتَلأَتْ صُدُورُنَا مِنْهُ ، فإِذَا صَاحِبِي الأَنْصَارِيُّ يَدُقُّ البَابَ ، فقَالَ : افْتَحْ . افْتَحْ . فَقُلْتُ : جَاءَ الغَسَّانِيُّ ؟ فَقَالَ : بَلْ أَشَدُّ مِنْ ذَلِكَ ، اعْتَزَلَ رَسُولُ اللهِ صلى اللهُ عليه وسلّم أَزْوَاجَهُ فَقُلْتُ : رَغِمَ أَنْفُ حَفْصَةَ وعَائِشَةَ . فأَخَذْتُ ثَوْبِي فأَخْرُجُ حَتَّى جِئْتُ ، فإِذَا رَسُولُ اللهِ صلى اللهُ عليه وسلّم في مَشْرُبَةٍ لَهُ يَرْقَى عَلَيْهَا بِعَجَلَةٍ ، وغُلامٌ لِرَسُولِ اللهِ صلى اللهُ عليه وسلّم أَسْوَدُ عَلَى رَأْسِ الدَّرَجَةِ . فَقُلْتُ لَهُ : قُلْ هَذَا عُمَرُ بنُ الخَطَّابِ ، فأَذِنَ لي. قَالَ عُمَرُ : فَقَصَصْتُ عَلَى رَسُولِ اللهِ صلى اللهُ عليه وسلّم هَذَا الحَدِيثَ ، فلَمَّا بَلَغْتُ حَدِيثَ أُمِّ سَلَمَةَ تَبَسَّمَ رَسُولُ اللهِ صلى اللهُ عليه وسلّم وإِنَّهُ لَعَلَى حَصِيرٍ

ما بينه وبينه شيء، وتحت رأسه وسادة من أدم حشوها ليف، وأن عند رجليه قرظا مضبورا، وعند رأسه أهب معلقة. فرأيت أثر الحصير فى جنبه فبكيت، فقال: ما يبكيك؟ فقلت: يا رسول الله، إن كسرى وقيصر فيما هما فيه، وأنت رسول الله، فقال: أما ترضى أن تكون لهم الدنيا ولنا الآخرة؟.

(313) CHAPTER. And (remember) 'When the Prophet disclosed a matter in confidence to one of his wives......' (66:3)

باب ـ وإذ أسر النبي إلى بعض أزواجه حديثا ـ إلى ـ الخبير ـ فيه عائشة عن النبي صلى الله عليه وسلم.

436. Narrated Ibn 'Abbās : I intended to ask 'Umar so I said, "Who were those two ladies who tried to back each other against the Prophet ?" I hardly finished my speech when he said, They were 'Āisha and Ḥafṣa."

٤٣٦ ـ حدثنا علي: حدثنا سفيان: حدثنا يحيى بن سعيد قال: سمعت عبيد بن حنين قال: سمعت ابن عباس رضي الله عنهما يقول: أردت أن أسأل عمر رضي الله عنه فقلت: يا أمير المؤمنين، من المرأتان اللتان تظاهرتا على رسول الله صلى الله عليه

وسلَّم؟ فمَا أتممْتُ كَلامي حتَّى قالَ عائشةُ وحفصةُ.

(318) CHAPTER. If you two (wives of the Prophet ﷺ namely 'Āisha and Ḥafṣa) turn in repentence to Allāh, your hearts are indeed so inclined (to oppose what the Prophet ﷺ likes) but if you help one another against him (the Prophet ﷺ) then, truly, Allāh is his Protector, and Gabriel and righteous among the believers and furthermore, the Angels are his aiders. (66:4)

بابُ - إنْ تتُوبا إلى اللهِ فقدْ صغَتْ قلُوبُكما - صَغَوْتُ وأصغَيْتُ: مِلْتُ. لِتَصْغَى: لِتَميلَ. - وإنْ تظاهرَا عليْهِ فإنَّ اللهَ هوَ مولاهُ وجبْريلُ وصالِحُ المؤْمنينَ والملائكةُ بعْدَ ذلكَ ظهيرٌ - عوْنٌ. تظاهرُونَ: تعاوَنُونَ. وقالَ مُجاهِدٌ - قُوا أنفُسكم - أوْصُوا أهْليكمْ بتقْوَى اللهِ وأدِّبُوهُمْ.

437. Narrated Ibn 'Abbās ﷺ: I intended to ask 'Umar about those two ladies who back each other against 'Allāh's Messenger ﷺ. For one year I was seeking the opportunity to ask this question, but in vain, until once when I accompanied him for Ḥajj. While we were in Ẓahrān, 'Umar went to answer the call of nature and told me to follow him with some water for ablution. So I followed him with a container of water and started pouring water for him. I found it a good opportunity to ask him, so I said, "O chief of the Believers! Who were those two ladies who had backed each other (against the Prophet ﷺ)?" Before I could complete my question, he replied, "They were 'Āisha and Ḥafṣa."

٤٣٧ - حدَّثنا الحُمَيْديُّ: حدَّثنا سُفْيانُ: حدَّثنا يحْيَى بنُ سعيدٍ قالَ: سمِعْتُ عُبَيْدَ بنَ حُنَيْنٍ يقُولُ: سمِعْتُ ابنَ عبَّاسٍ يقُولُ: أرَدْتُ أنْ أسألَ عُمرَ عنِ المرْأتَيْنِ اللَّتَيْنِ تظاهرَتا علَى رسُولِ اللهِ صلى اللهُ عليهِ وسلَّم، فمكثْتُ سنَةً فلَمْ أجِدْ لهُ موْضِعًا حتَّى خرَجْتُ معَهُ حاجًا. فلمَّا كُنَّا بظَهْرانَ ذهَبَ عُمرُ لحاجتِهِ فقالَ: أدْرِكْنِي بالوَضُوءِ. فأدْرَكْتُهُ بالإدَاوةِ، فجعَلْتُ أسْكُبُ علَيْهِ، ورأيْتُ موْضِعًا فقُلْتُ: يا أميرَ المؤْمنينَ، منِ المرْأتانِ اللَّتانِ تظاهرَتا؟ قالَ ابنُ عبَّاسٍ: فمَا أتممْتُ كَلامي حتَّى قالَ: عائشةُ وحفْصةُ.

(319) CHAPTER. It may be, if he divorced you all, that his Lord (Allāh) will give him instead of you, wives better than you. ....:(66:5)

بابُ - عَسَى رَبُّهُ إِنْ طَلَّقَكُنَّ أن يُبْدِلَهُ أَزْوَاجًا خَيْرًا مِنْكُنَّ - الآيَة .

438. Narrated 'Umar رضي الله عنه : The wives of the Prophet ﷺ, out of their jealousy, backed each other against the Prophet ﷺ, so I said to them, "It may be, if he divorced you all, that Allāh will give him, instead of you wives better than you." So this Verse was revealed. (66:5)

٤٣٨ - حدَّثنا عَمْرُو بنُ عَوْنٍ : حدَّثنا هُشَيمٌ، عَنْ حُمَيْدٍ، عَنْ أنسٍ قالَ: قالَ عُمَرُ رَضِيَ اللهُ عَنْهُ : اجْتَمَعَ نِساءُ النَّبِيِّ صلى اللهُ عليهِ وسلَّم في الغَيْرَةِ عَلَيْهِ فَقُلْتُ لَهُنَّ - عَسَى رَبُّهُ إِنْ طَلَّقَكُنَّ أَنْ يُبْدِلَهُ أَزْوَاجًا خَيْرًا مِنْكُنَّ - فَنَزَلَتْ هَذِهِ الآيَةُ.

SŪRAT AL-MULK (The Dominion)
No. LXVII

In the Name of Allāh,
the Most Beneficent, the Most Merciful

(Blessed be He in Whose Hand is the dominions.)

(No Ḥadīths were mentioned here).

سورة تبارك الذى بيده الملك

التَّفَاوُتُ : الاخْتِلافُ. والتَّفاوُتُ والتَّفَوُّتُ واحِدٌ. تَمَيَّزُ : تَقَطَّعُ. مَنَاكِبِها: جَوَانِبِها. تَدَّعُونَ وَتَدْعُونَ واحِدٌ، مِثْلُ تَذَكَّرُونَ وَتَذْكُرُونَ. وَيَقْبِضْنَ : يَضْرِبْنَ بأَجْنِحَتِهِنَّ ، وَقالَ مُجاهِدٌ: صَافَّاتٍ : بَسْطُ أَجْنِحَتِهِنَّ. وَنُفُورٌ : الكُفُورُ .

SŪRAT NŪN (The Pen) LXVIII

**In the Name of Allāh,
the Most Beneficent, the Most Merciful**

سورة نٓ

بِسْمِ اللهِ الرَّحْمَنِ الرَّحِيمِ

وَقَالَ ابْنُ عَبَّاسٍ: يَتَخَافَتُونَ: يَنْتَجُونَ السِّرَارَ وَالكَلامَ الخَفِيَّ. وَقَالَ قَتَادَةُ: حَرْدٍ: جِدٍّ فِي أَنْفُسِهِمْ. وَقَالَ ابْنُ عَبَّاسٍ: لَضَالُّونَ: أَضْلَلْنَا مَكَانَ جَنَّتِنَا. وَقَالَ غَيْرُهُ: كَالصَّرِيمِ: كَالصُّبْحِ انْصَرَمَ مِنَ اللَّيْلِ، وَاللَّيْلِ انْصَرَمَ مِنَ النَّهَارِ. وَهُوَ أَيْضًا كُلُّ رَمْلَةٍ انْصَرَمَتْ مِنْ مُعْظَمِ الرَّمْلِ. وَالصَّرِيمُ أَيْضًا المَصْرُومُ مِثْلُ قَتِيلٍ وَمَقْتُولٍ.

(320) CHAPTER. 'Cruel after all that, base-born (of illegitimate birth). (68:13)

بابٌ - عُتُلٍّ بَعْدَ ذَلِكَ زَنِيمٍ -.

439. Narrated Ibn 'Abbās: (regarding the Verse):—

'Cruel after all that, base-born (of illegitimate birth).' (68:13)

It was revealed in connection with a man from Quraish who had a notable sign (Zanamah) similar to the notable sign which usually hung on the neck of a sheep (to recognise it).

٤٣٩ - حَدَّثَنَا مَحْمُودٌ: حَدَّثَنَا عُبَيْدُ اللهِ بْنُ مُوسَى، عَنْ إِسْرَائِيلَ، عَنْ أَبِي حَصِينٍ، عَنْ مُجَاهِدٍ، عَنِ ابْنِ عَبَّاسٍ رَضِيَ اللهُ عَنْهُمَا - عُتُلٍّ بَعْدَ ذَلِكَ زَنِيمٍ - قَالَ: رَجُلٌ مِنْ قُرَيْشٍ لَهُ زَنَمَةٌ مِثْلُ زَنَمَةِ الشَّاةِ.

440. Narrated Hāritha bin Wahb Al-Khuzā'ī: I heard the Prophet

٤٤٠ - حَدَّثَنَا أَبُو نُعَيْمٍ: حَدَّثَنَا سُفْيَانُ، عَنْ مَعْبَدِ بْنِ خَالِدٍ قَالَ:

saying. "May I tell you of the people of Paradise? Every weak and poor obscure person whom the people look down upon but his oath is fulfilled by Allāh when he takes an oath to do something. And may I inform you of the people of the Hell-Fire? They are all those violent, arrogant and stubborn people."

سَمِعْتُ حارِثَةَ بنَ وَهْبٍ الخُزَاعِيَّ قالَ: سَمِعْتُ النَّبِيَّ صلى اللهُ عليهِ وسلَّمَ يقُولُ: ألا أُخْبِرُكُمْ بأهْلِ الجَنَّةِ؟ كُلُّ ضَعِيفٍ مُتَضَعَّفٍ لَوْ أقْسَمَ علىَ اللهِ لأَبَرَّهُ، ألا أُخْبِرُكُمْ بأهْلِ النَّارِ؟ كُلُّ عُتُلٍّ جَوَّاظٍ مُسْتَكْبِرٍ.

(321) CHAPTER. (Remember) 'The Day when the severest Hour will befall. (68:42)

بابُ ـ يَوْمَ يُكْشَفُ عَنْ ساقٍ ـ.

441. Narrated Abū Sa'īd (رضي الله عنه): I heard the Prophet (صلى الله عليه وسلم) saying, "Allāh will bring forth the severest Hour, and then all the Believers, men and women, will prostrate themselves before Him, but there will remain those who used to prostrate in the world for showing off and for gaining good reputation. Such people will try to prostrate (on the Day of Judgement) but their backs will be as stiff as if it is one bone (a single vertebra)."

٤٤١ ـ حدَّثَنا آدَمُ: حدَّثَنا اللَّيْثُ، عَنْ خالِدِ بنِ يَزِيدَ، عَنْ سَعِيدِ بنِ أبي هِلالٍ، عَنْ زَيْدِ ابنِ أسْلَمَ، عَنْ عَطاءِ ابنِ يَسارٍ، عَنْ أبي سَعِيدٍ رَضِيَ اللهُ عَنْهُ قالَ: سَمِعْتُ النَّبِيَّ صلى اللهُ عليهِ وسلَّمَ يقُولُ: يَكْشِفُ رَبُّنا عَنْ ساقِهِ، فيَسْجُدُ لهُ كُلُّ مُؤْمِنٍ وَمُؤْمِنَةٍ، وَيَبْقَى مَنْ كانَ يَسْجُدُ في الدُّنْيا رِياءً وسُمْعَةً فيَذْهَبُ لِيَسْجُدَ فيَعُودُ ظَهْرُهُ طَبَقاً واحِداً.

SŪRAT AL-ḤĀQQA (The Sure Reality) LXIX

سورة الحاقة

In the Name of Allāh, the Most Beneficent, the Most Merciful

بِسْمِ اللهِ الرَّحْمٰنِ الرَّحِيمِ

No Ḥadīths were mentioned here

عِيشَةٍ رَاضِيَةٍ: يُرِيدُ فيها الرِّضا. القاضِيَةَ: المَوْتَةَ الأُولى التي مُتُّها، لمْ أُحْيَ بَعْدَها، مِنْ أحَدٍ عَنْهُ حاجِزِينَ:

أَحَدٌ يَكُونُ لِلْجَمِيعِ وَلِلْوَاحِدِ . وَقَالَ ابنُ عَبَّاسٍ : الوَتِينَ : نِيَاطُ القَلْبِ . قَالَ ابنُ عَبَّاسٍ : طَغَى : كَثُرَ وَيُقَالُ بِالطَّاغِيَةِ بِطُغْيَانِهِمْ . وَيُقَالُ طَغَتْ عَلَى الخُزَّانِ كَمَا طَغَى المَاءُ عَلَى قَوْمِ نُوحٍ .

سورة سأل سائل

SŪRAT SĀ'ALA SĀ'ILUN (A Question asked) LXX

In the Name of Allāh, the Most Beneficent, the Most Merciful

بِسْمِ اللهِ الرَّحْمَنِ الرَّحِيمِ

الفَصِيلَةُ : أَصْغَرُ آبَائِهِ القُرْبَى : إِلَيْهِ يَنْتَمِي مَنِ انْتَمَى : لِلشَّوَى : اليَدَانِ وَالرِّجْلَانِ وَالأَطْرَافُ ، وَجِلْدَةُ الرَّأْسِ يُقَالُ لَهَا شَوَاةٌ . وَمَا كَانَ غَيْرَ مَقْتَلٍ فَهُوَ شَوًى . عِزِينَ ، وَالعِزُونَ : الحِلَقُ وَالجَمَاعَاتُ ، وَوَاحِدُهَا عِزَةٌ .

(No Ḥadīths were mentioned here).

سورة نوح

SŪRAT NOAH LXXI

In the Name of Allāh, the Most Beneficent, the Most Merciful

بِسْمِ اللهِ الرَّحْمَنِ الرَّحِيمِ

أَطْوَارًا : طَوْرًا كَذَا وَطَوْرًا كَذَا ، يُقَالُ عَدَا طَوْرَهُ ، أَيْ قَدْرَهُ . وَالكُبَّارُ : أَشَدُّ مِنَ الكِبَارِ ، وَكَذَلِكَ جُمَّالٌ وَجَمِيلٌ لِأَنَّهَا أَشَدُّ مُبَالَغَةً . وَكَذَلِكَ كُبَّارٌ الكَبِيرُ . وَكُبَارًا أَيْضًا بِالتَّخْفِيفِ

والعَرَبُ تَقُولُ رَجُلٌ حُسَّانٌ وجُمَّالٌ وحُسَانٌ مُخَفَّفٌ. وجُمَالٌ مُخَفَّفٌ. دَيَّاراً مِنْ دَوْرٍ ولَكِنَّهُ فَيْعالٌ مِنَ الدَّوَرانِ كما قرأ عُمَرُ - الحَيُّ القَيَّامُ - وهِيَ مِنْ قُمْتُ. وقالَ غَيْرُهُ: دَيَّاراً: أحَداً. تَبَاراً: هَلاكاً. وقالَ ابنُ عَبَّاسٍ: مِدْرَاراً: يَتْبَعُ بَعْضُها بَعْضاً. وقاراً: عَظَمَةً.

(322) CHAPTER. Forsake not Wadd nor Suwā' nor Yaghūth.' (71:23)

باب - وَدّاً ولا سُواعاً ولا يَغُوثَ ويَعُوقَ -.

442. Narrated Ibn 'Abbās (may Allah be pleased with him): All the idols which were worshipped by the people of Noah were worshipped by the Arabs later on. As for the idol Wadd, it was worshipped by the tribe of Kalb at Daumat-al-Jandal; Suwā' was the idol of the Bani-Ḥudhail, and Yaghūth was the idol of (the tribe of) Murād and then by Banī Ghuṭaif at Al-Jurf near Sabā; Ya'ūq was the idol of Hamdān, and Nasr was the idol of Ḥimyr, the branch of Dhi-al-Kalā.' The names (of the idols) formerly belonged to some pious men of the people of Noah, and when they died, Satān inspired their people to (prepare) and place idols at the places where they used to sit, and to call those idols by their names. The people did so, but the idols were not worshipped till those people (who initiated them) had died

٤٤٢ - حَدَّثَنا إبْرَاهِيمُ بنُ مُوسَى: أخبرَنا هِشامٌ، عَنِ ابنِ جُرَيْجٍ. وقالَ عَطاءٌ، عَنِ ابنِ عَبَّاسٍ رَضِيَ اللهُ عَنْهُما صارَتِ الأوْثانُ الَّتي كانَتْ في قَوْمِ نُوحٍ في العَرَبِ بَعْدُ. أمَّا وَدٌّ كانَتْ لِكَلْبٍ بِدَوْمَةِ الجَنْدَلِ، وأمَّا سُواعٌ كانَتْ لِهُذَيْلٍ، وأمَّا يَغُوثُ فَكانَتْ لِمُرادٍ ثُمَّ لِبَني غُطَيْفٍ، بالجُرُفِ عِنْدَ سَبَإٍ. وأمَّا يَعُوقُ فَكانَتْ لِهَمْدانَ. وأمَّا نَسْرٌ فَكانَتْ لِحِمْيَرَ، لآلِ ذي الكَلاعِ. أسْماءُ رِجالٍ صالِحِينَ مِنْ قَوْمِ نُوحٍ. فَلَمَّا هَلَكُوا أوْحَى الشَّيْطانُ إلى قَوْمِهِمْ أنْ

and the origin of the idols had become obscure, whereupon people began worshipping them.

انصبوا إلى مجالسهم التي كانوا يجلسون أنصابا وسموها بأسمائهم. ففعلوا فلم تُعبد حتى إذا هلك أولئك وتنسخ العلم عُبدت.

SŪRAT QUL–UḤIYĀ ILAIYA (or SŪRAT–AL JINN) LXXII

سورة قل أوحي إلى

قال ابن عباس: لبدا: أعوانا.

443. Narrated Ibn 'Abbās ﷺ: Allāh's Messenger ﷺ went out along with a group of his companions towards 'Ukāẓ Market. At that time something intervened between the devils and the news of the Heaven, and flames were sent down upon them, so the devils returned. Their fellow-devils said, "What is wrong with you? " They said, "Something has intervened between us and the news of the Heaven, and fires (flames) have been shot at us." Their fellow-devils said, "Nothing has intervened between you and the news of the Heaven, but an important event has happened. Therefore, travel all over the world, east and west, and try to find out what has happened." And so they set out and travelled all over the world, east and west, looking for that thing which intervened between them and the news of the Heaven. Those of the devils who had set out towards

٤٤٣ - حدثنا موسى بن إسماعيل: حدثنا أبو عوانة، عن أبي بشر، عن سعيد بن جبير، عن ابن عباس قال: انطلق رسول الله صلى الله عليه وسلم في طائفة من أصحابه عامدين إلى سوق عكاظ، وقد حيل بين الشياطين وبين خبر السماء، وأرسلت عليهم الشهب فرجعت الشياطين. فقالوا: ما لكم؟ فقالوا: حيل بيننا وبين خبر السماء، وأرسلت علينا الشهب قال: ما حال بينكم وبين خبر السماء إلا ما حدث، فاضربوا مشارق الأرض ومغاربها فانظروا ما هذا الأمر الذي حدث. فانطلقوا فضربوا مشارق الأرض ومغاربها ينظرون ما هذا

Tihāma, went to Allāh's Messenger ﷺ at Nakhla (a place bwteeen Mecca and Ṭā'if) while he was on his way to 'Ukāẓ Market. (They met him) while he was offering the Fajr prayer with his companions. When they heard the Holy Qur'ān being recited (by Allāh's Messenger ﷺ), they listened to it and said (to each other). This is the thing which has intervened between you and the news of the Heavens." Then they returned to their people and said, "O our people! We have really heard a wonderful recital (Qur'ān). It gives guidance **to the right way and we have believed therein. We shall not join in worship, any-thing with our Lord." (See 72 :1-2)**

Then Allāh عزوجل revealed to His Prophet (Sūrat al-Jinn):

'Say: It has been revealed to me that a group (3 to 9) of Jinns listened (to the Qur'ān). (72:1)

The statement of the Jinns was revealed to him.

الأمرُ الذي حالَ بينَهم وبينَ خبرِ السماءِ. قالَ: فانطلقَ الذينَ توجَّهوا نحوَ تِهامةَ إلى رسولِ اللهِ صلى اللهُ عليه وسلّم بنخلةَ وهوَ عامدٌ إلى سوقِ عُكاظٍ وهوَ يُصلّي بأصحابِه صلاةَ الفجرِ. فلمّا سمعوا القرآنَ تسمّعوا لهُ، فقالوا: هذا الذي حالَ بينَكم وبينَ خبرِ السماءِ. فهنالكَ رجعوا إلى قومِهم فقالوا: ـ يا قومَنا إنّا سمعنا قرآنا عجبا يهدي إلى الرُّشدِ فآمنّا به ولنْ نُشركَ بربِّنا أحدًا ـ وأنزلَ اللهُ عزَّ وجلَّ على نبيِّه صلى اللهُ عليه وسلّم قُلْ أُوحيَ إليَّ أنّهُ استمعَ نفرٌ منَ الجنِّ ـ وإنّما أُوحيَ إليه قولُ الجنِّ.

SŪRAT AL–MUZZAMMIL (Folded in Garments): LXXIII

No Hadith were mentioned here)

سورة المزمل والمدثر

وقالَ مُجاهدٌ: وتبتَّلْ: أخلِصْ. وقالَ الحسنُ: أنكالاً: قيودًا. منفطرٌ

بِهِ : مُثْقَلَةٌ بِهِ . وَقَالَ ابْنُ عَبَّاسٍ : كَثِيبًا مَهِيلاً : الرَّمْلُ السَّائِلُ . وَبِيلاً : شَدِيدًا .

SŪRAT AL–MUDDAT͟HT͟HIR (The One Wrapped-up) LXXIV

سورة المدثر

In the Name of Allāh, the Most Beneficent, the Most Merciful

بِسْمِ اللهِ الرَّحْمَنِ الرَّحِيمِ

قَالَ ابْنُ عَبَّاسٍ : عَسِيرٌ : شَدِيدٌ . قَسْوَرَةٌ : رِكْزُ النَّاسِ وأَصْوَاتُهُمْ . وكُلُّ شَدِيدٍ قَسْوَرَةٌ ، وَقَالَ أَبُو هُرَيْرَةَ : القَسْوَرَةُ ، قَسْوَرٌ : الأَسَدُ . الرِّكْزُ : الصَّوْتُ . مُسْتَنْفِرَةٌ : نَافِرَةٌ مَذْعُورَةٌ .

444. Narrated Yaḥyā bin Abī Kat͟hīr: I asked Abā Salama bin 'Abdur-Raḥmān about the first Sūra revealed of the Qur'ān. He replied. " 'O you, wrapped-up (i.e. Al-Muddat͟ht͟hir)." I said, "They say it was, 'Read, in the Name of your Lord Who created,' (i.e. Sūrat Al-'Alaq (the Clot)." On that, Abū Salama said, "I asked Jābir bin 'Abdullāh about that, saying the same as you have said, whereupon he said, 'I will not tell you, except what Allāh's Messenger ﷺ had told us. Allāh's Messenger ﷺ said, "I was in seclusion in the cave of Ḥirā', and after I completed the limited period of my seclusion. I came down (from the cave) and heard a voice calling me. I looked to my right, but

٤٤٤ ـ حدَّثني يَحْيَى : حدَّثنا وَكيعٌ : عَنْ عَلِيِّ بنِ المُبَارَكِ ، عَنْ يَحْيَى بنِ أَبي كَثِيرٍ : سَأَلْتُ أَبا سَلَمَةَ ابنَ عَبْدِ الرَّحْمَنِ عَنْ أَوَّلِ مَا نَزَلَ مِنَ القُرآنِ قالَ ـ يا أيُّها المُدَّثِّرُ ـ قُلْتُ : يَقُولُونَ ـ اقْرأْ باسْمِ رَبِّكَ الَّذي خَلَقَ ـ فَقَالَ أَبُو سَلَمَةَ : سَأَلْتُ جابِرَ بنَ عَبْدِ اللهِ رَضِيَ اللهُ عَنْهُما عَنْ ذَلكَ وَقُلْتُ لَهُ مِثْلَ الَّذي قُلْتَ ، فَقالَ جابِرٌ : لا أُحَدِّثُكَ إلاَّ ما حدَّثنا رَسُولُ اللهِ صلى اللهُ عليهِ وسلَّم ، قالَ : جاوَرْتُ بِحِراءَ فَلَمَّا قَضَيْتُ جِوَاري هَبَطْتُ

saw nothing. Then I looked up and saw something. So I went to Khadīja (the Prophet's wife) and told her to wrap me up and pour cold water on me. So they wrapped me up and poured cold water on me." Then,

'O you,(Muhammad ﷺ) wrapped-up! Arise and warn,' (Sūrat Al-Muddaththir) was revealed.' "

(74:1)

فَنُودِيتُ فَنَظَرْتُ عَنْ يَمِينِي فَلَمْ أَرَ شَيْئًا ، وَنَظَرْتُ عَنْ شِمَالِي فَلَمْ أَرَ شَيْئًا ، وَنَظَرْتُ أَمَامِي فَلَمْ أَرَ شَيْئًا ، وَنَظَرْتُ خَلْفِي فَلَمْ أَرَ شَيْئًا . فَرَفَعْتُ رَأْسِي فَرَأَيْتُ شَيْئًا ، فَأَتَيْتُ خَدِيجَةَ فَقُلْتُ : دَثِّرُونِي وَصُبُّوا عَلَيَّ مَاءً بَارِدًا . قَالَ : فَدَثَّرُونِي وَصَبُّوا عَلَيَّ مَاءً بَارِدًا ، قَالَ : فَنَزَلَتْ ـ يَا أَيُّهَا الْمُدَّثِّرُ قُمْ فَأَنْذِرْ ـ .

445. Narrated Jābir bin 'Abdullāh (رضي الله عنهما): The Prophet ﷺ said, "I was in a seclusion in the cave of Hirā............."(similar to the narration related by 'Alī bin Al-Mubārak, 444 above).

٤٤٥ ـ حَدَّثَنِي مُحَمَّدُ بْنُ بَشَّارٍ : حَدَّثَنَا عَبْدُ الرَّحْمَنِ بْنُ مَهْدِيٍّ وَغَيْرُهُ قَالَا : حَدَّثَنَا حَرْبُ ابْنُ شَدَّادٍ ، عَنْ يَحْيَى بْنِ أَبِي كَثِيرٍ ، عَنْ أَبِي سَلَمَةَ ، عَنْ جَابِرِ بْنِ عَبْدِ اللَّهِ رَضِيَ اللَّهُ عَنْهُمَا ، عَنِ النَّبِيِّ صلى الله عليه وسلم قَالَ : جَاوَرْتُ بِحِرَاءَ ، مِثْلَ حَدِيثِ عُثْمَانَ بْنِ عُمَرَ عَنْ عَلِيِّ بْنِ الْمُبَارَكِ .

(323) CHAPTER. The Statement of Allāh (تعالى): "And your Lord magnify."

(74:3)

بَابُ قَوْلِهِ وَرَبَّكَ فَكَبِّرْ ـ .

446. Narrated Yahyā: I asked'

٤٤٦ ـ حَدَّثَنَا إِسْحَاقُ بْنُ مَنْصُورٍ :

Abā Salama, "Which Sūra of the Qur'ān was revealed first?" He replied, " 'O you, wrapped-up' (Al-Muddaththir)." I said, "I have been informed that it was, 'Read, in the Name of your Lord who created........ (i.e. Sūrat Al-'Alaq).' " Abū Salama said, " 'I asked Jābir, 'Which Sūrat of the Qur'ān was revealed first?" He said, "O you, wrapped-up' " "I said, "I have been told that it was 'Read, in the Name of your Lord who created." He said, "I will not tell you but what Allāh's Messenger ﷺ said. Allāh's Messenger ﷺ said, "I was in seclusion in the cave of Ḥirā' and when I completed the limited period of my seclusions, I came down till I reached the valley. I heard a voice calling me, so I looked in front of me, behind me, to my right, and to my left, and behold! I saw (an angel) sitting on a throne between the sky and the earth. So I went to Khadīja and told her to wrap me up and pour cold water on me. Then,

> 'O you, wrapped-up' arise and warn and your Lord magnify. . . ..'
> (74:1-2-3)

(i.e. Sūrat Al-Muddaththir) was revealed to me.' "

حدثنا عبد الصمد : حدثنا حرب : حدثنا يحيى قال : سألت أبا سلمة : أي القرآن أنزل أول ؟ فقال - يا أيها المدثر - فقلت ، أنبئت أنه - اقرأ باسم ربك الذي خلق - فقال أبو سلمة : سألت جابر بن عبد الله : أي القرآن أنزل أول ؟ فقال : يا أيها المدثر - فقلت : نبئت أنه - اقرأ باسم ربك الذي خلق - فقال : لا أخبرك إلا بما قال رسول الله صلى الله عليه وسلم ، قال رسول الله صلى الله عليه وسلم : جاورت في حراء فلما قضيت جواري هبطت فاستبطنت الوادي ، فنوديت فنظرت أمامي وخلفي وعن يميني وعن شمالي فإذا هو جالس على عرش بين السماء والأرض . فأتيت خديجة فقلت : دثروني وصبوا علي ماء باردا . وأنزل علي - يا أيها المدثر قم فأنذر وربك فكبر - .

(324) CHAPTER. 'And your garments purify. (74:4)

باب - وثيابك فطهر - .

447. Narrated Jābir bin 'Abdullāh : I heard the Prophet describing the period of pause of the Divine Inspiration. He said in his talk, "While I was walking, I heard voices from the sky. I looked up, and behold! I saw the same Angel who came to me in the cave of Ḥirā',sitting on a chair between the sky and the earth. I was too much afraid of him (so I returned to my house) and said, 'Wrap me up in garments!' They wrapped me up. Then Allāh revealed:—

'O you wrapped. . . . . .and desert the idols

before the prayer became compulsory. 'Rujz means idols.

٤٤٧ - حدثنا يحيى بن بكير: حدثنا الليث، عن عقيل، عن ابن شهاب. وحدثني عبد الله ابن محمد: حدثنا عبد الرزاق: أخبرنا معمر، عن الزهري فأخبرني أبو سلمة بن عبد الرحمن، عن جابر بن عبد الله رضي الله عنهما قال: سمعت النبي صلى الله عليه وسلم وهو يحدث عن فترة الوحي فقال في حديثه: فبينا أنا أمشي إذ سمعت صوتا من السماء فرفعت رأسي فإذا الملك الذي جاءني بحراء جالس على كرسي بين السماء والأرض فجئثت منه رعبا فقلت: زملوني زملوني، فدثروني، فأنزل الله تعالى - يا أيها المدثر - إلى - والرجز فاهجر - قبل أن تفرض الصلاة وهي الأوثان

(325) CHAPTER. 'And desert the idols.' . . . . (74:5)
It is said that 'Rujz' and 'Rijs' means punishment (i.e. the worshipping of idols that leads to punishment).

باب - والرجز فاهجر - يقال الرجز والرجس: العذاب.

448. Narrated Jābir bin 'Abdullāh

٤٤٨ - حدثنا عبد الله بن يوسف:

that he heard Allāh's Messenger ﷺ describing the period of pause of the Divine Inspiration, and in his description he said, "While I was walking I heard a voice from the sky. I looked up towards the sky, and behold! I saw the same Angel who came to me in the Cave of Ḥirā', sitting on a chair between the sky and the earth. I was so terrified by him that I fell down on the ground. Then I went to my wife and said, 'Wrap me in garments! Wrap me in garments!' They wrapped me, and then Allāh revealed:–

> 'O you, (Muḥammad ﷺ) wrapped-up! Arise and warn.......
> .... and desert the idols.' " (74:1-5)

Abū Salama said. ...Rujz' means idols." After that, the Divine Inspiration started coming more frequently and regularly.

حدثنا الليث، عن عقيل قال ابن شهاب: سمعت أبا سلمة قال: أخبرني جابر بن عبد الله أنه سمع رسول الله صلى الله عليه وسلم يحدث عن فترة الوحي: فبينا أنا أمشي إذ سمعت صوتا من السماء، فرفعت بصري قبل السماء فإذا الملك الذي جاءني بحراء قاعد على كرسي بين السماء والأرض، فجئثت منه حتى هويت إلى الأرض، فجئت أهلي فقلت: زملوني، زملوني، فزملوني، فأنزل الله تعالى - يا أيها المدثر قم فأنذر - إلى قوله - فاهجر - قال أبو سلمة: والرجز: الأوثان، ثم حمي الوحي وتتابع.

SŪRAT AL–QIYĀMA (The Resurrection): LXXV

In the Name of Allāh, the Most Beneficent, the Most Merciful

سورة القيامة

بسم الله الرحمن الرحيم

(326) CHAPTER. The Statement of Allāh تعالى :–

> 'Move not your tongue concerning (the Qur'ān) to make haste therewith.' (75:16)

وقوله - لا تحرك به لسانك لتعجل به - وقال ابن عباس - ليفجر أمامه - سوف أتوب: سوف أعمل. لا وزر: لا حصن. سدى: هملا.

449. Narrated Ibn 'Abbās ﵄: The Prophet ﷺ used to move his tongue when the Divine Inspiration was being revealed to him. (Sufyān, a sub-narrator, demonstrated (how the Prophet ﷺ used to move his lips) and added. "In order to memorize it." So Allāh revealed:

> 'Move not your tongue concerning (the Qur'ān) to make haste therewith." (75:16)

٤٤٩ - حَدَّثَنَا الحُمَيْدِيُّ: حَدَّثَنَا سُفْيَانُ: حَدَّثَنَا مُوسَى بْنُ أَبِي عَائِشَةَ، وَكَانَ ثِقَةً عَنْ سَعِيدِ ابْنِ جُبَيْرٍ، عَنِ ابْنِ عَبَّاسٍ رَضِيَ اللهُ عَنْهُمَا قَالَ: كَانَ النَّبِيُّ صلى الله عليه وسلم إِذَا نَزَلَ عَلَيْهِ الوَحْيُ حَرَّكَ بِهِ لِسَانَهُ. وَوَصَفَ سُفْيَانُ يُرِيدُ أَنْ يَحْفَظَهُ فَأَنْزَلَ اللهُ - لَا تُحَرِّكْ بِهِ لِسَانَكَ لِتَعْجَلَ بِهِ -.

(327) CHAPTER. 'It is for us to collect it (in your mind) (O Muḥammad), and to give you the ability to recite it (by heart).' (75:17)

باب - إِنَّ عَلَيْنَا جَمْعَهُ وَقُرْآنَهُ -.

450. Narrated Mūsā bin Abī 'Āisha that he asked Sa'īd bin Jubair regarding (the statement of Allāh). 'Move not your tongue concerning (the Qur'ān) to make haste therewith.' He said, "Ibn 'Abbās said that the Prophet ﷺ used to move his lips when the Divine Inspiration was being revealed to him. So the Prophet ﷺ was ordered not to move his tongue, which he used to do, lest some words should escape his memory. 'It is for Us to collect it' means, We will collect it in your chest;' and its recitation' means, We will make you recite it. 'But when We recite it (i.e. when it is revealed to you), follow its recital; it is for Us to explain it and make it clear,' (i.e. We will explain it through your tongue).

٤٥٠ - حَدَّثَنَا عُبَيْدُ اللهِ بْنُ مُوسَى، عَنْ إِسْرَائِيلَ، عَنْ مُوسَى بْنِ أَبِي عَائِشَةَ: أَنَّهُ سَأَلَ سَعِيدَ ابْنَ جُبَيْرٍ عَنْ قَوْلِهِ تَعَالَى - لَا تُحَرِّكْ بِهِ لِسَانَكَ - قَالَ: وَقَالَ ابْنُ عَبَّاسٍ: كَانَ يُحَرِّكُ شَفَتَيْهِ إِذَا أُنْزِلَ عَلَيْهِ، فَقِيلَ لَهُ - لَا تُحَرِّكْ بِهِ لِسَانَكَ - يَخْشَى أَنْ يَنْفَلِتَ مِنْهُ - إِنَّ عَلَيْنَا جَمْعَهُ - أَنْ نَجْمَعَهُ فِي صَدْرِكَ - وَقُرْآنَهُ - أَنْ تَقْرَأَهُ فَإِذَا قَرَأْنَاهُ - يَقُولُ أُنْزِلَ عَلَيْهِ - فَاتَّبِعْ قُرْآنَهُ ثُمَّ إِنَّ عَلَيْنَا بَيَانَهُ - أَنْ نُبَيِّنَهُ عَلَى لِسَانِكَ.

(328) CHAPTER. When We have revealed it to (O Muḥammad ﷺ through Gabriel) then follow you its recital.' (75-18)

And Ibn 'Abbās said: 'We recite it' means 'We explain it'. 'Follow its recital' means, 'Act on its order.'

باب - فإذا قرأناه فاتبع قرآنه -

قال ابن عباس: قرأناه: بيناه. فاتبع: اعمل به.

451. Narrated Ibn 'Abbās (as regards) Allāh's Statement,

> 'Move not your tongue concerning (the Qur'ān) to make haste there-with. (75:16)

When Gabriel descended with the Divine revelation to Allāh's Messenger ﷺ, he (Allāh's Messenger ﷺ) moved his tongue and lips, and that state used to be very hard for him, and that movement indicated that he was being inspired Divinely. So Allāh revealed in Sūrat Al-Qiyāma which begins:

> 'I do swear by the Day of Resurrection ....' (75)

the Verses:–

> 'Move not your tongue concerning (the Qur'ān) to make haste there-with. It is for Us to collect it (Qur'ān) in your mind, and give you the ability to recite it by heart. (75:16-17)

Ibn 'Abbās added: It is for Us to

٤٥١ - حدثنا قتيبة بن سعيد: حدثنا جرير، عن موسى بن أبي عائشة، عن سعيد بن جبير، عن ابن عباس في قوله - لا تحرك به لسانك لتعجل به - قال: كان رسول الله صلى الله عليه وسلم إذا نزل جبريل بالوحي وكان مما يحرك به لسانه وشفتيه فيشتد عليه وكان يعرف منه. فأنزل الله الآية التي في لا أقسم بيوم القيامة - لا تحرك به لسانك لتعجل به إن علينا جمعه وقرآنه - قال: علينا أن نجمعه في صدرك وقرآنه، فإذا قرأناه فاتبع قرآنه. فإذا أنزلناه فاستمع - ثم إن علينا بيانه - علينا أن نبينه بلسانك. قال: فكان إذا أتاه جبريل أطرق فإذا ذهب قرأه كما وعده الله - أولى لك فأولى - توعد.

collect it (Qur'ān) (in your mind), and give you the ability to recite it by heart means, "When We reveal it, listen.' 'Then it is for Us to explain it,' means, 'It is for us to explain it through your tongue.' So whenever Gabriel came to Allāh's Messenger ﷺ he would keep quiet (and listen), and when the Angel left, the Prophet ﷺ would recite that revelation as Allāh promised him.

SŪRAT HAL—ATA—'ALAL INSĀNI (i.e. SŪRAT AD-DAHR) LXXVI

In the Name of Allāh, the Most Beneficent, the Most Merciful
(No Ḥadīths were mentioned here)

سورة هل أتى على الإنسان

يقالُ معناهُ أتى على الإنسانِ، وهَلْ تكونُ جَحْدًا وتكونُ خَبَرًا. وهذا من الخبرِ، يقولُ: كان شيئًا فلم يكن مذكورًا، وذلك من حينِ خلقهُ من طينٍ إلى أن يُنفخَ فيهِ الروحُ. أمشاجٍ: الأخلاطُ، ماءُ المرأةِ وماءُ الرجلِ، الدمُ والعلقةُ. ويقالُ إذا خُلطَ مَشيجٌ، كقولكَ خليطٌ، وممشوجٌ مثلُ مخلوطٍ. سلاسلاً وأغلالاً ولم يَجِزْ بعضُهم. مُستطيرًا: ممتدًا. البلاءُ والقمطريرُ: الشديدُ، يقالُ يومٌ قمطريرٌ ويومٌ قُماطرٌ، والعَبُوسُ والقُماطرُ، والعصيبُ أشدُّ ما يكونُ من الأيامِ في البلاءِ. وقال الحسنُ:

النَّضْرَةُ فِي الوَجْهِ، والسُّرُورُ فِي القَلْبِ
وَقالَ ابنُ عَبَّاسٍ: الأَرائِكُ: السُّرُرُ.
وَقالَ مُقاتِلٌ: السُّرُرُ: الحِجالُ والدُّرُّ
وَالياقُوتُ. وَقالَ البَرَاءُ - وَذُلِّلَتْ
قُطُوفُها - يَقْطِفُونَ كَيْفَ شاءُوا. وَقالَ
مُجاهِدٌ: سَلْسَبِيلاً: حَدِيدُ الجِرْيَةِ.
وَقالَ مَعْمَرٌ: أَسْرَهُمْ: شِدَّةُ الخَلْقِ،
وكُلُّ شَيْءٍ شَدَدْتَهُ مِنْ قَتَبٍ فَهُوَ
مأْسُورٌ.

SŪRAT WAL–MURSALĀT (Those Who Sent Forth) LXXVII

سورة والمرسلات

In the Name of Allāh, the Most Beneficent, the Most Merciful

بِسْمِ اللهِ الرَّحْمَنِ الرَّحِيمِ

جُمالاتٌ: جِبالٌ وَقالَ مُجاهِدٌ: ارْكَعُوا:
صَلُّوا. لا يَرْكَعُونَ: لا يُصَلُّونَ، وَسُئِلَ
ابنُ عَبَّاسٍ - لا يَنْطِقُونَ - واللهِ رَبِّنا ما
مـا كُنَّا مُشْرِكِينَ، اليَوْمَ نَخْتِمُ عَلَى
أَفْوَاهِهِمْ - فَقالَ: إِنَّهُ ذُو أَلْوَانٍ، مَرَّةً
يَنْطِقُونَ، وَمَرَّةً يُخْتَمُ عَلَيْهِمْ.

452. Narrated 'Abdullāh (may Allah be pleased with him): We were with the Prophet (peace be upon him) when Sūrat Wal-Mursalāt was revealed to him. While we were receiving it from his mouth, a snake suddenly came and we ran to kill it, but it outstripped us and entered its hole quickly. Allāh's

٤٥٢ - حَدَّثَنا مَحْمُودٌ: حَدَّثَنا
عُبَيْدُ اللهِ، عَنْ إِسْرائِيلَ، عَنْ مَنْصُورٍ،
عَنْ إِبْراهِيمَ، عَنْ عَلْقَمَةَ، عَنْ
عَبْدِ اللهِ رَضِيَ اللهُ عَنْهُ قالَ: كُنَّا مَعَ
النَّبِيِّ صَلَّى اللهُ عَلَيْهِ وسَلَّمَ وأُنْزِلَتْ عَلَيْهِ

Messenger ﷺ said, "It has escaped your evil, and you too, have escaped its evil."

والمرسلات، وإنا لنتلقاها من فيه فخرجت حية فابتدرناها فسبقتنا فدخلت جحرها. فقال رسول الله صلى الله عليه وسلم: وقيت شركم كما وقيتم شرها.

453. Narrated 'Abdullāh رضي الله عنه : (Similarly—as no. 452 above.)

٤٥٣ - حدثنا عبدة بن عبد الله: أخبرنا يحيى بن آدم، عن إسرائيل، عن منصور بهذا. وعن إسرائيل، عن الأعمش، عن إبراهيم، عن علقمة، عن عبد الله مثله. وتابعه أسود بن عامر، عن إسرائيل. وقال حفص وأبو معاوية وسليمان بن قرم، عن الأعمش، عن إبراهيم، عن الأسود. وقال يحيى بن حماد: أخبرنا أبو عوانة، عن مغيرة، عن إبراهيم، عن علقمة، عن عبد الله. وقال ابن إسحاق، عن عبد الرحمن ابن الأسود، عن أبيه، عن عبد الله.

454. Narrated 'Abdullāh رضي الله عنه : While we were with Allāh's Messenger ﷺ in a cave, Sūrat "wal Mursalāt" was revealed to him and we received it directly from his mouth as soon as he had received the revelation. Suddenly a snake came out and Allāh's Messenger ﷺ said, "Get at it and kill it!" We ran to kill it but it outstripped us.

٤٥٤ - حدثنا قتيبة: حدثنا جرير، عن الأعمش، عن إبراهيم، عن الأسود قال: قال عبد الله: بينما نحن مع رسول الله صلى الله عليه وسلم في غار، إذ نزلت عليه والمرسلات، فتلقيناها من فيه وإن فاه لرطب بها، إذ خرجت حية فقال رسول

Allāh's Messenger ﷺ said, "It has escaped your evil, as you too, have escaped its."

اللهُ صلى الله عليه وسلم : عَلَيْكُمْ اقْتُلُوهَا ، قَالَ : فابْتَدَرْنَاهَا فَسَبَقَتْنَا . قَالَ : فَقَالَ : وُقِيَتْ شَرَّكُمْ كَمَا وُقِيتُمْ شَرَّهَا .

(329) CHAPTER. The Statement of Allāh ﷻ :—

'Indeed, it (Hell) throws about sparks (huge) as Forts.' (77:32)

بابُ قَوْلِهِ ـ إِنَّها تَرْمِى بِشَرَرٍ كالقَصْرِ ـ

455. Narrated Ibn 'Abbās (as regards the explanation of)

'Indeed, it (Hell) throws about sparks (huge) as Forts.'

We used to collect wood in the form of logs, three cubits long or shorter. for heating purposes in winter., and we used to call such wood, the Qaṣr.

٤٥٥ ـ حدَّثَنا مُحَمَّدُ بنُ كَثِيرٍ : أخبَرَنا سُفْيانُ : حدَّثَنا عبدُ الرَّحْمنِ ابنُ عَابِسٍ قالَ : سَمِعْتُ ابنَ عبَّاسٍ : إِنَّها تَرْمِى بِشَرَرٍ كالقَصْرِ ، قالَ : كُنَّا نَرْفَعُ الخَشَبَ بِقَصْرٍ ثلاثةَ أذْرُعٍ أو أقَلَّ فَنَرْفَعُهُ للشِّتاءِ فَنُسَمِّيهِ القَصْرَ .

(330) CHAPTER. The Statement of Allāh ﷻ :—

'As if they were yellow camels.' (77:33)

Narrated Ibn 'Abbās ﷺ (regarding) the explanation of

'It throws about sparks (huge) as Forts.''

We used to collect logs of wood, three cubits long or longer, to store for heating purposes in winter, and we used to call it, the "Qaṣr," (i.e. the castle or Fort).

بابُ قَوْلِهِ ـ كأنَّهُ جِمالاتٌ صُفْرٌ ـ
حدَّثَنا عمرُو بنُ عليٍّ : حدَّثَنا يَحْيى : أخبَرَنا سُفْيانُ : حدَّثَني عبدُ الرَّحْمنِ ابنُ عَابِسٍ : سَمِعْتُ ابنَ عبَّاسٍ رضيَ اللهُ عنهُما ـ تَرْمِى بِشَرَرٍ كالقَصْرِ ـ قالَ : كُنَّا نَعْمِدُ إلى الخَشَبَةِ ثلاثةَ أذْرُعٍ وفوقَ ذلكَ فَنَرْفَعُهُ للشِّتاءِ فَنُسَمِّيهِ القَصْرَ ـ كأنَّهُ جِمالاتٌ صُفْرٌ ـ حِبالُ السُّفُنِ تُجْمَعُ حتى تكونَ

'As if they were yellow camels.' (77:33)

means the ropes of a ship which are made in bundles till it become as wide as men's waists.

كأوساط الرجال .

(331) CHAPTER. 'That will be a Day when they shall not speak (during some part of it).' (77:35)

باب - هذا يوم لا ينطقون .

456. Narrated 'Abdullāh: While we were with the Prophet in a cave, Sūrat wal-Mursalāt was revealed to him and he recited it, and I heard it directly from his mouth as soon as he recited its revelation. Suddenly a snake sprang at us, and the Prophet said, "Kill it!" We ran to kill it but it escaped quickly. The Prophet said. "It has escaped your evil, and you too have escaped its evil."

٤٥٦ - حدثنا عمر بن حفص بن غياث : حدثنا أبي : حدثنا الأعمش : حدثني إبراهيم ، عن الأسود ، عن عبد الله قال : بينما نحن مع النبي صلى الله عليه وسلم في غار إذ نزلت عليه والمرسلات . فإنه ليتلوها وإني لأتلقاها من فيه ، وإن فاه لرطب بها ، إذ وثبت علينا حية . فقال النبي صلى الله عليه وسلم اقتلوها . فابتدرناها فذهبت . فقال النبي صلى الله عليه وسلم : وقيت شركم كما وقيتم شرها . قال عمر : حفظته من أبي في غار بمنى .

SŪRAT 'AMMA YATASĀ'ALŪN (SŪRAT AN-NABĀ') (The Great News) LXXVIII

In the Name of Allāh, the Most Beneficent, the Most Merciful

سورة عم يتساءلون

لا يرجون حسابا : لا يخافونه . لا

يَمْلِكُونَ مِنْهُ خِطابا : لايَمْلِكُونَ إلاَّ أنْ يأذَنَ لَهُمْ . صَوَابا : حَقّا فى الدُّنيا وَعَمِلَ بِهِ . وَقالَ ابنُ عبّاسٍ : وَهاجا : مُضِيئا . وَقالَ غَيرُهُ : غَسّاقا : غَسَقَتْ عَيْنُهُ . وَيَغْسِقُ الجُرْحُ يَسِيلُ كَأنَّ الغَسِيقَ وَاحِدٌ . عطاءً حِسابا : جَزَاءً كافِيا أعْطَانى ما أحْسَبَنى : أىْ كَفانى

(332) CHAPTER. 'The Day when the Trumpet will be blown, and you shall come forth in crowds (groups).' (78:18)

بابُ - يَوْمَ يُنْفَخُ فى الصُّورِ فَتَأْتُونَ أفْوَاجا - زُمَرًا .

457. Narrated Al-'Amash: Abū Huraira said, "Allāh's Messenger said, 'Between the two sounds of the Trumpet, there will be forty.' " Somebody asked Abū Huraira, "Forty days?" But he refused to reply. Then he asked, "Forty months?" He refused to reply. Then he asked, "Forty years?" Again, he refused to reply. Abū Huraira added. "Then (after this period) Allāh will send water from the sky and then the dead bodies will grow like vegetation grows, There is nothing of the human body that does not decay except one bone; that is the little bone at the end of the coccyx of which the human body will be recreated on the Day of Resurrection."
(See Hadīth No. 338)

٤٥٧ - حدَّثَنِى مُحَمَّدٌ : أخبرَنا أبُو مُعاوِيَةَ ، عَنِ الأعْمَشِ ، عَنْ أبى هُرَيْرَةَ رَضِىَ اللهُ عَنْهُ قالَ : قالَ رَسُولُ اللهِ صلى اللهُ عليهِ وسلَّم : ما بَيْنَ النَّفْخَتَيْنِ أرْبَعُونَ . قالَ : أرْبَعُونَ يَوْما ، قالَ : أبَيْتُ ، قالَ : أرْبَعُونَ شَهْرًا ، قالَ : أبَيْتُ ، قالَ : أرْبَعُونَ سَنَةً ، قالَ : أبَيْتُ : قالَ : ثُمَّ يُنْزِلُ اللهُ مِنَ السَّماءِ ماءً فَيَنْبُتُونَ كَمَا يَنْبُتُ البَقْلُ ، لَيْسَ مِنَ الإنْسانِ شَىْءٌ إلاَّ يَبْلَى ، إلاَّ عَظْما وَاحِدًا وَهُوَ عَجْبُ الذَّنَبِ وَمِنْهُ يُرَكَّبُ الخَلْقُ يَوْمَ القِيامَةِ .

SŪRAT WAN–NĀZI'ĀT (Those Who Tear Off) LXXIX

In the Name of Allāh, the Most Beneficent, the Most Merciful

سورة والنازعات

وَقَالَ مُجَاهِدٌ: الآيَةَ الكُبْرَى عَصَاهُ وَيَدُهُ. يُقَالُ النَّاخِرَةُ وَالنَّخِرَةُ سَوَاءٌ مِثْلُ الطَّامِعِ وَالطَّمِعِ، وَالبَاخِلِ وَالبَخِيلِ. وَقَالَ بَعْضُهُمْ: النَّخِرَةُ: البَالِيَةُ، وَالنَّاخِرَةُ العَظْمُ المُجَوَّفُ الَّذِي يَمُرُّ فِيهِ الرِّيحُ فَيَنْخَرُ، وَقَالَ ابْنُ عَبَّاسٍ: الحَافِرَةِ: إلى أمْرِنا الأوَّلِ: إلى الحَيَاةِ، وَقَالَ غَيْرُهُ: أيَّانَ مُرْسَاهَا: مَتَى مُنْتَهَاهَا، وَمُرْسَى السَّفِينَةِ حَيْثُ تَنْتَهِي.

458. Narrated Sahl bin Sa'd (ﷺ): I saw Allāh's Messenger ﷺ pointing with his index and middle fingers, saying. "The time of my Advent and the Hour are like these two fingers." The Great Catastrophy will overwhelm everything.

٤٥٨ - حدَّثنا أحْمَدُ بنُ المِقْدَامِ: حدَّثنا الفُضَيْلُ بنُ سُلَيْمَانَ: حدَّثنا أبُو حَازِمٍ: حدَّثنا سَهْلُ بنُ سَعْدٍ رَضِيَ اللهُ عَنْهُ قالَ: رأيْتُ رَسُولَ اللهِ صلى الله عليه وسلَّم قالَ بإصْبَعَيْهِ هكَذا بالوُسْطَى وَالَّتي تَلِي الإبْهامَ، بُعِثْتُ وَالسَّاعَةَ كَهَاتَيْنِ، الطَّامَّةُ تَطِمُّ عَلَى كُلِّ شَيْءٍ.

SŪRAT 'ABASA (He Frowned): IXXX

سورة عبس

In the Name of Allāh, the Most Beneficent, the Most Merciful

بسم الله الرحمن الرحيم

- عبس وتولى - كلح وأعرض .
وقال غيره : مطهرة : لا يمسها إلا المطهرون وهم الملائكة . وهذا مثل قوله - فالمدبرات أمرا - جعل الملائكة والصحف مطهرة ، لأن الصحف يقع عليها التطهير فجعل التطهير لمن حملها أيضا . سفرة : الملائكة ، واحدهم سافر . سفرت : أصلحت بينهم . وجعلت الملائكة إذا نزلت بوحي الله وتأديته كالسفير الذي يصلح بين القوم . وقال غيره : تصدى : تغافل عنه . وقال مجاهد لما يقض لا يقضي أحد ما أمر به . وقال ابن عباس : ترهقها : تغشاها شدة . مسفرة : مشرقة بأيدي سفرة . وقال ابن عباس : كتبة : أسفارا : كتبا . تلهى : تشاغل . يقال واحد الأسفار سفر .

459 Narrated 'Āisha (رضي الله عنها) : The Prophet ﷺ said, "Such a person as recites the Qur'ān and masters it by heart, will be with the noble righteous scribes (in Heaven). And such a person

٤٥٩ - حدثنا آدم : حدثنا شعبة : حدثنا قتادة قال : سمعت زرارة بن أوفى يحدث عن سعد بن هشام ،

as exerts himself to learn the Qur'ān by heart, and recites it with great difficulty, will have a double reward."

عَنْ عائِشَةَ ، عَنِ النَّبِيِّ صلى اللهُ عليهِ
وسلَّم قالَ : مَثَلُ الَّذِي يَقْرأُ القُرآنَ
وهُوَ حافِظٌ لهُ مَعَ السَّفَرَةِ الكِرامِ
البَرَرَةِ ، وَمَثَلُ الَّذِي يَقْرأُ وَهُوَ
يَتَعاهَدُهُ وَهُوَ عَلَيْهِ شَدِيدٌ فَلَهُ
أجْرانِ .

SŪRAT IDHA-SH-SHAMSU KUWIRAT (SŪRAT AL-TAKWĪR) (The Folding up) LXXXI

In the Name of Allāh, the Most Beneficent, the Most Merciful

No Ḥadīths were mentioned in this Chapter.

سورة إذا الشمس كورت

بِسْمِ اللهِ الرَّحْمَنِ الرَّحِيمِ

انْكَدَرَتْ : انْتَثَرَتْ . وَقالَ الحَسَنُ :
سُجِّرَتْ : يَذْهَبُ ماؤُها فَلا يَبْقَى
قَطْرَةٌ . وَقالَ مُجاهِدٌ : المَسْجُورُ
المَمْلُوءُ . وَقالَ غَيْرُهُ : سُجِرَتْ : ١
أفْضَى بَعْضُها إلى بَعْضٍ فَصارَتْ بَحْرًا
وَاحِدًا . والخُنَّسُ : تَخْنِسُ في مَجْراها،
تَرْجِعُ . وَتَكْنِسُ : تَسْتَتِرُ كَما
تَكْنِسُ الظِّباءُ . تَنَفَّسَ : ارْتَفَعَ
النَّهارُ . والظَّنِينُ : المُتَّهَمُ . والضَّنِينُ :
يَضَنُّ بِهِ . وقال عُمَرُ ، النُّفُوسُ زُوِّجَتْ :
يُزَوَّجُ نَظِيرَهُ مِنْ أهْلِ الجَنَّةِ والنَّارِ ،
ثُمَّ قَرأ - احْشُرُوا الَّذِينَ ظَلَمُوا
وأزْواجَهُمْ - عَسْعَسَ : أدْبَرَ .

SŪRAT AI–INFIṬĀR
(The Cleaving Asunder):
LXXXII
In the Name of Allāh, the Most Beneficent, the Most Merciful

(No Ḥadīths were mentioned here)

سورة إذا السماء انفطرت

بِسْمِ اللهِ الرَّحْمَنِ الرَّحِيمِ

وَقَالَ الرَّبِيعُ بنُ خُثَيْمٍ : فُجِّرَتْ : فَاضَتْ . وَقَرَأَ الأَعْمَشُ وَعَاصِمٌ - فَعَدَلَكَ - بالتَّخْفِيفِ ، وقرأ أهْلُ الحِجازِ بالتَّشْدِيدِ . وأَرَادَ مُعْتَدِلَ الخَلْقِ . وَمَنْ خَفَّفَ يَعْنِي فى أىْ صُورَةٍ شاءَ . إمَّا حَسَنٌ ، وإمَّا قَبِيحٌ ، أوْ طَوِيلٌ أوْ قَصِيرٌ .

SŪRAT AL–MUṬAFFIFĪN
(Woe on those Dealing in Fraud):
LXXXIII
In the Name of Allāh, the Most Beneficent, the Most Merciful

سورة ويل للمطففين

بِسْمِ اللهِ الرَّحْمَنِ الرَّحِيمِ

وَقَالَ مُجَاهِدٌ - بَلْ رَانَ - ثَبْتُ الخَطَايا : ثُوِّبَ : جُوزِىَ . الرَّحِيقُ : الخَمْرُ . خِتامُهُ مِسْكٌ : طِينُهُ : التَّسْنِيمُ : يَعْلُو شَرَابَ أهْلِ الجَنَّةِ . وَقَالَ غَيْرُهُ : المُطَفِّفُ لا يُوَفِّى غَيْرَهُ .

(333) CHAPTER. The Statement of Allāh تعالى :-
'A Day when (all) mankind will stand before the Lord of the Worlds.' (83:6)

يَوْمَ يَقُومُ النَّاسُ لِرَبِّ العالمِينَ .

460. Narrated 'Abdullāh bin 'Umar : The Prophet said, "On the Day when all mankind will stand before the Lord of the Worlds, some of them will be enveloped in their sweat up to the middle of their ears."

٤٦٠ - حدثنا إبراهيم بن المنذر: حدثنا معن قال: حدثني مالك، عن نافع، عن عبد الله ابن عمر رضي الله عنهما: أن النبي صلى الله عليه وسلم قال: يوم يقوم الناس لرب العالمين - حتى يغيب أحدهم في رشحه إلى أنصاف أذنيه.

SŪRAT AL-INSHIQĀQ
(The rendering assunder) LXXXIV
In the Name of Allāh,
the Most Beneficent, the Most Merciful

سورة إذا السماء انشقت

قال مجاهد: كتابه بشماله، يأخذ كتابه من وراء ظهره. وسق: جمع من دابة. ظن أن لن يحور: لا يرجع إلينا.

(334) CHAPTER. He surely will receive an easy reckoning.' (84:8)

باب - فسوف يحاسب حسابا يسيرا -.

461. Narrated 'Āisha : I heard the Prophet saying . . . .

٤٦١ - حدثنا عمرو بن علي: حدثنا يحيى، عن عثمان بن الأسود قال: سمعت ابن أبي مليكة: سمعت عائشة رضي الله عنها قالت: سمعت النبي صلى الله عليه وسلم.

462. Narrated 'Āisha : I heard the Prophet saying. . . . .

٤٦٢ - حدثنا سليمان بن حرب: حدثنا حماد بن زيد، عن أيوب، عن ابن أبي مليكة، عن عائشة، عن

النَّبِيِّ صلى اللهُ عليهِ وسلَّم

463. Narrated 'Āisha : Allāh's Messenger said," (On the Day of Resurrection) any one whose account will be taken will be ruined (i.e. go to Hell)." I said, "O Allāh's Messenger! May Allāh make me be sacrificed for you! Doesn't Allāh say:

> 'Then as for him who will be given his record in his right hand, he surely will receive an easy reckoning.?" (84:7 and 8)

He replied, "That is only the presentation of the accounts; but he whose record is questioned, will be ruined."

٤٦٣ - حدَّثنا مُسَدَّدٌ، عَنْ يَحْيَى، عَنْ أبي يُونُسَ حاتِمِ بنِ أبي صَغِيرَةَ، عَنِ ابنِ أبي مُلَيْكَةَ، عَنِ القاسِمِ، عَنْ عائِشَةَ رَضِيَ اللهُ عَنْها قالَتْ: قالَ رَسُولُ اللهِ صلى اللهُ عليهِ وسلَّم: لَيْسَ أحَدٌ يُحاسَبُ إلاَّ هَلَكَ، قالَتْ: قُلْتُ يا رَسُولَ اللهِ، جَعَلَنِي اللهُ فِداءَكَ. ألَيْسَ يَقُولُ اللهُ عَزَّ وَجَلَّ - فأمَّا مَنْ أُوتِيَ كِتابَهُ بِيَمِينِهِ فَسَوْفَ يُحاسَبُ حِساباً يَسِيراً - قالَ: ذاكِ العَرْضُ يُعْرَضُونَ. وَمَنْ نُوقِشَ الحِسابَ هَلَكَ.

(335) CHAPTER. The Statement of Allāh :-

> 'You shall surely travel form stage to stage (in this life and in the Hereafter.) ....(84:19)

بابٌ - لَتَرْكَبُنَّ طَبَقاً عَنْ طَبَقٍ -.

464. Narrated Ibn 'Abbās (as regards the Verse):-

> 'You shall surely travel from stage to stage (in this life and in the Hereafter) (It means) from one state to another. That concerns your Prophet .

٤٦٤ - حدَّثنا سَعِيدُ بنُ النَّضْرِ، أخْبَرَنا هُشَيْمٌ: أخْبَرَنا أبُو بِشْرٍ جَعْفَرُ ابنُ إياسٍ، عَنْ مُجاهِدٍ قالَ: قالَ ابنُ عَبَّاسٍ - لَتَرْكَبُنَّ طَبَقاً عَنْ طَبَقٍ - حالاً بَعْدَ حالٍ. قالَ: هَذا نَبِيُّكُمْ صلى اللهُ عليهِ وسلَّم.

SŪRAT AL-BURŪJ (ZODIACAL SIGNS) LXXXV

سورة البروج

In the Name of Allāh, the Most Beneficent, the Most Merciful

(No Ḥadīths were mentioned here)

وَقَالَ مُجَاهِدٌ: الأُخْدُودُ: شَقٌّ فِى الأَرْضِ: فَتَنُوا: عَذَّبُوا. وَقَالَ ابْنُ عَبَّاسٍ: الوَدُودُ: الحَبِيبُ. المَجِيدُ: الكَرِيمُ

SŪRAT AṬ-ṬĀRIQ (The Night Visitant) LXXXVI

سورة الطارق

In the Name of Allāh, the Most Beneficent, the Most Merciful

(No Ḥadīths were mentioned here)

هُوَ النَّجْمُ، وَمَا أَتَاكَ لَيْلاً فَهُوَ طَارِقٌ. النَّجْمُ الثَّاقِبُ: المُضِىءُ. وَقَالَ مُجَاهِدٌ: ذَاتِ الرَّجْعِ: سَحَابٌ يَرْجِعُ بِالمَطَرِ. وَذَاتِ الصَّدْعِ: الأَرْضُ تَتَصَدَّعُ بِالنَّبَاتِ. وَقَالَ ابْنُ عَبَّاسٍ: لَقَوْلٌ فَصْلٌ: لَحَقٌّ. لَمَّا عَلَيْهَا حَافِظٌ: إِلاَّ عَلَيْهَا حَافِظٌ.

SŪRAT AL-A'LĀ (THE MOST HIGH) LXXXVII (GLORIFY THE NAME OF YOUR LORD, MOST HIGH.)

سورة سبح اسم ربك الأعلى

In the Name of Allāh, the Most Beneficent, the Most Merciful

وَقَالَ مُجَاهِدٌ: قَدَّرَ فَهَدَى: قَدَّرَ لِلإِنْسَانِ الشَّقَاءَ وَالسَّعَادَةَ، وَهَدَى الأَنْعَامَ لِمَرَاتِعِهَا.

465. Narrated Al-Barā' ﷺ : The first of the companions of the Prophet ﷺ who came to us (in Medīna), were Muṣ'ab bin 'Umair and Ibn Um Maktūm,

٤٦٥ - حَدَّثَنَا عَبْدَانُ قَالَ: أَخْبَرَنِى أَبِى عَنْ شُعْبَةَ، عَنْ أَبِى إِسْحَاقَ، عَنِ البَرَاءِ رَضِىَ اللهُ عَنْهُ قَالَ: أَوَّلُ

and they started teaching us the Qur'ān. Then came 'Ammār, Bilāl and Sa'd. Afterwards 'Umar bin Al-Khaṭṭāb came along with a batch of twenty (men): and after that the Prophet came. I never saw the people of Medīna so pleased with anything as they were with his arrival, so that even the little boys and girls were saying, "This is Allāh's Messenger who has come." He (the Prophet) did not come (to Medīna) till I had learnt Sūrat Al-A'lā and also other similar Sūras.

مَنْ قَدِمَ عَلَيْنا مِنْ أصحابِ النَّبِيِّ صلى اللهُ عليهِ وسلَّم مُصْعَبُ بنُ عُمَيْرٍ وَابنُ أُمِّ مَكْتُومٍ فَجَعَلا يُقْرِئانِنا القُرْآنَ . ثُمَّ جاءَ عَمَّارٌ وَبِلالٌ وَسَعْدٌ ، ثُمَّ جاءَ عُمَرُ بنُ الخَطَّابِ فى عِشْرِينَ ، ثُمَّ جاءَ النَّبِيُّ صلى اللهُ عليهِ وسلَّم فَمَا رأيْتُ أهْلَ المَدِينَةِ فَرِحُوا بِشَىْءٍ فَرَحَهُمْ بِهِ حَتَّى رَأيْتُ الوَلائِدَ والصِّبْيانَ يَقُولُونَ : هَذا رَسُولُ اللهِ صلى اللهُ عليهِ وسلَّم قَدْ جاءَ ، فَمَا جاءَ حَتَّى قَرأتُ - سَبِّحِ اسْمَ رَبِّكَ الأعْلَى - فى سُوَرٍ مِثْلِها .

SŪRAT GHĀSHIYA (The Overwhelming Event) LXXXVIII

In the Name of Allāh, the Most Beneficent, the Most Merciful

(No Ḥadīths were mentioned here)

سورة هل أتاك

بِسْمِ اللهِ الرَّحْمَنِ الرَّحِيمِ

وَقالَ ابنُ عَبَّاسٍ - عامِلَةٌ ناصِبَةٌ - النَّصارَى وَقالَ مُجاهِدٌ - عَيْنٌ آنِيَةٌ - بَلَغَ إناها وَحانَ شُرْبُها - حَمِيمٍ آنٍ - بَلَغَ إناهُ - فيها لاغِيَةٌ - شَتْمًا ، وَيُقالُ الضَّرِيعُ : نَبْتٌ يُقالُ لَهُ الشِّبْرِقُ يُسَمِّيهِ أهْلُ الحِجازِ الضَّرِيعَ إذا يَبِسَ وَهُوَ سُمٌّ . بِمُسَيْطِرٍ : بِمُسَلَّطٍ ، وَيُقْرأُ بالصَّادِ والسِّينِ . وقالَ ابنُ عَبَّاسٍ : إيابَهُمْ : مَرْجِعَهُمْ .

SŪRAT AL-FAJR (The Break of Day)
LXXXIX

**In the Name of Allāh,
the Most Beneficent, the Most Merciful**

(No Ḥadīths were mentioned here)

سورة والفجر

بِسْمِ اللهِ الرَّحْمَنِ الرَّحِيمِ

وَقَالَ مُجَاهِدٌ: وَالْوَتْرُ: اللهُ. إِرَمَ ذَاتِ الْعِمَادِ: يَعْنِي الْقَدِيمَةَ. وَالْعِمَادُ: أَهْلُ عَمُودٍ لَا يُقِيمُونَ. سَوْطَ عَذَابٍ: الَّذِي عُذِّبُوا بِهِ. أَكْلًا لَمًّا: السَّفُّ. وَجَمًّا: الْكَثِيرُ، وَقَالَ مُجَاهِدٌ: كُلُّ شَيْءٍ خَلَقَهُ فَهُوَ شَفْعٌ، وَالْوَتْرُ: اللهُ تَبَارَكَ وَتَعَالَى. وَقَالَ غَيْرُهُ: سَوْطَ عَذَابٍ كَلِمَةٌ تَقُولُهَا الْعَرَبُ لِكُلِّ نَوْعٍ مِنَ الْعَذَابِ يَدْخُلُ فِيهِ السَّوْطُ. لَبِالْمِرْصَادِ: إِلَيْهِ الْمَصِيرُ. تَحَاضُّونَ: تُحَافِظُونَ، يَأْمُرُونَ بِإِطْعَامِهِ. الْمُطْمَئِنَّةُ: الْمُصَدِّقَةُ بِالثَّوَابِ. وَقَالَ الْحَسَنُ - يَا أَيَّتُهَا النَّفْسُ الْمُطْمَئِنَّةُ - إِذَا أَرَادَ اللهُ عَزَّ وَجَلَّ قَبْضَهَا اطْمَأَنَّتْ إِلَى اللهِ وَاطْمَأَنَّ اللهُ إِلَيْهِ، وَرَضِيَتْ عَنِ اللهِ وَرَضِيَ اللهُ عَنْهُ، فَأَمَرَ بِقَبْضِ رُوحِهَا وَأَدْخَلَهَا اللهُ الْجَنَّةَ وَجَعَلَهَا مِنْ عِبَادِهِ الصَّالِحِينَ. وَقَالَ غَيْرُهُ: جَابُوا: نَقَبُوا، مِنْ جِيبِ الْقَمِيصِ قُطِعَ لَهُ جَيْبٌ. يَجُوبُ الْفَلَاةَ يَقْطَعُهَا، لَمَّا لَمَمْتُهُ أَجْمَعَ: أَتَيْتُ عَلَى آخِرِهِ.

SŪRAT:AL-BALAD (The City)
XC

In the Name of Allāh,
the Most Beneficent, the Most Merciful

(No Ḥadīths were mentioned here)

سورة لا أقسم

وَقَالَ مُجَاهِدٌ ـ وأنتَ حِلٌّ بهذا البَلَدِ ـ مَكَّةَ لَيْسَ عَلَيْكَ ما عَلَى النَّاسِ فيهِ مِنَ الإثمِ. وَوَالِدٍ: آدَمَ، وَمَا وَلَدَ. لُبَدًا: كَثِيرًا. والنَّجْدَيْنِ: الخَيرُ والشَّرُّ. مَسْغَبَةٍ: مَجَاعَةٍ. مَتْرَبَةٍ: السَّاقِطُ فى التُّرَابِ: يُقَالُ ـ فَلا اقْتَحَمَ العَقَبَةَ ـ فَلَمْ يَقْتَحِمِ العَقَبَةَ فى الدُّنيا، ثُمَّ فَسَّرَ العَقَبَةَ فقالَ ـ وَمَا أَدْرَاكَ ما العَقَبَةُ فَكُّ رَقَبَةٍ ـ أَوْ إطْعامٌ فى يَوْمٍ ذِى مَسْغَبَةٍ ـ فى كَبَدٍ: شِدَّةٍ.

SŪRAT ASH-SHAMS (The Sun)
XCI

In the Name of Allāh,
the Most Beneficent, the Most Merciful

سورة والشمس وضحاها

بِسْمِ اللهِ الرَّحْمنِ الرَّحِيمِ

وَقَالَ مُجَاهِدٌ: ضُحاها: ضَوْءُهَا. إذَا تَلاهَا: تَبِعَهَا. وَطَحَاهَا: دَحَاهَا وَدَسَّاهَا: أَغْوَاهَا. فَأَلْهَمَهَا: عَرَّفَهَا الشَّقَاءَ والسَّعَادَةَ. وَقَالَ مُجَاهِدٌ: بِطَغْوَاهَا: بِمَعَاصِيهَا. وَلا يَخَافُ عُقْبَاهَا: عُقْبَى أَحَدٍ.

466. Narrated 'Abdullāh bin Zam'a that he heard the Prophet ﷺ delivering a sermon, and he mentioned the she-camel and the one who hamstrung it.

٤٦٦ ـ حَدَّثَنَا مُوسَى بنُ إسْمَاعِيلَ: حَدَّثَنَا وُهَيْبٌ: حَدَّثَنَا هِشَامٌ، عَنْ أَبِيهِ: أَنَّهُ أَخْبَرَهُ عَبْدُ اللهِ بنُ زَمْعَةَ أَنَّهُ

Allāh's Messenger ﷺ recited:—

'When, the most wicked man among them went forth (to hamstrung the she-camel).' (91:12.)

Then he said, "A tough man whose equal was rare and who enjoyed the protection of his people, like Abī Zam'a, went forth to (hamstrung) it." The Prophet ﷺ then mentioned about the women (in his sermon). "It is not wise for anyone of you to lash his wife like a slave, for he might sleep with her the same evening." Then he advised them not to laugh when somebody breaks wind, and said, "Why should anybody laugh at what he himself does?"

سَمِعَ النَّبِيَّ صلى الله عليه وسلم يَخْطُبُ وَذَكَرَ النَّاقَةَ وَالَّذِي عَقَرَ، فَقَالَ رَسُولُ اللهِ صلى الله عليه وسلم - إِذِ انْبَعَثَ أَشْقَاهَا - انْبَعَثَ لَهَا رَجُلٌ عَزِيزٌ عَارِمٌ مَنِيعٌ فِي رَهْطِهِ مِثْلُ أَبِي زَمْعَةَ. وَذَكَرَ النِّسَاءَ فَقَالَ: يَعْمِدُ أَحَدُكُمْ يَجْلِدُ امْرَأَتَهُ جَلْدَ الْعَبْدِ فَلَعَلَّهُ يُضَاجِعُهَا مِنْ آخِرِ يَوْمِهِ، ثُمَّ وَعَظَهُمْ فِي ضَحِكِهِمْ مِنَ الضَّرْطَةِ، وَقَالَ: لِمَ يَضْحَكُ أَحَدُكُمْ مِمَّا يَفْعَلُ؟ وَقَالَ أَبُو مُعَاوِيَةَ: حَدَّثَنَا هِشَامٌ، عَنْ أَبِيهِ، عَنْ عَبْدِ اللهِ بْنِ زَمْعَةَ قَالَ النَّبِيُّ صلى الله عليه وسلم: مِثْلُ أَبِي زَمْعَةَ عَمِّ الزُّبَيْرِ بْنِ الْعَوَّامِ

SŪRAT: BY THE NIGHT AS IT CONCEALS..........XCII

In the Name of Allāh, the Most Beneficent, the Most Merciful

سورة والليل إذا يغشى

بِسْمِ اللهِ الرَّحْمَنِ الرَّحِيمِ

وَقَالَ ابْنُ عَبَّاسٍ - وَكَذَّبَ بِالْحُسْنَى - بِالْخَلَفِ. وَقَالَ: مُجَاهِدٌ: تَرَدَّى مَاتَ. وَتَلَظَّى: تَوَهَّجَ. وَقَرَأَ عُبَيْدُ بْنُ عُمَيْرٍ: تَتَلَظَّى.

(336) CHAPTER. 'By the day as it appears in brightness, (92:2)

بَابٌ - وَالنَّهَارِ إِذَا تَجَلَّى -.

467. Narrated 'Alqama: I went to Shā'm with a group of the companions of 'Abdullāh (bin Mas'ūd). Abū Ad-Dardā' heard of our arrival so he came to us and said, "Is there anybody among you who can recite (Qur'ān)?" We replied in the affirmative. Then he asked, "Who is the best reciter?" They pointed at me. Then he told me to recite, so I recited the Verse:—

'By the night as it envelops
'By the day as it appears in brightness;
By (Him Who created) male and the female.' (92:1-3)

Abū Ad-Dardā' then said to me, "Did you hear it (like this) from the mouth of your friend ('Abdullāh bin Mas'ūd)?" I said, "Yes." He said, "I too, heard it (like this) from the mouth of the Prophet ﷺ, but these people do not consider this recitation as the correct one."

٤٦٧ - حدثنا قبيصة بن عقبة: حدثنا سفيان، عن الأعمش، عن إبراهيم، عن علقمة: قال: دخلت في نفر من أصحاب عبد الله الشام فسمع بنا أبو الدرداء فأتانا فقال: أفيكم من يقرأ؟ فقلنا: نعم. قال: فأيكم أقرأ؟ فأشاروا إلي، فقال: اقرأ. فقرأت - والليل إذا يغشى والنهار إذا تجلى والذكر والأنثى - قال: أنت سمعتها من في صاحبك؟ قلت: نعم. قال: وأنا سمعتها من في النبي صلى الله عليه وسلم وهؤلاء يأبون علينا.

(337) CHAPTER. 'By Him Who Created male and female.' (92:3)

باب - وما خلق الذكر والأنثى -.

468. Narrated Ibrāhīm: The companions of 'Abdullāh (bin Mas'ūd) came to Abī Dardā', (and before they arrived at his home), he looked for them and found them. Then he asked them,:'Who among you can recite (Qur'ān) as 'Abdullāh recites it?" They replied, "All of us." He asked, "Who among you knows it by heart?" They pointed at 'Alqama.

٤٦٨ - حدثنا عمر: حدثنا أبي: حدثنا الأعمش، عن إبراهيم قال: قدم أصحاب عبد الله على أبي الدرداء فطلبهم فوجدهم فقال: أيكم يقرأ على قراءة عبد الله؟ قال: كلنا. قال: فأيكم يحفظ؟ وأشاروا إلى علقمة،

Then he asked Alqama. "How did you hear 'Abdullāh bin Mas'ud reciting Sūrat Al-Lail (The Night)?" 'Alqama recited:–

'By the male and the female.'

Abū Ad-Dardā said, "I testify that I heard the Prophet ﷺ reciting it likewise, but these people want me to recite it:–

'And by Him Who created male and female.'

but by Allāh, I will not follow them."

قَالَ: كَيْفَ سَمِعْتَهُ يَقْرَأُ ـ وَاللَّيْلِ إِذَا يَغْشَى ـ؟ قَالَ عَلْقَمَةُ ـ وَالذَّكَرِ وَالأُنْثَى ـ قَالَ: أَشْهَدُ أَنِّي سَمِعْتُ النَّبِيَّ صلى الله عليه وسلم يَقْرَأُ هَكَذَا وَهَؤُلَاءِ يُرِيدُونَنِي عَلَى أَنْ أَقْرَأَ ـ وَمَا خَلَقَ الذَّكَرَ وَالأُنْثَى ـ وَاللهِ لَا أُتَابِعُهُمْ.

(338) CHAPTER. The Statement of Allāh تعالى :–

'As for him who gives (in charity) and keeps his duty to Allāh.'

(92:5)

بَابٌ قَوْلُهُ ـ فَأَمَّا مَنْ أَعْطَى وَاتَّقَى ـ.

469. Narrated 'Alī رضي الله عنه : We were in the company of the Prophet ﷺ in a funeral procession at Baqī Al-Gharqad. He said, "There is none of you but has his place written for him in Paradise or in the Hell-Fire." They said, "O Allāh's Messenger! Shall we depend (on this fact and give up work)?" He said, "Carry on doing (good deeds), for every body will find it easy to do (what will lead him to his destined place)." Then he recited:–

'As for him who gives (in charity) and keeps his duty to Allāh, and believes in the Best reward from Allāh (i.e. Allāh will compensate him

٤٦٩ ـ حَدَّثَنَا أَبُو نُعَيْمٍ: حَدَّثَنَا سُفْيَانُ، عَنِ الأَعْمَشِ، عَنْ سَعْدِ بْنِ عُبَيْدَةَ، عَنْ أَبِي عَبْدِ الرَّحْمَنِ السُّلَمِيِّ. عَنْ عَلِيٍّ رَضِيَ اللهُ عَنْهُ قَالَ: كُنَّا مَعَ النَّبِيِّ صلى الله عليه وسلم فِي بَقِيعِ الْغَرْقَدِ فِي جَنَازَةٍ، فَقَالَ: مَا مِنْكُمْ مِنْ أَحَدٍ إِلَّا وَقَدْ كُتِبَ مَقْعَدُهُ مِنَ الْجَنَّةِ وَمَقْعَدُهُ مِنَ النَّارِ. فَقَالُوا: يَا رَسُولَ اللهِ، أَفَلَا نَتَّكِلُ؟ فَقَالَ: اعْمَلُوا فَكُلٌّ مُيَسَّرٌ، ثُمَّ قَرَأَ ـ فَأَمَّا مَنْ أَعْطَى وَاتَّقَى وَصَدَّقَ بِالْحُسْنَى ـ إِلَى قَوْلِهِ ـ لِلْعُسْرَى ـ.

for what he will spend in Allāh's way). So, We will make smooth for him the path of ease. But he who is a greedy miser.....for him, the path for evil.' (92:5-10)

(339) CHAPTER. The Statement of Allāh تعالى :–

باب قوله ـ وصدق بالحسنى ـ .

......and believes in the Best reward.' ....(92:6)

470. Narrated Abū 'Abdur-Raḥmān: 'Alī رضي الله عنه said, "We were sitting with the Prophet ﷺ ," (He then mentioned the Ḥadīth above (469).

٤٧٠ ـ حدثنا مسدد، حدثنا عبد الواحد: حدثنا الأعمش، عن سعد بن عبيدة، عن أبي عبد الرحمن، عن علي رضي الله عنه قال: كنا قعودا عند النبي صلى الله عليه وسلم فذكر الحديث .

(340) CHAPTER. 'We will make smooth for him, the path of ease.' (92:7)

باب ـ فسنيسره لليسرى ـ .

471. Narrated 'Alī رضي الله عنه :While the Prophet ﷺ was in a funeral procession, he took a small stick and started scraping the earth with it and said, "There is none among you but has his place written for him, either in the Hell-Fire or in Paradise." They (the people) said, "O Allāh's Messenger! Shall we depend on this (and leave work)?" He

٤٧١ ـ حدثنا بشر بن خالد: أخبرنا محمد بن جعفر: حدثنا شعبة، عن سليمان، عن سعد بن عبيدة، عن أبي عبد الرحمن السلمي، عن علي رضي الله عنه، عن النبي صلى الله عليه وسلم أنه كان في جنازة فأخذ

replied. "Carry on doing (good deeds), for everybody will find easy (to do) such deeds as will lead him to his destined place." The Prophet ﷺ then recited:–

> 'As for him who gives (in charity) and keeps his duty to Allāh, and believes in the Best Reward.' . . .
> . . . . (92:5-10)

عوداً ينكت في الأرض فقال: ما منكم من أحد إلا وقد كتب مقعده من النار، أو من الجنة. قالوا: يا رسول الله، أفلا نتكل؟ قال: اعملوا فكل ميسر. فأما من أعطى واتقى وصدق بالحسنى. الآية، قال شعبة: حدثني به منصور فلم أنكره من حديث سليمان.

(341) CHAPTER. The Statement of Allāh تعالى :–

> 'But he who is a greedy miser and thinks himself self-sufficient...'
> (92:8)

باب قوله وأما من بخل واستغنى.

472. Narrated 'Alī رضي الله عنه : We were in the company of the Prophet ﷺ and he said, "There is none among you but has his place written for him, either in Paradise or in the Hell-Fire." We said, "O Allāh's Messenger! Shall we depend (on this fact and give up work)?" He replied, "No! Carry on doing good deeds, for everybody will find easy (to do) such deeds as will lead him to his destined place." Then the Prophet ﷺ recited:

> 'As for him who gives (in charity) and keeps his duty to Allāh, and believes in the Best reward. We will make smooth for him the path of ease . . . . the path for evil.'
> (92:5–10)

٤٧٢ - حدثنا يحيى: حدثنا وكيع، عن الأعمش، عن سعد بن عبيدة، عن أبي عبد الرحمن عن علي رضي الله عنه قال: كنا جلوساً عند النبي صلى الله عليه وسلم فقال: ما منكم من أحد إلا وقد كتب مقعده من الجنة ومقعده من النار، فقلنا: يا رسول الله أفلا نتكل؟ قال: لا، اعملوا فكل ميسر. ثم قرأ - فأما من أعطى واتقى وصدق بالحسنى فسنيسره لليسرى - إلى قوله - فسنيسره للعسرى -.

(342) CHAPTER. The Statement of Allāh تعالى :—

'And gives the lie to the Best reward from Allāh. . . . .(92:9)

باب قوله ـ وكذب بالحسنى ـ.

473. Narrated 'Alī رضي الله عنه : While we were in a funeral procession in Baqī' Al-Gharqad, Allāh's Messenger ﷺ came and sat down, and we sat around him. He had a small stick in his hand and he bent his head and started scraping the ground with it. He then said, "There is none among you, and no created soul but has his place written for him either in Paradise or in the Hell-Fire, and also has his happy or miserable fate (in the Hereafter) written for him." A man said, "O Allāh's Messenger! Shall we depend upon what is written for us and give up doing (good) deeds? For whoever among us is destined to be fortunate (in the Hereafter), will join the fortunate people, and whoever among us is destined to be miserable will do such deeds as are characteristic of the people who are destined to misery." The Prophet ﷺ said, "Those who are destined to be happy (in the Hereafter) will find it easy and pleasant to do the deeds characteristic of those destined to happiness, while those who are to be among the miserable (in the Hereafter), will find it easy to do the deeds characteristic of those destined to misery." Then he

٤٧٣ ـ حدثنا عثمان بن أبي شيبة: حدثنا جرير، عن منصور، عن سعد ابن عبيدة، عن أبي عبد الرحمن السلمي، عن علي رضي الله عنه قال: كنا في جنازة في بقيع الغرقد، فأتانا رسول الله صلى الله عليه وسلم فقعد وقعدنا حوله ومعه مخصرة فنكس فجعل ينكت بمخصرته. ثم قال: ما منكم من أحد، وما من نفس منفوسة إلا كتب مكانها من الجنة والنار، وإلا قد كتبت شقية أو سعيدة. قال رجل: يا رسول الله، أفلا نتكل على كتابنا وندع العمل؟ فمن كان منا من أهل السعادة فسيصير إلى أهل السعادة. ومن كان منا من أهل الشقاء فسيصير إلى عمل أهل الشقاوة. قال: أما أهل السعادة فييسرون لعمل أهل السعادة، وأما

recited:—

'As for him who gives (in charity) and keeps his duty to Allāh and believes in the Best reward from Allāh, We will make smooth for him the path of ease. But he who is a greedy miser and thinks himself self sufficient, and gives the lie to the Best reward from Allāh we will make smooth for him the path for evil.'

(92:5-10)

أَهْلُ الشَّقَاوَةِ فَيُيَسَّرُونَ لِعَمَلِ أَهْلِ الشَّقَاوَةِ. ثُمَّ قَرَأَ - فَأَمَّا مَنْ أَعْطَى وَاتَّقَى وَصَدَّقَ بِالْحُسْنَى - الآيَةَ.

(343) CHAPTER. 'We will make smooth for him the path for evil.' (92:10)

بَابٌ - فَسَنُيَسِّرُهُ لِلْعُسْرَى -.

474. Narrated 'Alī ﷺ :While the Prophet ﷺ was in a funeral procession. he picked up something and started scraping the ground with it, and said, "There is none among you but has his place written for him either in the Hell-Fire or in Paradise." They said, "O Allāh's Messenger! Shall we not depend upon what has been written for us and give up deeds? He said, "Carry on doing (good) deeds, for everybody will find easy to do such deeds as will lead him to his destined place for which he has been created. So he, who is destined to be among the happy (in the Hereafter), will find it easy to do the

٤٧٤ - حَدَّثَنَا آدَمُ: حَدَّثَنَا شُعْبَةُ، عَنِ الأَعْمَشِ قَالَ: سَمِعْتُ سَعْدَ بْنَ عُبَيْدَةَ يُحَدِّثُ عَنْ أَبِي عَبْدِ الرَّحْمَنِ السُّلَمِيِّ، عَنْ عَلِيٍّ رَضِيَ اللهُ عَنْهُ قَالَ: كَانَ النَّبِيُّ صلى اللهُ عليه وسلَّم فِي جَنَازَةٍ فَأَخَذَ شَيْئًا فَجَعَلَ يَنْكُتُ بِهِ الأَرْضَ فَقَالَ: مَا مِنْكُمْ مِنْ أَحَدٍ إِلاَّ وَقَدْ كُتِبَ مَقْعَدُهُ مِنَ النَّارِ وَمَقْعَدُهُ مِنَ الْجَنَّةِ. قَالُوا: يَا رَسُولَ اللهِ أَفَلا نَتَّكِلُ عَلَى كِتَابِنَا وَنَدَعُ الْعَمَلَ؟ قَالَ: اعْمَلُوا

deeds characteristic of such people, while he who is destined to be among the miserable ones, will find it easy to do the deeds characteristic of such people." Then he recited:

'As for him who gives (in charity) and fears Allāh, and believes in the best........ '(92:5–10)

فَكُلٌّ مُيَسَّرٌ لِمَا خُلِقَ لَهُ . أَمَّا مَنْ كَانَ مِنْ أَهْلِ السَّعَادَةِ فَيُيَسَّرُ لِعَمَلِ أَهْلِ السَّعَادَةِ . وَأَمَّا مَنْ كَانَ مِنْ أَهْلِ الشَّقَاءِ فَيُيَسَّرُ لِعَمَلِ أَهْلِ الشَّقَاوَةِ ثُمَّ قَرَأَ ـ فَأَمَّا مَنْ أَعْطَى وَاتَّقَى وَصَدَّقَ بِالْحُسْنَى ـ الآيَةَ .

SŪRAT WAḌ-ḌUḤĀ (By the fore noon): XCIII

In the Name of Allāh,
the Most Beneficent, the Most Merciful

سورة والضحى

بِسْمِ اللهِ الرَّحْمَنِ الرَّحِيمِ

وَقَالَ مُجَاهِدٌ ـ إِذَا سَجَى ـ اسْتَوَى . وَقَالَ غَيْرُهُ : سَجَى : أَظْلَمَ وَسَكَنَ . عَائِلاً : ذُو عِيَالٍ .

(344) CHAPTER. The Statement of Allāh :–

'Your Lord (O Muḥammad) has neither forsaken you nor hated you.' (93:3)

بَابُ قَوْلِهِ مَا وَدَّعَكَ رَبُّكَ وَمَا قَلَى ـ .

475. Narrated Jundub bin Sufyān : Once Allāh's Messenger became sick and could not offer his night prayer (Tahajjud) for two or three nights. Then a lady (the wife of Abū Lahab) came and said, "O Muḥammad! I think that your Satan has forsaken you, for I have not seen him with you for two or three nights!"

٤٧٥ ـ حَدَّثَنَا أَحْمَدُ بْنُ يُونُسَ : حَدَّثَنَا زُهَيْرٌ : حَدَّثَنَا الأَسْوَدُ بْنُ قَيْسٍ قَالَ : سَمِعْتُ جُنْدَبَ ابْنَ سُفْيَانَ رَضِيَ اللهُ عَنْهُ قَالَ ، اشْتَكَى رَسُولُ اللهِ صلى الله عليه وسلم فَلَمْ يَقُمْ لَيْلَتَيْنِ أَوْ ثَلاثاً ، فَجَاءَتِ امْرَأَةٌ فَقَالَتْ : يَا

محمد، إني لأرجو أن يكون شيطانك قد تركك لم أره قربك منذ ليلتين أو ثلاثا، فأنزل الله عز وجل - والضحى والليل إذا سجى ما ودعك ربك وما قلى - .

On that Allāh عزوجل revealed:–

'By the fore-noon, and by the night when it darkens, your Lord (O Muḥammad) has neither forsaken you, nor hated you.' (93:1–3)

باب قوله - ما ودعك ربك وما قلى - تقرأ بالتشديد والتخفيف بمعنى واحد: ما تركك ربك. وقال ابن عباس: ما تركك وما أبغضك.

(345) CHAPTER. The statement of Allāh تعالى:

"Your Lord (O Muḥammad) has neither forsaken you, nor hated you.' (93: 1–3)

(The Arabic word that is translated as 'has forsaken you' can be read in two ways: with emphasis (i.e., Wadda'aka) or without emphasis (i.e. Wada'aka). The meaning of both is the same, i.e., (your Lord) has (not) forsaken you.) Ibn 'Abbās said: The Verse means, 'He has not forsaken you, nor does He hate you.'

٤٧٦ - حدثنا محمد بن بشار: حدثنا محمد بن جعفر غندر: حدثنا شعبة، عن الأسود ابن قيس قال: سمعت جندبا البجلي: قالت امرأة: يا رسول الله، ما أرى صاحبك إلا أبطأك، فنزلت - ما ودعك ربك وما قلى - .

476. Narrated Jundub Al-Bajalī: A lady said, "O Allāh's Messenger! I see that your friend has delayed. (in conveying Qur'ān) to you." So there was revealed:

Your Lord (O Muḥammad) has neither forsaken you, not hated you.' (93:1–3)

SŪRAT ALAM-NASHRAḤ (The Expansion) XCIV

In the Name of Allāh,

the Most Beneficent, the Most Merciful

(No Ḥadīths were mentioned here)

سورة ألم نشرح

بِسْمِ اللهِ الرَّحْمَنِ الرَّحِيمِ

وَقَالَ مُجَاهِدٌ: وِزْرَكَ فِي الْجَاهِلِيَّةِ. أَنْقَضَ: أَثْقَلَ. مَعَ الْعُسْرِ يُسْرًا، قَالَ ابْنُ عُيَيْنَةَ: أَيْ إِنَّ مَعَ ذَلِكَ الْعُسْرِ يُسْرًا آخَرَ. كَقَوْلِهِ - هَلْ تَرَبَّصُونَ بِنَا إِلَّا إِحْدَى الْحُسْنَيَيْنِ - وَلَنْ يَغْلِبَ عُسْرٌ يُسْرَيْنِ. وَقَالَ مُجَاهِدٌ: فَانْصَبْ فِي حَاجَتِكَ إِلَى رَبِّكَ. وَيُذْكَرُ عَنِ ابْنِ عَبَّاسٍ أَلَمْ نَشْرَحْ لَكَ صَدْرَكَ: شَرَحَ اللهُ صَدْرَهُ لِلْإِسْلَامِ.

SŪRAT AT–TĪN (The Fig) XCV

In the Name of Allāh,

the Most Beneficent, the Most Merciful

سورة والتين

بِسْمِ اللهِ الرَّحْمَنِ الرَّحِيمِ

وَقَالَ مُجَاهِدٌ: هُوَ التِّينُ وَالزَّيْتُونُ الَّذِي يَأْكُلُ النَّاسُ، يُقَالُ: فَمَا يُكَذِّبُكَ، فَمَا الَّذِي يُكَذِّبُكَ بِأَنَّ النَّاسَ يُدَانُونَ بِأَعْمَالِهِمْ، كَأَنَّهُ قَالَ: وَمَنْ يَقْدِرُ عَلَى تَكْذِيبِكَ بِالثَّوَابِ وَالْعِقَابِ؟

477. Narrated Al-Barā' رضي الله عنه: While the Prophet ﷺ was on a journey, he recited Sūrat At-Tīni waz-Zaitūni (95) in one of the first two Rak'āt of the 'Ishā prayer.

٤٧٧ - حَدَّثَنَا حَجَّاجُ بْنُ مِنْهَالٍ: حَدَّثَنَا شُعْبَةُ قَالَ: أَخْبَرَنِي عَدِيٌّ قَالَ: سَمِعْتُ الْبَرَاءَ رَضِيَ اللهُ عَنْهُ: أَنَّ النَّبِيَّ صلى اللهُ عليهِ وسلَّم كَانَ فِي سَفَرٍ

فقرأ في العشاء في إحدى الركعتين بالتين والزيتون تقويم الخلق.

SŪRAT AL-'ALAQ (The Clot) XCVI

سورة اقرأ باسم ربك الذى خلق

وقال قتيبة: حدثنا حماد، عن يحيى بن عتيق، عن الحسن قال: اكتب في المصحف في أول الإمام: بسم الله الرحمن الرحيم، واجعل بين السورتين خطا. وقال مجاهد: ناديه: عشيرته. الزبانية: الملائكة، وقال معمر: الرجعى: المرجع. لنسفعن: قال لنأخذن، ولنسفعن بالنون وهي الخفيفة. سفعت بيده: أخذت.

CHAPTER:–

باب: –

478. Narrated 'Āisha , the wife of the Prophet : The commencement (of the Divine Inspiration) to Allāh's Messenger was in the form of true dreams in his sleep, for he never had a dream but it turned out to be true and clear as the bright daylight. Then he began to like seclusions, so he used to go in seclusion in the cave of Ḥirā' where he used to worship Allāh continuously for many nights before going back to his family to take the necessary provision (of food) for the stay. He

٤٧٨ - حدثنا يحيى بن بكير: حدثنا الليث، عن عقيل، عن ابن شهاب. وحدثني سعيد بن مروان: حدثنا محمد بن عبد العزيز بن أبي رزمة: أخبرنا أبو صالح سلمويه: حدثني عبد الله، عن يونس بن يزيد قال: أخبرني ابن شهاب: أن عروة بن

would come back to (his wife) Khadīja again to take his provision (of food) likewise, till one day he received the Guidance while he was in the cave of Hirā'. An Angel came to him and asked him to read. Allāh's Messenger ﷺ replied, "I do not know how to read." The Prophet ﷺ added, "Then the Angel held me (forcibly) and pressed me so hard that I felt distressed. Then he released me and again asked me to read, and I replied, 'I do not know how to read.' Thereupon he held me again and pressed me for the second time till I felt distressed. He then released me and asked me to read, but again I replied. 'I do not know how to read.' Thereupon he held me for the third time and pressed me till I got distressed, and then he released me and said, 'Read, in the Name of your Lord Who has created (all that exists), has created man out of a clot, Read! And your Lord is the Most Generous. Who has taught (the writing) by the pen, has taught man that which he knew not.' " (96:1-5)

Then Allāh's Messenger ﷺ returned with that experience; and the muscles between his neck and shoulders were trembling till he came upon Khadīja (his wife) and said, "Cover me!" They covered him, and when the state of fear was over, he said to Khadīja, "O Khadīja! What is wrong with me? I was afraid that something bad might happen to me." Then he told her the story. Khadīja said, "Nay! But receive the good tidings! By Allāh, Allāh will never disgrace you, for by Allāh, you keep good relations with your kith and kin, speak the truth, help the poor and the destitute, entertain your guests generously and assist those who are stricken with calamities." Khadīja then took him to

الزُّبَيْرِ أَخْبَرَهُ: أَنَّ عَائِشَةَ زَوْجَ النَّبِيِّ صلى اللهُ عليهِ وسلَّم قَالَتْ: كَانَ أَوَّلُ مَا بُدِئَ بِهِ رَسُولُ اللهِ صلى اللهُ عليهِ وسلَّم الرُّؤْيَا الصَّادِقَةُ فِي النَّوْمِ فَكَانَ لا يَرَى رُؤْيَا إِلاَّ جَاءَتْ مِثْلَ فَلَقِ الصُّبْحِ. ثُمَّ حُبِّبَ إِلَيْهِ الخَلاءُ فَكَانَ يَلْحَقُ بِغَارِ حِرَاءٍ فَيَتَحَنَّثُ فِيهِ. قَالَ: وَالتَّحَنُّثُ التَّعَبُّدُ اللَّيَالِي ذَوَاتِ العَدَدِ قَبْلَ أَنْ يَرْجِعَ إِلَى أَهْلِهِ. وَيَتَزَوَّدُ لِذَلِكَ ثُمَّ يَرْجِعُ إِلَى خَدِيجَةَ. فَيَتَزَوَّدُ بِمِثْلِهَا حَتَّى فَجِئَهُ الحَقُّ وَهُوَ فِي غَارِ حِرَاءٍ فَجَاءَهُ المَلَكُ فَقَالَ اقْرَأْ فَقَالَ: رَسُولُ اللهِ صلى اللهُ عليهِ وسلَّم: مَا أَنَا بِقَارِئٍ، قَالَ فَأَخَذَنِي فَغَطَّنِي حَتَّى بَلَغَ مِنِّي الجُهْدُ. ثُمَّ أَرْسَلَنِي فَقَالَ: اقْرَأْ، قُلْتُ: مَا أَنَا بِقَارِئٍ فَأَخَذَنِي فَغَطَّنِي الثَّانِيَةَ حَتَّى بَلَغَ مِنِّي الجُهْدُ، ثُمَّ أَرْسَلَنِي فَقَالَ: اقْرَأْ، قُلْتُ: مَا أَنَا بِقَارِئٍ فَأَخَذَنِي فَغَطَّنِي الثَّالِثَةَ حَتَّى بَلَغَ مِنِّي الجُهْدُ، ثُمَّ أَرْسَلَنِي فَقَالَ - اقْرَأْ بِاسْمِ رَبِّكَ الَّذِي خَلَقَ خَلَقَ الإِنْسَانَ مِنْ عَلَقٍ اقْرَأْ وَرَبُّكَ الأَكْرَمُ الَّذِي عَلَّمَ بِالقَلَمِ - الآيَاتِ إِلَى قَوْلِهِ - عَلَّمَ الإِنْسَانَ مَا لَمْ يَعْلَمْ - فَرَجَعَ بِهَا رَسُولُ اللهِ صلى اللهُ عليهِ وسلَّم تَرْجُفُ بَوَادِرُهُ حَتَّى دَخَلَ عَلَى خَدِيجَةَ، فَقَالَ: زَمِّلُونِي، فَزَمَّلُوهُ حَتَّى ذَهَبَ عَنْهُ الرَّوْعُ، قَالَ لِخَدِيجَةَ:

Waraqa bin Naufil, the son of Khadija's paternal uncle. Waraqa had been converted to Christianity in the Pre-Islāmic Period and used to write Arabic and write of the Gospel in Arabic as much as Allāh wished him to write. He was an old man and had lost his eyesight. Khadija said (to Waraqa), "O my cousin! Listen to what your nephew is going to say." Waraqa said, "O my nephew! What have you seen?" The Prophet then described whatever he had seen. Waraqa said, "This is the same Angel (Gabriel) who was sent to Moses. I wish I were young." He added some other statement. Allāh's Messenger asked, "Will these people drive me out?" Waraqa said, "Yes, for nobody brought the like of what you have brought, but was treated with hostility. If I were to remain alive till your day (when you start preaching). then I would support you strongly." But a short while later Waraqa died and the Divine Inspiration was paused (stopped) for a while so that Allāh's Messenger was very much grieved.

Narrated Jābir bin 'Abdullāh: While Allāh's Messenger was talking about the period of pause in revelation. he said in his narration. "Once while I was walking, all of a sudden I heard a voice from the sky. I looked up and saw to my surprise, the same Angel as had visited me in the cave of Ḥirā.' He was sitting on a chair between the sky and the earth. I got afraid of him and came back home and said, Wrap me! Wrap me!" So they covered him and then Allāh revealed:—

'O you, wrapped up! Arise and warn and your Lord magnify, and your garments purify and desert

أيْ خَدِيجَةُ، مَا لِي لَقَدْ خَشِيتُ عَلَى نَفْسِي فَأَخْبَرَهَا الخَبَرَ، قَالَتْ خَدِيجَةُ كَلَّا أَبْشِرْ. فَوَاللَّهِ لا يُخْزِيكَ اللَّهُ أَبَدًا، فَوَاللَّهِ إِنَّكَ لَتَصِلُ الرَّحِمَ، وَتَصْدُقُ الحَدِيثَ، وَتَحْمِلُ الكَلَّ، وَتَكْسِبُ المَعْدُومَ، وَتَقْرِي الضَّيْفَ، وَتُعِينُ عَلَى نَوَائِبِ الحَقِّ. فَانْطَلَقَتْ بِهِ خَدِيجَةُ حَتَّى أَتَتْ بِهِ وَرَقَةَ بْنَ نَوْفَلٍ وَهُوَ ابْنُ عَمِّ خَدِيجَةَ أَخِي أَبِيهَا، وَكَانَ امْرَأً تَنَصَّرَ فِي الجَاهِلِيَّةِ، وَكَانَ يَكْتُبُ الكِتَابَ العَرَبِيَّ وَيَكْتُبُ مِنَ الإِنْجِيلِ بِالعَرَبِيَّةِ مَا شَاءَ اللَّهُ أَنْ يَكْتُبَ، وَكَانَ شَيْخًا كَبِيرًا قَدْ عَمِيَ، فَقَالَتْ خَدِيجَةُ: يَا عَمِّ اسْمَعْ مِنَ ابْنِ أَخِيكَ. قَالَ وَرَقَةُ: يَا ابْنَ أَخِي، مَاذَا تَرَى؟ فَأَخْبَرَهُ النَّبِيُّ صَلَّى اللَّهُ عَلَيْهِ وَسَلَّمَ خَبَرَ مَا رَأَى، فَقَالَ وَرَقَةُ: هَذَا النَّامُوسُ الَّذِي أُنْزِلَ عَلَى مُوسَى، لَيْتَنِي أَكُونُ حَيًّا، ذَكَرَ حَرْفًا. قَالَ رَسُولُ اللَّهِ صَلَّى اللَّهُ عَلَيْهِ وَسَلَّمَ: أَوَمُخْرِجِيَّ هُمْ؟ قَالَ وَرَقَةُ: نَعَمْ. لَمْ يَأْتِ رَجُلٌ بِمَا جِئْتَ بِهِ إِلَّا أُوذِيَ، وَإِنْ يُدْرِكْنِي يَوْمُكَ حَيًّا أَنْصُرْكَ نَصْرًا مُؤَزَّرًا. ثُمَّ لَمْ يَنْشَبْ وَرَقَةُ أَنْ تُوُفِّيَ وَفَتَرَ الوَحْيُ فَتْرَةً حَتَّى حَزِنَ رَسُولُ اللَّهِ صَلَّى اللَّهُ عَلَيْهِ وَسَلَّمَ. قَالَ مُحَمَّدُ ابْنُ شِهَابٍ: فَأَخْبَرَنِي أَبُو سَلَمَةَ بْنُ

the idols.' (74:1–5)

Abū Salama said, "(Rijz) are the idols which the people of the Pre-Islāmic period used to worship." After this the revelation started coming frequently and regularly.

عَبْدِ الرَّحْمَنِ أَنَّ جَابِرَ ابْنَ عَبْدِ اللهِ الأَنْصَارِيَّ رَضِيَ اللهُ عَنْهُما قَالَ : قَالَ رَسُولَ اللهُ صلى اللهُ عليهِ وسلَّم وَهُوَ يُحَدِّثُ عَنْ فَتْرَةِ الوَحْيِ ، قَالَ فِي حَدِيثِهِ : بَيْنَا أَنا أَمْشِي سَمِعْتُ صَوْتاً مِنَ السَّماءِ فَرَفَعْتُ بَصَرِي فَإِذَا المَلَكُ الَّذِي جَاءَنِي بِحِرَاءٍ جَالِسٌ عَلَى كُرْسِيٍّ بَيْنَ السَّماءِ والأَرْضِ ، فَفَرِقْتُ مِنْهُ فَرَجَعْتُ فَقُلْتُ : زَمِّلُونِي زَمِّلُونِي ، فَدَثَّرُوهُ . فَأَنْزَلَ اللهُ تَعالى - يا أَيُّها المُدَّثِّرُ قُمْ فَأَنْذِرْ وَرَبَّكَ فَكَبِّرْ وَثِيابَكَ فَطَهِّرْ وَالرُّجْزَ فاهْجُرْ - قَالَ أَبُو سَلَمَةَ : وَهِيَ الأَوْثانُ الَّتِي كانَ أَهْلُ الجاهِلِيَّةِ يَعْبُدُونَ . قالَ : ثُمَّ تَتابَعَ الوَحْيُ .

(346) CHAPTER. The Statement of Allāh تعالى :–
'Has created man from a clot.' (96:2)

بابٌ قَوْلُهُ - خَلَقَ الإِنْسانَ مِنْ عَلَقٍ - .

479. Narrated 'Āisha رضي الله عنها : The commencement of the Divine Inspiration to Allāh's Messenger ﷺ was in the

٤٧٩ - حدَّثَنا ابنُ بُكَيرٍ : حدَّثَنا اللَّيْثُ ، عَنْ عُقَيْلٍ ، عَنِ ابنِ شِهابٍ ، عَنْ عُرْوَةَ : أَنَّ عائِشَةَ رَضِيَ اللهُ عَنْها

form of true dreams. The Angel came to him and said, "Read, in the Name of your Lord Who has created (all that exists), has created man from a clot. Read! And your Lord is Most Generous."
(96:1,2,3)

قالت: أول ما بدئ به رسول الله صلى الله عليه وسلم الرؤيا الصالحة فجاءه الملك، فقال - اقرأ باسم ربك الذى خلق خلق الانسان من علق اقرأ وربك الاكرم -

(347) CHAPTER. The Statement of Allāh :-
'Read! And your Lord is Most Generous." (96:3)

باب قوله - اقرأ وربك الاكرم -.

480. Narrated 'Āisha : The commencement of (the Divine Inspirations to) Allāh's Messenger was in the form of true dreams. The Angel came to him and said, "Read! In the Name of your Lord Who has created all exists), has created man from a clot. Read! And your Lord is Most Generous, Who has taught (the writing) by the pen (the first person to write was Prophet Idris . (96:1–4)

٤٨٠ - حدثنا عبد الله بن محمد: حدثنا عبد الرزاق: أخبرنا معمر، عن الزهرى ح. وقال الليث: حدثنى عقيل: قال محمد: أخبرنى عروة، عن عائشة رضى الله عنها: أول ما بدئ به رسول الله صلى الله عليه وسلم الرؤيا الصادقة، جاءه الملك فقال - اقرأ باسم ربك الذى خلق خلق الانسان من علق اقرأ وربك الاكرم الذى علم بالقلم -.

(348) CHAPTER. 'Who has taught (the writing) by the pen.' (96:4)

باب - الذى علم بالقلم -.

481. Narrated 'Āisha : The Prophet returned to Khadīja and

٤٨١ - حدثنا عبد الله بن يوسف: حدثنا الليث عن عقيل، عن ابن

said, "Wrap me! Wrap me!" (Then the sub-narrator narrated the rest of the narration.)

شهاب قال: سمعت عروة: قالت عائشة رضي الله عنها: فرجع النبي صلى الله عليه وسلم إلى خديجة فقال: زملوني زملوني، فذكر الحديث.

(349) CHAPTER. The Statement of Allāh :–

'Let him beware if he (Abū Jahl) does not cease. We will drag him by the forelock, a lying and sinful forelock!' (96: 15–16)

باب قوله تعالى - كلا لئن لم ينته لنسفعا بالناصية ناصية كاذبة خاطئة -.

482. Narrated Ibn 'Abbās : Abū Jahl said, "If I see Muhammad praying at the Ka'ba, I will tread on his neck." When the Prophet heard of that, he said, "If he does so, the Angels will snatch him away."

٤٨٢ - حدثنا يحيى: حدثنا عبد الرزاق، عن معمر، عن عبد الكريم الجزري، عن عكرمة: قال ابن عباس: قال أبو جهل: لئن رأيت محمدا يصلي عند الكعبة لأطأن على عنقه، فبلغ النبي صلى الله عليه وسلم فقال: لو فعله لأخذته الملائكة، تابعه عمرو بن خالد، عن عبيد الله عن عبد الكريم.

SŪRAT AL-QADR (The Night of Decree) XCVII

"Verily, We have sent it (the Qur'ān) down in the Night of Decree." (97:1)

سورة إنا أنزلناه

يقال المطلوع، هو والطلوع، والمطلع: الموضع الذي يطلع منه. أنزلناه: الهاء كناية عن القرآن. إنا أنزلناه خرج مخرج الجميع،

والمُنْزِلُ هوَ اللهُ ، والعرَبُ تُؤَكِّدُ
فِعْلَ الواحدِ فتَجْعَلُهُ بِلَفْظِ الجَمِيعِ
لِيَكُونَ أثبتَ وأَوْكَدَ .

SŪRAT LAM YAKUN (i.e. AL-BAIYINA) (The Clear Evidence) XCVIII

In the Name of Allāh, the Most Beneficent, the Most Merciful

سورة لم يكن

بِسمْ اللهِ الرَّحْمَنِ الرَّحِيمِ

مُنْفَكِّينَ : زَائِلِينَ . قَيِّمَةٌ : القائمةُ ، دِينُ القَيِّمَةِ . أضافَ الدِّينَ إلى المُؤَنَّث .

483. Narrated Anas bin Mālik : The Prophet said to Ubai (bin Ka'b). "Allāh has ordered me to recite to you:—

> 'Those who disbelieve among the people of the Scripture and among the idolators are not going to stop (from their disbelief.') (Sūra 98)

Ubai said, "Did Allāh mention me by name?" The Prophet said, "Yes." On that, Ubai wept.

٤٨٣ ـ حدَّثَنا مُحَمَّدُ بنُ بَشَّارٍ : حدَّثَنا شُعْبَةُ قالَ : سَمِعْتُ قَتادَةَ ، عَنْ أنَسِ ابنِ مالكٍ رَضِيَ اللهُ عَنْهُ : قالَ النَّبِيُّ صلى اللهُ عليه وسلَّم لأُبَيٍّ : إنَّ اللهَ أمرَنِي أنْ أقرأَ عليكَ ـ لَمْ يَكُنِ الَّذِينَ كَفَرُوا ـ قالَ : وسَمَّانِي ؟ قالَ : نَعَمْ ، فَبَكَى

484. Narrated Anas bin Mālik : The Prophet said to Ubai, "Allāh has ordered me to recite Qur'ān to you." Ubai asked, "Did Allāh mention me by name to you?" The

٤٨٤ ـ حدَّثَنا حَسَّانُ بنُ حَسَّانٍ : حدَّثَنا هَمَّامٌ ، عَنْ قَتادَةَ ، عَنْ أنَسٍ رَضِيَ اللهُ عَنْهُ قالَ : قالَ النَّبِيُّ صلى

Prophet ﷺ said, "Allāh has mentioned your name to me." On that Ubai started weeping. (The sub-narrator) Qatāda added: I have been informed that the Prophet ﷺ recited:—

> "Those who disbelieve among the people of the Scripture," ....to Ubai.

اللهُ عليهِ وسلَّم لأُبيٍّ : إنَّ اللهَ أمرَني أنْ أقرأ عليكَ القرآنَ ، قالَ أُبيٌّ : آللهُ سمَّاني لكَ ؟ قالَ : اللهُ سمَّاكَ لي ، فجعَلَ أبيٌّ يبكي . قالَ قتادَةُ : فأُنبِئتُ أنَّهُ قرأ عليهِ ـ لمْ يكُنِ الذينَ كفَرُوا مِنْ أهلِ الكِتابِ ـ .

485. Narrated Anas bin Mālik (رضي الله عنه): Allāh's Prophet ﷺ said to Ubai bin Ka'b, "Allāh has ordered me to recite Qur'ān to you." Ubai said, "Did Allāh mention me by name to you?" The Prophet ﷺ said, "Yes." Ubai said, "Have I been mentioned by the Lord of the Worlds?" The Prophet ﷺ said, "Yes." Then Ubai burst into tears.

٤٨٥ ـ حدثنا أحمدُ بنُ داوُدَ أبو جعفرٍ المُنادي : حدثنا رَوْحٌ : حدثنا سعيدُ بنُ أبي عرُوبةَ ، عنْ قتادَةَ ، عنْ أنسِ بنِ مالكٍ : أنَّ نبيَّ اللهِ صلى اللهُ عليهِ وسلَّم قالَ لأُبيِّ بنِ كعْبٍ : إنَّ اللهَ أمرَني أنْ أُقرِئكَ القرآنَ ، قالَ : آللهُ سمَّاني لكَ ؟ قالَ : نعَمْ ، قالَ : وقدْ ذُكِرْتُ عِندَ ربِّ العالمينَ ؟ قالَ : نعَمْ ، فذَرَفتْ عيناهُ .

SŪRAT IDHĀ-ZULZILAT (The Convulsion) XCIX

In the Name of Allāh, the Most Beneficent, the Most Merciful

سورة إذا زلزلت

بِسْمِ اللهِ الرَّحْمَنِ الرَّحِيمِ

(350) CHAPTER. The Statement of Allāh تعالى :—

> 'So whoever does good equal to the weight of an atom (or a smallest ant) shall see it (its reward).' (99:7)

بابٌ قوْلُهُ ـ فمَنْ يعْمَلْ مِثْقالَ ذَرَّةٍ خيرًا يرَهُ ـ يُقالُ أوْحَى إليْها ، ووَحَى لها ، ووَحَى إليْها واحِدٌ .

486. Narrated Abū Huraira رضي الله عنه : Allāh's Messenger ﷺ said, "Horses are kept for one of three purposes: A man may keep them (for Allāh's Cause) to receive a reward in the Hereafter; another may keep them as a means of protection; and a third may keep them to be a burden for him. As for the man for whom the horse is a source of reward, he is the one who ties it for Allāh's Cause, and he ties it with a long rope in a pasture or a garden, then, whatever it eats or drinks in that pasture or garden will be added to his good deeds. And if it breaks its rope and jumps over one or two hills, then, for all its footsteps and its manure, good deeds will be written for him. And if it passes by a river and drinks of its water though its owner had no intention to water it from that river, even then he will have good deeds written for him. So that horse will be (a source of) reward for such a man.

If a man ties a horse for earning his livelihood and abstaining from asking others for help and he does not forget Allāh's right, i.e. pays its Zakāt and gives it to be used in Allāh's Cause, then that horse will be a means of protection for him.

But if a man ties it out of pride and to show off and to excite others, then that horse will be a burden (of sins) for him." Then Allāh's Messenger ﷺ was asked regarding donkeys. He replied, "Nothing has been revealed to me except this comprehensive Verse which includes everything:—

'So whoever does good equal to

٤٨٦ ـ حدَّثنا إسماعيلُ بنُ عبدِ الله: حدَّثنا مالكٌ، عن زيدِ بنِ أسلمَ عن صالحٍ السَّمان، عن أبي هريرةَ رضيَ اللهُ عنهُ: أنَّ رسولَ اللهِ صلى اللهُ عليه وسلَّم قال: الخيلُ لثلاثةٍ: لرجلٍ أجرٌ، ولرجلٍ سِترٌ، وعلى رجلٍ وِزرٌ. فأمَّا الذي له أجرٌ فرجلٌ ربطَها في سبيلِ اللهِ فأطالَ في مرجٍ أو روضةٍ فما أصابتْ في طِيَلِها ذلك في المرجِ والروضةِ كان له حسناتٍ، ولو أنَّها قطعتْ طِيَلَها فاستنَّتْ شَرَفاً أو شرفينِ كانتْ آثارُها وأرواثُها حسناتٍ له، ولو أنَّها مرَّتْ بنهرٍ فشربتْ منه ولم يُرِدْ أنْ يَسقيَ به كان ذلك حسناتٍ له، فهيَ لذلكَ الرجلِ أجرٌ. ورجلٌ ربطَها تغنِّياً وتعفُّفاً ولم ينسَ حقَّ اللهِ في رقابِها ولا ظهورِها فهيَ له سِترٌ. ورجلٌ ربطَها فخراً ورِئاءً ونِواءً فهيَ على ذلك وِزرٌ. فسُئلَ رسولُ اللهِ صلى اللهُ عليه وسلَّم عن الحُمُرِ، قال: ما أنزلَ اللهُ عليَّ فيها إلَّا هذه الآيةَ الفاذَّةَ الجامعةَ ـ فمنْ يعملْ مثقالَ ذرَّةٍ خيراً يرَهُ ومنْ يعملْ مثقالَ ذرَّةٍ شرًّا يرَهُ ـ.

the weight of an atom (or a smallest ant) shall see it; and whoever does evil equal to the weight of an atom (or a smallest ant,) shall see it.' (99:7-8)

(351) CHAPTER. 'And whoever does evil (even) equal to the weight of an atom (or a smallest ant), shall see it.' (99:8)

باب - وَمَنْ يَعْمَلْ مِثْقَالَ ذَرَّةٍ شَرًّا يَرَهُ -.

487. Narrated Abū Huraira ﷺ: The Prophet ﷺ was asked about donkeys and he replied, "Nothing has been revealed to me regarding donkeys except this comprehensive Verse which includes everything:—

'So whoever does good equal to the weight of an atom (or a smallest ant) shall see it; And whoever, does evil equal to the weight of an atom (or a smallest ant) shall see it.' (99:7-8)

٤٨٧ - حدثنا يحيى بن سليمان قال: حدثني ابن وهب قال: أخبرني مالك، عن زيد بن أسلم، عن أبي صالح السمان عن أبي هريرة رضي الله عنه: سُئِلَ النبي صلى الله عليه وسلم عن الحُمُر فقال: لم يُنْزَلْ عليَّ فيها شيء إلا هذه الآية الجامعة الفاذة - فمن يعمل مثقال ذرة خيرا يره ومن يعمل مثقال ذرة شرا يره -.

SŪRAT AL-'ĀDIYĀT (THOSE WHO RUN):

C

(No Ḥadīths were mentioned here)

سورة والعاديات

وقال مجاهد الكنود: الكفور، يقال - فأثرن به نقعا - رفعنا به غبارا -.

لحُبُّ الخَيْرِ - مِنْ أَجْلِ حُبِّ الخَيْرِ ، لَشَدِيدٌ : لَبَخِيلٌ ، وَيُقَالُ لِلْبَخِيلِ : شَدِيدٌ . حُصِّلَ مُيِّزَ .

SŪRAT AL-QĀRIʻA
(The Striking (Hour)):
CI
(No Ḥadīths were mentioned here)

سورة القارعة

كالفَرَاشِ المَبْثُوثِ :كَغَوْغاءِ الجَرَادِ يَرْكَبُ بَعْضُهُ بَعْضًا، كَذَلِكَ النَّاسُ يَجُولُ بَعْضُهُمْ فِى بَعْضٍ . كالعِهْنِ : كأَلْوانِ العِهْنِ ، وَقَرَأَ عَبْدُاللهِ كالصُّوفِ .

SŪRAT–ALHĀKUM (AT–TAKĀTHUR):
CII
In the Name of Allāh,
the Most Beneficent, the Most Merciful
Ibn ʻAbbās said,"'At-Takāthur' (piling up) means piling up money and children."

سورة ألهاكم

بِسْمِ اللهِ الرَّحْمَنِ الرَّحِيمِ
وَقَالَ ابنُ عَبَّاسٍ : التَّكاثُرُ مِنَ الأَمْوَالِ والأَوْلادِ .

SŪRAT AL-ʻAṢR
(The time)
CIII
No' CIII

سورة والعصر

وَقَالَ يَحْيَى : العَصْرُ : الدَّهْرُ ، أَقْسَمَ بِهِ .

SŪRAT AL–HUMAZA
(The Slanderer)
CIV
In the Name of Allāh,
the Most Beneficent, the Most Merciful

سورة ويل لكل همزة

بِسْمِ اللهِ الرَّحْمَنِ الرَّحِيمِ

Al-Ḥuṭama is the name of the Fire, similar to Saqar and Laẓā.

الحُطَمَةُ : اسْمُ النَّارِ ، مِثْلُ سَقَرَ وَلَظَى .

SŪART–AL–FĪL
(The Elephant)
CV
(No. Ḥadīths were mentioned here)

سورة ألم تر

قالَ مُجَاهِدٌ : ألمْ تَرَ : ألم تَعلَمْ . قالَ مُجَاهِدٌ : أبابِيلَ : مُتَتَابِعَةً ، مُجْتَمِعَةً . وَقَالَ ابنُ عَبَّاسٍ : مِنْ سِجِّيلٍ : هِيَ سَنْكِ وكِيلْ .

SŪRAT (QURAISH)
(For the taming):
CVI
(No Ḥadīths were mentioned here)

سورة لإيلاف

وَقَالَ مُجَاهِدٌ : لإيلافِ : ألِفُوا ذَلكَ فَلا يَشُقُّ عَلَيْهِمْ فِي الشِّتاءِ والصَّيْفِ . وآمَنَهُمْ مِنْ كُلِّ عَدُوِّهِم فِي حَرَمِهِمْ .

SŪRAT–AL–MĀ'ŪN
(Neighbourly needs)
(Small Kindnesses):
CVII
(No Ḥadīths were mentioned here)

سورة أرأيت

وَقَالَ ابنُ عُيَيْنَةَ - لإيلافِ - لِنِعْمَتِي عَلَى قُرَيْشٍ . وَقَالَ مُجَاهِدٌ : يَدُعُّ : يَدْفَعُ عَنْ حَقِّهِ ، يُقَالُ هُوَ مِنْ دَعَعْتُ . يُدَعُّونَ : يُدْفَعُونَ . ساهُونَ : لاهُونَ . وَالمَاعُونَ : المَعْرُوفَ كُلُّهُ . وَقَالَ بَعْضُ العَرَبِ : المَاعُونُ : المَاءُ . وقال عِكْرِمَةُ : أعْلاها الزَّكَاةُ المَفْرُوضَةُ،

وَأَدَّاهَا عَارِيَةُ الْمَتَاعِ.

SŪRAT AL-KAUTHAR
(Abundance):
CVIII

سورة إنا أعطيناك الكوثر

وَقَالَ ابْنُ عَبَّاسٍ: شَانِئَكَ: عَدُوُّكَ.

488 Narrated Anas ﷺ: When the Prophet ﷺ was made to ascend to the Heavens, he said (after his return), "I came upon a river the banks of which were made of tents of hollow pearls. I asked Gabriel. What is this (river)?' He replied, 'This is the Kauthar.'

٤٨٨ - حَدَّثَنَا آدَمُ: حَدَّثَنَا شَيْبَانُ: حَدَّثَنَا قَتَادَةُ، عَنْ أَنَسٍ رَضِيَ اللهُ عَنْهُ قَالَ: لَمَّا عُرِجَ بِالنَّبِيِّ صلى الله عليه وسلم إِلَى السَّمَاءِ قَالَ: أَتَيْتُ عَلَى نَهَرٍ حَافَتَاهُ قِبَابُ اللُّؤْلُؤِ مُجَوَّفٌ، فَقُلْتُ: مَا هَذَا يَا جِبْرِيلُ؟ قَالَ: هَذَا الْكَوْثَرُ.

489. Narrated Abū 'Ubaida: I asked 'Āisha ﷺ regarding the verse:— 'Verily we have granted you the Kauthar.' She replied, "The Kauthar is a river which has been given to your Prophet ﷺ on the banks of which there are (tents of) hollow pearls and its utensils are as numberless as the stars."

٤٨٩ - حَدَّثَنَا خَالِدُ بْنُ يَزِيدَ الْكَاهِلِيُّ: حَدَّثَنَا إِسْرَائِيلُ، عَنْ أَبِي إِسْحَاقَ، عَنْ أَبِي عُبَيْدَةَ، عَنْ عَائِشَةَ رَضِيَ اللهُ عَنْهَا قَالَ: سَأَلْتُهَا عَنْ قَوْلِهِ تَعَالَى - إِنَّا أَعْطَيْنَاكَ الْكَوْثَرَ - قَالَتْ: هُوَ نَهَرٌ أُعْطِيَهُ نَبِيُّكُمْ صلى الله عليه وسلم، شَاطِئَاهُ عَلَيْهِ دُرٌّ مُجَوَّفٌ، آنِيَتُهُ كَعَدَدِ النُّجُومِ. رَوَاهُ زَكَرِيَّا وَأَبُو الْأَحْوَصِ وَمُطَرِّفٌ عَنْ أَبِي إِسْحَاقَ.

490. Narrated Abū Bishr: Sa'īd bin Jubair said that Ibn 'Abbās said about Al-Kauthar. "That is the good which Allāh has bestowed upon His Messenger." I said to Sa'īd bin Jubair. "But the people claim that it is a river in Paradise." Sa'īd said, "The river in Paradise is part of the good which Allāh has bestowed on His Messenger."

٤٩٠ ـ حدثنا يعقوب بن إبراهيم : حدثنا هشيم : حدثنا أبو بشر ، عن سعيد بن جبير ، عن ابن عباس رضى الله عنهما أنه قال فى الكوثر : هو الخير الذى أعطاه الله إياه . قال أبو بشر : قلت لسعيد بن جبير : فإن الناس يزعمون أنه نهر فى الجنة ، فقال سعيد : النهر الذى فى الجنة من الخير الذى أعطاه الله إياه .

SŪRAT "SAY! O YOU DISBELIEVERS." CIX

(No Ḥadīths were mentioned here)

سورة قل يا أيها الكفرون

يقال ـ لكم دينكم ـ الكفر ولى دين ـ الإسلام . ولم يقل دينى لأن الآيات بالنون فحذفت الياء كما قال يهدين ويشفين . وقال غيره :ـ لا أعبد ما تعبدون ـ الآن ولا أجيبكم فيما بقى من عمرى ـ ولا أنتم عابدون ما أعبد ـ وهم الذين قال : وليزيدن كثيرا منهم ما أنزل إليك من ربك طغيانا وكفرا ـ .

SŪRAT AN-NAṢR (The Help): CX

In the Name of Allāh, the Most Beneficent, the Most Merciful

"When comes the Help of Allāh (to you

سورة إذا جاء نصر الله

بسم الله الرحمن الرحيم

O Muḥammad against your enemies) and the conquest (of Mecca). (110:1)

491. Narrated 'Āisha : "When the "Sūrat-An-Naṣr", 'When comes the Help of Allāh and the conquest,' had been revealed to the Prophet he did not offer any prayer except that he said therein, "Subḥānka Rabbanā wa biḥamdika; Allāhumma ighfirlī (I testify the Uniqueness of our Lord, and all the praises are for Him: O Allāh, forgive me!")

٤٩١ - حدثنا الحسن بن الربيع: حدثنا أبو الأحوص، عن الأعمش، عن أبي الضحى، عن مسروق، عن عائشة رضي الله عنها قالت: ما صلى النبي صلى الله عليه وسلم صلاة بعد أن نزلت عليه - إذا جاء نصر الله والفتح - إلا يقول فيها: سبحانك ربنا وبحمدك، اللهم اغفر لي.

492. Narrated 'Āisha :Allāh's Messenger used to say very often in bowing and prostration (during his prayers), Subḥānka Allāhumma Rabbanā wa biḥamdika; Allāhumma ighfirlī," according to the order of the Qur'ān.

٤٩٢ - حدثنا عثمان بن أبي شيبة: حدثنا جرير، عن منصور، عن أبي الضحى، عن مسروق، عن عائشة رضي الله عنها قالت: كان رسول الله صلى الله عليه وسلم يكثر أن يقول في ركوعه وسجوده: سبحانك اللهم ربنا وبحمدك، اللهم اغفر لي، يتأول القرآن

(352) CHAPTER. The Statement of Allāh:

'And you see the people enter Allāh's religion (Islām) in crowds.' (110:2)

باب قوله - ورأيت الناس يدخلون في دين الله أفواجا -.

493. Narrated Ibn 'Abbās :
'Umar asked the people regarding Allāh's Statement: -

> 'When comes the Help of Allāh (to you O Muḥammad against your enemies) and the conquest of Mecca. (110:1)

They replied, "It indicates the future conquest of towns and palaces (by Muslims)." 'Umar said, "What do you say about it, O Ibn 'Abbās?" I replied, "(This Sūrat) indicates the termination of the life of Muḥammad .. Through it he was informed of the nearness of his death."

٤٩٣ ـ حدَّثنا عبدُ الله بنُ أبي شيبةَ : حدَّثنا عبدُ الرحمنِ ، عن سفيانَ ، عن حبيبِ بنِ أبي ثابتٍ ، عن سعيدِ بنِ جُبيرٍ ، عن ابنِ عبّاسٍ : أنّ عمرَ رضيَ اللهُ عنه سألهم عن قوله تعالى ـ إذا جاءَ نصرُ اللهِ والفتحُ ـ قالوا : فتحُ المدائنِ والقصورِ . قالَ : ما تقولُ يا ابنَ عبّاسٍ ؟ قالَ : أجلٌ أو مثلٌ ضُربَ لمحمّدٍ صلى الله عليه وسلّم . نُعيتْ لهُ نفسُهُ .

(353) CHAPTER. The Statement of Allāh :–

> 'So, celebrate the Praises of your Lord, And ask for His forgiveness. Verily! He is the One Who accepts the repentance and forgives.
> (110:3)

بابُ قولِه ـ فسبِّحْ بحمدِ ربِّكَ واستغفرْهُ إنّهُ كانَ توّابا ـ توّابٌ على العبادِ . والتوّابُ منَ النّاسِ : التائبُ منَ الذّنبِ .

494. Narrated Ibn 'Abbās :
'Umar used to make me sit with the elderly men who had fought in the Battle of Badr. Some of them felt it (did not like that) and said to 'Umar "Why do you bring in this boy to sit with us while we have sons like him?" 'Umar replied, "Because of what you know of his position (i.e. his religious knowledge.)" One day 'Umar called me and made me sit in the gathering of those people; and I think that he called me just to show them. (my religious know ledge). 'Umar then asked them (in

٤٩٤ ـ حدَّثنا موسى بنُ إسماعيلَ : حدَّثنا أبو عوانةَ ، عن أبي بشرٍ ، عن سعيدِ بنِ جُبيرٍ ، عن ابنِ عبّاسٍ قالَ : كانَ عمرُ يُدخلُني معَ أشياخِ بدرٍ فكأنَّ بعضَهم وجدَ في نفسِه فقالَ : لمَ تُدخلُ هذا معنا ولنا أبناءٌ مثلُهُ ؟ فقالَ عمرُ : إنّهُ منْ حيثُ علمتُم ، فدعا ذاتَ يومٍ فأدخلَهُ معَهم فما رُؤيتُ أنّهُ دعاني يومئذٍ إلاّ ليُريَهم ،

my presence). "What do you say about the interpretation of the Statement of Allāh ﷻ :–

> 'When comes Help of Allāh (to you O, Muḥammad ﷺ against your enemies) and the conquest (of Mecca). (110:1)

Some of them said, "We are ordered to praise Allāh and ask for His forgiveness when Allāh's Help and the conquest (of Mecca) comes to us." Some others kept quiet and did not say anything. On that, 'Umar asked me, "Do you say the same, O Ibn 'Abbās?" I replied, "No." He said, "What do you say then?" I replied, "That is the sign of the death of Allāh's Messenger ﷺ which Allāh informed him of. Allāh said:–

> '(O Muḥammad) When comes the Help of Allāh (to you against your enemies) and the conquest (of Mecca) (which is the sign of your death)– – – 'You should celebrate the praises of your Lord and ask for His Forgiveness, and He is the One Who accepts the repentance and forgives.' " (110:3)

On that 'Umar said, "I do not know anything about it other than what you have said."

قالَ : ما تَقُولُونَ فى قَوْلِ اللهِ تَعالى - إِذَا جاءَ نَصْرُ اللهِ والفَتْحُ - فقالَ بَعْضُهُمْ : أُمِرْنا نَحْمَدُ اللهَ وَنَسْتَغْفِرُهُ إذا جاءَ نَصْرُنا وفُتِحَ علَيْنا. وسَكَتَ بَعْضُهُمْ فلَمْ يَقُلْ شَيْئًا . فقالَ لى : أكَذَاكَ تَقُولُ يا ابنَ عبّاسٍ ؟ فقُلْتُ : لا ، قالَ : فمَا تَقُولُ ؟ قُلْتُ : هُوَ أجَلُ رَسُولِ اللهِ صلى اللهُ عليه وسلّم أعْلَمَهُ لهُ . قالَ - إِذَا جاءَ نَصْرُ اللهِ والفَتْحُ - وَذَلكَ عَلامَةُ أجَلِكَ - فَسَبِّحْ بِحَمْدِ رَبِّكَ وَاسْتَغْفِرْهُ إنّهُ كانَ تَوّابًا - فقالَ عُمَرُ : ما أعْلَمُ مِنْها إلاّ ما تَقُولُ .

SŪRAT: 'PERISH THE HANDS OF ABŪ LAHAB' CXI

سورة تبت يدا أبي لهب

In the Name of Allāh, the Most Beneficent, the Most Merciful

بِسْمِ اللهِ الرَّحْمَنِ الرَّحِيمِ

تَبَابٌ : خُسْرَانٌ . تَتْبِيبٌ : تَدْمِيرٌ .

495. Narrated Ibn 'Abbās : When the Verse:—

'And warn your tribe of near kindred.' (26:214)

was revealed. Allāh's Messenger went out, and when he had ascended Aṣ-Ṣafā mountain, he shouted, "O Ṣabāḥāh! (1)" The people said, "Who is that?" "Then they gathered around him, whereupon he said, "Do you see? If I inform you that cavalrymen are proceeding up the side of this mountain, will you believe me?" They said, "We have never heard you telling a lie." Then he said, "I am a plain warner to you of a coming severe punishment." Abū Lahab said, "May you perish! You gathered us only for this reason?" Then Abū Lahab went away. So the "Sūrat:—ul—LAHAB"

'Perish the hands of Abū Lahab!' was revealed. (111:1)

٤٩٥ ـ حَدَّثَنَا يُوسُفُ بْنُ مُوسَى: حَدَّثَنَا أَبُو أُسَامَةَ : حَدَّثَنَا الأَعْمَشُ : حَدَّثَنَا عَمْرُو بْنُ مُرَّةَ ، عَنْ سَعِيدِ بْنِ جُبَيْرٍ ، عَنِ ابْنِ عَبَّاسٍ رَضِيَ اللهُ عَنْهُمَا قَالَ : لَمَّا نَزَلَتْ ـ وَأَنْذِرْ عَشِيرَتَكَ الأَقْرَبِينَ ـ وَرَهْطَكَ مِنْهُمُ الْمُخْلَصِينَ ، خَرَجَ رَسُولُ اللهِ صلى الله عليه وسلَّم حَتَّى صَعِدَ الصَّفَا فَهَتَفَ يَا صَبَاحَاهُ ، فَقَالُوا: مَنْ هَذَا؟ فَاجْتَمَعُوا إِلَيْهِ فَقَالَ : أَرَأَيْتُمْ إِنْ أَخْبَرْتُكُمْ أَنَّ خَيْلاً تَخْرُجُ مِنْ سَفْحِ هَذَا الْجَبَلِ أَكُنْتُمْ مُصَدِّقِيَّ؟ قَالُوا: مَا جَرَّبْنَا عَلَيْكَ كَذِبًا . قَالَ : فَإِنِّي نَذِيرٌ لَكُمْ بَيْنَ يَدَيْ عَذَابٍ عَظِيمٍ . قَالَ أَبُو لَهَبٍ : تَبًّا لَكَ ، مَا جَمَعْتَنَا إِلاَّ لِهَذَا؟ ثُمَّ قَامَ فَنَزَلَتْ ـ تَبَّتْ يَدَا أَبِي لَهَبٍ وَتَبَّ ـ وَقَدْ تَبَّ هَكَذَا قَرَأَهَا الأَعْمَشُ يَوْمَئِذٍ .

(1) "O Ṣabāḥāh!" is an Arabic expression used when one appeals for help or draws the attention of others to some danger.

(354) CHAPTER. The Statement of Allāh تعالى :–

'And perish he! His wealth and his children will not benefit him.

(111:1–2)

باب قوله - وتب ما أغنى عنه
ماله وما كسب - .

496. Narrated Ibn 'Abbās رضي الله عنهما : The Prophet صلى الله عليه وسلم went out towards Al-Baṭ-ḥā' and ascended the mountain and shouted, "O Ṣabāḥāh!" So the Quraish people gathered around him. He said, "Do you see? If I tell you that an enemy is going to attack you in the morning or in the evening, will you believe me?" They replied, "Yes." He said, "Then I am a plain warner to you of a coming severe punishment." Abū Lahab said, "Is it for this reason that you have gathered us? May you perish!" Then Allāh عزّ وجلّ revealed:–

'Perish the hands of Abū Lahab!'

٤٩٦ - حدثنا محمد بن سلام :
أخبرنا أبو معاوية : حدثنا الأعمش ،
عن عمرو بن مرة ، عن سعيد بن
جبير ، عن ابن عباس : أن النبي صلى الله
عليه وسلم خرج إلى البطحاء فصعد إلى
الجبل فنادى : يا صباحاه ، فاجتمعت
إليه قريش ، فقال : أرأيتم إن
حدثتكم أن العدو مصبحكم أو
ممسيكم ، أكنتم تصدقوني ؟ قالوا :
نعم ، قال : فإني نذير لكم بين يدي
عذاب شديد . فقال أبو لهب : ألهذا
جمعتنا ؟ تبا لك ، فأنزل الله عز وجل -
تبت يدا أبي لهب - إلى آخرها .

(355) CHAPTER. The Statement of Allāh تعالى :–

'He (Abū Lahab) will be burnt in a fire of blazing flame!'

(111:3)

باب قوله - سيصلى نارا ذات
لهب - .

497. Narrated Ibn 'Abbās رضي الله عنهما : Abū Lahab said, "May you perish! Is it'

٤٩٧ - حدثنا عمر بن حفص :
حدثنا أبي : حدثنا الأعمش : حدثني عمرو

for this that you have gathered us?" So there was revealed:—

'Perish the hands of Abū Lahab!'

ابنُ مُرَّةَ، عَنْ سَعِيدِ ابنِ جُبَيْرٍ، عَنِ ابنِ عَبَّاسٍ رَضِيَ اللهُ عَنْهُما: قالَ أَبُو لَهَبٍ: تَبًّا لَكَ، أَلِهَذَا جَمَعْتَنا؟ فَنَزَلَتْ ـ تَبَّتْ يَدَا أَبِي لَهَبٍ ـ.

(356) CHAPTER. 'And his wife too, who carries wood as fuel.' (111:4)
Mujāhid said, 'Carries the wood means that she used to slander (the Prophet ﷺ):—

"In her neck is a twisted rope of palm-leaf fibre (111:5)
i.e. the chain which is in the Fire."

باب ـ وَامْرَأَتُهُ حَمَّالَةُ الحَطَبِ ـ

وَقَالَ مُجاهِدٌ: حَمَّالَةُ الحَطَبِ تَمْشِي بِالنَّمِيمَةِ ـ فِي جِيدِها حَبْلٌ مِنْ مَسَدٍ ـ يُقالُ مِنْ مَسَدٍ: لِيفِ المُقْلِ وَهِيَ السِّلْسِلَةُ الَّتِي فِي النَّارِ.

SURAT (The Unity): SAY: HE IS ALLĀH, THE ONE CXII

In the Name of Allāh,
the Most Beneficent, the Most Merciful

(It is said that 'Aḥad' in Arabic in the Verse, cannot be pronounced as 'Aḥdun', i.e. 'Wāḥdun')

سورة قل هو الله أحد

بِسْمِ اللهِ الرَّحْمَنِ الرَّحِيمِ

يُقالُ: لا يُنَوَّنُ أَحَدٌ: أَيْ وَاحِدٌ.

498. Narrated Abū Huraira رضي الله عنه : The Prophet ﷺ said, "Allāh said: 'The son of Ādam tells a lie against Me, though he hasn't the right to do so. He abuses me though he hasn't the right to do so. As for his telling a lie against Me, it is his saying that I will not recreate him as I created him for the first time. In fact, the

٤٩٨ ـ حَدَّثَنا أَبُو اليَمانِ: حَدَّثَنا شُعَيْبٌ: حَدَّثَنا أَبُو الزِّنادِ، عَنِ الأَعْرَجِ، عَنْ أَبِي هُرَيْرَةَ رَضِيَ اللهُ عَنْهُ، عَنِ النَّبِيِّ صلى اللهُ عليهِ وسلَّمَ قالَ: قالَ اللهُ كَذَّبَنِي ابنُ آدَمَ وَلَمْ يَكُنْ لَهُ ذَلِكَ وَشَتَمَنِي وَلَمْ يَكُنْ ذَلِكَ لَهُ فَأَمَّا تَكْذِيبُهُ إِيَّايَ فَقَوْلُهُ لَنْ يُعِيدَنِي

first creation was not easier for Me than new creation. As for his abusing Me, it is his saying that Allāh has begotten children, while I am the One, the Self-Sufficient Master Whom all creatures need, I beget not, nor was I begotten, and there is none like unto Me."

كما بدأني، وليس أول الخلق بأهون علي من إعادته. وأما شتمه إياي فقوله اتخذ الله ولدا، وأنا الأحد الصمد لم ألد ولم أولد ولم يكن لي كفوا أحد

(357) CHAPTER. The Statement of Allāh ﷻ :–

"Allāh, the Self-Sufficient Master Whom all creatures need."

(112:2)

باب قوله - الله الصمد - والعرب تسمي أشرافها الصمد. قال أبو وائل: هو السيد الذي انتهى سودده.

499. Narrated Abū Huraira رضي الله عنه : Allāh's Messenger ﷺ said, "Allāh said:– 'The son of Adam tells a lie against Me and he hasn't the right to do so; and he abuses me and he hasn't the right to do so. His telling a lie against Me is his saying that I will not recreate him as I created him for the first time; and his abusing Me is his saying that Allāh has begotten children, while I am the Self-Sufficient Master, Whom all creatures need, Who begets not nor was He begotten, and there is none like unto Me."

٤٩٩ - حدثنا إسحاق بن منصور: حدثنا عبد الرزاق: أخبرنا معمر، عن همام، عن أبي هريرة قال: قال رسول الله صلى الله عليه وسلم: كذبني ابن آدم ولم يكن له ذلك، وشتمني ولم يكن له ذلك. أما تكذيبه إياي أن يقول إني لن أعيده كما بدأته، وأما شتمه إياي أن يقول اتخذ الله ولدا. وأنا الصمد الذي لم ألد ولم أولد ولم يكن لي كفوا أحد.

(358) CHAPTER. 'He begets not nor was He begotten, and there is none for

باب لم يلد ولم يولد ولم يكن له كفوا أحد - كفوا وكفيئا

like unto Him.' (112:3–4)

وكفاء واحد.

SŪRAT AL-FALAQ (The Dawn): CXIII

سورة قل أعوذ برب الفلق

In the Name of Allāh, the Most Beneficent, the Most Merciful

بسم الله الرحمن الرحيم

وقال مجاهد: الفلق: الصبح. غاسق: الليل - إذا وقب - غروب الشمس، يقال أبين من فرق وفلق الصبح، وقب: إذا دخل فى كل شىء وأظلم.

500. Narrated Zirr bin Ḥubaish: I asked Ubaī bin Ka'b regarding the two Mu'wwidhāt (Sūrats of taking refuge with Allāh). He said, "I asked the Prophet ﷺ about them, He said, 'These two Sūrats have been recited to me and I have recited them (and are present in the Qur'ān).' So, we say as Allāh's Messenger ﷺ said (i.e., they are part of the Qur'ān)."

٥٠٠ - حدثنا قتيبة بن سعيد: حدثنا سفيان، عن عاصم وعبدة عن زر بن حبيش قال: سألت أبى بن كعب عن المعوذتين فقال: سألت النبى صلى الله عليه وسلم فقال: قيل لى فقلت فنحن نقول كما قال رسول الله صلى الله عليه وسلم:

SŪRAT AN–NĀS (Mankind) CXIV

سورة قل اعوذ برب الناس

وقال ابن عباس: الوسواس: إذا ولد خنسه الشيطان فإذا ذكر الله عز وجل ذهب. وإذا لم يذكر الله ثبت على قلبه.

501. Narrated Zirr bin Ḥubaish: I asked Ubai bin Ka'b, "O Abū Al-Mundhir! Your brother, Ibn Mas'ūd said so-and-so (i.e., the two Mu'awwidhāt do not belong to the Qur'ān)." Ubai said, "I asked Allāh's Messenger ﷺ about them, and he said, 'They have been revealed to me, and I have recited them (as a part of the Qur'ān),' " So Ubai added, "So we say as Allāh's Messenger ﷺ has said."

٥٠١ ـ حَدَّثَنَا عَلِيُّ بْنُ عَبْدِ اللهِ : حَدَّثَنَا سُفْيَانُ : حَدَّثَنَا عَبْدَةُ بْنُ أَبِي لُبَابَةَ ، عَنْ زِرِّ بْنِ حُبَيْشٍ . وَحَدَّثَنَا عَاصِمٌ ، عَنْ زِرٍّ قَالَ : سَأَلْتُ أُبَيَّ بْنَ كَعْبٍ قُلْتُ : أَبَا الْمُنْذِرِ إِنَّ ، أَخَاكَ ابْنَ مَسْعُودٍ يَقُولُ كَذَا وَكَذَا ، فَقَالَ أُبَيٌّ : سَأَلْتُ رَسُولَ اللهِ صلى اللهُ عليهِ وسلَّم فَقَالَ لِي : قِيلَ لِي فَقُلْتُ ، قَالَ : فَنَحْنُ نَقُولُ كَمَا قَالَ رَسُولُ اللهِ صلى اللهُ عليهِ وسلَّم .

In the Name of Allāh,
the Most Beneficent, the Most Merciful

بسم الله الرحمن الرحيم

LXI THE BOOK OF THE VIRTUES OF THE QUR'ĀN:

كتاب فضائل القرآن

(1) CHAPTER. How the Divine Inspirations used to be revealed and what was the first thing revealed (to the Messenger ﷺ).

باب كيف نزل الوحي وأول ما نزل؟ قال ابن عباس: المهيمن: الأمين، القرآن أمين على كل كتاب قبله.

502. Narrated ‘Āisha and Ibn ‘Abbās (رضي الله عنهم): The Prophet ﷺ remained in Mecca for ten years, during which the Qur'ān used to be revealed to him; and he stayed in Medīna for ten years.

٥٠٢ - حدثنا عبيد الله بن موسى، عن شيبان، عن يحيى، عن أبي سلمة قال: أخبرتني عائشة وابن عباس رضي الله عنهم قالا: لبث النبي صلى الله عليه وسلم بمكة عشر سنين ينزل عليه القرآن، وبالمدينة عشر سنين.

503. Narrated Abū ‘Uthmān: I was informed that Gabriel came to the Prophet ﷺ while Um Salama was with him. Gabriel started talking (to the Prophet ﷺ). Then the Prophet ﷺ asked Um Salama, "Who is this?" She replied, "He is Diḥya (al-Kalbi)." When Gabriel

٥٠٣ - حدثنا موسى بن إسماعيل: حدثنا معتمر قال: سمعت أبي، عن أبي عثمان قال: أنبئت أن جبريل أتى النبي صلى الله عليه وسلم وعنده أم سلمة فجعل يتحدث فقال لأم

had left, Um Salama said, "By Allāh, I did not take him for anybody other than him (i.e. Diḥya) till I heard the sermon of the Prophet ﷺ wherein he informed about the news of Gabriel." The sub-narrator asked Abū 'Uthmān: From whom have you heard that? Abū 'Uthmān said: From Usāma bin Zaid.

سَلَمَةَ: مَنْ هَذَا؟ أَوْ كما قال. قالَتْ: هَذَا دِحْيَةُ، فَلَمَّا قَامَ قالَتْ: وَاللهِ ما حَسِبْتُهُ إلاَّ إيَّاهُ حَتَّى سَمِعْتُ خُطْبَةَ النَّبِيِّ صلى اللهُ عليه وسلَّم يُخْبِرُ بِخَبَرِ جِبْرِيلَ أَوْ كَمَا قالَ، قالَ أبي: قُلْتُ لأَبِي عُثْمانَ: مِمَّنْ سَمِعْتَ هَذَا؟ قالَ: مِنْ أُسامَةَ بنِ زَيْدٍ.

504. Narrated Abū Huraira (رضي الله عنه): The Prophet ﷺ said, "Every Prophet was given miracles because of which people believed, but what I have been given, is Divine Inspiration which Allāh has revealed to me. So I hope that my followers will outnumber the followers of the other Prophets on the Day of Resurrection."

٥٠٤ ـ حدَّثَنا عَبْدُ اللهِ بنُ يُوسُفَ: حدَّثَنا اللَّيْثُ: حدَّثَنا سَعِيدٌ المَقْبُرِيُّ، عَنْ أبيهِ، عَنْ أبي هُرَيْرَةَ قالَ: قالَ النَّبِيُّ صلى اللهُ عليه وسلَّم: ما مِنَ الأَنْبِياءِ نَبِيٌّ إلاَّ أُعْطِيَ مِنَ الآياتِ ما مِثْلُهُ آمَنَ عَلَيْهِ البَشَرُ، وَإِنَّما كانَ الَّذِي أُوتِيتُ وَحْيًا أَوْحاهُ اللهُ إِلَيَّ، فَأَرْجُو أَنْ أَكُونَ أَكْثَرَهُمْ تابِعًا يَوْمَ القِيامَةِ.

505. Narrated Anas bin Mālik (رضي الله عنه): Allāh sent down His Divine Inspiration to His Messenger ﷺ continuously and abundantly during the period preceding his death till He took him unto Him. That was the period of the greatest part of revelation; and Allāh's Messenger ﷺ died after that.

٥٠٥ ـ حدَّثَنا عَمْرُو بنُ مُحَمَّدٍ: حدَّثَنا يَعْقُوبُ بنُ إبْراهِيمَ: حدَّثَنا أبي عَنْ صالِحِ بنِ كَيْسانَ، عَنِ ابنِ شِهابٍ قالَ: أَخْبَرَنِي أَنَسُ بنُ مالِكٍ رَضِيَ اللهُ عَنْهُ: أَنَّ اللهَ تابَعَ عَلَى رَسُولِهِ صلى اللهُ عليه وسلَّم قَبْلَ وَفاتِهِ حَتَّى تَوَفَّاهُ أَكْثَرَ ما كانَ الوَحْيُ، ثُمَّ تُوُفِّيَ رَسُولُ اللهِ صلى اللهُ عليه وسلَّم بَعْدُ.

506. Narrated Jundub: Once the Prophet ﷺ fell ill and did not offer the night prayer (Tahajjud prayer) for a night or two. A woman (the wife of Abū Lahab) came to him and said, "O Muhammad! I do not see but that your Satan has left you." Then Allāh عزّ وجلّ revealed (Sūrat-Ad-Duhā):

> 'By the fore-noon, and by the night when it darkens (or is still); Your Lord has not forsaken you, nor hated you.' (93)

٥٠٦ ـ حدّثنا أبو نعيم : حدّثنا سفيان ، عن الأسود بن قيس قال : سمعت جندبا يقول : اشتكى النبي صلى الله عليه وسلم فلم يقم ليلة أو ليلتين فأتته امرأة فقالت : يا محمّد ، ما أرى شيطانك إلاّ قد تركك . فأنزل الله عزّ وجلّ ـ والضحى والليل إذا سجى ما ودّعك ربّك وما قلى ـ .

(2) CHAPTER. The Qur'ān was revealed in the language of Qur'aish and the Arabs:

> '(An Arabic Qur'ān) In the plain Arabic tongue.' (26:195)

باب نزل القرآن بلسان قريش والعرب قرآنا عربيّا بلسان عربي مبين ـ .

507. Narrated Anas bin Mālik رضي الله عنه: (The Caliph 'Uthmān ordered Zaid bin Thābit, Sa'īd bin Al-'Āṣ, 'Abdullāh bin Az-Zubair and 'Abdur-Rahmān bin Al-Hārith bin Hishām to write the Qur'ān in the form of a book (Mushafs) and said to them. "In case you disagree with Zaid bin Thābit (Al-Anṣāri) regarding any dialectic Arabic utterance of the Qur'ān, then write it in the dialect of Quraish, for the Qur'ān was revealed in this dialect." So they did it.

٥٠٧ ـ حدّثنا أبو اليمان : أخبرنا شعيب ، عن الزهري ، وأخبرني أنس بن مالك قال : فأمر عثمان زيد ابن ثابت ، وسعيد بن العاص ، وعبد الله ابن الزبير ، وعبد الرحمن بن الحارث ابن هشام أن ينسخوها في المصاحف وقال لهم : إذا اختلفتم أنتم وزيد ابن ثابت في عربية من عربية القرآن ، فاكتبوها بلسان قريش ، فإنّ القرآن أنزل بلسانهم ، ففعلوا .

508. Narrated Safwān bin Ya'lā bin

٥٠٨ ـ حدّثنا أبو نعيم : حدّثنا

Umaiya. Ya'lā used to say, "I wish I could see Allāh's Messenger ﷺ at the time he is being inspired Divinely." When the Prophet ﷺ was at Al-Ja'rāna and was shaded by a garment hanging over him and some of his companions were with him, a man perfumed with scent came and said, "O Allāh's Messenger! What is your opinion regarding a man who assumes Iḥrām and puts on a cloak after perfuming his body with scent?" The Prophet ﷺ waited for a while, and then the Divine Inspiration descended upon him. 'Umar pointed out to Ya'lā, telling him to come. Ya'lā came and pushed his head (underneath the screen which was covering the Prophet ﷺ) and behold! The Prophet's face was red and he kept on breathing heavily for a while and then he was relieved. Thereupon he said, "Where is the questioner who asked me about 'Umra a while ago?" The man was sought and then was brought before the Prophet ﷺ who said (to him), "As regards the scent which you perfumed your body with, you must wash it off thrice, and as for your cloak, you must take it off; and then perform in your 'Umra all those things which you perform in Ḥajj."

همام: حدثنا عطاء، وقال مسدد: حدثنا يحيى، عن ابن جريج قال: أخبرني عطاء قال: أخبرني صفوان بن يعلى بن أمية: أن يعلى كان يقول: ليتني أرى رسول الله صلى الله عليه وسلم حين ينزل عليه الوحي. فلما كان النبي صلى الله عليه وسلم بالجعرانة وعليه ثوب قد أظل عليه ومعه الناس من أصحابه إذ جاءه رجل متضمخ بطيب فقال: يا رسول الله، كيف ترى في رجل أحرم في جبة بعدما تضمخ بطيب؟ فنظر النبي صلى الله عليه وسلم ساعة فجاءه الوحي فأشار عمر إلى يعلى أي تعال، فجاء يعلى فأدخل رأسه فإذا هو محمر الوجه يغط كذلك ساعة. ثم سري عنه فقال: أين الذي يسألني عن العمرة آنفا؟ فالتمس الرجل فجيء به إلى النبي صلى الله عليه وسلم فقال: أما الطيب الذي بك فاغسله ثلاث مرات. وأما الجبة فانزعها ثم اصنع في عمرتك كما تصنع في حجك.

(3) CHAPTER. The collection of the Qur'ān.

باب جمع القرآن.

509. Narrated Zaid bin Thābit: Abū Bakr As-Ṣiddīq sent for me when the people of Yamā-ma had been killed (i.e., a number of the Prophet's Companions who fought against Musailama). (I went to him) and found 'Umar bin Al-Khaṭṭāb sitting with him. Abū Bakr then said (to me), "Umar has come to me and said: "Casualties were heavy among the Qurrā' of the Qur'ān (i.e. those who knew the Qur'ān by heart) on the day of the Battle of Yamāma, and I am afraid that more heavy casualties may take place among the Qurrā' on other battlefields, whereby a large part of the Qur'ān may be lost. Therefore I suggest, you (Abū Bakr) order that the Qur 'ān be collected." I said to 'Umar, "How can you do something which Allāh's Messenger did not do?" 'Umar said, "By Allāh, that is a good project." "Umar kept on urging me to accept his proposal till Allāh opened my chest for it and I began to realise the good in the idea which 'Umar had realised." Then Abū Bakr said (to me). 'You are a wise young man and we do not have any suspicion about you, and you used to write the Divine Inspiration for Allāh's Messenger. So you should search for (the fragmentary scripts of) the Qur'ān and collect it (in one book)." By Allāh! If they had ordered me to shift one of the mountains, it would not have been heavier for me than this ordering me to collect the Qur'ān. Then I said to Abū Bakr, "How will you do something which Allāh's Messenger did not do?" Abū Bakr replied, "By Allāh, it is a good project." Abū Bakr kept on urging me to accept his idea until Allāh opened my chest for what He had opened the chests of Abū Bakr and 'Umar. So I

٥٠٩ - حدثنا موسى بن إسماعيل، عن إبراهيم ابن سعد: حدثنا ابن شهاب، عن عبيد بن السباق: أن زيد بن ثابت رضي الله عنه قال: أرسل إلى أبو بكر الصديق مقتل أهل اليمامة فإذا عمر بن الخطاب عنده. قال أبو بكر رضي الله عنه: إن عمر أتاني فقال. إن القتل قد استحر يوم اليمامة بقراء القرآن، وإني أخشى أن يستحر القتل بالقراء بالمواطن فيذهب كثير من القرآن. وإني أرى أن تأمر بجمع القرآن. قلت لعمر: كيف تفعل شيئا لم يفعله رسول الله صلى الله عليه وسلم؟ قال عمر: هذا والله خير، فلم يزل عمر يراجعني حتى شرح الله صدري لذلك ورأيت في ذلك الذي رأى عمر. قال زيد: قال أبو بكر: إنك رجل شاب عاقل لا نتهمك وقد كنت تكتب الوحي لرسول الله صلى الله عليه وسلم فتتبع القرآن فاجمعه. فوالله لو كانوا كلفوني نقل جبل من الجبال ما كان أثقل علي مما أمرني به من جمع القرآن. قلت: كيف تفعلون شيئا لم يفعله رسول الله صلى الله عليه وسلم؟ قال: هو والله خير. فلم يزل

started looking for the Qur'ān and collecting it from (what was written on) palm-leaf stalks, thin white stones and also from the men who knew it by heart, till I found the last Verse of Sūrat At-Tauba (Repentance) with Abī Khuzaima Al-Anṣārī, and I did not find it with anybody other than him. The Verse is:

> Verily there has come unto you an Messenger(Muḥammad) from amongst yourselves. It grieves him that you should receive any injury or difficulty......(till the end of "Sūrat-Barā'a (At-Tauba) (9:128-129)

Then the complete manuscripts (copy) of the Qur'ān remained with Abū Bakr till he died, then with 'Umar till the end of his life, and then with Ḥafṣa, the daughter of 'Umar .

أَبُو بَكْرٍ يُرَاجِعُنِي حَتَّى شَرَحَ اللهُ صَدْرِي لِلَّذِي شَرَحَ لَهُ صَدْرَ أَبِي بَكْرٍ وَعُمَرَ رَضِيَ اللهُ عَنْهُمَا ، فَتَتَبَّعْتُ الْقُرْآنَ أَجْمَعُهُ مِنَ الْعُسُبِ وَاللِّخَافِ وَصُدُورِ الرِّجَالِ حَتَّى وَجَدْتُ آخِرَ سُورَةِ التَّوْبَةِ مَعَ أَبِي خُزَيْمَةَ الأَنْصَارِيِّ لَمْ أَجِدْهَا مَعَ أَحَدٍ غَيْرِهِ ـ لَقَدْ جَاءَكُمْ رَسُولٌ مِنْ أَنْفُسِكُمْ عَزِيزٌ عَلَيْهِ مَا عَنِتُّمْ ـ حَتَّى خَاتِمَةِ بَرَاءَةَ . فَكَانَتِ الصُّحُفُ عِنْدَ أَبِي بَكْرٍ حَتَّى تَوَفَّاهُ اللهُ ، ثُمَّ عِنْدَ عُمَرَ حَيَاتَهُ ، ثُمَّ عِنْدَ حَفْصَةَ بِنْتِ عُمَرَ رَضِيَ اللهُ عَنْهُ .

510. Narrated Anas bin Mālik : Ḥudhaifa bin Al-Yamān came to 'Uthmān at the time when the people of Shām and the people of 'Irāq were waging war to conquer Ārmīnya and Ādhar-

٥١٠ ـ حَدَّثَنَا مُوسَى : حَدَّثَنَا إِبْرَاهِيمُ : حَدَّثَنَا ابْنُ شِهَابٍ : أَنَّ أَنَسَ ابْنَ مَالِكٍ حَدَّثَهُ : أَنَّ حُذَيْفَةَ بْنَ الْيَمَانِ قَدِمَ عَلَى عُثْمَانَ ، وَكَانَ يُغَازِي

bījān. Hudhaifa was afraid of their (the people of Shā'm and 'Irāq) differences in the recitation of the Qur'ān, so he said to 'Uthmān, "O chief of the Believers! Save this nation before they differ about the Book (Qur'ān) as Jews and the Christians did before." So 'Uthmān sent a message to Hafsa saying, "Send us the manuscripts of the Qur'ān so that we may compile the Qur'ānic materials in perfect copies and return the manuscripts to you." Hafsa sent it to 'Uthmān. 'Uthmān then ordered Zaid bin Thābit, 'Abdullāh bin Az-Zubair, Sa'īd bin Al-'Āṣ and 'Abdur-Raḥmān bin Ḥārith bin Hishām to re-write the manuscripts in perfect copies. 'Uthmān said to the three Quraishī men, "In case you disagree with Zaid bin Thābit on any point in the Qur'ān, then write it in the dialect of Quraish as the Qur'ān was revealed in their tongue." They did so, and when they had written many copies, 'Uthmān returned the original manuscripts to Hafsa. 'Uthmān sent to every Muslim province one copy of what they had copied, and ordered that all the other Qur'ānic materials, whether written in fragmentary manuscripts or whole copies, be burnt. Zaid bin Thābit added, "A Verse from Sūrat Aḥzāb was missed by me when we copied the Qur'ān and I used to hear Allāh's Messenger ﷺ reciting it. So we searched for it and found it with Khuzaima bin Thābit Al-Anṣārī. (That Verse was):

> 'Among the Believers are men who have been true in their covenant with Allāh.' (33:23)

أهل الشام فى فتح إرمينية وأذربيجان
مع أهل العراق . فأفزع حذيفة
اختلافهم فى القراءة ، فقال حذيفة
لعثمان : يا أمير المؤمنين ، أدرك هذه
الأمة قبل أن يختلفوا فى الكتاب
اختلاف اليهود والنصارى . فأرسل
عثمان إلى حفصة أن أرسلى إلينا
بالصحف ننسخها فى المصاحف ثم
نردها إليك . فأرسلت بها حفصة
إلى عثمان ، فأمر زيد بن ثابت ، وعبد
الله بن الزبير ، وسعيد بن العاص .
وعبد الرحمن بن الحارث بن هشام
فنسخوها فى المصاحف . وقال عثمان
للرهط القرشيين الثلاثة : إذا اختلفتم
أنتم وزيد بن ثابت فى شيء من
القرآن فاكتبوه بلسان قريش فإنما
نزل بلسانهم ، ففعلوا حتى إذا نسخوا
الصحف فى المصاحف رد عثمان
الصحف إلى حفصة وأرسل إلى كل
أفق بمصحف مما نسخوا . وأمر
بما سواه من القرآن فى كل صحيفة
أو مصحف أن يحرق قال ابن شهاب :
وأخبرنى خارجة بن زيد بن ثابت
قال : فقدت آية من الأحزاب حين
نسخنا المصحف قد كنت أسمع
رسول الله صلى الله عليه وسلم يقرأ بها
فالتمسناها فوجدناها مع خزيمة بن

ثابت الأنصاري ـ مِنَ المُؤْمِنِينَ رِجالٌ صَدَقُوا ما عاهَدُوا اللهَ عَلَيْهِ ـ فألحقناها في سُورَتِها في المُصْحَفِ .

(4) CHAPTER. The scribe of the Prophet ﷺ :-

بابٌ كاتِبِ النَّبِيِّ صلى اللهُ عليه وسلَّم .

511. Narrated Zaid bin Thābit: Abū Bakr sent for me and said, "You used to write the Divine Revelations for Allāh's Messenger ﷺ : So you should search for (the Qur'ān and collect) it." I started searching for the Qur'ān till I found the last two Verses of Sūrat At-Tauba with Abī Khuzaima Al-Anṣārī and I could not find these Verses with anybody other than him. (They were):—

> 'Verily there has come unto you an Messenger (Muḥammad ﷺ) from amongst yourselves. It grieves him that you should receive any injury or difficulty ....
> (9:128-129)

٥١١ ـ حدَّثَنا يَحْيَى بنُ بُكَيْرٍ : حدَّثَنا اللَّيْثُ ، عَنْ يُونُسَ ، عَنِ ابنِ شِهابٍ : أنَّ ابنَ السَّبَّاقِ قالَ : إنَّ زَيْدَ ابنَ ثابِتٍ قالَ : أرْسَلَ إليَّ أبُو بَكْرٍ رَضِيَ اللهُ عَنْهُ قالَ : إنَّكَ كُنْتَ تَكْتُبُ الوَحْيَ لِرَسُولِ اللهِ صلى اللهُ عليه وسلَّم فاتَّبِعِ القُرْآنَ ، فَتَتَبَّعْتُ حتَّى وَجَدْتُ آخِرَ سُورَةِ التَّوْبَةِ آيَتَيْنِ مَعَ أبي خُزَيْمَةَ الأنْصارِيِّ لَمْ أجِدْهُما مَعَ أحَدٍ غَيْرِهِ ـ لَقَدْ جاءَكُمْ رَسُولٌ مِنْ أنْفُسِكُمْ عَزِيزٌ عَلَيْهِ ما عَنِتُّمْ ـ إلى آخِرِها .

512. Narrated Al-Barā': There was revealed:

> 'Not equal are those believers who sit (at home) and those who strive and fight in the Cause of Allāh.'
> (4:95)

٥١٢ ـ حدَّثَنا عُبَيْدُ اللهِ بنُ مُوسَى ، عَنْ إسْرائِيلَ ، عَنْ أبي إسْحاقَ ، عَنِ البَراءِ ، قالَ : لمَّا نَزَلَتْ ـ لا يَسْتَوِي القاعِدُونَ مِنَ المُؤْمِنِينَ والمُجاهِدُونَ في سَبِيلِ اللهِ ـ قالَ النَّبِيُّ صلى اللهُ عليه

The Prophet ﷺ said, "Call Zaid for me and let him bring the board, the inkpot and the scapula bone (or the scapula bone and the inkpot)." Then he said, "Write: 'Not equal are those Believers who sit......'", and at that time 'Amr bin Um Maktūm, the blind man, was sitting behind the Prophet ﷺ. He said, "O Allāh's Messenger! What is your order for me (as regards the above Verse) as I am a blind man?" So, instead of the above Verse, the following Verse was revealed:

> 'Not equal are those believers who sit (at home) except those who are disabled (by injury or are blind or lame etc.) and those who strive and fight in the cause of Allāh.' (4:95)

وسلَّم: ادْعُ لي زَيْداً ولْيَجِئْ باللَّوْحِ والدَّواةِ والكَتِفِ، أوِ الكَتِفِ والدَّواةِ. ثُمَّ قالَ: اكْتُبْ - لا يَسْتَوِي القاعِدُونَ - وخَلْفَ ظَهْرِ النَّبِيِّ صلى الله عليه وسلَّم عَمْرُو بنُ أُمِّ مَكْتُومٍ الأعمَى فقالَ: يا رَسُولَ اللهِ، فما تأمُرُني؟ فإني رَجُلٌ ضَرِيرُ البَصَرِ، فنَزَلَتْ مَكانَها - لا يَسْتَوِي القاعِدُونَ مِنَ المُؤْمِنِينَ والمُجاهِدُونَ في سَبِيلِ اللهِ غَيْرُ أُولي الضَّرَرِ -.

(5) CHAPTER. The Qur'ān was revealed to be recited in seven different ways.(1)

بابٌ أُنْزِلَ القُرآنُ عَلى سَبْعَةِ أَحْرُفٍ.

513. Narrated 'Abdullāh bin 'Abbās : Allāh's Messenger ﷺ said, "Gabriel recited the Qur'ān to me in one way. Then I requested him (to read it in another way), and continued asking him to recite it in other ways, and he recited it in several ways till he ultimately recited it

٥١٣ - حدَّثَنا سَعِيدُ بنُ عُفَيْرٍ: حدثَنِي اللَّيْثُ: حدَّثَنِي عُقَيْلٌ، عَنِ ابنِ شِهابٍ قالَ: حدثَنِي عُبَيْدُ اللهِ بنُ عَبْدِ اللهِ: أنَّ ابنَ عَبَّاسٍ رَضِيَ اللهُ

(1) This does not mean that everything in it can be recited in seven different ways, but it means that some of its words can be read in seven different ways which is the maximum number of variation.

in seven different ways."

عنهما حدثه أن رسول الله صلى الله عليه وسلم قال أقرأنى جبريل على حرف فراجعته فلم أزل أستزيده ويزيدنى حتى انتهى إلى سبعة أحرف.

514. Narrated 'Umar bin Al-Khattab : I heard Hishām bin Ḥakīm reciting Sūrat Al-Furqān during the life-time of Allāh's Messenger ﷺ and I listened to his recitation and noticed that he recited in several different ways which Allāh's Messenger ﷺ had not taught me. I was about to jump over him during his prayer, but I controlled my temper, and when he had completed his prayer, I put his upper garment around his neck and seized him by it and said, "Who taught you this Sūra which I heard you reciting?" He replied, "Allāh's Messenger ﷺ taught it to me." I said, "You have told a lie, for Allāh's Messenger ﷺ has taught it to me in a different way from yours." So I dragged him to Allāh's Messenger and said (to Allāh's Messenger ﷺ), "I heard this person reciting Sūrat Al-Furqān in a way which you haven't taught me!" On that Allāh's Messenger ﷺ said, "Release him, (O 'Umar !) Recite, O Hishām!" Then he recited in the same way as I heard him reciting. Then Allāh's Messenger ﷺ said, "It was revealed in this way," and added , "Recite, O 'Umar!" I recited it as he had taught me. Allāh's Messenger ﷺ then said, "It was revealed in this way. This Qur'ān has been revealed to be recited in seven different ways, so recite of it whichever (way) is easier for you (or read as much of it as may be easy for you)."

٥١٤ - حدثنا سعيد بن عفير: حدثنى الليث: حدثنى عقيل، عن ابن شهاب قال: حدثنى عروة بن الزبير: أن المسور بن مخرمة، وعبد الرحمن بن عبد القارى حدثاه: أنهما سمعا عمر بن الخطاب يقول: سمعت هشام بن حكيم يقرأ سورة الفرقان فى حياة رسول الله صلى الله عليه وسلم فاستمعت لقراءته فإذا هو يقرأ على حروف كثيرة لم يقرئنيها رسول الله صلى الله عليه وسلم فكدت أساوره فى الصلاة فتصبرت حتى سلم فلببته بردائه فقلت: من أقرأك هذه السورة التى سمعتك تقرأ؟ قال: أقرأنيها رسول الله صلى الله عليه وسلم، فقلت: كذبت فإن رسول الله صلى الله عليه وسلم قد أقرأنيها على غير ما قرأت، فانطلقت به أقوده إلى رسول الله صلى الله عليه وسلم فقلت: إنى سمعت هذا يقرأ بسورة الفرقان على حروف لم تقرئنيها، فقال رسول الله صلى الله عليه وسلم أرسله اقرأ يا هشام

فقرأ عليه القراءة التي سمعته يقرأ فقال رسول الله صلى الله عليه وسلم: كذلك أنزلت. ثم قال: اقرأ يا عمر، فقرأت القراءة التي أقرأني، فقال رسول الله صلى الله عليه وسلم: كذلك أنزلت، إن هذا القرآن أنزل على سبعة أحرف فاقرءوا ما تيسر منه.

(6) CHAPTER. The compilation of the Qur'ān (i.e. the arrangement of its Sūras).

باب تاليف القرآن.

515. Narrated Yūsuf bin Māhk: While I was with 'Āisha, the mother of the Believers, a person from 'Irāq came and asked, "What type of shroud is the best?" 'Āisha said, "May Allāh be merciful to you! What does it matter?" He said, "O mother of the Believers! Show me (the copy of) your Qur'ān," She said, "Why?" He said, "In order to compile and arrange the Qur'ān according to it, for people recite it with its Sūras not in proper order." 'Āisha said, "What does it matter which part of it you read first? (Be informed) that the first thing that was revealed thereof was a Sūra from Al-Mufassal, and in it was mentioned Paradise and the Fire. When the people embraced Islām, the Verses regarding legal and illegal things were revealed. If the first thing to be revealed was: 'Do not drink alcoholic drinks.' people would have said, 'We will never leave alcoholic drinks,' and if there had been revealed, 'Do not commit illegal

٥١٥ - حدثنا إبراهيم بن موسى: أخبرنا هشام بن يوسف أن ابن جريج أخبرهم قال: وأخبرني يوسف بن ماهك قال: إني عند عائشة أم المؤمنين رضي الله عنها إذ جاءها عراقي فقال: أي الكفن خير؟ قالت: ويحك، وما يضرك؟ قال: يا أم المؤمنين أريني مصحفك، قالت: ولم؟ قال: لعلي أؤلف القرآن عليه فإنه يقرأ غير مؤلف. قالت: وما يضرك أيه قرأت قبل؟ إنما نزل أول ما نزل منه سورة من المفصل فيها ذكر الجنة والنار، حتى إذا ثاب الناس إلى الإسلام نزل الحلال والحرام. ولو نزل أول شيء - لا

sexual intercourse, 'they would have said, 'We will never give up illegal sexual intercourse.' While I was a young girl of playing age, the following Verse was revealed in Mecca to Muḥammad ﷺ :

> 'Nay! But the Hour is their appointed time (for their full recompense), and the Hour will be more grievous and more bitter.'
>
> (54:46)

Sūra Al-Baqara (The Cow) and Sūrat An-Nisā' (The Women) were revealed while I was with him." Then 'Āisha took out the copy of the Qur'ān for the man and dictated to him the Verses of the Sūras (in their proper order).

تَشْرَبُوا الخَمْرَ - لقالُوا لا نَدَعُ الخَمْرَ أبَدًا: ولَوْ نَزَلَ: لا تَزْنُوا، لقالُوا لا نَدَعُ الزِّنا أبَدًا، لَقَدْ نَزَلَ بِمَكَّةَ عَلى مُحَمَّدٍ صلى الله عليه وسلّمَ وإنّي لَجارِيَةٌ ألْعَبُ - بَلِ السّاعَةُ مَوْعِدُهُمْ والسّاعَةُ أدْهى وأمَرُّ - وما نَزَلَتْ سُورَةُ البَقَرَةِ والنِّساءِ إلّا وأنا عِنْدَهُ. قالَ: فأخْرَجَتْ لَهُ المُصْحَفَ فأمْلَتْ عَلَيْهِ آيَ السُّوَرِ.

516. Narrated 'Abdullāh bin Mas'ūd: Sūrat Banī-Isrāel, Al-Kahf (The Cave), Maryam, Ṭāhā, Al-Anbiyā' (The prophets) are amongst my first earnings and my old property, and (in fact) they are my old property.

٥١٦ - حَدَّثَنا آدَمُ: حَدَّثَنا شُعْبَةُ، عَنْ أبي إسحاقَ قالَ: سَمِعْتُ عَبْدَ الرَّحْمَنِ بنَ يَزِيدَ قالَ: سَمِعْتُ ابنَ مَسْعُودٍ يَقُولُ في بَني إسْرائِيلَ والكَهْفِ ومَرْيَمَ وطَهَ والأنْبِياءِ إنَّهُنَّ مِنَ العِتاقِ الأُوَلِ وهُنَّ مِنْ تِلادي.

517. Narrated Al-Barā' ﷺ : I learnt, 'Glorify the Name of your Lord the Most High' (Sūrat al-A'lā) No 87, before the Prophet ﷺ came (to

٥١٧ - حَدَّثَنا أبُو الوَلِيدِ: حَدَّثَنا شُعْبَةُ: أنْبأنا أبُو إسحاقَ: سَمِعَ البَراءَ رَضِيَ اللهُ عَنْهُ قالَ: تَعَلَّمْتُ - سَبِّحِ

Medina).

اسْمَ رَبِّكَ - قَبْلَ أنْ يَقْدَمَ النَّبِيُّ صلى اللهُ عليهِ وسلَّمَ.

518. Narrated Shaqīq: 'Abdullāh said, "I learnt An-Naẓā'ir (1) which the Prophet ﷺ used to recite in pairs in each Rak'a." Then 'Abdullāh got up and 'Alqama accompanied him to his house, and when 'Alqama came out, we asked him (about those Sūras). He said, "They are twenty Sūras that start from the beginning of Al-Mufaṣṣal, according to the arrangement done by Ibn Mas'ūd, and end with the Sūras starting with Ḥā Mīm, e.g., Ḥā 'Mīm the Smoke,' and "About what they question one another ?" (78:1)

٥١٨ - حدَّثنا عَبْدَانُ، عَنْ أبي حَمْزَةَ، عَنِ الأعمَشِ، عَنْ شَقِيقٍ قالَ: قالَ عَبْدُ الله: قَدْ عَلِمْتُ النَّظائِرَ الَّتِي كانَ النَّبِيُّ صلى اللهُ عليهِ وسلَّمَ يَقْرَؤُهُنَّ اثْنَيْنِ في كُلِّ رَكْعَةٍ، فقامَ عَبْدُ الله وَدَخَلَ مَعَهُ عَلْقَمَةُ وَخَرَجَ عَلْقَمَةُ فَسألْناهُ فقالَ: عِشْرُونَ سُورَةً مِنْ أوَّلِ المُفَصَّلِ عَلى تَأْلِيفِ ابنِ مَسْعُودٍ، آخِرُهُنَّ الحَوامِيمُ: حم الدُّخان، وعَمَّ يتَساءَلُونَ.

(7) CHAPTER. Gabriel used to present (recite) the Qur'ān to the Prophet ﷺ. Fāṭima said, "The Prophet ﷺ told me secretly, " 'Gabriel used to recite the Qur'ān to me and I to him once a year, but this year he recited the whole Qur'ān with me twice. I don't think but that my death is approaching.' "

باب كانَ جِبريلُ يَعْرِضُ القُرآنَ عَلى النَّبِيِّ صلى اللهُ عليهِ وسلَّمَ وقالَ مَسرُوقٌ، عَنْ عائِشَةَ، عَنْ فاطِمَةَ عَلَيْها السَّلامُ: أسَرَّ إلَيَّ النَّبِيُّ صلى اللهُ عليهِ وسلَّمَ أنَّ جِبريلَ يُعارِضُنِي بالقُرآنِ كُلَّ سَنَةٍ، وإنَّهُ عارَضَنِي العامَ مَرَّتَيْنِ، ولا أُراهُ إلاَّ حَضَرَ أجَلِي.

(1) An-Naẓā'ir is the Sūras that deal with the same topic or that are equal in length.'

519. Narrated Ibn 'Abbās: The Prophet was the most generous person, and he used to become more so (generous) particularly in the month of Ramaḍān because Gabriel used to meet him every night of the month of Ramaḍān till it elapsed. Allāh's Messenger used to recite the Qur'ān for him. When Gabriel met him, he used to become more generous than the fast wind in doing good.

٥١٩ - حدَّثنا يحيى بن قزعة: حدَّثنا إبراهيم بن سعد، عن الزهري، عن عبيد الله بن عبد الله، عن ابن عباس رضي الله عنهما قال: كان النبيُّ صلى الله عليه وسلم أجود الناس بالخير، وأجود ما يكون في شهر رمضان لأنَّ جبريل كان يلقاه في كل ليلة في شهر رمضان حتى ينسلخ، يعرض عليه رسول الله صلى الله عليه وسلم القرآن فإذا لقيه جبريل كان أجود بالخير من الريح المرسلة.

520. Narrated Abū Huraira: Gabriel used to repeat the recitation of the Qur'ān with the Prophet once a year, but he repeated it twice with him in the year he died. The Prophet used to stay in I'tikāf for ten days every year (in the month of Ramaḍān), but in the year of his death, he stayed in I'tikāf for twenty days.

٥٢٠ - حدَّثنا خالد بن يزيد: حدَّثنا أبو بكر، عن أبي حصين، عن أبي هريرة قال: كان يعرض على النبي صلى الله عليه وسلم القرآن كل عام مرة، فعرض عليه مرتين في العام الذي قبض، وكان يعتكف كل عام عشرًا، فاعتكف عشرين في العام الذي قبض.

(8) CHAPTER. (What is said regarding) the Qurrā' (the reciters of the Qur'ān by heart) from among the companions of the Prophet.

باب القرّاء من أصحاب النبي صلى الله عليه وسلم.

521. Narrated Masrūq: 'Abdullāh

٥٢١ - حدَّثنا حفص بن عمر:

bin 'Amr mentioned 'Abdullāh bin Mas'ūd and said, "I shall ever love that man, for I heard the Prophet ﷺ saying, 'Take (learn) the Qur'ān from four: 'Abdullāh bin Mas'ūd, Sālim, Mu'ādh and Ubai bin Ka'b.' "

حدثنا شعبة، عن عمرو، عن إبراهيم، عن مسروق: ذكر عبد الله بن عمرو عبد الله بن مسعود فقال: لا أزال أحبه، سمعت النبي صلى الله عليه وسلم يقول: خذوا القرآن من أربعة، من عبد الله بن مسعود، وسالم، ومعاذ، وأبي بن كعب.

522. Narrated Shaqīq bin Salama: Once 'Abdullah bin Mas'ūd delivered a sermon before us and said, "By Allāh, I learnt over seventy Sūras direct from Allāh's Messenger ﷺ. By Allāh, the companions of the Prophet ﷺ came to know that I am one of those who know Allāh's Book best of all of them, yet I am not the best of them." Shaqīq added: I sat in his religious gathering and I did not hear anybody opposing him (in his speech).

٥٢٢ - حدثنا عمر بن حفص: حدثنا أبي: حدثنا الأعمش: حدثنا شقيق ابن سلمة، قال: خطبنا عبد الله فقال: والله لقد أخذت من في رسول الله صلى الله عليه وسلم بضعا وسبعين سورة، والله لقد علم أصحاب النبي صلى الله عليه وسلم أني من أعلمهم بكتاب الله وما أنا بخيرهم، قال شقيق: فجلست في الحلق أسمع ما يقولون فما سمعت رادا يقول غير ذلك.

523. Narrated 'Alqama: While we were in the city of Ḥimṣ (in Syria), Ibn Mas'ūd recited Sūrat Yūsuf. A man said (to him), "It was not revealed in this way." Then Ibn Mas'ūd said, "I recited it in this way before Allāh's Messenger ﷺ and he confirmed my recitation by saying, 'Well done!' " Ibn Mas'ūd detected the smell of wine from the man's mouth, so he said to him, "Aren't you ashamed of telling a lie about Allāh's Book and (along with this)

٥٢٣ - حدثني محمد بن كثير، أخبرنا سفيان، عن الأعمش، عن علقمة قال: كنا بحمص فقرأ ابن مسعود سورة يوسف فقال رجل: ما هكذا أنزلت، قال: قرأت على رسول الله صلى الله عليه وسلم فقال: أحسنت. ووجد منه ريح الخمر فقال: أتجمع أن تكذب بكتاب الله

you drink alcoholic liquors too?" Then he lashed him according to the law.

وتشرب الخمر؟ فضربه الحد.

524. Narrated 'Abdullāh (bin Mas'ūd) : By Allāh other than Whom none has the right to be worshipped! There is no Sūra revealed in Allāh's Book but I know at what place it was revealed; and there is no Verse revealed in Allāh's Book but I know about whom it was revealed. And if I know that there is somebody who knows Allāh's Book better than I, and he is at a place that camels can reach, I would go to him.

٥٢٤ - حدثنا عمر بن حفص: حدثنا أبي: حدثنا الأعمش: حدثنا مسلم، عن مسروق قال: قال عبد الله رضي الله عنه: والله الذي لا إله غيره ما أنزلت سورة من كتاب الله إلا أنا أعلم أين أنزلت. ولا أنزلت آية من كتاب الله إلا أنا أعلم فيمن أنزلت. ولو أعلم أحدا أعلم مني بكتاب الله تبلغه الإبل لركبت إليه.

525. Narrated Qatāda: I asked Anas bin Mālik , "Who collected the Qur'ān at the time of the Prophet ?" He replied, "Four, all of whom were from the Anṣār: Ubaī bin Ka'b, Mū'adh bin Jabal, Zaid bin Thābit and Abū Zaid."

٥٢٥ - حدثنا حفص بن عمر: حدثنا همام: حدثنا قتادة قال: سألت أنس بن مالك رضي الله عنه: من جمع القرآن على عهد النبي صلى الله عليه وسلم؟ قال: أربعة كلهم من الأنصار: أبي بن كعب، ومعاذ بن جبل، وزيد بن ثابت، وأبو زيد. تابعه الفضل، عن حسين بن واقد، عن ثمامة، عن أنس.

526. Narrated Anas (bin Mālik) : When the Prophet died,

٥٢٦ - حدثنا معلى بن أسد: حدثنا عبد الله بن المثنى: حدثني

none had collected the Qur'ān but four persons: Abū Ad-Dardā'. Mu'ādh bin Jabal, Zaid bin Thābit and Abū Zaid. We were the inheritors (of Abū Zaid) as he had no offspring .

ثابتٌ البُنانيُّ وثُمامةُ عن أنسٍ قالَ: ماتَ النبيُّ صلى اللهُ عليهِ وسلَّم ولم يَجمعِ القرآنَ غيرُ أربعةٍ: أبو الدَّرْداءِ، ومُعاذُ بنُ جبلٍ، وزيدُ ابنُ ثابتٍ، وأبو زيدٍ. قالَ: ونحنُ ورِثناهُ.

527. Narrated Ibn 'Abbās : 'Umar said, "Ubai was the best of us in the recitation (of the Qur'ān) yet we leave some of what he recites." Ubai says, "I have taken it from the mouth of Allāh's Messenger and will not leave for anything whatever." But Allāh said:

> None of Our Revelations do We abrogate or cause to be forgotten but We substitute something better or similar. (2:106)

٥٢٧ - حدَّثنا صدقةُ بنُ الفضلِ: أخبرَنا يحيى، عن سُفيانَ، عن حبيبِ بنِ أبي ثابتٍ، عن سعيدِ بنِ جُبيرٍ، عن ابنِ عبّاسٍ قالَ: قال عُمرُ: أُبيٌّ أقرؤُنا وإنّا لندَعُ مِن لَحنِ أُبيٍّ، وأُبيٌّ يقولُ أخذتُهُ مِن في رسولِ اللهِ صلى اللهُ عليهِ وسلَّم فلا أتركُهُ لشيءٍ، قالَ اللهُ تعالى - ما ننسخْ مِن آيةٍ أو نُنسِها نأتِ بخيرٍ منها أو مثلِها -.

(9) CHAPTER. The superiority of Fātiḥa-Al-Kitāb (The Opening Sūrah of the Book).

بابُ فضلِ فاتحةِ الكتابِ.

528. Narrated Abū Sa'īd Al-Mu'allā: While I was praying, the Prophet called me but I did not respond to his call. Later I said, "O Allāh's Messenger! I was praying." He said, "Didn't Allāh say:

> 'O you who believe! Give your response to Allāh (by obeying Him) and to His Messenger when He calls you'?" (8:24)

٥٢٨ - حدَّثنا عليُّ بنُ عبدِ اللهِ: حدَّثنا يحيى بنُ سعيدٍ: حدَّثنا شُعبةُ قال: حدَّثني خُبيبُ ابنُ عبدِ الرَّحمنِ، عن حفصِ بنِ عاصمٍ، عن أبي سعيدِ ابنِ المُعلَّى، قالَ: كُنتُ أُصلِّي فدعاني النبيُّ صلى اللهُ عليهِ وسلَّم فلم أُجِبْهُ،

He then said, "Shall I not teach you the most superior Sūrah in the Qur'ān?" He said, '(It is),

'Praise be to Allāh, the Lord of the worlds.'

(i.e., Sūrat-Al-Fātiḥa) which consists of seven repeatedly recited Verses and the Magnificent Qur'ān which was given to me."

قُلْتُ: يا رَسُولَ اللهِ إني كُنْتُ أُصَلِّي، قالَ: ألم يَقُلِ اللهُ - اسْتَجِيبُوا للهِ وللرَّسُولِ إذَا دَعَاكُمْ - ثُمَّ قالَ: ألا أُعَلِّمُكَ أعْظَمَ سُورَةٍ في القُرْآنِ قَبْلَ أنْ تَخْرُجَ مِنَ المَسْجِدِ؟ فأخَذَ بِيَدِي فَلَمَّا أرَدْنَا أنْ نَخْرُجَ قُلْتُ: يا رَسُولَ اللهِ، إنَّكَ قُلْتَ ألا أُعَلِّمُكَ أعْظَمَ سُورَةٍ في القرآنِ؟ قالَ - الحَمْدُ للهِ رَبِّ العالمينَ - هِيَ السَّبْعُ المَثَانِي، والقُرْآنُ العَظِيمُ الذي أُوتِيتُهُ.

529. Narrated Abū Sa'īd Al-Khudrī: While we were on one of our journeys, we dismounted at a place where a slave girl came and said, "The chief of this tribe has been stung by a scorpion and our men are not present; is there anybody among you who can treat him (by reciting something)?" Then one of our men went along with her though we did not think that he knew any such treatment. But he treated the chief by reciting something, and the sick man recovered whereupon he gave him thirty sheep and gave us milk to drink (as a reward) When he returned, we asked our friend,"Did you know how to treat with the recitation of something?" He said, "No, but I treated him only with the recitation of the Mother of the Book (i.e., Al-Fātiḥa)." We said, "Do not say anything (about it) till we reach or ask the Prophet ﷺ .So when we reached Medīna, we mentioned that to the Prophet ﷺ (in order to know whether the sheep which we had taken were lawful to take or not). The Prophet ﷺ said, "How

٥٢٩ - حَدَّثَنِي مُحَمَّدُ بنُ المُثَنَّى: حَدَّثَنا وَهْبٌ: حَدَّثَنا هِشامٌ، عَنْ مُحَمَّدٍ، عَنْ مَعْبَدٍ، عَنْ أبي سَعِيدٍ الخُدْرِيِّ قالَ: كُنَّا في مَسِيرٍ لَنا فَنَزَلْنا، فَجاءَتْ جارِيَةٌ فَقالَتْ: إنَّ سَيِّدَ الحَيِّ سَلِيمٌ وإنَّ نَفَرَنا غَيَبٌ فَهَلْ مِنْكُمْ رَاقٍ؟ فَقامَ مَعَها رَجُلٌ ما كُنَّا نَأْبُنُهُ بِرُقْيَةٍ فَرَقاهُ فَبَرَأَ. فَأَمَرَ لَهُ بِثَلاثِينَ شاةً وَسَقانا لَبَنًا. فَلَمَّا رَجَعَ قُلْنا لَهُ أكُنْتَ تُحْسِنُ رُقْيَةً أوْ كُنْتَ تَرْقِي؟ قالَ: لا، ما رَقَيْتُ إلاَّ بِأُمِّ الكِتابِ، قُلْنا: لا تُحْدِثُوا شَيْئًا حَتَّى نَأْتِيَ أوْ نَسْأَلَ النَّبِيَّ صلى اللهُ عليهِ وسلَّم. فَلَمَّا قَدِمْنا المَدِينَةَ ذَكَرْناهُ للنَّبِيِّ صلى اللهُ عليهِ وسلَّم فَقالَ: وَما كانَ يُدْرِيهِ أنَّها رُقْيَةٌ، اقْسِمُوا واضْرِبُوا لي بِسَهْمٍ

did he come to know that it (Al-Fātiḥa) could be used for treatment? Distribute your reward and assign for me one share thereof as well."

وَقَالَ أَبُو مَعْمَرٍ: حَدَّثَنَا عَبْدُ الْوَارِثِ: حَدَّثَنَا هِشَامٌ: حَدَّثَنَا مُحَمَّدُ بْنُ سِيرِينَ: حَدَّثَنَا مَعْبَدُ بْنُ سِيرِينَ، عَنْ أَبِي سَعِيدٍ الْخُدْرِيِّ بِهَذَا.

(10) CHAPTER. The superiority of Sūrat-Al-Baqara (The Cow). No. (2)

بَابُ فَضْلِ سُورَةِ الْبَقَرَةِ

530. Narrated Abū Mas'ūd: The Prophet ﷺ said, "Whosoever recited the last two Verses of Sūrat-Al-Baqara at night, that will be sufficient for him."

Narrated Abū Huraira ؓ: Allāh's Messenger ﷺ ordered me to guard the Zakāt revenue of Ramaḍān. Then somebody came to me and started stealing of the foodstuff. I caught him and said, "I will take you to Allāh's Messenger ﷺ!" Then Abū Huraira described the whole narration and said:) That person said (to me), "(Please don't take me to Allāh's Messenger ﷺ and I will tell you a few words by which Allāh will benefit you.) When you go to your bed, recite Āyat-al-Kursī, (2:255) for then there will be a guard from Allāh who will protect you all night long, and Satan will not be able to come near you till dawn." (When the Prophet ﷺ heard the story) he said (to me), "He (who came to you at night) told you the truth although he is a liar; and it was Satan."

٥٣٠ ـ حَدَّثَنَا مُحَمَّدُ بْنُ كَثِيرٍ: أَخْبَرَنَا شُعْبَةُ، عَنْ سُلَيْمَانَ، عَنْ إِبْرَاهِيمَ، عَنْ عَبْدِ الرَّحْمَنِ، عَنْ أَبِي مَسْعُودٍ، عَنِ النَّبِيِّ صلى الله عليه وسلم قَالَ: مَنْ قَرَأَ بِآيَتَيْنِ. وَحَدَّثَنَا أَبُو نُعَيْمٍ: حَدَّثَنَا سُفْيَانُ، عَنْ مَنْصُورٍ، عَنْ عَبْدِ الرَّحْمَنِ بْنِ يَزِيدَ، عَنْ أَبِي مَسْعُودٍ رَضِيَ اللهُ عَنْهُ قَالَ: قَالَ النَّبِيُّ صلى الله عليه وسلم: مَنْ قَرَأَ بِالْآيَتَيْنِ مِنْ آخِرِ سُورَةِ الْبَقَرَةِ فِي لَيْلَةٍ كَفَتَاهُ. وَقَالَ عُثْمَانُ بْنُ الْهَيْثَمِ: حَدَّثَنَا عَوْفٌ، عَنْ مُحَمَّدِ بْنِ سِيرِينَ، عَنْ أَبِي هُرَيْرَةَ رَضِيَ اللهُ عَنْهُ قَالَ: وَكَّلَنِي رَسُولُ اللهِ صلى الله عليه وسلم بِحِفْظِ زَكَاةِ رَمَضَانَ، فَأَتَانِي آتٍ فَجَعَلَ يَحْثُو مِنَ الطَّعَامِ، فَأَخَذْتُهُ فَقُلْتُ: لَأَرْفَعَنَّكَ إِلَى رَسُولِ

صلى الله عليه وسلم فقصَّ الحديثَ فقال: إذا أويتَ إلى فراشِكَ فاقرأ آيةَ الكرسيِّ، لم يزل معك من الله حافظٌ ولا يقربْكَ شيطانٌ حتى تصبحَ، وقال النبيُّ صلى الله عليه وسلم: صدقكَ وهو كذوبٌ، ذاكَ شيطانٌ.

(11) CHAPTER. The superiority of Sūrat-Al-Kahf (The Cave), No. (18)

بابُ فضلِ الكهفِ

531. Narrated Al-Barā': A man was reciting Sūrat Al-Kahf and his horse was tied with two ropes beside him. A cloud came down and spread over that man, and it kept on coming closer and closer to him till his horse started jumping (as if afraid of something). When it was morning, the man came to the Prophet ﷺ and told him of that experience. The Prophet ﷺ said, "That was As-Sakīna (tranquillity) which descended because of (the recitation of) the Qur'ān."

٥٣١ـ حدثنا عمرو بن خالد: حدثنا زهيرٌ: حدثنا أبو إسحاقَ، عن البراءِ قال: كان رجلٌ يقرأُ سورةَ الكهفِ وإلى جانبِهِ حصانٌ مربوطٌ بشطنينِ، فتغشَّتْهُ سحابةٌ فجعلت تدنو وتدنو وجعل فرسُهُ ينفرُ، فلمّا أصبح أتى النبيَّ صلى الله عليه وسلم فذكرَ ذلك لَهُ، فقال: تلكَ السكينةُ تنزَّلتْ بالقرآنِ.

(12) CHAPTER. The superiority of Sūrat-Al-Fath (The Victory). No. (48)

بابُ فضلِ سورةِ الفتحِ

532. Narrated Aslam: Allāh's Messenger ﷺ was travelling on one of his journeys,

٥٣٢ـ حدثنا إسماعيلُ قال: حدثني مالكٌ، عن زيدِ بن أسلمَ،

and 'Umar bin Al-Khattab was travelling along with him at night. 'Umar asked him about something, but Allāh's Messenger ﷺ did not answer him. He asked again, but he did not answer. He asked for the third time, but he did not answer. On that, 'Umar said to himself, "May your mother lose you! You have asked Allāh's Messenger ﷺ three times, but he did not answer at all!" 'Umar said, "So I made my camel go fast till I was ahead of the people, and I was afraid that something might be revealed about me. After a little while I heard a callmaker calling me, I said, 'I was afraid that some Qur'ānic Verse might be revealed about me.' So I went to Allāh's Messenger ﷺ and greeted him. He said, 'Tonight there has been revealed to me a Sūrah which is dearer to me than that on which the sun shines (i.e. ,the world).' Then he recited:

> 'Verily! We have given you (O Muḥammad ﷺ, a manifest victory.' " (Sūrat-al-Fatḥ).

No. (48:1)

عَنْ أَبِيهِ : أَنَّ رَسُولَ اللهِ صلى اللهُ عليه وسلَّم كانَ يَسِيرُ فِى بَعْضِ أَسْفارِهِ وعُمَرُ بنُ الخَطَّابِ يَسِيرُ مَعَهُ لَيْلاً فَسأَلَه عُمَرُ عَنْ شَىْءٍ فَلَمْ يُجِبْهُ رَسُولُ اللهِ صلى اللهُ عليه وسلَّم . ثُمَّ سأَلَهُ فَلَمْ يُجِبْهُ ، ثُمَّ سأَلَهُ فَلَمْ يُجِبْهُ . فقالَ عُمَرُ : ثَكِلَتْكَ أُمُّكَ . نَزَرْتَ رَسُولَ اللهِ صلى اللهُ عليهِ وسلَّمَ ثَلاثَ مَرَّاتٍ كُلَّ ذَلكَ لا يُجِيبُكَ . قالَ عُمَرُ : فحرَّكْتُ بَعِيرِى حتَّى كُنْتُ أَمامَ النَّاسِ وَخَشِيتُ أَنْ يَنزِلَ فِىَّ قُرآنٌ ، فَمَا نَشِبْتُ أَنْ سَمِعْتُ صارِخاً يَصْرُخُ ، قالَ : فَقُلْتُ لَقَدْ خَشِيتُ أَنْ يَكُونَ نَزَلَ فِىَّ قُرآنٌ ، قالَ : فَجِئْتُ رَسُولَ اللهِ صلى اللهُ عليهِ وسلَّم فَسَلَّمْتُ عَلَيْهِ فَقالَ : لَقَدْ أُنْزِلَتْ عَلَىَّ اللَّيْلَةَ سُورَةٌ لَهِىَ أَحَبُّ إِلَىَّ مِمَّا طَلَعَتْ عَلَيْهِ الشَّمْسُ ، ثُمَّ قَرأَ ـ إِنَّا فَتَحْنا لكَ فَتْحاً مُبِيناً ـ .

(13) CHAPTER. The superiority of: 'Say: He is Allāh, (the) One.' (i.e.' Sūrat - al-Ikhlāṣ). No. (112)

بابُ فَضْلِ . قُلْ هُوَ اللهُ أَحَدٌ

فِيهِ عَمْرَةُ عَنْ عائشةَ عَنِ النَّبِىِّ صلى اللهُ عليهِ وسلَّم .

533. Narrated Abū Sa'īd Al-Khudrī ﷺ: A man heard another man reciting: (Sūrat-Al-Ikhlāṣ)

٥٣٣ ـ حدَّثَنا عَبْدُ اللهِ بنُ يُوسُفَ : أَخْبَرَنا مالكٌ ، عَنْ عَبْدِ الرَّحْمَنِ بنِ

'Say He is Allāh, (the) One.'
(112: 1)

repeatedly. The next morning he came to Allāh's Messenger and informed him about it as if he thought that it was not enough to recite. On that Allāh's Messenger said, "By Him in Whose Hand my life is, this Sūrah is equal to one-third of the Qur'ān!"
Narrated Abū Sa'īd Al-Khudrī : My brother, Qatāda bin An-Nauman said, "A man performed the night prayer late at night in the lifetime of the Prophet and he read:

'Say: He is Allāh, (the) One,'
(112:1)

and read nothing besides that. The next morning a man went to the Prophet and told him about that. (The Prophet replied the same as (in Ḥadīth 533) above.)

عَبْدِ اللهِ بنِ عَبْدِ الرَّحْمَنِ ابنِ أبي
صَعْصَعَةَ، عَنْ أبِيهِ، عَنْ أبي سَعِيدٍ
الخُدْرِيِّ: أنَّ رَجُلاً سَمِعَ رَجُلاً يَقْرَأُ -
قُلْ هُوَ اللهُ أحَدٌ - يُرَدِّدُها. فَلَمَّا
أصْبَحَ جاءَ إلى رَسُولِ اللهِ صلى اللهُ عليهِ
وسلَّم فَذَكَرَ ذَلِكَ لَهُ وكأنَّ الرَّجُلَ
يَتَقالُّها، فَقالَ رَسُولُ اللهِ صلى اللهُ عليهِ
وسلَّم: والَّذِي نَفْسِي بِيَدِهِ إنَّها لَتَعْدِلُ
ثُلُثَ القُرآنِ. وَزادَ أبُو مَعْمَرٍ: حدَّثَنا
إسْماعِيلُ بنُ جَعْفَرٍ، عَنْ مالِكِ بنِ
أنَسٍ، عَنْ عَبْدِ الرَّحْمَنِ بنِ عَبْدِ اللهِ
ابنِ عَبْدِ الرَّحْمَنِ بنِ أبي صَعْصَعَةَ،
عَنْ أبِيهِ. عَنْ أبي سَعِيدٍ الخُدْرِيِّ:
أخْبَرَنِي أخِي قَتادَةُ ابنُ النُّعْمانِ: أنَّ
رَجُلاً قامَ في زَمَنِ النَّبِيِّ صلى اللهُ عليهِ
وسلَّم يَقْرَأُ مِنَ السَّحَرِ - قُلْ هُوَ اللهُ
أحَدٌ - لايَزِيدُ عَلَيْها، فَلَمَّا أصْبَحْنا
أتَى رَجُلٌ النَّبِيَّ صلى اللهُ عليهِ وسلَّم،
نَحْوَهُ.

534. Narrated Abū Sa'īd Al-Khudrī : The Prophet said to his companions, "Is it difficult for any of you to recite one third of the Qur'ān in one night?" This suggestion was difficult for them so they said, "Who among us has the power to do so, O Allāh's Messenger?" Allāh Messenger replied, " 'Allāh (the) One, the Self-Suffi-

٥٣٤ - حدَّثَنا عُمَرُ بنُ حَفْصٍ:
حدَّثَنا أبي: حدَّثَنا الأعْمَشُ: حدَّثَنا
إبْراهِيمُ والضَّحَّاكُ المِشْرَقِيُّ، عَنْ
أبي سَعِيدٍ الخُدْرِيِّ رَضِيَ اللهُ عَنْهُ
قالَ: قالَ النَّبِيُّ صلى اللهُ عليهِ وسلَّم
لأصْحابِهِ: أيَعْجِزُ أحَدُكُمْ أنْ يَقْرَأَ

cient Master Whom all creatures need.' (Sūrat-Al-Ikhlāṣ 112:1—to the End) is equal to one third of the Qur'ān."

ثُلُثَ الْقُرْآنِ فِي لَيْلَةٍ ؟ فَشَقَّ ذَلِكَ عَلَيْهِمْ وَقَالُوا : أَيُّنَا يُطِيقُ ذَلِكَ يَا رَسُولَ اللهِ ؟ فَقَالَ : اللهُ الوَاحِدُ الصَّمَدُ ، ثُلُثُ الْقُرْآنِ . قَالَ أَبُو عَبْدِ اللهِ ، عَنْ إِبْرَاهِيمَ : مُرْسَلٌ ، وَعَنِ الضَّحَّاكِ الْمَشْرِقِيِّ مُسْنَدٌ .

(14) CHAPTER. The superiority of Al-Mu'awwidhāt (Sūrat al-Falaq and Sūrat-An-Nās). (113 and 114).

بَابُ فَضْلِ الْمُعَوِّذَاتِ

535. Narrated 'Āisha (رضي الله عنها) : Whenever Allāh's Messenger ﷺ became sick, he would recite Mu'awwidhāt (Sūrat-Al-Falaq and Sūrat-An-Nās) and then blow his breath over his body. When he became seriously ill, I used to recite (these two Sūras) and rub his hands over his body hoping for its blessings.

٥٣٥ - حَدَّثَنَا عَبْدُ اللهِ بْنُ يُوسُفَ : أَخْبَرَنَا مَالِكٌ ، عَنِ ابْنِ شِهَابٍ ، عَنْ عُرْوَةَ ، عَنْ عَائِشَةَ رَضِيَ اللهُ عَنْهَا : أَنَّ رَسُولَ اللهِ صلى الله عليه وسلم كَانَ إِذَا اشْتَكَى يَقْرَأُ عَلَى نَفْسِهِ بِالْمُعَوِّذَاتِ وَيَنْفُثُ . فَلَمَّا اشْتَدَّ وَجَعُهُ كُنْتُ أَقْرَأُ عَلَيْهِ وَأَمْسَحُ بِيَدِهِ رَجَاءَ بَرَكَتِهَا .

536 (A). Narrated 'Āisha (رضي الله عنها) : Whenever the Prophet ﷺ went to bed every night, he used to cup his hands together and blow over it after reciting Sūrat-Al-Ikhlāṣ, Sūrat-Al-Falaq and Sūrat-An-Nās, and then rub his hands over whatever parts of his body he was able to rub, starting with his head, face and front of his body. He used to do that three times.

٥٣٦ (ا) حَدَّثَنَا قُتَيْبَةُ بْنُ سَعِيدٍ : حَدَّثَنَا الْمُفَضَّلُ بْنُ فَضَالَةَ ، عَنْ عُقَيْلٍ ، عَنِ ابْنِ شِهَابٍ ، عَنْ عُرْوَةَ ، عَنْ عَائِشَةَ : أَنَّ النَّبِيَّ صلى الله عليه وسلم كَانَ إِذَا أَوَى إِلَى فِرَاشِهِ كُلَّ لَيْلَةٍ جَمَعَ كَفَّيْهِ ثُمَّ نَفَثَ فِيهِمَا - فَقَرَأَ فِيهِمَا - قُلْ هُوَ اللهُ أَحَدٌ - وَ - قُلْ أَعُوذُ بِرَبِّ الْفَلَقِ - وَ - قُلْ أَعُوذُ بِرَبِّ

لنَّاسِ - ثُمَّ يَمْسَحُ بِهِمَا مَا اسْتَطَاعَ مِنْ جَسَدِهِ يَبْدَأُ بِهِمَا عَلَى رَأْسِهِ وَوَجْهِهِ وَمَا أَقْبَلَ مِنْ جَسَدِهِ ، يَفْعَلُ ذَلِكَ ثَلَاثَ مَرَّاتٍ .

(15) CHAPTER, The descent of tranquillity and Angels at the time of the recitation of the Qur'ān.

536 (B). Narrated Usaid bin Ḥuḍair that while he was reciting Sūrat Al-Baqara (The Cow) at night, and his horse was tied beside him, the horse was suddenly startled, and troubled. When he stopped reciting, the horse became quiet, and when he started again, the horse was startled again. Then he stopped reciting and the horse became quiet too. He started reciting again and the horse was startled and troubled once again. Then he stopped reciting and his son, Yaḥyā was beside the horse. He was afraid that the horse might trample on him. When he took the boy away and looked towards the sky, he could not see it. The next morning he informed the Prophet ﷺ who said, "Recite, O Ibn Ḥuḍair! Recite, O Ibn Ḥuḍair!" Ibn Ḥuḍair replied, "O Allāh's Messenger! My son, Yaḥyā was near the horse and I was afraid that it might trample on him, so I looked towards the sky, and went to him. When I looked at the sky, I saw something like a cloud containing what looked like lamps, so I went out in order not to see it." The Prophet ﷺ said, "Do you know what that was?" Ibn Ḥuḍair replied, "No." The Prophet ﷺ said, "Those

بابُ نُزُولِ السَّكِينَةِ وَالْمَلَائِكَةِ عِنْدَ قِرَاءَةِ الْقُرْآنِ .

٥٣٦ (ب) - وَقَالَ اللَّيْثُ : حَدَّثَنِي يَزِيدُ بْنُ الْهَادِ ، عَنْ مُحَمَّدِ بْنِ إِبْرَاهِيمَ ، عَنْ أُسَيْدِ بْنِ حُضَيْرٍ قَالَ : بَيْنَمَا هُوَ يَقْرَأُ مِنَ اللَّيْلِ سُورَةَ الْبَقَرَةِ وَفَرَسُهُ مَرْبُوطٌ عِنْدَهُ إِذْ جَالَتِ الْفَرَسُ فَسَكَتَ فَسَكَنَتْ فَقَرَأَ فَجَالَتِ الْفَرَسُ فَسَكَتَ وَسَكَنَتِ الْفَرَسُ ثُمَّ قَرَأَ فَجَالَتِ الْفَرَسُ فَانْصَرَفَ وَكَانَ ابْنُهُ يَحْيَى قَرِيبًا مِنْهَا فَأَشْفَقَ أَنْ تُصِيبَهُ ، فَلَمَّا اجْتَرَّهُ رَفَعَ رَأْسَهُ إِلَى السَّمَاءِ حَتَّى مَا يَرَاهَا ، فَلَمَّا أَصْبَحَ حَدَّثَ النَّبِيَّ صلى الله عليه وسلّم فَقَالَ : اقْرَأْ يَا ابْنَ حُضَيْرٍ ، اقْرَأْ يَا ابْنَ حُضَيْرٍ ، قَالَ : فَأَشْفَقْتُ يَا رَسُولَ اللهِ أَنْ تَطَأَ يَحْيَى وَكَانَ مِنْهَا قَرِيبًا . فَرَفَعْتُ رَأْسِي فَانْصَرَفْتُ إِلَيْهِ فَرَفَعْتُ رَأْسِي إِلَى السَّمَاءِ ، فَإِذَا مِثْلُ الظُّلَّةِ فِيهَا أَمْثَالُ الْمَصَابِيحِ فَخَرَجْتُ حَتَّى لَا أَرَاهَا . قَالَ : وَتَدْرِي مَا ذَاكَ ؟ قَالَ : لَا ، قَالَ : تِلْكَ الْمَلَائِكَةُ

were Angels who came near to you for your voice, and if you had kept on reciting till dawn, it would have remained there till morning when people would have seen it as it would not have disappeared."

دَنَتْ لِصَوْتِكَ، وَلَوْ قَرَأْتَ لأَصْبَحَتْ يَنْظُرُ النَّاسُ إِلَيْهَا، لا تَتَوَارَى مِنْهُمْ. قَالَ ابْنُ الْهَادِ: وَحَدَّثَنِي هَذَا الْحَدِيثَ عَبْدُ اللهِ بْنُ خَبَّابٍ: عَنْ أَبِي سَعِيدٍ الْخُدْرِيِّ عَنْ أُسَيْدِ بْنِ حُضَيْرٍ.

(16) CHAPTER. Whoever said that the Prophet ﷺ did not leave anything after his death, except what is between the two binders (of the Qur'ān).

بَابُ مَنْ قَالَ لَمْ يَتْرُكِ النَّبِيُّ صلى الله عليه وسلم إِلاَّ مَا بَيْنَ الدَّفَّتَيْنِ.

537. Narrated 'Abdul 'Azīz bin Rufai': Shaddād bin Ma'qil and I entered upon Ibn 'Abbās. Shaddād bin Ma'qil asked him, "Did the Prophet ﷺ leave anything (besides the Qur'ān)?" He replied. "He did not leave anything except what is between the two bindings (of the Qur'ān)." Then we visited Muḥammad bin Al-Ḥanafiyya and asked him (the same question). He replied, "The Prophet did not leave except what is between the two bindings (of the Qur'ān)."

٥٣٧ - حَدَّثَنَا قُتَيْبَةُ بْنُ سَعِيدٍ: حَدَّثَنَا سُفْيَانُ، عَنْ عَبْدِ الْعَزِيزِ بْنِ رُفَيْعٍ قَالَ: دَخَلْتُ أَنَا وَشَدَّادُ بْنُ مَعْقِلٍ عَلَى ابْنِ عَبَّاسٍ رَضِيَ اللهُ عَنْهُمَا، فَقَالَ لَهُ شَدَّادُ بْنُ مَعْقِلٍ: أَتَرَكَ النَّبِيُّ صلى الله عليه وسلم مِنْ شَيْءٍ؟ قَالَ: مَا تَرَكَ إِلاَّ مَا بَيْنَ الدَّفَّتَيْنِ، قَالَ: وَدَخَلْنَا عَلَى مُحَمَّدِ بْنِ الْحَنَفِيَّةِ فَسَأَلْنَاهُ فَقَالَ: مَا تَرَكَ إِلاَّ مَا بَيْنَ الدَّفَّتَيْنِ.

(17) The Superiority of the Qur'ān above

بَابُ فَضْلِ الْقُرْآنِ عَلَى سَائِرِ

other kinds of speech.

الكلام .

538. Narrated Abū Mūsā Al-'Ash 'arī: The Prophet ﷺ said, "The example of him (a believer) who recites the Qur'ān is like that of a citron which tastes good and smells good. And he (a believer) who does not recite the Qur'ān is like a date which is good in taste but has no smell. And the example of a dissolute wicked person who recites the Qur'ān is like the Raiḥāna (sweet basil) which smells good but tastes bitter. And the example of a dissolute wicked person who does not recite the Qur'ān is like the colocynth which tastes bitter and has no smell.

٥٣٨ - حدثنا هدبة بن خالد أبو خالد : حدثنا همام : حدثنا قتادة : حدثنا أنس بن مالك ، عن أبي موسى الأشعري ، عن النبي صلى الله عليه وسلم قال : مثل الذي يقرأ القرآن كالأترجة طعمها طيب ، وريحها طيب ، والذي لا يقرأ القرآن كالتمرة طعمها طيب ولا ريح فيها . ومثل الفاجر الذي يقرأ القرآن كمثل الريحانة ريحها طيب وطعمها مر . ومثل الفاجر الذي لا يقرأ القرآن كمثل الحنظلة ، طعمها مر ولا ريح لها .

539. Narrated Ibn 'Umar (رضي الله عنهما): The Prophet ﷺ said, "Your life in comparison to the lifetime of the past nations is like the period between the time of 'Aṣr prayer and sunset. Your example and the example of the Jews and Christians is that of person who employed labourers and said to them, "Who will work for me till the middle of the day for one Qīrāṭ (a special weight)?' The Jews did. He then said, "Who will work for me from the middle of the day till the 'Aṣr prayer for one Qīrāṭ each?" The

٥٣٩ - حدثنا مسدد ، عن يحيى ، عن سفيان : حدثني عبد الله بن دينار قال : سمعت ابن عمر رضي الله عنهما ، عن النبي صلى الله عليه وسلم قال : إنما أجلكم في أجل من خلا من الأمم كما بين صلاة العصر ومغرب الشمس . ومثلكم ومثل اليهود والنصارى كمثل رجل استعمل عمالا ، فقال : من يعمل لي ، إلى

Christians worked accordingly. Then you (Muslims) are working from the 'Asr prayer till the Maghrib prayer for two Qirāṭs each. They (the Jews and the Christians) said, 'We did more labour but took less wages.' He (Allāh) said, 'Have I wronged you in your rights?' They replied, 'No.' Then He said, 'This is My Blessing which I give to whom I wish.' "

نِصْفِ النَّهارِ عَلَى قِيراطٍ ؟ فَعَمِلَتِ اليَهُودُ ، فَقالَ : مَنْ يَعْمَلُ لِى مِنْ نِصْفِ النَّهارِ إلى العَصْرِ عَلَى قِيراطٍ ؟ فَعَمِلَتِ النَّصارَى . ثُمَّ أَنْتُمْ تَعْمَلُونَ مِنَ العَصْرِ إلى المَغْرِبِ بِقِيراطَيْنِ قِيراطَيْنِ ، قالُوا : نَحْنُ أَكْثَرُ عَمَلاً وأَقَلُّ عَطاءً . قالَ : هَلْ ظَلَمْتُكُم مِنْ حَقِّكُمْ ؟ قالُوا : لا ، قالَ : فَذاكَ فَضْلِى أُوتِيهِ مَنْ شِئْتُ .

(18) CHAPTER. To recommend the Book of Allāh عزّوجلّ :-

بابُ الوَصاةِ بِكِتابِ اللهِ عَزَّ وجَلَّ .

540. Narrated Ṭalḥa: I asked 'Abdullāh bin Abī 'Aufā. ' Did the Prophet ﷺ make a will (to appoint his successor or bequeath wealth)?" He replied, "No." I said, "How is it prescribed then for the people to make wills, and they are ordered to do so while the Prophet ﷺ did not make any will?" He said, "He made a will wherein he recommended Allāh's Book."

٥٤٠ ـ حدَّثنا مُحَمَّدُ بنُ يُوسُفَ : حدَّثنا مالكُ بنُ مِغْوَلٍ : حدَّثنا طَلْحَةُ قالَ : سأَلْتُ عَبْدَ اللهِ بنَ أبي أَوْفَى : أَوْصَى النَّبِيُّ صلى اللهُ عليه وسلَّمَ ؟ فقالَ : لا ، فقُلْتُ : كَيْفَ كُتِبَ عَلَى النَّاسِ الوَصِيَّةُ أُمِرُوا بِها ولَمْ يُوصِ ؟ قالَ : أَوْصَى بِكِتابِ اللهِ .

(19) CHAPTER. Whoever does not recite the Qur'ān in a pleasant tone. And the Statement of Allāh تعالى :—

'Is it not sufficient for them that We have sent down to you the Book (the Qur'ān) which is re-

بابُ مَنْ لَمْ يَتَغَنَّ بالقُرْآنِ ، وَقَوْلُهُ تَعالَى ـ أَوَلَمْ يَكْفِهِمْ أَنَّا أَنْزَلْنا عَلَيْكَ الكِتابَ يُتْلَى عَلَيْهِمْ ـ .

cited to them?' (29:51)

541. Narrated Abū Huraira : Allāh's Messenger said, "Allāh does not listen to a prophet as He listens to a prophet who recites the Qur'ān in a pleasant tone." The companion of the sub-narrator (Abū Salama) said, "It means, reciting it aloud."

٥٤١ - حدثنا يحيى بن بكير قال: حدثني الليث، عن عقيل، عن ابن شهاب قال: أخبرني أبو سلمة بن عبد الرحمن، عن أبي هريرة رضي الله عنه: أنه كان يقول: قال رسول الله صلى الله عليه وسلم: لم يأذن الله لنبي ما أذن لنبي أن يتغنى بالقرآن. وقال صاحب له يريد يجهر به.

542. Narrated Abū Huraira : The Prophet said, "Allāh does not listen to a prophet as He listens to a prophet who recites the Qur'ān in a loud and pleasant tone." Sufyān said, "This saying means: a prophet who regards the Qur'ān as something that makes him dispense with many worldly pleasures."

٥٤٢ - حدثنا علي بن عبد الله، عن سفيان، عن الزهري، عن أبي سلمة بن عبد الرحمن، عن أبي هريرة، عن النبي صلى الله عليه وسلم قال: ما أذن الله لنبي ما أذن لنبي أن يتغنى بالقرآن، قال سفيان: تفسيره يستغني به.

(20) CHAPTER. Wish to be the like of the one who recites the Qur'ān.

باب اغتباط صاحب القرآن.

543. Narrated 'Abdullāh bin 'Umar : Allāh's Messenger said, "Not

٥٤٣ - حدثنا أبو اليمان: أخبرنا شعيب، عن الزهري قال: حدثني

to wish to be the like except of two men. A man whom Allāh has given the knowledge of the Book and he recites it during the hours of the night, and a man whom Allāh has given wealth, and he spends it in charity during the night and the hours of the day."

سالم بن عبد الله بن عمر رضي الله عنهما قال: سمعت رسول الله صلى الله عليه وسلم يقول لا حسد إلا على اثنتين، رجل آتاه الله الكتاب وقام به آناء الليل، ورجل أعطاه الله مالا فهو يتصدق به آناء الليل وآناء النهار.

544. Narrated Abū Huraira رضي الله عنه: Allāh's Messenger ﷺ said, "Not to wish to be the like of except two men: A man whom Allāh has taught the Qur'ān and he recites it during the hours of the night and during the hours of the day, and his neighbour listens to him and says, 'I wish I had been given what has been given to so-and-so, so that I might do what he does; and a man whom Allāh has given wealth and he spends it on what is just and right, whereupon an other man may say, 'I wish I had been given what so-and-so has been given, for then I would do what he does.' "

٥٤٤ - حدثنا علي بن إبراهيم: حدثنا روح: حدثنا شعبة، عن سليمان قال: سمعت ذكوان، عن أبي هريرة: أن رسول الله صلى الله عليه وسلم قال: لا حسد إلا في اثنتين: رجل علمه الله القرآن فهو يتلوه آناء الليل وآناء النهار، فسمعه جار له فقال: ليتني أوتيت مثل ما أوتي فلان فعملت مثل ما يعمل. ورجل آتاه الله مالا فهو يهلكه في الحق، فقال رجل: ليتني أوتيت مثل ما أوتي فلان، فعملت مثل ما يعمل.

(21) CHAPTER. "The best among you(Muslims) are those who learn the Qur'ān and teach it.

باب خيركم من تعلم القرآن وعلمه.

545. Narrated 'Uthmān رضي الله عنه: The Prophet ﷺ said, "The best among you

٥٤٥ - حدثنا حجاج بن منهال: حدثنا شعبة قال: أخبرني علقمة بن

(Muslims) are those who learn the Qur'ān and teach it."

مرثد : سمعت سعد ابن عبيدة ، عن أبي عبد الرحمن السلمي ، عن عثمان رضي الله عنه ، عن النبي صلى الله عليه وسلم قال : خيركم من تعلم القرآن وعلمه . قال : وأقرأ أبو عبد الرحمن في إمرة عثمان حتى كان الحجاج ، قال : وذاك الذي أقعدني مقعدي هذا .

546. Narrated 'Uthmān bin 'Affān ﷺ : The Prophet ﷺ said, "'The most superior among you (Muslims) are those who learn the Qur'ān and teach it."

٥٤٦ ـ حدثنا أبو نعيم : حدثنا سفيان ، عن علقمة بن مرثد ، عن أبي عبد الرحمن السلمي عن عثمان بن عفان رضي الله عنه قال : قال النبي صلى الله عليه وسلم : إن أفضلكم من تعلم القرآن وعلمه .

547. Narrated Sahl bin Sa'd: A lady came to the Prophet ﷺ and declared that she had decided to offer herself to Allāh and His Messenger ﷺ .The Prophet ﷺ said, "I am not in need of women." A man said (to the Prophet ﷺ), "Please marry her to me." The Prophet ﷺ said (to him), "Give her a garment." The man said, "I cannot afford it." The Prophet ﷺ said, "Give her anything, even if it were an iron ring." The man apologised again. The Prophet ﷺ then asked him, "What do you know by

٥٤٧ ـ حدثنا عمرو بن عون : حدثنا حماد ، عن أبي حازم ، عن سهل ابن سعد قال : أتت النبي صلى الله عليه وسلم امرأة فقالت : إنها قد وهبت نفسها لله ولرسوله صلى الله عليه وسلم فقال : ما لي في النساء من حاجة ، فقال رجل : زوجنيها ، قال : أعطها ثوبا ، قال : لا أجد ، قال : أعطها ولو خاتما من حديد ، فاعتل له . فقال : ما معك

heart of the Qur'ān?" He replied, "I know such-and-such portion of the Qur'ān (by heart)." The Prophet ﷺ said, "Then I marry her to you for that much of the Qur'ān which you know by heart."

مِنَ الْقُرْآنِ؟ قَالَ كَذَا وَكَذَا، قَالَ: فَقَدْ زَوَّجْتُكَهَا بِمَا مَعَكَ مِنَ الْقُرْآنِ.

(22) CHAPTER. The recitation of the Qur'ān by heart.

بَابُ الْقِرَاءَةِ عَنْ ظَهْرِ الْقَلْبِ.

548 . Narrated Sahl bin Sa'd: A lady came to Allāh's Messenger ﷺ and said, "O Allāh's Messenger! I have come to you to offer myself to you." He raised his eyes and looked at her and then lowered his head. When the lady saw that he did not make any decision, she sat down. On that, a man from his companions got up and said. "O Allāh's Messenger! If you are not in need of this woman, then marry her to me." Allāh's Messenger ﷺ said, "Do you have anything to offer her?" He replied. "No, by Allāh, O Allāh's Messenger!" The Prophet ﷺ said to him, "Go to your family and see if you can find something.' The man went and returned, saying, "No, by Allāh, O Allāh's Messenger! I have not found anything." The Prophet ﷺ said, "Try to find something, even if it is an iron ring." He went again and returned, saying, "No, by Allāh, O Allāh's Messenger, not even an iron ring, but I have this waist sheet of mine." The man had no upper garment, so he intended to give her, half his waist sheet. So Allāh's Messenger ﷺ

٥٤٨ - حَدَّثَنَا قُتَيْبَةُ بْنُ سَعِيدٍ: حَدَّثَنَا يَعْقُوبُ بْنُ عَبْدِ الرَّحْمَنِ، عَنْ أَبِي حَازِمٍ، عَنْ سَهْلِ ابْنِ سَعْدٍ: أَنَّ امْرَأَةً جَاءَتْ رَسُولَ اللهِ صلى اللهُ عليه وسلَّم فَقَالَتْ: يَا رَسُولَ اللهِ: جِئْتُ لأَهَبَ لَكَ نَفْسِي، فَنَظَرَ إِلَيْهَا رَسُولُ اللهِ صلى اللهُ عليه وسلَّم فَصَعَّدَ النَّظَرَ إِلَيْهَا وَصَوَّبَهُ ثُمَّ طَأْطَأَ رَأْسَهُ. فَلَمَّا رَأَتِ الْمَرْأَةُ أَنَّهُ لَمْ يَقْضِ فِيهَا شَيْئًا جَلَسَتْ، فَقَامَ رَجُلٌ مِنْ أَصْحَابِهِ فَقَالَ: يَا رَسُولَ اللهِ، إِنْ لَمْ يَكُنْ لَكَ بِهَا حَاجَةٌ فَزَوِّجْنِيهَا، فَقَالَ: هَلْ عِنْدَكَ مِنْ شَيْءٍ؟ فَقَالَ: لاَ وَاللهِ يَا رَسُولَ اللهِ، قَالَ: اذْهَبْ إِلَى أَهْلِكَ فَانْظُرْ هَلْ تَجِدُ شَيْئًا. فَذَهَبَ ثُمَّ رَجَعَ فَقَالَ: لاَ وَاللهِ يَا رَسُولَ اللهِ مَا

said, "What would she do with your waist sheet? If you wear it, she will have nothing of it over her body, and if she wears it, you will have nothing over your body." So that man sat for a long period and then got up, and Allāh's Messenger ﷺ saw him going away, so he ordered somebody to call him. When he came, the Prophet ﷺ asked him, "How much of the Qur'ān do you know?" He replied, "I know such Sūrah and such Sūrah and such Sūrah," and went on counting them. The Prophet ﷺ asked him, "Can you recite them by heart?" he replied, "Yes." The Prophet ﷺ said "Go, I have married this lady to you for the amount of the Qur'ān you know by heart."

وجدت شيئا. قال: انظر ولو خاتما من حديد، فذهب ثم رجع فقال: لا والله يا رسول الله، ولا خاتما من حديد ولكن هذا إزاري، قال سهل: ماله رداء فلها نصفه، فقال رسول الله صلى الله عليه وسلم: ما تصنع بإزارك، إن لبسته لم يكن عليها منه شيء، وإن لبسته لم يكن عليك شيء، فجلس الرجل حتى طال مجلسه، ثم قام فرآه رسول الله صلى الله عليه وسلم موليا فأمر به فدعي، فلما جاء قال: ماذا معك من القرآن؟ قال: معي سورة كذا وسورة كذا وسورة كذا عددها، قال: أتقرؤهن عن ظهر قلبك؟ قال: نعم، قال: اذهب فقد ملكتكها بما معك من القرآن.

(23) CHAPTER. The learning of the Qur'ān by heart and the reciting of it repeatedly.

باب استذكار القرآن وتعاهده.

549. Narrated Ibn 'Umar : Allāh's Messenger ﷺ said, "The example of the person who knows the Qur'ān by heart is like the owner of tied camels. If he keeps them tied, he will control them, but if he releases them, they will run

٥٤٩ - حدثنا عبد الله بن يوسف: أخبرنا مالك، عن نافع، عن ابن عمر رضي الله عنهما: أن رسول الله صلى الله عليه وسلم قال: إنما مثل صاحب

away."

القُرآنِ كَمَثَلِ صَاحِبِ الإِبِلِ المُعَقَّلَةِ ، إِنْ عَاهَدَ عَلَيْهَا أَمْسَكَهَا ، وَإِنْ أَطْلَقَهَا ذَهَبَتْ .

550. Narrated 'Abdullāh : The Prophet ﷺ said, "It is a bad thing that some of you say, 'I have forgotten such-and-such Verse of the Qur'ān,' for indeed, he has been caused (by Allāh) to forget it. (1) So you must keep on reciting the Qur'ān because it escapes from the hearts of men faster than camel do."

٥٥٠ - حَدَّثَنَا مُحَمَّدُ بْنُ عَرْعَرَةَ : حَدَّثَنَا شُعْبَةُ ، عَنْ مَنْصُورٍ ، عَنْ أَبِي وَائِلٍ ، عَنْ عَبْدِ اللهِ قَالَ : قَالَ النَّبِيُّ صلى اللهُ عليهِ وسلَّم : بِئْسَ مَا لأَحَدِهِمْ أَنْ يَقُولَ نَسِيتُ آيَةَ كَيْتَ وَكَيْتَ ، بَلْ نُسِّيَ وَاسْتَذْكِرُوا القُرْآنَ فَإِنَّهُ أَشَدُّ تَفَصِّيًا مِنْ صُدُورِ الرِّجَالِ مِنَ النَّعَمِ .

551. Narrated 'Abdullāh: I heard the Prophet ﷺ saying... (as above, no. 550).

٥٥١ - حَدَّثَنَا عُثْمَانُ : حَدَّثَنَا جَرِيرٌ ، عَنْ مَنْصُورٍ مِثْلَهُ . تَابَعَهُ بِشْرٌ ، عَنِ ابْنِ المُبَارَكِ ، عَنْ شُعْبَةَ . وَتَابَعَهُ ابْنُ جُرَيْجٍ ، عَنْ عَبْدَةَ ، عَنْ شَقِيقٍ : سَمِعْتُ عَبْدَ اللهِ : سَمِعْتُ النَّبِيَّ صلى اللهُ عليهِ وسلَّم .

552. Narrated Abū Mūsā: the Prophet ﷺ said, "Keep on reciting the Qur'ān, for, by Him in Whose Hand my life is, Qur'ān runs away (is forgotten) faster than camels that are released from

٥٥٢ - حَدَّثَنَا مُحَمَّدُ بْنُ العَلاءِ : حَدَّثَنَا أَبُو أُسَامَةَ ، عَنْ بُرَيْدٍ ، عَنْ أَبِي بُرْدَةَ ، عَنْ أَبِي مُوسَى عَنِ النَّبِيِّ صلى

(1) Because of neglecting the Qur'ān and not reciting it frequently.

their tying ropes."

اللهُ عليهِ وسلَّم قالَ: تَعاهَدُوا القُرآنَ فَوَالَّذى نَفْسِى بِيَدِهِ لَهُوَ أشَدُّ تَفَصِّيًا مِنَ الإبِلِ فى عُقُلِها .

(24) CHAPTER. The recitation of the Qur'ān on an animal.

بابُ القِرَاءَةِ عَلى الدَّابَّةِ .

553. Narrated 'Abdullāh bin Mughaf-fal: I saw Allāh's Messenger ﷺ reciting Sūrat-al-Fatḥ on his she-camel on the day of the Conquest of Mecca.

٥٥٣ ـ حدَّثَنا حَجّاجُ بنُ مِنْهالٍ : حدَّثَنا شُعْبَةُ قالَ : أخبَرَنِى أبو إياسٍ قالَ : سَمِعْتُ عَبْدَ اللهِ ابنَ مُغَفَّلٍ قالَ : رَأيْتُ رَسُولَ اللهِ صلى اللهُ عليهِ وسلَّم يَوْمَ فَتْحِ مَكَّةَ وَهُوَ يَقرَأُ عَلى راحِلَتِهِ سُورَةَ الفَتْحِ .

(25) CHAPTER. Teaching the Qur'ān to the children.

بابُ تَعْلِيمِ الصِّبْيانِ القُرآنَ .

554. Narrated Sa'id bid Jubair: Those Sūras which you people call the Mufaṣṣal, (1) are the Muḥkam. (2) And Ibn 'Abbās said, "Allāh's Messenger ﷺ died when I was a boy of ten years, and I had learnt the Muḥkam (of the Qur'ān).

٥٥٤ ـ حدَّثَنِى مُوسَى بنُ إسْماعيلَ : حدَّثَنا أبو عَوانَةَ ، عَنْ أبى بِشْرٍ ، عَنْ سَعيدِ بنِ جُبَيْرٍ قالَ : إنَّ الَّذى تَدْعُونَهُ المُفَصَّلَ هُوَ المُحْكَمُ ، قالَ : وَقالَ

(1) The Muḥkam are those Sūras which contain no abrogated decrees or orders.

(2) The Mufaṣṣal are the Sūras which start with Sūrat-al-Ḥujurāt to the end of the Qur'ān.

ابنُ عبّاسٍ: تُوُفّيَ رسولُ اللهِ صلى اللهُ
عليهِ وسلّم وأنا ابنُ عشرِ سنينَ وقد
قرأتُ المُحكَمَ .

555. Narrated Sa'īd bin Jubair: Ibn 'Abbās said, "I have learnt all the Muḥkam Sūras during the life time of Allāh's Messenger." I said to him, 'What is meant by the Muḥkam?" He replied,"The Mufaṣṣal."

٥٥٥ ـ حدّثنا يعقوبُ بنُ إبراهيمَ:
حدّثنا هُشَيمٌ: أخبرَنا أبو بِشرٍ، عن
سعيدِ بنِ جُبَيرٍ، عنِ ابنِ عبّاسٍ رضيَ
اللهُ عنهُما: جمعتُ المُحكَمَ في عهدِ
رسولِ اللهِ صلى اللهُ عليهِ وسلّمَ، فقلتُ
لهُ: وما المُحكَمُ؟ قالَ: المُفصَّلُ .

(26) CHAPTER. Forgetting the Qur'ān. And can one say: 'I forgot such-and-such a Verse'? And the Statement of Allāh :–

'We shall make you (O Muḥammad) recite (the Qur'ān) so that you shall not forget it except what Allāh will.' (87:6-7)

بابُ نسيانِ القرآنِ، وهل يقولُ
نسيتُ آيةَ كذا وكذا؟ وقولِ اللهِ تعالى-
سنُقرِئُكَ فلا تنسى إلاّ ما شاءَ اللهُ - .

556. Narrated 'Āisha : The Prophet heard a man reciting the Qur'ān in the mosque and said, "May Allāh bestow His Mercy on him, as he has reminded me of such-and-such Verses of such a Sūrah."

٥٥٦ ـ حدّثنا ربيعُ بنُ يحيى:
حدّثنا زائدةُ: حدّثنا هشامٌ، عن عروةَ،
عن عائشةَ رضيَ اللهُ عنها قالت:
سمعَ النبيُّ صلى اللهُ عليهِ وسلّمَ رجلاً
يقرأُ في المسجدِ فقالَ: يرحمُهُ اللهُ
لقد أذكرَني كذا وكذا آيةً من

سُورَةِ كَذَا

557. Narrated Hishām : (The same Ḥadīth, adding): which I missed from such and such "Sura".

٥٥٧ ـ حدَّثنا مُحمَّدُ بنُ عُبَيْدِ اللهِ ابنِ مَيْمُونٍ : حدَّثنا عِيسَى ، عَنْ هِشامٍ وقالَ أسقَطْتُهُنَّ مِنْ سُورَةِ كَذا. تابَعَهُ عَلِيُّ بنُ مُسْهِرٍ ، وعَبْدَةُ عَنْ هِشامٍ .

558. Narrated 'Āisha :Allāh's Messenger heard a man reciting the Qur'ān at night, and said, "May Allāh bestow His Mercy on him, as he has reminded me of such-and-such Verses of such-and-such Sūras, which I was caused to forget."

٥٥٨ ـ حدَّثنا أحمَدُ بنُ أبي رَجاءٍ : حدَّثنا أبُو أُسامَةَ ، عَنْ هِشامِ بنِ عُرْوَةَ ، عَنْ أبيهِ ، عَنْ عائِشَةَ قالَتْ : سَمِعَ رَسُولُ اللهِ صلى الله عليه وسلَّمَ رَجُلاً يَقْرَأُ في سُورَةٍ باللَّيْلِ فقالَ : يَرْحَمُهُ اللهُ لقَدْ أذْكَرَنِي آيَةَ كَذا وكَذا كُنْتُ أُنْسِيتُها مِنْ سُورَةِ كَذا وكَذا .

559. Narrated 'Abdullāh :The Prophet said, "Why does anyone of the people say, 'I have forgotten such-and-such Verses (of the Qur'ān)?' He, in fact, is caused (by Allāh) to forget."

٥٥٩ ـ حدَّثنا أبُو نُعَيْمٍ : حدَّثنا سُفْيانُ ، عَنْ مَنْصُورٍ ، عَنْ أبي وائِلٍ ، عَنْ عَبْدِ اللهِ قالَ : قالَ النَّبيُّ صلى الله عليه وسلَّمَ : مالأَحَدِهِمْ يَقُولُ نَسِيتُ آيَةَ كَيْتَ وكَيْتَ ؟ بَلْ هُوَ نُسِّيَ .

(27) CHAPTER. Whoever thinks that there is no harm in saying: "Sūrat-al-Baqara (The Cow) or Sūrat so-and-so."

بابُ مَنْ لَمْ يَرَ بأساً أنْ يَقُولَ سُورَةُ البَقَرَةِ ، وسُورَةُ كَذا وكَذا.

560. Narrated Abū Mas'ūd Al-Anṣārī : The Prophet ﷺ said, "Whosoever recited the last two Verses of Sūrat-al-Baqara at night, that will be sufficient for him (for that night)."

٥٦٠ ـ حدثنا عمر بن حفص : حدثنا أبي: حدثنا الأعمش قال : حدثني إبراهيم، عن علقمة، وعبد الرحمن ابن يزيد، عن أبي مسعود الأنصاري قال : قال النبي صلى الله عليه وسلم : الآيتان من آخر سورة البقرة من قرأ بهما في ليلة كفتاه .

561. Narrated 'Umar bin Khaṭṭāb (رضي الله عنه) : I heard Hishām bin Ḥakīm bin Ḥizām reciting Sūrat-al-Furqān during the lifetime of Allāh's Messenger ﷺ, and I listened to his recitation and noticed that he recited it in several ways which Allāh's Messenger ﷺ had not taught me. So I was on the point of attacking him in the prayer, but I waited till he finished his prayer, and then I seized him by the collar and said, "Who taught you this Sūrah which I have heard you reciting?" He replied, "Allāh's Messenger ﷺ taught it to me." I said, "You are telling a lie; By Allāh! Allāh's Messenger ﷺ taught me (in a different way) this very Sūrah which I have heard you reciting." So I took him, leading him to Allāh's Messenger ﷺ and said, "O Allāh's Messenger! I heard this person reciting Sūrat-al-Furqān in a way that you did not teach me, and you have taught me Sūrat-al-Furqān." The Prophet ﷺ said, "O Hishām, recite!" So he recited in the same way as I heard him recite it before. On that Allāh's Messenger ﷺ said, "It was revealed to be recited in this way." Then Allāh's Messenger ﷺ said, "Recite, O 'Umar!" So I recited it as he had taught me. Allāh's

٥٦١ ـ حدثنا أبو اليمان : أخبرنا شعيب، عن الزهري قال : أخبرني عروة بن الزبير، عن حديث المسور ابن مخرمة، وعبد الرحمن بن عبد القاري أنهما سمعا عمر بن الخطاب رضي الله عنه يقول : سمعت هشام بن حكيم بن حزام يقرأ سورة الفرقان في حياة رسول الله صلى الله عليه وسلم فاستمعت لقراءته فإذا هو يقرؤها على حروف كثيرة، لم يقرئنيها رسول الله صلى الله عليه وسلم فكدت أساوره في الصلاة، فانتظرته حتى سلم فلببته، فقلت : من أقرأك هذه السورة التي سمعتك تقرأ ؟ قال : أقرأنيها رسول الله صلى الله عليه وسلم، فقلت : كذبت فو الله إن رسول الله صلى الله عليه وسلم لهو أقرأني هذه السورة التي سمعتك، فانطلقت به إلى رسول الله صلى الله عليه وسلم

Messenger then said, "It was revealed to be recited in this way." Allāh's Messenger added, "The Qur'ān has been revealed to be recited in seven different ways, so recite of it that which is easier for you."

أَقُودُهُ فَقُلْتُ: يَا رَسُولَ اللهِ إِنِّي سَمِعْتُ
هَذَا يَقْرَأُ سُورَةَ الْفُرْقَانِ عَلَى حُرُوفٍ
لَمْ تُقْرِئْنِيهَا، وَإِنَّكَ أَقْرَأْتَنِي سُورَةَ
الْفُرْقَانِ، فَقَالَ: يَا هِشَامُ اقْرَأْهَا، فَقَرَأَهَا
الْقِرَاءَةَ الَّتِي سَمِعْتُهُ، فَقَالَ رَسُولُ اللهِ
صلى اللهُ عليه وسلَّمَ: هَكَذَا أُنْزِلَتْ،
ثُمَّ قَالَ: اقْرَأْ يَا عُمَرُ، فَقَرَأْتُهَا الَّتِي أَقْرَأَنِيهَا.
فَقَالَ رَسُولُ اللهِ صلى اللهُ عليه وسلَّمَ:
هَكَذَا أُنْزِلَتْ، ثُمَّ قَالَ رَسُولُ اللهِ
صلى اللهُ عليه وسلَّمَ: إِنَّ الْقُرْآنَ أُنْزِلَ
عَلَى سَبْعَةِ أَحْرُفٍ فَاقْرَءُوا مَا تَيَسَّرَ
مِنْهُ

562. Narrated 'Āisha : The Prophet heard a reciter reciting the Qur'ān in the mosque at night. The Prophet said, "May Allāh bestow His Mercy on him, as he has reminded me of such-and-such Verses of such-and-such Sūras, which I missed!"

٥٦٢ - حَدَّثَنَا بِشْرُ بْنُ آدَمَ: أَخْبَرَنَا
عَلِيُّ بْنُ مُسْهِرٍ: أَخْبَرَنَا هِشَامٌ عَنْ أَبِيهِ،
عَنْ عَائِشَةَ رَضِيَ اللهُ عَنْهَا قَالَتْ:
سَمِعَ النَّبِيُّ صلى اللهُ عليه وسلَّمَ قَارِئًا
يَقْرَأُ مِنَ اللَّيْلِ فِي الْمَسْجِدِ فَقَالَ:
يَرْحَمُهُ اللهُ، لَقَدْ أَذْكَرَنِي كَذَا وَ
كَذَا آيَةً أَسْقَطْتُهَا مِنْ سُورَةِ كَذَا وَ
كَذَا.

(28) CHAPTER. The Recitation of Qur'ān in 'Tartīl' (clearly and in a slow style). And the Statement of Allāh :–

'And recite the Qur'ān in slow style.' (73:4)

بَابُ التَّرْتِيلِ فِي الْقِرَاءَةِ، وَقَوْلِهِ

تَعَالَى - وَرَتِّلِ الْقُرْآنَ تَرْتِيلًا - وَقَوْلِهِ -
وَقُرْآنًا فَرَقْنَاهُ لِتَقْرَأَهُ عَلَى النَّاسِ عَلَى
مُكْثٍ - وَمَا يُكْرَهُ أَنْ يُهَذَّ كَهَذِّ

And also His Statement:—

> 'And (it is) a Qur'ān which We have divided (into parts) in order that you might recite it to mankind at intervals.' (17:106)

And it is hated to recite Qur'ān very quickly as one recites poetry.

الشِّعْرِ - فِيهَا يُفْرَقُ - يُفَصَّلُ ، قَالَ ابْنُ عَبَّاسٍ : فَرَقْنَاهُ : فَصَّلْنَاهُ .

563. Narrated Abū Wā'il: We went to 'Abdullāh in the morning and a man said, "Yesterday I recited all the Mufaṣṣal Sūras." On that 'Abdullāh said, "That is very quick, and we have the (Prophet's) recitation, and I remember very well the recitation of those Sūras which the Prophet ﷺ used to recite, and they were eighteen Sūras from the Mufaṣṣal, and two Sūras from the Sūras that start with Ḥā Mīm.

٥٦٣ - حَدَّثَنَا أَبُو النُّعْمَانِ : حَدَّثَنَا مَهْدِيُّ بْنُ مَيْمُونٍ : حَدَّثَنَا وَاصِلٌ ، عَنْ أَبِي وَائِلٍ ، عَنْ عَبْدِ اللهِ قَالَ : غَدَوْنَا عَلَى عَبْدِ اللهِ فَقَالَ رَجُلٌ : قَرَأْتُ الْمُفَصَّلَ الْبَارِحَةَ فَقَالَ : هَذًّا كَهَذِّ الشِّعْرِ ؟ إِنَّا قَدْ سَمِعْنَا الْقِرَاءَةَ وَإِنِّي لأَحْفَظُ الْقُرَنَاءَ الَّتِي كَانَ يَقْرَأُ بِهِنَّ النَّبِيُّ صلى اللهُ عليه وسلّمَ ثَمَانِيَ عَشْرَةَ سُورَةً مِنَ الْمُفَصَّلِ ، وَسُورَتَيْنِ مِنْ آلِ حم .

564. Narrated Ibn 'Abbās رضي الله عنهما regarding His (Allāh's) Statement:—

> 'Move not your tongue concerning (the Qur'ān) to make haste therewith.' (75:16)

And whenever Gabriel descended to Allāh's Messenger ﷺ with the Divine Inspiration, Allāh's Messenger ﷺ used to move his tongue and lips, and that used to be hard for him, and one could easily recognise that he was being inspired Divinely. So Allāh revealed the Verse

٥٦٤ - حَدَّثَنَا قُتَيْبَةُ بْنُ سَعِيدٍ : حَدَّثَنَا جَرِيرٌ ، عَنْ مُوسَى بْنِ أَبِي عَائِشَةَ ، عَنْ سَعِيدِ بْنِ جُبَيْرٍ ، عَنِ ابْنِ عَبَّاسٍ رَضِيَ اللهُ عَنْهُمَا فِي قَوْلِهِ - لاَ تُحَرِّكْ بِهِ لِسَانَكَ لِتَعْجَلَ بِهِ - قَالَ : كَانَ رَسُولُ اللهِ صلى اللهُ عليه وسلّمَ إِذَا نَزَلَ عَلَيْهِ جِبْرِيلُ بِالْوَحْيِ ، وَكَانَ مِمَّا يُحَرِّكُ بِهِ لِسَانَهُ وَشَفَتَيْهِ فَيَشْتَدُّ عَلَيْهِ وَكَانَ

which occurs in the Sūrah starting with:
"I do swear by the Day of Resurrection.' (75:1)

i.e. 'Move not your tongue concerning (the Qur'ān) to make haste there with. It is for Us to collect it (in your mind) (O Muḥammad) and give you the ability to recite it 'by heart.' (75:16–17)

which means: It is for us to collect it (in your mind) and give you the ability to recite it by heart. And when We have recited it to you (O Muḥammad) through Gabriel then follow you iṭs recital.(75:18) means:

'When We reveal it (the Qur'ān) to you, Listen to it.'

for then:

'It is for Us to explain it and make it clear to you (75:19)

i.e. It is up to Us to explain it through your tongue. So, when Gabriel came to him, Allāh's Messenger ﷺ would listen to him attentively, and as soon as Gabriel left, he would recite the Revelations, as Allāh had promised him.

يعرف منه، فأنزل الله الآية التي في - لا أقسم بيوم القيامة - لا تحرك به لسانك لتعجل به إن علينا جمعه وقرآنه - فإن علينا أن نجمعه في صدرك وقرآنه - فإذا قرأناه فاتبع قرآنه - فإذا أنزلناه فاستمع - ثم إن علينا بيانه - قال: إن علينا أن نبينه بلسانك . قال : وكان إذا أتاه جبريل أطرق ، فإذا ذهب قرأه كما وعده الله

(29) CHAPTER. Prolonging certain sounds while reciting the Qur'ān.

باب مد القراءة .

565. Narrated Qatāda: I asked Anas bin Mālik about the recitation of the Prophet ﷺ. He said, "He used to prolong (certain sounds) very much.

٥٦٥ - حدثنا مسلم بن إبراهيم : حدثنا جرير بن حازم الأزدي : حدثنا قتادة قال : سألت أنس بن مالك عن

قِراءَةِ النَّبِيِّ صلى اللهُ عليهِ وسلَّمَ فقالَ: كانَ يَمُدُّ مَدًّا .

566. Narrated Qatāda: Anas was asked, "How was the recitation (of the Qur'ān) of the Prophet ﷺ?' He replied, "It was characterised by the prolongation of certain sounds." He then recited:

In the Name of Allāh,
the Most Beneficent, the Most Merciful
prolonging the pronunciation of 'In the Name of Allāh, 'the most Beneficent,' and 'the Most Merciful.'

٥٦٦ ـ حدَّثنا عَمْرُو بنُ عاصِمٍ: حدَّثنا هَمَّامٌ، عَنْ قَتادَةَ قالَ: سُئِلَ أنَسٌ: كَيْفَ كانَتْ قِراءَةُ النَّبِيِّ صلى اللهُ عليهِ وسلَّمَ؟ فقالَ: كانَتْ مَدًّا، ثُمَّ قَرَأَ- بِسْمِ اللهِ الرَّحْمَنِ الرَّحيمِ يَمُدُّ بِبِسْمِ اللهِ. ويَمُدُّ بالرَّحْمَنِ، ويَمُدُّ بالرَّحيمِ.

(30) CHAPTER. At-Tarjī' (to recite Qur'ān in a sort of attractive vibrating tone.)

بابُ التَّرْجيعِ .

567. Narrated 'Abdullāh bin Mughaffal: I saw the Prophet ﷺ reciting (Qur'ān) while he was riding on his she-camel or camel which was moving, carrying him. He was reciting Sūrat Fatḥ or part of Sūrat Fatḥ very softly and in an attractive vibrating tone.

٥٦٧ ـ حدَّثنا آدَمُ بنُ أبي إياسٍ: حدَّثنا شُعْبَةُ: حدَّثنا أبو إياسٍ قالَ: سَمِعْتُ عَبْدَ اللهِ بنَ مُغَفَّلٍ قالَ: رأيْتُ النَّبِيَّ صلى اللهُ عليهِ وسلَّمَ يَقْرَأُ وَهُوَ عَلى ناقَتِهِ أوْ جَمَلِهِ وَهِيَ تَسيرُ بِهِ وَهُوَ يَقْرَأُ سُورَةَ الفَتْحِ أوْ مِنْ سُورَةِ الفَتْحِ قِراءَةً لَيِّنَةً، يَقْرَأُ وَهُوَ يُرَجِّعُ .

578. Narrated Abū Sa'īd Al-Khudrī رضي الله عنه : I heard Allāh's Messenger ﷺ saying, "There will appear some people among you whose prayer will make you look down upon yours, and whose fasting will make you look down upon yours, but they will recite the Qur'ān which will not exceed their throats (they will not act on it) and they will go out of Islām as an arrow goes out through the game whereupon the archer would examine the arrowhead but see nothing, and look at the unfeathered arrow but see nothing, and look at the arrowfeathers but see nothing, and finally he suspects to find something in the lower part of the arrow."

٥٧٨ - حدثنا عبد الله بن يوسف : أخبرنا مالك ، عن يحيى بن سعيد ، عن محمد بن إبراهيم ابن الحارث التيمي ، عن أبي سلمة بن عبد الرحمن ، عن أبي سعيد الخدري رضي الله عنه أنه قال : سمعت رسول الله صلى الله عليه وسلم يقول : يخرج فيكم قوم تحقرون صلاتكم مع صلاتهم ، وصيامكم مع صيامهم ، وعملكم مع عملهم ، ويقرءون القرآن لا يجاوز حناجرهم ، يمرقون من الدين كما يمرق السهم من الرمية ، ينظر في النصل فلا يرى شيئا ، وينظر في القدح فلا يرى شيئا ، وينظر في الريش فلا يرى شيئا ، ويتمارى في الفوق .

579. Narrated Abū Mūsā: The Prophet ﷺ said, "The example of a believer who recites the Qur'ān and acts on it, like a citron which tastes nice and smells nice. And the example of a believer who does not recite the Qur'ān but acts on it, is like a date which tastes good but has no smell. And the example of a hypocrite who recites the Qur'ān is like a Raihāna (sweet basil) which smells good but tastes bitter. And the example of a hypocrite who does not recite the Qur'ān is like a colocynth which tastes bitter and has a bad smell."

٥٧٩ - حدثنا مسدد : حدثنا يحيى ، عن شعبة ، عن قتادة ، عن أنس بن مالك ، عن أبي موسى ، عن النبي صلى الله عليه وسلم قال : المؤمن الذي يقرأ القرآن ويعمل به كالأترجة ، طعمها طيب وريحها طيب . والمؤمن الذي لا يقرأ القرآن ويعمل به كالتمرة طعمها طيب ، ولا ريح لها . ومثل المنافق الذي يقرأ القرآن كالريحانة ريحها

طيّبٌ، وطعمُها مرٌّ. ومثلُ المنافقِ الذي لا يقرأُ القرآنَ كالحنظلةِ، طعمُها مرٌّ. أو خبيثٌ، وريحُها مرٌّ.

(37) CHAPTER. Recite (and study) the Qur'ān together as long as you agree about its interpretation.

باب اقرءوا القرآنَ ما ائتلفتْ عليه قلوبُكم.

580. Narrated 'Abdullāh: The Prophet ﷺ said, "Recite (and study) the Qur'ān as long as you agree about its interpretation, but if you have any difference of opinion (as regards its interpretation and meaning) then you should stop reciting it (for the time being)."

٥٨٠ - حدّثنا أبو النُّعمانِ: حدّثنا حمّادٌ، عنْ أبي عمرانَ الجونيِّ، عنْ جُندبِ بنِ عبدِ اللهِ، عنِ النبيِّ صلى اللهُ عليهِ وسلّم قالَ: اقرءوا القرآنَ ما ائتلفتْ قلوبُكم، فإذا اختلفتم فقوموا عنه.

581. Narrated Jundub: The Prophet ﷺ said, "Recite (and study) the Qur'ān as long as you agree about its interpretation, but when you have any difference of opinion (as regards its interpretation and meaning) then you should stop reciting it (for the time being)"

٥٨١ - حدّثنا عمرُو بنُ عليٍّ: حدّثنا عبدُ الرحمنِ بنُ مهديٍّ: حدّثنا سلّامُ بنُ أبي مُطيعٍ، عنْ أبي عمرانَ الجونيِّ، عنْ جُندبٍ: قالَ النبيُّ صلى اللهُ عليهِ وسلّم: اقرءوا القرآنَ ما ائتلفتْ عليهِ قلوبُكم، فإذا اختلفتم فقوموا عنهُ. تابعهُ الحارثُ ابنُ عُبيدٍ وسعيدُ بنُ زيدٍ، عنْ أبي عمرانَ، ولم يرفعْهُ حمّادُ بنُ سلمةَ وأبانُ. وقالَ غُندرٌ، عنْ شُعبةَ، عنْ أبي عمرانَ: سمعتُ جُندبًا قولَهُ. وقالَ ابنُ عونٍ عنْ أبي عمرانَ عنْ

عَبْدِ اللهِ بنِ الصَّامِتِ عَنْ عُمَرَ قَوْلَهُ .
وَجُنْدَبٌ أصَحُّ وأكْثرُ .

582. Narrated 'Abdullāh that he heard a man reciting a Qur'ānic Verse which he had heard the Prophet reciting in a different way. So he took that man to the Prophet ﷺ (and told him the story). The Prophet ﷺ said, "Both of you are reciting in a correct way, so carry on reciting." The Prophet ﷺ further added, "The nations which were before you were destroyed (by Allāh) because they differed."

٥٨٢ - حدَّثنا سُلَيْمانُ بنُ حَرْبٍ : حدَّثنا شُعْبَةُ ، عَنْ عَبْدِ المَلِكِ بنِ مَيْسَرَةَ ، عَنِ النَّزَّالِ ابنِ سَبْرَةَ ، عَنْ عَبْدِ اللهِ : أنهُ سَمِعَ رَجُلاً يقرأُ آيةً سَمِعَ النَّبِيَّ صلى اللهُ عليهِ وسلَّم قرأ خِلافَها فأخَذْتُ بيَدِهِ فانطَلَقْتُ بِهِ إلى النَّبِيِّ صلى اللهُ عليهِ وسلَّم فقالَ : كِلاكُما مُحْسِنٌ فاقرآ أكبَرُ عِلمي ، قالَ فإنَّ مَنْ كانَ قَبْلَكُمْ اخْتَلَفوا فأهْلَكَهُمْ

End of Volume 6

بحمد الله تعالى تمت الجزء السادس